The Handbook of
COMMUNITY PRACTICE

*To those current and future students who will carry on community
practice—in work to foster social and economic development, in mutual work
with people to improve the conditions and quality of their lives, to advance the profession's
mission to press unwaveringly for human rights, and to work always toward social justice.*

The Handbook of

COMMUNITY PRACTICE

Edited by

Marie Weil
University of North Carolina, Chapel Hill

Associate Editors:

Michael Reisch
University of Michigan

Dorothy N. Gamble
University of North Carolina, Chapel Hill

Lorraine Gutiérrez
University of Michigan

Elizabeth A. Mulroy
University of Maryland

Ram A. Cnaan
University of Pennsylvania

SAGE Publications
Thousand Oaks ■ London ■ New Delhi

For information:

 Sage Publications, Inc.
2455 Teller Road
Thousand Oaks, California 91320
E-mail: order@sagepub.com

Sage Publications Ltd.
1 Oliver's Yard
55 City Road
London EC1Y 1SP
United Kingdom

Sage Publications India Pvt. Ltd.
B-42, Panchsheel Enclave
Post Box 4109
New Delhi 110 017 India

Printed in the United States of America

Library of Congress Cataloging-in-Publication Data

Handbook of community practice / Marie Weil, editor; associate editors,
Michael Reisch . . . [et al.]
      p. cm.
Includes bibliographical references and index.
ISBN 0-7619-2177-X (cloth)
   1. Community—based social services, 2. Community organization. 3. Community development. 4. Community psychology. I. Weil, Marie, 1941- II. Reisch, Michael, 1948-
HV41. H323 2004
361—dc22

                                                              2004009280

04   10   9   8   7   6   5   4   3   2   1

Acquiring Editor:	Arthur T. Pomponio
Editorial Assistant:	Veronica Novak
Production Editor:	Diana E. Axelsen
Copy Editors:	Julie Guin, Jacqueline A. Tasch
Typesetter/Designer:	C&M Digitals (P) Ltd.
Indexer:	David Luljak
Cover Designer:	Michelle Lee Kenny

Contents

D. Social Change: People, Systems, and Societies

PART III Issues, Areas, and Fields of Community Practice   339

A. Issues and Areas

Preface

Marie Weil
University of North Carolina, Chapel Hill

Community practice has been an integral part of social work since its inception in the Settlement House Movement and the Charity Organization Societies. In its grassroots organizing, interagency planning, and social action aspects, this method of practice engages citizens in problem solving, works to improve the quality of life for vulnerable groups and communities, and enacts the profession's social justice mission through a variety of practice models from policy practice to political action. While practice emphases varied over the course of the 20th century—sometimes with greater focus on organizing services, on grassroots organizing, on planning, on social action—the essential purposes to strengthen communities and services, and to press for access, equality, empowerment, and social justice have not wavered.

Indeed, community practice is expanding in the early decades of the 21st century in the United States and around the world. At the same time, major new contexts are developing that will have an impact on community practice work everywhere: the increasing interaction of multiple cultures within and among nations; the continuing struggle to make human rights for everyone—including women and children—a reality throughout the world; and the far-reaching impacts of globalization on the poor and working classes in Western democracies and the Global South alike. Many practice strategies are likely to prove tried and true, others will need modifications for diverse settings or changing populations, and doubtless other strategies will be conceived in the future as needed.

All communities are and will continue to be affected by the global economy and the social, economic, and political shifts that will continue interactively. Community practitioners will need to be cognizant, proactive, and seriously engaged to bring forth closer global connections that support human and sustainable development rather than witnessing the risks and damage to local economies, social structures, and environments that are already evident. Community practice approaches from community development to social action must take into account new complexities, challenges, and opportunities in this period of unparalleled global change. Indeed, community practice is the critical component of the profession that can help citizens, groups, communities, and organizations enlarge civil society, increase grassroots political clout, advocate for human rights, and work for positive social change to support those most disadvantaged by macro changes.

This book is intended to assist current and future social work students, faculty, and practitioners as they confront the challenges posed in the coming decades. For these reasons, this handbook places significant emphasis on social, economic, and sustainable development. Themes in this book emphasize organizing, planning, and development perspectives—from policy, through multiple practice models and strategies, to work focused on building people's skills for local, regional, and international projects as well as on knowledge development to respond effectively to changing and challenging macro contexts. Social work has much to be proud of in the history of community practice, and we now face major challenges to move values and purposes forward to support human flourishing in the 21st century (Friedmann, 1992). For this reason, it seems a vital time for a handbook of community practice to help lay out the agendas and consider directions for our future work.

The Handbook of Community Practice is the fifth work in a major series undertaken by Sage to establish the current state of the art—knowledge, theory, and research—in major areas of social work practice and to point the way to the future. Initially, I was asked to take on this project by Jim Nageotte, Sage's social work editor at that time, and Charles Garvin of the University of Michigan. Jim birthed and nurtured this series with great support from Charles, to determine areas, editors, and major topics needed for such a series. I am immensely grateful for their support and this opportunity to work with colleagues to lay the groundwork for community practice in the coming decades.

The *Handbook* series is a major accomplishment for the social work literature—a landmark in some ways as significant as the Council on Social Work Education's development and documentation of social work education issues in the thirteen-volume *Social Work Curriculum Study* (1959) coordinated by Werner Boehm nearly a half-century ago. That important effort served to clarify methods and models for all social work education. In contrast, the current *Handbook* series demonstrates both how central values have been maintained and how far we have come in knowledge development.

The previous publications in the *Handbook* series are *The Handbook of Direct Social Work Practice,* edited by Paula Allen-Meares and Charles Garvin; *The Handbook of Social Policy,* edited by James Midgley, Martin Tracy, and Michelle Livermore; *The Handbook of Social Welfare Management,* edited by Rino Patti; and *The Handbook of Social Work Research Methods,* edited by Bruce Thyer. I am honored to be a part of this effort and have greatly enjoyed bringing together the strongest company of community practice scholars working in its diverse aspects to examine and present the state of the art and directions for community practice.

I am especially appreciative of the support, concern, and assistance that have been offered by Arthur Pomponio, Sage's editor for social work, who stepped in to assist with a work in progress and encouraged the vision and direction of the book with great enthusiasm, and that of Veronica Novak and Diana Axelsen, who have made working with Sage a highly enjoyable experience.

I am also very appreciative of the advice, support, and skillful work undertaken in the early stages of this effort by the Associate Editors who agreed to contribute to the book and to review and prepare initial recommendations to authors. Having two sounding boards for chapter development was, I think, extremely useful for a considerable number of authors. I extend great thanks to them and to the authors who saw the need for this volume and worked with creative diligence to document where we are and where we need to be going in a wide range of community practice arenas. Many of the authors are members of the Association for Community Organization and Social Administration, others have written for the *Journal of Community Practice,* and many have major books as well as definitive professional articles to their credit. I have been pleased to extend the range of perspectives on community practice in this volume, and have particularly relished not only the diversity of perspectives but also the great diversity of authors engaged in this project—by generation, ethnicity, gender, geography, and specialization. This diversity helps to make this volume more representative of community practice across the nation. Three "generations" of scholars are represented in the volume: the majority are stellar senior scholars, long-term leaders in our field, who have helped to shape the community practice literature since the 1970s and 1980s. Other authors are extraordinary mid-career scholars, widely recognized and respected as leaders in their specializations, many of whom have made building partnerships with community organizations and particular populations the focus of their service as well as scholarly careers. Finally, some are rising stars—close to the pressing realities of current practice and carrying forward commitment to the future of community practice scholarship. It has been an extraordinary experience to work with such a talented and committed group of scholars. My thanks and admiration to them all.

Development of the literature. There is a growing historical literature in community practice (Addams, 1960; Betten & Austin, 1990; Deegan, 1990; Fisher, 1984; Garvin & Cox, 2001; Lewis, 1973; Rothman, 1999; Weil, 1996), and a rich and varied literature about practice (Brager & Specht, 1973; Cox, Erlich, Rothman, & Tropman, 1970, 1984; Harper & Dunham, 1959; Kramer & Specht, 1983; Murphy, 1954; Rivera & Erlich, 1992; Ross, 1955, 1958; Rothman, Erlich, & Tropman, 2001; Taylor & Roberts, 1985) and a rapidly growing periodical literature—particularly in the *Journal of Community Practice,* and also in *Social Development Issues, Administration in Social Work, Sociology and Social Welfare,* the *Progressive Journal of Social Work,* and the *Journal of Social Policy,* among others. This volume, however, adds to the literature an opportunity to survey the scope of community practice perspectives, approaches, methods, skills, and research strategies in a comprehensive way that has not before been undertaken. While there are several community practice entries in the most recent *Encyclopedia of Social Work, 19th Edition* (Edwards, 1995) and several chapters in the *Social Workers' Desk Reference* (Roberts & Greene, 2002), this volume represents an encyclopedia of community practice documenting the strong development of the knowledge base and the state of the art in practice.

A number of significant textbooks about community practice have been published over the last twenty years, covering major approaches or specializing in one method such as planning or organizing. Some have been edited collections (Cox, Erlich, Rothman, & Tropman, 1970, 1984; Kramer & Specht, 1983), while others have been texts undertaken by a single or small number of authors (Brager & Specht, 1973; Ecklein & Lauffer, 1972; Hardcastle, Wenocur, & Powers, 1997; Homan, 2004; Lauffer, 1978; Rubin & Rubin, 1992). *The Handbook of Community Practice* builds on all these earlier works and presents both the scope and depth of community practice. The authors have had the welcome opportunity to compose a comprehensive summary of their favorite subjects and methods.

As a result, this volume provides unprecedented opportunities (1) to examine the range of practice methods focused on community interventions; (2) to consider the political, economic, social, and global shifts that are changing the context of practice; (3) to explore theory; and (4) to analyze the ways in which knowledge, methodology, and research can provide direction and inform leaders, facilitators, and practitioners of ways to strengthen communities and service systems as well as organize, plan, and act for needed change. Authors have critically examined knowledge, theory, practice, and methods, and have worked to define and interpret emerging issues that future students, practitioners, community leaders, scholars, and researchers will need to confront in coming years.

Organization of the book. The handbook is organized into four sections. Part I provides views on the context of community practice and covers central issues that impact practitioners' work. It provides an historical grounding for community practice and an overview of emerging trends, as well as an in-depth treatment of issues of diversity and challenges related to practice in communities of color—both areas that are essential to understanding American society and identifying directions for future practice. It continues with an innovative perspective on theory and theorizing for community practice—illustrating the range of theories and the kind of critical thinking needed to enlighten and guide practice. This section also includes an analysis of the conditions of persistent poverty and possibilities of asset-building, and concludes with a discussion of the evolution of community practice and an analysis of practice models in light of the changing contexts of the 21st century. These chapters reaffirm the values and purposes of community practice and identify challenges for the future.

Part II provides a panorama of the range and levels of community practice, exploring the major approaches—development, organizing, planning, and social change—and levels—grassroots engagement, political and legislative action, radical organizing, coalitions, system reform, and policy practice. These chapters focus on the methods and strategies of practice employed in each of these arenas.

Part III examines a variety of issues, areas, and fields of community practice. Section A, "Issues and Areas," explores the importance of multiculturalism and intergroup empowerment strategies, feminist community practice, faith-based organizing, and program development and service coordination. Section B, "Fields," addresses the topics of rural practice, health and mental health settings, child mental health, community building, economic and social development, and investing in socially and economically distressed communities. This section illustrates the breadth of community practice and its specializations in many settings. Section C, "Global Approaches and Local Issues," expands the focus with treatises on global change and use of social indicators, practice challenges in the global economy, and local and international strategies for engagement of women in economic development through microcredit strategies.

Part IV addresses supports for community practice. Among topics examined are management, resource development, research methodologies and empowerment research, practice in the electronic community, and use of administrative data to support community change. These chapters treat operational and strategic issues, explore the expansion of practice into virtual communities, and advocate for increased efforts in research and evaluation by expanding the range of methodologies, engaging citizens in empowerment research, building partnerships among researchers, agencies, and communities, and by using administrative data to plan, evaluate, and support community change efforts. The concluding chapters then deal with trends, advances in technology, and the challenges of program development and of engaging in stronger partnerships with community members, as well as advancing the research and knowledge base through evolving methodologies.

Acknowledgments

I extend great appreciation to my colleagues who served as associate editors of this volume. Each is a renowned scholar in multiple areas of community practice. Many special thanks to Michael Reisch and Lorraine Gutiérrez of the University of Michigan, Elizabeth Mulroy of the University of Maryland, Ram Cnaan of the University of Pennsylvania, and Dorothy Gamble, my colleague and scholarly partner at the University of North Carolina, Chapel Hill. All were of great help in reviewing chapters and advising and encouraging authors, thus ensuring the quality of the volume.

My deep thanks to Jennie Vaughn and Margaret Morse of the UNC Chapel Hill School of Social Work, copy editors *par excellence*. Special thanks also to Tezita Negussie, Karen Smith Rotabi, and Jennifer Hemingway-Foday for their help with research and logistics and their generous support. Finally, I express great appreciation to my partner, Charles Weil, who has endured this long process and remained stalwart and loving.

Dedication

This volume is personally dedicated to the lives, memories, and accomplishments of extraordinary mentors in community practice with whom I have had the great good fortune to work: Anne E. Queen of the University of North Carolina, Chapel Hill, who opened my eyes and my heart to community work through engagement in the civil and human rights movements and to community development on the Tule River Reservation; Eleanor Ryder of the University of Pennsylvania School of Social Work, who engaged me in community theory and methods; Michael Blum of University Settlement and Nationality Services Center of Philadelphia, who imparted strategies and skills; Paul Schreiber, former Dean of the Hunter College School of Social Work, CUNY, who was and is my model of scholarship and integrity; and Barbara Solomon of the University of Southern California, who has brilliantly led social work toward empowerment practice. I offer special thanks also to David Austin, Rino Patti, and Shanti Khinduka for their early and consistent encouragement and their exemplary scholarship.

References

Addams, J. (1960). *A centennial reader*. New York: Macmillan.

Betten, N., & Austin, M. J. (Eds.). (1990). *The roots of community organizing, 1917–1939*. Philadelphia: Temple University Press.

Boehm, W. W. (Ed.), (1959). *Social work curriculum study.* New York: Council on Social Work Education.

Brager, G., & Specht, H. (1973). *Community organizing.* New York: Columbia University Press.

Cox, F. M., Erlich, J. L., Rothman, J., & Tropman, J. E. (Eds.). (1970). *Strategies of community organization.* Itasca, IL: F. E. Peacock.

Cox, F. M., Erlich, J. L., Rothman, J., & Tropman, J. E. (Eds.). (1984). *Tactics and techniques of community organization* (2nd ed.). Itasca, IL: F. E. Peacock.

Deegan, M. J. (1990). *Jane Addams and the men of the Chicago School, 1892–1918.* New Brunswick, NJ: Transaction.

Ecklein, J. L., & Lauffer, A. A. (1972). *Community organizers and social planners.* New York: John Wiley & CSWE.

Edwards, R. L. (Ed.). (1995). *Encyclopedia of social work* (19th ed.). Washington, DC: NASW Press.

Fisher, R. (1984). *Let the people decide: Neighborhood organizing in America.* Boston: Twayne.

Friedmann, J. (1992). *Empowerment: The politics of alternative development.* Cambridge: Blackwell.

Garvin, C. D., & Cox, F. M. (2001). A history of community organizing since the Civil War with special reference to oppressed communities. In J. Rothman, J. L. Erlich, & J. E. Tropman (Eds.), *Strategies of community intervention* (pp. 65–100). Itasca, IL: F. E. Peacock.

Hardcastle, D. A., Wenocur, S., & Powers, P. R. (1997). *Community practice: Theories and skills for social workers.* New York: Oxford University Press.

Harper, E. B., & Dunham, A. (1959). *Community organization in action.* New York: Association Press.

Homan, M. S. (2004). *Promoting community change: Making it happen in the real world* (3rd ed.). Belmont, CA: Brooks Cole/Thompson.

Journal of Community Practice. (1990–). New York: Haworth Press.

Kramer, R., & Specht, H. (1983). *Readings in community organization practice* (3rd ed.). Englewood Cliffs, NJ: Prentice Hall.

Lauffer, A. (1978). *Social planning at the community level.* Englewood Cliffs, NJ: Prentice Hall.

Lewis, V. S. (1973). Charity organization society. In R. Morris (Ed.), *Encyclopedia of social work* (16th ed., pp. 94–98). Washington, DC: NASW Press.

Murphy, C. G. (1954). *Community organization practice.* Boston: Houghton Mifflin.

Rivera, F. G., & Erlich, J. L. (1992). *Community organizing in a diverse society.* Needham Heights, MA: Allyn & Bacon.

Roberts, A. R., & Greene, G. J. (Eds.). (2002). *Social workers' desk reference.* New York: Oxford University Press.

Ross, M. G. (1955). *Community organization: Theory, principles and practice.* New York: Harper & Row.

Ross, M. G. (1958). *Case histories in community organization.* New York: Harper & Row.

Rothman, J. (Ed.). (1999). *Reflections on community organization: Enduring themes and critical issues.* Itasca, IL: F. E. Peacock.

Rothman, J., Erlich, J. L., & Tropman, J. E. (2001). *Strategies of community intervention* (6th ed.). Itasca, IL: F. E. Peacock.

Rubin, H. J., & Rubin, I. S. (2000). *Community organizing and development.* Columbus, OH: Merrill.

Taylor, S. H., & Roberts, R. W. (Eds.). (1985). *Theory and practice of community social work.* New York: Columbia University Press.

Weil, M. (1996). Model development in community practice: An historical perspective. In M. Weil (Ed.), *Community practice: Conceptual models* (pp. 5–67). New York: Haworth Press.

PART I

The Context of Community Practice

In the introduction to *The Handbook of Community Practice*, I seek to lay out the current context and range of community practice and illustrate new challenges in the 21st century. In order to promote social justice and the positive development of under-resourced areas, practitioners, scholars, researchers, and students need to understand the context of specific communities, how to identify community assets, and how to engage people in their own goals for development. The introduction also traces the development of education for community practice in social work, examines the positioning of community practice and macro practice in current curricula, argues for an expanded role for community practice in social work education, and concludes with current issues and challenges facing community practitioners, faculty and students.

The chapters in Part I of the *Handbook* examine the contexts of community practice and central social and political issues underlying the work that practitioners do. History is important, and in "History, Context, and Emerging Issues for Community Practice," Robert Fisher provides a trenchant and engaging history of community organizing and practice and outlines emerging issues and challenges that we will face in the 21st century. The second chapter focuses on diverse populations and illuminates challenging realities of our multicultural society that has not yet enacted its positive potential. The authors advocate more extensive organizing within and across cultural groups in intergroup or multicultural organizations, to gain strength for political influence and for social change. John Erlich and Teiahsha Bankhead present a cutting-edge view of these issues that must be effectively solved, resolved—if we are to settle the question raised by W. E. B. DuBois and Gunner Myrdal—whether the race issue will destroy America, or whether a pluralistic and equitable society can be its direction and salvation. Beth Glover Reed presents an exciting and newly formed framework for "Theorizing in Community Practice." Reed draws on theories most frequently treated in the community practice literature—general systems and ecological theories. However, she emphasizes how and why using theories is an important aspect of community practice. Drawing from a range of theories, she illustrates their utility in informing processes of assessment, planning, implementation and evaluation. Her new framework for theorizing about community practice is both useful and challenging for faculty, practitioners and practitioners.

In "Communities and Social Policy Issues: Persistent Poverty, Economic Inclusion, and Asset Building," Yolanda Padilla and Michael Sherraden analyze the conditions that curtail opportunity and propose strategies for asset development for the poor and for the expansion of civil society in the 21st century. This section concludes with "Evolution and Current Models of Community Practice for the 21st Century," in which Dorothy Gamble and I describe some of the current challenges to social work values and emphasize the increasing importance of three central contexts for practice in the next several decades: multiculturalism, human rights, and globalism.

CHAPTER 1

Introduction

Contexts and Challenges for 21st-Century Communities

Marie Weil

University of North Carolina, Chapel Hill

A nexus of serious challenges faces community practitioners and educators in the 21st century. Some of these entangled issues, such as the persistence of poverty, are ancient, whereas others, such as globalization, have only recently emerged. The connections among these problems are becoming increasingly complex. Today's community practitioners must deal with the combined effects of global economics and escalating poverty in both postindustrial societies and developing economies; other challenges include wars internal to nations and terrorism across borders, massive movements of refugees, rising tensions caused by increasingly multicultural populations, the continued existence of slavery, and the realities of racial and ethnic discrimination in many societies. There are continuing struggles to build democracies where they have not been established and corollary efforts to make existing democracies representative of their citizenry. This intersection of major social issues offers challenges on every level, from the local to the international.

In a period of unprecedented speed of communication, access to information, and increased knowledge, major work to build and rebuild democratic civil societies is central to take on these problems at multiple levels. Although these issues may seem daunting, apathy, withdrawal, or disillusionment can only promote their invidiousness. Instead, a proactive effort is essential. Community practitioners and the people they serve at the local, state, national, and international levels can address this nexus of social challenges at least partially by strengthening civil society at home and abroad through work in social and economic development as well as community and service system organizing and by planning to treat new facets of problems in innovative ways. One approach to dealing with these new challenges is to focus on five central practice issues:

1. *Expanding and refining practice approaches* that can build toward social and economic justice

2. Focusing practice on the *expansion of basic human rights* for women, children, and men

3. *Building opportunity structures* for disadvantaged populations, and working to *build multicultural strategies and coalitions* for positive social change based on specific situations and common human needs

4. Focusing community practice activities on *social and economic development, strengthening civil society,* and *enlarging civic and political participation*

5. *Finding effective multinational approaches to reducing absolute poverty* (Drake, 2001; Figueira-McDonough, 2001; Friedmann, 1992; Gil, 1988).

In the United States, major demographic shifts are a central component of the new context of practice. Our nation is rapidly becoming a minority-majority population (U.S. Bureau of the Census, 2000). The United States has always been multicultural, but it is not yet fully pluralistic; the future direction of civil society is largely dependent on bridging the great divide between racial and ethnic populations and closing the ever-widening gulf in socioeconomic status. All social workers, and community practitioners in particular, need to be better prepared to address conflicts within and across racial and cultural groups so they can focus on social and economic achievement for all groups that have been marginalized (Longres, 1997). As we work with specific groups and communities, we need to foster the building of horizontal connections necessary to construct larger multicultural coalitions and communities of interest, and we must reclaim and establish a basic concern for common human needs (Longres, 1997; Towle, 1965; Weil, 1994).

The income gap among U.S. citizens continues to grow, the result of policies that produce increasing economic and social distance between the very rich and everyone else (Rose, 1997). As a result, the severity of poverty increases not only for the long-term poor but also for the near-poor and for many working-class families, as the policy safety net is dismantled and millions of jobs are moved offshore. The global economy has strengthened the power of multinational corporations, increased poverty in postindustrial states, and created unsafe working conditions in many parts of the Third World. Increased poverty in the United States also relates to the evolution of a postindustrial state characterized by a split between high-tech and service economies.

The unprecedented loss of jobs through globalization and corporate restructuring has greatly expanded unemployment and underemployment and carries a high risk of increasing racism—even while racial discrimination in employment practices still persists in the United States (Rose, 1997; Stern, 1997). These tightly interwoven issues illustrate the need for short-term action and long-term vision to combat structural, persistent poverty and to promote human rights.

Globalization has increased deprivation and poverty worldwide through both structural adjustment and the massive movement of political and economic refugees (Midgley & Sherraden, 2000; World Bank, 1991). Violence based in racism and economic competition has escalated in the older democracies of Western Europe, in postcolonial areas of the developing world, and in Eastern Europe as well as North America (Midgley, 1997).

Economic globalization has also played a primary role in the spread of urban decay, increased isolation of the poor, and decreased government propensity to address large-scale unemployment (Wilson, 1987). Midgley (1997) and others urge social work to respond to this escalating problem by engaging in serious social and economic development with low-income, immigrant, and refugee populations. There is much in terms of practice and perspectives that Western nations can learn from the developing world to ameliorate serious social and economic dislocation, to build on the knowledge base of international social work, and to transfer innovative social interventions (Gamble, Castelloe, & Varma, 2003; Mayadas & Elliott, 1997; Mayadas, Watts, & Elliott, 1997).

Although we need to be responsive to the results of massive social, economic, and political shifts at home, we also need to be attentive to the global connections of social work and to learn from other nations. Sarri (1997, p. 387) states four major benefits of studying international examples:

1. Greater understanding of alternative economic, political, and social welfare systems

2. Enhanced appreciation for diverse cultures

3. Exposure to comparative options for addressing economic and social issues

4. Increased possibilities for innovation and change in practice and education

Each of these concerns about mutual learning and practice foci—on social and economic justice, human rights, multicultural coalitions, and social, economic, and political development—underscores the importance of community practitioners increasing their efforts in establishing and enlarging civil society as a central means of coping with current and future economic and social challenges.

Economic and policy changes in the United States have also shifted the relationships among public and nonprofit agencies. Philosophies of practice have become more community based and family centered; however, medical and mental health services are increasingly rationed. As a result, at-risk families often are unable to secure supportive services at a time when prevention methods would work and become clients only when their situations are very serious and they may be drawn into the child welfare system. To build responsive and responsible practice for the 21st century, Brilliant (1997) holds that social work must take significant responsibility in determining the changing roles of public- and nonprofit-sector human services. She argues that in this effort, practitioners will need to focus sharply on group participation and community processes. Expanded participation and broadly shared leadership should be central to practice approaches and should guide policy development and promote more significant engagement in political processes (Brilliant, 1997).

In analyzing development and empowerment approaches, Friedmann (1992) holds that popular struggle takes place in four overlapping spheres or domains: the state, the political community, the corporate economy, and civil society. Each sphere has its own core of institutions and also overlaps in functions with the others. Community practitioners and the groups, communities, coalitions, and systems with which they work increasingly need to have clearer goals and strategies to influence the power of the state and the ever-increasing strength of the multinational corporate economy. However, to have humanizing and potent effects in these spheres, it is necessary first to strengthen and expand civil society and the participation of groups, progressive organizations, and communities in the political sphere. These are time-honored community practice activities—and they must now be revitalized with a broader range of strategies to foster civic and political participation, building power in both areas.

Figueira-McDonough (2001) defines civil society as follows:

> Civil society encompasses the associations in which we conduct our lives and which owe their existence to our needs and initiatives rather than to the state. The crisscrossing network of such volunteer associations—their creative chaos—makes up the reality of civil society. . . . Civil society, then, refers to collaboration between intermediate organizations, informal and formal, to deal with common local problems. (p. 108)

Friedmann (1992) believes that the strengthening of low-wealth communities through the building of internal and external associational contacts is a central means to build civil society, and he holds that the state must invest in this development. Figueira-McDonough (2001) agrees that the "flourishing of these associations is essential" to promote progressive local politics and build resources but she adds that although dense associational networks are necessary, they are not a "sufficient condition for a civil society" (p. 108). Additional conditions, she says, are finding means to balance the interests of multicultural groups and devising a "new localism" framed in economic policy activism. Figueira-McDonough sees new localism as taking on aspects of the global issues discussed above, noting:

> A local economy needs to develop "a dynamic reciprocity" with other communities, with the city at large, and with global businesses. If local communities are to protect themselves successfully, they need to engage in trade with large outside firms, without being controlled by them. (p.110)

Logan and Swanstrom (1990) identify conditions that could help local communities function in the global economy: inventive leadership; development of new processes to replace traditional business and labor patterns; grassroots political support; and national and international networking among pioneers of the new localism for sharing information, experience, and support. Essential to this new formulation of localism is intensive work to develop and increase both bonding and bridging social capital (Gittell & Vidal 1998). A central caution that Figueira McDonough (2001) offers community practitioners is that although new and emerging strategies for revitalizing and renewing civil society are available, it is equally important to assess (with residents) the capacities of any economically and politically vulnerable community to initiate strategies responsive and appropriate to current situations.

In addition to focusing on multilevel strategies of social and economic development related to specific community capacity, practitioners also need to be ready to support and enhance organizing, social action, and political action—preferably in coalitions that are multicultural and that have broad-based membership, including service providers and progressive neighborhood organizations, to have an effect on local polity and therefore on continuing political and economic interactions (Shragge, 2003). Figueira-McDonough (2001), Shragge (2003), and Fisher (2001) discuss the need to engage women in this work. Figueira-McDonough presents examples representing "an invisible, resilient grassroots force" composed of women engaged in collective activism. Shragge and Fisher speak of learning new organizing lessons from feminist organizations, literature, and connections, most specifically emphasis on process and long-term goals. New as well as old conceptions of power need to be employed—power *with* rather than power *over;* power as a resource that grows with use, rather than authoritarian power that can diminish as used; power as *empowerment* to take on the tasks needed to rebuild and bring solidarity to the social community as it seeks to form viable economic power internally and externally; and power and conviction to take on work for progressive political change. Clearly, the minds, efforts, and energy of both "halves" of the gendered world are needed to meet today's challenges to the world community.

Development and empowerment are processes that increase the likelihood of effective use of social, economic, and political power for change directed to social justice. As always, there now exists a need for community practitioners and allies to work within the state system and as intermediaries to promote these goals (Friedmann, 1992) and to promote the means and the will to implement a social development policy perspective that could provide local, national, and international incentives for needed change. Midgley and Sherraden (2000) urge a social development perspective that provides a partial fit with Friedmann's (1992) alternative development/empowerment approach. This alternative policy approach transcends the century-long debates regarding residual versus institutional approaches to welfare "by encouraging the adoption of social programs that are primarily concerned not with providing social services but with enhancing the capacities of needy people to participate in the productive economy" (Midgley & Sherraden, 2000, p. 437).

As Friedmann (1992), Midgley and Sherraden (2000), and others have argued, this perspective requires not only grassroots work but also state investment and commitment to assure that the benefits of economic development actually "bring tangible benefits to ordinary people" (Midgley & Sherraden, 2000, p. 437). Such efforts must combine social and economic policy. Human development, that is, should have the same priority as economic development. The social development perspective should encourage projects, programs, and policies that are "productivist, investment-oriented, and committed to enhancing economic participation" (Midgley & Sherraden, 2000, p. 438) among those people, groups, and communities that, as Friedmann emphasizes, have been structurally disempowered and excluded from economic, social, and political participation. Internationally, these perspectives on development efforts are encapsulated in central concepts, a number of which have been explored by Sen (1999) and encoded in the United Nations' *Human Development Reports* initiated by Mahbub ul Haq (United Nations Development Programme, 1999). Human development is increasingly discussed as human capital—increasing the skills and capacities of individuals and groups.

Additional investments by development-oriented states would promote employment, self-employment, and workers' cooperatives and would focus on social capital investment to form and strengthen social networks both within and external to a community. Friedmann discusses this process as promoting access to bases of social power that can lead to increased economic viability. Development-oriented states should "foster civic engagement and promote community solidarity . . . because they have positive implications for economic development" (Friedmann, 1992, p. 35; see also Midgley & Sherraden, 2000). These activities interface in communities to encourage economic development through credit opportunities, local enterprise development that can increase employment, asset building, and the multifunctional work of community development corporations and comprehensive community initiatives (Brisson, 2003; Sherraden & Ninacs, 1998). Diverse strategies, from individual development accounts to workers' cooperatives to comprehensive community initiatives, can build functional economic structures that, over time, can increase both social and political power (Friedmann, 1992). Community practitioners need to increase and expand the range of skills that can be used to build economic footholds and later economic stability in communities that have been marginalized.

Many social workers already engage in social and economic development, but many more are needed who possess both the development skills and the political and organizing skills necessary to move to stronger community economic status and to increased political clout. Examples are Bethel New Life (n.d.) in Chicago and the Dudley Street Initiative in Boston (Medoff & Sklar, 1994), each of which has achieved a number of the following outcomes: cultural and multicultural coalitions, housing development, employment training, enterprises and an enterprise incubator, increased economic opportunities, social and political solidarity, and youth development programs. Community strength of this kind can translate into political clout and enable communities to engage more successfully in politics, wield power in conflictual situations, and press for needed changes in policies. Successful models offer much hope, even in the face of major local, national, and international challenges.

Communities, Values, and Community Practice

Communities are the context of all social work practice, and community practice is recognized as a major means to carry forward the profession's long-standing ethical commitment to social justice (Netting, Kettner, & McMurty, 2004). *Justice* essentially means *fairness*. As *social* refers to our human relations and interconnections in society, *social justice* implies commitment to fairness in our dealings with each other in the major public aspects of our lives—the political, economic, social, and civil realms. In society, social justice should foster equal human rights, distributive justice, and a structure of opportunity and be grounded in representative and participatory democracy.

Given social work's mission, the value of social justice implies that the profession should display commitment and actions to increase fairness in the political and economic arenas, as well as social access and equality in the civil realm (Gil, 1988;

Rawls, 1970; Weil, 2000). Improving the quality of life for people and communities relates to direct work with communities to build resources and develop social and political power. A practical extension of Rawls's (1970) exposition of distributive justice would argue for providing the most attention, redress, and resources to those who are least advantaged.

Community practice encompasses four central processes: development, organizing, planning, and action for progressive social change. Together, these processes form social work's major method of actively working for social justice. Community practice emphasizes working mutually with citizens groups, cultural and multicultural groups and organizations, and human service organizations to improve life options and opportunities in communities—and to press for the expansion of civil and human rights, political equality, and distributive justice. These efforts range from grassroots work to social action and legislative advocacy to change systems that fail to support these values.

Community practice is grounded in values of "democratic process, citizen participation, group determination, empowerment, multiculturalism, and leadership development" (Weil, 1994, p. xxvii). Democratic revitalization is a central purview of community practice in all its forms and is expressed through transformation that supports social and economic development and brings complex political economies and administrative structures under democratic scrutiny through increased citizen knowledge and understanding of economic and political problems. Four major processes that can aid in this revitalization reflect the realities and scope of community practice and can be defined as follows:

Development: The processes of community social and economic development that focus on enabling and empowering citizens to work in united ways to change their lives and environments in relation to living conditions, economic conditions, and social, employment, and opportunity structures. Development includes the models of community, social, and economic development and sustainable development.

Organizing: The processes of empowerment and community organizing that engage citizens in projects to change social, economic, and political conditions. Organizing includes locality development, neighborhood organizing, organizing in communities of interest, development of local leadership, and coalition development.

Planning: The processes of social planning engaged in by citizens, advocacy groups, advocate planners, and public and voluntary sector planners to design programs and services that are appropriate to given communities, counties, or regions. Planning also relates to the design of more effective services, the coordination of services, and the major reform of human service systems. It includes the models for social planning and program development and coordination.

Progressive change: The actions taken by groups to effect positive social, economic, and political change. Social change includes the models of political and social action, pluralism and participation, leadership development, coalitions, and engagement in social movements. It embraces levels of change from local to global. (adapted from Weil, 1994, pp. xxx–xxxi)

Community practice, then, is work to improve quality of life and increase social justice through social and economic development, community organizing, social planning, and progressive social change. It is a cooperative effort between practitioners and affected individuals, groups, organizations, communities, and coalitions. Improving the quality of life for impoverished and vulnerable persons and communities requires helping people help themselves to build resources and develop social and political power.

Clearly, work to expand the rights and opportunities of the poor requires efforts to change systems and institutions as well as negative life conditions. To promote social justice and the positive development of under-resourced areas, practitioners, scholars, and researchers need to understand the context of specific communities (Fisher & Karger, 2000), how to identify community assets (Kretzmann & McKnight, 1993), and how to engage people in their own goals for development and increase of social, economic, and political power (Figueira-McDonough, 2001; Mondros & Wilson, 1994; Reisch, 1997; Ross, 1967).

Communities can be understood either as geographic entities or as groups that share a special concern or identity—functional communities. Although a geographic community can range from a small neighborhood to a large city and its environs, most of the existing community research begins at the neighborhood or territorial level (Netting et al., 2004). Both of these major types of communities—geographic and functional—share the characteristics of face-to-face communication, exchange, and interaction (Fellin, 2001). A variety of geographic and functional communities, therefore, will exist in a metropolitan setting or a rural area.

Community has been a central aspect of both human life and social thought throughout history, and concerns about community have been the subject of major philosophical debate throughout Western history—at least from the time of Socrates' dialogues focusing on the individual and the polity. Early sociologists, most notably Tönnies (1889/1955) and Durkheim (1895/1964), and later 19th-century students of society, including Weber, Spencer, and Marx, introduced widely divergent views and conceptions of economy, society, and justice that are under debate even today (Scott, 1995). Many of our current questions about community can be traced back to earlier conceptions of what it means to be human and to be part of a social, economic, and political collective. These questions are perennial, and each society and each era casts its own reflection or Hegelian *Zeitgeist* (spirit, meaning, and purposes) on its study of society.

Tönnies (1889/1955) provided the essential distinction between *Gemeinschaft* (reciprocity; informal, mutual, and interdependent bonds; shared norms; and face-to-face, relationship-oriented interaction) and *Gesellschaft* (formal, larger-scale, associational, task-oriented interaction), which is still a central rubric in contemporary sociology. Writers of the Scottish Enlightenment developed the concept of *civil society*, then considered to be an arena of "market exchange" and "contractual relations" that had emerged in Europe with increasing commercialism and industrial means of production (Scott, 1995, p. 4). Hegel saw civil society as a product of the decline of *Gemeinschaft* and as a central organizing force with the rise of individual self-interest expressed in interdependent commercial exchange and the increasing differentiation of social strata or classes (Marcuse, 1941). Today, our conception of civil society has shifted so that it represents a nongovernmental and nonbusiness sphere of society that is home, among other societal factors, to intermediary organizations, citizen involvement, social action, the nonprofit sector, the arts, and other community practice concerns (Figueira-McDonough, 2001; Friedmann, 1992).

Current theory and practice still grapple with the complexities and changes in the connections of the individual to society and with heightened concerns about the decline in influence of face-to-face communities, which is accompanied by the increasingly mechanistic, technological, and electronic effects on formal economic, social, and political structures that further distance people from their local and larger geographic communities (Figueira-McDonough, 2001; Fisher & Karger, 1997; Kretzmann & McKnight, 1993; McKnight, 1997; Putnam, 2000; Putnam & Feldstein, 2003; Rifkin, 2000). Now we face the added challenge of viewing the individual citizen in a global context, facing further decline in the supportive community and the impact of international and global economic and political forces on the local community (Fisher & Karger, 1997; Rifkin, 2000). Understanding ourselves and our communities in this complex new context is a major current challenge.

Classical theory and sociological approaches have been subject to much greater scrutiny in recent years and have increasingly been critiqued (by critical theorists, among others) as being culture bound, vested in current political power structures, ignoring many aspects of power (except for Marx and neo-Marxists), providing little if any focus on women's actions and contributions in society, and most typically, not making efforts to hear or understand the views of groups that have been marginalized—with the notable exception, of course, of W. E. B. DuBois (1896, 1935). Although 19th- and early to mid 20th-century theories still offer useful concepts, it is critically important to develop, investigate, and apply newer perspectives grounded in the current and emerging societal and international milieu. Current scholars and practitioners need to be engaged in continual examination and modification of theories to take account of changing political, economic, and social conditions. Communities are "where we live"—where the realities of political, social, and economic change shape and reshape our environment. Therefore, organizing, community development, planning, and progressive change are major means through which community residents and community practitioners should seek to guide the way to the future.

Community Practice and Societal Change: Academic and Professional Roots

In America, community practice emerged at a time of great societal change. Both the Settlement Movement and the rapid expansion of charity organization societies (COSs) were created in response to changes brought about by industrialization and by the vast waves of immigrants coming from Europe to the United States, followed by the "Great Migration" of African Americans to northern cities. The COSs were established to provide coordinated support services for the greatly increasing numbers of urban poor—thus establishing the forerunner of today's federated funding and service coordination efforts (Betten & Austin, 1990). In many cities, and perhaps most influentially in New York, Chicago, and Philadelphia, the

Settlement Movement was a response to pressures of industrialization, the large immigrant population, and the changing nature of cities. Across the nation, the settlement workers' approach was to settle in poor neighborhoods and come to know the neighbors, and then to work with and for them on projects as diverse as the creation of recreational opportunities and surveys of public health problems (Addams, 1902).

The development of programs, advocacy, and research at Hull-House is particularly interesting because of its vivid representation of intellectual history: the initial conjoining and subsequent separation of social work from the discipline of sociology. The Department of Sociology at the University of Chicago was the incubator for the emerging field of urban sociology, and early sociologists and a number of women associated with Hull-House who taught in that department pioneered research on and with communities in America. Jane Addams and several of her female colleagues taught in the Sociology Department, where much work was being done on development of ecological theory applied to human society (Deegan, 1988; Park, 1936).

In several cities, especially Chicago, both sociologists and settlement workers were seriously engaged in analyses of community conditions during the period of rapid urbanization and immigration that created large and concentrated low-income urban neighborhoods of workers and their families. In Chicago, the work by Addams (1902) and her colleagues and other University of Chicago sociology faculty, which initially was somewhat collaborative, began to diverge as the pressures to establish sociology solidly within the academic disciplines conflicted with the settlement-associated faculty's commitment not only to study communities but also to work to change deplorable living conditions. For example, the University of Chicago's Department of Sociology became well-known for the development of studies of deviancy, as exhibited, for example, in juvenile delinquency and prostitution. The sociologists examined and documented these social problems; workers in the Settlement Movement and later in the School of Social Services Administration not only documented but also sought to change the living conditions of impoverished youth and young adults (Deegan, 1988). Workers at some settlements sought to find legitimate employment opportunities for prostitutes, many of whom were young women migrating to Chicago from rural areas or other countries, and Hull-House residents were particularly instrumental in developing methods of community analysis as well as in providing forums, services, and neighborhood supports.

Comparable efforts were carried out in other cities. Lillian Wald (Edwards, 1995) of the Henry Street Settlement initially focused on public health issues on the Lower East Side of Manhattan but rapidly broadened into concerns about child labor and welfare as well as a range of neighborhood activities. It is well documented that settlement workers were oriented toward social reform—toward working *with* people and moving local causes into the public policy arena (Adams, 1902; Carson, 1990; Philpott, 1991).

These activities and other community social work carried out within the COSs and settlements marked the yoking of social research and social action—to document social needs and test interventions and, in the case of many settlements, to build social connections and promote civic participation in poor communities. Although community-focused social work has continued to draw from the social sciences—sociology, psychology, and political science, in particular—it has also from its earliest beginnings sought to develop assessment and research methods to support community practice and to build a knowledge base to guide interventions.

The women of Hull-House actively engaged in community mapping. For their 1895 book, *Hull-House Maps and Papers, by Residents of Hull-House, A Social Settlement, A Presentation of Nationalities and Wages in a Congested District of Chicago, Together With Comments and Essays on Problems Growing Out of the Social Conditions,* Addams and her colleagues worked with community residents to map the low-income ethnic communities surrounding Hull-House. Workers in the COSs and settlement houses in major urban areas initiated aspects of practice and community engagement that continue to evolve today. Community practice has continued to draw on social science theory and has concomitantly developed a broad range of practice theory and practice and research approaches. This volume presents the state of theory, practice, and research knowledge in the first decade of the 21st century. To understand the development of the field, it is useful to compare the early and current state of education for community practice in order to carry forward this proud tradition in social work.

Early Macro Practice Specializations: Challenges and Enduring Themes

Training in community practice (largely through hands-on learning, or apprenticeship) began well before the existence of courses, much less formal schools of social work attached to universities. Early community practitioners learned by doing, whether within the Settlement Movement or in organizational and administrative work in COSs. As demand escalated for a more scientific and research-based approach to learning for community practice, specialized courses were brought under the umbrella of universities. Most early social work programs within or sponsored by universities were connected to departments of sociology—a social science seeking to rapidly establish its credentials in the American academy as coequal with the longer-established natural sciences. In a struggle that lasted 14 years, the Hull-House settlement-connected faculty sought to retain a place for the applied sociology and research they had helped to establish. However, in 1920, "all of the women sociologists in the Department of Sociology were moved en masse out of sociology and into social work" in the School of Social Service Administration (Deegan, 1988, p. 309). This trend to establish separate programs and schools of social work or social welfare was mirrored at a number of other universities.

The mid to late 1920s was a time of rapid advancement in formal, university-based social work education. Social work educators across the nation joined together to form the American Association of Training Schools for Social Work. Macro practice was a central part of these early curricula, both because community work was a major form of engagement to help improve the living and working conditions of immigrant populations and the poor and because new types of social agencies—both public and nonprofit—were being formed to address both specific and complex overlapping social issues.

The early university-based schools clearly were pioneers in establishing the canon of knowledge that master's- and doctoral-level social workers were expected to acquire. An early forum for development of knowledge in sociology, applied sociology, and social work was *The Journal of Social Forces,* founded in 1923. This periodical publication was edited by Howard Odum of the University of North Carolina, Chapel Hill, founder of that university's School of Public Welfare and a scholar committed to development of research and intervention knowledge for social work.

During its first year of publication, *Social Forces* provided a listing of schools offering bachelor's, master's, and doctoral degrees in social work, along with descriptions of their curriculum specializations. Table 1.1 depicts the macro specializations offered; these selections raise interesting questions about change and continuity in our present systems of social work education.

Table 1.1   Early Macro Practice Concentrations

Members of the American Association of Training Schools for Social Work, as Reported in *Social Forces,* September 1923

Bryn Mawr College
Graduate department of social economy and social research
Community organization
Organizations and industrial problems
Social and industrial research
M.A. and Ph.D.

University of Minnesota
Course for social and civic work
Group work and rural social work
Four- and five-year courses
B.S. and A.M. degrees

University of Missouri
Missouri School of Social Economy
Community organization and fieldwork
Public health

New York School of Social Work
Social research
Community organization
Industry

University of North Carolina
School of Public Welfare
Community organization
Social research and fieldwork
Master's degree and certificate

Ohio State University
Department of Social Work
Social administration
Community organization
Americanization and industry
B.A. and one-year M.A.

University of Pennsylvania
School of Social and Health Work
Community social work
Community organization
Social research
Public health

Smith College
Training School for Social Work
Community service work

University of Toronto
Department of Social Service
Social science and practice

College of William and Mary
School of Social Work and Public Health
Community work
Public health nursing

University of Wisconsin
Courses in social casework
Organization and administration
Publicity and public speaking

Source: The Journal of Social Forces, 1(5), 262-267.

Six schools did not note any specialized areas of work. The University of Chicago's concentrations were not listed; however, its School of Social Service Administration did offer programs in both community organization and social administration at that time. It is interesting to see the early connection to public health, with 4 of the 20 schools listing a specialization in public health. Nine of the programs offer community organization or community social work as specializations. It is quite likely that much of the work related to specializations in industrial problems, rural social work, and perhaps public speaking were also largely community focused in their application.

While this company of university-based social work programs provided specialized, advanced work in community social work and community organization, the late 1920s also witnessed the rapid advance of psychoanalytic theory in American social work following Freud's landmark visit to Clark University in 1909 (Ellis, 1965). Many professional social work leaders in academia and practice rapidly adopted a psychoanalytic approach to diagnosing and treating the problems of individuals—thus retrenching from Mary Richmond's (1901) focus on the family in a neighborhood context, presented in her article, "Charitable Co-Operation." They began to promulgate a radical separation of the methods of work with individuals and families from the community-based and frequently group-focused work in the Settlement Movement. Administrators and workers in the COSs increasingly found themselves raising funds and coordinating services focused on treatment of individuals, as social agencies began a major move toward individual treatment based on the new psychoanalytic theory and method. These actions were part of a major response to Abraham Flexner's (1915) critique that social work did not have its own discrete knowledge and research base. Between the 1920s and 1930s, the intellectual divide between faculty who focused on "the social in social work" and those who focused on individual adjustment had established a divide that current educators and practitioners must still confront. Although it is of critical importance for social work to give attention to individual emotional and social well-being, it seems clear that the rapid adoption of the psychoanalytical approach to helping moved the profession and its students further into the psychological realm and further from the field's origins in community practice. After community practice was pushed out of the nest by mainstream sociologists, a large part of the emerging social work profession was increasingly allied with psychological knowledge and treatment methods. Nevertheless, community practice has held its ground and continued to develop its own base of knowledge: Practice theory and research focused on a range of efforts to strengthen communities and service systems and to build empowerment and social change. Numerous community-focused scholars support the need for empowerment-oriented services for individuals, families, groups, and communities and have proposed several means to unite these various approaches in a full continuum of social work interventions (Delgado, 2000; Fisher & Karger, 2000; Gil, 1988; Lee, 2001; Weil, 2000; Wood & Middleman, 1989). It is hoped that today's emerging focus on community-based social work (for direct practitioners) can effectively bridge this divide—uniting case and cause, private troubles and public needs (Adams & Nelson, 1995; Delgado, 2000; Longres, 1997; Towle, 1965).

Community Theory and Community Change

As community practice continued to evolve, it benefited from the development of theories that focused more intently on factors of larger community structure and community change. The earliest sociologists in Europe established themselves in the academy through studies of the changes in all aspects of community life that were wrought by the industrial revolution and the rapid expansion of cities; similar events shaped the development of sociology as a discipline in America.

Just as early sociological knowledge formed part of the base of early social work knowledge, the community theory developed by sociologists in the 1960s and 1970s remains a central touchstone for much of community practice theory. Roland Warren is perhaps the foremost theorist of this period and had a major impact on education for community practice. Warren (1978) elaborated concepts and interactions such as horizontal and vertical relationships, internal and external linkages, nested systems, and interacting systems that carry out various functions that support or constrain community life. Warren's work, his collaboration with Lyon (Warren & Lyon, 1988), and the studies by Floyd Hunter (1953) provide greater recognition of the normal and constant reality of diverse interests and community conflict than did Parsons and earlier sociologists (Park et al., 1925; Parsons, 1951; Scott, 1995).

A major aspect of Warren's (1978) work was his delineation of the "Great Change in American Communities." If one were unaware of the original publication date, 1963, of Warren's *The Community in America,* some of his discussion of change might sound eerily contemporary:

> Changes on the community level are taking place at such a rapid rate and in such drastic fashion that they are affecting the entire structure and function of community living. How shall we grasp and analyze this vast, complex, many sided, interrelated process of change? (p. 52)

It is perhaps worth noting that some of Warren's (1978) concerns described in the last half of the 20th century echo those raised by Durkheim (1895/1964; 1893/1984) and Weber (1904-1905/1930) during the rise of industrial society nearly a century before. Community theory is perhaps needed most at times of major social and economic change. Then, as now, conditions of life and livelihood were changing—requiring a new framework for thoughts and ideas about ourselves and our world.

The factors that Warren (1978) identified as characterizing the "Great Change" in American communities occurred over a long period of time, but in combination, they constituted extraordinary societal shifts. These factors included: (a) division of labor, (b) differentiation of interests and association, (c) increasing systemic relationships to the larger society, (d) bureaucratization and impersonalization, (e) transfer of functions to profit enterprise and government, (f) urbanization and suburbanization, and (g) changing values (p. 53). Although these factors are still aspects of ongoing social change, emerging issues and the new global context have both complicated and accelerated the changes we face. The following list updates Warren's (1978) factors to take account of current challenges:

Major Factors of Escalating Societal Change—Early 21st Century

Division of labor evolving into postindustrial poles of high-tech and service economies; global division of labor rendering the United States a consumer society and the nations of the developing world industrial producers; major dislocation of workers, including unemployment and underemployment; a great increase in the number of women in the labor force and realities of racial discrimination in hiring together with an astounding divergence between compensation for workers and CEOs.

Differentiation of interests and association further separating the population through the escalating wage gap, with increasing poverty and the increasing concentration of wealth in the top 5% of the U.S. population; the dismantling of the social policy safety net; large-scale housing segregation between suburbs and inner cities, increased privatization and lessened focus on community life.

Increasing relationships to larger society now experienced not only nationally but in the unprecedented impact of the global economy, resulting in the loss of jobs for millions of American working-class and low-wage earners; the increasing power of multinational corporations; changing international alliances; and overall effects of globalization.

Bureaucratization continuing apace, and impersonalization accelerating with increasing density of population. The impact of devolution, however, has resulted in the federal government passing on responsibilities for services to state and local governments without funding to adequately respond to changing needs.

Transfer of functions among voluntary groups, government, and private enterprise. While Warren (1978) wrote at a time of transfer of previous family and community voluntary functions to government and for-profit enterprises, the current context is the federal government's divesting service functions and implementing and encouraging privatization and for-profit services in many arenas. States likewise are seeking to outsource or privatize a range of services and programs that have for decades been considered basic public services—for example, foster care, community mental health services, and in at least one state, child abuse investigation.

Urban decay and suburbanization continuing unabated. Central business districts of cities large and small have greatly deteriorated (Halpern, 1995; Wilson, 1987) and have been replaced by shopping malls in ever-widening suburban rings, as closer rings of early suburbs become new low-income communities. The distance between the workplace and home increases, particularly for low-income workers, and racial and economic segregation in housing is increasingly prevalent.

Changing values: Our current period is a time of disturbing value flux in areas related to community practice. Whereas Warren (1978) earlier discussed issues of race and class and expressed concern regarding the decline of the sense of community, our current period reveals continuing racism, despite the gains of the civil rights movement, and the exacerbation of class differences (Halpern, 1995; Wilson, 1987). A growing literature (Bellah, Madsen, Sullivan, Swidler, & Tipton, 1996; Etzioni, 1996; Putnam, 2000) describes a much more serious decline of sense of community and the common good. The current period also seems to be a time of value flux. Some progress has been achieved for women and minorities through legal and social changes, but there is much left to accomplish. Current values issues include rampant global capitalism (Fisher & Karger, 1997), increasingly polar political ideologies, further decline of sense of community, privatization, acquiescence to the dismantling of the social policy safety net, and insufficient political will to strive for the common good.

Also undergoing substantial change are the "major functions" of communities that Warren (1978) identified in the 1960s: (a) production, distribution, consumption; (b) socialization; (c) social control; (d) social participation; and (e) mutual support (p. 9).

Community Functions and Changes—Early 21st Century

Production: Manufacturing moving offshore; distribution much more rapid; America, now a nation of consumers rather than producers, must rely on other nations for basic production.

Socialization: Increasingly a function of schools and media, not the family; an upsurge of "popular culture"; considerable concern about education for citizenship and lack of participation in civil society; broad-scale change in family structure.

Social control: More stringent, with a high proportion of minority males in prison; the United States has the largest number of incarcerated people in any Western democracy; efforts to privatize prisons; class and race divergence in convictions and sentencing; and increases in major fraud, theft, and scandal in major corporate entities.

Social participation: Very low, according to Putnam and Feldstein (2003), Putnam (2000), and Chaskin (2001); U.S. voting rate lowest of any Western democracy; efforts to reemphasize associational connections and community supports undertaken, but to date insufficient. Low participation remains a serious social problem (Chaskin, 2001; Coleman, 1988; Kretzmann & McKnight, 1993; Putnam & Feldstein, 2003; Rubin, 2000).

Mutual support: Although much desired, traditional support from extended family is increasingly compromised by mobility; middle and upper classes purchase "support"; lower-income families expected to provide support but often have few resources to exchange.

Major context changes: Reality of multicultural society, with the United States soon to be a minority-majority nation composed primarily of combined groups of minorities of color; necessity of expanding human rights and civil rights for minorities of color and for women; and finding workable responses to globalization, privatizing, and dismantling of the social safety net.

Worldwide pandemics and famine: HIV/AIDS and risks of quick spread of diseases (SARS) without effective treatments through pervasive travel and migration, and famine in many parts of the developing world.

More political and economic refugees: Numbers larger than at any other time in history due to famine, war, the continued existence of slavery, and increased trafficking in women and children.

Crises of global economy: World Bank and World Trade Organization; expansion of terrorism to the United States and numerous other nations, and increase of "democratic" states without basic freedoms and rights.

Clearly, contemporary society in North America (and throughout the world) is experiencing another major shift to a massive global economy, with increasing privatization, shifting national alliances, and cyber-communication. Communities now must grapple with larger-scale and much more rapid change in the Western postindustrial societies and in the industrializing economies of the Global South.

Recognizing that wisdom often comes with hindsight, Hegel (1807/1971) claimed that "the owl of Minerva flies only at sunset." However, given the seriousness of current challenges at community, state, national, and international levels, we must make every effort to have our knowledge, wisdom, practice, and research "fly" with expanded vision during the present time to see where we are and understand where we are going. There is too much at stake to do otherwise.

Current Situation and Community Practice

Community practice in social work has entered its second century, and although it flourishes in many aspects and many places throughout the world, there are significant and difficult challenges ahead. The shifting geopolitical context presents national and international challenges for the further development of democracy around the world, especially where democratic procedures such as voting are implemented but without the liberty to freely choose or to participate in civil society (Zakaria, 2003). In the long-established Western democracies, particularly the United States, there are major challenges of reduced participation in democratic processes and risks of dangerous identification of national interests with multinational corporate interests. In both these areas, then, the possibilities of either the advance or diminution of true democracy are real. In addition, many countries—and most explicitly the United States—are multicultural nations, but citizens have not yet learned how to appreciate, negotiate, and work together toward societal improvement and the common good. Traditional societies and old democracies alike are challenged by pressures to ensure full human rights for women and girls. Human rights worldwide are of increasing concern as we learn more about limitations and infringements. The United Nations *Universal Declaration of Human Rights* offers direction, but within and across nations, peaceful means of expanding human rights are not in practice.

Globalization poses challenges not only to economic systems but also to the very existence of the world's poorest and most vulnerable citizens. People perish for lack of food and water, and infrastructure is often insufficient or even nonexistent in postindustrial and developing states alike. We witness the lack of social justice and the lack of economic opportunity every day—in our own communities and across the globe through multimedia communications. These are major social problems requiring governmental policy changes, stronger international compacts, and intensive social and economic development through public and nonprofit auspices. People from multiple disciplines are needed to work on these issues; however, these escalating needs also call for more and better prepared community practitioners skilled to work at home and abroad.

Preparation for Community Practice: Increasing Needs and New Opportunities

Locally and globally, there is increasing need for community practitioners who can facilitate and assist community leaders and organizations in strengthening community bonds, developing resources, and dealing with governmental structures to improve the quality of life for their residents in ways that enhance inclusion and social justice and decrease the barriers of exclusion, racism, and classism. Workers in other fields have recognized the need for community-focused interventions and have increased their efforts; social workers need to continue and expand involvement in this important push to strengthen communities, build civil society, and increase democracy from local to national levels.

Direct Practice and Community Practice: Infusion and Expansion

The practice community increasingly recognizes the need for community-based practice and social workers who can meet that need (Adams & Nelson, 1995; Johnson, 2004). Several national organizations and numerous authors (Adams & Nelson, 1995; Delgado, 2000; Fisher & Karger, 1997; Lee, 2001; Weil, 2000) have recently reassessed that impact locally and nationally and have determined that for direct social work practice, they need a community-based approach (Johnson, 2004). Family Services America (FSA) is one such organization; it has expressed strong concern and has sought to develop training for its staff in community-focused work. FSA also seeks to encourage schools of social work to increase the community focus in their direct/micro and mezzo level practice courses. Newer practices in services for children and families and for the aged increasingly use community-based service models. Across the nation, much of the rhetoric about reform in the mental health system calls for a greatly expanded focus on community services. In neighborhoods and communities, Community Development

Corporations (CDCs), faith-based service programs, and comprehensive community initiatives are all grounded in community practice.

Some schools are responding to this concern expressed from the field and are increasing their curriculum focus on community-based practice. The rapidly expanding focus on strengths-based and resiliency perspectives and empowerment perspectives directly calls for a community-oriented basis of practice that puts the social environment and change within it on a par with direct work with individuals, families, and groups. Increasing the understanding of economics and the political system is also necessary to engage with global impacts on local communities (Fisher & Karger, 2000; Prigoff, 2001; Reisch, 1997). The 1999–2000 Council on Social Work Education (CSWE) Summary Report on MSW Programs documents that a total of 21 MSW programs have as their single advanced-practice specialization either an advanced generalist curriculum or a variation on that focus. Fifteen of the programs specify that their advanced curriculum is "advanced generalist practice," while four other programs offer a combination of direct and macro practice—sometimes with offerings in two or more fields of practice. Two programs specifically note that their advanced curriculum focuses on family and community (CSWE, 2000).

Tulane University's School of Social Work has recently presented an evolving model of community-based practice dealing with family and community issues in low-income neighborhoods in New Orleans; Georgia State University focuses on intervention with a community focus; the School of Social Work at Washington University, St. Louis, provides a specialization in building community capacity, and Monmouth University's social work program provides specializations in community and international work. Paul Adams and Kristy Nelson urge expanded family- and community-based practice in their 1995 book, *Reinventing Human Services: Community- and Family-Centered Practice,* and provide ample illustration of how this newly revived form of practice can contribute to improving the lives of families and increasing the strengths of communities they inhabit.

One approach to this considerable task seeks to integrate the structural perspective as articulated by Wood and Middleman (1989) and Withorn (1984) with the empowerment perspective originated by Barbara Solomon (1985, 1986), one that has been elaborated by many authors—perhaps most fully by Judith Lee (2001) in her book, *The Empowerment Approach to Social Work Practice.* Solomon's (1985) initial work, *Black Empowerment,* emerged from her work with the African American community in Los Angeles and called for practice strategies to assist people with any internalized barriers and to bring the full range of macro strategies to bear on the external barriers they face—to address issues of oppression and marginalization, to build a stronger community, and to foster full participation in society. Empowerment practice as articulated by Lee provides a number of examples of empowering strategies that connect individuals to groups and to community efforts, all with a focus on expanding connections and sense of community in marginalized or low-wealth communities.

Structurally focused social work practice as articulated by Withorn (1984) and Wood and Middleman (1989) focuses on the issues of work grounded in social justice and on the need for changes in organizations, structures, and environments to promote thriving families and communities. Wood and Middleman divide social work into four quadrants, the first being direct work with clients; the second, work with clients and others like themselves for their own benefit; the third, work with others on behalf of classes of clients; and the fourth, work with others on behalf of clients. In each of these areas, the authors hold, practitioners should engage with structural change and focus on increasing justice and fairness. Structural approaches are the best defense against blaming clients and the most useful for making positive changes in people's lives and accomplishing structural change at both small and large scales. These two approaches are further amplified by the strategies of the strengths perspective (Saleebey, 1997) and perspectives on risk and resiliency, which can target specific means of increasing resiliency in the face of serious problems (Fraser, 1997).

At the request of the editors of *The Handbook of Social Work Direct Practice* (Allen-Meares & Garvin, 2000), I sought to design a structural/empowerment model that posits a holistic view of social work and challenges those focused on direct and macro practice alike to gain the needed skills to move across arenas of practice to see that people "get what they need" rather than a professionally pre-ferred practice intervention (Weil, 2000). All social workers need skills and abilities to move across several levels and to make needed connections for macro app-roaches or for direct interpersonal assistance. Empowerment practice strategies and a structural approach that encompasses issues of power, politics, and change from individual to policy levels can assist students not only in understanding these crit-ical connections but also in working effectively with people at multiple levels guided by values of social justice.

Fisher and Karger (2000) recommend establishing an integrated social work practice that focuses education on macro social work analysis and practice as the "base of social work practice" on which different levels of intervention can be built. As they see it, "an inclusive and egalitarian public good are principles by which social work [and social work education] can be organized" (Fisher & Karger, 2000, p. 20). Fisher and Karger argue that social work practice at all levels can (and must) be linked to the macro context and hold that when this is done, the boundaries that have been placed between methods of practice become permeable (Fisher & Karger, 2000). Reisch (1997) and Figueira-McDonough (2001) also urge education that focuses on the political nature and context of social work and includes social change theory and ideology. Figueira-McDonough sees work on strengthening civil society as a central means of reconstructing democracy.

In considering the need for direct practice social workers to be knowledgeable and skilled in community-based practice and community work skills, Alice Johnson (1998) conducted an extensive literature search and identified six characteristics of community-based service delivery that can assist in this holistic approach. The liter-ature indicates that community-based practice is: (a) neighborhood based and family focused, (b) oriented to strengths and empowerment, (c) culturally sensitive with competencies in multicultural practice, (d) carried out through comprehensive services, (e) designed to promote access to integrated services and supports, and (f) grounded in teamwork and leadership skills (p. 56). These characteristics provide guidance for curriculum development in community-based practice for both bachelor's and master's degree programs for social workers. Johnson documented courses used to integrate these skills and found various foci, including multiculturalism, empowerment, service delivery, service continua, feminism, and environmentalism. In efforts to ensure that direct practice-oriented students engage intellectually with community practice material, these courses often employed emphases on experiential work in the classroom, social investigation in the community, and group projects as major class experiences. Those of us who specialize in community practice should work with colleagues toward grounding direct practice in evolving community contexts.

Current Macro and Community Practice Education: Challenges and Themes

Currently, the CSWE requires schools of social work to provide a first-year generalist curriculum that places equal emphasis on macro and micro practice. Although most MSW programs offer a first-year practice course in macro practice or social work with organizations and communities, generalist macro content may not be adequately covered in field placements, perhaps because the majority of field instructors are clinically trained (Gamble, Shaffer, & Weil, 1994). Generally, there is need for increased macro content and experiences in first-year field placements and in foundation practice and theory courses.

Macro faculty face considerable challenges to put together a 1-year advanced curriculum that can fully prepare students for the current realities of community and management practice. Most small- and medium-size MSW programs that have macro concentrations are likely to mix macro intervention methods in one concentration, combining management and community practice, for example, or policy, planning, and administration. Programs differentially combine planning, organizing, development, management/administration, and policy. Although some faculty might prefer to sponsor separate specialized tracks in policy practice, planning, community organizing and development, management and administration, or program evaluation and community research, the reality of faculty and fiscal resources dictates that most schools will provide some combination of these methods.

Macro practice faculty frequently discuss the insufficiency of a 1-year advanced curriculum to fully prepare MSW students for macro practice, and given the increasingly complex realities of practice, schools need to consider options to develop and provide advanced certificates (concurrent with or following the MSW program) in, for example, nonprofit management; social and economic development; international development and social change; advocacy, lobbying, and policy practice; or other community practice areas that present special needs in local areas. Faculty also need to consider means to expand continuing education offerings to provide both management and community practice skills post-MSW for direct practice graduates who realize belatedly that a broader range of skills is needed in their work in the community, nonprofit, or public sector.

With regard to current approaches to macro practice curricula, some core models are most typically offered, and they show considerable variation in the combinations adopted by MSW programs. As McNutt reported in a 1995 research report on macro education in graduate social work programs, 70% of MSW programs offer an advanced specialization in combined macro practice methods—such as community organization, planning, and administration; community organization and social administration; or policy practice, community organization, and administration. Furthermore, he notes, most of the macro curricula are 1-year concentrations (in keeping with CSWE requirements for a generalist micro/macro focus in the first year of MSW work), and the average number of advanced specialization courses offered is nearly 8 (with a standard deviation of 6.29). The number of faculty teaching advanced specialized macro courses per MSW program (that offered macro specializations) was 5 (standard deviation of 2.67).

The CSWE tracks the advanced concentrations offered by all MSW programs. Their *Summary Information on Master of Social Work Programs, 1999–2000* (CSWE, 2000) provides the most recent list of offerings through individual descriptions of each program. To obtain a useful picture of the range of macro concentrations, I compiled the following charts to illustrate the range and types. Table 1.2 illustrates the range of macro curricula offerings focusing on how many schools provide from one to four macro methods in their advanced concentrations. The chart also includes programs that offer "unspecified" macro practice concentrations (7) and programs that combine micro and macro practice, primarily through advanced generalist concentrations (21). The largest number of programs offer a two-method macro advanced concentration, closely followed by three-method concentrations, with somewhat fewer programs offering either a four-method concentration or one macro method advanced specialization. Given the brief profile of curriculum information that each MSW program provides for the *Summary,* it is not possible to gauge how much emphasis is placed on each method or how many courses are offered in each within specific programs. Also, because the data were compiled in 2000, doubtless there are already some changes in this configuration; still, it represents a useful format to consider the current status of social work education with regard to macro practice concentration offerings.

The data can also be viewed by how many programs offer specific methods, although in this aggregation, as in Table 1.2, it is not possible to ascertain which combinations of methods each program offers. Table 1.3 presents the frequency with which each macro practice model listed in the CSWE *Summary* is offered in MSW programs.

As noted in Table 1.2, the community concentrations are described as community practice, community organization, community social work, and communities. If social and economic development is combined with this set, the total number of community concentrations offered is 33. Although some differences are likely in programs' definitions and foci between administrative and management practice, there is sufficient similarity to group them together, which yields a total of 54 MSW programs that offer a concentration in administration/management.

The decision to offer a combined-methods macro concentration that focuses both on management and community practice depends most likely on the financial and faculty resources of particular programs. This decision is, however, also quite logical because of the likelihood that MSW graduates will switch from positions with more of an administrative focus to positions with more emphasis on community practice, or vice versa (Jansson, 1987; Starr, Mizrahi, & Gurzinsky, 1999). With the increasing emphasis on "managing out," as documented by Austin (2002), the community practice roles and responsibilities of many managers are greatly expanding, as

Table 1.2   Macro Specializations in Schools of Social Work—2000

Number of Macro Methods Offered in All Schools of Social Work That Offer Advanced Macro Specializations

74 MSW Programs Offer at Least One Macro Practice Advanced Specialization

21 MSW Programs Offer Advanced Generalist or Another Combination of Micro With Macro Practice

Direct Practice Combined With Macropractice	Single Macro Method Offered	Two Macro Methods Offered	Three Macro Methods Offered	Four Macro Methods Offered	Macro Practice Unspecified
N = 21	N = 18	N = 28	N = 15	N = 5	N = 7
Advanced Generalist, 15 Programs	Administration, 10 Programs	Community, 17 Programs • community practice, 5 • communities or community social work, 4 • community development, 3 • community organization, 4 • community,1	Planning, 11 Programs	Community, 5 Programs • community organization, 4 • community development, 1	Macro Practice—Unspecified, 5 Programs
Other Combinations of Direct and Macropractice, 3 Programs	Community, 5 Programs • community social work, 3 • community partnerships, 1 • community development, 1	Administration, 15 Programs	Administration, 11 Programs	Administration, 4 Programs	Indirect Practice—Methods Unspecified, 2 Programs
Family & Community, 2 Programs	Social & Economic Development, 1 Program	Policy, 3 Programs	Policy, 7 Programs	Policy, 5 Programs	
Specialized Field of Practice, plus electives in Policy, Planning, & Administration, 1 Program	Political Social Work, 1 Program	Management, 7 Programs	Community or Community Organization, 5 Programs	Planning, 4 Programs	
	Management, 1 Program	Planning, 7 Programs; Organizations, 3 Programs; Program Development, 1 Program; Supervision, 1 Program; International, 1 Program; Social Action, 1 Program; Program Evaluation, 1 Program	Management, 5 Programs; Program Development, 2 Programs; Research, 2 Programs; Community Mental Health, 1 Program	Management, 1 Program; Evaluation, 1 Program	

Source: Data compiled from CSWE *Summary Information on MSW Programs, 1999-2000.*

Table 1.3   Advanced Concentration Macro Methods Offered by MSW Programs

Administration	40
Community practice	32
Planning	22
Policy	15
Management	14
Organizations	3
Program development	3
Program evaluation	2
Research	2
Community mental health	1
International	1
Political	1
Social action	1
Social and economic development	1
Supervision	1

are responsibilities and involvement in coalitions or other combined service operations. In addition, community practitioners also often develop programs, start and manage nonprofits, and are engaged in a range of financial, management, and planning functions, so it is useful to master essential management skills.

It has been argued elsewhere recently that it might be to social work's advantage to limit MSW macro concentrations to a focus on management and administration in order to meet the need for administrators with social work training and to produce enough management graduates to maintain a strong social work presence (Patti, 2000). I would argue, in contrast, that it is important for macro graduates to have skills in community and management practice as well as in planning and policy practice. It would seem that the means to secure more macro professionals for both management and community practice is first to increase the macro content that all MSWs receive—because their advancement into supervision, program management, community outreach, planning, and coalitions, as well as full-time community or administrative practice, increases following several years of post-MSW work. The increasing numbers of BSW graduates only makes this MSW transition more probable.

Second, in relation to the issues just cited and to the needs of the field, it would be quite logical for schools and departments of social work to actively recruit and admit more students with macro practice interests along with students who have an established interest in community-based, family-centered services. The nature and context of these services is rapidly changing, and we need to ensure we are not left behind. Public and nonprofit agencies need planners, program developers, and skilled evaluators. The shifting nature of public and private partnerships requires staff who can handle contracts, outreach, and marketing, as well as organize communities and services and establish new nonprofits. Devolution has promoted rapid changes in the provision of community-based services to families and children, to people with mental health issues, and to older people. Public social service agencies are outsourcing not only prevention programs and case management but also foster care and other child welfare functions; as such services are contracted out, the need for advocacy and organizing for these and other at-risk populations is likely to increase. The need for competent macro practitioners to handle both the community and management aspects of community-based services, as well as service development, advocacy, and coalitions, will increase.

Educational Responses and Challenges

The changing context indicates that macro concentrations should offer more opportunity for advanced specialization in economic and social development, with additional emphasis on issues of sustainability and global change. The need continues for work in organizing as well as development of macro methods to support and strengthen civil society. Increased focus is greatly needed on recruitment and retention of students of color and students with low incomes whose goal is to work toward investment in local communities and in multicultural work. Planning can bridge direct and macro practice as a method in itself and as a necessary adjunct to organizing, program development, and management. Policy practice with increasing attention to human rights, globalization, economics, and strategies to combat persistent poverty should be required coursework for all macro students.

I would argue that the best educational response to pressing social issues is combined method macro practice concentrations that offer sufficient electives to specialize in community practice, management, or social and economic development with options to tailor macro education to the regional needs and career development goals of students.

Larger MSW programs will be able to continue offering multiple tracks in macro practice as well as advanced specializations and electives in related areas. The most critical aspect seems to be the challenge to increase the numbers of macro-oriented students recruited by schools of social work and to provide challenging and cutting-edge content to prepare students for the realities of current practice and emerging societal changes.

In addition, it is particularly important to recruit more students of color into macro practice. The need to have students with primary or secondary connections to communities of color and communities of low wealth increases along with the poverty rates, the disengagement of the governmental sector from the poor, and the quickly arriving demographic shift of the United States to a combined minority-majority population (U.S. Bureau of the Census, 2000). Students of all backgrounds are needed for community practice, yet it is increasingly important for members of disenfranchised communities to see people with whom they identify as organizers, planners, managers, and policymakers.

Clearly, a wide variety of courses are appropriate for macro and community practice students, and curricula should provide a good fit with community needs with an eye toward the future for emerging trends. In this period of great change, it is vitally important to provide students with opportunities to master skills that prepare them for expanded and flexible roles and for dealing with emerging social issues that should be addressed through community practice strategies. The list in Table 1.4 provides one view of the range of skills relevant to community practice in the 21st century.

Table 1.4   Skills for Current Community Practice

Practice Skills

policy practice
lobbying
advocacy
program design, implementation,
    and management
financial management
management
organizing
nonprofit development
social marketing
fundraising
facilitation
citizen participation
leadership
volunteer management
proposal development
contract management
human resources management
grassroots planning
sectorial planning
cross-sector planning
campaigns
public education
contest skills
confrontation tactics
negotiating
mediation
position-taking and -writing
group and intergroup development
economic and social development
social planning
political and social action

Research Skills

program evaluation
participatory research
use of administrative data
GIS
MIS
community assessments
community mapping and asset mapping
neighborhood analysis
policy and poverty research
cost benefit/cost-effectiveness analyses
community analysis

empowerment research
action research
statistics
use of social indicators

Specialized Content

social and economic development
community practice methods and models
political economy
economics and labor market
leadership models
leadership development
planning
sustainable development
coalition development
network development
system reform
globalization
transnational issues
asset development
microenterprise
rural and regional contexts
international development

Theory and Knowledge

community theory
organizational behavior
    and interorganizational theory
development theory
social change theory, political theory,
    and economic theory
organizing theory
planning theory
alternative development theory
theory of change
theories of planned change
diffusion of innovation theory
social development theory
social movement theory
ecological theory
systems theory
critical theory
feminist theory
anti-racist theory
ethics and emerging legal issues for practice
multicultural theory

Community practice is greatly needed to help communities, organizations, and nations deal with massive change and serious social issues including globalization, increased poverty, multiculturalism, feminist issues, and human rights concerns. Effective strategies to promote human flourishing in communities are needed to address these issues. In addition, the United States and a number of other nations are experiencing a great need to develop human investment programs that can truly move people out of poverty rather than simply off welfare rolls. This *Handbook* is designed to prepare students and practitioners to be proactive in dealing with the local and regional impact of the massive social changes we now face.

This *Handbook* is based on the principle that knowledge is a major form of power—for community members and for students and practitioners as well. The knowledge base for community practice provides a range of theories, methods, strategies, and skills to engage in effective community practice in the 21st century. Community practice is one of the instruments most needed for the expansion of civil society here and worldwide (Figueira-McDonough, 2001). All community practice approaches require multiple skills, particularly those of facilitation and leadership. The pursuit of democracy, civic participation, economic justice, and sustainable development will never be easy—but we must persevere. The future well-being of local communities and the global community depends on it.

References

Adams, P., & Nelson, K. (1995). *Reinventing human services: Community and family centered practice.* New York: Aldine de Gruyter.

Addams, J. (1902). *Democracy and social ethics.* New York: Macmillan.

Allen-Meares, P., & Garvin, C. (2000). *Handbook of social work direct practice.* Thousand Oaks, CA: Sage.

Austin, M. J. (2002). Managing out: The community practice dimensions of effective agency management. *Journal of Community Practice, 10*(4), 33–48.

Bellah, R., Madsen, R., Sullivan, W. M., Swidler, A., & Tipton, S. M. (1996). *Habits of the heart: Individualism and commitment in American life* (Rev. ed.). Berkeley: University of California Press.

Bethel New Life. (n.d.). *Our programs.* Retrieved July 15, 2003, from http://www.bethelnewlife.org/pgms.html

Betten, N., & Austin, M. J. (1990). *The roots of community organization, 1917–1939.* Philadelphia: Temple University Press.

Brilliant, E. L. (1997). Nonprofit organizations, social policy, and public welfare. In M. Reisch & Eileen Gambrill (Eds.), *Social work in the 21st century* (pp. 68–79). Thousand Oaks, CA: Pine Forge Press.

Brisson, D. S. (2003). *Neighborhood, comprehensive community initiatives, and social capital: How they work together for low-income households.* Unpublished paper, University of North Carolina, Chapel Hill, School of Social Work.

Carson, M. (1990). *Settlement folk: Social thought and the American settlement movement, 1885-1930.* Chicago: University of Chicago Press.

Chaskin, R. J. (2001). Building community capacity: A definitional framework and case studies from a comprehensive community initiative. *Urban Affairs Review 36*(3), 291–323.

Coleman, J. S. (1988). Social capital in the creation of human capital. *American Journal of Sociology, 94* (Supplement), S95-S120.

Council on Social Work Education. (2000). *Summary information on master of social work programs.* Alexandria, VA: Author.

Deegan, M. J. (1988). *Jane Addams and the men of the Chicago School, 1892–1918.* New Brunswick, NJ: Transaction Books.

Delgado, M. (2000). *Community social work in practice in an urban context.* New York: Oxford University Press.

Drake, R. F. (2001). *The principles of social policy.* New York: Palgrave.

DuBois, W. E. B. (1896). *The Philadelphia Negro: A social study.* New York: B. Blom.

DuBois, W. E. B. (1935). *Black reconstruction.* New York: Harcourt Brace.

Durkheim, E. (1964). *The rules of sociological method.* New York: Free Press. (Original work published 1895)

Durkheim, E. (1984). *The division of labour in society.* London: Macmillan. (Original work published 1893)

Edwards, L. M. (1995). Lillian Wald. In R. L. Edwards (Ed.), *Encyclopedia of social work* (19th ed., p. 2615). Washington DC: NASW Press.

Ellis, D. E. (1965). The origins of Frendianism in America. Unpublished master's thesis, University of North Carolina, Chapel Hill.

Etzioni, A. (1996). The responsive community: A communitarian perspective. *American Sociologial Review, 61*(1), 1–11.

Fellin, P. (2001). *The community and the social worker* (3rd ed.). Itasca, IL: F. E. Peacock.

Figueira-McDonough, J. (2001). *Community analysis and praxis: Toward a grounded civil society.* Philadelphia: Brunner-Routledge/Taylor & Francis.

Fisher, R. (2001). Political economy and public life: The context for community organizing. In J. Rothman, J. L. Erlich, & J. E. Tropman (Eds.), *Strategies of community intervention* (6th ed., pp. 100–117). Itasca, IL: F. E. Peacock.

Fisher, R., & Karger, H. (1997). *Social work and community in a private world: Getting out in public.* New York: Longman.

Fisher, R., & Karger, H. J. (2000). The context of social work practice. In P. Allen-Meares & C. Garvin (Eds.), *The handbook of social work direct practice* (pp. 5–22). Thousand Oaks, CA: Sage.

Flexner, A. (1915). *Is social work a profession? Proceedings of the National Conference of Charities and Correction.* Chicago: University of Chicago Press.

Fraser, M. W. (Ed.). (1997). *Risk and resilience in childhood: An ecological perspective.* Washington, DC: NASW Press.

Friedmann, J. (1992). *Empowerment: The politics of alternative development.* Cambridge, MA: Blackwell.

Gamble, D. N., Castelloe, P., & Varma, S. (2003). Women have their say: The meaning of sustainable development. *The Journal of Social Work Research and Evaluation, 4*(1), 121–135.

Gamble, D. N., Shaffer, G. L., & Weil, M. O. (1994). Assessing the integrity of community organization and administration content in field practice. *Journal of Community Practice 1*(3), 73–92.

Gil, D. G. (1988). *Confronting injustice and oppression: Concepts and strategies for social workers.* New York: Columbia University Press.

Gittell, R. J., & Vidal, A. (1998). *Community organizing: Building social capital as a development strategy.* Thousand Oaks, CA: Sage.

Halpern, R. (1995). *Rebuilding the inner city: A history of neighborhood initiatives to address poverty in the United States.* New York: Columbia University Press.

Hegel, G. W. F. (1971). *Hegel's philosophy of mind* [Die Philosophie des Geistes]. Oxford, UK: Oxford University Press. (Original work published 1807)

Hull-House maps and papers, by residents of Hull-House, a social settlement, a presentation of nationalities and wages in a congested district of Chicago, together with comments and essays on problems growing out of the social conditions. (1895). New York: Crowell.

Hunter, F. G. (1953). *Community power structure: A study of decision makers.* Chapel Hill: University of North Carolina Press.

Jansson, B. S. (1987). From sibling rivalry to pooled knowledge and shared curriculum: Relations among community organization, administration, planning, and policy. *Administration in Social Work, 11*(2), 5–18.

Johnson, A. K. (1998). The revitalization of community practice: Characteristics, competencies, and curricula for community-based services. *Journal of Community Practice, 5*(3), 37–62.

Johnson, A. K. (2004). Social work is standing on the legacy of Jane Addams, but we're sitting on the sidelines. *Social Work, 49* (2), 319–322.

Kretzmann, J. P., & McKnight, J. L. (1993). *Building communities from the inside out.* Evanston, IL: Northwestern University, Center for Urban Affairs.

Lee, J. (2001). *The empowerment approach to social work practice* (2nd ed.). New York: Columbia University Press.

Logan, J. R., & Swanstrom, T. (1990). Urban restructuring: A critical view. In J. R. Logan & T. Swanstrom (Eds.), *Beyond the city limits: Urban policy and economic restructuring in comparative perspective* (pp. 37–52). Philadelphia: Temple University Press.

Longres, J. F. (1997). The impact and implications of multiculturalism. In M. Reisch & Eileen Gambrill (Eds.), *Social work in the 21st century* (pp. 39–47). Thousand Oaks, CA: Pine Forge Press.

Lubove, R. (1969). *The professional altruist: The emergence of social work as a career (1880–1930).* New York: Atheneum.

Marcuse, H. (1941). *Reason and revolution.* New York: Humanities Press.

Mayadas, N. S., & Elliott, D. (1997). Lessons from international social work policies and practices. In M. Reisch & Eileen Gambrill (Eds.), *Social work in the 21st century* (pp. 175–185). Thousand Oaks, CA: Pine Forge Press.

Mayadas, N. S., Watts, T., & Elliott, D. (1997). *International handbook on social work theory and practice.* Westport, CT: Greenwood Press.

McKnight, J. L. (1997, March/April). A 21st-century map for healthy communities and families. *Families in Society,* 117–127.

McNutt, J. G. (1995). The macro practice curriculum in graduate social work education: Results of a national study. *Administration in Social Work, 19*(3), 59–74.

Medoff, P., & Sklar, H. (1994). *Streets of hope: The fall and rise of an urban neighborhood.* Boston: South End Press.

Midgley, J. (1997). Social work in international context: Challenges and opportunities for the 21st century. In M. Reisch & Eileen Gambrill (Eds.), *Social work in the 21st century* (pp. 59–67). Thousand Oaks, CA: Pine Forge Press.

Midgley, J., & Sherraden, M. (2000). The social development perspective in social policy. In J. Midgley, M. B. Tracy, & M. Livermore (Eds.), *The handbook of social policy* (pp. 435–446). Thousand Oaks, CA: Sage.

Mondros, J. B., & Wilson, S. M. (1994). *Organizing for power and empowerment.* New York: Columbia University Press.

Netting, F. E., Kettner, P. M., & McMurty, S. L. (2004). *Social work macro practice* (3rd ed.). Boston: Pearson.

Park, R. E. (1936). Human ecology. *American Journal of Sociology, 62*(1), 1–15.

Park, R., Burgess, E. W., & McKenzie, R. D. (Eds.). (1925). *The city*. Chicago: University of Chicago Press.

Parsons, T. (1951). *The social system*. New York: Free Press.

Patti, R. J. (2000). *The handbook of social welfare management*. Thousand Oaks, CA: Sage.

Philpott, T. L. (1991). *The slum and the ghetto*. Belmont, CA: Wadsworth.

Prigoff, A. (2001). *Economics for social workers: Social outcomes of economic globalization with strategies for community action*. Belmont, CA: Brooks/Cole.

Putnam, R. (2000). *Bowling alone: The collapse and revival of American community*. New York: Simon & Schuster.

Putnam, R. D., & Feldstein, L. M. (2003). *Better together: Restoring the American community*. New York: Simon & Schuster.

Rawls, J. (1970). *A theory of justice*. Cambridge, MA: Harvard University Press.

Reisch, M. (1997). The political context of social work. In M. Reisch & Eileen Gambrill (Eds.), *Social work in the 21st century* (pp. 80–92). Thousand Oaks, CA: Pine Forge Press.

Richmond, M. E. (1901). Charitable co-operation. In I. C. Barrows (Ed.), *Proceedings of the National Conference on Charities and Correction*. Boston: George H. Ellis.

Rifkin, J. (2000). *The age of access: The new culture of hypercapitalism, where all of life is a paid-for experience*. New York: J. P. Tarcher/Putnam.

Rose, N. (1997). The future economic landscape: Implications for social work practice and education. In M. Reisch & Eileen Gambrill (Eds.), *Social work in the 21st century* (pp. 28–38). Thousand Oaks, CA: Pine Forge Press.

Ross, M. G., with Lappin, B. (1967). *Community organization: Theory, principles, and practice* (2nd ed.). New York: Harper & Row.

Rothman, J., Erlich, J. L., & Teresa, J. G. (1976). *Promoting innovation and change in organizations and communities: A planning manual*. New York: John Wiley.

Rubin, H. (2000). *Renewing hope within neighborhoods of despair: The community-based development model*. Albany: SUNY Press.

Saleebey, D. (Ed.). (1997). *The strengths perspective in social work practice* (2nd ed.). New York: Macmillan.

Sarri, R. (1997). International social work at the millennium. In M. Reisch & Eileen Gambrill (Eds.), *Social work in the 21st century* (pp. 387–395). Thousand Oaks, CA: Pine Forge Press.

Scott, J. (1995). *Sociological theory: Contemporary debates*. Cheltenham, UK: Edward Elgar.

Sen, A. (1999). *Development as freedom*. New York: Knopf.

Sherraden, M. S., & Ninacs, W. A. (Eds.). (1998). *Community economic development and social work*. New York: Haworth.

Shragge, E. (2003). *Activism and social change: Lessons for community and local organizing*. Peterborough, Ontario, Canada: Broadview.

Solomon, B. B. (1985). Community social work practice in oppressed minority communities. In S. H. Taylor & R. W. Roberts (Eds.), *Theory and practice of community social work* (pp. 217–257). New York: Columbia University Press.

Solomon, B. B. (1986). *Black empowerment: Social work in oppressed communities*. New York: Columbia University Press.

Starr, R., Mizrahi, T., & Gurzinsky, E. (1999). Where have all the organizers gone? The career paths of community organizing social work alumni. *Journal of Community Practice* 6(3), 23–48.

Stern, M. J. (1997). Poverty and postmodernity. In M. Reisch & Eileen Gambrill (Eds.), *Social work in the 21st century* (pp. 48–58). Thousand Oaks, CA: Pine Forge Press.

Tönnies, F. (1955). *Community and association*. London: Routledge & Kegan Paul. (Original work published 1889)

Towle, C. (1965). *Common human needs.* Washington, DC: NASW Press.

United Nations Development Programme [UNDP]. (1999). New York: Oxford University Press.

U.S. Bureau of the Census. (2000). *Population projections of the total resident population by 5-year age groups, race, and Hispanic origin with special age categories: Middle series, 2050–2070.* Washington, DC: Department of Commerce.

Warren, R. J. (1978). *The community in America* (3rd ed.). Chicago: Rand McNally.

Warren, R. L., & Lyon, L. (1988). *New perspectives on the American community.* Chicago: Dorsey.

Weber, M. (1930). *The Protestant ethic and the spirit of capitalism.* London: George, Allen and Unwin. (Original work published 1904–1905).

Weil, M. (1994). Editor's introduction. *Journal of Community Practice, 1*(1), xxi-xxxiii.

Weil, M. (2000). Social work in the social environment: Integrated practice—an empowerment/structural approach. In P. Allen-Meares & C. Garvin (Eds.), *The handbook of social work direct practice* (pp. 373–410). Thousand Oaks, CA: Sage.

Wilson, W. J. (1987). *The truly disadvantaged: The inner city, the underclass, and public policy.* Chicago: University of Chicago Press.

Withorn, A. (1984). *Serving the people: Social services and social change.* New York: Columbia University Press.

Wood, G. G., & Middleman, R. R. (1989). *The structural approach to direct practice in social work.* New York: Columbia University Press.

World Bank. (1991). *World development report 1990: Poverty.* New York: Oxford University Press.

Zakaria, F. (2003). *The future of freedom: Illiberal democracy at home and abroad.* New York: W. W. Norton.

CHAPTER 2

History, Context, and Emerging Issues for Community Practice

Robert Fisher

History provides a collective memory, historical shoulders to stand on, and roots for contemporary practice. Historical knowledge also puts practice into comparative perspective, as the similarities and differences of efforts in prior eras force comparison with contemporary practice. We dismiss the past—for its provincialism, naïveté, or worse—at our own peril. It isn't simply, as Santayana warned, that those who fail to heed the past are condemned to repeat it. There is no present without the past. Because we in community organization are overwhelmed by the demands of the present, we think we have little time for history, that reviewing and understanding the past is a luxury. But history matters.

Certainly, issues of human agency—defining the very nature of a community organization, its goals, methods, daily choices—play a critical role in the life of any community organization effort. But the larger historical context heavily influences which conceptualizations and choices are available or encouraged, as well as which goals and strategies seem salient and likely to succeed. The renowned English social historian E. P. Thompson (1971) referred to history as the discipline of context. Because organizing efforts and writings about organizing are always specific to a particular time and place, a history of community organization situates practice in the context of the varied social sites that generated it. To that end, what follows is a framework for understanding the changes over time in the history of community practice. It is obviously not a definitive history. It offers a model for appreciating major historical roots and currents. As the analysis approaches the present, it reveals continuing historical trends as well as emerging critical issues for community practice.

The Model

This chapter contextualizes the study of contemporary community practice in a cyclical model, which proposes that the transformation of community organization practice occurred less as a linear process and more as a periodic shifting back and forth in response to two dominant influences: (a) changes in the national political economy and (b) developments and pressures in the social work profession. In terms of political economy, throughout the history of community practice, there has been a direct and dialectical relationship between the national political economy and local community efforts.[1] In each era since the late 19th century, the national political-economic context—which includes economic power and relations, on the one hand, and the political power to affect or change it, on the other— has given shape to a dominant type of organizing practice. Organizing is always shaped by a myriad of factors, including the work of predecessors, local context, leadership, and resources. Nevertheless, whether it was interorganizational efforts in the charity organization societies in the late 19th century; service delivery, community building, and social action work in settlement houses during the first decades of the 20th century; professional reevaluation and strengthening in the 1920s; social welfare programming and social action efforts in the 1930s; or other trends during other eras, discourse, policies, and programs at the national level substantially determined which types of community practice would develop, survive, attract attention, and succeed (Fisher, 1994).

Local efforts and social movements also played a critical role in affecting national developments. The social reform work of the settlement houses and the significant leadership of settlement workers such as Jane Addams, Lillian Wald, Mary Simkhovitch, and Florence Kelley, to name but a few, had a profound impact on the events and movements of their day. The national political economy of the Progressive Era, as well as the social movements of the day, which shaped that political economy and responded to it, profoundly structured the broader context for and nature of community organization practice. The larger political economy presses itself on community practice in this way: identifying and legitimizing conditions, encouraging endeavors and actions, promoting particular conceptualizations of community organization, and discouraging others.

Community practice is not only affected by events, politics, and movements of the day, but also heavily influenced by being part of the social work profession. Community organization occurs within the norms, boundaries, and processes of overall social work practice. Ties to the social work profession improve the practice of community organization through such professional processes as systematic discussion, debate, analysis, and evaluation. The sophisticated efforts in the history of social work to define and conceptualize community organization demonstrate these virtues. Being situated within the social work profession also constrained community organization, both in regard to demands placed on the subfield to be like the rest of social work and by tensions resulting from being a stepchild of the profession.[2] For example, Jack Rothman recalls that when he was in graduate school in the early 1950s, "the *au courant* view in social work at the time was that you had to work a good eight to ten years in casework or group work before you could possibly go into CO [community organization]" (Rothman, 1999b, p. 221). Of course, the relationship to the social work profession is complex. The point here is that this relationship and changes in this relationship are seminal in the history of social work community practice.

Critically, community practice also occurred outside of social work.[3] In a nutshell, efforts inside social work, historically called *community organization,* expand social work practice to the community realm, whether a geographic community, cultural community, or community of agencies and service providers. Links to the social work profession usually make community organization more institutionalized, formalized, tied to an academic discourse, and agency-based than its counterparts outside of social work. Community practice outside social work, historically called *community organizing,* expands, reconceptualizes, and applies models of union organizing and political activism to the community. Although the latter approaches share a number of aspects with social work community practice, they exist independent of the social work profession and are heavily influenced by shifts in the political economy and social movements. Community organization and community organizing sometimes merge and overlap, as in Mobilization for Youth (MFY) and other efforts in the 1960s or, more recently, in feminist organizing and work in the gay and lesbian communities. Much of the time, however, community workers inside and outside of social work have been aware of but generally ignored each other. In some instances, they have seen themselves in competition and at odds. This chapter, unlike most histories, incorporates both strands of community practice, although the focus is on community organization in social work.[4]

The Gilded Age and Charity Organization Society

The emerging urban-industrial order that developed after the Civil War presented unprecedented social conditions and challenges. In the late 19th century, the United States witnessed a dramatic acceleration of its transition from an agrarian, rural, and traditional society to one that was industrial, urban, heterogeneous, and modern. The Gilded Age, so named by Mark Twain to reflect many Americans' single-minded quest for individual wealth during that time, brought about fierce competition among big businessmen, workers, and farmers to see who would benefit from the transformation to an urban-industrial society. In a nutshell, the laissez-faire and Social Darwinist political economy of the day encouraged only social interventions that were oriented to improving individual behavior and benefiting business. Pro-labor and pro-farmer organizers were unable during this period to win many concessions or force government to intercede on their behalf.

The first Charity Organization Society (COS) in the United States, founded in Buffalo, New York, was added to this mix in 1877. COSs quickly spread across the nation as their leaders sought to develop a new form of social welfare that could bring order, through scientific means, to the disordered state of charitable enterprises at the time. The "scientific approach" of the COS sought to bring business principles of efficiency, management, and consolidation to the administration of charity. The COS idea of scientific philanthropy was consistent with other efforts in the larger society such as civil service reform, which sought to bring order to government employment and counteract corrupt systems. As community practice, COS sought through interorganizational efforts to coordinate existing charity efforts. The goal was to "bring about some order in relationships among numerous agencies and organizations [and to this end COSs] were the forerunners of all modern social work development" (McNeil, 1951, p. 122). But COS practice emphasized more than interagency coordination. The structure of COS services also rested firmly on the self-help ethos of the Gilded Age. It presumed that poverty and other social problems resulted from individual character defects and therefore should be resolved through individual improvement. The "friendly visitor," more a caseworker than community organizer, sought through home visits to help those in need *and* to discriminate between the truly deserving and undeserving poor.

Progressive Era and Social Settlements

Although the 1880s and 1890s was an era absorbed by the business credos of Social Darwinism and laissez-faire capitalism, many saw it as a time of crisis (Bannister, 1979; Hays, 1957; Hofstadter, 1948). Society seemed to be coming apart at its class and ethnic seams (Fisher, 1994; Husock, 1990; Kogut, 1972). Settlement leader Vida Scudder saw the turn-of-the-century city as a "cleavage of classes, cleavage of races, cleavage of faiths: an inextricable confusion" (cited in Shapiro, 1978, p. 215). In response, reformers began to develop a counterideology and social movement which argued that society, not simply the individual, was responsible for social conditions, and that the environment, not simply one's personal characteristics, heavily shaped life experience (Quandt, 1970). Many reformers in the national progressive movement believed in large, centralized initiatives, but the essence of progressivism was a variant of communitarian reform, best epitomized by the social Settlement Movement, which advocated for community-based initiatives and interventions.

The Settlement Movement began on the American side of the Atlantic on the lower East Side of New York City with the founding in 1886 of Neighborhood Guild (later University Settlement) by Stanton Coit (1974; see also Kendall, 2000; Reinders, 1982; Skocpol, 1992). Three years later, Hull-House was established in Chicago, and in 1892, Lillian Wald helped create the Nurses Settlement in New York, which soon became Henry Street Settlement (Wald, 1915, 1934). These were only the most famous settlements. The decade saw a proliferation of social settlements, so that by 1910, there were as many as 400 nationwide. Although they were predominantly initiated by affluent Whites for the benefit of European immigrants, community work and settlements for African Americans also proliferated and contributed to community practice in the Progressive Era (Carlton-LaNey, 2001a, 2001b; Rouse, 1984). Nowhere was the expansion of settlement house community work more evident than in the nation's two premier cities, New York and

Chicago (Kraus, 1980). These cities were the sites of the most important social innovations of the era because they were at the confluence of the massive challenges of the time: industrialization, urbanization, immigration, and the development of finance capitalism (Hays, 1957; Still, 1974; Warner, 1972).

Community organization practice in the settlement houses responded to the obvious limits of COS. "To begin with, charity workers emphasized the individual causes of poverty while settlement workers stressed the social and economic conditions that made people poor. . . . The settlement workers tried desperately to disassociate their movement from charity in the public mind" (Davis, 1967, pp. 18–19). Settlement workers were social reformers and social scientists, not charity workers (Crunden, 1982; Deegan, 1991). Theirs was a form of community organization tied to responding to the excesses of the Gilded Age and the massive needs of the new immigrants. They saw community organization as social reform practice at the community level.

Building on the settlement workers' sense of the interconnectedness between individual problems and social betterment, their practice method included three core elements: (a) an integrated collaborative practice that delivered desperately needed services, intervened at the individual as well as community level, and sought to develop solidarity between settlement workers and neighborhood residents; (b) a sense of the essential importance of community and community building; and (c) a willingness to organize and advocate for social, political, and economic justice (Fabricant & Fisher, 2002b). Mary Simkhovitch said, "The aim of the settlement or neighborhood house is to bring about a new kind of community life" (cited in Kennedy, Farra, et al., 1935). Jane Addams sought to "arouse" a neighborhood's "civic and moral energy" (cited in Holden, 1922, p. 77). At their most progressive, settlement houses fought to improve local health conditions, develop small parks and public recreation, reform municipal politics, upgrade public schools by promoting their extended use after school hours, and establish public nursing and school social worker systems in the public schools. Settlement leaders lobbied for legislation, served on public boards, promoted political candidates, occasionally ran for office themselves, conducted social research, and participated in broad campaigns for tenement house reform, defense of labor unions, and the rights of workers, women, and children. Settlements fought to revitalize the local community by reforming the local political economy and providing social services (Lasch-Quinn, 1993). The larger settlement houses, especially in New York and Chicago, tended to be more involved in social action. Although their daily program of child care, medical care, recreation, and education gave the settlements viability and permanence (Rothman, 1973), it was the combination of collaborative practice, community building, and social action that signified their practice at the time and for later generations.

And the settlements were not alone. Workers and immigrants organized countless similar projects, efforts at community-based self-empowerment (Spain, 2000). Moreover, other contemporary efforts, such as the Community Center Movement to use public schools as social centers in every neighborhood, and the Social Unit Plan, a block-by-block plan for community health, reflect concepts and practice built on the settlement house model (Fisher, 1994; Halpern, 1995; Mattson, 1998;

Melvin, 1987). After World War I, social work professionals would debate whether social work was a cause or function and whether it was about social reform or service provision. But the integrated and pluralistic community organization practiced prior to the 1920s transcended this dualism. In this period, aiding individuals, building community, and changing society were all integral parts of the community organization practice pyramid (Berry, 1999).

The Return to Normalcy, 1918–1929

The political economy of the 1920s dramatically altered the practice of community organization. Settlements and community centers did not decline in numbers as much as they seemed to fade in significance. They persisted in the 1920s, but not as vital institutions. Settlement programs continue today in many cities but struggle to maintain funding (Fabricant & Fisher, 2002b). During the 1920s, an intersection of pressures helped account for changes in the dominant form of community organization practice. Within the newly emerging field of social work, federated funding structures such as community chests (precursors to the United Way) were established throughout the nation (see Brilliant, Chapter 12, this volume). Their fundraising efforts promoted their power in the service community, and they engaged in larger-scale service planning and assumed increasing responsibility for coordinating and vetting services. These new structures, which grew out of the COSs, had a profound impact. However, it was the conservative political economy—the return to pre–Progressive Era politics and the rejection of the reform impulse—that gave these and other developments particular salience and legitimacy.

In the cyclical model, the economy of the 1920s is an archetypal conservative political economy. With the close of World War I, right-wing repression against social activism, exemplified by the Red Scare of 1918, delegitimized prior reform projects and victories. The Red Scare was followed by a so-called "return to normalcy," in which the business ethic of the 1920s replaced the social reform impulse of the Progressive Era. Heightened individualism replaced concerns about social cohesion. A resurfacing of laissez-faire ideology replaced analyses of structural causation. Society drew back from concern with social issues into more individualist and materialist pursuits, including the consumption of new consumer durables such as radios and cars. To increase demand for these new products and stimulate economic growth, businesses began to invest heavily in advertising and to encourage purchasing on credit, which had been taboo up to that point in American history. Right-wing social movements resurfaced as well, such as religious fundamentalism, the Ku Klux Klan, and other nativist organizations (Carter, 1975; Chambers, 1963; Fisher, 1994).[5]

World War I was a watershed for Progressive Era community organization practice. Some, like Jane Addams (who later received the Nobel Prize for Peace) and Lillian Wald, opposed the war, and many Progressives saw antiwar activities as an opportunity to increase social solidarity and complete the Progressive agenda. Instead, the war delivered a traumatic shock to liberal and collective sensibilities.

With the postwar Red Scare and attacks on Progressive reformers and immigrants, key aspects of community practice were forced to retreat. In place of the core settlement elements of collaborative practice, community building, and social action, the 1920s institutionalized a much more restrictive and confined practice. Jane Addams said that social work reflected the "symptoms of this panic and with a kind of protective instinct, carefully avoided any identification with the phraseology of social reform" (quoted in Lundblad, 1995, p. 667). The atmosphere of social work changed in the 1920s (Lubove, 1975). The newly emerging profession of social work thought that it needed to reject the romantic "do-goodism" of the Progressive Era to gain credibility as a profession. Among social workers, there was a new emphasis on being disengaged, that is, being objective experts rather than social reformers (Tobin, 1988). Social work students in the 1920s were said to scoff at the very idea of community service.[6]

This was not, however, entirely true. Social action tended to fade during the 1920s; community building was no longer primary, but community practice did not disappear (Chambers, 1963; Ehrenreich, 1985). In the field, as the COSs had done earlier, efforts such as the newly emerging community chest movement focused on interorganizational coordination and administration, that is, building and managing federations of social service agencies that sought to bring greater order, efficiency, effectiveness, and power to voluntary sector welfare efforts (Bowman, 1929; Trolander, 1975; see also Brilliant, Chapter 12, this volume). By linking charitable efforts, by developing a centralized mechanism for collecting and distributing charitable giving, and by being more attentive to issues of funding and record keeping, social planning efforts such as community chests and welfare councils fit closely with the business-minded, efficiency-seeking, and professional temper of the time (Fabricant & Fisher, 2002a).

Related changes can be seen in the emerging literature on community organization. As the field of social work began to professionalize, so did the subfield of community organization (Lubove, 1975). The writings of Bowman, Hart, Lindeman, McClenahan, Pettit, and Steiner, although not all of a single piece, began to emphasize a more rigorous and exacting approach to the study and practice of community organization (Rothman, 1999b; Schwartz, 1965). The writings of this period, for example, are much more scholarly in tone and approach than the earlier writings of settlement house workers (Rothman, 1999b). Some authors strongly rejected what they saw as the naïve romanticism of community organization in the Progressive Era (Fisher, 1994). These writers recognized that community was an ideal, not an actuality (Schwartz, 1965). But most authors, influenced by the writings of John Dewey and the emerging field of urban sociology, sought a more professional and systematic method to guide community organization practice. The varied works of Steiner and McClenahan (Betten & Austin, 1990), for example, offered a "study-diagnosis-treatment schema" that, according to Schwartz (1965, p. 177), was intended to help workers understand a community's uniqueness as well as how its problems were shared generally with other communities. At the same time, community organization theorists were increasingly focused on the tensions in the relationship between expert and citizen. While committed to the idea of democratic participation, they increasingly searched for an essential place in community organization for the "expert or professional."

Depression, New Deal, and War

The Depression and the vigorous public reaction to it, at both the grassroots level and in Washington, D.C., dramatically altered community organization yet again. When the social reform impulse resurfaced in the 1930s, it was different than in the Progressive Era. The 1930s response to economic disaster and social need was much more centralized and national, not community based. In the 1930s, community organizing surfaced with a strong class- and union-based model of social action. Within social work agencies, too, including settlement houses, the struggles of the period restored social policy advocacy and social action to the community organization equation. However, the focus of social reform and social action was clearly at the national level during this era. Former settlement workers, such as Harry Hopkins, Frances Perkins, Henry Morgenthau, Jr., and Herbert Lehman, were involved in implementing large-scale social policy and welfare programs rather than community-based organizing projects. Helen Hall, the head worker at the Henry Street Settlement in New York, was often invited to Washington, where she testified and acted as adviser on a variety of social issues.

In terms of the larger political economy, the massive problems of poverty and unemployment forced society and social workers to see and confront, once again, the structural dimensions of individual problems. "All around the social workers of Hull-House," commentator Edmund Wilson wrote in 1932, "there today stretches a sea of misery more appalling even than that which discouraged Miss Addams in the nineties" (quoted in Davis & McCree, 1969, p. 177). Environmental factors rather than character deficits regained prominence as the primary explanation for social problems. As social problems and needs worsened in the 1930s, with all the attendant pain and human suffering, the era revived a sense of public life and a need for social change.

Within social work, debates raged. Some argued that the 1920s' emphasis on casework was inappropriate, as it denied the relationship between social context and individual problem. Harry Lurie, director of the Bureau of Jewish Social Research, criticized his fellow social workers for being as responsible for the Depression as the country's industrial and political leaders because social workers had turned away in the 1920s from the social dimensions of problems and had focused instead on issues of professionalism and technique (Trattner, 1999).

> The message was clear: Social workers could best make their contributions by allying themselves with those groups in society working for political, social, and economic change. This, in turn, of course, tended to politicize social workers once again, a sharp contrast to their nonpartisanship of the prior decade. (Trattner, 1999, p. 297)

These social forces prompted the field of community organization within social work to reevaluate its mission, hoping to put community organization on a firmer professional footing and at the same time meet pressing contemporary demands. A report at the 1939 meeting of the National Conference of Social Work, "The Field of Community Organization," delivered by community chest executive Robert Lane, intended to define community organization as a field of social work comparable to casework and group work. Based on discussion groups in six cities, the Lane Report reflected both the nature and the aspirations of community organization during the 1930s. Continuing from the 1920s was social work's emphasis on professional standing and legitimacy. Within a broad definition of community organization, the report specified a typology of the kinds of practice that constitute community organization. Among them were fact-finding for social action and social planning; initiating and developing social welfare services and programs; facilitating interrelationships between and among individuals, organizations, and groups; and developing public understanding of and public support for social welfare activities, programs, and objectives (Schwartz, 1965). But the Lane Report determined that the "core function" of community organization was achieving adjustment between social welfare resources and social welfare needs. The focus here was on social service planning and coordination, program development, and administration (Rothman, 1999b). The 1930s' distinguishing characteristic, which differed from some earlier and later periods, was an emphasis on task over process goals. This was an era of social planning and getting things done to confront the Depression; community building and more participatory processes were seen as less central to the field and certainly less pressing. As the Depression subsided and World War II began, community organization continued its emphasis on "maintaining adjustment between social welfare resources and social welfare needs" (Dunham, 1943, p. 138) and proposed that "community organization was a social work process comparable to social casework and social group work and that the community was a client in a distinctive sense" (Schwartz, 1965, p. 179).

Outside of social work, community organizing tended to be more engaged in social action, often of the confrontational and direct action variety. From the Unemployed Councils of the Communist Party, protesting against hunger and eviction, to the founding of Saul Alinsky's Back of the Yards effort in a stockyard neighborhood of Chicago, community organizing took on the militant and even ideological tone of contemporary labor struggles, specifically that of the emerging Congress of Industrial Organizations (CIO). The class-based democratic organizing of the more radical unions in the CIO was transferred to the neighborhoods where these workers and their families lived. Settlements and other community organization efforts were also involved in comparable efforts around social security and welfare relief. Outside of social work, the community organizing of the day, unburdened by professional constraints and sometimes proposing a revolutionary, rather than incremental, program, went beyond middle-class advocacy and leadership on these issues to mobilizing and politicizing those most affected by the Great Depression. Compare the tone, politics, and tactics of the statement by Clarence King in the *Encyclopedia of Social Work*—"In general, community organization for social work may be said to comprise social welfare planning, organization, and coordination" (King, 1941, pp. 128–29)—to those of Saul Alinsky, who at about the same time encouraged community organizers to "rub raw people's resentments" to build a people's movement (Alinsky, 1946).

To be sure, there were those in social work who used a social justice movement approach during the Depression. The rank-and-file movement within social work, led by Jacob Fisher, Bertha Reynolds, Mary van Kleeck, and others, picked up on the radical politics and the militant union model of the day. These leaders sought dramatic changes inside and outside the profession. Although these changes were not exclusively in the area of community organization (Bertha Reynolds, for example, was a clinician), their analysis and work proceeded from a class-based structural perspective of both the profession and the relation between social workers and their clients (Burghardt & Fabricant, 1987). This approach changed as World War II put the brakes on social action efforts. After the war ended, however, militancy returned. In 1946, there emerged a wave of local and national strikes, demands for better wages and conditions for workers, and a general demand for equality for which the war against fascism had been fought. But this was short-lived. Actually, it was crushed. Another wave of conservative political economy was about to constrain community practice, pushing community organization into more professional concerns once again, and pushing social action organizing into near oblivion. During the Depression, however, whether community practice occurred within or without social work, there was a general focus on the larger issues of social welfare and a sense of reaching larger aims through political action (Magee, 1943).

Cold War and the Fifties

The years from about 1945 until 1973 were ones of tremendous economic growth and opportunities as well as political and cultural change. Initially, there was the enthusiasm of the postwar atmosphere—returning to peace and civilian life after years of delaying school and work and disturbing personal life. The atmosphere was buoyed for social workers by the social justice *spirit of the times.* Fascism had been defeated abroad; democracy had prevailed. Of about 3 million students in universities after the war, one third were there on the GI bill. Many were studying to become social workers, as social work, like other professions, was about to undergo a major expansion. At the same time, however, elites sought to cement U.S. economic and political power worldwide and fashion a conservative consensus for the Cold War at home through economic growth and political repression. Economic growth opened up opportunities and career advancement for young adults, but political repression heavily curtailed social justice work. Social action community organization was largely put on hold for a decade, when a context more interested in social work and social justice fed it and gave it room to grow.

   Equally important, the postwar era was a difficult time for those in and outside of social work interested in community organizing. Community practitioners found it nearly impossible, in the reactionary context of the day, to sustain their social action work. Once again, as in the Red Scare after World War I, social change and democratic dissent were widely perceived as a threat to the nation. This was an era of highly conservative Cold War politics, dominated by the fear of communism abroad and at home (Fisher, 1994; Fried, 1996; Pells, 1994). Equally as important, the architects of this conservative post-World War II political economy feared another economic depression. There was deep concern about the fragility of the American economy and capitalism in general. Federal deficit spending for war and defense—what President Eisenhower later called the "military-industrial complex"—appeared to be the only answer to economic depression. Insecure about

American prospects at home and abroad, cold warriors in both political parties sought to silence those who raised concerns about the direction and priorities of postwar America (Kolko, 1976). In such a context, quite similar to the period directly after World War I and during the 1920s, issues of poverty, social problems, and urban slums were as absent from public discussion as they had been omnipresent just a decade or so before (Galbraith, 1958/1998; Harrington, 1962). In response to a context of repression and intimidation, most community work, whether inside or outside the field of social work, withdrew from the political scene or fell dormant (Andrews & Reisch, 1997; Fabricant & Fisher, 2002b). As David Rosenstein, then president of the National Federation of Settlements, put it in 1953, at the height of the repression: "People in the neighborhoods are afraid to join anything" (cited in Fisher, 1994, p. 70). Arthur Dunham at the University of Michigan remained the only continuing university professor in the field of community organization. Meyer Schwartz was just helping to develop the first 2-year concentration in community organization at the University of Pittsburgh. But these exceptions proved the rule of constrained community organization in this era.

Community organizing had little public impact in the late 1940s and 1950s. For example, Alinsky's work essentially lay fallow for more than a decade until the civil rights movement took off in the 1960s and drew attention once again to community-based social action (Horwitt, 1990). Social workers involved in community practice, in the field and in academic settings, had greater viability because they responded to the postwar context in a greater variety of ways and sought a wider variety of funding sources (Fabricant & Fisher, 2002b). The United Community Defense Services, a community organization project in defense industry–related sites in the United States during the Korean War, secured funding for community organization in a climate hostile to social change by promoting community organization as a means for "lubricating the social machine," helping people in "critical defense areas," and thereby supporting the Cold War and the struggle against communism (Fisher, 1994). During this period, academics and practitioners also worked hard to develop "a conceptual framework for social work practice in the field of community work" (Schwartz, 1999, p. 264). According to Kenneth Pray, the focus of community work should be on developing a "direct helping relationship with individual people and groups of people," much like casework (cited in Schwartz, 1965, p. 181). Newstetter (1947) was more interested in the process of intergroup work; he viewed community to be essentially the interaction and adjustment relation of groups. John Hill warned practitioners "to distinguish between their responsibilities as citizens and their responsibilities as members of a profession" (Hill, 1951, p. 459).

Writing toward the end of this period, Murray Ross (1955) offered a more expanded conceptualization of community organization, which included process, reform, and planning orientations. His work rested more heavily on contemporary social science research and used a more systematic and social-scientific approach than others writing about community organization at the time. But ultimately, like most of his contemporaries, Ross concluded that community organization should focus on community organization as a process and the community worker as an enabler, rather than on social action and more advocacy-related forms of community work or more top-down planning models (Rothman, 2001; Schwartz, 1965). Austin recalls the dominant trend in community organization at this time:

CO, like group work and casework, was primarily focused on interpersonal processes—that is, how inclusively self-help groups were organized and how democratic decisions were made, not with specific outcomes impacting poverty, racial segregation, or general patterns of discrimination. (Austin, 1999, p. 196)

The Sixties: 1960–1975

The period from 1960 to 1975 was a heyday for social action the world over. Resistance began in the Third World, with nationalist and socialist rebellion against Western imperialism following World War II. It percolated in the United States in the 1950s, then dominated public discourse for the next decade. In the United States, mass social movements—by people of color for civil rights and power, by students against the war in Vietnam, and later by women against sexism and for gender equality—resisted oppression of people based on class, race, politics, values, and gender. This period is remembered as a time of mass insurgence, radical politics, and youthful experimentation. It was a time when the notion of democracy was reinvigorated with participatory content. Community-based work—from that of Students for a Democratic Society (SDS) and the Student Nonviolent Coordinating Committee (SNCC) to Mobilization for Youth (MFY) and the Community Action Program—was central to sixties activism. (Breines, 1982; Carson, 1982; Chafe, 1980; Evans, 1979; Polletta, 2002). The social movements and programs of the era incorporated community organizing, especially social action, into the equation of urban social change to an even greater extent than in the Progressive Era (Halpern, 1995).

This massive interest in community organization and participation resulted from three primary sources: (a) civil rights and student movement initiatives, (b) foundations seeking new models in the late 1950s to address juvenile delinquency, and (c) liberal elites who came to power in the 1960s seeking to address, at least modestly, social problems and the growing unrest in the United States. In a nutshell, social disorder and mass movements, which sprang up in response to the gross inequities and inconsistencies between the ideal and de facto practice of democracy in the United States, pushed political and federal leadership to develop a wide array of programs that would provide both needed resources and services at a decentralized level and the opportunity to increase community-based organization and participation.

What made the period even more exciting and important was the quantity of funding and social space available for varied forms of political participation and social change (Fabricant & Fisher, 2002b; Halpern, 1995). Public initiatives in the War on Poverty committed extensive federal support to organizations working with the poor, addressing the social causes of poverty, and pursuing a decentralized strategy of working to address poverty at the neighborhood level (Marris & Rein, 1967; Moynihan, 1969; Peterson & Greenstone, 1977). The Office of Economic Opportunity, developed in 1964 to administer the War on Poverty, dramatically expanded the amount of money available for community-based nonprofit programs (Kravitz, 1969). Programs under the new Office of Economic Opportunity included Operation Head Start, Job Corps, Neighborhood Youth Corps, Upward Bound, VISTA, and the Community Action Program, which established community action agencies throughout the nation (Marris & Rein, 1967; Piven & Cloward, 1971). Poverty was once again seen as a federal problem, but many of the key programs defined the federal role as helping to initiate and fund such community-based efforts as participation, planning, and power. From the mid-1960s onward, the Great Society, limits aside, wrought profound changes and brought massive funding for neighborhood work and social change (Halpern, 1995). Federal expenditures for social welfare services tripled in only 5 years, increasing from $812 million in 1965 to $2.2 billion in 1970.

Community workers were not passive recipients in this process. The Henry Street Settlement, for example, was an initiator of MFY, an experiment in community-based response to poverty and powerlessness. In 1957, Helen Hall and others first began work in neighborhoods with MFY planning, which was a precursor to later projects under the War on Poverty. MFY achieved such prominence that President Kennedy initiated a federally recognized project in May 1962. Activist academics at Columbia University's School of Social Work, among them Lloyd Ohlin, Richard Cloward, and George Brager (Brager, 1999; see also Hall, 1971), revised the model to heighten community activism and development of power (and activism). Tensions at MFY reflected significant splits in community organization strategy and tactics: a more activist movement strategy versus a more professional incremental approach. Many community workers had used the latter approach with success in the Progressive Era and especially during the New Deal, when they had a good deal of access to power and were influential participants in policy development. For example, Margaret Berry, director of the National Federation of Settlements in the 1960s, opposed the transformation of a community organization into a "protest agency for the poor," because she felt Blacks could make significant gains by bridging rather than exacerbating class and racial tensions (Lasch-Quinn, 1993, p. 161). But whether community work was more militant and revolutionary or more engaged in advocacy and social reform, community-based efforts attracted a great deal of attention and provided many people with jobs and social change experience. Of course, it was not an easy time to achieve social change; victory never comes easily. But for community organization, it was an unusually supportive and exciting era.

Within the field of social work, the enormous growth and transformation that began after World War II reached fruition in the 1960s (Rothman, 1999a). More progressive and macro-minded social workers were primed to expand on the egalitarian values and political experiences of the Depression and the Second World War, but they were stymied in the postwar decade by a reactionary context and a social work profession that pursued more traditional (micro) and more conservative (adjustment-oriented) forms of social work practice and preferred more psychosocial and behavioral forms of research. The reform context of the 1960s, however, expanded the audiences and opportunities for community organization theory and practice. In this more liberal context, a new generation of community organization professionals found a more comfortable and supportive home. Some—such as Richard Cloward, George Brager, and Harry Specht at MFY—were key architects and players in the newly emerging social movements and projects, and many educators—Jack Rothman, David Austin, John Turner, Robert Perlman, and Irving Spergel, to name just a few—were practitioners who also developed careers in social change as university educators. However, most of the social workers who became involved in community organization were less heralded, grassroots professionals involved in a wide variety of agencies, organizations, and movement efforts.

Community practice continued to occur in the same arenas and with similar methods as before, but those involved in community building, social planning, and social action increasingly became much more interested in issues of power and much more willing to consider expanding strategies and tactics to include more social action and political advocacy and even militant, confrontational strategies and tactics. John Turner stated it mildly when he wrote, "Over the years we learned much more about power" (Turner, 1999, p.100). Burghardt and Fabricant (1987) emphasize that during this era, community organization emphasized the refinement of particular skills, especially the democratic intergroup process, coalition work, the understanding of political and power structures, and the confrontation of racism and sexism. The programs and funding of the era offered job opportunities and experience to those interested in community organization. Of course, it wasn't entirely a heyday for those interested in social change. Warren Haggstrom's program in radical community organizing at Syracuse University was aborted, leading to his move to UCLA. But the overall atmosphere was one of greater support and legitimacy for social action and democratic dissent.

Related developments occurred in community-organizing efforts outside of social work. SNCC's community-organizing work around Black civil rights in the Deep South was perhaps the most compelling model of the period. Participatory democracy served as the core vision, goal, and method for student activist work in SNCC and SDS. Saul Alinsky, distancing himself from the New Left as he had done earlier from the field of social work, found in the new, more liberal context support for his work as a "professional radical." A pariah only a few years earlier, he was heralded as "the prophet of power to the people" by *Time* magazine in the mid-1960s (Horwitt, 1990). The essence of 1960s social action community organizing, especially that of the New Left, often is summarized in the phrase "power to the people" and can be captured in a number of basic working principles:

- The organizer is a catalyst rather than a leader.
- Participatory democracy is the prime thrust of community organizing with a mission to "let the people decide."
- Finding and developing advocacy and other skills among indigenous leaders is a central goal for long-term change.

In following these principles, an effective community organizer will:

- Develop informal organization structures to encourage participation and attract participants
- Find and develop social spaces in the community that are free of constraint in which people can meet and organize
- Create supportive personal relations within and across community groups
- Recognize that grassroots efforts are not simply an end in themselves, but part of a larger movement for social, economic, and political justice (Fisher, 1994; Frost, 2001; Polletta, 2002)

In the late 1960s and early 1970s, a number of key developments both expanded interest in community work and undermined its future. Government repression, such as COINTELPRO, a covert counterintelligence effort of the FBI designed to eliminate radical political opposition inside the United States, began to destabilize movement efforts. Great Society programs were significantly derailed as early as 1967. The student movement became increasingly absorbed by the struggle against the Vietnam War and felt increasingly pressured to escalate strategies and tactics. Simultaneously, women within the movements began to develop a gender analysis of contemporary problems and American life, ultimately helping to birth the women's movement. The women's movement came partly out of the tensions within the New Left but much more significantly out of the activist fervor and lessons in democracy learned by the women in the organizing projects. With the success of the mobilization to end the war and the repression of movement activism, many activists had withdrawn from nationally oriented, mass movement work by the early 1970s and returned to grassroots community organizing as a means to build a more participatory, egalitarian, and communal society. Some of these grassroots organizations, such as ACORN and the Industrial Areas Foundation, continue today. Many of these efforts seemed to experience a heyday in the late 1970s—a veritable "backyard revolution" (Boyte, 1981). As the animus for such work declined, however, these efforts, while still important, receded from public consciousness, and their significance faded.

Since 1975: Community Practice in a Private World

Referring back to the historical cycles model, which has guided the analysis in this chapter, in the last generation, we have witnessed a shift to a conservative, corporate-dominated context on a global scale (Barnet, 1994; Bauman, 1998; Brecher & Costello, 1994; Eisenstein, 1998). Key indicators underscore this shift: the turn to greater individualism, conservative politicians, right-wing discourse and social movements, laissez-faire economic orientation, and corporate hegemony. This set of conditions is the context for most of the chapters in this handbook on contemporary practice. Because the other chapters flesh out the varied nature of practice and challenges in our contemporary context, this one highlights the significance of the shift in context and its broad impact on emerging trends in community practice. In a nutshell, the contemporary context is characterized by three central challenges: (a) the private marketplace and the practices of global corporations dominate and permeate almost all areas of life; (b) issues become increasingly private and individual rather than public and social; and (c) people are increasingly isolated and less able to build community and social solidarity. I have referred elsewhere to these as the political economy of private institutions, the culture of private individualism, and the privatization of physical space (Fisher & Karger, 1997, 2000).

First, the post-1975 era exalts private institutions. They are seen as the engines of economic and technological progress and as the primary instruments to address and resolve social problems. Likewise, the post-1975 era disparages public-sector institutions and unrequested intervention in the global marketplace. The corporate bottom line, prerogatives, and process come to dominate all sectors of life. The public sector declines as a significant force. Such tendencies increasingly translate into a withdrawal from social problems that do not affect the business community and marginalization of those who try to raise them as public issues. The efforts in the 1980s and 1990s to dismantle the welfare state of the 1930s and 1960s underscores the hostility of this private era toward the public policies and programs of prior reform eras. In this new context, policies and programs of the welfare state are dramatically undermined. Increasingly, instead of addressing contemporary inequities, the new privatized political economy exacerbates or ignores them (Block, Cloward, Ehrenreich, & Piven, 1987; Greider, 1992). Public issues are framed by marketplace discourse, and the marketplace increasingly becomes the final arbiter of public life. As public life dissolves into private life, social change becomes much more difficult. Society is reduced to marketplace cause and function, and community organizations are dominated by corporate processes and objectives.

Second, and obviously related to the first trend, we live in a world that increasingly emphasizes a culture of private individualism rather than a sense of public good and public participation (Bellah, Madsen, Sullivan, Swidler, & Tipton, 1985; Lasch, 1978; Putnam, 1996, 2000; Sennett, 1974, 1990; Specht & Courtney, 1994). People focus even more than before on their own individual needs and growth, and those of their family, to the exclusion of concern about, let alone participation in, public life (Habermas, 1989; Madsen, Bellah, Madsen, & Tipton, 1991; Ryan, 1992). Increasingly this leads to a preoccupation with individual deficits as opposed to social problems and a belief that if all problems are caused by the individual, then solutions also rest within that person. The very sense of social problems and social solutions disappears as issues of poverty, violence, education, and environmental pollution are redefined as individual problems with individual solutions (Fisher & Karger, 1997, 2000; Schram, 2000).

Third, private space increasingly replaces public space (Blakely & Snyder, 1997; Boyte, 1992; Davis, 1992; McKenzie, 1994; Sorkin, 1992). The restructured urban landscape removes people from public spaces (e.g., streets, parks, beaches, libraries, mass transit, dense city neighborhoods, and downtown street shopping) and encourages them to inhabit the private sphere (e.g., private homes and backyards, country clubs, private bookstores, private cars, fortified gated and suburban communities, and shopping malls). In such a world, the very act of building social solidarity with others, of building community, let alone public life, is dramatically diminished (Boyte, 1989; Eisenstein, 1998; Fisher & Karger, 1997; Putnam, 1993, 2000; Sandel, 1996; Suarez, 1999) at the same time that increasing corporatization, individualization, and globalization force people to seek solidarity and empowerment at the community level (Fisher & Karger, 1997; Sirianni & Friedland, 2001.

In such a context, a number of emerging trends in community practice seem most salient. Within the field of social work, the last few decades have seen a dramatic turn away from macro analysis and interventions and toward more individualistic and intrapsychic work. Paradoxically, social work places greater and greater emphasis on professionalization at the same time that the practice of social service work becomes increasingly deskilled by the corporatized economy of managed care and contracting. In the subfield of community organization, there has been a general turn toward more conservative approaches because these are the ones most likely to receive acceptance, support, and funding. Within schools of social work, education has shifted away from social action to a revival of interest in "traditional forms of process-oriented, interagency planning and coordination" (Kramer, 1999, p. 281). As in all historical periods since the COS, a great deal of social planning continues to occur in large service agencies, although in the past few decades these agencies have been driven more by contract availability and requests for proposals than internal goal-setting (Fabricant & Fisher, 2002b; see also Brilliant, Chapter 12, this volume). In the 1980s, community practice emphasized management and administration. In the past decade, as individual therapy approaches and family-based interventions have proven unable to impact deep and despair-provoking social and community conditions, community-based work of the community-building and community development types, with a focus on asset-building and social capacity strategies, is experiencing a miniboom in terms of financial support and attention (Saegert, Thompson, & Warren, 2001; Sherraden, 2003). Reflecting on an era that emphasizes goodwill and harmony with the private sector, the emphasis is on building partnerships and consensus and getting to the table with those who wield economic and political power. Unfortunately, these efforts, although significant in a world of diminishing social cohesion and resources for poor communities, are limited in terms of addressing larger issues of social, economic, and political justice.

On a related note, one of the contributions of the feminist movement of this period was to underscore the political and social change nature of service work (Stout & McPhail, 1998; Withorn, 1984). Another contribution of the feminist movement was to reinstate women in more leadership roles in community organization; after a heyday of female leadership during the Progressive Era, the leadership of community organization and community organizing became a male bastion. The delivery of services to victims of male battering or AIDS, in a context disinterested in both, was part of the larger feminist and gay/lesbian movements (Hyde, 1989; Weil, 1986). But the delivery of services in community-based organizations and agencies is about social change only as long as there remains a larger vision and project that not only includes but extends beyond service delivery (Armstrong, 2002). The same is true for various approaches in community practice. It is the politics of the effort that matters (Burghardt, 1982).

Accordingly, in the conservative political economy since 1975, social action efforts, inside and outside of social work, have been viewed by many as inappropriate vestiges of a prior era. The price of corporate support for social planning, community building, or community development—the price of sitting at the table—is often the exclusion of confrontation or even the potential for an adversarial role. This has a huge impact on whether or not the causes of social problems and conditions can be met or even addressed. It also has an impact on whether public-sector programs, such as those to address poverty, racism, hunger, and low-income housing, can be pressured or leveraged (Calpotura, 2000; Fisher & Shragge, 2000; Shragge, 2003; Williams, 1999).

While militant social action community work has declined dramatically, there seems to have been more political advocacy and electoral-oriented work around service budget cuts and policy initiatives since the 1980s, especially in response to the most recent fiscal crisis facing many states (Burghardt & Fabricant, 1987; Fabricant & Fisher, 2002b). In addition, in a context in which power has become highly concentrated, democracy more constrained, and life more individualized, community practice has featured a greater emphasis on democratic process and voice and on defining organizing as being about building relationships (Warren, 2001). The obvious neoconservative and neoliberal politics of the era have made people more aware of the structural dimensions and implications of contemporary problems. In addition to increasing organizing with the poor around welfare rights, a great deal of work has developed in communities, particularly the organizing work within the women's and gay and lesbian communities as well as among functional communities of people with disabilities and older adults; these groups previously were not involved in issues of community organization or advocacy. Thousands of community-based efforts are organized around particular cultural identities and, as always, around specific local community issues (Sirianni & Friedland, 2001). In addition, an anti-globalization youth movement is emerging, which seeks to build ties with labor and grassroots organizations and which, prior to the September 11, 2001, attacks on the World Trade Center and the Pentagon and the war on Iraq, seemed to be developing into a critical source of an alternative vision and democratic opposition (Brecher, Costello, & Smith, 2000; Polletta, 2002; Prokosch & Raymond, 2002). The challenge to all those who are doing good work in communities throughout the nation is to develop an ideological and philosophical gel and programmatic base that can begin to unite the diversity and proliferation of community work across the United States and enable diverse groups to contend together for political, economic, and social power. In the 1980s, it seemed that feminism would be the gel and the base to challenge the neoconservative politics of our time; in the 1990s, it seemed that perhaps organizing around the environment or visions of a multicultural society would unite and mobilize the fragmented world of community practice and social change; in the late 1990s and early 21st century, it looked more like the direct-action, anti-globalization movement would be a vanguard of change. Any of these, or a combination thereof, might still create the gel and the base.

Clearly, however, the Bush and Cheney regime and the events of September 11, 2001, have moved the political economy of the nation further to the right, dismantling public life and the public sector and challenging and reshaping community practice once again. Perhaps our current challenge is akin to that faced by community activists in the early 1950s. But with the pervasively conservative political economy merging with the privatizing trends of the past two decades, perhaps what we observe now is a much more formidable obstacle than even the early 1950s to the democratic politics and ideal of an inclusive and equalitarian public good. This ideal incorporates concerns for participatory democracy, equalitarian citizenship and access, community building, and diminished racism and sexism with progressive political, social, and economic programs. Focused on a constant goal of moving society toward social, economic, and political justice, such ideals and initiatives have characterized the best of community practice inside and outside social work. Only through continued struggle and practice will we discover the depth of the opposition to and the potential of our work. To that end, the chapters that follow should help.

Notes

1. Cyclical interpretations of American social welfare and political history are common. Schlesinger (1986) describes the past century as a series of cycles between eras that are more public regarding and those that are more private regarding. Piven and Cloward (1971; Cloward & Piven, 1999) discuss the shifts in terms of periods of contraction and expansion of civil, labor, and social welfare rights. For them, history shifts between periods of consensus and dissensus politics. Schlesinger thinks the shifts are generational; Cloward and Piven, offering a more dialectical model, think it reflects the state of social struggle, "the balance of power between people and their rulers" (Cloward & Piven, 1999, p. 186). Most recently, Putnam sees it in terms of ups and downs in "civic engagement" (Putnam, 2000, p. 25). Many other social welfare historians, social scientists, social workers, and others agree in general on the periodization of this model. See, for example, Reisch (1998) and Ehrenreich (1985). Periods of public investment and social activism include the Progressive Era (1900–1918), the New Deal and World War II period (1933–1946), and the sixties (1960–1975). Private contexts are the Gilded Age (1877–1896), the twenties (1920–1929), the fifties (1948–1959), and our contemporary world (1975–present). The years in between are times of transition. The model provides a single lens to put in context more than 100 years of community practice. Clearly, all models have limits. They conflate historical specificity. They risk becoming mechanical and running counter to lived experience. Historical change usually comes slowly and incrementally, rather than in sudden shifts. The dates offered are obviously not absolute but designed to emphasize a general change in national political atmosphere and a shift in the context for social investment. Equally important, continuities in American history, such as a broad consensus on private property and individualism, the persistence of class and racial domination, and the hegemony of capitalist development, are certainly as significant as the changes this model emphasizes (Crocker, 1992; Dowd, 1974; Hofstadter, 1948; Walkowitz, 1999). These and other caveats acknowledged, the cyclical model continues to have salience, not only for understanding the past but also, as this chapter hopes to demonstrate, for understanding the present.

2. Michael Reisch (personal communication, 2001) reminds that this view of stepchild is inaccurate, as community organization, in such efforts as the COSs and the settlements, actually antedated the development of casework within the field. COSs had to organize communities prior to creating a distinct form of individualized service.

3. Regarding terminology, this chapter reflects the historical record. *Community organization* is the term used for community practice in social work agencies and by social workers. *Community organizing* is used for community practice in organizations and by organizers outside of social work. Clearly, the two overlap; for example, social workers engaged in social action community practice refer to their work as both community organizing and community organization. *Community practice* is a contemporary term to cover the broad range of work done both inside and outside social work.

4. Not all would agree with these definitions or the exclusive use of the terms. For example, Irving Spergel (1999) sees the definitions differently, with both occurring within the domain of social work. Community organization relates to structures and processes of organizations and to interorganizational, and citizen relationships. Organizing emphasizes how structures and institutions are purposefully changed to enhance their capacity to address their issues. Certainly, this chapter cannot cover all varieties of community organization, no matter how defined. In this chapter, therefore, important work in terms of coalition building, community economic development, social policy, and administration work takes a back seat to the dominant forms of community building, social planning, and social action (Rothman, 2001).

5. None of these shifts occur absolutely. It's not as though society experiences a total or instant overhaul. A multiplicity of currents and efforts are present in every time period. But in each era, a dominant zeitgeist prevails. This "spirit of the time" is largely the result of interactions between the economic base, political initiatives, and social struggle. Of course, the shift does not affect all people in the same ways. The Progressive Era, for example, has been called "the nadir" of Black history because it institutionalized de jure segregation and turned its back on the oppression of African Americans.

6. Of course, there are exceptions to this general historical model at almost every turn. Despite the conservatism of the 1920s, Chambers (personal communication, September 30, 2000) notes the experience of a Black settlement in Minneapolis, which served as a safe haven for the efforts of A. Phillip Randolph to organize Pullman porter workers in the Twin Cities.

References

Alinsky, S. (1946). *Reveille for radicals.* New York: Random House.

Andrews, J., & Reisch, M. (1997). Social work and anti-communism: A historical analysis of the McCarthy era. *Journal of Progressive Human Services, 8*(2), 29–47.

Armstrong, E. (2002). *Forging gay identities: Organizing sexuality in San Francisco, 1950-1994.* Chicago: University of Chicago.

Austin, D. (1999). The impact of politics, economics, and race on social work community organization. In J. Rothman (Ed.), *Reflections on community organization: Enduring themes and critical issues* (pp. 194–214). Itasca, IL: F. E. Peacock.

Bannister, R. (1979). *Social Darwinism.* Philadelphia: Temple University Press.

Barnet, R. J. (1994, December). Lords of the global economy. *The Nation, 190,* 754–757.

Bauman, Z. (1998). *Globalization: The human consequences.* New York: Columbia University Press.

Bellah, R., Madsen, R., Sullivan, W., Swidler, A., & Tipton, S. (1985). *Habits of the heart: Individualism and commitment in American life.* New York: Harper & Row.

Berry, M. (1999). Service and cause: Both sides of the coin. In J. Rothman (Ed.), *Reflections on community organization: Enduring themes and critical issues* (pp. 106–122). Itasca, IL: F. E. Peacock.

Betten, N., & Austin, M. J. (1990). *The roots of community organizing: 1917–1939.* Philadelphia: Temple University Press.

Blakely, E., & Snyder, M. (1997). *Fortress America: Gated communities in the United States.* Washington, DC: Brookings Institution.

Block, F., Cloward, R., Ehrenreich, B., & Piven, F. F. (1987). *The mean season: The attack on the welfare state.* New York: Pantheon.

Bowman, L. (1929). Community organization. In F. Hall (Ed.), *Social work yearbook* (p. 100). New York: Russell Sage Foundation.

Boyte, H. (1981). *The backyard revolution.* Philadelphia: Temple University Press.

Boyte, H. (1989). *Commonwealth: A return to citizen politics.* New York: Free Press.

Boyte, H. (1992). The pragmatic ends of popular politics. In C. Calhoun (Ed.), *Habermas and the public sphere* (pp. 109–135). Boston: MIT Press.

Brager, G. (1999). Agency under attack: The risks, demands, and rewards of community activism. In J. Rothman (Ed.), *Reflections on community organization: Enduring themes and critical issues* (pp. 57–74). Itasca, IL: F. E. Peacock.

Brecher, J., & Costello, T. (1994). *Global village or global pillage: Economic reconstruction from the bottom up.* Boston: South End Press.

Brecher, J., Costello, T., & Smith, B. (2000). *Globalization from below: The power of solidarity.* Boston: South End Press.

Breines, W. (1982). *Community organization and the new left, 1962–1968.* New York: Praeger.

Burghardt, S. (1982). *The other side of organizing.* Rochester, VT: Schenkman Books.

Burghardt, S., & Fabricant, M. (1987). Radical social work. In *Encyclopedia of social work* (Vol. 3, pp. 455–62). Silver Spring, MD: NASW Press.

Calpotura, F. (2000). The view from the ground: Organizers speak out on race. *Colorlines* 3(2), 12–19.

Carlton-LaNey, I. (Ed.). (2001a). *African American leadership: An empowerment tradition in social welfare history.* Washington, DC: NASW.

Carlton-LaNey, I. (2001b). Birdye Henrietta Haynes: A pioneer settlement house worker. In I. Carlton-LaNey (Ed.), *African American leadership: An empowerment tradition in social welfare history* (pp. 35–54). Washington, DC: NASW.

Carson, C. (1982). *In struggle: SNCC and the Black awakening of the 1960s.* New York: Oxford University Press.

Carter, P. (1975). *The twenties in America.* Wheeling, IL: Harlan-Davidson.

Chafe, W. (1980). *Civilities and civil rights: Greensboro, North Carolina, and the Black struggle for freedom.* New York: Oxford University Press.

Chambers, C. A. (1963). *Seedtime of reform: American social service and social action, 1918–1933.* Minneapolis, MN: University of Minneapolis Press.

Cloward, R., & Piven, F. F. (1999). Disruptive dissensus: People and power in the industrial age. In J. Rothman (Ed.), *Reflections on community organization: Enduring themes and critical issues* (pp. 165–193). Itasca, IL: F. E. Peacock.

Coit, S. (1974). *Neighbourhood guilds: An instrument of social reform.* New York: Arno Press.

Crocker, R. H. (1992). *Social work and social order: The settlement movement in two industrial cities: 1889–1930.* Urbana: University of Illinois Press.

Crunden, R. M. (1982). *Ministers of reform: The progressives' achievement in American civilization, 1889–1920.* New York: Basic Books.

Davis, A. F. (1967). *Spearheads for reform: The social settlements and the progressive movement, 1890–1914.* New Brunswick, NJ: Rutgers University Press.

Davis, A. F., & McCree, M. L. (1969). *Eighty years at Hull House.* New York: Quadrangle Books.

Davis, M. (1992). *City of quartz.* New York: Vintage.

Deegan, M. J. (Ed.). (1991). *Women in sociology.* New York: Greenwood Press.

Dowd, D. (1974). *The twisted dream: Capitalist development in the United States.* Cambridge, MA: Winthrop.

Dunham, A. (1943). Community organization for social work. In R. Kurtz (Ed.), *Social work yearbook* (pp. 137–142). New York: Russell Sage.

Ehrenreich, J. (1985). *The altruistic imagination: A history of social work and social policy in the United States.* Ithaca, NY: Cornell University Press.

Eisenstein, Z. (1998). *Global obscenities.* New York: New York University Press.

Evans, S. (1979). *Personal politics: The roots of women's liberation in the civil rights movement and the new left.* New York: Random House.

Fabricant, M., & Fisher, R. (2002a). Agency-based community building in low income neighborhoods: A praxis framework. *Journal of Community Practice, 10*(2), 1–22.

Fabricant, M., & Fisher, R. (2002b). *Settlement houses under siege: The struggle to sustain community organization in New York.* New York: Columbia University Press.

Fisher, R. (1994). *Let the people decide: Neighborhood organizing in America.* Boston: Twayne.

Fisher, R., & Karger, H. (1997). *Social work and community in a private world: Getting out in public.* New York: Longman.

Fisher, R., & Karger, H. (2000). The context of social work practice. In P. A. Meares & C. Garvin (Eds.), *Handbook of social work practice* (pp. 5–22). Thousand Oaks, CA: Sage.

Fisher, R., & Shragge, E. (2000). Challenging community organizing: Facing the 21st century. *Journal of Community Practice, 8*(3), 1–19.

Fried, A. (Ed.). (1996). *McCarthyism: The great American red scare: A documentary history.* New York: Oxford University Press.

Frost, J. (2001). *An interracial movement of the poor: Community organizing and the New Left in the 1960s.* New York: New York University Press.

Galbraith, J. K. (1998). *The affluent society.* New York: Houghton Mifflin. (Original work published 1958)

Greider, W. (1992). *Who will tell the people?* New York: Simon & Schuster.

Habermas, J. (1989). *The structural transformation of the public sphere.* Boston: Harvard University Press.

Hall, H. (1971). *Unfinished business in neighborhood and nation.* New York: MacMillan.

Halpern, R. (1995). *Rebuilding the inner city: A history of neighborhood initiatives to address poverty in the United States.* New York: Columbia University Press.

Harrington, M. (1962). *The other America: Poverty in the United States.* New York: MacMillan.

Hays, S. (1957). *The response to industrialism.* Chicago: University of Chicago Press.

Hill, J. (1951). Social action. In M. Hodges (Ed.), *Social work yearbook* (pp. 455–460). New York: American Association of Social Workers.

Hofstadter, R. (1948). *Social Darwinism in American thought.* Philadelphia: J. D. Lippincott.

Holden, A. C. (1922). *The settlement idea: A vision of social justice.* New York: MacMillan.

Horwitt, S. D. (1990). *Let them call me rebel: Saul Alinsky, his life and legacy.* New York: Knopf.

Husock, H. (1990). Fighting poverty the old-fashioned way. *Wilson Quarterly* (14), 79–91.

Hyde, C. (1989). A feminist model for macro-practice. *Administration in Social Work, 13,* 145–181.

Kendall, K. (2000). *Social work education: Its origins in Europe.* Alexandria, VA: Council on Social Work Education.

Kennedy, A., Farra, K., et al. (1935). *Social settlements in New York City: Their activities, policies, and administration.* New York: Columbia University Press.

King, C. (1941). Community organization for social work. In R. Kurtz (Ed.), *Social work yearbook* (pp. 128–133). New York: Russell Sage.

Kogut, A. (1972). The settlements and ethnicity, 1890–1914. *Social Work, 17,* 99–108.

Kolko, G. (1976). *Main currents in modern American history.* New York: Harper & Row.

Kramer, R. (1999). The rise and decline of community organization at Berkeley. In J. Rothman (Ed.), *Reflections on community organization: Enduring themes and critical issues* (pp. 277–289). Itasca, IL: F. E. Peacock.

Kraus, A. (1980). *The settlement house movement in New York City, 1886–1914.* New York: Arno Press.

Kravitz, S. (1969). The community action program: Past, present, and future. In J. Sundquist (Ed.), *On fighting poverty* (pp. 52–69). New York: Basic Books.

Lasch, C. (1978). *The culture of narcissism.* New York: Norton.

Lasch-Quinn, E. (1993). *Black neighbors: Race and the limits of reform in the American settlement house movement, 1890–1945.* Chapel Hill: University of North Carolina Press.

Lubove, R. (1975). *The professional altruist: The emergence of social work as a career, 1880–1930.* New York: Atheneum.

Lundblad, K. S. (1995). Jane Addams and social reform: A role model for the 1990s. *Social Work, 40,* 661–669.

Madsen, R., Bellah, R., Madsen, R., & Tipton, S. (1991). *The good society.* New York: Knopf.

Magee, E. (1943). Social action. In R. Kurtz (Ed.), *Social work yearbook* (pp. 478–482). New York: Russell Sage.

Marris, P., & Rein, M. (1967). *Dilemmas of social reform: Poverty and community action in the United States.* New York: Atherton.

Mattson, K. (1998). *Creating a democratic republic: The struggle for urban participatory democracy during the Progressive Era.* University Park: Pennsylvania University Press.

McKenzie, E. (1994). *Privatopia: Homeowners associations and the rise of residential private government.* New Haven, CT: Yale University Press.

McNeil, C. F. (1951). Community organization for social welfare. In M. Hodges (Ed.), *Social work yearbook* (pp. 122–128). New York: American Association of Social Workers.

Melvin, P. M. (1987). *The organic city: Urban definition and neighborhood organization, 1880–1920.* Lexington: University of Kentucky Press.

Moynihan, D. (1969). *Maximum feasible misunderstanding: Community action in the War on Poverty.* New York: Free Press.

Newstetter, W.I. (1947). The social intergroup work process. In *Proceedings of the National Conference of Social Work.* New York: Columbia University Press.

Pells, R. (1994). *The liberal mind in a conservative age: American intellectuals in the 1940s and 1950s.* Middletown, CT: Wesleyan University Press.

Peterson, P., & Greenstone, D. (1977). The mobilization of low-income communities through community action. In R. Haveman (Ed.), *A decade of federal antipoverty programs: Achievements, failures, and lessons* (pp. 241–278). New York: Academic Press.

Piven, F. F., & Cloward, R. (1971). *Regulating the poor: The functions of public welfare.* New York: Pantheon.

Polletta, F. (2002). *Freedom is an endless meeting: Democracy in American social movements.* Chicago: University of Chicago Press.

Prokosch, M., & Raymond, L. (2002). *The global activist's manual: Local ways to change the world.* New York: Nations Books.

Putnam, R. (1993). *Making democracy work.* Princeton, NJ: Princeton University Press.

Putnam, R. (1996, Winter). The strange disappearance of civic America. *American Prospect, 24,* 22–38.

Putnam, R. (2000). *Bowling alone: The collapse and revival of American community.* New York: Simon & Schuster.

Quandt, J. (1970). *From the small town to the great community.* New Brunswick, NJ: Rutgers University Press.

Reinders, R. C. (1982). Toynbee Hall and the American settlement movement. *Social Service Review, 56*(1), 39–54.

Reisch, M. (1998). The sociopolitical context and social work method, 1890–1950. *Social Service Review, 72*(2), 161–181.

Ross, M. G. (1955). *Community organization: Theory and principles.* New York: Harper.

Rothman, J. (1999a). Intent and content. In J. Rothman (Ed.), *Reflections on community organization: Enduring themes and critical issues* (pp. 3–26). Itasca, IL: F. E. Peacock.

Rothman, J. (1999b). A very personal account of the intellectual history of community organization. In J. Rothman (Ed.), *Reflections on community organization: Enduring themes and critical issues* (pp. 215–234). Itasca, IL: F. E. Peacock.

Rothman, J. (2001). Approaches to community intervention. In J. Rothman, J. Ehrlich, & J. Tropman (Eds.), *Strategies of community intervention* (6th ed., pp. 27–64). Itasca, IL: F. E. Peacock.

Rothman, S. (1973, Winter). Other people's children: The day care experience in America. *The Public Interest, 30,* 11–27.

Rouse, J. (1984). The legacy of community organizing: Lugenia Burns Hope and the Neighborhood Union. *The Journal of Negro History, 69*(3/4), 114–133.

Ryan, M. (1992). Gender and public access: Women's politics in nineteenth century America. In C. Calhoun (Ed.), *Habermas and the public sphere* (pp. 259–288). Boston: MIT Press.

Saegert. S., Thompson, J. P., & Warren, M. (Eds.). (2001). *Social capital and poor communities.* New York: Russell Sage Foundation.

Sandel, M. (1996). *Democracy's discontent.* Cambridge, MA: Harvard University Press.

Schlesinger, A., Jr. (1986). *The cycles of American history.* Boston: Houghton Mifflin.

Schram, S. (2000). *After welfare: The culture of postindustrial social policy.* New York: New York University Press.

Schwartz, M. (1965). Community organization. In H. L. Lurie, (Ed.), *Encyclopedia of social work* (19th ed., pp. 177–190). New York: NASW Press.

Schwartz, M. (1999). Development of a specialized curriculum in community organization. In J. Rothman (Ed.), *Reflections on community organization: Enduring themes and critical issues* (pp. 259–276). Itasca, IL: F. E. Peacock.

Sennett, R. (1974). *The fall of public man.* New York: Norton.

Sennett, R. (1990). *The conscience of the eye.* New York: Norton.

Shapiro, E. S. (1978). Robert A. Woods and the settlement house impulse. *Social Service Review, 52,* 215–226.

Shragge, E. (2003). *Activism and social change: Lessons for community and local organizing.* Ontario, Canada: Broadview Press.

Sherraden, M. (2003). From the social welfare state to the social investment state. *Shelterforce, 25*(2), 16–17.

Sirianni, C., & Friedland, L. (2001). *Civic innovation in America: Empowerment, public policy, and the movement for civic renewal.* Berkeley: University of California Press.

Skocpol, T. (1992). *Protecting soldiers and mothers: The political origins of social policy in the United States.* Cambridge, MA: Harvard University Press.

Sorkin, M. (Ed.). (1992). *Variation on a theme park: The new American city and the end of public space.* New York: Noonday Press.

Spain, D. (2000). *How women saved the city.* Minneapolis: University of Minnesota Press.

Specht, H., & Courtney, M. (1994). *Unfaithful angels: How social work has abandoned its mission.* New York: Free Press.

Spergel, I. (1999). Gangs and community organization. In J. Rothman (Ed.), *Reflections on community organization: Enduring themes and critical issues* (pp. 123–144). Itasca, IL: F. E. Peacock.

Still, B. (1974). *Urban America.* Boston: Little, Brown.

Stout, K., & McPhail, B. (1998). *Confronting sexism and violence against women: A challenge for social work.* New York: Longman.

Suarez, R. (1999). *The old neighborhood: What we lost in the great suburban migration, 1966–1999.* New York: Free Press.

Thompson, E. P. (1971). Anthropology and the discipline of historical context. *Midland History, 3,* 41–55.

Tobin, E. (1988). From Jane Addams to Saul Alinsky. *Reviews in American History, 16*(3), 117–124.

Trattner, W. I. (1999). *From Poor Law to welfare state: A history of social welfare in America.* New York: Free Press.

Trolander, J. A. (1975). *Settlement houses and the Great Depression.* Detroit: Wayne State University Press.

Turner, J. (1999). Neighborhood organization: How well does it work? In J. Rothman (Ed.), *Reflections on community organization: Enduring themes and critical issues* (pp. 91–105). Itasca, IL: F. E. Peacock.

Wald, L. (1915). *The house on Henry Street.* New York: Dover.

Wald, L. (1934). *Windows on Henry Street.* Boston: Little, Brown.

Walkowitz, D. (1999). *Working with class: Social workers and the politics of middle-class identity.* Chapel Hill: University of North Carolina Press.

Warner, S. B., Jr. (1972). *The urban wilderness: A history of the American city.* New York: Harper & Row.

Warren, M. (2001). *Dry bones rattling: Community building to revitalize American democracy.* Princeton, NJ: Princeton University Press.

Weil, M. O. (1986). Women, community, and organizing. In N. Van Der Bergh & L. Cooper (Eds.), *Feminist visions for social work* (pp. 187–210). Silver Spring, MD: NASW Press.

Williams, J. (1999). Alinsky discovered organizing like Columbus discovered America. *Third Force, 4*(1), 14–17.

Withorn, A. (1984). *Serving the people.* New York: Columbia University Press.

CHAPTER 3

Diverse Populations and Community Practice

Teiahsha Bankhead

John L. Erlich

"A way of seeing," British statesman Edmund Burke suggested, "is a way of not seeing." Taking this admonition to heart, we will offer some nontraditional perspectives on organizing with communities of color. On the other hand, doing so means that we will give short shrift to some expected explorations of community practice. Addressed are aspects of the evolution of community practice with diverse populations, current and changing issues in this practice arena, and an emerging model of practice consisting of related cultural competency views and personal qualities needed for successful organizing.

Ethno-Racial Context for Organizing in Communities of Color

> *The depth of white fear is underestimated and misunderstood by progressive thinkers and the media. . . . The best that can be hoped for is a multiracial capitalist society without a white majority.*
>
> Maharidge, 1996, pp. 11, 21

Racial and ethnic demographic changes in the United States have resulted in a landscape in which White people are becoming a numeric minority and people of color, in aggregate, are becoming the majority (Grieco & Cassidy, 2001). The 2000 U.S. Census revealed that the current population is 75% White, 12% Black, 4% Asian or Pacific Islander, 1% American Indian or Alaskan Native, 8% multiracial or some other race, and 13% Hispanic (Grieco & Cassidy, 2001). Hispanic respondents can be counted as White or non-White for census purposes. In either case, the Hispanic population doubled nationwide from 1980 to 2000 (Hobbs & Stoops, 2002). The race and Hispanic origin categories together constitute a minority category growing at a rate that will quickly outpace White population growth (Perry & Mackun, 2001; U.S. Bureau of the Census, 2001). The minority population is significantly younger, concentrated in urban centers in states along the coastal borders of the nation, and experiencing disproportionately high birthrates. Projections for the future suggest that by the year 2050, the entire country will follow California, Hawaii, New Mexico, and the District of Columbia, all of which are currently inhabited by a majority of minorities (Hicks, 1997; Hobbs & Stoops, 2002; Nelson & O'Reilly, 2000; U.S. Bureau of the Census, 2001). This reality has sparked reactions from widespread fear to anxiety and resentment among White people, all along the continuum from racists to well-intentioned liberals who have never thoroughly examined their personal motivations for social justice positions. Not only low-income, but also angry middle-class White males have expressed feelings of encroachment and fear of losing economic ground; they blame civil rights equity-building policies for creating a more competitive marketplace where White skin privilege is increasingly challenged (Chappell, 1995; Gibbs & Bankhead, 2001; Lynch, 2000; Maharidge, 1996; Tempest, 2003; Webber, 2003). Recently governmental leadership has evidenced disinterest and invidious contempt for the particular needs of people of color—related to economic and civic exclusion. Policy changes, indeed, have limited protections and affirmative action for minorities of color. These policy changes accompany increasingly negative public sentiment, with some Whites assuming that any earlier issues of discrimination have been solved, while others express active hostility, viewing people of color as competitors who threaten "White jobs" rather than deserving equal treatment.

During this enormous shift in both demographics and mainstream perceptions of people of color, racially motivated hate crime has increased (U.S. Department of Justice, 1997). A series of regressive public policy initiatives has targeted people of color across the nation in an attempt to turn back the hands of time on progress, access, and mobility opportunities (Gibbs & Bankhead, 2001).

Backlash Against the Progressive Politics of the 1960s and 1970s

Our society needs formation and social action by multiethnic, multiracial, multicultural coalitions to improve access to education, employment, and health care for all people, particularly minorities of color and all people who are poor. Equally, there is need to respond to the disproportionately high rates of HIV/AIDS, homicide, poverty, teenage pregnancy, low-birthweight babies, and substance abuse in diverse communities. Instead of public policy and social responses to these egregious problems, we are experiencing a backlash against the political and socially progressive politics of the 1960s and 1970s. In this climate, people of color are blamed for the injustices affecting their communities. Once again, people of color and low-income people are made the scapegoat of irrational blame and fear-driven attacks. One impact of this "blaming of victims" is evidenced by clients of human service agencies who present with shame and guilt about circumstances that are beyond their control, apologizing for simply being themselves. Barbara Solomon, in her groundbreaking book *Black Empowerment* (1986), documented these structural conditions that create internal personal barriers as well as enforce external barriers to resources and opportunities.

A right-wing Republican, conservative political agenda has become organized against affirmative action, bilingual education, immigration, and crime definition. These efforts have resulted in the criminalization of young Black and Latino males, the demonization of immigrants, an assault on bilingual education, English-only crusades, and anti-affirmative action efforts (Gibbs & Bankhead, 2001). These actions together constitute a neoconservative backlash against the progress of the civil rights era, a backlash that began with the conservative 1980s and gained momentum during subsequent Republican presidencies (Fisher, 1994). Although in periods of major elections, neoconservative politicians may court the votes of people of color, their policy proposals often further disadvantage minority communities.

This capitalist nation remains ambivalent about responding to the uprising of low income, disenfranchised, ethnically diverse, and oppressed people. Although class, gender, sexual orientation, and income status create constellations of diversity in American society, race continues to be an enduring, significant, and defining characteristic that limits access to opportunity. In the American capitalist context, oppressed people struggle at the margins of society and are vilified, often viewed as dysfunctional, incapable, and damaged. The civil rights movement of the late 1960s and early 1970s, which advocated for people of color, is a foundation for all subsequent grassroots and national social activism. The feminist and gay and lesbian rights movements followed closely in time. White feminists, however, took a long time to recognize the specific and unique aspects of Black feminist/womanist thought and engagement (Weil, 1986). As Barbara Smith, a prominent Black lesbian social activist, has pointed out, the mainstream gay rights movement has sometimes alienated people of color with a narrow, single focus while ignoring that people of color who are gay or lesbian most often have strong social justice concerns in multiple spheres (Diehl, 2000). In both these instances, Black activists have been acutely aware of insufficient attention to issues of race, poverty, homelessness, and police brutality in both the mainstream feminist and gay rights movements. Indeed, notable Black feminist writers Paula Giddings, bell hooks, and Audre Lorde have commented clearly on the historical and current exclusion from the center of mainstream feminist politics the concerns of women of color, ranging from the omission of Black women's rights during the suffrage movements (Giddings, 1988) to polarization of women of color and White women's issues (hooks, 1989; Lorde, 1984). While the civil rights, feminist, and gay and lesbian movements together paved the way for later organizing efforts for populations such as the aging and people with disabilities, one shortcoming in the aftermath of the civil rights movement was the absence of a flexible blueprint for use when addressing future injustices as they arise (Ladner, 2000).

Beyond Cultural Awareness, Appreciation, and Competence

Is Harriet Tubman, architect of the underground railroad, the visual image we conjure when considering a community organizer in American society? Did Saul Alinsky (1971) fully consider people of color in diverse populations when he proposed the rules for radicals? From the Gilded Age to the Progressive Era, during the Settlement Movement, throughout the New Deal and World War II, most visibly during the civil rights era and more sporadically during the current conservative backlash, at every point of societal development in the last century, diverse populations have been organizing for freedom from oppression and for increased access to social, political, and economic opportunity. However, in the community organizing literature, people of color have all too often been ignored, overlooked, and disregarded, their issues minimized and viewed as not deserving special attention or a unique political or theoretical approach (Betten & Austin, 1990; Gittell & Vidal, 1998; Lubove, 1965; Rothman, Erlich, & Tropman, 2001; Rubin & Rubin, 2001; Warren, 1998).

Although the history of community organizing in the social work profession can be traced prior to the Gilded Age, not until the recent American interest in its expanding multicultural society have serious scholarly works been dedicated to the unique community organizing needs of diverse populations (Bradshaw, Soifer, & Gutiérrez, 1994; Edwards, Drews, & Seaman, 1994; Garvin & Cox, 2001; Glugoski, Reisch, & Rivera, 1994; Gutiérrez & Alvarez, 2000; Gutiérrez, Alvarez, Nemon, & Lewis, 1996; Gutiérrez & Lewis, 1994; Rivera & Erlich, 1998). As a result, despite rhetoric to the contrary, community organizing with people from oppressed groups (people of color, women, gays and lesbians, people with disabilities, and those with low incomes) has been marginalized for much of social work's past. These people represent the very populations that today we think of as the center, those who carry the burden of disenfranchisement in our society through the real-life experiences of targeted oppression and discrimination.

Effective Community Organizing With People of Color

Basic tenets of community organizing with diverse populations follow the canon of organizing protocol with special considerations related to the historical, sociopolitical, racial, ethnic, gender, sexual orientation, economic, and ability/disability experience of the community members. It is, however, more important with diverse populations to recognize the sociopolitical and historical context of the organizational effort because it may be inextricably connected to a community experience of marginalization in another social, political, or historical realm. Research with these populations also requires knowledge of community organizing history, admission through gatekeepers, and development of trust (Gibbs & Bankhead-Greene, 1997).

Many of our most successful examples of community organizing in the United States are found in communities of color (Rivera & Erlich, 1998). Equity-building activities that occurred during the civil rights era and union organizing by farm workers are two clear examples. Black and brown people have frequently engaged successfully in collective action resulting in community empowerment.

Considerations for Organizing in Communities of Color

It is important for organizers in communities of color to be familiar with certain historical assumptions and current realities. Throughout much of the literature, there is an unacknowledged assumption of color blindness. More specific is the assumption that universal strategies and tactics may be applied when organizing diverse communities (Betten & Austin, 1990; Gittell & Vidal, 1998; Lubove, 1965; Rothman et al., 2001; Rubin & Rubin, 2001; Warren, 1998). The focus on low-income status as a contributing factor to disempowerment in communities has resulted in an overemphasis on social class, along with inadequate attention to the particular and harmful consequences of racism (Rivera & Erlich, 1998). White activists have been caught in a double bind when organizing in communities of color, in that they are alternately seen as able to infuse the struggle into a larger (White) community and often are unable to be fully trusted because of their outsider status. Dissent by people of color has been viewed by the mainstream as a threat to the social order, in part because people of color in the United States remain engaged in an ongoing struggle to be recognized as fully human. Confrontational empowerment historically has been the most successful tactic employed by communities of color in the fight for social justice, where community members have relied on informal networks, the value of insider status, and adherence to hierarchical mobilization efforts. The following is an expanded discussion of concerns for organizing in communities of color.

1. Assumption of effective color-blind strategies and tactics. The history of community organizing is replete with the arrogant assumption that a single set of strategies and tactics can be wrapped around an infinite set of problems. This one-size-fits-all approach to organizing communities disrespects the unique challenges, triumphs, cultural values, and real and powerful experiences with oppression that create cohesion within and shape boundaries around a community.

2. Inadequate emphasis on the impact of racism in society. Historically, economic status and class struggle have been overemphasized with corresponding neglect of the significance of the deleterious impact of racism on people of color. Community organizers themselves are much to blame for framing this debate through a White middle-class view of capitalist society. The age-old debate among organizers regarding whether poverty or racism is the worst problem deflects attention from the intricacies of the interaction of the two (Rivera & Erlich, 1998). Race, class, and gender are all significant; however, it remains reasonable to focus on race, as it continues to be a leading motivating factor not only for discrimination but for violence, hate crimes, exclusion, abuse, and incarceration.

3. Double bind for White activists. Historically, White middle-class liberal community organizers have been thought of by members of communities of color as engaging in a cathartic process of clearing their own consciences, particularly with regard to being undeserving beneficiaries of white skin and often economic privilege. These liberal, sometimes progressive thinkers may be well-intentioned organizers, but they are also ensnared in a double bind—carrying with them their own struggles, issues, and complexities, which may diminish their effectiveness as social change agents with culturally different populations. Although the authors strongly encourage White activists to stand up, comfortably and with a clear conscience and passionate heart, to counter injustices in communities of color, it is essential that they be aware of the often problematic legacy of historical cross-cultural organizing efforts and that they tailor strategies and tactics to honor those realities.

4. Democratic dissent as a threat to the social order. At the heart of the struggle for people of color has been a cry for their humanity to be fully recognized. In this nation, women, people of color, and the poor have historically been seen as not fully human—as not possessing the capacity, credibility, or worth to hold dissenting views. Marginalized people in the United States have thus always been engaged in an equity-building agenda that will ultimately admit them to full status in the human race as credible, capable, and worthy to be complete, vocal, and respected participants in civil society.

In the 1960s, a focus in organizing efforts was on teaching and sharing tactics. Of central import was a political and theoretical perspective that argued for recognition of the humanity of people of color, particularly young Black men. One common slogan adopted from Malcolm X was "by any means necessary." This militant approach served a dual purpose both to inspire other people of color to get in touch with the power they possessed and to create shock and awe in mainstream White society. Although many people, both Black and White, were alienated by this aspect of the movement, these images are some of the most potent, memorable, and powerful from the period.

5. Confrontational empowerment. The civil rights era's model of social justice organizing for people of color is rooted in a militant, public-protest framework. Actions such as public demonstrations, sit-ins, marches, and, in rare cases, a call to arms have challenged legal limits of the social order and created some fears and anxieties for all involved in this style of protest. Unfortunately, this legacy has alienated would-be activists who fear association with groups that could be considered lawless, groups that sometimes engage in illegal activity even if it is to challenge unjust laws. In addition, this style of confrontational empowerment has courageously relied heavily on an analysis of power, privilege, and the pathway to compromise.

6. Informal networks. Although all of community organizing might be thought of as occurring in loosely formed networks, diverse populations may have more skepticism, resistance, and caution about formal organizing efforts, especially when initiated by an outsider or when providing material resources for some limited special segment of community members is a goal. For example, if an affordable housing campaign, marketed as helping the whole community, is in fact designed to benefit only a few investors, community activists will understand the marginal benefits to the community, but they may not want to erect barriers to a questionable project because it will at least provide a needed service to some community members. This reliance on and trust in loosely formed, informal, and kinship networks is related to the historical experiences of diverse communities, wherein a heightened degree of guardedness and reasonable suspicion of outsiders is warranted.

7. Insider status valued. Since the height of the civil rights era, the trust of outsiders has eroded among members of communities of color. This mistrust developed following widespread negative experiences with organizers who had their own unstated agendas. In the case of the environmental movement, mainstream environmental organizations, claiming to care about environmental racism, have narrowly defined environmental justice to focus on air, water, land, and pesticides and have actively excluded the race factor in location of these hazards, even though several studies conducted in communities of color since the late 1980s have found disproportionate amounts of toxic waste, polluted water, and environment-related public health concerns (Chang & Hwang, 2000). For example, before the South West Organizing Project (SWOP) began the environmental justice movement targeting environmental racism in New Mexico, mainstream environmental organizers would contribute to the problem by dispassionately and inaccurately advocating on behalf of communities of which they were not members (Calpotura & Wing, 2000). These more recent out-group activists sometimes acted as informants who posed as organizers but who were more interested in gathering intelligence to counter organizing efforts within communities of color. Some aimed to sabotage or dismantle plans from within community groups, as did segregationists in earlier periods, who were deceptively working to cause harm to communities under the guise of offering assistance. What emerged in the late 1970s and early 1980s was increased emphasis on single-issue, single-race, single-gender, single-ethnic group organizing efforts because common cultural understanding, in-group membership, and a more intimate connection to the specific issue result in a deeper investment in both the process of organizing and the outcome. For example, a low-income Latina living in New Mexico may not have to worry about the *possibility* of toxic waste; she has to organize her neighborhood because the toxic dump is already there. Single-issue, single-group organizing efforts minimize need for suspicion of outsiders and may create greater solidarity.

8. People of color's hierarchical relation to community organizing. People of color are likely to become impassioned about issues central to increasing the value, equity, and quality of life for all people. Perhaps the reason people of color have been less likely to become involved in animal rights is because of this pragmatic sensibility that places human welfare first. People of color may desire a more hierarchical structure for mobilizing organizing campaigns. Such a model would have strong leadership, a clear outcome, and a shared vision. Consensus decision making and participatory democracy would precede a more linear command structure to operationalize the plan. This model suggests that multiple demands on the lives of people of color in modern society may place value on efficiency in implementing an organizing plan.

Considerations for Organizing in an Evolving and Diverse Society

Community organization with diverse populations has evolved to cover many macro practice activities. These include community-based organization and corporate economic coalitions, community building through public social action, fact-finding for social planning, organizational development, and social justice demonstrations in the form of marches, sit-ins, and organized civil disobedience. In this section, we will discuss trends that may suggest changes needed in community organizing approaches as society is diversified through the introduction of new technologies, as some members of communities of color strengthen their economic base and attain greater socioeconomic status, and as tolerance for violence in society increases.

Hate Groups Flourish

Technology, in a number of ways, creates social and physical distance between individuals, organizations, and communities of color. There is the appearance of intimacy because of the sheer volume of electronic communication many receive; however, this substitute for face-to-face contact often leads to distortion in our perception of the world around us. Recent rapid technological advancement has paved the way for nonphysical communities to organize, exchange information, and spread messages anonymously. The emergence of the faceless virtual community can be witnessed in the fearless proliferation of Internet-based hate groups that advertise messages encouraging attacks of African Americans, Asians, Latinos, and gays and lesbians. Such technology is powerful in its ability to support racially motivated hate groups by offering them a faceless voice. The Internet has, therefore, become a vehicle for negative coalition building of conservative and neoconservative group members wishing to share ideas in private that they might not feel justified sharing openly in their physical communities.

Rise in Acceptable Injustices

With the increasing population of middle-class people of color has come a corresponding increase in physical isolation and a kind of apathy that could not be held when communities of color more typically lived in the same neighborhoods regardless of class status. The relocation of many middle-class people of color to the suburbs has created physical and social distance from their low-income counterparts, who have largely been left in urban centers. The result is fewer physical boundaries for communities and a transformation to cultural communities that are organized around identity with reference to race, gender, ethnicity, and sexual orientation. This reality has changed the face of organizing in communities of color such that today's organizing efforts are less connected to physical place and more concerned with the politics of identity (Delgado, 1994). With the absence of physical boundaries to designate a community, we find fewer positions on which community members are able to interact enough to find agreement. As a result, there seems to be increased tolerance for "acceptable injustices." Small and large everyday hassles, annoying insults, and other racially motivated inconveniences are routinely tolerated. Injustices such as the disproportionately high rate of Black and Latino incarceration and inadequate police response in communities of color are accepted as endemic. Insufficient access to positions of power—for example, the disproportionately low rate of people of color who are top business executives and run successful large businesses—is seen as an intractable problem, firmly rooted in racism. These injustices are viewed by professionals of color as things that likely will not change in their lifetimes.

Independence Valued Above Interdependence

The American cultural promotion of radical individualism and its concomitant devaluing of interdependence are in stark contrast to the traditional cultural experiences of many people of color. This major difference in orientation to life can create cultural conflict as members of communities of color struggle to maintain their social and community responsibilities emphasizing interconnectedness while they increasingly have to accommodate to efficiency-based models in other aspects of their lives. Increasingly, they experience external cultural pressure to emphasize private benefit and independence over community advancement (Gibbs & Huang, 1989; Lum, 2003).

Violence as an Acceptable Means of Resolving Conflict

Violence in America as a whole, and even more so in some communities of color, is too often seen as an acceptable means of resolving conflict (Children's Defense Fund, 1995). This unfortunate reality disproportionately impacts people in communities of color, the same people who are discriminated against in our legal system (Adams, Onek, & Riker, 1998; American Civil Liberties Union, 1999; Davis, Estes, & Schiraldi, 1996; Koetting & Schiraldi, 1994; Males & Macallair, 2000; Poe-Yamagata & Jones, 2000).

Ignorance or Amnesia? Current Issues in Organizing Diverse Communities

It is unclear if post-civil rights era generations are misinformed and uneducated about the historic challenges and hard-won advances of large-scale community organizing efforts, or if these struggles simply have been forgotten or ignored with the lapse of time and distance from media coverage. Regardless, this dulling of memory has resulted in a complacency through which some people of color are willing to tolerate an inordinate number of acceptable injustices. Contemporary organizing efforts within oppressed populations are plagued by deception and disloyalty. For example, a large multiservice public-benefit organization in San Francisco, with an $8 million annual budget, received a substantial city grant to provide education about violence against women and self-protection for children of color. However, the funding was primarily used to cover the organization's existing overhead expenses. The case was complex; however, the agency was largely administered by and for low-income people of color during a time of dwindling government grants. Nevertheless, the targeted issue of violence against women and girls of color in this community went largely unaddressed because of a deceptive and disloyal use of funds.

Competing and conflicting alliances occur, often both inside and outside community organizing efforts. An example internal to an organizing effort would be the conflict that some low-income women of color feel about their economic advancement, which often facilitates their ability to move out of a community that they have helped transform into a healthier place. This phenomenon happened several times in the Girls After School Academy (GASA), a women's and girls' economic and social justice empowerment project located in a large public housing development in San Francisco. The organization provided weekend and after-school education support, tutorial services, and recreation and leadership training for girls; organized public forums and justice campaigns for the community; and offered training and testing for community mothers seeking high school equivalency diplomas. One conflicting effect of such a successful program is that talent can be drained from the community because as the most capable participants become more empowered and self-sufficient, they often move out of the community and disengage as a community resource. There are also many competing agendas outside of communities of color, such as the current resurgent conservative political agenda.

A nationwide deceptive backlash is under way in the United States, which aims to advance a conservative political agenda by using progressive key words and phrases such as civil rights, racial privacy, law and order, and increased educational opportunity (Gibbs & Bankhead, 2001). This backlash has a different and negative impact on communities of color. These efforts pander to fearful, conservative, uneducated, and older people, and even to average professionals who are too exhausted and overwhelmed by the demands of daily living (overcrowded cities, difficulty with transportation, challenges negotiating goods and services, high housing costs, and inadequate leisure time) to thoroughly investigate changing public policies, consider ballot initiatives, and think about how they might actively participate in civic life. Through convoluted media misinformation using progressive labels for regressive policies, an overall deceptive message has emerged that advances conservative causes (Armbruster, Geron, & Bonacich, 1995; Brimelow, 1995; Gibbs & Bankhead, 2001; Muller, 1997; Preston & Lai, 1998; Taqi-Eddin, Macallair, & Schiraldi, 1998). After the September 11, 2001, terrorist attacks, we witnessed an emergence of nativist ideologies that were exploited by conservative politicians and spokespersons, who stretched the truth and used fear to aid in violating civil rights and overstepping boundaries of protection, free speech, and privacy (O'Leary, 1999; O'Leary & Platt, 2002; Scraton, 2002; Thomas, 2002). In communities of color as diverse as South Central Los Angeles and emerging Southeast Asian immigrant communities in San Francisco, we are experiencing a wartime hysteria that supports public belief in very thinly veiled exaggeration. This tendency to stretch the truth is described in Daniel Ellsberg's new book, *Secrets: A Memoir of Vietnam and the Pentagon Papers,* in which he concludes, "The President's men think they have a license to lie that never expires" (quoted in Mirsky, 2003, p. 46). This sentiment is nowhere more apparent than in conservative political leaders' pronouncements about communities of color.

Competing and conflicting alliances among ethnic group members on issues such as whether to support Rodney King or O. J. Simpson are resulting in perceived disloyalty and side-switching on issues, which compromises the potential efficacy of multiethnic, multiracial coalitions. As a consequence, issue-oriented coalition building has emerged among communities of color. For example, a select community group might get behind an effort that monitors police for racial profiling; however, that same watch group may not be able to unite in pressing for a better transportation infrastructure and clean air. These coalitions are fragile and dependent solely on the degree to which each represented community can benefit. The guiding principles in the new age of organizing are less dependent on what is the right thing to do and more a reflection of who will benefit the most.

Not Your Average Hippie's Struggle

An emerging theme in community organizing combines a rise in apathy, concerns about deception, and a neoconservative political agenda. Deceit takes advantage of elders, people who are uneducated, and middle-class citizens who advocate only for policies that offer private rather than public benefit. The neoconservative, covert assault on affirmative action, bilingual education, immigrants, the unemployed, people of color, and addicts puts a modern cloak on a vintage problem. The current conservative political agenda and the response to it will likely not follow a 1960s-style confrontational empowerment model. Response to political manipulation of capitalist values requires being prepared for cynical misrepresentations of public issues by neoconservative strategists, who routinely put a colored face, like that of Ward Connerly (the Black man who is a University of California Regent and the major sponsor of that state's Proposition 209, the anti-affirmative action initiative, and Proposition 54, the so-called racial privacy initiative) or Linda Chavez (a Latina who has campaigned for anti-immigrant initiatives) on the latest conservative crusade. The new racist policies benefit the diminishing White majority and result in dwindling opportunity for all. Some of these regressive policies, such as Proposition 209, could result in sanctions through reduced federal support for state violation of federal equal opportunity mandates. Proposition 187, the so-called Save Our State Initiative, demonized immigrants and overstepped the boundaries of California's jurisdiction in its effort to set federal immigration policy (Gibbs & Bankhead, 2001).

An alarming trend related to individualism and privatization is disinterest and emotional distancing by middle-class people of color as well as Whites on issues that contribute to the strengthening of civil society and the common good. The not-in-my-back-yard (NIMBY) mentality has been widely adopted by middle-class would-be activists who in prior generations may have lent a hand to protesting social injustices. For example, during the 1960s, many people across racial lines committed to equity activism. However, during the 1990s, there was much less support for social action, particularly among the middle class and others not immediately impacted by particular injustices or social problems.

The aftermath of the tragedy of September 11, 2001, created and has maintained a vision of America under attack. This sparked in the American people an unexpected level of reactive patriotism, prompted by widespread fear that accompanied a long-delayed recognition of the vulnerability of this nation and the consequences of world domination (O'Leary & Platt, 2002). In this light, the emerging model that we propose for work with diverse populations in the 21st century is a mixture of uncommon sense and current realities of racial, ethnic, class, and sexual politics. There are two aspects of this paradigm. The first addresses cultural competence; the second explicates qualities of organizers that we believe are intimately related to organizing success.

The Cultural Incompetence Reality

Few issues in the recent history of social work and social work education, to say nothing of community organization, have generated as much difficulty and confusion as cultural competence. For individuals and organizations alike, cultural competence goals have become badges of honor. Unfortunately, the rhetoric of commitment is rarely matched by the reality of knowledge and sensitivities.

A bit of history is instructive here. In the face of the civil rights revolution of the 1960s, the Council on Social Work Education (CSWE) structured meetings around the issues of diversity. One of the raging debates was whether a single course devoted exclusively to diversity was better than a commitment to address diversity questions throughout the social work curriculum. Over time, it became increasingly clear to people in the field and in the classroom that both were necessary, especially because it appeared that if either approach became primary, the other could be more easily ignored. (It is interesting to note that despite CSWE members' noble goals to address diversity, they often did not follow through in action; during meetings, White, Asian, African American, and Latino groups each had their own place to congregate.)

The current status of cultural competence and awareness in the field is hardly cause for celebration. Of the enormous number of problematic examples that might be cited, perhaps a simple one will suffice. A bilingual Latina student of one of the authors was placed with a small-town rural family agency serving a population that was about 55% primarily or exclusively Spanish-speaking. She was the only Spanish-speaking staff member in the agency. With instructor support and encouragement, she raised this issue with the agency. The response was the all-too-typical, "We would like to hire more bilingual staff, but we just can't find any."

Over the next 7 months of her placement, nothing more was said. Although there certainly is a lack of bilingual staff in the region, benign neglect is not likely to turn up possible recruits.

In an effort to contain costs and increase efficiency, the ideological commitment to cultural competence has been trumpeted while infrastructure to support it has been absent or starved for resources. A well-delivered annual 2-hour in-service on cultural competence cannot possibly keep a staff sharp in this arena. The illusion is maintained, inexpensively and with little challenge to the status quo. Consider the observations of Lecca, Quervalu, Nunes, and Gonzales (1998):

> Look . . . at the number of minority faculty in our institutions of higher learning, our research programs, and in the management and administration of both private and public entities . . . the numbers are dismal. (p. 254)

Surely, when social work practitioners and students look around them in most agencies, the underrepresentation of culturally relevant staff (in relation to the groups represented in the populations served), especially bilingual staff, is apparent. This representation is even more evident in top-level positions in a wide range of agencies. Unfortunately, this problem appears to be even more evident among organizers working in communities of color. The simple answer, "Well, I guess we're just going to have to use White organizers," is self-limiting. That is, although there are roles that White organizers can usefully play (as noted below), to deny the absolute necessity to recruit and train African American, Latino, Asian, and Native American organizers is to avoid one fundamental challenge of cultural competence.

The standard view of current cultural competence within social work, if such may be said to exist, is significantly based in the 2002 diversity standards of the CSWE's *Educational Policy and Accreditation*. As Lum (2003, p. 1) summarizes, curricula are expected to contain and/or encourage:

> Content that promotes understanding, affirmation, and respect for people from diverse backgrounds

> Content that emphasizes the interlocking and complex nature of culture and personal identity

> Social services that are culturally relevant and able to meet the needs of groups served

> Diversity within and between groups that may influence assessment, planning, intervention, and research

> Skills on how to define, design, and implement strategies for effective practice with persons of diverse backgrounds

For us, this is a place to initiate, not end a search for true cultural competence as it relates to working with communities of color. Our core objective must be empowerment. Much as we might prefer it otherwise, there is no way to go directly from sensitive awareness to equality-based, cross-cultural interaction and social justice. The issue of who can do what for whom under what circumstances is neither simple nor easy. There has been extensive documentation of indigenously led, successful organizing efforts in African American, Latino, Asian, and Native American communities (Rivera & Erlich, 1998). There is, however, no guarantee of success for people whose background is the same as or similar to that of community residents. As Rivera and Erlich (1998) note, by way of example, in certain Mexican American communities, there are conflicting loyalties to different leaders in Mexico's complex revolutionary history. Ignorance of this history or preconceived ideas about presumed identification with certain leaders can lead to awkward moments for an otherwise exceptionally sensitive Mexican American organizer. Likewise, many immigrants from Southeast Asia over the last few decades have arrived with long-standing political and social loyalties that put them in conflict with longer-term residents or newly arriving countrymen.

For a variety of complicated reasons, most community organizers and people teaching about community organization have been White males. Many of the teachers bring with them the organizing experience of the student, anti-war, and civil rights movements of the 1960s and early 1970s. Liberal and radical alike, it is their credo and gut-level sense that White people can be effective organizers in communities of color. Freire (1994) talks about "naïve consciousness," or a tendency to take a romanticized view of intensely rewarding past events (like fighting the "good fight" for justice, brotherhood, and truth) and trying to force that view into the future without adequately taking account of not only the more subtle dimensions noted above, but also the racial and ethnic uniqueness of a particular population; differences in kinship structures, power, and subsystem patterns; and, perhaps most important, the development of critical consciousness and the process of empowerment.

For the authors, then, cultural competence in community organizing needs to be viewed differently than it might be in work with individuals, families, and small groups. Zuniga (2003) notes that workers in the latter context need knowledge of culturally relevant, community-based agencies and resources. For organizers, this is only one place for important investigation. Stopping at that depth, organizers risk being regarded as culturally incompetent. Both knowledge of and identification with the community must be addressed. Successful strategies and tactics depend on the nature and intensity of the contacts the organizer has with the community, as well as the constraints these contacts place on the organizer, no matter how much like the people in the community the organizer may be. Rivera and Erlich (1998) have developed a multi-tier model that we believe is useful in exploring both the meaning of cultural competence in organizing and the essential roles that can be played by culturally varied organizers. The authors have, it should be noted, taken some conceptual liberties with the model and altered it to meet their view of current political and social realities. Rivera and Erlich posit a three-tier design of "contact intensity and influence." The authors suggest the model might more properly be termed to encompass "contact intensity and patterns of influence" at the primary, secondary, and tertiary levels of community involvement (see Figure 3.1).

The primary level requires racial, cultural, and linguistic identity with the community. Thus, full ethnic solidarity with the community is needed for intimate entry at this level. A Puerto Rican in a Mexican American community, a Haitian in

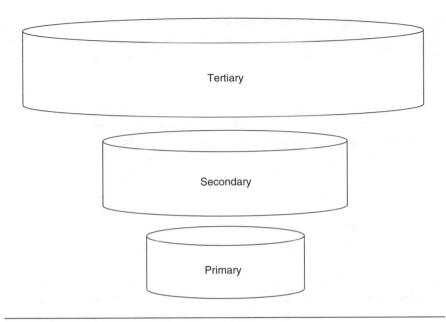

Figure 3.1   Contact Intensity and Patterns of Influence

NOTE: As the figure illustrates, primary intensity indicates greatest identification, possibility of influence, and connection to a specific community of color, while tertiary workers would not be members of that group but would be able to provide advocacy, perhaps technical assistance, and supportive influence in the broader community. The primary cylinder indicates the likelihood that workers having these primary connections will be fewer in number while the broader community will have a large number of social workers carrying out diverse functions.

an African American community, or a Turkish Muslim in an Afghani-American community would not qualify.

The secondary level requires a similarity of culture and experience but not language fluency (of course, the more language skill the better). Particularly when the organizing functions are likely to stress serving as a bridge between the organizing community and broader communities, this level of contact intensity seems viable. However, a sensitive and thorough awareness of community culture is necessary if the organizer is to be effective in helping to interpret the needs of the organizing community to the broader community, and interpreting the service perspectives of the broader community to the organizing community. Here the Puerto Rican, Haitian, and Turk described above might well have an important role.

The third or tertiary level would involve someone who is easily and clearly identified as an outsider working for the welfare of the community. Linguistic, cultural, ethnic, or racial similarity is not required. The brokerage, advocacy, and information-gathering and -dissemination functions would need to be especially significant. Technical skills in appropriate roles are highly desirable. Both dissimilar people of color (e.g., the Puerto Rican in an African American community) and Whites may be particularly effective at this level.

What if no people of color are available? The frequently heard lament, "What if no people of color are available?" in many parts of the United States is more an excuse for avoiding serious recruitment efforts than a statement of absolute reality. There are, however, places in the country—many rural areas and some areas dominated by small cities or towns—where communities of color are currently very small in number, and often composed of newly arrived immigrants or migrants with little experience with English or with organizing. In these areas, organizers of color are often in short supply and are greatly needed. Academic programs in or near these places have a challenging balancing act to manage. On the one hand, social work academic programs need to educate their current students to provide needed and relevant services, programs, outreach, information, brokering, bridging, and advocacy for communities of color. On the other hand is the even greater professional responsibility to seriously strengthen recruitment and retention efforts and to provide financial and other resources for students of color. Of particular importance is to recruit, retain, and engage students from established and emerging communities of color in community practice so that they can take on the primary and secondary contact intensity roles requiring racial, cultural, and linguistic identity with the communities they serve, as well as the secondary roles of bridging between communities of color and the broader community. In our view, as long as Whites take on roles in which people of color are clearly to be preferred (as noted above), the efforts toward empowerment, self-determination, and local control will be blunted. Education in cultural competency is important for all students—but the greater the distance, the greater the risks of cultural incompetence. Communities of color are most likely to engage more quickly and more closely with workers who share their culture and concerns. The three-tier conceptualization of contact intensity and patterns of influence offers a partial guiding framework for organizer effectiveness.

Emerging Practice Model of Organizing in Diverse Communities

What should an organizer bring to the organizing task? The model we offer for work with diverse populations is about organizer qualities that we believe are intimately related to organizing success. Following the work of Rivera and Erlich (1998), we suggest certain qualities of sensitivity, knowledge, skills, abilities, experience, and attributes that are most likely to lead to success. In a sense, our model is more of a statement of goals to be mutually explored between community and organizer than it is an expression of absolutes on which the fate of organizing efforts absolutely depends.

1. Similar Cultural and Racial Identification

There is no stronger identification with a community than truly being part of it. The most successful organizers, at least since the 1960s, are people who resemble the community in their own culture, race, language, and sexual identity. To some degree, this may also be true of the class identification of the organizer.

2. Familiarity With Traditions, Customs, Values, and Social Networks

A solid and thoughtful grounding in the traditions and customs of the community being organized is vital. This is particularly the case for people with racial, cultural, linguistic, and sexual (as appropriate) identification but who, like many graduate students, may have been away from their own communities for a significant period of time. One of the core problems is often generational and cultural. That is, younger, more formally educated organizers may find themselves at odds with community elders in a variety of ways. Elders may be much more conservative than the organizers and prefer discussion and various forms of mediation to confrontation and other forms of direct action. Respect for the elders' culture and traditions will go a long way toward reducing the likelihood of unnecessary struggles and battles. Patience with what G. K. Chesterton called "the thunder of the authority of human habit" is required. A typical issue is the dynamics of organized religion in the target community, and how that has changed in the recent past. Ignoring this area can put the organizer at perceived spiritual odds with the community in a way that can completely undermine an organizing effort.

3. Intimate Knowledge of Language and Group/Subgroup Slang

Although this is clearly related to the cultural dimensions already listed, we regard it as being of such importance that it requires specific attention. True understanding of the group or subgroup language style is indispensable when engaged with communities that are mono- or bilingual. Idiomatic expressions that are acceptable in some communities may be highly offensive in others. Terms with sexual overtones come immediately to mind. The pejorative way homosexuals, bisexuals, and transgendered individuals are referred to in many Latino, Asian, and African American communities suggests another significant example.

4. Leadership Development and Style

Although organizers must be leaders to be effective, an essential part of that leadership is working with established and emerging leaders in an ongoing training process. Many individual attributes, such as roles, values, and political perspectives, need to be nourished and explored. A key for both organizers and community leaders is the respectful use of power, which often seems at odds with the disrespectful way power is expressed by nonindigenous leaders in relation to communities of color.

5. A Framework for Political and Economic Analysis

Although an analysis of the dynamics of oppression is desirable for community leaders, it is essential for organizers. This includes social class as well as structures of authority within the ethnic community and the systems of internal power (both formal and informal). Without this framework, points of political leverage and access tend to remain obscure if not completely mysterious. What, also, are the sources of mediating influences between the local and wider communities? Understanding the economic status of the community is vital in appraising its roles and functions (however limited they may be) in the greater community. Kinds of employment and the extent of under- and unemployment are examples. One important aspect of this is for organizers to let the community know about their willingness to offer information about the interaction between the economics of the community and the broader economic and social systems.

6. Knowledge of Past Organizing Efforts and Plans for Sustainability

We believe it is imperative that organizers educate themselves about past organizing efforts (and their relative success or failure) in the communities in which they work. This information needs to be archived so that future organizers can have the benefit of it. Unfortunately, the tendency is for most community organizers to treat history as an impediment to action. Although we do not believe that those who ignore history are always doomed to repeat it, there is much to be learned from what worked and did not work in the past, especially if illuminating explanations can be found.

The organizer must make a commitment to communities of color that goes beyond the immediate and short-term goals of the present organizing effort. Too often, communities that have experienced an organizing campaign were left in the aftermath without support for much-needed additional organizing efforts. It is essential that a plan for sustainability be articulated so that community members have relative assurance that their efforts will have a long-lasting effect.

7. Skills in Empowerment Through Conscientization

Disenfranchised communities need to be supported in developing the kind of critical consciousness that can lead to empowerment. Problem solving without building power, as Alinsky (1971) so importantly noted, is likely to have limited medium- or long-term consequences. The consciousness that leads to power involves an understanding of personal experience and political processes and how they affect each other.

Emerging community power may take many additional forms. Developing trust between organizer and community, as well as mutual reliance on each other's commitment to change, is one important form of this power building. It is also to be seen in a special kind of love—of family, of community, of everyday life—that motivates organizer and community.

8. Skills in Assessing Community Psychology

With the recent proliferation of interest in and materials about diversity and cultural competence, there has been an unfortunate tendency to lock in on what appear to be progressive concern stereotypes, as with the expectation of male dominance in certain Asian cultures. Although rooted in cultural traditions, these can be stereotypes nonetheless. On the other hand, ignoring information about traditional cultures can have equally deleterious consequences. The balance needs to be aimed at appraising what the community is as an organic entity. Is it growing, mature, or declining—or are different parts at different stages? Are there families that have roots extending back generations? Are there new arrivals or waves of recent arrivals? Does language serve as a cohesive force within the community or a divisive one? Is this an area of conflict between generations? Does the community feel somewhat frustrated and powerless? Has it lost (or won) a recent effort at community improvement? Is the sense that "you can't fight city hall" pervasive? Or is there anger focused on a particular problem or issue that can be a catalyst for mobilization?

9. Organizational Behavior and Decision Making

Although an understanding of organizational behavior is currently regarded as a necessity in training human service professionals, the views presented tend to be theoretical and conceptual rather than truly digging into the reality of the complex tangle created when people join together in organizations. This important understanding may apply equally to both the organizational targets of change and whatever kind of community-based organization is being created. Special attention needs to be drawn to how the established patterns of decision making impact organizational effectiveness and change. Problematic issues of the use and accumulation of dysfunctional personal power should not be ignored by organizers; nor should efforts to control dissemination of information for personal gain. Organizers have the responsibility to coach and assist group members in "keeping their eyes on the prize" and on the common good of the organization and the community.

Often disregarded are what Bachrach and Baratz (1970) call "decisionless decisions"—when nondecisions are actually decisions in terms of impact on decision-making processes. A frequent explanation is that "things just happen." Bachrach and Baratz (p. 247) suggest that nondecisions as decisions may be defined as

> a means by which demands for change in the existing allocation of benefits and privileges in the community can be suffocated before they are even voiced or kept covert; or killed before they can gain access to the relevant decision-making arena; or, failing all these things, maimed or destroyed in the decision-implementing stage of the policy process.

10. Skills in Participatory and Evaluative Research

Communities of color have often been victimized by research that has defined their problems and needs without any significant community participation. Who, for example, should control the understanding and meaning of rates of teen pregnancy? Frequently, the data are used to support action that is politically expedient in the wider community or meets the operational needs of the most powerful service providers in the community. What is needed is an expanded role for organizers in analyzing demographic data, population projections, and social problem specification. At the same time, a vital context for current research must explore the strengths and resilience of communities, which enable them to survive in the face of declining social, economic, and political bases, as well as open hostility from majority communities, restricted employment opportunities, and encroachment on civil rights and liberties. Crime, especially drug-related crime, must be addressed in this context. Participatory approaches to research, in which organizers and community members come together as equal partners, need to be sought.

Skills in evaluation research should become part of the organizer's tool kit. This includes both appraisal of programs intended to benefit the community, as well as assessment of the effectiveness of organizing strategies and tactics. This is also an area where groups of organizers from different communities can get together to share information and experiences that might reduce major mistakes and increase effectiveness. In this regard, full advantage needs to be taken of new technologies, particularly the Internet and specialized databases.

11. Proficiency in Management, Program Development, and Planning

Reasonable levels of expertise in these arenas are important to provide guidance for community-based organizations so they can function effectively and serve as a training ground for community members to prepare to take on administrative and managerial responsibilities inside and outside the community. Mentoring may turn out to be a much more important function than previously recognized.

12. A Strong and Flexible Vision of the Future

One important aspect of power building is belief in the possibility of a better future. Although it is often said that community activists must be optimists or they would quit in frustration, too often this adage is not effectively communicated to the community members with whom they work. Part of the problem is that most organizers feel they have to appear "tough" and skeptical to be credible, but that should not preclude a shared vision that things truly can get better. That sense of hope for transforming the future is part of what makes organizing possible.

Both for themselves and for the community, it is important that organizers have a view of what a stronger, healthier, more empowered place could look and feel like in the future for the people who live there. This means not a high-minded, simplistic laundry list of all the things that should be improved, but a clear and concrete vision of how, for example, safer streets might feel to the people who live on them, or what the old crack house might look like as an employment opportunity center. The vision must, however, remain flexible in the face of the ever-changing reality of community politics and the broad influences to which they are subject.

13. The Myth of Superorganizer

Where can one find the "superorganizer" who has all the characteristics and skills described in this list? It would be unreasonable to expect that one individual could excel in all these areas. Like models of strategy and tactics, this is a design to be worked with and modified as each situation requires. Perhaps most important is that organizers recognize that they may lack vital knowledge and skills and then work hard to obtain them for the community's benefit. Being a good organizer also means being willing to ask for help and being able to step aside in favor of someone who may bring more of what is needed to a particular situation.

Organizers must be keenly aware of their own limitations, especially in relation to handling frustration and high stress. The consequences of burnout are too well documented to require additional repetition, but even the strongest organizers must be prepared to catch themselves taking out their distress on the communities they are trying to serve. Care should be taken to provide for one's own rest and relaxation.

Finally, great care should be taken not to assume a position of "doing it for the community"—or to allow others to cast the organizer in this role. This can destroy or seriously limit the effort toward empowerment, as well as create an organizer who risks feeling "eaten alive." Organizers who withdraw from a community because they have put themselves in this position do a great disservice not only to themselves but also to communities whose reputation as a place where change can occur may be seriously compromised.

Conclusion

In our discussion, we have tried to illustrate that organizing in communities of color is not static but rather a complex, difficult, and always evolving practice that must flexibly meet the needs of the community of interest. Organizing in communities of color offers practitioners a moving target, where they must be concerned with history, biography, labor, and policy in response to rapidly shifting political, economic, and social conditions. To be effective, not only must organizers be compassionate, culturally competent, and aware of subtle cultural as well as racial differences, stereotypes, and the legacy of historic organizing efforts, but also they must critically assess their relationship to power, the future vision of the community of interest, and the long-term meaning of the work. They must also articulate why community members should trust them and invest time and talents in the organizing effort. It is essential in this organizing process that people of color are not blamed, even inadvertently, for circumstances beyond their control, for their values and attitudes, or for simply being themselves. All too often, low-income people of color who seek assistance are put in the position of feeling they must begin by apologizing for who they are. We believe that it is part of the mission of social work to truly preserve human dignity by affirming people with the skins they are in.

Community organizing with people of color is at a crossroads. The aftermath of the wars in Afghanistan and Iraq, tight budgetary constraints, increasing political polarization and cultural conflicts highlighted in the media support a broad political dominance of right-wing ideology. The resulting racial tensions are very much part of our daily lives, and little resolution is in sight. In this context, the question of appropriate roles for White people in organizing communities of color takes on special meaning.

Clearly, people of color and White people must work together to challenge the oppression of people of color, or what Garland (2003), in relation to imprisonment, has aptly termed "the culture of control." Yet, in many ways, the powerful social movement toward individualism deems this scenario less likely now than at any time since the 1960s. So in a period where profound racial tensions are boiling just below the surface, as well as out in the open, there is an urgent need to fill leadership roles in community organizing with people who have the closest possible "contact intensity" in relation to communities of interest. Most often, this will mean people of color who are primary or secondary participants in these communities as we have suggested. The challenge to encourage and assist people of color in taking leadership roles in their own communities is intense. Vitally important is to inspire White people to be engaged in the struggle and to genuinely value their efforts in standing up for the concerns of communities of color, even though they are playing supporting roles. For the future of our struggling communities of color, we can do no less.

References

Adams, R., Onek, D., & Riker, A. (1998). *Double jeopardy: An assessment of the felony drug provision of the welfare reform act.* Washington, DC: Justice Policy Institute.

Alinsky, S. D. (1971). *Rules for radicals: A pragmatic primer for realistic radicals.* New York: Random House.

American Civil Liberties Union. (1999). *Driving while Black: Racial profiling on our nation's highways.* New York: Author.

Armbruster, R., Geron, K., & Bonacich, E. (1995). The assault on California's Latinos immigrants: The politics of Proposition 187. *International Journal of Urban and Regional Research, 19*(4), 655–663.

Bachrach, P., & Baratz, M. (1970). *Power and poverty: Theory and practice.* New York: Oxford University Press.

Betten, N., & Austin, M. (1990). *The roots of community organizing, 1917–1939.* Philadelphia: Temple University Press.

Bradshaw, C., Soifer, S., & Gutiérrez, L. (1994). Toward a hybrid model for effective organizing in communities of color. *Journal of Community Practice, 1*(1), 25–41.

Brimelow, A. (1995). *Alien nation: Common sense about America's immigration disaster.* New York: Random House.

Calpotura, F., & Wing, B. (2000, Summer). The view from the ground: Organizers speak out on race. *Colorlines, 3*(2). Retrieved October 12, 2003, from http://www.arc.org/C_Lines/CLArchive/CL3_2.html.

Chang, J., & Hwang, L. (2000, Summer). It's a survival issue: The environmental justice movement faces the new century. *Colorlines, 3*(2). Retrieved October 12, 2003, from http://www.arc.org/C_Lines/CLArchive/CL3_2.html.

Chappell, K. (1995). What they don't tell you about affirmative action. *Ebony, 50*(10), 46–52.

Children's Defense Fund. (1995). *A Black community crusade and covenant for protecting children.* Washington, DC: Author.

Delgado, G. (1994). *Beyond the politics of place: New directions in community organizing in the 1990s.* Oakland, CA: Applied Research Center.

Davis, C., Estes, R., & Schiraldi, V. (1996). *"Three Strikes": The new apartheid.* San Francisco: Center on Juvenile and Criminal Justice.

Diehl, K. (2000). Here's the movement, let's start building: An interview with Barbara Smith. *Colorlines, 3*(3), 28–30.

Edwards, E. D., Drews, J., & Seaman, J. R. (1994). Community organizing in support of self-determination within Native American communities. *Journal of Multicultural Social Work, 3*(4), 43–60.

Fisher, R. (1994). Community organizing in the conservative '80s and beyond. *Social Policy, 25*(1), 11–21.

Freire, P. (1994). *The pedagogy of hope.* New York: Continuum.

Garland, D. (2003). *The culture of control: Crime and social order in contemporary society.* Chicago: University of Chicago Press.

Garvin, C. D., & Cox, F. M. (2001). A history of community organizing since the Civil War with special reference to oppressed communities. In J. Rothman, J. Erlich, & J. Tropman (Eds.), *Strategies of community intervention* (6th ed., pp. 65-100). Itasca, IL: F. E. Peacock.

Gibbs, J. T., & Bankhead, T. (2001). *Preserving privilege: California politics, propositions, and people of color.* Westport, CT: Praeger.

Gibbs, J. T., & Bankhead-Greene, T. (1997). Issues of conducting qualitative research in an inner-city community: A case study of black youth in post-Rodney King Los Angeles. *Journal of Multicultural Social Work, 6*(1/2), 41–57.

Gibbs, J. T., & Huang, L. N. (1989). *Children of color: Psychological interventions with minority youth.* San Francisco: Jossey-Bass.

Giddings, P. (1988). *In search of sisterhood: Delta Sigma Theta and the challenge of the Black sorority movement.* New York: William Morrow.

Gittell, R., & Vidal, A. (1998). *Community organizing: Building social capital as a development strategy.* Thousand Oaks, CA: Sage.

Glugoski, G., Reisch, M., & Rivera, F. G. (1994). A wholistic ethno-cultural paradigm: A new model for community organization teaching and practice. *Journal of Community Practice, 1*(1), 81–98.

Grieco, E. M., & Cassidy, R. C. (2001). *Overview of race and Hispanic origin.* Washington, DC: U.S. Bureau of the Census.

Gutiérrez, L., & Alvarez, A. R. (2000). Educating students for multicultural community practice. *Journal of Community Practice, 7*(1), 39–56.

Gutiérrez, L., Alvarez, A. R., Nemon, H., & Lewis, E. A. (1996). Multicultural community organizing: A strategy for change. *Social Work, 41*(5), 501–508.

Gutiérrez, L. M., & Lewis, E. A. (1994). Community organizing with women of color: A feminist approach. *Journal of Community Practice, 1*(2), 23–44.

Hicks, J. R. (1997, July 20). The changing face of America [Letter to the editor]. *Los Angeles Times*, p. M1.

Hobbs, F., & Stoops, N. (2002). *Demographic trends in the 20th century: Census 2000 special reports.* Washington, DC: U.S. Census Bureau.

hooks, b. (1989). *Talking back: Thinking feminist, thinking Black.* Boston: South End Press.

Koetting, M., & Schiraldi, V. (1994). *Singapore West: The incarceration of 200,000 Californians.* San Francisco: Center on Juvenile and Criminal Justice.

Ladner, J. A. (2000). A new civil rights agenda. *The Brookings Review, 18*(2), 26–28.

Lecca, P., Quervalu, I., Nunes, J., & Gonzales, H. (1998). *Cultural competency in health, social, and human services.* New York: Garland.

Lorde, A. (1984). *Sister outsider: Essays and speeches.* Freedom, CA: The Crossing Press.

Lubove, R. (1965). *The professional altruist: The emergence of social work as cause, 1880–1930.* Cambridge, MA: Harvard University Press.

Lum, D. (Ed.). (2003). *Culturally competent practice* (2nd ed.). Pacific Grove, CA: Brooks/Cole-Thomson Learning.

Lynch, F. R. (2000, September 18). Rainbow rhetoric does nothing for the forgotten majority [Letter to the editor]. *Los Angeles Times,* p. B7.

Maharidge, D. (1996). *The coming white minority: California, multiculturalism and America's future.* New York: Vintage.

Males, M., & Macallair, D. (2000). *The color of justice: An analysis of juvenile adult court transfers in California.* Washington, DC: Building Blocks for Youth.

Mirsky, J. (2003, October 9). Wartime lies [Review of the book *Secrets: A memoir of Vietnam and the Pentagon papers*]. *The New York Review of Books,* p. 46.

Muller, T. (1997). Nativism in the mid-1990s: Why now? In J. F. Perea (Ed.), *Immigrants out! The new nativism and the anti-immigrant impulse in the United States* (pp. 105–118). New York: New York University Press.

Nelson, S. S., & O'Reilly, R. (2000, August 30). Minorities become majority in state, census officials say. *Los Angeles Times* [Orange County edition], p. A1.

O'Leary, C. E. (1999). *To die for: The paradox of American patriotism.* Princeton, NJ: Princeton University Press.

O'Leary, C., & Platt, T. (2002). Pledging allegiance: The revival of prescriptive patriotism. In P. Scraton (Ed.), *Beyond September 11: An anthology of dissent* (pp. 173–176). Sterling, VA: Pluto.

Perry, M. J., & Mackun, P. J. (2001). *Population change and distribution 1990 to 2000. U.S. Census Bureau* (Report No. C2KBR/01–2). Washington, DC: U.S. Department of Commerce, Economics and Statistics Administration.

Poe-Yamagata, E., & Jones, M. A. (2000). *And justice for some: Differential treatment of minority youth in the justice system.* Washington, DC: Youth Law Center.

Preston, M. B., & Lai, J. S. (1998). The symbolic politics of affirmative action. In M. B. Preston, B. E. Cain, & S. Bass (Eds.), *Racial and ethnic politics in California* (Vol. 2, pp. 61–198). Berkeley: University of California, Berkeley, Institute of Governmental Studies Press.

Rivera, F. G., & Erlich, J. L. (1998). *Community organizing in a diverse society* (3rd ed.). Needham Heights, MA: Allyn & Bacon.

Rothman, J., Erlich, J., & Tropman, J. (Eds.). (2001). *Strategies of community intervention* (6th ed.). Itasca, IL: F. E. Peacock.

Rubin, H. J., & Rubin, I. S. (2001). *Community organizing and development* (3rd ed.). Needham Heights, MA: Allyn & Bacon.

Scraton, P. (2002). In the name of a "just war." In P. Scraton (Ed.), *Beyond September 11: An anthology of dissent* (pp. 216–233). Sterling, VA: Pluto.

Taqi-Eddin, K., Macallair, D., & Schiraldi, V. (1998). *Class dismissed: Higher education vs. corrections during the Wilson years.* Washington, DC: Justice Policy Institute.

Tempest, R. (2003, March 7). Tearing it up. *Los Angeles Times,* p. E1.

Thomas, P. A. (2002). Legislative responses to terrorism. In P. Scraton (Ed.), *Beyond September 11: An anthology of dissent* (pp. 93–102). Sterling, VA: Pluto.

U.S. Bureau of the Census. (1999). *Statistical abstract of the United States* (119th ed.). Washington, DC: U.S. Department of Commerce.

U.S. Bureau of the Census. (2001). *Population projections of the total resident population by 5-year age groups, race, and Hispanic origin with special age categories: Middle series, 2050 to 2070.* Washington, DC: U.S. Department of Commerce.

U.S. Department of Justice. (1997). *Criminal victimization 1996: Changes 1995–96 with trends 1993–1996* (Bulletin NCJ-165812). Washington, DC: Bureau of Justice Statistics.

Warren, M. P. (1998). Community building and political power. *The American Behavioral Scientist, 42*(1), 78–92.

Webber, A. M. (2003, September 8). Beware of angry, jobless men. *USA Today,* p. A17.

Weil, M. (1986). Women, community, and organizing. In N. Van Den Bergh & L. B. Cooper (Eds.), *Feminist visions for social work practice* (pp. 187–210). Washington, DC: NASW Press.

Zuniga, M. (2003). Latino needs: Flexible and empowering interventions. In L. Gutiérrez, M. Zuniga, & D. Lum (Eds.), *Education for multicultural social work practice* (pp. 185-199). Alexandria, VA: NASW.

CHAPTER 4

Theorizing in Community Practice

*Essential Tools
for Building Community,
Promoting Social Justice,
and Implementing Social Change*

Beth Glover Reed

W riting a chapter on theories and/or theorizing for community practice is a daunting task because huge numbers of theories can have relevance for some type of community practice. Despite this, many texts on the community or community practice in social work do not have separate chapters or sections on theories or theoretical work relevant for community practice. Theoretical assumptions often are not explicitly identified or explained, and they remain implicit. Authors who discuss theories tend to focus on general systems or ecological theories (e.g., Fellin, 2000), or they categorize broadly the types of theories that social workers use in community practice (e.g., Hardcastle, Wenocur, & Powers, 1997; Hardina, 2002). In this chapter, although I will draw on this work, my emphasis is on why and how using theories is important in community practice, describing how practitioners *could* use theory, and how theorizing can inform assessment, planning, implementation, and evaluation. I assume that different theories are relevant for different purposes, and I will pose a set of broad topics and questions that are important for community practice. I discuss some theories to illustrate how theorizing is essential for community practitioners, but they are illustrative, and many others could be included.

What Do We Mean by Theories and Theorizing?

Various authors and dictionaries define theories in similar ways, as sets of systematically related propositions or statements used to explain and/or predict phenomena. These propositions are thought to be applicable in a relatively wide variety of circumstances. They comprise a system of assumptions, accepted principles, and rules of procedure devised to analyze, and sometimes to predict, or otherwise explain the nature or behavior of a specified set of phenomena. Theories usually involve abstract reasoning and analysis and structured ways of organizing and making sense of information. Concepts are the building blocks in theories and form symbols that allow communication about phenomena.

Theories are based on underlying assumptions about the nature of human social life—what Kuhn (1962/1970) called *paradigms* and other authors have called *perspectives* (e.g., Hardina, 2002; Payne, 1997). Kuhn argued that theories are developed not only from our systematic observations of nature but also from paradigms used to guide observations. Paradigms are basic beliefs or axioms, and within these are the methods and approaches for viewing and understanding nature. Paradigms direct and organize theory constructions, shape how nature is perceived according to theories, and direct how we find out about nature. They can constrain our view of nature as we follow particular rules.

In social work, Mullaly (1997) and Hardcastle et al. (1997) describe paradigms as taken-for-granted assumptions that we often do not recognize or examine, including beliefs, values, and techniques. The concept of paradigms allows us to analyze the relationship between scientific thought in a discipline and the social context in which it arises. Paradigms help those who hold them to locate and organize information, select methods for their work, and shape meaning from the results. Paradigms are grounded in ideology—they represent certain idea sets and values about the way things are and ought to be. They organize and order our perceptions of nature according to their rules. Theories are developed by following the paradigm's rules, and when viewed through the ideological lens of the paradigm, these theories appear reasonable to scientists, scholars, and others who share the paradigm. Practices that arise from a particular paradigm may not appear to be valid or reasonable to observers who do not follow the paradigm's rules or ideology.

Kuhn (1962/1970) proposed the concept of paradigm from his investigation and theorizing about how scientific knowledge develops, arguing that we assume that knowledge develops as a linear accumulation of facts and insights about phenomena. In fact, major disagreements often exist among scientists about both the nature of their work and the methods they use; periodically, basic frameworks are altered substantially when new information challenges dominant assumptions and competing paradigms become too strong to ignore.

Thus, theories are not static: They change and grow with new evidence and new ideas; studies may gather data supporting conflicting views; and theorists may disagree substantially about elements of the theory, with debates and controversies occurring at professional meetings and in published literature. Theorists often contribute to more than one theory, sometimes at different stages of their career and sometimes simultaneously. Every textbook captures a body of knowledge and theory at a single point in time and may not describe how a theory has developed over time or the current controversies and disagreements within a theoretical tradition. The theories cited in this chapter are continuing to change and evolve.

Theorizing refers to the processes of formulating or analyzing theories or using theoretical frameworks to make sense of particular phenomena. I will use the term *theorizing* more often than *theory* in this chapter to depict the movement and change described above.

The theories noted in this chapter arise from many sources. They represent different ontological assumptions about humankind and different epistemologies about the nature and sources of knowledge, and they were developed using multiple methodologies and methods. Most are linked to the social sciences, although I have also deliberately included some that began in the humanities and physical sciences and that are just beginning to influence social work and community practice. Theories relevant for community practice lie at every level of understanding, from those at the individual level to those that focus on global concerns.

Basic Assumptions About Community Practice Underlying This Chapter

I will emphasize mostly theories that explicitly focus on change in this chapter for two major reasons. The first assumes that community practice, whatever its other goals, should be about promoting social justice and challenging and changing sources of injustice along the way. Social justice cannot occur without fundamental and continual change because we are clearly far away from having socially just institutions or communities. We must also develop and implement modes of practice that can help us to learn about socially just relationships and processes.

Second, all forms of community practice ought to promote social participation and human health and well-being and work to prevent the development of problems. Theories and knowledge exist about what causes and sustains many types of social problems. Reducing problems may be the focus of a particular community practice, but prevention of problems and promotion of community capacity requires more than the identification and reduction of problems. One must also identify and intervene with those factors that either put communities at risk for developing problems or help protect them from problems. This usually includes developing leadership and capacity—among individuals, groups, communities, and institutions.

Why Is Theorizing Important for Community Practitioners?

Although many reasons exist for a stronger theoretical emphasis within community practice, I emphasize primarily three: (a) Theorizing is an important tool for effective practice; (b) theorizing helps practitioners to learn and improve their practice and knowledge about what is effective; and (c) theorizing is essential for community practice that has social justice goals.

Theorizing improves practice. Theories are important to help guide assessment, analysis, planning, implementation, and evaluation, and they can help to organize information and a person's thinking. Some theories can illuminate the goals and domains of a particular community practice situation in relation to the origins of particular types of problems and what is known about how to achieve a desired goal or prevent or reduce a particular problem. Theories can illuminate areas and consider options that otherwise might not be considered, and they can help us to anticipate what we might expect and develop ways to react to potential options. Theories can assist the practitioner to decide what information should be gathered to evaluate progress and problems encountered. Moreover, theorizing is a way to understand why progress is or is not happening and to recognize unintended negative consequences as quickly as possible.

Many community practitioners believe that practice models and the knowledge and skills useful in community practice are mostly atheoretical, and the primary task is to match particular strategies with the situation. Because some sort of paradigm underlies all forms of social work practice, explicit theorizing can help to identify nonconscious (Bem, 1970) assumptions. Many practitioners, especially those concerned with ameliorating social problems or challenging social injustices, are impatient with theories they perceive as too abstract to be relevant *and* the time required for theorizing and planning based on systematic theorizing. They want to move right to "doing things" and "making a difference." Moving too quickly to action, however, without theorizing about the goals and the situation and gathering information based on that theorizing, can and often does have many limitations in terms of missing possible options and encountering unexpected negative consequences. As many wise practitioners have said, there is no more important tool for practice than a good theory. I say more later about ways that theorizing can be limiting and ways to guard against this.

Theorizing facilitates learning and growth among community practitioners. Existing bodies of knowledge and theoretical frameworks will evolve; thus, practitioners need to be oriented toward continuous updating of relevant knowledge and theories and to amending and expanding personal epistemologies and paradigms. Theorizing is an important way for practitioners to deepen and expand their knowledge and skills and, when engaged in community practice with others, to expand or change the knowledge and skills of those who are collaborators in practice. These include not only the core leadership in a community practice situation but also those who will benefit from changes and those who may be targets of change.

Theorizing is necessary for community practice with social justice goals. If we assume that all community-based practice in social work, whatever its other emphases or goals, should be conceptualized also as increasing social justice, we must guard against unintended consequences that can create or sustain injustices and power imbalances and must strengthen forces that can promote social transformation to a more just society and societal processes. In general, most of us are better at recognizing instances of discrimination than we are at envisioning what a just world could be. Surprisingly little is available in the social work literature that defines economic or social justice, despite the emphasis on these topics in social work ethics and education guidelines. Because our environments are not socially just, we have little experience to inform our visions of what could be. Freire (1995) stressed that developing and deepening critical consciousness is an important part of working for social justice because we all have learned *not* to see how all but the most obvious injustices occur. He proposed *praxis* as a major means for this. Praxis requires theorizing in a tripartite interactive model: (a) learning about and applying existing knowledge and theory, (b) enacting that knowledge through action, and (c) reflecting on that action to revise our knowledge and theories (the process of theorizing).

How Theorizing Can Inform Community Practice

Some theories can help us to understand how things work and anticipate and predict what to expect in general practice situations. These approaches to theorizing began after the enlightenment to move from religious and mystical explanations of the world to those based on scientific observation. Agger (1998) describes these types of theories as originating from "positivist" assumptions—that underlying truths can be discovered and research methods can be used to ensure the objective study of social phenomena. The goals of these theories are often to predict and ultimately influence social and natural phenomena (Brodsky, 2001).

Other types of theorizing can help us to explore the impact of particular contexts and unrecognized underlying assumptions. Postmodern critiques of totalizing and "objective" searches for truth argue that all theorizing is limited and shaped by existing knowledge and methods and by the historical and cultural contexts in which the work was conducted. Postmodern approaches assume that all knowledge is socially constructed and represents only an approximation of reality at any given time (e.g., Pease & Fook, 1998; Taylor, 1998). Thus, many "truths" are possible, which vary depending on the vantage point of the observer and the particular circumstances. These approaches are useful for illuminating the impact of contexts and bringing to the surface underlying assumptions. They can also help the practitioner and evaluator examine situations from multiple perspectives.

Theorizing about how change happens in society can help us to understand the sources of and barriers to change in ways that can inform assessment, planning, interventions, and evaluation. Theories can help us to understand society and social change in general and can guide our analyses, assessments, planning, and evaluation. Table 4.1 depicts several different types of explanatory theories about society and social change drawn from multiple sources (e.g., Hardcastle et al., 1997; Hardina, 2002; Vago, 1999). The questions in the third column raise issues relevant to community practice that arise from each category of theories. Space does not allow explanation

Table 4.1   Illustrative Types of Explanatory Theories About Society and Social Change

Type of Theorizing	Brief Description	Relevant Questions/Functions
Evolutionary—society and communities make progress over time	Assumes that change occurs in multilinear progressions, usually from more simple to more complex; some assume that changes improve society	What types of change are currently under way? What is the history of particular issues in a community and the society as a whole? What are the patterns and sources of change?
Political economy—concerned with polity (political processes), and economic systems	Assumes that economic and political bases of the global, national, and other external environments can create conditions for either change or stability	What are the consequences of the current political economic system and the political and economic circumstances that are impacting a particular situation and context?
Structural/functional, open systems, ecological (from theorizing about natural and social systems; could place role theory here)	Describes/analyzes structures and their functions, also processes within and between structures and boundaries. Tends to focus on what keeps things stable	What structures exist? What is the nature of their boundaries and relationships between and within them? What are the processes that occur within and among components of the system?
Conflict theories (strain, competing interests, scarce resources, power differences; competition among groups)	Focuses on group differences, stresses and strains between societal and community components; assumes that conflict creates conditions that promote change	What groups in the community have conflicting interests and approaches? Who is competing for existing resources? What power differentials exist across group boundaries?
Construction of meaning (symbolic interactionism, some aspects of culture, theories about ideology, interpretive theories)	Focuses on how ideologies (religious, political, cultural, and personal) are created and maintained, and internalized; includes how they explain and justify existing social and power arrangements	What rationales are given by whom about the existing state of affairs and the causes of perceived problems? What latent and manifest meanings can be discerned? What cultural and subcultural symbols and norms are operating?
Social psychological, social learning; exchange, rational choice	Focuses at the personal and interpersonal levels, how individuals develop and learn, and influence each other	What community members are involved or could be? What characterizes them psychologically and relationally? What motivates their interests?
Co-construction: How everyday interactions shape behavior and institutions—each co-constructing and mediating the others	Examines how social structures and relationships co-construct each other; how everyday actions sustain social systems and vice versa; roles of human agency	How do social systems regulate and structure options for their members and vice versa? How do routines and transactions create/sustain the status quo? What sources of agency exist?
Critical, feminist, and critical race theories (emphasize power and oppression, with an advocacy stance)	Have explicit goals for promoting improved situations for those most disadvantaged in society, seek to understand and challenge sources of oppression	How are existing power and inequality differences being created and sustained? What will disrupt, challenge, and change these? What would social justice look like?

of the sources and variability within each category on this table. Many would classify theories differently and would contest aspects of this framework. My purpose is not to portray a totality of theories. Instead, I wish to illustrate how using multiple forms of theorizing creates multiple lenses. These can raise questions that guide practitioners to different levels of analysis and sources of information. Multiple forms of theorizing open more potential avenues for change than might be considered otherwise. Considering factors at all levels of this table can enrich a practitioner's options: Each illuminates different aspects of complex situations.

Each set of theories comprises approaches by different theorists, with often conflicting assumptions, some of which will be discussed later. They are grouped loosely by their level of analysis and/or focus. I will describe each briefly.

Earlier *evolutionary* approaches assumed that change is equated with progress and growth and is linear (usually moving from more simple to more complex and "sophisticated"). Most current approaches in this category are more nuanced and multifaceted; they focus the practitioner's attention on the historical progression of change and the evolution of current circumstances (quite aside from whether people think these changes are for the better). *Political economy* analyses could provide a lens for understanding the impact of the larger macro environment, including the global economy and larger political processes, but they could also focus on these issues within the community in question.

Structural/functional approaches could guide the identification and assessment of component structures, the purposes they serve, and the way they work. Some approaches in this category came from studies of biological systems; others originated in other types of science and the study of social and organizational systems.

• *Conflict theories* (usually associated with Marx) focus on differences and power associated with those differences, assuming that change often is created when conflict arises about goals or the allocation of resources.

Theories focusing on *how meaning is created* are especially important in understanding how issues are understood and can be framed or reframed to consider new possibilities. One form of theorizing here is symbolic interactionism (e.g., Deegan & Hill, 1987; Denzin, 1992), which focuses on how people develop shared symbols and understandings and the impact of these. Many postmodern approaches focus on this area (e.g., Pease & Fook, 1998). *Social psychological* approaches focus at the level of the individual and transactions among people and across groups. They might include notions of how people learn, change, and grow and also on how people and groups of people make decisions and negotiate within and across boundaries.

The next category (*co-construction*) emphasizes how human and everyday interactions shape individual and group behaviors *and* social structures, with each contributing to the development and maintenance of the other. Theorists here recognize the active agency of individuals and groups within environments (including oppressive ones) and study how these environments are sustained through everyday actions. These approaches help to illuminate how meanings, status hierarchies, and power relationships are re-created and sustained in work and every community setting. If we can recognize these forces and acts of agency, we are more able to influence them in desired directions. Theorists here include Giddens (structuration; Giddens & Pierson, 1998), Foucault (disciplinary surveillance; Chambon,

1999; Collins, 1998; 2000), and Habermas (communicative action; Agger, 1998). I describe *critical theories* in the next section.

Particular types of theories are especially helpful for identifying and achieving social justice goals and addressing barriers to reaching those goals. Theorizing and theorists are important in relation to social justice in many ways. Theorizing can help us to understand what creates and perpetuates injustice, to recognize injustices and their sources, and to implement our community practice in socially just ways. Theorizing can help us to identify, define, and examine our assumptions and potential biases. Some theories can help us to recognize, surface, and monitor power dynamics and inequities, as well as cultural and other differences that must be built upon if we are to implement socially just processes. Below I emphasize three particular purposes for theorizing.

First, theories can help us to define social justice (e.g., Reisch, 2002). Statements and theories about social and economic justice arise from philosophy, religion, government, social change activists, and numerous types of critical writers and thinkers. Iris Marion Young (1990), a feminist philosopher, and others argue that distributive paradigms (those that argue for equal access or more fair distribution of resources in society) are insufficient frames for social justice for a number of reasons, especially because different groups have different desires and needs. Distributive paradigms also fail to take into account differential barriers that groups face to access and use resources, exercise rights and responsibilities, and participate in decisions that affect them. Young also describes five ways in which oppression is maintained, all of which can be understood theoretically: powerlessness, marginalization/exclusion, hegemonic ideologies, exploitation, and violence and threats of violence. She asserts that strategies for undermining these forces also need to be part of our conceptualization of social justice.

Second, theorizing about power is especially important within a social justice frame. Most of the theories in Table 4.1 can illuminate some aspects of power. For instance, structural/functional theorizing would be useful to identify where power is located at different levels and positions within societal structures and what types of power are found in each area. Those concerned with "making meaning" could focus on whose versions of meaning dominate in particular institutions, for example, who has the power to influence which meanings prevail. Conflict theorists could focus on the differential access to power among conflicting groups and the impact of different amounts and types of power. Foucault proposed more fluid notions of power, constructed through everyday interactions (Chambon, 1999). These concepts can help practitioners evaluate how power is operating in the processes that take place among those engaged in community change work.

Third, theorizing can help us to understand barriers to social justice and sources of oppression and privilege within society and within our community practice endeavors. Although much theorizing purports to be neutral about the goals, impact, or effects of the society it endeavors to understand, some theories are overtly concerned with those who fare the least well within society. A cluster of theories often called *critical theories* (last row in Table 4.1) are centrally concerned with oppression and with what creates and what can disrupt or change forces that create and sustain inequities (Agger, 1998; Held, 1980). Critical theorists assume that existing power and inequality arrangements within society are influential and that theorizing reflects dominant paradigms. Thus, although they agree that we must uncover the influence of these paradigms, they caution against forms of postmodern scholarship that Agger (1998) calls interpretive. These focus heavily on the uses of language and symbols (and would be included in the "making meaning" category in Table 4.1), but within very relativistic frameworks. In other words, these approaches may be useful in uncovering previously unrecognized patterns within discourses and theories, but they are neutral as to the consequences of these patterns.

Critical theorists take sides—they wish to discover patterns that can be challenged and changed to reduce inequality and challenge power inequities. Within this, they may be concerned with many types of issues. Macarov (2003) focuses on economic class and poverty; Foucault addressed health care, prisons, and sexuality (Chambon, 1999); Habermas developed a theory of communicative action, unpacking how the use of language both obscures power and inequality or can be used to illuminate previously unrecognized patterns (Agger, 1998).

A number of other bodies of knowledge and theorizing are relevant for addressing social justice issues. Feminist theorists have been especially important in conceptualizing sources of inequities, a range of desired goals for change, and strategies for reaching those goals (e.g., Tong, 1998). Feminist thought also has proposed the possibility of "power with" rather than "power over" (e.g., Freeman & Bourque, 2001). Collins (2000) proposes four domains of power, focusing on four of the categories in Table 4.1 (institutional, making of meaning, co-constructive, and social psychological). She argues that the forces in these different domains act together to socialize, "discipline," and monitor people; create structural barriers; and marginalize some members because of lack of fit with dominant norms and cultural practices and through everyday transactions among people. Critical race theories (e.g., Crenshaw, Gotanda, Peller, & Thomas, 1998) are creating frameworks for understanding how conceptions of race are embedded in and influence our institutions, laws, and social norms. Queer theorizing is challenging binary notions of gender and sexuality, fundamental constructs within most societies (e.g., Beemyn & Eliason, 1996). Some of these works are coming from law and the humanities.

Theories about differences are also important: How can we negotiate differences, work together despite differences, and use differences to enhance our knowledge and broaden our approaches? Earlier approaches focused on particular groups and characteristics. More recently, theorists who occupy multiple marginalized identities have developed concepts of intersectionality to describe how various identity dimensions work together and must be considered together (e.g., Collins, 1998; Crenshaw, 1995; Gutiérrez & Lewis, 1999; Hurtado, 1996). In addition, most of us also occupy some positions of privilege in society, in addition to whatever stigmatized and disadvantaged group memberships we may have. We cannot "unpack" how our group memberships intersect or how we may be consciously or inadvertently contributing to the oppression of others without recognizing the ways in which we experience unearned privilege from some group memberships (Johnson, 2001). The implications of this work are only beginning to be addressed within community practice contexts.

Theorizing can focus on what creates and sustains stability within social systems or focus more on what creates change and instability. Most theories have implications for both stability and change—they are most often opposite sides of the same coin—but different theories and theorists emphasize one side more than the other. For instance, in sociology, much theorizing about organizations has focused on what creates stable and productive structures and processes, whereas social movement theorists have focused more on what creates and sustains change (McAdam & Scott, 2002). Critiques of general systems and ecological frameworks note the emphasis in these theories on adaptation to one's environment, the implications of maintaining the status quo in the concepts of stability and homeostasis, and the relative lack of attention to proactive efforts to change one's environment and to seek more optimal and socially just conditions. On the other hand, theories the focus primarily on stability and centrality are also important in many community practice situations: Achieving sufficient stability and sense of membership is necessary for a community to act on its own behalf. Also, those who are concerned with change may need to destabilize conditions of equilibrium or harmony in order to promote alternative points of view, to allow those with less power to challenge the status quo, or to create the option for new possibilities.

Theorizing can be relevant in defining and understanding multiple forms of community in ways that illuminate practice issues and possibilities. Hardcastle et al. define community practice as "the application of practice skills to alter the behavioral patterns of community groups, organizations, and institutions or people's relationships and interactions with these entities" (1997, p. 1). Theorizing must acknowledge that communities provide sources of support and meaning in people's lives as well as being sites for change. As noted elsewhere in this volume, many definitions of community are possible. Community is most often defined in three ways: communities of place (people who live or work together); communities of identity (people who share common circumstances and issues); and communities of interest (people who share common goals or interests). Different theories may be more or less relevant depending on the type of community.

Work with communities of geography, for instance, should be informed by knowledge and theories about neighborhoods: for example, how to define them and what characterizes different types of neighborhoods (Chaskin, 1997; Smith, 1997). Within a village, city, or county, it will be important to understand its various component social systems and how they work; multiple theories are available to inform these tasks. Systems and ecological theories may be especially useful here to identify key community components and their relationships, but they are less likely to identify preventive and social justice goals or potential sources of social capital (e.g., Breton, 2001).

With communities of identity, other theories become more important—for instance, theories about identity development and the impact of marginalized identities (e.g., Swigonski, 1994). Theories inform using consciousness-raising methods to develop knowledge about the impact of identities and societal reactions to those identities (Carr, 2003) and understanding the dynamics among people working together on issues related to their identities (Bernstein, 1997; Laraña, Johnston, & Gusfield, 1994; Taylor, 1998).

Communities of affiliation are those drawn together because of common interests. These may be related not only to identities but also to values and social problems of concern. For instance, some may be drawn to become part of a community practice project focused on family planning options whereas others are more interested in violence against women or police profiling, protecting children, fostering human rights, or stopping urban sprawl to protect natural resources. Theories about interest groups are particularly relevant here (e.g., Baumgartner & Leech, 1998). These "communities" may be able to meet face to face but increasingly more "virtual" connections are possible.

In addition to general theories about stability and change, practice models are derived from theories about how to effect change in particular types of practice. Various authors writing about theories of change (e.g., Hardina, 2002; Payne, 1997; Vago, 1999) distinguish between analytic or explanatory theories (why and how society and societal change happens, Table 4.1) from those concerned with *planned* change. In social work, these are called theories or models for practice and intervention design and implementation. Payne (1997) describes a model as "an organized prescription for action," or a system of principles that attempts to explain the form and structure of practice in the social services. Community practice models have been characterized various ways. Rothman (1996) empirically derived three basic models: locality development, social planning, and social action; he argues that practitioners tend to mix and match elements depending on the circumstances, their own backgrounds, and the stages of the practice. Checkoway (1997) proposes five types of community practice, and Weil (1996) presents an eight-component typology (described more fully in other chapters of this book).

Different types of community practice are likely to have different goals and bodies of knowledge. Thus, different theories are likely to be relevant for particular models. Working to create or support a community to define and achieve its own goals is important in locality development and neighborhood organizing. Useful theories are those about what creates a sense of community, what helps people feel a sense of belonging, and what comprises a competent or resilient community. Other models facilitate community input and community oversight of governmental planning. In this case, various theories of community participation, social planning, and policy analysis are relevant (Parsons, 1995). Social action models assume that a power imbalance exists and that those in power are unlikely to support the goals of those being organized. Theories about power and conflict become especially important for social action—different types and sources of power and their implications, the way power works, ways to mobilize and increase power, sources of conflict, different types of conflict, ways to escalate and reduce conflict, and also theories about different types of actions, political processes, and how they work.

Knowledge of interorganizational relations, boundary spanning, and conflict at organizational interfaces (Brown, 1983; Halley, 1997; Reitan, 1998) is likely to be especially important when working with coalitions whose members represent different organizations and groups. Knowledge about human motivation is important in all community practice to understand what leads people to become engaged in work on behalf of their community, but this kind of knowledge is likely to be especially important for community practitioners who are working to promote and increase citizen participation.

Prevention of problems and promotion of health, well-being, and resilience require knowledge about causes of problems and what facilitates positive change. Theorizing can guide the identification of community and environmental risk and protective factors and how these interact with other forces that impact health and well-being. Concepts such as social capital (Breton, 2001) and theories about contributors to particular problems are invaluable tools for prevention planning and design (Center for Substance Abuse Prevention, 2002; Institute of Medicine, 1994).

Theorizing can inform community practice assessment and planning in particular practice situations and settings. Theories can be classified in many ways. One way is by the scope of the phenomena that the theory attempts to explain. Payne (1997) and Vago (1999) describe some theories as comprehensive or inclusive, but others strive to be neither—they seek to understand particular phenomena, within a bounded context. Many of these types of theories are relevant for community practice. For instance, many community practice projects are focused on goals related to particular domains of society or particular social problem areas. Theorizing about the sources of such problems can help us to understand what sustains the problems or to identify the forces that could be mobilized to change them and to imagine what the world might look like absent those problems. For instance, community practice focused on domestic violence should be informed by the various theories about causes of domestic violence and how these theories and research based on them agree and disagree with each other. Community practice focused on environmental concerns or environmental justice will need to be informed by knowledge not only about human ecology but also about larger bio-ecosystems, environmental toxins, agricultural practices, and multiple other areas of knowledge and theory.

Organization theories (e.g., Powell & DiMaggio, 1991) are relevant for many types of community practice because practitioners usually work from some organizational base, and the targets of change can be organizations. New work is illuminating ways in which organizations are gendered and raced (Britton, 2003; Fletcher, 2001). This theorizing is important to help us recognize and change these dynamics in our organizing structures and in the organizations we work in, collaborate with, or are trying to change. Many theories and bodies of knowledge also exist about leadership—types of leadership and how to match leadership strategies and styles with needed tasks and situations.

Theories can assist us to determine what is needed to create, strengthen, or change a community. Sometimes a community already exists with a common identity, goals, and leadership, and the practitioner must determine how best to enter and work with this community. Sometimes a community must be created—potential members and common interests identified, membership defined and stimulated, goals and agendas developed. Sometimes a community has been damaged or diminished in some way or is not working effectively, and the community practitioner will need to assess and deal with the causes of this and help the community to rebuild or change before other tasks can be tackled. Sometimes the goal is to create an action group to challenge existing structures, practices, and policies. Theories have a lot to say about what leads to a sense of community cohesiveness among community members under different circumstances and barriers to such cohesiveness and action. There are also theories about how too much cohesiveness limits diversity and can lead to bad decisions (e.g., groupthink; Janis, 1972). How can you create a community with enough stability so that people can work together and pursue mutual goals, but without so much stability that it becomes stagnant and inflexible? How can you create core values and a mission that can accommodate different cultural values and styles, as well as procedures and processes that allow a group to get things done, but that also allow people with different cultural styles and agendas to be heard and to contribute?

Theories are also relevant for particular stages or elements of community practice and the tasks and challenges faced during that stage or component. For instance, community practitioners must consider how to frame the goals and issues in a particular project to motivate people to support them. Theories about how communication occurs, how to interest and motivate people, and how cultural meaning is constructed can all be relevant here. Every community practitioner needs to know how to create opportunities for change—this can involve destabilizing a stagnant system, using the media to create awareness of an issue, or taking advantage of change that is already occurring by steering it in particular directions or making other changes while the system is in transition. Community practitioners must conduct different types of meetings and implement events (conferences, rituals, community presentations, demonstrations) that are enhanced by theories and knowledge about small and larger groups, human development, and social relationships.

Theories about resistance to change are particularly important in community practice, especially with social justice goals. One cannot work toward any kind of personal, group, institutional, or societal change without understanding sources of resistance to these changes and engaging with this resistance. Understanding and working with resistance at all levels is an important way to initiate and sustain transformative changes. Resistance is an expected component of work toward change—a way that all organisms and systems maintain their integrity and stability. They are a natural and normal set of processes. Lewin (1947) applied field theory to considering change and developed the force field analysis, a common tool used in community practice. Its assumptions are that forces are working for and against desired changes in every situation and that working to reduce restraining forces will ultimately be more effective than simply increasing forces for change. This is the case within organizations (e.g., Dent & Goldberg, 1999) as in all forms of community practice. Moreover, uncovering and reflecting on our own resistances can lead us to discover new capacities and options for ourselves, our practice, and social change.

Resistance can also be defined in another way: as actions undertaken by those in oppressed categories to fight back or undermine the forces that diminish self-esteem and agency. Without understanding this context, these actions can be construed as lack of cooperation, "acting out," or destructive behaviors. Reframed and harnessed in community practice situations, they become potential sources of positive power and change.

The complexities of practice require complex theories and mixing and matching of theories. Community practitioners are most often concerned with planned change—in which goals are developed, interventions planned, and steps taken to implement them. Often, however, change is already occurring in multiple ways, some of them desired and others not, and the practitioner's tasks then include trying to shape or guide the change in desired directions. Sometimes this involves creating new goals and options, sometimes challenging or trying to eliminate some components, accelerating an ongoing change, or slowing a change down to decrease resistance and allow time to build support for and reduce barriers to the change. Some changes are totally unplanned; they happen through no efforts of the community practitioner (losing major sources of employment, a natural disaster, an unexpected source of funds for particular purposes). The practitioner then must help to deal with the consequences of that change and assist communities to respond to or shape changes to reduce negative consequences and achieve desired ends.

A number of multifaceted theoretical frameworks are especially relevant for the complexities of community practice. For instance, complex systems/chaos theories (Hudson, 2000; Mace, 1997; Warren, Franklin, & Streeter, 1998) are just beginning to be considered by social work. They focus explicitly on complex patterns of change, including why change is slow and difficult at some times and fast and coming from multiple sources at other times. These theories arose from the physical sciences—working to understand such phenomena as ocean currents and the movement of celestial objects—but are now being applied in the social sciences. Most natural and social phenomena (like communities) are dynamically nonlinear and complex with many potentially synergistic effects (many forces multiplying each other's effects). These theories view the system as more than the sum of its parts. Using these theories, a practitioner can begin to identify potential "lever points" where small amounts of change can lead to large effects (the butterfly effect) and to consider the influence of multiple sources for change happening simultaneously. These theories stress the importance of initial conditions and assessment of changes and forces that are already operating.

Gladwell (2002) has popularized some aspects of these, as well as another set of helpful theories—those concerned with how innovations are created and spread (Osbourne, 1998; Rogers, 1995). Some models of community practice focus on implementing community-based programs or getting a particular policy adopted. This theorizing is based on studies of whether or not an innovation is adopted in particular settings and situations. Many types of innovations have been studied (including policy and organizational), and researchers have delineated factors that facilitate or are barriers to adopting new practices. These include characteristics of the desired change, how the change is introduced, forces operating at different levels of the structures in which the change must be implemented, how compatible the change is with existing practices, and whether or not someone champions the change in different locations.

Another complex of theories has been constructed from the study of social movements. Relatively recent formulations of this theorizing discuss the importance and interrelatedness of political opportunities, resources, organizing structures, and cultural framings in social change work (McAdam, McCarthy, & Zald, 1996) and how the state has adopted many social movement techniques (Meyer & Tarrow, 1998). Some social work community practitioners (e.g., Castelloe & Prokopy, 2001) have used aspects of social movement theories. Castelloe (1999) has also proposed a complex model for place-based organizing, combining knowledge from many types of research to focus on predicting what will increase community capacity.

The Strengths, Limitations, and Potential Biases of Theory

Theories and theorizing either can be allies in community work toward social justice goals, or they can obscure forces that perpetuate injustices and be part of our inability to make needed changes. Theories are only as informed as those who create and use them. They reflect the available knowledge, research methods, and worldviews extant within particular historical conditions. As noted earlier, theories are usually created by those privileged enough in a society to have access to debates within higher education and the professions and, usually, to publishing venues. Thus, many theories are likely to reflect the biases and worldviews of those with more power in society. In fact, knowledge and theory may be a force in marginalizing those who don't "fit" with dominant modes of thinking and being. Thus, we need to be able to be analytic about various theories, to identify their advantages and their limitations. De Anda (1997) argues that culture-free theories are unlikely and proposes ways to determine the cross-cultural utility of theories. Nicholson (1993) depicts most grand theories as being very ethnocentric. Thus, theorizing may not facilitate social justice without precautions.

An important question to ask when encountering a new theory is whether the theorizer is transparent about underlying assumptions and methods for collecting and analyzing information. Do the theories implicitly accept the status quo or assume adaptation to an environment that may be unjust? How does the theorizing address circumstances that disempower and disenfranchise? Does the theorizing make any assumptions about social justice?

Stanton and Stewart (1995) suggest a number of strategies to follow to identify omissions and biases in theories and in your use of them. First, identify what has been left out or what is not known in the context of a particular theory. Second, place yourself in relation to the issue or topic relevant for a particular theory—how does it fit or not with your own worldview and experiences? What does this mean in relation to how you are likely to use this theory or components of it? Third, consider how the theoretical framework can be used to identify agency, acts of resistance, and uses of power among those typically left out of theorizing and examine the constraints to agency in the theory. Fourth, consider how the basic concepts within a theory have been socially constructed—what assumptions underlie them? How has this theory considered those not involved in constructing the theory—women, people of color, those less able to participate because of disability, social resources, or exclusion. Fifth, consider how power works in particular theories. Is power defined explicitly? How does power work within this framework, or how could it work? Sixth, consider what other types of social problems and populations are relevant within particular approaches and the implications of their inclusion or exclusion. Finally, consider the risks and benefits of making generalizations for particular types of individuals or groups.

Summary and Conclusions

This chapter has argued that theorizing in community practice is extremely important for effective practice, practitioner learning, and social justice goals, and it has outlined some of the ways in which theorizing can be beneficial, with illustrative examples of relevant theories. I argued that theorizing can help the practitioner to address many key questions in practice: What is sustaining the status quo and what can be mobilized to create desired change? What should be assessed and incorporated into planning and evaluation? What kinds of leadership are needed? How is power operating and how can we build on this? What kinds of alternative structures and processes can we envision and work to create? Why isn't the desired change already happening? Theorizing can also help to frame goals and create a common understanding among practitioners and community members about what a project is about, and more important, *why* particular strategies are being proposed and how they are expected to work. As in all practice, however, the usefulness of theorizing is limited by our ability to keep learning about theories and to learn to see the benefits and limitations of different theories. This is difficult for the active community practitioner, who has to make the time to actively theorize and to learn more about approaches that can be helpful for particular situations and projects. We cannot learn all potential theories at once, but much of the learning and benefit comes from structuring in time for community practitioners to theorize together. Theorizing might involve discussing a particular reading or two and considering how those readings may apply to particular practice goals. A group can invite someone knowledgeable about a theory to explain the approach and help the group theorize from that framework to determine its relevance for practice. One way to learn about a theory is to begin to use it, with whatever imperfect level of knowledge you have. Different aspects will become clearer over time.

Academic-community partnerships can be invaluable here. Academically based collaborators can help to identify and translate different theoretical approaches and help to construct evaluations that are theoretically grounded. Those who are community-based can help to determine the relevance of different modes of theorizing in community contexts. They can also provide practical examples and information to inform classroom teaching, which also may lead to modifications and further development of the theories.

Ultimately, theorizing expands our horizons about what is possible and is invaluable in envisioning a socially just community and working toward this end. This chapter was intended to provide some useful frameworks and resources for using theories to improve community practice in multiple ways.

References

Agger, B. (1998). *Critical social theories: An introduction.* Boulder, CO: Westview.

Baumgartner, F. R., & Leech, B. L. (1998). *Basic interests: The importance of groups in politics and in political science.* Princeton, NJ: Princeton University Press.

Beemyn, B., & Eliason, M. (Eds.). (1996). *Queer studies: A lesbian, gay, bisexual, and transgender anthology.* New York: New York University Press.

Bem, D. (1970). *Beliefs, attitudes, and human affairs.* Monterey, CA: Brooks/Cole.

Bernstein, M. (1997) Celebration and suppression: The strategic uses of identity by the lesbian and gay movements. *American Journal of Sociology, 103*(3), 531–565.

Breton, M. (2001). Neighborhood resiliency. *Journal of Community Practice, 9*(1), 21–36.

Britton, D. M. (2003). *At work in the iron cage: The prison as gendered organization.* New York: New York University Press.

Brodsky, A. E. (2001). More than epistemology: Relationships in applied research with underserved communities. *Journal of Social Issues, 57*(2), 323–335.

Brown, L. D. (1983). *Managing conflict at organizational interfaces.* Reading, MA: Addison-Wesley.

Carr, E. S. (2003). Rethinking empowerment theory using a feminist lens: The importance of process. *Affilia, 18*(1), 8–20.

Castelloe, P. E. (1999). *Community change and community practice: A qualitative inquiry into an organic model of community practice.* Digital Dissertation AAT 9943191.

Castelloe, P., & Prokopy, J. (2001). Recruiting participants for community practice interventions: Merging practice theory and social movement theory. *Journal of Community Practice, 9*(2), 31–48.

Center for Substance Abuse Prevention. (2002). *Science-based prevention programs and principles* (DHHS Publication No. [SMA] 03–3764). Rockville, MD: Substance Abuse and Mental Health Services Administration.

Chambon, A. S. (1999). Foucault's approach: Making the familiar visible. In A. S. Chambon, A. Irving, & L. Epstein (Eds.), *Reading Foucault for social work* (pp. 51–81). New York: Columbia University Press.

Chaskin, R. J. (1997, December). Perspectives on neighborhood and community: A review of the literature, *Social Services Review, 521*–547.

Checkoway, B. (1997). Core concepts for community change. *Journal of Community Practice, 4*(1), 11–29.

Collins, P. H. (1998). Some group matters: Intersectionality, situated standpoints, and Black feminist thought. In *Fighting words: Black women and the search for justice* (pp. 201–228). Minneapolis: University of Minnesota Press.

Collins, P. H. (2000). Toward a politics of empowerment. In *Black feminist thought: Knowledge, consciousness, and the politics of empowerment* (pp. 273–290). New York: Routledge.

Crenshaw, K. W. (1995). The intersection of race and gender. In K. Crenshaw, G. Gotanda, G. Peller, & K. Thomas (Eds.) *Critical race theory* (pp. 357–383). New York: The New Press.

Crenshaw, K, Gotanda, G., Peller, G., & Thomas, K. (Eds.). (1998). *Critical race theory.* New York: The New Press.

De Anda, D. (1997). Are there theories that are sufficiently "culture-free" to be appropriate and useful for practice with multicultural clients? In *Controversial issues in multiculturalism* (pp. 143–152). Boston: Allyn & Bacon.

Deegan, M. J., & Hill, M. R. (1987). *Women and symbolic interactionism.* Boston: Allen & Unwin.

Dent, E. B., & Goldberg, S. G. (1999). Challenging: Resistance to change. *The Journal of Applied Behavioral Science, 35*(1), 25–41.

Denzin, N. K. (1992). *Symbolic interactionism and cultural studies: The politics of interpretation.* Oxford, UK: Blackwell.

Fellin, P. (2000). *The community and the social worker* (3rd ed.). Itasca, IL: F. E. Peacock.

Fletcher, J. (2001). *Disappearing acts: Gender, power, and relational practice at work.* Cambridge: MIT Press.

Freeman, S. J. M., & Bourque, S. C. (2001). Leadership and power: New conceptions. In S. J. M. Freeman, S. C. Bourque, & C. M. Shelton (Eds.), *Women on power: Leadership redefined* (pp. 3–24). Boston: Northeastern University Press.

Freire, P. (1995). *Pedagogy of hope: Reliving pedagogy of the oppressed.* New York: Continuum.

Giddens, A., & Pierson, C. (1998). *Conversations with Anthony Giddens: Making sense of modernity.* Stanford, CA: Stanford University Press.

Gladwell, M. (2002). *The tipping point: How little things can make a big difference.* Boston: Little, Brown.

Gutiérrez, L. M., & Lewis, E. L. (1999). *Empowering women of color.* New York: Columbia University Press.

Halley, A. A. (1997). Applications of boundary theory to the concept of service integration in the human services. *Administration in Social Work, 21*(3/4), 145–168.

Hardcastle, D. A., Wenocur, S., & Powers, P. R. (1997). Theories for community practice for direct service practitioners. In *Community practice: Theories and skills for social workers.* (pp. 37–57), New York: Oxford University Press.

Hardina, D. (2002). Theoretical frameworks for practice. In *Analytical skills for community organization practice* (pp. 44–64). New York: Columbia University Press.

Held, D. (1980). *Introduction to critical theory: Horkheimer to Habermas.* Berkeley: University of California Press.

Hudson, C. G. (2000). At the edge of chaos: A new paradigm for social work? *Journal of Social Work Education, 36*(2), 215–230.

Hurtado, A. (1996). *The color of privilege: Three blasphemies on race and feminism.* Ann Arbor: University of Michigan Press.

Institute of Medicine. (1994). *Reducing risks for mental disorders: Frontiers for preventive intervention research.* Washington, DC: National Academy Press.

Janis, I. L. (1972). *Victims of groupthink.* Boston: Houghton Mifflin.

Johnson, A. G. (2001). *Privilege, power, and difference.* Mountain View, CA: Mayfield.

Kuhn, Thomas S (1970). *The structure of scientific revolutions.* Chicago: University of Chicago Press. (Original work published 1962)

Laraña, E., Johnston, H., & Gusfield, J. R. (Eds.). (1994). *New social movements: From ideology to identity.* Philadelphia: Temple University Press.

Lewin, K. (1947). Frontiers in group dynamics: Concept, method, and reality in social science; social equilibria and social change. *Human Relations, 1*(1), 5–41.

Macarov, D. (2003) *What the market does to people: Privatization, globalization, and poverty.* Atlanta, GA: Clarity Press.

Mace, J. P. (1997). Introduction of chaos and complexity theory to social work. In D. Tucker, C. Garvin, & R. Sarr (Eds.), *Integrating knowledge and practice: The case of social work and social science* (pp. 149–163). Westport, CT: Praeger.

McAdam, D., McCarthy, J. D., & Zald, M. N. (Eds.). (1996). *Comparative perspectives on social movements: Political opportunities, mobilizing structures, and cultural framings.* Cambridge, UK: Cambridge University Press.

McAdam, D., & Scott, W. R. (2002, May). *Organizations and movements: Toward a synthetic framework.* Paper presented at the Social Movement and Organizations Conference, University of Michigan Business School.

Meyer, D. S., & Tarrow, S. (1998). *The social movement society: Contentious politics for a new century,* Lanham, MD: Rowman & Littlefield.

Mullaly, B. (1997). *Structural social work: Ideology, theory, and practice* (2nd ed.). Toronto: Oxford University Press.

Nicholson, L. (1993). Ethnocentrism in grand theory. In R. S. Gottlieb (Ed.), *Radical philosophy: Tradition, counter tradition, politics* (pp. 48–64). Philadelphia: Temple University Press.

Osborne, S. P. (1998). Innovations, innovators, and innovating. In *Voluntary organizations and innovation in public services* (pp. 20–68). London & New York: Routledge.

Parsons, W. (1995). Varieties of analytical frameworks. *Public policy: An introduction to the theory and practice of policy analysis* (pp. 32–83). Northhampton, MA: Edward Elgar.

Payne, M. (1997). *Modern social work theory* (2nd ed.). Boston: Lyceum Press.

Pease, B., & Fook, J. (1998). *Transforming social work practice: Postmodern critical perspectives.* London: Routledge.

Powell, W. W., & DiMaggio, P. J. (1991). *The new institutionalism in organizational analysis.* Chicago: University of Chicago Press.

Reisch, M. (2002). Defining social justice in a socially unjust world. *Families in Society: The Journal of Contemporary Human Services, 83*(4), 343–354.

Reitan, T. C. (1998, September). Theories of interorganizational relations in the human services. *Social Service Review,* 287–309.

Rogers, E. M. (1995). *Diffusion of innovations* (4th ed.). New York: Free Press.

Rothman, J. (1996). The interweaving of community intervention approaches. *Journal of Community Practice, 3*(3/4), 69–99.

Smith, D. H. (1997) Grassroots associations are important: Some theory and a review of the impact literature. *Nonprofit and Voluntary Sector Quarterly, 26*(3), 269–306.

Stanton, D., & Stewart, A. (1995). *Feminisms in the academy.* Ann Arbor: University of Michigan Press.

Swigonski, M. E. (1994). The logic of feminist standpoint theory for social work research. *Social Work, 39*(4), 387–393.

Taylor, D. (1998) Social identity and social policy: Engagements with postmodern theory. *Journal of Social Policy, 27*(3), 329–350.

Tong, R. P. (1998). *Feminist thought* (2nd ed.). Boulder, CO: Westview.

Vago, S. (1999). Theories of change. In *Social change* (4th ed., pp. 44–77). Englewood Cliffs, NJ: Prentice Hall.

Warren, K., Franklin, C., & Streeter, C. L. (1998). New directions in systems theory: Chaos and complexity. *Social Work, 43*(3), 357–372.

Weil, M. (1996). Model development in community practice: An historical perspective. *Journal of Community Practice, 3*(3/4), 5–67.

Young, I. M. (1990). Introduction: Displacing the distributive paradigm, five faces of oppression. In *Justice and the politics of difference* (pp. 3–65). Princeton, NJ: Princeton University Press.

CHAPTER 5

Communities and Social Policy Issues

Persistent Poverty, Economic Inclusion, and Asset Building

Yolanda C. Padilla

Michael Sherraden

The struggle against poverty, and more broadly, the pursuit of social and economic justice, is an important element of community practice. For this reason, an understanding of social policy addressing poverty and social inequality is essential. Such an understanding informs community practice in several ways. First, it incorporates an analysis of the values and interests that shape the various perspectives on the causes and consequences of poverty and thus the structure of antipoverty policy (Parsons, 1995). Equipped with knowledge concerning the policy environment, community practitioners are in a better position to plan viable strategies for social change. According to Fisher, to be effective, "every organizer should have as good a grasp as possible of the challenges and opportunities in the larger political economic context" (2001, p. 100). Second, information related to the policy context helps us ascertain how to integrate community practice and social policy approaches to alleviate poverty and social inequality. Of particular interest in this chapter are approaches encompassing economic opportunity and asset building. Asset building is a new direction in public policy and community development for expanding economic opportunity. Its goal is to connect the poor to the kind of asset-based policies and community strategies that already benefit the non-poor, such as home ownership and retirement savings accounts.

The reasoning is that, like everyone else, people who are poor must save and invest if they are to develop out of poverty.

This chapter characterizes the policy context of community practice by providing an analysis of antipoverty policy in the United States. We begin by describing the current prevalence of poverty in the country, including dominant factors framing the demographic profile of people in poverty. Next, we explore the political discourse on poverty and consider the ramifications for community practice. Finally, we provide a brief evaluation of social policies designed to address poverty in the current context of welfare reform and devolution. We show that strategies to address poverty in the current policy environment have failed to accomplish the goal of increasing self-sufficiency among the poor. The emphasis has been on getting welfare recipients to work and off welfare assistance, with no provisions to help them achieve long-term economic independence or to address the problems of the persistently poor. In the second part, we introduce an alternative approach to helping people escape from poverty, one that incorporates a community-level component to expand their economic potential. This approach focuses on asset building through a program of matched savings called individual development accounts (IDAs).

Analysis of Antipoverty Policy

Political Discourse on Poverty and Implications for Community Practice

Poverty rates in the United States decreased significantly at the end of the last decade of the 20th century (Dalaker & Proctor, 2000). According to census data reports, the overall poverty rate dropped to 11.8% in 1999 from 12.7% in 1998. Child poverty experienced an even sharper drop, from a high of 20.8% in 1995 and 18.9% in 1998 to 16.9% in 1999, the lowest child poverty rate since 1979 (Baugher & Lamison-White, 1996; Dalaker & Proctor, 2000). Although poverty rates declined for all groups, the demographic profile of the poor in the United States continues to be sharply demarcated by age, race and ethnicity, nativity, and family composition (Dalaker & Proctor, 2000).

Children are far more likely to be poor than adults. Almost 17% of children are poor, in comparison to 10% of the rest of the population. Poverty among African Americans (23.6%) and Hispanics (22.8%) is nearly three times higher than it is among non-Hispanic Whites (7.7%). Among Asians and Pacific Islanders, the poverty rate is 10.7%. Immigrants (16.8%) tend to have a much higher poverty rate than do their U.S.-born counterparts (11.2%). However, immigrants who have become naturalized citizens are slightly less likely to be poor than the U.S.-born population. Only 9.1 percent of naturalized citizens are poor. Among immigrants, those who are not citizens, representing 63% of the total immigrant population, have the highest poverty rate, 21.3%. However, the largest differences in poverty rates are related to family composition. A full 27.8% of female householder families (families with no husbands present) are in poverty compared to only 4.8% of married couple families. Employment does not equalize these poverty rates. Even when comparing families in which there is at least one worker, the family type differential remains substantially unchanged.

Attention to these disparities drives the current policy perspectives on poverty in the United States. Among these, concerns with family composition as a cause of poverty and a preoccupation with *welfare reform,* narrowly defined to focus on female-headed households, have dominated the social policy debate for nearly half a century (Bane & Ellwood, 1994; Duncan & Brooks-Gunn, 1999; Edin & Lein, 1997; Jennings, 1999; Kelso, 1994; Lawson, 1995; Mead, 1986). This policy environment has far-reaching ramifications for community practice. Although structural theories of poverty have been proposed, recent social welfare history reveals that discourse at a federal level on neighborhood and community-based interventions did not progress much beyond the War on Poverty era of the 1960s. Programs created by the Area Redevelopment Act, the Committee on Juvenile Delinquency and Youth Crime (such as the Mobilization for Youth in New York City), and the community action programs emphasized community-based approaches to poverty. Members of the community were to organize and make decisions concerning how they wanted to use government resources to design programs that best fit the needs of their own communities. Programs focused on increasing educational and employment opportunities. Nevertheless, a major policy objective was to prevent dependency on welfare (Patterson, 2000). Indeed, the political rhetoric in social welfare policy throughout U.S. history has been characterized by an individualistic rather than a collectivist vision (Skocpol, 1995).

After the 1960s, strong interest in scholarly perspectives on poverty was not revived again until the late 1980s, with the introduction of the influential underclass theory by sociologist William Julius Wilson (1987). Community (or neighborhood) was viewed very differently from this perspective—not as a possible source of activism but rather as a place extensively devastated by economic problems. The foundation of the neighborhood, its social institutions, was rendered ineffective. Wilson's underclass theory, modeled largely on his studies of inner-city Chicago, brought together a comprehensive theory of poverty encompassing psychological, neighborhood, and larger societal factors. Wilson proposed that broad economic restructuring trends, in which manufacturing jobs for low-skilled workers were being replaced by service-producing jobs, had caused significant out-migration of middle-class families from inner cities. As a consequence, poverty became concentrated in these neighborhoods, causing social dislocation: an increase in out-of-wedlock births, drug use, school dropout rates, and crime. Loss of employment and social networks had strong negative effects on neighborhood residents on a psychological level, Wilson argued, isolating them from mainstream behaviors and making them incapable of practicing norms and behaviors associated with steady employment. Despite his focus on neighborhood, however, Wilson did not view these problems as amenable to neighborhood or community-level approaches. Instead, his focus was on macroeconomic policy designed to promote economic growth.

Although the underclass theory became a central focus of scholarly discourse for nearly a decade, generating numerous national studies on the effects of living in highly disadvantaged neighborhoods (Jencks & Peterson, 1991; Ricketts & Sawhill, 1988), it failed to influence social policy substantially. Rather, in its wake, several reactionary perspectives on poverty came to the forefront, which were to reshape current social welfare policy in the United States in fundamental ways. Given the failure of previous social welfare policies to eliminate poverty, theorists like Murray (1984) and Mead (1986) maintained that poverty was caused by personal inadequacies deeply rooted not in the lack of opportunities but in psychological weakness and inertia—and by the very public assistance system that had been created to combat poverty. Poverty was to be viewed as a personal problem, not as a community or social problem. In the end, this view came to dominate the political discourse during the Reagan-Bush years and fully shaped social welfare legislation at the end of the 20th century during the Clinton administration (Patterson, 2000). This discourse culminated in the passage of a new welfare reform law, the Personal Responsibility and Work Opportunity Reconciliation Act of 1996.

The 1996 welfare reform legislation was touted as a return to local control of federal public assistance. It called for the establishment of state block grants, putting an end to the idea that people in need were entitled to financial benefits. In addition, under the program of Temporary Assistance to Needy Families (TANF), strict time limits for public financial assistance were established, and states were forced to initiate work requirements. Provisions for job training and placement and support services were severely curtailed compared to the provisions of the Job Opportunities and Basic Skills (JOBS) program, which had been established by the Family Support Act of 1988. The new policy was designed primarily to end welfare, rather than to end poverty, and as such, there are significant limitations on what it can achieve.

On the other hand, the current pressure of devolution presents some opportunities for community-based problem solving. The reasoning behind recent welfare reform legislation is that block grants will be provided to each state so that they can design programs to meet their own particular needs. The current social policy provides communities with some avenues to advocate on how programs will be implemented locally. The forms that community participation will take are still uncertain. However, some community-based efforts have been implemented. In Texas, for example, local boards, called Local Workforce Development Boards, were developed (Texas Workforce Commission, 2000). The boards are located in communities throughout the state and are made up of local citizens, elected officials, and business representatives. These members of the community recommend policies that address local employment issues. Thus, at a time of decreasing federal responsibility, a window of opportunity is being created for community initiatives to play a role in setting new policy directions (NASW, 1996). The extent to which community-level intervention will evolve in this new era of welfare reform, however, remains to be seen.

Evaluation of Welfare Reform Policy: Gaps in Addressing Poverty

To assess the potential of community practice to combat poverty within the current policy environment, it is helpful to analyze the success of existing welfare legislation. What still needs to be done, and how might community practice strategies offer alternative solutions? Measured by its principal intent, a significant reduction in welfare assistance, the 1996 welfare reform legislation has been successful. In

2000, 4 years after its enactment, President Clinton reported that the number of people on welfare had been cut in half (U.S. Department of Health and Human Services, 2000). In addition, the proportion of Americans on welfare was down to 2.3%, the lowest in 35 years, and 33% of welfare recipients were now working, compared to 7% in 1992. On the other hand, according to the Council of Economic Advisors, a strong economy may have accounted for as much as 40% of the reduction in welfare caseloads (DiNitto, 2000), which suggests that these outcomes may be closely associated with the economic conditions of the country. It must be noted as well that being off the welfare rolls does not mean that people have achieved incomes above the poverty level.

Overall, however, comprehensive policy evaluation of the impact of welfare reform legislation shows some significant gaps in addressing poverty. According to the Center on Budget and Policy Priorities (Lazere, 2000), families leaving welfare for work typically have very low earnings and remain in poverty. Among this population, employment is characterized by part-time or intermittent work, non-standard hours and/or changing schedules, and poor or no benefits (Strawn & Martinson, 2000). Furthermore, extensive research shows that both current and former welfare recipients face multiple barriers to work, which can be categorized as low human capital, poor accessibility to the labor market, or medical and mental health disabilities. Inadequate preparation for the workforce (low human capital) includes low education, poor job skills, and limited work experience. Limited accessibility to the labor market includes lack of transportation and responsibility for an infant or presence of a child with disabilities. A national survey (Zedlewski, 1999) revealed that a year after the implementation of the welfare reform act, 43% of welfare recipients had not worked for 3 or more years, 41% did not have a high school diploma or equivalent, and 10% lived outside metropolitan areas and did not have a car to drive to work. Caring for an infant or having a child with disabilities was a barrier for 15% and 4% of recipients, respectively. Furthermore, a survey of welfare mothers in Michigan showed that those who face these types of obstacles are significantly less likely to be working at least 20 hours per week (Danziger et al., 1999).

Underlying human capital limitations and job accessibility restrictions of welfare recipients are often complex problems related to mental health and medical disabilities. A comprehensive review of studies examining this issue provides some important information (Sweeney, 2000). Mental impairments, including serious depression, posttraumatic stress disorder, and general anxiety disorder, affect as many as one quarter of parents who receive welfare assistance. As many as 1 in 20 may have physical impairments, and between 2% and 20% report substance abuse problems. In addition, studies show that one fifth to one half of welfare recipients have learning disabilities. A related problem that has received less attention and that affects the functioning of welfare families is domestic violence. One study showed that 15% of welfare mothers experienced severe domestic violence (Danziger et. al., 1999). All in all, research shows that families who face multiple barriers related to mental and physical impairments, coupled with other obstacles to work, are less likely to be successful in the labor market (Danziger et. al., 1999; Sweeney, 2000).

In sum, the current policy approach to poverty, with its narrow emphasis on "personal responsibility" in place of social responsibility, is clearly antithetical to community practice approaches of locally focused social and economic development. Nevertheless, given the findings of welfare reform evaluations, policy analysts agree that increasing employment and ending welfare dependency is not enough. Policies are needed to improve access to better jobs and to promote the well-being of families and children. Despite this understanding and given the over-whelming emphasis that social policy currently places on *women* in poverty, what stands out is the paucity of discussion on alternative strategies to increase the ability of the poor to sustain themselves economically. These include pay equity, employer-provided supports related to family responsibilities (e.g., child care), and opportunities to begin micro enterprises. Thus, current social welfare policy in the United States calls for a consideration of community practice approaches to the problems of persistent poverty and economic opportunity. Part of the challenge is to create innovative community practice strategies that can operate within the opportunities and constraints that are presented by the current policy environment.

Asset Building: A Public Policy and Community Development Strategy

In this section, we examine in greater detail one emerging community develop-ment strategy, asset building, and show its relationship to policy. This may be an example of how a new policy direction can be forged via community development applications. The vision and framework is for a large-scale, inclusive, and progres-sive policy, but the pathway has turned out to be essentially through community development.

The Trend Toward Individual Asset Accounts

Income support has been the signal idea of the welfare state of the 20th century. The goal has been to support people when they did not have income from indus-trial labor markets. The primary form of income support for the people who are not in poverty has been social insurance, and for those in poverty, it has been means-tested transfers or "welfare." In the "developed" economies, income-based policy typically constitutes most of social policy, and social policy constitutes most of federal spending. On reflection, it is somewhat remarkable that one idea has defined so much public policy for so long (Sherraden, 2001b, 2001c).

The world has changed considerably since income-based policies were initiated. To be sure, people still require income security when they are not employed, but income alone is no longer enough. The labor market of the information age requires that people have resources to invest in themselves throughout their life-times. In effect, people will require greater control in making their own "social policy" decisions across the lifespan. With less stable employment, workers will need to carry fully portable benefits with them in and out of the labor market, from employer to employer, even across national boundaries. Retirement is likely to be redefined so that it will no longer be such a rigid period of the life course, and

Americans will want greater flexibility in how they live in their older years (Morrow-Howell, Hinterlong, & Sherraden, 2001). Also, policy should promote wealth accumulation across generations, so that more children begin life in households with at least some financial resources. Asset accounts are, in many respects, well suited to accomplish this goal (Sherraden, 1991, 1997).

In part for these reasons, a shift to asset-based policy is under way. For example, in the United States, this can been seen in the introduction and growth of 401(k)s, 403(b)s, IRAs, Roth IRAs, the federal thrift savings plan, educational savings accounts, medical savings accounts, individual training accounts, college savings plans in the states, and proposed individual accounts in Social Security. Some of these are public, and some are called private, but the private plans are typically defined by public policies, are regulated by government, and receive substantial subsidies through the tax system (the fact that the expenditures are through the tax system does not make them any less real or any less public). All of these asset-based policies have been introduced in the United States since 1970. Overall, asset accounts, for various purposes, are the most rapidly growing form of domestic policy in the United States, and it seems likely that the shift to asset-based policy will continue (Sherraden, 2001a).

Individual account policies are regressive. Unfortunately, most asset-based policies are considerably more regressive than income-based policies. The reasons for this are twofold: First, the poor often do not participate in asset-based policies that currently exist; and second, subsidies for asset-based policies operate primarily through tax benefits (tax expenditures) and thus cannot benefit people with insufficient income to pay taxes. Asset-based policies, that is, have the potential to exacerbate inequality because people in poverty are left behind. Asset building in homes, retirement accounts, and investments is funded through the tax system at more than $300 billion per year in the United States. These social benefits are extraordinarily regressive, with more than 90% of benefits going to households earning more than $50,000 (Sherraden, 2001a). For example, in 1999, two thirds of tax benefits for pensions in the United States accrued to the top 20% of households, while only 2.1% went to the bottom 40% (Orszag & Greenstein, 2000).

In other words, *public policy is part of the structure of wealth inequality.* We emphasize this point because the common perception of social policy in the United States is that resources are redistributed downward from the rich to the poor by the federal government. This is to some extent true for direct expenditures, but it is decidedly not true for tax expenditures. There is a large and somewhat "hidden" asset-based policy in the United States (Howard, 1997; Sherraden, 1991). The pattern in the United States is typical. Looking around the world, no country has instituted a substantial asset-based policy that is inclusive and progressive. To date, on a global scale, these policies have greatly favored the rich and middle class over the poor (Sherraden, 2001c).

Why not asset building for people in poverty? This pattern of publicly supported inequality in policies of individual accounts has fundamental ideological and political explanations (Midgley, 2000), and these must be studied and better understood. It is also important to address inclusion in asset-based policy from a practical perspective by asking the simple question: If assets can be successfully transferred to the non-poor, why not also to the poor?

Large-Scale Policy via Community Development

Individual development accounts (IDAs) were introduced in the United States about a decade ago as a policy strategy for inclusive and progressive asset building. IDAs are savings accounts for designated purposes, such as home purchase, post-secondary education, and small-business capitalization, with deposit subsidies for people in poverty (Sherraden, 1991). A large IDA policy demonstration sponsored by a consortium of private foundations began in 1997. Today in the United States, more than 400 IDA programs are operating at the local level. At least 32 states have IDA legislation; 9 additional states have unlegislated IDA projects; and 32 states have IDAs in their TANF plans (Edwards, 2001). IDAs were incorporated as a state option in the federal welfare reform act of 1996, allowing states to use TANF funding for IDAs and making IDA savings exempt from asset tests for any federal program. A large-scale federal demonstration, the Assets for Independence Act (Public Law 101-285, 1998), provided $125 million to test IDAs (Sherraden, 2000, provides a summary of IDA policy development). A federal proposal for a larger IDA policy nearly passed in 2000 and 2001 in the form of the Savings for Working Families Act, which appears to have a good chance of being enacted in the future.

Although IDAs were designed as a policy tool, their character until now has been as a community development strategy, fitting into the general category of community economic development (Sherraden & Ninacs, 1998; see also Rubin and Sherraden, Chapter 26, this volume). State and federal IDA legislation provides funding for IDA programs to operate out of community-based organizations, such as social service agencies and housing organizations, in cooperation with a local financial institution. In fact, progressive policies to relieve poverty are rarely enacted at large scale at the outset. They must first be tested. Compare the policy development of IDAs with that of 401(k)s. In the case of 401(k)s, which benefit the non-poor almost exclusively, large-scale policy was enacted in one fell swoop. There was never a call to test the policy and no requirement for rigorous research. It was just assumed to be a good idea. Alas, the non-poor get large-scale policy, while the poor get "demonstrations." Owing to their small size and limited applications, demonstrations do not have the same character as large-scale policy. They are local and often take the form of community development strategies. The major challenges of policy demonstrations are to undertake thorough and sound research that might demonstrate success at the community level and then to aim for large-scale applications. Progressive policy is often a long road that goes through community development. This is an old story in the United States. Some of the best historical examples are the projects of the women of Hull-House in the early 20th century, many of which laid the groundwork for important social policies later in the century (Addams, 1910).

A large demonstration and research project on IDAs, known as the American Dream Demonstration (ADD), began in 1997. ADD is funded by 11 private foundations: the Ford Foundation, Charles Stewart Mott Foundation, Joyce Foundation, Citigroup Foundation, John D. and Catherine T. MacArthur Foundation, Ewing Marion Kauffman Foundation, F. B. Heron Foundation, Fannie Mae Foundation, Levi Strauss Foundation, Rockefeller Foundation, and the Moriah Fund. ADD ran through 2002, with research extending at least to 2005. ADD may be the largest applied social research project in the United States at this writing. As of June 2000, there were 2,378 ADD participants at 14 IDA program sites around the country. IDA programs are located in a variety of community organizations, including social service agencies, housing organizations, and credit unions. The Corporation for Enterprise Development in Washington, D.C., developed and implemented ADD. The Center for Social Development at Washington University in St. Louis, Missouri, designed an extensive research agenda for ADD, including monitoring of all saving and withdrawal transactions, interviews with participants, and an experiment with randomly assigned controls. Abt Associates in Cambridge, Massachusetts, is collecting and reporting on the experimental data. Below we summarize some of the key findings from ADD to date.

IDA savings. As of June 30, 2000, IDA participants in ADD had net savings of an average of $25.42 per month (this average includes dropouts, who by definition have net savings of zero). IDAs are matched an average of 2:1 in ADD, so that participants had accumulated about $75 per month or $900 per year. The average use of match eligibility was 67 cents of every dollar. In other words, ADD participants were saving two thirds of the amount they could save and have matched. The average participant had made a deposit in 7 of every 12 months. Deposits increased sharply in March, possibly reflecting income tax returns and the impact of the earned income tax credit. There was no statistical difference in saving amount by income. The savings rate (savings/monthly income) for the lowest income decile (about half the poverty line and below) was 5.6%, and the savings rate for the highest income decile (about twice the poverty line) was 1.2%. Our interpretation is that IDA participants, regardless of income level, are responding to program characteristics, including the matching incentive and expectations of a monthly savings amount (detailed data and analyses on IDA savings patterns are in Schreiner et al., 2001).

Sources of savings. In a survey of 298 ADD participants, we asked where they got the money to save. The primary source was changes in consumption behavior. For example, 70% said they shopped more carefully for food; 68% said they ate out less often; and 64% said they spent less on leisure. Some respondents (29%) said that they worked more hours to generate the money for saving in IDAs. Few (7%) said they borrowed from family or friends, and few (3%) said they borrowed on credit cards to save in IDAs (Moore et al., 2001).

Uses of saving in IDAs. As of June 30, 2000, 318 (13%) of ADD participants had taken a matched withdrawal. The average total was $603 ($1,698 with the match). Looking at uses, 24% of withdrawals were for home purchase, 24% were for micro enterprise (small business) development, 21% were for postsecondary education, and 20% were for home repair. Among ADD participants who had not yet taken a matched withdrawal, 57% indicated that the intended use was home purchase (Schreiner et al., 2001).

Program characteristics and saving performance. Controlling for many program and individual factors in regression analysis, up to 12 hours of financial education at the community level has a positive effect on saving performance, but after 12 hours there is no clear effect. Unobserved program characteristics account for a great deal of variance in saving performance among IDA programs (Schreiner et al., 2001).

Effects of saving in IDAs. Reported economic effects are as follows: Respondents *strongly agree* or *agree* that because of their participation in the IDA program, they are more likely to work or stay employed (59%); they are likely to work more hours (41%); and they plan to buy or renovate a home (73%). Reported psychological effects are as follows: Respondents *strongly agree* or *agree* that participation in the IDA program makes them more confident about the future (93%), more economically secure (84%); and more in control of their lives (85%). Turning to human capital development, 60% *strongly agree* or *agree* that participation in the IDA program makes it more likely that they will make educational plans for their children, and 59% indicated that they would make educational plans for themselves (Moore et al., 2001).

In summary, based on these results, it would be incorrect to assume that low-income people, even those far below the poverty line, cannot save and accumulate assets if they have a structure and incentives to do so. Also, there is reason to believe that asset accumulation has positive effects on well-being beyond deferred consumption.

Policy directions based on community-level IDA research. The following recommendations follow from research on IDAs (Sherraden, 2001b, 2001c, 2001d):

1. Based on IDA research results, it would be incorrect to assume that people with low incomes, even those far below the poverty line, cannot save and accumulate assets. Everyone should have the opportunity to be included in asset-building policy initiatives.

2. Savings policies for the poor should aim to capture lump sum distributions, such as the earned income tax credit.

3. There appears to be a large demand for home ownership among the poor. Given that monthly mortgage payments are no higher than rental payments in many parts of the country, saving for home ownership should be a priority.

4. More generally, a progressive saving policy for people in poverty should focus on more than retirement security. Access to home ownership, education, and business ownership is necessary for household development and, at the same time, these will contribute in the long run to retirement security.

5. IDA participants are willing to sacrifice immediate consumption to save, and we see little evidence that these sacrifices are harmful to well-being. The policy principle should be that everyone deserves similar opportunities to make these choices.

6. A small curriculum of financial education at the community level in conjunction with IDAs may be a good investment.

7. Effects of saving and asset accumulation appear to be multiple and positive in areas such as work behavior, home ownership, confidence and control, and plans for education. These broader definitions of well-being should be acknowledged, studied, and taken into consideration in community development and public policy (see especially Sen, 1985, 1993).

8. Looking at the data overall, poor people, like everyone else, should have structured opportunities and incentives to save and accumulate assets. Any public policy that is based on individual asset accounts should include the poor and provide progressive matching deposits.

Toward large-scale policy. Among other impacts, IDA research from ADD has influenced large-scale proposals for universal savings accounts in the United States (Clinton, 1999) and a universal and progressive child trust fund (children's savings accounts) in the United Kingdom (Blair, 2001; H.M. Treasury, 2001; Sherraden, 2001d). Thinking about the future, possibilities for children's accounts look promising (Curley & Sherraden, 2000; Goldberg & Cohen, 2000), especially the potential of 529 plans (state college savings plans) to include the poor (Clancy, 2001). Progressive and universal systems might also be based on the federal thrift savings plan (Fisher, 2000) or a variety of other policy pathways (Friedman & Boshara, 2000). If someday there are to be individual accounts in Social Security, they should be funded progressively, with deposit subsidies for the poor (Sherraden, 2001b).

Conclusion

Connections between policy and community development are rich and multifaceted. Most basically, all community development occurs within a policy context that facilitates or hinders community endeavors. It behooves social workers and other community-level practitioners to understand these contexts if they are to take utmost advantage of positive policies, avoid or subvert negative policies, and identify priorities for policy change in the future. As the analysis of welfare reform demonstrates, it is not possible to practice at the community level with welfare recipients in the absence of a thorough understanding of this policy environment.

From a different perspective, public policy, especially for people in poverty, is often enacted only after a long "try out" period at the community level. This policy process is fundamentally unjust because policies for the non-poor seldom go through these tests; nevertheless, it is a political fact of life in America. Community development professionals and scholars thus have extraordinary responsibility to practice well and conduct sound research because the context and meaning of their work often extends beyond the boundaries of the community. The example of IDAs may be instructive. At the outset, IDAs were a policy concept, which was later implemented as a community development strategy. Data from IDA research, in turn, are having policy impacts in the United States and elsewhere.

Complex interactions of policy and community development are basic to American social work, perhaps more than in any other nation. These interactions are born of federalism (distribution of policy responsibility between federal and state governments), entrepreneurialism (Americans like to try things out), a relatively vital democracy (local examples and voices can genuinely influence larger policies), and long-standing skepticism about people in poverty (some are "worthy", others not; and in this country, no one has to be poor). Overall, the current mix of public policy positions and community development strategies is far from an ideal situation; there are enormous complexities and barriers to both community development and progressive public policy that would create more economic opportunities for the poor and for low-income communities. On the other hand, the system is wide open to both inquiry and action; indeed, it literally invites action. Understanding and appreciating the role of community development and opportunities in the policy context is often the beginning point of social change.

References

Addams, J. (1910). *Twenty years at Hull-House.* New York: MacMillan.

Assets for Independence Act (AFIA). (1998). P.L. 105–385, U.S.C.

Bane, M. J., & Ellwood, D. T. (1994). *Welfare realities: From rhetoric to reform.* Cambridge, MA: Harvard University Press.

Baugher, E., & Lamison-White, L. (1996). *Poverty in the United States: 1995* (U.S. Census Bureau, Current Population Reports Series P60–194). Washington, DC: Government Printing Office.

Blair, T. (2001, April 26). *Savings and assets for all* [speech]. London: 10 Downing Street. Retrieved July 2, 2002, from http://www.pm.gov.uk/output/page2952.asp.

Clancy, M. (2001). *College savings plans: Implications for policy and for a children and youth saving account policy demonstration* (Research background paper). St. Louis, MO: Washington University, Center for Social Development.

Clinton, W. J. (1999). *State of the union address.* Retrieved July 2, 2002, from http://www.washingtonpost.com/wp-srv/politics/special/states/docs/sou99.htm.

Curley, J., & Sherraden, M. (2000). Policy lessons from children's allowances for children's savings accounts. *Child Welfare, 79*(6), 661–687.

Dalaker, J., & Proctor, B. D. (2000). *Poverty in the United States: 1999* (U.S. Census Bureau, Current Population Reports Series P60–210). Washington, DC: Government Printing Office.

Danziger, S., Corcoran, M., Danziger, S., Heflin, C., Kalil, A., Levine, J., Rosen, D., Seefeldt, K., Siefert, K., & Tolman, R. (1999). Barriers to employment among welfare recipients. *Focus, 20*(2), 30–34.

DiNitto, D. M. (2000). *Social welfare: Politics and public policy.* Needham Heights, MA: Allyn & Bacon.

Duncan, G., & Brooks-Gunn, J. (Eds.). (1999). *Consequences of growing up poor.* New York: Russell Sage Foundation.

Edin, K., & Lein, L. (1997). *Making ends meet: How single mothers survive welfare and low-wage work.* New York: Russell Sage Foundation.

Edwards, K. (2001). *State IDA policy profiles.* St. Louis, MO: Washington University, Center for Social Development.

Family Support Act of 1988. (1988). P. L. 100-485, U.S.C.

Fisher, E. R. (2000, September). *The thrift saving experience: Implications for a universal asset account initiative.* Paper presented at the Inclusion in Asset-Building: Research and Policy Symposium, Center for Social Development, Washington University, St. Louis, MO.

Fisher, R. (2001). Political economy and public life: The context for community organizing. In J. Rothman, J. L. Erlich, & J. E. Tropman (Eds.), *Strategies of community intervention* (pp. 100–117). Itasca, IL: F. E. Peacock.

Friedman, R., & Boshara, R., Jr. (2000, September). *Going to scale: Principles and policy options for an inclusive asset-building policy.* Paper presented at the Inclusion in Asset

Building: Research and Policy Symposium, Center for Social Development, Washington University, St. Louis, MO.

Goldberg, F., & Cohen, J. (2000, September). *The universal piggy bank: Designing and implementing a system of savings accounts for children.* Paper presented at Inclusion in Asset Building: Research and Policy Symposium, Center for Social Development, Washington University, St. Louis, MO.

H. M. Treasury. (2001, November). *Delivering saving and assets: The modernization of Britain's tax and benefit system.* London: Author.

Howard, C. (1997). *The hidden welfare state: Tax expenditures and social policy in the United States.* Princeton, NJ: Princeton University Press.

Jencks, C., & Peterson, P. E. (Eds). (1991). *The urban underclass.* Washington, DC: Brookings Institution.

Jennings, J. (1999). Persistent poverty in the United States: Review of theories and explanations. In L. Kushnick & J. Jennings (Eds.), *A new introduction to poverty: The role of race, power, and politics* (pp. 13–38). New York: New York University Press.

Kelso, W. A. (1994). *Poverty and the underclass: Changing perceptions of the poor in America.* New York: New York University Press.

Lawson, R. (1995). The challenge of "new poverty": Lessons from Europe and North America. In K. Funken & P. Cooper (Eds.), *Old and new poverty: The challenge for reform* (pp. 5–28). London: Rivers Oram Press.

Lazere, Ed. (2000). *Welfare balances after three years of TANF Block Grants: Unspent TANF funds at the end of the federal fiscal year 1999.* Washington, DC: Center on Budget and Policy Priorities.

Mead, L. M. (1986). *Beyond entitlement: The social obligations of citizenship.* New York: Free Press.

Mead, L. M. (1992). *The new politics of poverty: The nonworking poor in America.* New York: Basic Books.

Midgley, J. (2000, September). *Assets in the context of welfare theory: A developmentalist interpretation.* Paper presented at the Inclusion in Asset-building: Research and Policy Symposium, Center for Social Development, Washington University, St. Louis, MO.

Moore, A., Beverly, S., Schreiner, M., Sherraden, M., Lombe, M., Cho, E., Johnson, L., & Vonderlack, R. (2001). *Saving, IDA programs, and effects of IDAs: A survey of participants.* St. Louis, MO: Washington University, Center for Social Development.

Morrow-Howell, N., Hinterlong, J., & Sherraden, M. (Eds.). (2001). *Productive aging: Concepts and controversies.* Baltimore: Johns Hopkins University Press.

Murray, C. A. (1984). *Losing ground: American social policy, 1950–1980.* New York: Basic Books.

National Association of Social Workers. (1996). Social work in an era of diminishing federal responsibility [Special issue]. *Social Work, 41*(5).

Orszag, P., & Greenstein, R. (2000, September). *Toward progressive pensions: A summary of the U.S. pension system and proposals for reform.* Paper presented at the Inclusion in Asset-Building: Research and Policy Symposium, Center for Social Development, Washington University, St. Louis, MO.

Parsons, W. (1995). *Public policy: An introduction to the theory and practice of policy analysis.* Northampton, MA: Edward Elgar.

Patterson, J. T. (2000). *America's struggle against poverty in the twentieth century.* Cambridge: Harvard University Press.

Personal Responsibility and Work Opportunity Reconciliation Act of 1996. (1996). P.L. 104–193, U.S.C. (G.P.O., 1996). Retrieved September 6, 2002, from http://thomas.loc. gov/cgi-bin/t2GPO/http://frwebgate.access.gpo.gov/cgi-bin/getdoc.cgi?dbname=104_ cong_bills&docid=f:h3734enr.txt.pdf

Ricketts, E. R., & Sawhill, I. V. (1988). Defining and measuring the underclass. *Journal of Policy Analysis & Management, 7*(2), 316–326.

Schreiner, M., Sherraden, M., Clancy, M., Johnson, E., Curley, J., Grinstein-Weiss, M., Zhan, M., & Beverly, S. (2001). *Savings and asset accumulation in IDAs.* St. Louis, MO: Washington University, Center for Social Development.

Sen, A. (1985). *Commodities and capabilities.* Amsterdam: North-Holland.

Sen, A. (1993). Capability and well-being. In M. Nussbaum & A. Sen (Eds.), *The quality of life* (pp. 30–53). Oxford, UK: Clarendon Press.

Sherraden, M. (1991). *Assets and the poor. A new American welfare policy.* Armonk, NY: M. E. Sharpe.

Sherraden, M. (1997). Conclusion: Social security in the twenty-first century. In J. Midgley & M. Sherraden (Eds.), *Alternatives to social security: An international inquiry* (pp. 121–140). Westport, CT: Auburn House.

Sherraden, M. (2000). From research to policy: Lessons from individual development accounts. [Colston Warne Lecture.] *Journal of Consumer Affairs, 34*(2), 159–181.

Sherraden, M. (2001a). Asset building policy and programs for the poor. In T. M. Shapiro & E. N. Wolff (Eds.), *Assets for the poor: The benefits of spreading asset ownership* (pp. 302–323). New York: Russell Sage Foundation.

Sherraden, M. (2001b, October 18). *Assets and the poor: Implications for individual accounts in Social Security* [Testimony]. Washington, DC: The President's Commission to Strengthen Social Security.

Sherraden, M. (2001c, December). *Individual accounts in Social Security: Can they be progressive?* Paper presented at the international symposium, The Uncertain Future of Social Security, University of California, Berkeley.

Sherraden, M. (2001d, October 2). *Toward a universal and progressive asset-based domestic policy* [Speech at the meeting of the Labour Party]. Brighton, United Kingdom.

Sherraden, M. S., & Ninacs, W. A. (1998). Introduction: Community economic development and social work. In M. S. Sherraden & W. A. Ninacs (Eds.), *Community economic development and social work* (pp. 1–10). New York: Haworth.

Skocpol, T. (1995). *Social policy in the United States: Future possibilities in historical perspective.* Princeton, NJ: Princeton University Press.

Strawn, J., & Martinson, K. (2000). *Steady work and better jobs: How to help low-income parents sustain employment and advance in the workforce.* New York: Manpower Demonstration Research Corporation.

Sweeney, E. (2000, February 29). *Recent studies indicate that many parents who are current or former welfare recipients have disabilities or other medical conditions.* Washington, DC: Center on Budget and Policy Priorities.

Texas Workforce Commission. (2000). *Local Workforce Development Board integrated program guidelines, program year 2000–2004.* Austin: Texas Workforce Commission, Workforce Development Division.

U.S. Department of Health and Human Services. (2000). *Temporary Assistance for Needy Families (TANF) program, third annual report to Congress.* Washington, DC: Administration for Children and Families, Office of Planning, Research and Evaluation.

Wilson, W. J. (1987). *The truly disadvantaged: The inner city, the underclass, and public policy.* Chicago: University of Chicago Press.

Zedlewski, S. R. (1999). *Work-related activities and limitations of current welfare recipients. Assessing the New Federalism* (Discussion Paper 96–06). Washington, DC: Urban Institute.

CHAPTER 6

Evolution, Models, and the Changing Context of Community Practice

Marie Weil

Dorothy N. Gamble

Human organizations and social relationships form the basic domains of social work practice. Collective human activity occurs in a range of human groups, including, for example, villages, neighborhoods, women's cooperatives, a worldwide coalition focusing on HIV/AIDS, a national environmental group, and a farm workers' union, all of which are communities. Social workers, responding to the "importance of human relationships . . . engage people as partners in the helping process" as they "strive to ensure access to needed information, services, and resources; equality of opportunity; and meaningful participation in decision-making for all people" (National Association of Social Workers [NASW], 1996, pp. 5–6). Community practice, a concept developed in some depth through the work of members of the Association for Community Organization and Social Administration (ACOSA), is currently discussed in the *Journal of Community Practice*, which ACOSA sponsors. The journal, along with the burgeoning community practice literature and historical treatments, provides a focus and documentation of the varied models and approaches to social work with communities that have evolved throughout social work history.

Community Practice in Social Work History

During different historical periods we have referred to aspects of community practice as settlement house work, community organization, locality and community development, Community Chest and United Way work, agricultural and economic development, community planning, civic and social action, social development, community intervention, and social administration (Betten & Austin, 1990; Brager & Specht, 1973; Christenson & Robinson, 1989; Cox, Erlich, Rothman, & Tropman, 1970; Ecklein & Lauffer, 1972; Fisher, 1994; Garvin & Cox, 2001, pp. 65–100; Harper & Dunham, 1959; Kramer, 1966; Murphy, 1954; Ross, 1955, 1958; Rothman, 2001, pp. 27–64). The process and purpose of community practice has a focus on four primary concepts: development, organizing, planning, and change (Weil, 1996). As a major method of social work, community practice embodies the profession's empowerment tradition and social justice values (International Federation of Social Workers [IFSW], 2003; NASW, 1996; Simon, 1994).

The traditions of community practice are rooted in the settlement house movement, the Charity Organization Society movement, the rural development movement, theories of democratic participation, and the organizing and development histories of diverse ethnic and racial groups (Betten & Austin, 1990; Carleton-LaNey, 2001; Rivera & Erlich, 1998; Rubin & Rubin, 2001; Weil & Gamble, 2002).

Murray Ross (1955, 1958), Canadian community scholar, was one of the first scholars to formulate differential social work approaches in community-focused practice. He grounded his work in social science theory and formulated principles of practice with communities. His presentation of approaches or models provided clarity of focus and defined purposes for social work community practice. Differentiation in approaches provides useful guidance for workers in selection of planning, organizing, and action methods. Ross notes,

> There are numerous goals and consequently numerous approaches which are useful in community work. Only when we have decided what we are trying to accomplish can we decide which approach is the proper one and which methods are consistent with the end we have in mind. (1958, p. ix)

Ross discusses variation in philosophies and delineates values and methods that will direct the selection of goals. He describes a "reform orientation" that encompasses both social action and policy practice efforts. His "planning orientation" differentiates between (a) "exploration with people," which promotes grassroots planning as a major responsibility for community workers, and (b) a "technical study of welfare needs," which "encourages balanced welfare programs" and is undertaken by welfare councils or other planning bodies (Ross, 1958, p. 21). Ross's "process orientation" is akin to approaches to community organization and community development in which members of the community are the clear leaders and direction setters for work to strengthen community ties and engage in organizing to improve local conditions. This process orientation would be the guide for most neighborhood or functional community organizing and relates clearly to later conceptions of popular education and community empowerment strategies (Ross, 1958, pp. 5–12). Ross provides interesting and still applicable examples of international development work as well as North American neighborhood organization (1955, 1958).

Many macro practitioners are grounded in the three major approaches to community intervention introduced as models by Jack Rothman in 1968. Rothman has extensively revised his original framework of locality development, social planning, and social action to provide a more complex, interwoven view of the mixed and phased modes of community intervention (see Figure 6.1). In addition to discussion of 12 characteristics of these three major modes of community intervention, Rothman provides significant analysis of the dilemmas presented by each intervention as one tries to apply these ideal types to the real world. These dilemmas relate to the implications of internal and external (horizontal and vertical) linkages in locality development, the locus of decision making and community participation in community planning, and the relative kind of goals and tactical means, along a continuum from normative to radical, adopted for social action interventions (Rothman, 2001, pp. 53–58). Rothman's (1968) original models provided useful guidance for new community practitioners emerging from schools of social work in the 1960s and 1970s to work in the rapidly growing nonprofit sector and in antipoverty programs, numerous social planning efforts, and political and social action.

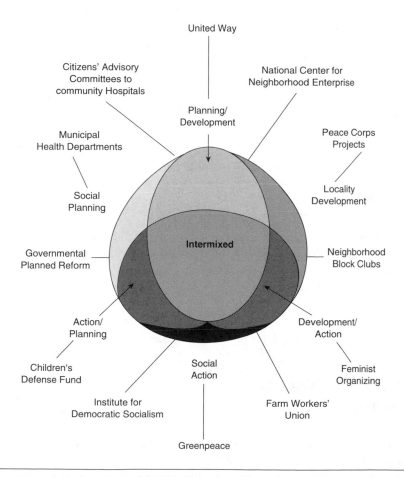

Figure 6.1   Rothman's Models With Examples of Organizational Types Interwoven

Taylor and Roberts elaborated five models of community social work in 1985. The models, program development and coordination, planning, community liaison, community development, and political empowerment, responded to some of the changes occurring in social work practice education in the early 1980s as education for the profession moved more in the direction of social administration and was less involved with grassroots organization (Patti, 1983; Slavin, 1985). Netting, Kettner, and McMurty (2004), drawing on an earlier conceptualization by Kramer (1966), developed the larger framework referred to as *macro practice,* encompassing both community practice and social administration, and defined it as "professionally directed intervention designed to bring about planned change in organizations and communities" (2004, p. 6).

This chapter focuses on eight models of community practice that are widely identifiable in community practice interventions in the first decade of the 21st century (Weil & Gamble, 2002). These models have evolved in practice and the literature over the last half-century (Brager & Specht, 1973; Ecklein & Lauffer, 1972; Harper & Dunham, 1959; Homan, 2004; Kramer & Specht, 1983; Lauffer, 1978, 1981; Lurie, 1959; Mizrahi & Rosenthal, 1993; Mondros & Wilson, 1994; Murphy, 1954; Netting et al., 2004; Ross, 1955, 1958; Rothman, 1968, 2001; Rubin, 2000; Rubin & Rubin 2001; Taylor & Roberts, 1985; Weil & Gamble, 2002). Although they may shift in emphasis with changing times and contexts, and although more progressive or more restraining political environments may impact methods and strategies, these models have stood the test of time as useful approaches for positive social change. In addition, these models can be mutually reinforcing as they are mixed or sequentially phased—for example, as a community group moves into economic development activities or as a functional community develops services for a stigmatized or underserved group (Weil, 1997; Weil & Gamble, 2002). The models treated in this chapter are:

- Neighborhood and community organizing
- Organizing functional communities
- Political and social action
- Community social and economic development
- Social planning
- Program development and community liaison
- Coalitions
- Social movements

These models are best made use of in the light of three changing contexts that are shaping the environment for practice in this new century.

Critical Contexts for Practice in the 21st Century

A set of factors critical in examining community practice in the 21st century are three significantly altered contexts that affect all practice in relation to social, economic, and political changes. For this discussion, we propose to consider these major changes in context as "spotlight" lenses that illuminate current practice, identify problems or tensions, and light the way for further practice development. We will analyze the eight models in light of these three critical contexts that are reshaping our world. These contexts are major changes sweeping the globe: (a) the increase of multicultural societies worldwide, (b) the expansion of rights for women and girls and further expansion of human rights, and (c) globalization, the major economic, political, and social shifts occurring throughout the world and creating complex interactive effects.

Multicultural Context

Although the United States has always been multicultural, it is now clearly recognized as such. Consequently, political, social, and economic policies are needed which take a more progressive and realistic view of this reality. Throughout the world, communication and commerce have broken through borders in positive and problematic ways. Chinese students are able to access the Internet, opening new if somewhat covert opportunities for international connections and information, while in some areas, the economic power of multinational corporations seems to dwarf national perspectives on development. In Africa alone, there are currently more than 15 million refugees who have fled war, starvation, and political oppression (United Nations High Commission for Refugees, 2003). The movement of refugees worldwide is the greatest it has ever been. An ever-increasing reality is that of migrants moving from the Global South to the United States and Western Europe, hoping to find jobs and freedom.

In all community interventions, a spotlight scrutinizing cultural and multicultural strategies (or lack thereof) must be used. Using a multicultural lens means pulling back from the traditional tight focus on a specific culture to gain a wide-angle view of the multiple cultural, racial, and economic groups in a geographic area or a functional community, then analyzing commonalities and differences in interests and perspectives between and among these groups and also between these groups and power elites (see Bankhead & Erlich, Chapter 3, this volume; Gutiérrez, Lewis, Nagda, Wernick, & Shore, Chapter 18, this volume).

With the dismantling of the federal and state policy safety nets that were hallmarks of the Western welfare state, the economic status of the poor from a variety of ethnic backgrounds has worsened. This increase in poverty and the effects of globalization on low- and moderate-wage workers has increased the need for multicultural/intergroup organizing and development. For the disenfranchised, now as ever, power comes in numbers—and community practitioners need to be sophisticated about potential political and economic strategies that may be used to divide diverse population groups and turn them against each other. The strength of the United States can be in its diversity, but only if its diverse populations and lower-income groups have opportunities for greater social and economic viability. The struggles of communities of color and those living in poverty or near poverty in the United States to attain civil and political equality, access to institutions, and economic opportunity are far from complete (Abromovitz, 1986; Blank, 1997; Gutiérrez & Lewis, 1999; Piven & Cloward, 1979; Rivera & Erlich, 1998). (See also

Bankhead & Erlich, Chapter 3, this volume; Gutiérrez et al., Chapter 18, this volume; Reisch, Chapter 15, this volume.)

Very few U.S. communities can be considered so homogeneous that a single cultural lens will be sufficient for analysis. Cultural awareness and cultural competence are necessary skills in social work (Fong & Furuto, 2001). However, as the literature on cultural competence and multiculturalism has become integrated into social work curricula and practice, it is critically important for these approaches not simply to focus on understanding and adapting direct practice skills to fit appropriately with diverse clients, but more important, to maintain a strong and clear focus on social and economic justice (Finn & Jacobson 2003; Hardy-Fanta, 1986; Longres, 1997) and on the need for community practice, political and social action, and policy practice to address issues of community (not just individual) empowerment, equity, and opportunity. It is equally critical to analyze any community practice model or planned intervention to assure that methods and approaches are relevant for diverse populations and perspectives.

A broad range of perspectives that are congruent with macro practice concerns are examined in Anderson and Carter's (2003) volume on diversity, including three major categories: ethnocultural, oppression, and vulnerable life situations. These are further divided into 12 more specific perspectives: strengths, empowerment, ethnic sensitive, value orientation, people of color, dual perspective, ethnic-centric, social justice, ethnographic, communication, feminist, and constructivist. These perspectives are helpful when analyzing community practice models for responsive approaches to diversity and multiculturalism.

Feminist and Human Rights Contexts

As long as half the world's population is women, gender issues will be a major focus through which all community practice models must be viewed and assessed. In most societies, women have always been involved in community issues and problem solving. In the United States, many women were among the early leaders in the development of community practice and have continued to be so in the major trajectories of both grassroots and interorganizational work. Until recently, most of the literature was written by men; however, during the second wave of American feminism, women scholars and activists have greatly added to the community and macro practice literature. To grasp the critical nature of inclusive structures and methods, some analysis of more recent developments is useful.

The history of feminism has been the long struggle in both the domestic and public spheres to claim or reclaim women's status as equal beings, citizens, and agents in society and in the world. Perspectives from the second wave of the feminist movement burst into the social work literature initially with the publication of *Women's Issues and Social Work Practice* (Norman & Mancuso) in 1980 and *Women, Power, and Change* (Weick & Vandiver) in 1981. The last 20 years of the 20th century saw the development and increasing application of feminist scholarship. The growth of this literature continues apace in the early decades of the 21st century as more women take on leadership positions in practice and academia and as more feminist literature is integrated into undergraduate and graduate curricula by male and female faculty.

Over this period of time, feminist social work literature has contributed significantly to development and analysis of the knowledge base regarding issues of women as clients, workers, leaders, and community practitioners (Abromovitz, 1986; Brandwein, 1981; Chandler, 1986; Ellsworth, Hooyman, Ruff, Stam, & Tucker, 1981; Gutiérrez & Lewis, 1999; Hyde, 1996, 2000, Chapter 19, this volume; Weil, 1986). Feminist approaches can be applied in all areas of community practice. In 1996, Hyde provided an analysis of Rothman's interwoven community intervention models and documented that rather than having a specific "place" in the "development-action" category, feminist models actually exist and thrive in all community practice models. For example, the National Council of Neighborhood Women relates to a development focus that includes planning; the Institute for Women's Policy Research is a classic social planning organization; Women's Way, a federated funding organization for feminist organizations, fits the development/planning model; the Women's Equity Action League focuses equally on planning and action; and the State Commissions on the Status of Women focus primarily on planning but also frequently engage in action strategies (Hyde, 1996).

As the above examples illustrate, the range of feminist community practice is wide. To analyze community practice approaches for consideration of gender issues, Weil, Gamble, and Williams (1998, pp. 256–263) have developed a set of questions that prompt the inclusion of feminist content, and the representation of women and girls, in all eight models of community practice.

The shifts in consciousness, policy, practice, and politics that are taking place worldwide as women overtly "claim half the human experience" (Figueira-McDonough, Netting, & Nichols-Casebolt, 1998) not only reveal women's capacities but also highlight the significant contributions that women have made in community practice from its earliest history. In *The Role of Gender in Practice Knowledge,* Figueira-McDonough and colleagues provide a full compendium of theory, knowledge, and research on gender to be integrated into the curricula of schools of social work. Gender is no longer an "added issue" or a footnote but a central factor in human interaction, community practice, and social change for social justice.

"Human rights are women's rights" is a clarion call that has been heard at many international convocations, from China to Africa and Latin America. Women across the globe seek equality and basic rights and will increasingly do so as education and economic opportunity become more accessible to girls and women in the Global South. Although the roots of the aforementioned community practice models bespeak a considerable history, new emphasis must be placed on the values and purposes of community practice, given the complex demographic, political, economic, and social changes faced by social workers in this new century. Ethnic and racial schisms, class and gender divisions, and the importance of access to support systems for the beginning and end of life in all societies require a focus on the most critical areas for understanding and engaging in community practice. These issues for community practice are echoed in the direct and dignified language of the *Universal Declaration of Human Rights* (United Nations, 1948). Community practice in the 21st century will need to focus intently at all levels to press for positive social change and expansion of human rights.

Globalization

All community practice models are subject to the effects of globalization, defined by the IFSW at its general meeting in July 2002 as "the process by which all people and communities around the world come to experience an increasingly common economic, social, and cultural environment" (2002, p. 3). As this definition indicates, globalization offers considerable long-term promise—for human rights, for sustainable development work, and for recognition of common humanity through communication and interaction (Burbidge, 1997; Henderson, 1996). However, in the early decades of the 21st century, the economic, political, and social risks seem high indeed for vulnerable populations such as refugees and immigrants, those sold into wage or sexual slavery (Cockburn, 2003), and the poor, lower-middle-class, and economically marginalized workers throughout the world. In short, globalization offers possibilities both for global human advancement and for increasing disparity of income and opportunity throughout the world.

The third lens for analyzing the models of community practice, therefore, is globalization. The process of globalization—the ability to quickly transmit information, the increasing interconnectedness between and among people and cultures, the diminishing significance of borders and national barriers, increased tribalism, and the increasing strength of global corporations (see Reisch, Chapter 29, this volume)—requires us to engage locally, connect to social problems and concerns nationally and internationally, and be able to understand and assess global issues.

No community is isolated from the issues and results of globalization, and questions such as the following abound: How and where are community members employed? What jobs have moved offshore? What is available to eat, and where does it come from? How will educational curricula be shaped? Who are the neighbors—and where are they from? How are family and organizational networks maintained? How can fair wages and working conditions be obtained? How are populations shifting demographically? All these issues are influenced by global changes. No community practice worker who expects to be able to engage in any of the eight models we describe could do so without knowledge of the global political, social, and economic contexts and their effects on the local economy and community. In addition, to become partners with social workers doing community practice in other countries, social workers in the United States need to understand the principles and provisions of the *UN Declaration of Human Rights,* the *UN Development Reports,* and the IFSW's international definition of social work, as well as substantive issues in their own arena of work. Indeed, the IFSW, in its *Ethics in Social Work: Statement of Principles,* proposes that "common standards of achievement" and recognized rights "accepted by the global community" as expressed in seven major international conventions should be known and understood by all social workers (IFSW, 2003). Perspectives on how we can think about global connections are now more regularly found in social work literature (Estes, Chapter 28, this volume; Gamble & Hoff, Chapter 8, this volume; Mayadas & Elliott, 1997; Mayadas, Watts, & Elliott, 1997; Prigoff, 2000; Reisch, Chapter 29, this volume; Sarri, 1997).

Finally, both gender and multicultural issues play into the inescapable reality of the global context of human existence in the 21st century. Current literature is replete with discussion of economic shifts, demographic shifts, and political and cultural shifts across the world. Community practice needs to take account of these three contexts in all its models, approaches, and practices. Later chapters in this volume specifically discuss these major shifts in detail (see Chapters 3, 8, 15, 18, 19, 28, 29, and 30).

Analyzing Eight Major Models of Community Practice in Light of 21st-Century Contexts

Guiding Values and Purposes of Community Practice

All social work community practice efforts must be guided by core values that are reflected in the NASW *Code of Ethics*, and reaffirmed in the international definition of social work (IFSW, 2003; NASW, 1996). These values, often criticized as having diminished power and loss of meaning from casual application (Gomory, 1997), have meaning only if they have been clearly defined and are implemented. In the most recent revision of the NASW *Code of Ethics*, general values are described as service, social justice, dignity and worth of the person, importance of human relationships, integrity, and competence (NASW, 1996, pp. 5–6). The IFSW emphasizes basic values in a draft for the 2004 general meeting, with a strong focus on human rights and human dignity, social justice, and professional conduct as defined by each national organization. In 2000, the IFSW (2003) agreed on a basic definition of social work, described below:

> The social work profession promotes social change, problem solving in human relationships, and the empowerment and liberation of people to enhance well-being. Utilising theories of human behaviour and social systems, social work intervenes at the points where people interact with their environments. Principles of human rights and social justice are fundamental to social work.

The value base of community practice not only respects the dignity of the individual but focuses on the interdependence of families and communities (e.g., human relationships) and the development of fairness, equity, and equality (e.g., social justice) (Allen-Meares & DeRoos, 1997; Drake, 2001; Flynn, 1995; IFSW, 2003; NASW, 1996; Weil & Gamble, 1995).

To engage with community groups, social workers must be able to define specific purposes for such engagement. These purposes should be developed in conjunction with those with whom the practitioner works and provide the central motivation for practitioners and community members to move toward a common, mutually supported goal. In work to strengthen human service systems, the work should be undertaken with representatives of the populations or groups being served. The purposes will not be a hidden or abstract reference point for the worker, but an open, transparent, and direct compact the worker has with community and organizational members. The set of purposes in Table 6.1 provides a basis for most community practice engagement.

Community practitioners can expect to engage with specific groups and with intergroup or multicultural groups who hold competing views on issues and often have divergent strategies for how to solve problems. The social worker who has a focus on values and purpose, and who makes those explicit with community

Table 6.1   Community Practice Purposes

Improving the quality of life from a single local issue such as securing a railroad crossing gate in a rural community, to complex social issues such as devising strategies to improve education and opportunities for African American youth or the design and implementation of global strategies for sustainable development.

Extending human rights by developing participatory structures and opportunities and deepening democracy for citizens who are excluded and feel powerless to influence policies that have an effect on their lives; responding to the needs of the substantial number of economic and political refugees in the world; ending slavery; and extending full human rights to women and children.

Advocacy for a community of interest such as children with severe emotional or behavioral problems; for a specific issue such as human rights for gays and lesbians; for resource attainment such as efforts to fund minority group economic development projects through the Community Reinvestment Act or to establish political and social rights for women and marginalized populations worldwide.

Human social and economic development to assure social support and economic viability and sustainability by expanding participation and building grassroots leadership locally, regionally, and globally; using business development tools such as cooperatives for American Indians and re-establishment of a greenbelt in Kenya by African women; building economic, social, and political assets for the poor in impoverished urban and rural areas across the world; implementing the United Nations Agenda 21 blueprint for sustainable social and economic development.

Service and program planning for a newly recognized or reconceptualized need or to serve an emerging population; efforts include health and social services for people with HIV/AIDS; development of alternative services for battered women; or design of adoption, foster care, mental health, or youth services within American Indian communities.

Service integration developing local to national and international means of coordinating human services for populations in need; examples include building the continuum of family support, preservation, and child welfare; building a network of well-connected services for healthy and frail senior citizens; and providing food, protection, relocation opportunities, and other services to refugees from national or international conflicts.

Political and social action to build political power for the economically and socially marginalized, protect the weak and the poor, foster institutional change for inclusion and equity, and increase participatory democracy and equality of access and opportunity in local, regional, and international efforts—such as political organizing in communities of color; national research and organizing for the rights, protection, and welfare of children by the Children's Defense Fund; and Amnesty International's efforts to prevent torture and secure release of political prisoners worldwide.

Social justice to build toward human equality and opportunity across race, ethnicity, gender, and nationality—for example, in securing the franchise for women, making reparations to Japanese Americans for internment, building the fabric of civil and human rights laws both nationally and globally, and incorporating the articles of the *Universal Declaration of Human Rights* (United Nations, 1948) as we develop social programs and interventions nationally and internationally.

Source: Adapted from Weil & Gamble, 1995.

groups, will have a greater capacity to develop mutually respectful relationships with the group members and to work as a facilitator to find sufficient common ground for consolidated action.

The three critical contexts described earlier, and the social work values and purposes outlined above, should provide spotlights for the analysis of the eight models. Although models, as Weber (1949) noted, are "ideal types," actual practice engagements can usefully be compared with models to ascertain if major aspects of the approaches are being applied and to check to see if important phases, components, or elements have been neglected and need to be factored into current work. As Netting et al. note: "Models provide guidance and direction for the practitioner. Theories provide the tools for thinking about a problem or need, whereas models provide guidelines for action and intervention" (2004, p. 11). Analysis of practice and use of the reflective processes of praxis can be significantly enhanced by analyzing not only the specific efforts in light of models and phases of work, but by careful analysis of the operation of the three contexts discussed above.

Practice Models for the 21st Century

Community practice encompasses approaches and methods ranging from popular education to grassroots organization and development, to human services planning and coordination, to policy practice. It employs the values of empowerment-based interventions to strengthen participation in democratic processes, reform human service systems, assist groups and communities in advancing their needs, and organizing for social justice. The eight models discussed here are drawn from surveys of practice, from communication with and case examples from faculty colleagues across the nation, from organizers and community practitioners, from alumni and students, and from continuous review of the literature for trends, differences, commonalities, and changes.

The following discussion details distinctions among the eight models that operate as major and continuing approaches for community practice. Examination of the models reveals overlap in some conceptual components, and essential community practice roles are employed in a number of approaches. Each model, however, is analytically discrete and often exists as a discrete approach in practice. Each model also represents a specific, coherent, and clear approach to community practice. Although, as Rothman and others (Hardcastle, Wenocur, & Powers, 1997; Homan, 2004) note, there is also considerable mixing and phasing of models in practice situations, it is useful to examine what components are critical in specific models for specific community interventions. Practitioners need to know what they are doing and why—and the targets of intervention, scope of work, and methodologies will differ with different models. This eight-model framework provides a typology that can be used in specifying different desired outcomes; clarifying constituencies, groups, or organizations targeted for change; and selecting strategies most likely to be successful, given the practice context and the selected model for engagement and intervention. With specification related to particular projects, the models can also be used to assess community practice situations and to frame comparative research.

The eight models depicted in Table 6.2 are presented in terms of purpose and scope, along with examples related to the 21st-century contexts of practice. Table 6.2 illustrates the examples and highlights: outcomes, change targets, constituencies, scope of concern, and primary social work roles for each model (Weil & Gamble, 2002).

Values and Purposes

Table 6.2 Models of Community Practice in 21st Century Contexts: Globalization, Human Rights, and Multicultural Societies

Comparative Characteristics	Neighborhood & Community Organizing	Organizing Functional Communities	Community Social & Economic Development	Social Planning	Program Development & Community Liaison	Political & Social Action	Coalitions	Social Movements
Desired Outcome	Develop capacity of members to organize, change the impact of negative planning and external development	Action for social justice focused on advocacy and on changing behaviors and attitudes; may also provide service	Initiate development plans from a grassroots perspective; prepare citizens to make use of social and economic investments	Citywide or regional proposals for action by (a) elected body or (b) human services planning councils	Expansion or redirection of agency program to improve community service effectiveness; organize new service	Action for social justice focused on changing policy or policy makers	Build a multi-organizational power base large enough to influence program direction or draw down resources	Action for social justice that provides a new paradigm for a particular population, group, or issue
System Targeted for Change	Municipal government; external developers;	General public; government institutions	Banks; foundations; external developers	(a) Perspectives of community leaders; (b) perspectives of human services leaders	Funders of agency programs; beneficiaries of agency services	Voting public; elected officials; inactive/potential participants	Elected officials; foundations; government institutions	General public; political systems
Primary Constituency	Residents of neighborhood, parish, or rural county	Like-minded people in a community, region, nation, or across the globe	Low-income, marginalized, or oppressed population groups in a city or region	(a) Elected officials; (b) social agencies and interagency organizations	Agency board or administrators; community representatives	Citizens in a particular political jurisdiction	Organizations and citizens that have a stake in the particular issue	Leaders, citizens, and organizations able to create new visions and images
Scope of Concern	Quality of life in the geographic area	Advocacy for particular issue or population	Income, resource, and social support development; improved basic education and leadership skills	(a) Integration of social needs into geographic planning in public arena; (b) human services network coordination	Service development for a specific population	Building political power; institutional change	Specified issue related to social need or concern	Social justice within society
Social Work Roles	Organizer Facilitator Educator Coach	Organizer Advocate Writer/communicator Facilitator	Negotiator Promoter Planner Educator Manager	Researcher Proposal writer Communicator Planner Manager	Spokesperson Planner Manager Proposal writer	Advocate Organizer Researcher Candidate	Mediator Negotiator Spokesperson Organizer	Advocate Facilitator

Values and Purposes

Neighborhood and Community Organizing

Even with the advent of e-mail and listservs, there is no substitute for face-to-face opportunities to engage together, find common ground, discuss issues, and plan strategies for action. People in geographic proximity—living in neighborhoods, rural communities, parishes, or counties—can capitalize on the synergy of exchanges with people of like mind and common concern for neighborhood action or improvement.

This model of community practice has a focus on activities that will increase the leadership, planning, and organization building skills of grassroots people. Civic engagement and community organizing constitute the bedrock of democratic institutions. When people at the grassroots of society can learn how to organize their efforts, be inclusive in their organization building, engage in democratic decision making, set priorities, access resources, and reach their goals, they have learned a basic lesson of all democracies. Increasing their capacity to work on basic community problems makes it possible for citizens to change community conditions to improve the quality of life for all residents (Mizrahi, 2002). This model of community practice can be seen in a variety of forms across the globe. It is a model used as effectively in older democracies as in the newly emerging democracies of Eastern Europe, Africa, and South America (CIVICUS, 1999; VeneKlasen & Miller, 2002; Weil & Gamble, 2002).

Neighborhood and community organizing has the dual focus of building the capacity of individuals to be able to lead and organize, while at the same time accomplishing a task that will enhance the quality of life for the geographic area (O'Donnell & Karanja, 2000). People may band together to carry out their own projects that address neighborhood development, safety, and educational concerns or other cooperative plans. They may also need to organize to place pressure on public officials or corporations to live up to legal or social responsibilities or to protect community institutions, environment, or the social fabric of the community. Elements of this model are found in any setting in which people who live in close proximity come together to create needed change.

An example is the Center for Community Action in Lumberton, North Carolina, a multicultural organization of Lumbee Indians, African Americans, and Whites that combines community learning and action on social, economic, political, multicultural, environmental, intergenerational, spiritual, and moral issues. Others include Project MASH (Make Something Happen) in the Stowe Village Housing Project of Hartford, Connecticut, engaged in community organizing as well as job and service development; COPS (Communities Organized for Public Service) of San Antonio, which has a focus on broad-based community development; and CARE (The Community and Resource Exchange) of Minneapolis and Hennepin County, Minnesota, established to fight drugs and crime.

There are as many international examples, especially from Africa, Asia, Latin America, and the newly independent states (VeneKlasen & Miller, 2002). In the western highlands of Peru, a neighborhood organization eventually expanded to three provinces when local farmers collaborated with the Center for Regional Development Studies to organize a dairy industry. The farmers, who own an average of six cows each, increased their milk production and also began making cheese, which provides additional employment for the community (Urday, 2003).

Partnerships along the Mexico-U.S. border have been formed among 20 community groups and foundations on both sides of the border. The communities are working to match $10 million committed from nine major foundations. According to the Inter American Foundation, "the goal is to root development efforts in local participation, build social capital and encourage cross-border collaboration" (2003, p. 52). Small nongovernmental organizations all along the border from Texas to California will be funded for projects that strengthen grassroots neighborhood social and economic development. For further examples of the methods and purposes of this model, see Rubin & Rubin, Chapter 9, this volume.

Organizing Functional Communities

The opportunity to organize functional communities, or communities of interest, has expanded in manifold ways with new communication technologies. Identity organizations, representing people across the globe with similar interests, have easy opportunities to be connected in loose interest groups or in tight organizational structures. Housing advocacy organizations, for example, hold "virtual" Internet-assisted meetings on a monthly basis. People with rare forms or leukemia regularly chat with each other about symptoms as scientists research the options for treatment.

Many people throughout the world have benefited enormously from the recent technology explosion, especially as computers have become cheaper and more commonplace. The cost of one megabit of storage fell from $5,257 in 1970 to 17 cents in 1999 (United Nations Development Program [UNDP], 2001). Although these advances have been useful for some poor and oppressed people, the United Nations suggests this is merely a happy coincidence: "Technology is created in response to market pressures—not the needs of poor people, who have little purchasing power" (UNDP, 2001, pp. 2–3). Community practitioners can link effortlessly to national nonprofit and macro websites across the country and around the world. We can communicate quickly with social work colleagues in South Africa, India, and Honduras to explore and share approaches, methods, and technologies for community practice.

Still, most of the identity groups and functional communities with whom we will work continue to use traditional means of communication, such as newsletters, flyers, campaigns, telephone trees, and letters, and meet face to face when possible. Feminist organizing has, for example, developed a range of service systems for women, including rape crisis centers, domestic violence programs, and programs for women's employment and economic development. Feminist models of community practice can be viewed as communities of interest; however, Hyde (1996) has demonstrated that feminist approaches appear not only in functional communities but throughout the range of community practice activities.

Community education is a significant focus of functional communities, helping the community at large understand and take action on behalf of such groups as the HIV/AIDS community, abused children, political prisoners, or people with disabilities. As functional communities organize and develop internal capacity, they may also conduct research about their issues to provide information for policy changes and advocacy activity. The Black Women's Health Imperative, for example, is committed to improving the health status of Black women and girls. Founded in 1983, it works to empower Black women through information about preventive health and health care services; it also advocates for health rights and functions as a source of research and resources on Black women's health (see website).

Oxfam America (see website), working to reduce poverty and hunger and to promote social justice worldwide, has a special campaign to support small coffee growers who use environmentally sustainable methods to produce and roast coffee. The organization provides information about the methods used and where to buy coffee that will support small holders in Latin America and Africa. The larger Make Trade Fair campaign (see website) pressures large coffee companies to pay a higher price for good-quality coffee. Oxfam is striving to bring the major players in the coffee industry to the table to support a more stable market. These kinds of campaigns provide like-minded citizens from anywhere in the world an opportunity to take action on global social justice issues.

Other examples of functional communities include local and national groups that are organized to improve services and advocate for the rights of children and adults with developmental disabilities; environmental organizations; and groups such as Amnesty International, which documents human rights violations and seeks protection and justice for political prisoners worldwide through local advocacy groups.

Community Social and Economic Development

Poverty and its causes have long been a primary concern of social work practitioners in direct, macro, and policy practice. Providing opportunities for people to increase their social and economic security is the other side of the equation and an equally important and growing arena for community practitioners. To be effective, social and economic development strategies must be brought together. Development efforts are currently framed under four rubrics: *economic development,* with recent helpful contributions from Arline Prigoff (2000) and Nancy Rose (1997); *social development,* as described in the *Journal of Social Development Issues* and the works of James Midgley (1995) and Midgley and Sherraden (2000); *sustainable development,* conceptualized in the 1987 report of the World Commission on Environment and Development with a focus on "development that meets the needs of the present without compromising the ability of future generations to meet their own needs" (p. 43; see Gamble & Hoff, Chapter 8, this volume); and *human development,* the focus of the United Nations Human Development Index, a measure of development progress using a composite index that takes into consideration life expectancy at birth, knowledge (based on literacy rate and school enrollment), and adjusted per capita income in purchasing power parity (UNDP, 1999). The need to bring together strategies for economic and social development was aptly expressed by Chilean president Ricardo Lagos when he said,

> Market forces alone mean that society is going to be as uneven as the market. You can have a market economy but not a market society. . . . I want a more egalitarian society, so that every Chilean has an opportunity in this century. (Yergin & Stanislaw, 2002, p. 241)

Historically, many community development programs have focused on either economic development or social capacity building. In recent years, there has been a growing focus on integrated development strategies to move people out of poverty through combined human capacity building, popular education, and locally controlled economic development (Rubin, 2000).

Some recent programs are targeted to build personal assets. Individual Development Accounts (IDAs) and Individual Training Accounts (ITAs) are local, statewide, and national programs that will match the savings of a low-wealth person who is saving to take a training or educational program, to start a small business, or to purchase a home (Center for Social Development, 2001). IDAs and ITAs are seen as ladders to help individuals climb out of poverty. Coupled with other workforce strategies, they may be especially helpful to those people who have been at the poverty borderline for many years. Although individuals need these kinds of programs to be able to develop creative entrepreneurial skills, individual strategies are insufficient without companion programs that focus on broader social and economic barriers to development. Securing capital in many societies is particularly difficult for women, so access to capital has been a major obstacle to advancement for many low-wealth communities (Squires, 2003).

Community development corporations (CDCs), of which there are thousands across the United States, often combine efforts to change the community by decreasing barriers to economic and social resources. Community reinvestment funds and community development block grants are used in these corporations to increase the availability of resources to broad groups of people in local communities. These strategies are used along with individual training to help people take advantage of resources such as home buyers' clubs and micro enterprise loan circles. When social and economic infrastructure is expanded by increasing affordable housing stocks and developing health clinics, day care, and after-school enrichment programs, the result is significant integrated development (Rubin, 2000; Rubin & Rubin, Chapter 9, this volume).

The scale of CDCs may range from small projects to comprehensive community initiatives (CCIs), which are complex, interorganizational groups seeking to build local capacity, revitalize a neighborhood's economy, develop affordable housing, design appropriate services for changing populations, build human and social capital, and increase civic engagement and participation in politics and neighborhood social and economic development. Such ventures are long-term change strategies requiring broad involvement from inside and outside the community, infusion of funds, and a vision for what the community should be. "Ambitiously, CCIs seek social, political, and economic change for individuals and families living in the neighborhood, for the neighborhood itself, and for the systems that impact the neighborhood" (Brisson, 2003, p. 73; see also Aspen Roundtable, 1995; Kubisch, Fullbright-Anderson, & Connell, 1998). The Dudley Street Initiative (Medoff & Sklar, 1994) and initiatives funded by the Annie E. Casey Foundation (2003) are current examples of these broad-based and far-reaching coalitions formed to develop a range of social and economic development projects. In these strategies it is not just the individual who is changing but the entire landscape of the community, with visible infrastructure and visible options for social and economic support.

Social Planning

Social planning takes place on scales from neighborhood to international and worldwide efforts. Planning efforts focus on improving quality of life; increasing opportunities for vulnerable, poor, and stigmatized populations; and developing programs, services, interventions, and processes that can meet these goals. This community practice model operates through a wide range of both nonprofit and public-sector agencies at local, state, national, or international levels (see Brilliant, Chapter 12, this volume). It is a method of practice that "refers to the development, expansion, and coordination of social services and social policies" (Lauffer, 1981, p. 583). Throughout most of the community practice literature, social planning is described as the most "technical" model, focused on the use of rational planning approaches carried out primarily by experts (Brager & Specht, 1973). Increasingly, however, current and emerging social planning models incorporate grassroots groups, citizens' organizations, and a broader range of community voices, making social planning more community based.

Social planning in the public sector is also often carried out through policy practice or initiative development, such as the federally sponsored Healthy Start Initiative, through statewide plans for mental health or juvenile justice reform, or through special demonstration programs. (See in this volume Cross & Friesen, Chapter 24; Jansson, Dempsey, McCroskey, & Schneider, Chapter 17; Padilla & Sherraden, Chapter 5; and Scheyett & Drinnen, Chapter 23.)

Historically, social planning has most often referred to the city or regional social planning efforts of charity organization societies and their descendants— Community Chests and United Ways. This approach engages a range of professionals and volunteers in larger scale, cross-sector service planning and resource allocation (see Brilliant, Chapter 12, this volume) that at its best assesses community needs and seeks to provide resources and programs appropriate to respond to those needs. In recent decades, the social planning function has been largely displaced in United Ways by fund allocation processes; however, currently, there are major efforts to revive and focus planning on specific unmet community needs. In response to the earlier narrowing of United Way focus, planning councils have reemerged that engage in long-range service planning and program development as well as federated funding. Examples include the local planning councils in Kansas, West Virginia, Massachusetts, and Jacksonville, Florida. Also, in response to the needs of specific populations, specialized funding federations such as Women's Way and United Black Funds have become firmly established in some communities.

Within smaller geographic areas or in specific service sectors, community action agencies, comprehensive community initiatives, community mental health boards, area agencies on aging, and human resource commissions engage in social planning to serve their particular populations through services, supports, and economic and social development efforts. These efforts are categorized as sectorial planning, which is focused on the needs of a particular population, such as the poor, the mentally ill, or the elderly (see Weil, Chapter 11, and Brilliant, Chapter 12, both in this volume).

Many social planning agencies operate at the international level, ranging from the massive projects of UNICEF, which are intended to improve the life chances and educational opportunities of impoverished children, to country-wide initiatives such as the installation of village pumps in many areas of Guinea or the development of health education and clean water systems in Guatemala by Peace Corps volunteers working with local planning committees. Other social planning agencies target their efforts toward a particular service sector. Rainbo (see website), an international organization working to promote and protect African women's and children's sexual and reproductive health and rights, engages in regional social planning approaches to address these health issues, setting agendas for action and providing financial assistance, training, and information to organizations, professionals, and networks engaged in the area of African women's sexual and reproductive health.

The Phoenix Futures Forum engaged in a broad-based, long-range planning and community building process that involved hundreds of residents during a period of rapid population and economic growth; outcomes included 21 major new initiatives and the eventual involvement of many forum participants on city boards and commissions (Plotz, 1992). In a community-directed, long-term social and economic planning project, members and staff of the Dudley Street Neighborhood Initiative (Medoff & Sklar, 1994) developed a comprehensive initiative that planned and developed new housing, parks, and youth programs, initially through a community organizing strategy that brought together neighbors from widely diverse ethnic and cultural backgrounds and progressing to broad-scale social and economic development.

Increasingly, planners are making use of conceptual models that can help them encompass the broad social, natural, and economic resources available in any community setting. For example, the Aspen Institute (1996) provides a community planning workbook that incorporates the strengths of planning strategies combining economic development, civic capacity building, and stewardship of natural and cultural resources. Community groups making use of this kind of guide can find an accessible path to more comprehensive planning with more inclusive participation. In addition, the work of Castelloe (1999) creates an integrated model of community change that can guide planners through a theoretical framework incorporating the characteristics and processes that could lead to community improvement and away from community deterioration over time. These kinds of conceptual tools are essential to social planning efforts.

Program Development and Community Liaison

A central shift in program development in the 21st century is the rapidly growing recognition and agreement that it is poor practice, wrong-headed, and increasingly ethically questionable to attempt to plan and implement social programs without the active participation and involvement of members of all communities and populations to be served. Armstrong (2001) describes strategizing to develop family-centered, neighborhood-based services as a process of organizational and community change. In Contra Costa County, California, as the Youth Services Board sought to expand a successful interagency family preservation program into system-wide change, it engaged in an agency and community interactive process of program development.

These steps were (a) develop a vision and strategic plan; (b) learn about targeted neighborhoods and engage residents in the program design planning process; (c) negotiate with staff and prepare them to work in neighborhood-based, family-centered, service integration teams; (d) negotiate with the state for waiver status to promote service integration; and (e) negotiate with community representatives—both potential clients and a broader range of community members (Armstrong, 2001, pp. 337–342). This project and others that follow similar processes (Mulroy & Shay, 1998; also see Mulroy, Nelson, & Gour, Chapter 25, this volume) are more challenging than traditional approaches operating from an expert/professional model, and they are proving to have staying power because of strong community engagement and ownership of the process and resulting programs.

Many nonprofit human service and advocacy agencies are almost constantly engaged in program design, implementation, evaluation, and program refinement. Agencies may open in neighborhoods new to them and need to adapt services to specific community needs. More frequently, agencies will expand services for emerging populations, as Jewish Family Services of Los Angeles did to develop broad-ranging training and support programs for Russian refugees. New programs and agencies will be formed by advocacy and action groups to provide services for underserved or stigmatized groups, such as the early efforts by activists across the nation to design appropriate programs and services to meet the needs of those living with HIV/AIDS.

Program design efforts may be as large-scale as the above-described Contra Costa County system reform, but often, program design is carried out in small non-profits or medium-sized multipurpose agencies. Whatever the scale, the orientation to program outcomes and the demands for accountability shape activities and encourage sound evaluation strategies. Program design typically begins with a needs assessment and comparisons of new ideas with existing programs (Schram, 1997). Determining the most appropriate intervention for a particular community is the most significant challenge and should engage community members in the process. Program design entails defining the service or services to be offered, setting goals, determining desired outcomes that can be measured, and specifying tasks for service provision, monitoring, and evaluation (Kettner, Moroney, & Martin, 1999). Program implementation will often involve proposal development or other means of securing funding and resources; developing plans, recruitment strategies, and training plans for staff; and implementing both process and outcome evaluations (Netting et al., 2004).

An international example illustrates the importance of designing an intervention mutually with community residents and, in this case, helping a village develop its own basic infrastructure. Healthy Students, also known as *Escuelas Saludables,* is a collaborative project between the Peace Corps and the Guatemala Ministry of Health and Education. Peace Corps volunteers assigned to rural schools teach health education lessons in addition to providing technical and material assistance with appropriate technology projects, emphasizing latrines, water sanitation, and improved cooking stoves. Teachers and Peace Corps volunteers improve the school sanitation and kitchen facilities with the assistance and labor of parent groups. From experience with the school-based changes, local families often initiate improvements of their own household sanitation and cooking facilities. These structural improvements, along with health education lessons, decrease childhood morbidity and mortality due to unsanitary water and related diseases.

Over the last two decades, community liaison has been increasingly recognized as not only a desirable but a necessary component for planning a successful program. Community outreach and liaison and joint service planning with community members, organizations, groups, and members of service populations are now rapidly becoming an integral aspect of program development. As community development and community-based programs grow, this component of serious community engagement (rather than tokenism) is becoming a sine qua non in the early years of the 21st century.

The central goal and desired outcome of this model is to design and implement a new or improved service that has been assessed as needed by a community or population (Kurzman, 1985; Netting et al., 2004; Taylor, 1985). A major means of assuring that community interests and needs are accurately addressed is to engage initially in participatory assessment processes to discern program and services that residents see as needed or that would invite their participation. Focus groups, or interviews conducted by community residents as well as staff, can be a sound means of achieving a program design that responds to real rather than imagined needs and interests. Community members can later become involved in program evaluation, advisory boards, and policy-making boards.

With all these efforts, the goal of program design is to lay out a sound plan for how to structure and operate effective human services. Plans must be made for the specific model of service—its goals, staffing plan, activities, budget, and the way that objectives will lead to desired outcomes. This design will be submitted to potential funders (foundations or governmental agencies) or to the existing agency's board of directors for financial support or legitimization. When implementation can begin, program planning proceeds with staff recruitment and training, outreach, and liaison to the community and to potential clients and referring organizations.

As a program is designed and implemented, mechanisms for feedback to and from the community are valuable in keeping new programs on target. Although new services are designed to serve vulnerable populations more effectively, program designers, planners, staff, and board members will also gain new perspectives as they are able to develop effective mutual planning strategies with community members.

System and service reform efforts increasingly emphasize the role of reflection and development of agencies into "learning organizations," the necessity for developing family-centered and community-based services, the need to move more child welfare services into the community, and creation of initiatives that fully engage residents and clients in service design, governance, and evaluation (Adams & Nelson, 1995; Weil, 2000a; Weil, 2000b; Weil, 2001; see also Cross and Friesen, Chapter 24, this volume; Mulroy, Nelson, & Gour, Chapter 25, this volume). The intensive work to develop the family preservation and support models of the Children's Bureau of Los Angeles presents one model of program development and community liaison that also stressed development of strong outcome evaluations of new programs (McCroskey & Meezan, 1992).

Political and Social Action

Political and social action efforts seek to develop powerful organizations that can change policy directions and public agendas so that opportunities and free spaces for development can take the place of oppressive and restrictive social institutions. During the last century, the world has seen significant political changes. Social democratic movements in the early 20th century were a response to the excesses of industrial capitalism and the needs of poor working classes in Western Europe and the United States. Social safety nets of policies and programs for the most vulnerable populations were developed with the creation of the modern welfare state. At the end of the century, the influence of neoconservative political theory and ideology moved national governments away from responsibility for the general welfare and toward the privatization of social services, with a significantly increased burden for social program responsibility devolving to state governments (Fisher & Karger, 1997). By reducing social spending and enacting huge tax cuts, conservative policies created severe budget crises for states and municipalities. Even Republicans began to warn that "the starve-government-at-the-source strategy is not only hypocritical, it is likely to fail—with great injury to the young" (Peterson, 2003, p. 15).

While these kinds of conservative political changes continue to evolve in the United States and much of Western Europe, major changes also have occurred as the effects of globalization swept across economic, cultural, and communications spheres. Throughout the world, democratic, social and economic changes have been both positive and negative. The UN Development Report of 2002 indicates that 33 military regimes have been replaced by civilian governments since 1980; however "only 82 countries, with 57 percent of the world's people, are fully democratic" (UNDP, 2002, p. 10). The worldwide mortality rate for children under the age of 5 fell from 96 to 56 per 1,000 live births between 1970 and 2000. On the other hand, "half of all civilian war casualties are children, and there are an estimated 300,000 child soldiers worldwide" (UNDP, 2002, p. 11). These kinds of conditions and situations seem to encourage the need for social action and political reform that will expand the opportunities for positive outcomes and diminish the negative outcomes.

Although significant international conventions respond to many of these issues—such as the International Convention on the Rights of the Child; the Convention on the Elimination of all Forms of Discrimination Against Women; the International Covenant on Economic, Social, and Cultural Rights; and the International Covenant on Civil and Political Rights—many countries still have failed to sign or ratify them. The United States has signed all four conventions but has ratified only the Covenant on Civil and Political Rights.

It is reasonable to expect community workers to be engaged with groups at home and abroad for the purpose of building democratic societies—societies that will nurture inclusive, supportive, nonracist, and nonsexist communities and institutions (Mondros, 2002). New attention to redefining and acting on the common good is emerging as a central tenet for community practice based on the emergence of democratic institutions for many countries, the achievement of some political freedoms, and the focus on human rights for all citizens (Burbidge, 1997; CIVI-CUS, 1999; Fisher & Karger, 1997; UNDP, 2000).

These issues of democratic revitalization and transformation are the central purview of community practice in all its forms. Of particular value are skills emerging from popular education and participatory methods, skills that echo the work of Murray Ross and Paulo Freire. These skills frame strategies for the practitioner to act as a partner with community members (Castelloe & Gamble, Chapter 13, this volume; Freire, 1970; Ross, 1958). One example of such activity is the Moorhead Justice Circle (see website), a multiracial group of community activists based in Moorhead, Minnesota, which draws on community organizing, advocacy, and education strategies to bring issues of equal opportunity and racial justice to the forefront of the public agenda. Another example is the South African Gender Advocacy Program (see website). Its slogan, "50/50 by 2005," reflects one of its many goals: to have 50% women representatives at all levels of government by the year 2005. A campaign brochure states, "At the heart of the underrepresentation of women in politics are age-old attitudes and stereotypes that confine women to the private, and men to the public domain. These attitudes are reinforced by custom, culture, religion, and the media" (Gender Advocacy Programme, 2003). Opportunities for political and social action enable community members to engage with government and to be elected to government posts.

Coalitions

At its simplest, the term *coalition* denotes a coming together of groups around a specific issue, concern, or problem to be solved. In much of the social work literature, coalitions are construed to be networks of organizations working together on specific social problems, such as coalitions to provide support, services, and housing for the homeless. However, coalitions can also operate at local, regional, state, national, or international levels and may seek to increase stability in areas of upheaval or to initiate progressive social change. One such international coalition is 50 Years Is Enough (see website), a group of more than 200 U.S.-based organizations working in consultation with economic justice organizations based in the Global South to advocate for reform of the International Monetary Fund and the World Bank. It should be noted that the purpose of some coalitions may be more closely connected to program development, social and economic development projects, or system reform activities than to any single specific social issue. Coalitions also may operate as precursors of social movements.

Increasingly, coalitions in neighborhoods, cities, or rural areas are more likely to have as members representatives of the groups likely to benefit from programs or system changes—as well as nonprofit organizations, civic groups, representatives from various faith communities, representatives from public agencies, members of business communities, and faculty and students from local colleges and universities. This deliberately broad and inclusive type of partnership has been defined by Berkowitz and Wolff as "a group involving multiple sectors of the community, coming together to address community needs and solve community problems" (2000, p. 2). Such coalitions may have a single goal to accomplish or a multistage and long-term project to implement.

Coalitions are developed among human service agencies and often their constituencies to strengthen services and make them more responsive to the range of needs of a specific population or community; or among community organizations and citizens' groups to press for needed political, economic, social, and human service system changes, or by combinations of these constituencies to improve the quality of life, opportunities, and supports for populations, groups, or communities with significant vulnerabilities (see Roberts-DeGennaro & Mizrahi, Chapter 16, this volume). Another growing trend is the community collaborative, which focuses on major work for service system reform, engages clients in planning processes, and produces new program models and methods of service system coordination (Bailey & Koney, 2000).

Coalitions make it possible for separate groups to work together for collective change. As defined by Mizrahi and Rosenthal, a "social change coalition is a group of diverse organizational representatives who join forces to influence external institutions on one or more issues affecting their constituencies while maintaining their own autonomy" (1993, p. 14). The authors describe coalitions as typically being filled with dynamic tensions resulting from simultaneous demands on organizational representatives to remain autonomous and anchored in their own organizations while at the same time building a new organization from the compatible interests of the diverse members. Coalitions may also evolve into long-term organizations engaged in social and economic development or system reform.

Rosenthal and Mizrahi (1994) present cogent arguments for the utility of coalitions when a larger group is needed for one or more of the following purposes: procuring resources; legitimizing a cause, issue, or organization; advocating in the political arena; managing tensions or problems in the external environment; responding to threats or intrusions from government or corporations; promoting interorganizational exchange; and influencing policy and the political economy.

The desired outcome for social change coalitions is to build multiorganizational power bases large enough to influence social program direction, with the potential to garner resources to respond to the common interests of the coalition. Elected officials are often the systems targeted for change, as they may be persuaded to adopt more favorable policies. Government institutions, which may have the authority to respond to a particular social concern but not the readiness to do so, are also the targets of coalition, advocacy, education, and action strategies.

Coalition building typically requires a major time commitment; for this reason, only organizations that have a stake in the particular issues will participate or continue longer-term involvement. Examples of coalitions found in many communities are those organized to promote affordable housing, service programs for the elderly, and environmentally safe economic development, and to work against the increase in teen pregnancy and domestic violence. To stay together, coalitions develop complex exchange relations and find ways to balance their commitment to the issues that hold them together with the individual agendas and perspectives of member groups (Roberts-DeGennaro, 1986, 1997). An emerging challenge in community practice will be to ascertain whether developing coalitions across national boundaries or other separations can be developed and sustained through Web-based technology.

Social workers are likely to be leaders and spokespersons in human service coalitions, using mediation and negotiation skills to balance internal tensions and maintain the coalition's focus. In coalitions of advocacy groups focused on alternative services, social workers will also have roles that emphasize group and organization facilitation, teaching or coaching, leadership development, conflict negotiation, and skills in interorganizational relations and planning (Roberts-DeGennaro, 1997). They can also seek to garner or maximize resources, develop strategies to tackle new issues, and promote integrated multisector planning (Berkowitz & Wolff, 2000).

Social Movements

Social movements occur when large numbers of people respond to social or environmental conditions by seeking a new paradigm for interpreting the condition or changing it. Wood and Jackson define social movements as groups "that attempt to produce or prevent radical or reformist type of change" (1982, p. 3). The economic and political changes that have evolved in the United States and across the globe during the 20th century have reconfigured the types of social movements organized for reform activity. According to Brueggemann, "Although modern social movements were large, single-issue, highly organized, mass movements, post-modern social movements are often small, loose, and open, tap local knowledge and resources, and respond to problems rapidly and creatively" (2002, p. 398). These small identity groups often form deep underground networks able to resurface to respond to issues as situations arise. Peace activists, for example, asking people to sign a petition urging restraint after the September 11 attacks on the World Trade Center and Pentagon, posted a letter on a website and received 120,000 signatures from people in 190 countries in 7 days (Packer, 2003).

The focus of social movements is to make significant changes in social institutions so that new relationships or new resources can emerge, contributing to an improved quality of life for a large population group. The U.S. civil rights movement of the late 1950s and early 1960s provided a model for rights movements that followed, including the American Indian movement, the women's movement, and the disabilities rights movement (MacNair, Fowler, & Harris, 2000). Community workers, in keeping with the values of the profession, were engaged in all these social movements to support the rights of minorities, individual dignity, the equality of women and girls, and the broad goals of human development and liberation.

In more recent years, social movements have often been organized to enlist a broad representation of coalitions from across the globe. The environmental movement and the Anti-Globalization Movement (see website), for example, seek to recruit support from a large base. The anti-globalization movement is a heterogeneous movement consisting of feminists, environmentalists, labor activists, socialists, and defenders of human rights and rights of indigenous people and cultures from all over the world. The movement is opposed to the unbridled increase and intensification of global movements of capital and finance. Although members' views are widely divergent, advocates are singularly opposed to the power of transnational corporations to move easily across borders, extract natural resources, and exploit human resources without regard to local needs or input. Within the business community itself, an international movement exists to persuade multinational corporations to develop "triple bottom line" production methods that will take into consideration protecting the environment and building social capital in communities as well as profit (World Business Council for Sustainable Development website). Fisher proposes that "the prime target for social movement mobilizing" is the electoral arena, and asserts that as coalitions build movements, it will become equally necessary to focus on "the local and the global" aspects of understanding and strategy development (2001, p. 359).

The buildup of oppression over time or significant developments that result in inequality in the social, economic, or political systems often set the stage for social movements. Protests may start small over a localized situation, but the climate may be established for such small protests to spread rapidly, generating widespread support and mass empathy. A social movement often emerges as a result. Piven and Cloward, in analyzing four different American social movements, have concluded that "both the limitations and opportunities for mass protest are shaped by social conditions" (1979, p. 36). Widespread social protest may offer only a brief opportunity for change as the social order is temporarily relaxed. A strategy to extend the window of opportunity for establishing change in systems would be a useful approach (Piven & Cloward, 1979).

The movement against apartheid in South Africa, for example, lasted for more than 40 years. The ability to maintain momentum and to enlarge the interest of the wider world in the oppression created by apartheid, as well as the prospect of economic sanctions against the country, eventually brought the government and the protest movement to the negotiation table. After spending 27 years in prison, Nelson Mandela was released to participate in the development of a new constitution and to become the president after the first free elections in the country in 1994. The social movement in South Africa was successful, resulting in a new constitution that created new political and social norms for all the citizens of the country (Mandela, 1994).

Conclusions

These eight models have been presented with new emphasis on three critical contexts that have emerged in the 21st century. The contexts focus on the increase of multicultural societies worldwide, the expansion of rights for women and girls and of human rights in general, and globalization, with resultant increasing interconnectedness of economic, political, social, and cultural spheres. Applying these three contexts as lenses or spotlights with which to view the eight models helps community practitioners recognize the complexities of practice in this new century. Many of the roles of community social workers continue to be useful in new circumstances, and both new roles and new role combinations are likely to emerge. Now and for the future, community workers need a strong international knowledge base and ability to analyze the complexity of local and global situations. Community social workers will still be called on to help communities build democratic institutions; facilitate individual, group, and organizational development; and engage in facilitating inclusive methods and structures that will model democratic outcomes. Whether community practitioners are teachers, coaches, advocates, organizers, facilitators, negotiators, mediators, planners, researchers, managers, proposal writers, spokespersons, promoters, or even political candidates, they must always use as their guide the value base of the national and international social work organizations and be grounded in their purpose for engagement and accountability to the people they serve.

Throughout the world for the next several decades, neighborhood and community organizing efforts will need to focus on the realities of multiculturalism within nations and small communities, as well as on the increasing involvement of women in organizing, assessing community needs, and working for change. Neighborhood economies will continue to be challenged by the incursions of the global economy; actions to create livelihoods, reclaim traditional practices, and determine and meet local needs will be critical to maintain the social and political fabric of small communities and urban neighborhoods.

Functional communities will see increased opportunities for nearly instant communication and response to policies and problems. Virtual community connections via the Internet will become commonplace. However, given economic ups and downs of human services funding here and abroad, the problems faced by many functional communities are likely to be exacerbated; and they will need increased skills in social action, service and program strategies, and leadership development to meet new challenges.

In the coming decades, small- and larger-scale community social and economic development projects will face a growing need to build human and social capital, develop employment and training opportunities, and ensure basics rights. Social capital bonding strategies and bridging connections to resources and opportunities will be at a premium to help those in or near poverty gain an economic foothold and a stake in society. Local efforts to forge means of sustainable development will loom large as communities strive to build economies and maintain natural resources.

Local social planning strategies will become more community driven, while regional plans for transportation and major economic centers are likely to become more centralized and complex. Diverse communities will need to come together to develop larger-scale plans and hold political bodies and corporate interests accountable for quality of life and environmental protection. Social workers' values and knowledge base, making use of new theoretical concepts and strategies for multicultural and gender inclusiveness in comprehensive planning, can make a significant contribution to a new era of social planning.

Program development, community liaison, and service coordination will continue as a primary method to respond to the needs of vulnerable populations. However, consumers of services and other community members are working with increasing strength and vigor as they actively take part in assessments, outreach, and engagement of citizens in service planning, monitoring, and evaluation. Community-based services and collaboratives will become more embedded in their service areas as more social workers learn skills of community practice and engagement. Coordinating services to meet broad community needs will reemerge as a service provision factor for both effectiveness and efficiency.

Given the impact of globalization, social workers will need to engage more vigorously in political and social action to advocate with and for client populations and community groups. Economic and social conditions causing the income gap to increase should promote citizen response to reassert rights and to press for political reform, respect for human rights, and economic opportunity. The challenges of the shifts in the world economy may well spur new coalitions with a focus on social justice. The NASW *Code of Ethics* makes it very clear that "social workers should engage in social and political action that seeks to ensure that all people have equal access to the resources, employment, services, and opportunities they require to meet their basic human needs and to develop fully" (1996, p. 27).

Social workers' skills in facilitation of groups and organizations will be key to enlarging the focus of coalitions to represent communities, not just service providers. Coalitions to respond to the crush of poverty, homelessness, and specific service needs are likely to gain even greater importance in securing and reforming services and responses to social needs.

Although social workers are not typically formal leaders of social movements, their skills as advocates and facilitators are particularly key in preparing groups, communities, and organizations to participate in social movements. National and international social movements are likely to be needed to press for responses to geopolitical and social problems and to the monumental dislocation of refugees; other movements may work to protest mass violence, to advocate for nonlethal solutions to cultural and international strife and to build social and political momentum to expand human rights.

In all these approaches to community practice, there is a need for high levels of interpersonal, process, task, and technical skills. In the current era of devolution, shifting demographics and economic upheaval, community practitioners need to be fully engaged in active strategies, from community building to policy practice. Community-based strategies for family and group development offer increasing opportunities for support and intervention. The needs for local and regional focus on planning and economic and social development will increase and become more complex, and practitioners need to be prepared with technical skills and knowledge to assist communities in responding to changing conditions. The need for stronger technical skills is accompanied by the need for more diverse and adaptable ways of working with changing communities. A particular skill needed by those working in community practice will be for facilitation methods that use popular education and participatory planning (Caroll & Minkler, 2000; Castelloe & Watson, 1999; Chambers, 1997; Freire, 1998; Gubbles & Koss, 2000; VeneKlasen & Miller, 2002). Recognizing that their work is often long and arduous, community practitioners in coming decades will need commitment to the development of stronger democratic and pluralistic societies, strong connections to communities and groups engaged in social development and change, and solidarity in the goal of building a world richer in compassion, civic engagement, and social justice.

References

Abromovitz, M. (1986). *Regulating the lives of women: Social welfare policy from colonial times to the present.* Boston: South End Press.

Adams, P., & Nelson, K. (1995). *Reinventing human services: Community- and family-centered practice.* New York: Aldine de Gruyter.

Allen-Meares, P., & DeRoos, Y. (1997). The future of the social work profession. In M. Reisch & E. Gambrill (Eds.), *Social work in the 21st century* (pp. 376–386). Thousand Oaks, CA: Pine Forge Press.

Anderson, J., & Carter, R. W. (Eds.). (2003). *Diversity perspectives for social work practice.* Boston: Allyn & Bacon.

Annie E. Casey Foundation. (2003). *Family economic success: Building strong financial futures for families and communities.* Retrieved July 1, 2003, from http://www.aecf.org/initiatives/fes.fes/index.htm

Armstrong, K. L. (2001). Launching a family-centered, neighborhood-based human services system: Lessons from working the hallways and street corners. In J. Rothman, J. L. Erlich, & J. E. Tropman (Eds.), *Strategies of community intervention* (5th ed., pp. 337–349). Itasca, IL: F. E. Peacock.

Aspen Institute. (1996). *Measuring community capacity building: A workbook in progress for rural communities.* Washington, DC: Author.

Aspen Roundtable. (1995). *Voices from the field: Learning from the early work of Comprehensive Community Initiatives.* Washington, DC: Aspen Institute.

Bailey, D., & Koney, K. M. (2000). *Strategic alliances among health and human service organizations.* Thousand Oaks, CA: Sage.

Berkowitz, B., & Wolff, T. (2000). *The spirit of the coalition.* Washington, DC: American Public Health Association.

Betten, N., & Austin, M. J. (Eds.). (1990). *The roots of community organizing, 1917–1939.* Philadelphia: Temple University Press.

Blank, R. M. (1997). *It takes a nation: A new agenda for fighting poverty.* Princeton, NJ: Princeton University Press.

Brager, G., & Specht, H. (1973). *Community organizing.* New York: Columbia University Press.

Brandwein, R. A. (1981). Toward androgyny in community and organizational practice. In A. Weick & S. T. VanDiver (Eds.), *Women, power, and change* (pp. 158–170). Washington, DC: NASW.

Brisson, D. (2003). *Neighborhoods, comprehensive community initiatives (CCIs), and social capital: How they work together for low-income households.* Unpublished paper, University of North Carolina, Chapel Hill, School of Social Work.

Brueggemann, W. G. (2002). *The practice of macro social work* (2nd ed.). Belmont, CA: Wadsworth/Thompson Learning.

Burbidge, J. (Ed.). (1997). *Beyond prince and merchant: Citizen participation and the rise of civil society.* New York: Pact.

Carleton-LaNey, I. B. (Ed.). (2001). *African American leadership: An empowerment tradition in social welfare history.* Washington DC: NASW Press.

Caroll, J., & Minkler, M. (2000). Freire's message for social workers: Looking back, looking ahead. *Journal of Community Practice, 8*(1), 21–36.

Castelloe, P. (1999). *Community change and community practice: An organic model of community practice.* Unpublished doctoral dissertation, University of North Carolina, Chapel Hill, School of Social Work.

Castelloe, P., & Watson, T. (1999). Participatory education as a community practice method: A case example from a Comprehensive Head Start program. *Journal of Community Practice, 6*(1), 71–89.

Center for Social Development. (2001). *Savings and assets accumulation in individual development accounts.* St. Louis, MO: George Warren Brown School of Social Work.

Chambers, R. (1997). *Whose reality counts? Putting the last first.* London: Intermediate Technology Publications.

Chandler, S. (1986). The hidden feminist agenda in social development. In N. VanDen Bergh & L. B. Cooper (Eds.), *Feminist visions for social work* (pp. 149–162). Washington, DC: NASW Press.

Christenson, J. A., & Robinson, J. W., Jr. (1989). *Community development in perspective.* Ames: Iowa State University Press.

CIVICUS. (1999). *Civil society at the millennium* (E. Mbogori, Ed.). West Hartford, CT: Kumarian Press.

Cockburn, A. (2003, September). 21st-century slaves. *National Geographic, 204*(3), 2–24.

Cox, F. M., Erlich, J. L., Rothman, J., & Tropman, J. E. (Eds.). (1970). *Strategies of community organization.* Itasca, IL: F. E. Peacock.

Drake, R. F. (2001). *The principles of social policy.* New York: Palgrave.

Ecklein, J. L., & Lauffer, A. A. (1972). *Community organizers and social planners.* New York: John Wiley.

Ellsworth, C., Hooyman, N., Ruff, R. A., Stam, S. B., & Tucker, J. H. (1981). Toward a feminist model for planning for and with women. In A. Weick & S. T. VanDiver (Eds.), *Women, power, and change* (pp. 146–157). Washington, DC: NASW Press.

Figueira-McDonough, J., Netting, F. E., & Nichols-Casebolt, A. (1998). *The role of gender in practice knowledge: Claiming half the human experience.* New York: Garland.

Finn, J. L., & Jacobson, M. (2003). *Just practice: A social justice approach to social work.* Peosta, IA: Eddie Bowers.

Fisher, R. (1994). *Let the people decide: Neighborhood organizing in America* (Rev. ed.). Boston: Twayne.

Fisher, R. (1998). Social action community organization: Proliferation, persistence, roots, and prospects. In M. Minkler (Ed.), *Community organizing and community building for health* (pp. 53–67). New Brunswick, NJ: Rutgers University Press.

Fisher, R. (2001). Social action community organization: Proliferation, persistence, roots, and prospects. In J. Rothman, J. L. Erlich, & J. E. Tropman (Eds.), *Strategies of community intervention* (6th ed.) Belmont, CA: Thompson, Brooks/Cole.

Fisher, R., & Karger, H. J. (1997). *Social work and community in a private world: Getting out in public.* New York: Longman.

Flynn, J. (1995). Social justice in social agencies. In R. L. Edwards (Ed.), *Encyclopedia of social work* (19th ed., pp. 2173–2179). Washington, DC: NASW Press.

Fong, R., & Furuto, S. B. C. L. (Eds.). (2001). *Culturally competent practice: Skills, interventions, and evaluations.* Needham Heights, MA: Allyn & Bacon.

Freire, P. (1970). *Pedagogy of the oppressed.* New York: Seabury.

Freire, P. (1998). *Teachers as cultural workers: Letters to those who dare to teach.* Boulder, CO: Westview.

Garvin, C. D., & Cox, F. M. (2001). A history of community organizing since the Civil War with special reference to oppressed communities. In J. Rothman, J. L. Erlich, & J. E. Tropman (Eds.), *Strategies of community intervention* (pp. 65–100). Itasca, IL: F. E. Peacock.

Gender Advocacy Program. (2003). *Women in government* [pamphlet]. Capetown, South Africa: Author.

Gomory, T. (1997). Social work and philosophy. In M. Reisch & E. Gambrill (Eds.), *Social work in the 21st century* (pp. 300–310). Thousand Oaks, CA: Pine Forge Press.

Gubbles, P., & Koss, C. (2000). *From the roots up: Strengthening organizational capacity through guided self-assessment.* Oklahoma City: World Neighbors.

Gutiérrez, L. M., & Lewis, E. A. (1999). *Empowering women of color.* New York: Columbia University Press.

Hardcastle, D. A., Wenocur, S., & Powers, P. R. (1997). *Community practice: Theories and skills for social workers.* New York: Oxford University Press.

Hardy-Fanta, C. (1986). Social action in Hispanic groups. *Social Work, 31*(2), 119–123.

Harper, E. B., & Dunham, A. (1959). *Community organization in action.* New York: Association Press.

Henderson, H. (1996). *Building a win-win world: Life beyond global economic warfare.* San Francisco: Barrett-Koehler.

Homan, M. S. (2004). *Promoting community change: Making it happen in the real world* (3rd ed.). Belmont, CA: Brooks Cole/Thompson.

Hyde, C. (1996). A feminist response to Rothman's "The interweaving of community intervention approaches." *Journal of Community Practice, 3*(3/4), 127–145.

Hyde, C. (2000). Feminist approaches to social policy. In J. Midgeley, M. S. Tracy, & M. Livermore (Eds.), *The handbook of social policy* (pp. 421–434). Thousand Oaks, CA: Sage.

Inter American Foundation. (2003). Partnership addresses poverty along the US-Mexican Border. *Grassroots Development, 24*(1), 52.

International Federation of Social Workers (IFSW). (2002). Countering the negative effects of globalisation. *IFSW News, 2*(3), 3.

International Federation of Social Workers (IFSW). (2003). *Ethics in social work: Statement of principles.* Retrieved September 5, 2003, from http://www.ifse.org?GM-2004//GM-Ethics-draft.html

Kettner, P. M., Moroney, R. M., & Martin, L. L. (1999). *Designing and managing programs: An effectiveness-based approach* (2nd ed.). Thousand Oaks, CA: Sage.

Kramer, R. M. (1966). Community organizing and administration: Integration or separate but equal? *Education for Social work, 2,* 48–56.

Kramer, R., & Specht, H. (1983). *Readings in community organization practice* (3rd ed.). Englewood Cliffs, NJ: Prentice-Hall.

Kubisch, A. C., Fullbright-Anderson, K., & Connell, J. P. (1998). Evaluating community initiatives: A progress report. In K. Fulbright-Anderson, A. C. Kubisch, & J. P. Connell (Eds.), *New approaches to evaluating community initiatives: Vol. 2. Theory, measurement, and analysis.* Queenstown, MD: Aspen Institute.

Kurzman, P. (1985). Program development and service coordination as components of community practice. In S. H. Taylor & R. W. Roberts (Eds.), *Theory and practice of community social work* (pp. 95–124). New York: Columbia University Press.

Lauffer, A. (1978). *Social planning at the community level.* Englewood Cliffs, NJ: Prentice-Hall.

Lauffer, A. (1981). The practice of social planning. In N. Gilbert & H. Specht (Eds.), *Handbook of the social services* (pp. 583–597). Englewood Cliffs, NJ: Prentice Hall.

Longres, J. F. (1997). The impact and implications of multiculturalism. In M. Reisch & E. Gambrill (Eds.), *Social work in the 21st century* (pp. 39–47). Thousand Oaks, CA: Pine Forge Press.

Lurie, H. L. (Ed.). (1959). *The community organization method in social work education: Vol. 4. A project report of the curriculum study* (W. W. Boehm, director and coordinator). New York: Council on Social Work Education.

MacNair, R. H., Fowler, L., & Harris, J. (2000). The diversity functions of organizations that confront oppression: The evolution of three social movements. *Journal of Community Practice, 7*(2), 71–88.

Mandela, N. (1994). *Long walk to freedom.* Boston: Little, Brown.

Mayadas, N. S., & Elliott, D. (1997). Lessons from international social work: Policies and practice. In M. Reisch & E. Gambrill (Eds.), *Social work in the 21st century* (pp. 175–185). Thousand Oaks, CA: Pine Forge Press.

Mayadas, N. S., Watts, T., & Elliott, D. (Eds.). (1997). *International handbook of social work theory and practice* (2nd ed.). Westport, CT: Greenwood.

McCroskey, J., & Meezan, W. (1992). Social work research in family and children's services. In J. Brown & M. Weil (Eds.), *Family practice* (pp. 199–213). Washington, DC: Child Welfare League of America.

Medoff, P., & Sklar, H. (1994). *Streets of hope: The fall and rise of an urban neighborhood.* Boston: South End Press.

Midgley, J. (1995). *Social development: The developmental perspective in social welfare.* Thousand Oaks, CA: Sage.

Midgley, J. (Ed.). (2000). *The handbook of social policy.* Thousand Oaks, CA: Sage.

Midgley, J., & Sherraden, M. (2000). The social development perspective in social policy. In J.Midgley, M. B. Tracy, & M. Livermore (Eds.), *The handbook of social policy* (pp. 435–446). Thousand Oaks, CA: Sage.

Mizrahi, T. (2002). Community organizing principles and practice guideline. In A. R. Roberts & G. J. Greene (Eds.), *Social workers' desk reference* (pp. 517–524). New York: Oxford University Press.

Mizrahi, T., & Rosenthal, B. (1993). Managing dynamic tensions in social change coalitions. In T. Mizrahi & J. D. Morrison (Eds.), *Community organization and social administration* (pp. 11–40). New York: Haworth.

Mondros, J. B. (2002). Principles and practice guidelines for social action. In A. R. Roberts & G. J. Greene (Eds.), *Social workers' desk reference* (pp. 534–539). New York: Oxford University Press.

Mondros, J. B., & Wilson, S. M. (1994). *Organizing for power and empowerment.* New York: Columbia University Press.

Mulroy, E., & Shay, S. (1998). Nonprofit organizations and innovation: A model of neighborhood-based collaboration to prevent child maltreatment. In P. A. Ewalt, E. M. Freeman, & D. L. Poole (Eds.), *Community building: Renewal, well-being, and shared responsibility* (pp. 95–106). Washington, DC: NASW Press.

Murphy, C. G. (1954). *Community organization practice.* Boston: Houghton Mifflin.

National Association of Social Workers (NASW). (1996). *Code of ethics.* Washington, DC: Author.

Netting, F. E., Kettner, P. M., & McMurtry, S. L. (2004). *Social work macro practice.* Boston: Allyn & Bacon.

Norman, E., & Mancuso, A. (1980). *Women's issues and social work practice.* Itasca, IL: F. E. Peacock.

O'Donnell, S., & Karanja, S. T. (2000). Transformative community practice: Building a model for developing extremely low-income African-American communities. *Journal of Community Practice, 7*(3), 67–84.

Packer, G. (2003, March 9). Smart-mobbing the war. *New York Times Magazine,* pp. 46–49.

Patti, R. J. (1983). *Social welfare administration: Managing social programs in a developmental context.* Englewood Cliffs, NJ: Prentice Hall.

Peterson, P. G. (2003, June 8). Deficits and dysfunction: How the Republicans (and Democrats) have sold out our future. *New York Times Magazine,* pp. 15–20.

Piven, F. F., & Cloward, R. S. (1979). *Poor people's movements: Why they succeed, how they fail.* New York: Vintage.

Plotz, D. A. (1992). *Community problem solving case summaries: Vol. 3.* Washington, DC: Program for Community Problem Solving.

Rigoff, A. (2000). *Economics for social workers: Social outcomes of economic globalization with strategies for community action.* Belmont, CA: Brooks/Cole.

Rivera, F. G., & Erlich, J. L. (Eds.). (1998). *Community organizing in a diverse society* (3rd ed.). Boston: Allyn & Bacon.

Roberts-DeGennaro, M. (1986). Factors contributing to coalition maintenance. *Journal of Sociology and Social Welfare, 13,* 248–264.

Roberts-DeGennaro, M. (1997). Conceptual framework of coalitions in an organizational context. In M. O. Weil (Ed.), *Community practice models in action* (pp. 91-l07). New York: Haworth.

Rose, N. (1997). The future economic landscape: Implications for social work practice and education. In M. Reisch & E. Gambrill (Eds.), *Social work in the 21st century* (pp. 28–38). Thousand Oaks, CA: Pine Forge Press.

Rosenthal, B., & Mizrahi, T. (1994). Should community-based organizations give priority to building coalitions rather than building their own membership? In M. Austin & J. Lowe

(Eds.), *Controversial issues in communities and organizations* (pp. 9-16). Boston: Allyn & Bacon.

Ross, M. G. (1955). *Community organization: Theory and principles.* New York: Harper & Brothers.

Ross, M. G. (1958). *Case histories in community organization.* New York: Harper & Row.

Rothman, J. (1968). Three models of community organization practice. In *National conference on social welfare, social work practice 1968.* New York: Columbia University Press.

Rothman, J. (2001). Approaches to community intervention. In J. Rothman, J. L. Erlich, & J. E. Tropman (Eds.), *Strategies of community intervention* (pp. 27–64). Itasca, IL: F. E. Peacock.

Rubin, H. J. (2000). *Renewing hope within neighborhoods of despair: The community-based development model.* Albany: SUNY Press.

Rubin, H. J., & Rubin, I. S. (2001). *Community organizing and development* (3rd ed.). Boston: Allyn & Bacon.

Sarri, R. (1997). International social work at the millennium. In M. Reisch & E. Gambrill (Eds.), *Social work in the 21st century* (pp. 387–395). Thousand Oaks, CA: Pine Forge Press.

Schram, B. (1997). *Creating small scale programs: Planning, implementation, and evaluation.* Thousand Oaks, CA: Sage.

Simon, B. L. (1994). *The empowerment tradition in American social work: A history.* New York: Columbia University Press.

Slavin, S. (Ed.). (1985). *Social administration: The management of the social services.* New York: Haworth.

Squires, G. D. (Ed.). (2003). *Organizing access to capital: Advocacy and democratization of financial institutions.* Philadelphia: Temple University Press.

Taylor, S. H. (1985). Community work and social work: The community liaison approach. In S. H. Taylor & R. W. Roberts (Eds.), *Theory and practice of community social work* (pp. 179–214). New York: Columbia University Press.

Taylor, S. H., & Roberts, R. W. (Eds.). (1985). *Theory and practice of community social work.* New York: Columbia University Press.

United Nations. (1948, December 10). *Universal declaration of human rights* (United Nations General Assembly Resolution 217 A[111]). Retrieved March 18, 2004, from http://www.un.org/Overview/rights.html

United Nations High Commission for Refugees. (2003) *Refugees,* No. 131, p. 15.

United Nations Development Program. (1999). New York: Oxford University Press.

United Nations Development Program. (2000). New York: Oxford University Press.

United Nations Development Program. (2001). New York: Oxford University Press.

United Nations Development Program. (2002). New York: Oxford University Press.

Urday, A. M. (2003). Development of the dairy industry in the Peruvian Andes. *Grassroots Development, 24*(1), 40–43.

VeneKlasen, L., & Miller, V. (2002). *A new weave of power, people, and politics: The action guide for advocacy and citizen participation.* Oklahoma City: World Neighbors.

Weber, M. (1949). *Methodology of the social sciences.* New York: Free Press.

Weick, A., & VanDiver, S. T. (Eds.). (1981). *Women, power, and change.* Washington, DC: NASW.

Weil, M. (1986). Women, community, and organizing. In N. VanDen Bergh & L. B. Cooper (Eds.), *Feminist visions for social work* (pp. 187–210). Washington, DC: NASW Press.

Weil, M. (1996). Model development in community practice: An historical perspective. In M. Weil (Ed.), *Community practice: Conceptual models* (pp. 5–68). New York: Haworth.

Weil, M. (1997). Community building: Building community practice. In P. L. Ewalt, E. M. Freeman, S. A. Kirk, & D. L. Poole (Eds.), *Social policy, reform, research, and practice* (pp. 35–61). Washington, DC: NASW Press.

Weil, M. (2000a). Services for families and children: The changing context and new challenges. In R. Patti (Ed.), *The handbook of social work management* (pp. 481–509). Thousand Oaks, CA: Sage.

Weil, M. (2000b). Social work in the social environment: Integrated practice—an empowerment/structural approach. In P. Allen-Meares & C. Garvin (Eds.), *The handbook of social work direct practice*. Thousand Oaks, CA: Sage.

Weil, M. (2001). Assessing community engagement in family group conferencing. In *Family group conferencing evaluation guidebook.* Denver CO: American Humane Association.

Weil, M., & Gamble, D. (1995). Community practice models. In R. L. Edwards (Ed.), *Encyclopedia of social work* (19th ed., pp. 577–593). Washington, DC: NASW Press.

Weil, M. O., & Gamble, D. N. (2002). Community practice models for the 21st century. In A. R. Roberts & G. J. Greene (Eds.), *Social workers' desk reference* (pp. 525–534). New York: Oxford University Press.

Weil, M., Gamble, D. N., & Williams, E. S. (1998). Women, communities, and development. In J. Figueira-McDonough, F. E. Netting, & A. Nichols-Casebolt (Eds.), *The role of gender in practice knowledge: Claiming half the human experience* (pp. 241–286). New York: Garland.

Wood, J. L., & Jackson, M. (1982). *Social movements: Development, participation, and dynamics.* Belmont, CA: Wadsworth.

World Commission on Environment and Development (WCED). (1987). *Our common future: From one earth to one world.* New York: Oxford University Press.

Yergin, D., & Stanislaw, J. (2002). *The commanding heights: The battle for the world economy.* New York: Touchstone, Simon & Schuster.

Web Sites

Anti-Globalization Movement. http://www/wikipedia.org/wiki/Anti-globalization-movement

Black Women's Health Imperative. http://www.blackwomenshealth.org

50 Years Is Enough. http:50years.org/

Gender Advocacy Prrogramme, http://www.gender.co.za

Make Trade Fair campaign. www.maketradefair.com

Moorhead Justice Circle. www.socservices.com/pdf/community.moorhead.pdf

Oxfam America. http://www.oxfamamerica.org/coffee

Rainbo. http://www.rainbo.org

World Business Council for Sustainable Development. http://www.wbcsd.ch

PART II

Major Approaches to Community Practice

In Part II, major approaches to community practice are presented, with two chapters each dealing with emerging issues in development, organizing, and planning. In addition, six chapters are devoted to various aspects of social change efforts in community practice. James Midgley and Michelle Livermore's analysis of development theory and its increasing importance for all community practice provides a perspective that is echoed in numerous chapters. As we learn more about development problems and issues in other parts of the world and about positive and empowering practices, we recognize the adaptability of development theory to our own society. As we move into the 21st century, social and economic development efforts alone will be insufficient responses to global changes. Increasingly, environmental and sustainable community development, as described and illustrated by Dorothy Gamble and Marie Hoff, will need to be woven into all community work, whether urban or rural, in the postindustrial and developing nations alike.

Herbert and Irene Rubin contribute Chapter 9, "The Practice of Community Organizing," illustrating essential practice skills for mobilization of people and resources to advocate for change and improve the quality of life in marginalized communities. They also provide useful theory to guide organizing and development. An area often insufficiently covered in social work literature and curricula is excitingly engaged by Steve Burghardt and Michael Fabricant in Chapter 10, "Which Side Are You On? Social Work, Community Organizing, and the Labor Movement." The need for community practitioners to connect more closely with workers and the labor movement is cogently argued—shifts in the global economy and the increasing income gap make the necessity for common cause with workers more obvious now than perhaps any time since the Great Depression.

Two approaches presenting current models of social planning conclude this section. In a practice that has become more current, sparked by devolution of federal funds to states and fostered by national and regional foundations, local community planning has again emerged as a critical form of community practice. In "Social Planning With Communities: Theory and Practice," Chapter 11, I illustrate this growing practice and provide supporting theory and examples of why this approach has become stronger in the late 20th century and in the early years of the 21st century. In Chapter 12, "From Community Planning to Changing Communities: Fundraising and Fund Allocation for Human Services," Eleanor Brilliant provides a sound critique of the growth of single-sector planning (dueling initiatives) and the difficulties experienced over the past two decades in federated fundraising and community-wide planning. The earlier retreat of United Way from community-focused planning and allocation is now shifting back to increasing efforts to rebuild city or regional federated fundraising and broad-based community planning for social needs. The recent rebirth of planning councils and their success in community-wide planning in a number of areas provides a positive example of an arena in which social work greatly needs to re-engage.

The fourth section of Part II, "Social Change: People, Systems, and Societies," presents six perspectives with methods and approaches for achieving positive change. Chapter 13, "Participatory Methods in Community Practice: Popular Education and Participatory Rural Appraisal," by Paul Castelloe and Dorothy Gamble, presents the methods and practices that need to be precursors to much of direct practice with communities. Using a range of facilitation methods developed by Freire and others in popular education efforts, local knowledge is shared; root-cause analyses are conducted; and people set their own goals, develop plans, and engage in community development, organizing, or action as their interests determine. These processes are mutual and grounded in values of shared participation as the basis for empowerment practice.

Jacqueline Mondros provides a powerful discussion of "Political, Social, and Legislative Action" in Chapter 14. Efforts are focused on engaging enough people to gain momentum and to influence the political and social power brokers and to promote political power for marginalized groups. Mondros emphasizes skills for advocacy and social action. In "Radical Community Organizing," Michael Reisch presents strategies needed for progressive social change addressing central problems of power and poverty. The chapter focuses on social justice and social change approaches to alter institutions, systems, conditions, and practices that are oppressive. Building on earlier studies of collaboration, Maria Roberts-DeGennaro and Terry Mizrahi focus productively on "Coalitions as Social Change Agents," presenting the skills needed to develop and maintain strong coalitions in difficult economic times and the factors involved in whether coalitions become long-term organizations or focus on short-term campaigns. Coalitions build a multiorganizational power base that can press effectively for changes in policies, programs, and services and develop resources for underserved populations. The final chapter in this section, "Four Models of Policy Practice: Local, State, and National Arenas," by Bruce Jansson, David Dempsey, Jacquelyn McCroskey, and Robert Schneider, analyzes and illustrates four major approaches to policy practice. Policy practice engages social workers in social change at local, state, and national levels employing skills for policy analysis, research, advocacy, and education as well as lobbying and negotiating.

CHAPTER 7

Development Theory and Community Practice

James Midgley

Michelle Livermore

E ffective community practice depends not only on professional skills but also on knowledge and values. Knowledge provides a testable basis for action, whereas values define desirable goals and the best ways to attain them. Both knowledge and values are, in turn, influenced by social science theory. Theory shapes conceptions of community life and, in its normative form, articulates the value assumptions of community practice strategies.

Despite the importance of theory in community practice, it remains neglected. Although community practitioners and scholars make frequent reference to concepts such as social change, participation, social justice, development, and self-determination, the complex ideas attending these terms have not been adequately debated. These terms are frequently used in a perfunctory way, and the theoretical basis for community practice is still relatively unsophisticated.

An example of this problem is the concept of *development,* a term widely used in community practice not only in the Global South but in industrial nations as well. Although community development is now a well-established form of community practice, its theoretical assumptions need to be more closely examined to ensure that the knowledge base for community development is sound and that its value assumptions are clarified. This is not merely an academic indulgence. An understanding of development theories and the ways these theories have been implemented will enhance the effectiveness of practice.

This chapter begins by tracing the conceptual roots of the idea of development and how this idea has been articulated over the last two centuries in economic, political, and social thought. Next, the relevance of development theories to community development practice is considered. Although community development has been influenced by a variety of analytic approaches over the years, the role of theory in shaping community development strategies is seldom made explicit. By examining the normative implications of competing theoretical frameworks, it may be possible to forge a sound theoretical basis for community development practice. This chapter concludes with a discussion of *developmentalism*, which, the authors believe, is a viable alternative to the currently popular neoliberal strategies, the intellectual offspring of both European classical liberalism (Drake, 2001) and the more recent phenomena of Reaganism and Thatcherism, which now characterize community development in many parts of the world.

Development and Development Theory

The notion of development is rooted in ancient beliefs about the nature of social change (Nisbet, 1980). For the Chinese, change was cyclical, finding expression in a never-ending series of progressive improvements and retrogressive declines. For the ancient Greeks and Hebrews and today's Christians, historical change is viewed as a regression from an original state of social perfection. Humanity, the Greeks believed, had descended into its present lamentable condition from a long-lost Golden Age. The advent of early Greek philosophy, with its cumulative focus on understanding the world from rational and empirical bases, altered traditional mythological views and provided the foundation for Western development of the natural and social sciences. Aristotle's work, particularly on the construct of teleology, embodies a sense of progression, growth, and progress. For Jews and Christians, history involved the fall from a virtuous state of grace that was characterized by the Garden of Eden, and although medieval philosophy's conception of building the "city of God" on earth promoted ideas of social intervention by the religious orders, traditional practice focused on preparation for the afterlife. However, for most of the world's people during their earliest days, social time was marked by a sense of sameness.

The concept of social change as involving the progressive improvement of social life is essentially a Western idea that appeared first in the optimism of the Renaissance but more significantly in the Enlightenment. Although this notion draws on Platonic and Augustinian ideas, its present popularity owes much to the Enlightenment-era idea that reason and knowledge can be applied to improve society. This idea found expression in numerous social theories, including social evolutionism, Marxism, and Adam Smith's articulation of a theory of market capitalism (Nisbet, 1980). The Judeo-Christian values of caring for and improving the lives of the poor intertwined with emerging ideas and strategies based on principles of social justice to form the beginnings of social work (Betten & Austin, 1990). In addition, the idea that society can be improved through human effort stimulated a variety of political movements, including progressive populism, Marxism, utopian socialism, and liberal interventionism. It also inspired the interventionist practices embodied in economic planning, social policy, and, of course, community practice.

Although contemporary theories of development differ in their conception of the dynamics and causes of social change and the best ways of promoting such change, they share many similarities. All are rooted in Enlightenment ideals and are part of the project of modernity. Most are characterized by the belief that progressive social change can be fostered through systematic social intervention. Many are inspired by a utopian belief in the possibility of progress and social perfectibility.

Modernization theory, which early on gave full expression to modernist thinking, evolved in the years after World War II to dominate views about how the new sovereign states in Africa, Asia, and Central and South America, which had secured political independence from European imperial rule, could become modern industrial nations (Hozelitz, 1960; Inkeles & Smith, 1974; Lerner, 1958; McClelland, 1964; Rostow, 1960). The modernists' goal was to transform the impoverished agrarian and traditional nations of the Global South into something approximating the prosperous liberal-democratic societies of Europe and, particularly, North America. Their means was rapid industrialization propelled by a vigorous market economy, accompanied by the transformation of traditional beliefs and practices into "modern" institutions and attitudes.

Marxism, which had formed the basis for the transformation of Imperial Russia and its neighboring territories into the Soviet Union, also gave expression to notions of modernity (Warren, 1980). However, it vigorously challenged the belief that progressive social change could be promoted by capitalist economic development. Instead, progress required the collectivization of the means of production, the harnessing of economic development for social ends, and centralized direction from technocratic and political elites committed to promoting the well-being of the masses. In addition, Marxists believed that progressive change was possible only through the apocalyptic destruction of the old order. Unlike modernization theorists who drew on Darwinian notions of gradual evolutionary change, Marxists predicated change on revolutionary action.

The Marxist critique of modernization theory was augmented in the 1960s and 1970s by radical populists, who made extensive use of Marxist rhetoric to formulate an alternative conception of development known as *international structuralism,* or more popularly as *dependency theory* (Amin, 1974; Cardoso, 1972; Frank, 1967; Sunkel, 1969). The *dependistas,* who originated in Latin America, regarded modernization theory as little more than a cloak for Western neo-imperialism and a legitimization of the continued economic exploitation and political manipulation of previously colonized nations. They advocated a radical "delinking" of these countries from the global economic system and the attainment of true independence through political struggle and "Third World solidarity" (Amin, 1974; Cardoso, 1972). Their ideas were enormously appealing and inspired many nationalist and anti-imperialist leaders in the Global South who sought to mobilize popular support for the struggle for "authentic" development. However, despite their Marxist rhetoric, few of these leaders advocated revolution or collectivization. Instead, they called for the regulation of the market, improved terms of trade for poor nations, and greater social and economic justice through domestic reforms. It is for this reason that many Marxists viewed their conception of development as essentially populist in inspiration.

The populism of the dependency writers can be contrasted with the statism of a group of development theorists known as the *institutionalists* (Chenery, Ahluwalia, Bell, Duloy, & Jolly, 1974; Griffin, 1978; Myrdal, 1970; Seers, 1972; Streeten, Burki, Ul Haq, Hicks, & Stewart 1981). Drawing from European social democratic and "New Liberal" ideas, American progressivism, and the writings of economists such as Veblen and Keynes, institutionalists argued that development required state intervention and central planning. Although their approach was highly critical of the excesses of unregulated capitalism, the pervasiveness of poverty, and the perpetuation of inequality and social injustice, they rejected the Marxist insistence on revolution and believed in the possibility of change through electoral efforts and social reform. Positive social change could be achieved if progressive political parties secured electoral power and implemented a range of reforms under the direction of a benevolent state. These reforms included economic regulation, redistribution of income and wealth, the collectivization of the "commanding heights" of the economy, substantial investments in education, and the provision of comprehensive social services designed to meet basic social needs. Although these ideas were abstracted from the successes of European social democratic political parties in the post–World War II period, it was thought that they could be applied to the developing nations of the Global South as well. Through planned economic and social development, it was believed that these nations could create prosperity for their citizens on a large scale.

Ecologism, or *sustainable development* (Pearce, Barbier, & Markandya, 1990; Redclift, 1987), is an increasingly influential approach to development. Although it does not constitute a development theory in the formal sense of the term, it has synthesized populist and institutional themes to offer a critique of the crass materialism and strident individualism of contemporary life. It also offers the prospect of creating an alternative social and cultural system that not only is sensitive to the environment but also promotes nonmaterial values (see Gamble & Hoff, Chapter 8, this volume). Ecologism offers an appealing alternative to development theories that stress the need for economic growth based on exclusively on industrialization.

Populist and communitarian ideas have also found expression in development strategies that stress the role of local communities and social movements in promoting positive social change (Kitching, 1982). These ideas have exerted a strong influence over the years, extolling the virtues of small communities, local identity, and traditional family ties. Originally, these ideas were associated with rural life and traditional peasant institutions, but in time they were extended to urban communities as well. Although urban squatter and slum communities were originally viewed in negative terms, they are regarded by communitarians as centers of cooperation and mutual support, dynamic activity, and developmental potential. Their role in promoting political change also has been recognized and often is associated with wider social and political movements that emerged in many developing countries to challenge oppressive power structures. The women's movement and other such current social movements have been inspired by populist and communitarian themes (Wilson & Whitmore, 2000).

Despite having been subjected to sustained criticism, modernization theory has proved to be enduring. Indeed, during the 1980s, with the electoral successes of the Conservatives in Britain under Prime Minister Thatcher and the Republicans in the United States under President Reagan, a reconstructed and more radical version of modernization theory took hold. The New Right had recently experienced political success in Chile when General Pinochet's regime set about ruthlessly eradicating Marxist and social democratic policies promoted by President Allende before his assassination. In addition to advocating a vigorous form of free market capitalism, Pinochet gave expression to a new strand in thinking about development that asserted the need for coercion and authoritarianism. Although not as overt, similar ideas were expressed in Reaganism and Thatcherism, whose proponents contended that development would occur more rapidly if the state used its authority to enforce marketization and the integration of the poor into the capitalist economy. Despite their frequent use of antistatist and *laissez-faire* rhetoric, neoliberal development theorists urged the state to use its power to deregulate the economy, privatize its assets, reduce taxes on the rich, retrench the social services, and actively promote the marketization of the economy and other aspects of social life. These ideas have now become the new orthodoxy for national and international development practitioners dependent on Western funds. The role of the International Monetary Fund (IMF) and World Bank in imposing a neoliberal development model on many countries of the Global South as a condition for much-needed development aid has been well documented (Gray, 1998).

Resistance to the neoliberal development model has come primarily from ecologists and radical populists who have mobilized to oppose the efforts of the IMF and the United States and its allies to impose these ideas on the poor nations of the world. Although the resisters' demonstrations at various important meetings have been well documented, it is not clear whether a reconstructed populist theory of development that extends the original ideas of the dependistas and world systems theory will emerge. The issue is further complicated by the growing popularity of *antidevelopmentalism* (Escobar, 1995; Munck & O'Hearn, 1999; Rahnema & Bawtree, 1997). Inspired by postmodernism, antidevelopment theory rejects the Enlightenment-era assumptions that characterize development theories. Because antidevelopmentalism is preoccupied with the critique of established thought, its proponents have not formulated viable policy prescriptions that incorporate their ideas. Indeed, some would claim that to do so would be oxymoronic. However, alternative development theory, as presented by John Friedmann (1992), provides an interesting model and antidote to both neoliberal and postmodernist views in its clear emphasis on the importance of development for low-wealth communities and recognition that both state intervention and local development efforts are needed to produce significant change.

Community Development and Development Theories

Development theories have been formulated largely in the context of conceptions of the nation-state and its international linkages that relate to issues of political economy. Most of the theories described here offer normative prescriptions for promoting social and economic well-being at the macro level. However, development theories have also provided a normative basis for community-level interventions. Infused into a form of community practice known as *community development,* these theories provide competing normative prescriptions for enhancing the economic and social well-being of local communities.

A distinctive form of community practice, community development emerged in the Global South in the context of European colonialism and Third World economic development during the middle decades of the last century (Brokensha & Hodge, 1969). It augmented earlier forms of community practice associated with the activities of the Charity Organization Societies and Settlement Houses. Canadian theorist Murray Ross (1955, 1958, 1967) wrote about local community development as a major approach to community practice, and the model has received considerable attention from subsequent writers as a way of strengthening low-income communities in the United States and internationally (Rothman, 1974, 1995; Taylor & Roberts, 1985; Weil & Gamble, 1995, 2001). Unlike community organizing and settlement work, and the subsequent Alinsky-esque emphasis on community activism (Alinsky, 1946, 1971), community development is primarily committed to raising the incomes of poor communities through local economic activities (Dore & Mars, 1981).

Although efforts to promote economic activities at the local level were rooted in traditional forms of rural cooperative endeavor, the idea that such activities could provide a basis for economic development was first formalized by indigenous leaders such as Tagore and Gandhi in India and by British colonial welfare officials in the rural areas of West Africa (Brokensha & Hodge, 1969). In fact, the term *community development* was invented by the British in the 1950s to connote small-scale rural development programs that combined local labor with government resources. These programs were typically concerned with agricultural improvements; the development of small industries and crafts; the provision of infrastructure; the construction of schools, clinics, and community centers; and the introduction of health services and safe drinking water. One of the earliest North American community social work texts (Ross, 1955) focused extensively on community development practice.

During the 1950s and 1960s, community development became something of a social movement, as it was championed by colonial powers, international development agencies, and increasingly by nationalist independence leaders. Leaders such as Gandhi stressed its indigenous roots and compatibility with traditional culture (Bhattacharyya, 1970). Echoing this idea, many nationalist leaders argued that economic and social progress depended not only on the industrialization of the national economy, but also on the simultaneous betterment of economic and social conditions in the rural areas through local self-help. These sentiments were reinforced by the colonial powers. The British government promoted the spread of community development throughout its colonial territories, and in the 1950s and 1960s, the French and other European powers also created community development programs known as *animation rurale* (Gow & VanSant, 1983). The United Nations and other international development agencies also became active proponents of community development. As many territories secured independence, community development was given prominence in nationalist rhetoric.

Known as *local economic development*, community development was also promoted by governments in the industrial countries. A major impetus for community development in these countries was the War on Poverty of the Johnson administration in the 1960s, which introduced local enterprises, employment training, job referral services, and similar programs in poor urban neighborhoods in the United States (Gillette, 1996; Ginzberg & Solow, 1974). However, these programs were not well funded, and they soon became embroiled in political struggles with established municipal leaders. Although the War on Poverty did not succeed in its goal of promoting economic prosperity at the local level, its role in enhancing political participation and civil rights has been very important. Similar community development programs were established in many other industrial nations but they never had the visibility or effect of this American experiment.

Theoretical Influences on Community Development

Community development in both the developing and industrial nations did not appear to be particularly influenced by theoretical ideas. Indeed, most of the literature on the subject gives little attention to theoretical issues, focusing instead on the techniques and strategies needed to create and sustain local economic initiatives. However, the atheoretical character of community economic development programs belies the subtle role that normative assumptions played in setting goals and shaping these activities. Although subtle, these theoretical and ideological conceptions exerted an important influence on community development practice.

Like other forms of community practice, community development is invariably influenced by populist and communitarian ideas that extol the virtues of the small community and argue for its centrality in social welfare. However, other conceptual themes also are infused into community practice. For example, the radical populism of much activist community practice frequently makes use of Marxist concepts. Similarly, the populist themes of community development have at different times been combined with ideas from modernization theory, traditionalism, institutionalism, religious social reform, and Marxism.

In its formative years in the Global South, community development was directly associated with modernization theory and, to a lesser extent, with traditionalism and institutionalism. Modernization theory not only provided the macroenvironment in which community development took place but also emphasized the role of local enterprise and material development in social welfare. Because community development also involved people's participation, however, many nationalist leaders stressed its compatibility with traditional culture, claiming that community development was an organic, rather than externally imposed, approach. The role of the state in providing fiscal and other resources to improve social conditions reflected the influence of institutional development theory. State involvement was widely regarded as an essential element in successful community development endeavors.

However, in many countries, state resources for community development remained meager, and it was clear that the modernization approach was promoting a Western, urban-based style of development that would require massive investments in industry rather than rural development. Indeed, budgetary allocations to rural projects were insignificant compared with those for urban development projects. By the 1970s, many critics were claiming that national development strategies favored the urban elite and did little to enhance the welfare of the rural majority (Lipton, 1977). Some argued that community development had become little more than a slogan for mobilizing rural electoral support and even that it was functioning as a mechanism for political control. Some critics claimed that governments were cynically using community development to co-opt rural people and secure their support against promoters of social change. These criticisms were not unfounded; indeed, in Southeast Asia and Latin America, community development's role as a means of combating insurgency and promoting rural pacification had become blatant.

It was in this climate that many proponents of community development began to emphasize the need for social and political activism. If authentic development were to take place, they argued, community development would need to challenge existing authority structures, advocate for increased resources, and address issues of social injustice and oppression. As community development became radicalized, it was increasingly associated with wider progressive movements. It drew inspiration from the dependistas, liberation theologians, Paulo Freire's (1972) theory of *conscientization*, and even the activities of Marxist and nationalist guerillas.

However, the commitment to activism did not reject the need for programs that addressed the material welfare of poor communities. Although terms such as *community participation* and *popular participation* were now used instead of *community development*, activists still sought to mobilize people's involvement in a variety of projects that were, in many ways, similar to those promoted by traditional community development. However, these activities were infused with a new dynamism, and in fields such as child nutrition and women's health, they achieved significant gains. They also incorporated new ideas from feminism and ecologism. Community activism also provided a new impetus for the involvement of local people in activities ranging from community forestry to mass literacy.

The rise of the political right in the 1980s and the formulation of a neoliberal development orthodoxy directly challenged the radical populism and institutional statism of community development. Indeed, in some countries of the Global South where community development had promoted left-progressive ideas, community leaders were harassed by the authorities, and in totalitarian states such as Apartheid-era South Africa, El Salvador, and Chile under Pinochet, their activities were brutally suppressed. However, the political right did not reject the need for community-level development. Rather, it regarded local development as a means of reducing the influence of statism and promoting self-reliance and local enterprise. As the writings of Hernan de Soto (1989) reveal, entrepreneurship and the infusion of a capitalist ethic into local economic development was actively encouraged. The neoliberal development orthodoxy has permeated community development not only in the Global South but in the industrial nations as well. Community or "bootstrap" capitalism (Stoesz, 2000; Stoesz & Saunders, 1999) is now providing a new and increasingly popular framework for community development in many parts of the world.

The neoliberal approach to community development offers an alternative both to the populist radicalism of community participation and the institutionalism of state-sponsored community development. The social democratic notion that government resources can be combined with local efforts to provide schools, clinics, cooperative enterprises, and community social services is believed by the political right to result not only in dependency and stagnation, but also in corruption, as local vested interests seek to appropriate public resources for their own ends. By fostering a vibrant culture of local capitalism, this view holds that as individual self-reliance increases, people are liberated from the oppressive influence of government intervention and they are empowered to realize their full potential.

The neoliberal approach regards local economic development as a mechanism for promoting capitalism at the local level and for integrating poor communities into the global capitalist culture (see Reisch, Chapter 29, this volume). The cooperative enterprise that long characterized traditional community development is being replaced with single-entrepreneur microenterprises. The privatization of community social services and assets is being advocated. The creation of individual asset accounts, rather than community-held assets, is preferred (see Padilla & Sherraden, Chapter 5, this volume). Marketization and commercialization of all aspects of community life are seen as new and highly desired goals.

The incorporation of the neoliberal orthodoxy into community development has been challenged from various perspectives. Vigorous opposition has come from radical populists and communitarians, but with the declining influence of Marxism, they have made increasing use of postmodernist ideas to frame their arguments. The postmodernist advocacy of social movements has also facilitated the articulation and expression of ecologism, feminism, and other ideas. Postmodernism has also provided an impetus for the expression of antidevelopment ideas. However, as suggested earlier, antidevelopmentalism has been concerned primarily with the critique of modernist development and does not provide a sound basis for reformulating community development in ways that maximize welfare and enhance social goals.

Another problem with the postmodernist challenge to neoliberal community development is that it downplays the contribution economic development makes to enhancing people's welfare. By rejecting community capitalism, it also rejects economic development. However, the promotion of economic development through a variety of local projects does not depend on the acceptance of neoliberalism. In their own ways, the different theories discussed previously all recognize the need for economic development. Marxism, institutionalism, and even ecologism all accept that economic development can dramatically raise incomes and transform impoverished communities and societies. However, these theories offer differing proposals for ways in which economic development can promote people's welfare. The struggle thus concerns how economic development is conceived in normative terms and the way its ultimate purpose is defined.

Toward Developmentally Focused Practice

The ascendancy of neoliberalism may not have obliterated traditional community development, but it has debilitated it. Neoliberals have portrayed traditional community development as old-fashioned, wasteful, and ineffective, and they have claimed that their advocacy of bootstrap or community capitalism offers a dynamic alternative. This approach has become pervasive in many parts of the world today.

However, community development has been weakened not only by the impetus of the neoliberal offensive but also by radical populists and postmodernists. This is because their rejection of neoliberalism not only fails to promote an alternative model for economic development, but also involves a rejection of local economic development. For example, activists have argued that community projects do not result in significant gains and that poverty can only be eradicated through international advocacy against global capitalism. Denny (2001) reported that Ann Pettifor, the head of the British aid organization Jubilee 2000, claimed that digging wells and engaging in other local social and economic activities was pointless. She said that "people concerned about development have got to concentrate on advocacy at the global level" (Denny, 2001, p. 23). Many development activists involved in antiglobalization campaigns have echoed these sentiments. By arguing that local community development has failed and that international activism offers the only prospect of bringing about meaningful change, these proponents of community development are left with few allies, and their ability to oppose the neoliberal challenge is weakened. Similarly, by downplaying or denouncing the idea that economic and social development can foster progress, postmodernists also undermine efforts by proponents of community development to counter the neoliberal offensive.

The postmodern and radical populist rejection of neoliberalism has thrown the proverbial baby out with the bathwater. Although it is true that traditional community development has many shortcomings and that it has not solved the problems of poverty and injustice, it has contributed to the achievement of desirable goals. There are many examples of successful community development programs that have combined government resources with the participation of local people. Indeed, it is not empirically true, as Pettifor asserted (Denny, 2001), that local development projects are a waste of time and effort. There is ample evidence to show that the wells and other safe water projects she so disdainfully derides have benefited many millions of children who otherwise would have sickened and perhaps died from waterborne diseases.

Nor is it true, as the neoliberal proponents of community capitalism assert, that community development can only be achieved by infusing a vigorous free market ethic into local development and integrating the poor into the capitalist system. Nevertheless, it is unfortunate that progressives have not been able to counter the neoliberal argument with a development theory that offers an appealing and workable alternative. A new rationale for community development that modernizes traditional community development thought, addresses its shortcomings, and provides a realistic basis for practice is urgently needed.

One possibility lies in applying the ideas of a small group of scholars known as the *developmentalists* to community development practice (Midgley, 1995, 1999; Midgley & Sherraden, 2000; Sherraden, 1991). Developmentalism is primarily concerned with macro-level issues of social policy, but its tenets can be applied to local-level interventions as well. Developmentalism is rooted in institutionalist thinking, but it differs from institutionalism in several respects, particularly in the way it promotes social investments rather than consumption-based income transfers. In this way, it emphasizes the role of productivist forms of social welfare in social policy. Unlike neoliberalism, developmentalism requires the allocation of substantial public resources for these investments. It is based on notions of redistribution and collective involvement (Midgley, 1999). However, as a neo-institutional project, developmentalism is more pluralistic than its predecessor. Although conventional institutionalism neglected the role of the market and civil society, contemporary developmentalism requires the coordination of state, market, and community efforts in the framework of what has been described as *managed pluralism* (Midgley, 1995).

Developmentalism is also based on the idea that governments, together with civil society, should purposefully promote economic development through a regulated market to achieve desirable social goals. Unlike postmodernist antidevelopment theory, developmentalism seeks to promote economic growth; equally influenced by ecologism, however, it embraces the notion of sustainable and renewal development (Estes, 1993). Reflecting the influence of social democratic thinking, developmentalists believe that the dynamism of the market can be used to raise standards of living. However, this requires judicious intervention, effective democratic institutions, and close cooperation with civil society to ensure that the bureaucratic tendencies toward statism and the excesses of the market are moderated. Although this is an optimistic vision, developmentalists are not sanguine about the challenges that current economic and political realities pose to the attainment of these ideals. As in the past, gains in social justice and welfare will not be achieved easily.

Applying Developmentalism to Community Development

The normative elements of developmentalist thinking can be applied at the community level to promote both sustainable local development and the well-being of local people. However, to be successful, community development must be effectively linked to national development strategies. A major reason for the failure of traditional community development projects was that leaders of the independence movements in the Global South extolled traditional agrarianism while supporting strategies that promoted urban industrialization, often disregarding the needs of people in the rural areas. The growing numbers of poor urban migrants who were concentrated in squatter settlements fared little better. Successful community development depends on linking local and national development strategies and on the effective mobilization and representation of local interests in national politics. This requirement also applies to industrial nations, where community development is often viewed as peripheral to national economic and social policy.

Successful community development also requires the allocation of substantial public resources in the form of investments that will stimulate local development activities. These investments include human capital programs, asset development projects, the mobilization of social capital, employment and self-employment strategies, microcredit projects, and the removal of barriers to effective economic participation. The neoliberal claim that local entrepreneurs together with external investors motivated exclusively by self-interest can transform poor communities without substantial government aid is either wishful thinking or a pretext for the colonization of these communities by outsiders. Urban renewal too often has involved gentrification that drives out poorer residents and keeps them from reaping the benefits of development. Authentic community development requires the infusion of resources that can promote the indigenous transformation of these communities. However, the need for investments, rather than unilateral transfers based on political and other considerations, must be emphasized. Indigenous assets can best be enhanced through investments that combine the resources of the state with those of local people.

Effective community development involves the creation of an authentic partnership between government and local people and the judicious use of the market to promote sustainable growth. Too often, traditional community development has involved a prescriptive, bureaucratic "top down" process that has stifled local initiative. Community development must institutionalize pluralism and recognize the right of local people to manage their own affairs. Local people should not merely participate in development projects but take effective control of them and, indeed, of local affairs. Past experience in the developing world reveals the tendency of the consensus-building strategies of community development to result in co-optation or manipulation when influenced by powerful external actors. These tendencies are also found in industrial countries, where current community development approaches have been criticized for abandoning their original commitment to social action (Fisher & Shragge, 2001). In this regard, community development needs to embrace a viable notion of empowerment that has political as well as economic dimensions. Friedmann's (1992) articulation of a theory of empowerment offers useful directions for a future synthesis that can effectively balance the developmental, communitarian, and radical populist elements in community practice to promote sustainable economic and social development based on authentic local participation.

Although these prescriptions offer a framework for a renewed commitment to community development, they do not claim to be a recipe that will magically result in the transformation of poor communities or solve all their social problems. Nevertheless, they do seek to offer a viable conceptual framework for community development today. In addition, there is growing evidence that local projects reflecting these ideas have enhanced standards of living and improved the well-being of poor communities. This is particularly true of initiatives that have made extensive use of the developmentalist notion of social investment.

Social Investment and Community Development

Increasingly, community development projects today emphasize the need for programs that transcend traditional schooling and develop human capital by improving skills, promoting literacy, and providing job experience. Although much of the literature on human capital focuses on individuals, investments in human capital can also be viewed as community assets because they provide a pool of skills that can be used to promote community welfare. Initiatives such as school-linked family resource centers provide community members with access to education through after-school and weekend tutoring for youth and lifelong learning programs (Dupper & Poertner, 1997). In fact, community schools initiatives are rebuilding the capacities of community members through school-based councils that promote leadership and skills (Lawson & Briar-Lawson, 1997; Surko, Lawson, & Muse-Lindemann, 1999). The development of local leadership is an important aid to community development efforts. The Pew Civic Entrepreneur Initiative, for example, targets individuals who do not necessarily see themselves as leaders, teaches them collaborative problem-solving skills, and brings them together to address pressing community problems (Pew Partnership, 2001). Such leadership development has been a primary target of agricultural extension programs in rural areas for years. The W. K. Kellogg Foundation has compiled a helpful resource list of leadership development material from such programs (2001).

Promoting social capital in communities is another important form of social investment advocated by developmentalists. *Social capital* refers to social networks and the trust and norms of reciprocity that exist among people. Community development interventions, such as those promoted by the Local Initiative Support Corporation (LISC), seek to increase community social capital not only for social but for economic development purposes as well. By strengthening community ties, LISC seeks to increase trust and cooperation to enhance solidarity and promote social and economic well-being (Gittell & Vidal, 1998). Midgley and Livermore (1998) suggested ways community social workers can use their skills to harness social capital to promote economic development, including forming community organizations that support local businesses, facilitating cooperative enterprises, and fostering local organizations that initiate economic development projects.

Another type of social investment that contributes to economic growth is the facilitation of productive employment and self-employment. Although often individualistic in focus, community-based versions of such activities have become increasingly common. For example, many churches and other faith-based organizations in the United States are now engaged in employment training, referral, placement, and mentoring programs through the provisions of the Personal Responsibility and Work Opportunity Reconciliation Act of 1996. The employment services provided by these community-based institutions are valuable because they link welfare recipients to the labor market through informal networks in the community (Griener, 2000).

Employment programs can be augmented with community-based microenterprise and microcredit programs (Balkin, 1989). These initiatives provide individuals with employment opportunities and also with goods and services needed locally, thus helping rebuild and strengthen local economies. Microenterprise development is a popular strategy used worldwide to build small-scale businesses owned and operated by people or groups with low incomes. The Grameen Bank, established in Bangladesh in 1983 by Mohammed Yunus (Holcombe, 1995; Wahid, 1994; Yunus, 1991), is an internationally emulated model for microenterprise development, in which small groups of individuals pool their efforts to create cooperative enterprises and guarantee loans (see Raheim, Noponen, & Alter, Chapter 30, this volume).

To be successful, these programs require public resources, the involvement of local people, and the opportunities afforded by regulated economic markets.

Incorporated into the wider normative system of developmentalist thinking, they offer the potential to reformulate community development, challenge the claims of neoliberal community capitalism, and enhance the economic and social well-being of poor communities that have, for too long, been excluded from the prosperity that many currently enjoy.

References

Alinsky, S. D. (1946). *Reveille for radicals.* Chicago: University of Chicago Press.

Alinsky, S. D. (1971). *Rules for radicals: A practical primer for realistic radicals.* New York: Random House.

Amin, S. (1974). *Accumulation on a world scale.* New York: Monthly Review Press.

Balkin, S. (1989). *Self-employment for low-income people.* New York: Praeger.

Betten, N., & Austin, M. J. (Eds.). (1990). *The roots of community organizing: 1917–1939.* Philadelphia: Temple University Press.

Bhattacharyya, S. N. (1970). *Community development: An analysis of the programme in India.* Calcutta, India: Academic.

Brokensha, D., & Hodge, P. (1969). *Community development: An interpretation.* San Francisco: Chandler.

Cardoso, F. H. (1972). Dependent capitalist development in Latin America. *New Left Review, 74,* 83–95.

Chenery, H., Ahluwalia, M., Bell, C., Duloy, J. H., & Jolly, R. (1974). *Redistribution with growth.* New York: Oxford University Press.

Denny, C. (2001, January 18–24). Tackling the system: Not just symptoms. *Guardian Weekly,* 23.

de Soto, H. (1989). *The other path: The invisible revolution in the Third World.* New York: Harper and Row.

Dore, R., & Mars, Z. (Eds.). (1981). *Community development.* London: Croom Helm.

Drake, R. F. (2001). *The principles of social policy.* New York: Palgrave Macmillan.

Dupper, D. R., & Poertner, J. (1997). Public schools and the revitalization of impoverished communities: School-linked, family resource centers. *Social Work, 42*(5), 415–422.

Escobar, A. (1995). *The making and unmaking of the Third World.* Princeton, NJ: Princeton University Press.

Estes, R. (1993). Towards sustainable development: From theory to praxis. *Social Development Issues, 15*(3), 1–29.

Fisher, R., & Shragge, E. (2001). Challenging community organizing: Facing the 21st century. *Journal of Community Practice, 8*(3), 1–19.

Frank, A. G. (1967). *Capitalism and underdevelopment in Latin America.* New York: Monthly Review Press.

Freire, P. (1972). *Pedagogy of the oppressed.* Harmondsworth, UK: Penguin.

Friedmann, J. (1992). *Empowerment: The politics of alternative development.* Cambridge, MA: Blackwell.

Gillette, M. (1996). *Launching the War on Poverty.* New York: Twayne.

Ginzberg, E., & Solow, R. M. (Eds.). (1974). *The Great Society: Lessons for the future.* New York: Basic Books.

Gittell, R., & Vidal, A. (1998). *Community organizing: Building social capital as a development strategy.* Thousand Oaks, CA: Sage.

Gow, D. D., & VanSant, J. (1983). Beyond the rhetoric of community development participation: How can it be done? *World Development, 11*(5), 427–446.

Gray, J. (1998). *False dawn: The delusions of global capitalism.* London: Granta.

Griener, G. M. (2000). Charitable choice and welfare reform: Collaboration between state and local governments and faith-based organizations. *Welfare Information Network: Issue Notes, 4*(12). Retrieved July 15, 2002, from www.welfareinfo.org/issuenotecharitablechoice.htm.

Griffin, K. (1978). *International inequality and national poverty.* London: Macmillan.

Holcolmbe, S. H. (1995). *Managing to empower: The Grameen Bank's experiment of poverty alleviation.* London: Zed Books.

Hozelitz, B. F. (1960). *Sociological factors in economic development.* New York: Free Press.

Inkeles, A., & Smith, D. H. (1974). *Becoming modern.* London: Heinemann.

Kitching, G. (1982). *Development and underdevelopment in historical perspective.* London: Methuen.

Lawson, H., & Briar-Lawson, K. (1997). *Connecting the dots: Progress toward the integration of school reform, school-linked services, parent involvement and community schools.* Oxford, OH: Danforth Foundation and Institute for Educational Renewal at Miami University.

Lerner, D. (1958). *The passing of traditional society.* New York: Free Press.

Lipton, M. (1977). *Why poor people stay poor: A study of urban bias in world development.* London: Temple Smith.

McClelland, D. (1964). A psychological approach to economic development. *Economic Development and Cultural Change, 12*(2), 320–324.

Midgley, J. (1995). *Social development: The developmental perspective in social welfare.* Thousand Oaks, CA: Sage.

Midgley, J. (1999). Growth, redistribution and welfare: Towards social investment. *Social Service Review, 77*(1), 3–21.

Midgley, J., & Livermore, M. (1998). Social capital and local economic development: Implications for community social work practice. *Journal of Community Practice, 5*(1/2), 29–40.

Midgley, J., & Sherraden, M. (2000). The social development perspective in social policy. In J. Midgley, M. B. Tracy, & M. Livermore (Eds.), *The handbook of social policy* (pp. 435–446). Thousand Oaks, CA: Sage.

Munck, R., & O'Hearn, D. (Eds.). (1999). *Critical development theory: Contributions to a new paradigm.* New York: Zed Books.

Myrdal, G. (1970). *The challenge of world poverty.* Harmondsworth, UK: Penguin.

Nisbet, R. (1980). *History of the idea of progress.* New York: Basic Books.

Pearce, D., Barbier, E., & Markandya, A. (1990). *Sustainable development: Economics and environment in the Third World.* Brookfield, VT: Edward Elgar.

Pew Partnership. (2001). *Pew Civic Entrepreneur Initiative.* Retrieved July 15, 2002, from www.pew-partnership.org/pcei/pcei.html.

Rahnema, M., & Bawtree, E. (Eds.). (1997). *The post-development reader.* New York: Zed Books.

Redclift, M. (1987). *Sustainable development: Exploring the contradictions.* London: Routledge.

Ross, M. G. (1955). *Community organization: Theory, principles, and practice.* New York: Harper.

Ross, M. G. (1958). *Case histories in community organization.* New York: Harper & Row.

Ross, M. G. (1967). *Community organization: Theory, principles, and practice* (2nd ed.). New York: Harper & Row.

Rostow, W. W. (1960). *The stages of economic growth: A non-Communist manifesto.* New York: Cambridge University Press.

Rothman, J. (1974). *Planning and organizing for social change.* New York: Columbia University Press.

Rothman, J. (1995). Approaches to community intervention. In J. Rothman, J. L. Erlich, & J. E. Tropman (Eds.), *Strategies of community intervention* (5th ed.). Ithaca, IL: F. E. Peacock.

Seers, D. (1972). The meaning of development. In N. T. Uphoff & W. F. Ilchman (Eds.), *The political economy of development* (pp. 123–129). Berkeley: University of California Press.

Sherraden, M. (1991). *Assets and the poor: A new American welfare policy*. Armonk, NY: M. E. Sharpe.

Stoesz, S. (2000). *Poverty of imagination: Bootstraps capitalism, sequel to welfare reform*. Madison: University of Wisconsin Press.

Stoesz, D., & Saunders, D. (1999). Welfare capitalism: A new approach to poverty policy? *Social Service Review, 73*(3), 381–399.

Streeten, P., Burki, S. J., Ul Haq, M., Hicks, N., & Stewart, F. (1981). *First things first: Meeting basic needs in developing countries*. New York: Oxford University Press.

Sunkel, O. (1969). National development policy and external dependence in Latin America. *Journal of Development Studies, 6*, 23–48.

Surko, M., Lawson, H., & Muse-Lindemann, E. (1999). Launching a journey: Analysis of a community school collaborative. *Universities and Community Schools, 6*(1-2), 25–48.

Taylor, S. H., & Roberts, R. (1985). *Theory and practice of community social work*. New York: Columbia University Press.

Wahid, A. (Ed.). (1994). *The Grameen Bank: Poverty relief in Bangladesh*. Boulder, CO: Westview.

Warren, B. (1980). *Imperialism: Pioneer of capitalism*. London: Verso.

Weil, M. O., & Gamble, D. N. (1995). Community practice models. In R. L. Edwards (Ed.), *Encyclopedia of social work* (Vol. 1, pp. 483–494). Washington, DC: National Association of Social Workers.

Weil, M. O., & Gamble, D. N. (2001). Community practice models for the 21st century. In A. R. Roberts & G. J. Greene (Eds.), *Social worker's desk reference* (pp. 525–534). New York: Oxford University Press.

Wilson, M., & Whitmore, E. (2000). *Seeds of fire: Social development in an era of globalism*. New York: Apex.

W. K. Kellogg Foundation. (2001). *W. K. Kellogg collection of rural community development resources*. Retrieved July 15, 2002, from www.libfind.unl.edu/kellogg/leaddevtitles.html.

Yunus, M. (1991). *Grameen Bank: Experiences and reflections*. Dhaka: Grameen Bank.

CHAPTER 8

Sustainable Community Development

Dorothy N. Gamble

Marie D. Hoff

Background

World population growth combined with resource depletion leads to a decreased capacity for social and economic development. These trends are not limited to the impoverished nations and cultures often designated as the Third World. All around the globe, water and soil, the basic foundation for production of food and fiber, are being depleted and polluted at rates far beyond nature's capacity to replenish and purify these essential resources (Pimentel, Westra, & Noss, 2000). The Earth is undergoing accelerated climate change, primarily owing to the use of fossil fuels that have made possible the modern industrial model of development. Climate change can be expected to contribute to the spread and increased rate of infectious diseases as well as severe threats to agricultural production; in turn, these effects will severely threaten cultural sustainability (Hoff, 2002; Intergovernmental Panel on Climate Change, 1996). The state of the natural environment is likely to be the primary economic and political factor influencing the development of peoples in the 21st century.

At the same time, through the human genome project, we are now aware more than ever that human beings are closely related to all living species on Earth. In the words of Swimme and Berry, "Every living being of earth is cousin to every other living being" (1994, p. 5). Scientific knowledge has opened our minds to more understanding of things we cannot see. It is, however, our willingness to accept responsibility for our role in environmental degradation and for changing the nature of development that allows us to have a salutary effect on the quality of survival for all Earth's species. Social work embraces the ethical principles that "social workers' primary goal is to help people in need and to address social problems" and that "social workers recognize the central importance of human relationships" (National Association of Social Workers [NASW], 1996, pp. 5–6). These ethical principles provide the grounds for social work practitioners in all fields—most especially for those in community practice—to become involved in local-to-global action in response to this unprecedented challenge to the quality of human life on Earth.

Concepts Underpinning Sustainable Development Practice

Concepts most often associated with sustainable development practice are *social development, human development,* and the term *sustainable development* itself. These concepts are widely used in the literature and have many overlapping, and sometimes contrasting, meanings.

Social development. This concept emerged after World War II, primarily to describe work to improve conditions in poor nations and societies newly liberated from colonial domination. In these societies, according to Midgley, social development was seen as "a process of planned social change designed to promote the well-being of the population as a whole in conjunction with a dynamic process of economic development" (1995, p. 25; see also Midgley & Livermore, this volume). In this approach, social services are intrinsically linked to economic development, and they are viewed more as investments than as a drain on the economy. Although social development as a concept and a process emerged primarily in poor nations, social workers in the United States have been among the leaders in applying its concepts, values, processes, and intervention strategies in the American context (Midgley & Livermore, 1997). Case studies, as well as theoretical debates and efforts to define social development, are regularly undertaken in many books, articles, and journals, including *Social Development Issues.* Some generally accepted principles and strategies include democratic procedures for decision making, intense intersectoral planning strategies (i.e., involvement of government, commerce, education, and civic groups), and broad participation by citizens in implementing programs.

Human development. Human development is defined as strategies aimed at the achievement of individual well-being and the opportunity to express personal capacities. In 1990, the United Nations Development Program (UNDP) published the first *Human Development Report,* in which they devised a composite index to measure human development (see Estes, Chapter 28, this volume). This index was a more comprehensive method than the gross national product (GNP) for measuring the development of people in both high-income and developing nations. Mahbub ul Haq was involved in the initial leadership for the creation of the UN's Human Development Index (HDI), which took into consideration life expectancy at birth, knowledge (based on the adult literacy rate and the combined school enrollment ratio), and adjusted per capita income in Purchasing Power Parity. Subsequently, each annual report provides the HDI for countries and regions and also focuses on a specific aspect of human development, highlighting barriers and support mechanisms for moving toward sustainable development policies that could improve human well-being. In the UNDP's 1992 report, for example, the 20:20 Initiative was introduced, proposing that every developing country allocate 20% of its domestic budget, and every donor country 20% of its official development assistance, to insuring basic health care, education, access to safe water and sanitation, and family planning packages for all couples. The UNDP's 1996 report was focused on the meaning of "growth," an important discussion that challenged traditional definitions.

Gender has become a particularly significant issue in sustainable development because of the role women play in nurturing families and preserving environmental resources. In response to this recognition, the UNDP's 1995 report introduced the Gender-Related Development Index and the Gender Empowerment Measure to track worldwide gender inequalities in human development. In the UNDP's 1997 report, human poverty was the focus of a new index. The Human Poverty Index was formulated as a composite measure for human poverty, including

> the percentage of people expected to die before age 40, the percentage of adults who are illiterate, and overall economic provisioning in terms of the percentage of people without access to health services and safe water, and the percentage of underweight children under 5. (UNDP, 1992, p. 14)

The annual update on these measures helps countries track the outcomes of economic and social policy changes.

Social work values are evident in the UNDP annual reports. In the 1999 report, for example, the writers focused on the concept they called

> caring labour—providing for children, the sick and the elderly, as well as all the rest of us, exhausted from the demands of daily life. . . . Without enough care, individuals do not flourish. Without attention and stimulus, babies languish, failing to reach their full potential. And without nurturing from their families, children underperform in school. (p. 7)

The HDI is a basic tool for measuring efforts toward sustainable community development. The concept of using a composite measure of human development rather than a simple income measure provides social workers engaged in community practice with a valuable resource.

Sustainable development. Sustainable development was conceptualized in 1987 in the report of the World Commission on Environment and Development (WCED), the United Nations' commission appointed to study the relationship between social development and the state of the world's natural environment. The WCED, chaired by Gro Harlem Brundtland, former prime minister of Norway, defined sustainability as "development that meets the needs of the present without compromising the ability of future generations to meet their own needs" (1987, p. 43).

A central idea of environmental sustainability is that of regeneration and continuity of the foundation of natural resources on which human society is necessarily built. Historical and anthropological research demonstrates that many societies have disappeared owing to depletion of their natural resources. Currently, all societies across the globe face this threat, as many natural resources are being used beyond rates of replenishment. Thus, environmental and social continuity are inextricably linked.

Estes (1993) provided an especially useful review of the theoretical and historical antecedents that contribute to "the power of the concept" (p. 1) of sustainable development, and he analyzed the actions and writings of a variety of recent social movements that have contributed to its meaning and evaluation. These include the environmental and ecological, antiwar and antinuclear, world order, world dynamics modeling, the European Green Party, alternative economics, women's, indigenous people's, and worldwide human rights movements.

Sustainable community development practice leads to a holistic development strategy that strives to integrate environmental, economic, and social factors in such a way, that, for example, biodiversity and cultural diversity can both be protected. Thus, environmental protection and conservative use of resources, along with investments in both human and social capital (e.g., education, health, civic capacity and leadership training, employment and entrepreneurial skills development, gender equity, and the elimination of racial and cultural oppression), are seen not as detrimental to national, regional, or local economic wealth, but as necessary components of economic production models for long-term viability to meet human needs and protect global resources.

Applications to Social Work Practice

The social work profession emerged in the United States during the early 20th century in response to conditions and problems generated by industrialization, urbanization, and mass immigration. The profession has a historical concern with alleviating poverty and developing healthy communities. NASW's (1996) Social Work Code of Ethics indicates that

> social workers should promote the general welfare of society, from local to global levels, and the development of people, their communities, and their environments. Social workers should advocate for living conditions conducive to the fulfillment of basic human needs and should promote social, economic, political, and cultural values and institutions that are compatible with the realization of social justice. (p. 26)

In recognition that human beings are intrinsically social and shaped by opportunities available in their social and physical environment, as well as by their genetic endowment, social work methods incorporate attention to sociocultural influences on the individual's capacity to develop as a person. Only in the past decade, however, has the profession begun to recognize explicitly and incorporate into practice the important influences of the natural environment on individuals and communities (Hoff & McNutt, 1994; NASW, 1999). Sustainable community development is probably still an unfamiliar practice framework for most social workers; however, as examples of sustainable community development emerge, we begin to see more and more social workers as significant participants.

Theoretical Foundations

In addition to the concepts described above, theoretical foundations in the natural and social sciences as well as the humanities help social workers gain more specific knowledge about human interaction with the environment.

Natural Sciences

Concepts of environmental sustainability are drawn from such natural sciences as biology and climatology, as well as from disciplines that cross the boundaries of natural and social sciences, such as geography and ecology. Ecological studies draw on many scientific disciplines to arrive at such concepts as *carrying capacity*, the number of a given species that an ecosystem can sustain without collapse; *biodiversity*, the dependence of the strength of an ecosystem on the variety of species within it—for example, monocultures or those with very limited diversity are less resistant to disease (Wilson, 1988); and *adaptivity and balance*, that is, in healthy ecosystems, species can creatively adapt for survival and tend to maintain an equilibrium in their numbers over time.

An important concept for sustainable community development in social work is *bioregionalism,* which emerges from biological studies of ecosystems and the articulation of the elements and interactions specific and sometimes unique to particular localities. Bioregional theory attempts to demonstrate how human activity, particularly work and economic production to meet basic human needs, is shaped by the natural elements of a region. Bioregional theory also subscribes to normative standards for human action, which are believed to be in harmony with how natural systems interact. Thus, according to Kirkpatrick Sale, a pioneer in the field, bioregional approaches to economy, polity, and society emphasize values such as cooperation, decentralization of authority, and diversity (1985, p. 50). Because of its focus on a geographic place, bioregional theory is compatible with the models for social work community practice that Jack Rothman identified as "locality development" (2001, p. 45) and Weil and Gamble identified as "community social and economic development" (1995, pp. 581–586). This theory goes beyond locality development in proposing that social planning should build on and integrate the distinctive aspects of a local ecosystem into proposals for economic and other social development. Experimental efforts to implement a bioregional vision are occurring in many regions of the United States (Bernard & Young, 1997), particularly in Appalachia (Scherch, 1998), the Pacific Northwest (Hoff, 1998), and along many major rivers and streams.

Perhaps the most comprehensive study of the global environment is the United Nations' commissioned Intergovernmental Panel on Climate Change (1996). This team of 2,500 scientists from around the world has developed an encyclopedic assessment of the effect of global warming on the world's ecological systems and the expected effects on human health and commerce. Immediately germane to social work practice are effects such as increases in weather-related disasters, reductions in food resources, and increases in the level and range of bacterial diseases. These conditions affect the quality of life for individuals, families, and communities. This research also helps us understand how human lifestyles and development activities create conditions that can contribute to more natural disasters.

Social Sciences

Sustainable development practice draws on economics, sociology, psychology, and anthropology, among other social sciences. Political theory and interdisciplinary fields, such as feminist and Native American studies, policy development, and urban/rural planning, also contribute to emerging perspectives on how to promote human development in an environmentally sustainable way.

Neither traditional free market (i.e., capitalist) nor Marxist economics addressed the costs of environmental pollution or depletion in assessing net improvements in the economic welfare of a society. E. F. Schumacher (1973), an English economist, was one of the first contemporary authors to appraise the deleterious effects of large-scale industrial production on both people and the environment. His widely hailed volume, *Small Is Beautiful: A Study of Economics as if People Mattered,* contributed significantly to the movement for new development approaches that sustain both people and the environment.

Economists and futurists such as Herman Daly (1996; Daly & Cobb, 1994), Costanza (1991); Hawken (1993); Hawken, Lovins, and Lovins (1999); Henderson (1996); and Lutz and Lux (1988) have developed articulate arguments for approaches to economic theory and practice that internalize environmental costs in economic equations and that make a distinction between sheer economic growth (expansion) and economic development that integrates an ecological component. The United States, for example, although perhaps the wealthiest nation in history, has an accelerated rate of soil and water depletion, the highest medical costs in the world, and a very high rate of physical violence among the population. Under older economic models, none of these costs of development would be calculated in assessing wealth.

Since the 1980s, when a sense of crisis became fairly widespread regarding the world's natural environment, researchers from almost every social discipline have pursued studies of the interactions between the natural world and human society. Paul Wachtel (1989), a psychologist, analyzed the negative psychological effects of the American way of life, devoted to the pursuit of affluence, which impels us to use extraordinary levels of natural resources, far beyond environmental sustainability. In their occasional "Earth Pulse" notes, *National Geographic* (2001) reported that the ecological footprint, representing the productive area of the Earth required to support the lifestyle of one individual, is, on average, 20 acres per person for industrialized countries, an amount four times the average in developing countries. In the United States, the figure is a high of 30.2 acres (an online "Ecological Footprint Quiz" is also available through the Redefining Progress Web site, www.rprogress.org).

Of special importance to social workers concerned with race, gender, and other bases of social and political inequality, multidisciplinary and action research have uncovered the relationships among environmental exploitation and race and gender inequities (Bullard, 1990; Harvey, 1996; Merchant, 1980, 1992; Shiva, 1993). This line of research has exposed the continuity of the logic behind exploitation of nature—based on power and acquisitive values—and the exploitation of poor neighborhoods and regions, often with a population disadvantaged by racial or class identity (Bullard, 1990; Bryant & Mohai, 1992). Critical theory that exposes unequal, unjust power relationships between rich and poor and demonstrates the logic that links human oppression to rapacious approaches to uses of environmental resources (Dickens, 1992; Korten, 1995) also informs sustainable development practice.

Feminist research has articulated the harmony between feminist values and environmental values (Harcourt, 1994; Merchant, 1980). Women make significant contributions to environmental causes and to the relationship between the environment and human well-being. Examples include Wangari Maathai of Kenya, whose tree-planting campaign has restored the landscape and improved the economic opportunities of women; Rachel Carson (1962), whose pioneering work *Silent Spring* on the lethal effects of pesticides was fought fiercely by chemical companies; and Lois Gibbs, the housewife whose concern for her son's health led her from a neighborhood safety campaign to national leadership in working-class citizens' fight against toxic pollution across the country (Breton, 1998). Recent United Nations conferences on the status of women have drawn more widespread attention to the need for the active involvement of women in both leadership and strategy development for the promotion of environmentally friendly development that also promotes human well-being (Weil, Gamble, & Williams, 1998, see especially pp. 269–270). Ecofeminism and development from a feminist perspective, especially in poor nations, notes that by stressing production for export, traditional (i.e., capitalist) models for development favor male workers and tend to destroy local agriculture and cultural traditions that in some countries (principally in Africa and Asia) were largely a woman's domain (Harcourt, 1994; Stoesz, Guzzetta, & Lusk, 1999). Feminist theory and studies of women's roles and action in development are significant resources for sustainable development strategies (Nussbaum & Glover, 1995; Rao, Stuart, & Kelleher, 1999).

Humanities

Philosophers (Partridge, 1981; Ralston, 1986) and theologians (Berry, 1988; Cobb, 1992; Hallman, 1994; Swimme & Berry, 1994) have delved into the cosmological beliefs and ethical values associated with various perspectives on the human relationship to the natural environment. Of particular merit is the partnership of economist Herman Daly with theologian John Cobb in their 1989 book, *For the Common Good* (revised in 1994). Their work critiqued current economic theory and the effect of its application on people and land, and they proposed a framework for reform by drawing on values derived from religious traditions such as community, justice, and a view of materialism (i.e., consumerism) as a form of idolatry (pp. 382–406). Based on these normative insights, many progressive religious organizations in the United States are developing individual initiatives and ecumenical partnerships for environmental action. The Web site of the National Religious Partnership for the Environment (www.nrpe.org) documents these endeavors, which frequently have a developmental character. They demonstrate, for example, environmental responsibility that also promotes human development, such as gardening projects for youth or water and forest restoration.

Principles, Concepts, and Skills for Social Workers in Sustainable Development

Principles

The advancement of sustainable development requires the involvement of many disciplines in cross-sectoral research, planning, and action. Estes referred to the tasks of rethinking and reorganizing the direction of human development as being "political, social, and moral in nature" (1993, p. 12). In his work, *This Endangered Planet: Prospects and Proposals for Human Survival,* Richard Falk (1972, pp. 293–312) provided a basic set of values to guide the work we might now call sustainable community development. Here are his principal points with rationales and notes on more recent developments:

- *Unity of humankind and unity of life on earth.* When we accept that all living creatures, plant life, water, and air are part of a common system, we are less likely to destroy parts of it carelessly.
- *The minimization of violence.* NASW engaged in a 3-year campaign to study and discuss how violence prevents and destroys gains in development (see Van Soest, 1997).
- *The maintenance of environmental quality.* This includes the need to reverse the damage that has already been done to water, soil, and air, when possible.
- *The satisfaction of minimum world welfare standards.* Poverty contributes to environmental degradation, violence, lost creativity, and lost productivity.
- *The primacy of human dignity.* With sustainable development, human beings require basic freedoms and should not be viewed as just consumers and expendable workers (see UNDP, 2000, p. 12; 2002).
- *The retention of diversity and pluralism.* Biodiversity and cultural diversity contribute to a healthy biosphere and a healthy society.
- *The need for universal participation.* Progress toward ecological preservation cannot be made if portions of the population are excluded because they are poor, dark-skinned, female, young, old, illiterate, or bereft of material resources (see Aspen Institute, 1996; Castelloe, 1999; Chambers, 1997).

These values offer guidance to social workers at the local, regional, national, and world-building levels, and they are congruent with the values of the NASW (1996) Code of Ethics.

Social workers may find roles for themselves at all levels of sustainable development practice. At the community level, social workers will most often begin by working with residents to explore the environmental problems and resources in the bioregion (or ecological niche) in which the community is located and then assisting the community in determining how several questions will be answered. How will goals be agreed on that can sustain human development (e.g., jobs, recreation, housing, transportation, cultural and religious diversity) while respecting the limits and natural character of the region? How can social and economic development be planned so that it will not deplete the natural resources beyond the natural restorative capacities of the region?

These are not questions that can be answered for the short term, and unfortunately, U.S. and world history is replete with examples of short-term community development that have produced bad consequences in the long term. For example, irrigated farming on the Great Central Plains of the United States is rapidly depleting the region's major aquifer, the Ogallala, while the rapid population growth in the Southwest, with its demand for water and electricity, is overwhelming the capacity of even the mighty Colorado River to regenerate itself. Social workers who are aware of such historical development will be more likely to ask questions and involve a wide spectrum of views in development planning.

Sustainable development practice also examines earlier or traditional social and economic practices of people to determine the ecological sustainability of an older practice and prospects for its current practical use. An example would be the effort in Hawaii to restore native Hawaiian cultural relationships to the land and sea in programs to reduce juvenile delinquency and increase economic security for working-class families (Matsuoka & McGregor, 1994).

Case Example 1

Restoring Hawaiian Connections to a Sacred Environment

Traditional Hawaiian culture was deeply rooted in spiritual and economic connections to the land and sea. Recent community development projects to increase the employment opportunities for native Hawaiian youth and ex-felons emphasized re-educating and reconnecting them with their cultural practices and beliefs related to their natural environmental heritage. "Participants are taught Hawaiian history, exchange feelings and perspectives on being Hawaiian, and through work programs, they are able to learn ancient technologies in cultivation, fishing, and food processing" (Matsuoka & McGregor, 1994, p. 114).

Concepts and Skills for Sustainable Development Practice

Master's-level social workers should have skills in the following areas, which are important for sustainable development practice at the community level.

Democratic and participatory planning. Democratic and participatory planning is both a value and a strategic approach to economic and social development (Lusk & Hoff, 1994). Democratic approaches to developing social services and economic development projects exemplify the profession's ethical commitment to "client's socially responsible self-determination" and "informed participation" (NASW, 1996, pp. 5, 29). Successful local economic development efforts in the United States confirm the importance of participation for the practical success of these undertakings (Betancur, Bennett, & Wright, 1991; Gittell, 1990; Gunn & Gunn, 1991; Guyette, 1996). Social work students and practitioners interested in sustainable development should become well versed in the participatory methods used in the assessment of community needs and priorities (see Castelloe & Gamble, Chapter 13, this volume), as well as in motivating groups and developing environmentally friendly projects. In addition, having studied oppression, social workers understand the need to identify and facilitate the inclusion of the missing voices in the planning process. They can advocate seeking diverse perspectives from the community, especially of people of color or women and girls (Gamble & Varma, 1999; Weil et al., 1998). Social work students and practitioners can develop skills in the application of Nominal Group Technique (Delbecq, Van de Ven, & Gustafson, 1975), "cardstorming" (Gamble & Varma, 1999), popular education methods (Freire, 1970, 1998), and Participatory Rural Appraisal (Chambers, 1997), which are a few of the techniques that can bring diverse, often excluded, voices to the planning table.

Currently, there is an explosion of civic activity in all corners of the globe (Burbidge, 1998). CIVICUS, the World Alliance for Citizen Participation, documented the contours of these efforts in *Civil Society at the Millennium* (Mbogori, 1999). Their Web site, http://www.civicus.org, connects advocates of democratic and participatory planning across national boundaries.

Capacity building and strengthening social capital. Capacity building and strengthening social capital are the building blocks for social and economic development. Capacity building is the ability to increase the leadership and organizational skills of local people for the purpose of strengthening their own organizations and networking capacities (Aspen Institute, 1996; Castelloe & Watson, 1999; Gubbels & Koss, 2000). The following example demonstrates ways of building community capacity.

Case Example 2

Restoring an Inner-City Neighborhood

In Baton Rouge, the Louisiana State University, under the leadership of social work faculty members and administrators, reached out to its impoverished African American neighbors to work in a true partnership to improve the physical environment (trash removal, tree and garden plantings), the skills and education levels of residents (human capital development), the level of social networks (social capital development), and the restoration of important historical buildings in the neighborhood (Livermore & Midgley, 1998). This community-university partnership entailed significant social work leadership and skills and enacted the principles of collaboration and networking (rather than hierarchical service-delivery models) and of human development as an investment rather than a cost. It also highlights that environmental sustainability is applicable to restoring or improving urban neighborhoods, not just rural areas or natural habitats.

Social workers can help build the capacities of people to lead, plan, set priorities, analyze economic and social conditions, engage with decision makers, develop alliances, access resources, and challenge injustice and undemocratic government. In developing these abilities—especially when analyzing the social and economic status of communities—social workers have the opportunity to incorporate the principles of sustainable development outlined previously.

Social capital is defined as the norms of trust and mutual obligation among community members (Castelloe, 1999; Midgley & Livermore, 1998; Putnam, 1993). It is particularly significant to community work, as Castelloe noted, because social capital reflects "the belief among community members that other community members, and the community as a whole, are worth the struggle and effort that collective action requires" (1999, p. 5). The primary skills needed by social workers to strengthen social capital are those required for developing networks and coalitions. Social work education stresses these skills for application in the development and delivery of traditional social service programs. In sustainable development, practitioners will also need to expand the range of networks to include partnerships with environmental organizations, religious and spiritual groups, community-based economic development organizations, political advocacy groups, government-appointed sustainable development groups, and progressive community-oriented businesses.

Intersectoral planning. Intersectoral planning for sustainable development strives to involve actively all the major institutional sectors of society—government, business, labor, religion, education (e.g., public schools, universities), and civic groups (e.g., environmental protection organizations, social agencies)—in a cooperative, integrated effort to promote economic improvements that maximize human development and minimize destruction to the physical environment. Urban renewal in the 1940s and 1950s crudely attempted to improve the physical infrastructure of cities without regard to effects on the people and their social and cultural sustainability. In later decades, beginning with the War on Poverty, social planners recognized the importance of people's participation. In the past two decades, local, regional, and national battles over environmental protection versus economic development have culminated in more widespread awareness that all parties must participate and plan together if they are to succeed in their goals for community development and environmental protection (Guyette, 1996; Schnurr & Holtz, 1998).

Bioregional planning for sustainable development takes into account the natural boundaries created by river drainage systems, mountain ranges, lakes, and soil types, which are a critical force in local climate, food production, shelter construction, and mobility. Bioregions demonstrate tenacious natural patterns. Recent natural disasters (e.g., flooding in North Carolina and along the U.S.–Canadian border, and Western forest fires) have occurred because community housing and commercial districts have been located in flood plains or too near forested areas. Coupled social and economic planning can take account of both the dangers and assets of working in the physical and environmental boundaries. Ecotourism, for example, can provide the impetus for developing yet preserving vulnerable mountain or coastal areas where community members prize the natural beauty by making it economically advantageous to incorporate environmentally responsible designs for hotel and housing construction, transportation, cultural and historical preservation, waste creation and disposal, and environmental renewal of forests and wetlands. Many coastal, mountain, and island communities are struggling with these issues.

Although social workers do not necessarily have technical skills for bioregional planning, they have the skills to facilitate interpersonal and intergroup processes and to mediate interactions among diverse representatives from communities seeking to explore the boundaries and meaning of bioregionalism. In addition, they can help community leaders establish linkages with such environmental experts as sustainable agriculture teachers at the community college, "green" business leaders, or state environmental leaders in water and air quality management. They can also help communities that have begun similar development efforts to create visions for sustainable community development to network with one another.

Sustainable community indicators. The use of sustainable community indicators will be an important skill for social workers to promote and use in the next several decades (see Estes, this volume). Many communities have already begun to map the baseline quality-of-life indicators they will follow in the next several decades to measure the results of development planning. For the global view, social workers can make use of the annual *United Nations Development Report* with its country-by-country indicators of human development, poverty, and gender development. This comparative information helps communities the world over explore their relative progress toward sustainable development.

On a local level, there are guides that will help communities prioritize their vision for development with a focus on environmental, social, economic, and cultural sustainability (Hart, 1999; Henderson, 1996). One example from a local effort involved the support of three municipalities and the county government to form a citizen group that worked for 4 years to develop a local vision and plan for sustainable development. Their shared set of values, presented to the public for open comment and discussion, was outlined as follows.

Case Example 3

Orange County, North Carolina: Vision Statement for Sustainable Development

- Sustainable, renewable use of resources and environmental stewardship through joint planning, cooperation and action; towns which are friendly and accessible, centers of education, culture and civic life; places where individuals and neighborhoods thrive along with institutions, organizations, and businesses which serve their needs; rural areas which retain natural, visual and economic resources by maintaining the integrity of forests, streams, and open space through voluntary incentives, thus preserving the land's continuing potential for agriculture and other appropriate uses.

- The development of children and youth, as well as adult citizens in various phases of their lives, by providing excellent elementary and secondary education, cultural experiences, and life-long learning opportunities all of which foster intellectual, social and spiritual growth, develop marketable skills, and contribute to the fulfillment of individual potential.

- A strong commitment to the well-being of all individuals, young and old, of any race or ethnicity, and with any disability, by providing for basic physical and social needs, including those which support children and families, in an atmosphere of safety, equity, dignity, justice and economic opportunity.

- Governance that provides necessary public services efficiently, proactively establishes collaborative ties within the region and state, encourages civic participation, and is fully representative of all the county's citizens, responsive to their needs, consistent and fair, socially just in decision-making, and accountable for the promises and obligations incurred on citizens' behalf.

- A shared sense of community, civil, collaborative, vibrant, friendly, caring and both diverse and inclusive; where citizens feel responsible to and for one another; where involvement in community life is both encouraged and anticipated; where the contributions of all are welcomed and respected. (Orange County, NC, 2000)

Henderson (1996) described the need to redefine wealth and progress and to develop a new set of indicators that will capture the progress of nations and communities. Guidelines for developing such indicators are available in many forms (Daly & Cobb, 1994; Hart, 1999).

Think globally, act locally. "Think globally, act locally" is perhaps an unexamined truism in development. Most of the scientific community agrees that the Earth's temperature is warming and that human activity is the primary cause. Greenhouse gasses such as carbon dioxide and methane are at the highest levels in recorded history, raising concerns about the dependence we have on nonrenewable fossil fuels for our energy sources. For those of us living in industrialized countries, our individual and collective behavior can make a difference to the global environment.

We not only have the scientific knowledge to understand how our local behavior affects the greater atmosphere, but through the use of electronic communication, we can also understand the conditions of small villages in countries around the globe. We have the ability to connect people in the industrialized world who have resources and skills with people in the developing world who can make use of such resources (whether political advocacy or material supports) from networks around the world (see, for example, the UNDP's NetAid, http://www.netaid.org). Some groups have called this kind of activity "thinking locally, acting globally." In addition, as individual citizens network with others throughout the world, they are able to see the role that individual families, communities, and regions play in decreasing behaviors that damage the social and environmental heritage of a place (Hoff, 1998). Communities have come to see how purchasing locally grown food products can both decrease the transport and processing costs and encourage the economic development of local farmers and the sustainability of local communities.

Social justice in development and accessibility. Social and economic justice in asset development and resource accessibility is a bold goal of sustainable development. For most people, deprivation and poverty in early childhood set them on a course of being deprived of assets and resources throughout life. One of Falk's principles speaks to the "satisfaction of minimum world welfare standards" (1972, p. 298). We cannot be equal in our abilities and resources; however, most sustainable development definitions outline a need to provide basic health, education, shelter, and food to all people. Today, in the United States and throughout the world, economies are deeply flawed by increasing inequities between the very rich and the very poor. According to the UNDP:

> Nearly 1.3 billion people live on less than a dollar a day, and close to 1 billion cannot meet their basic consumption requirements. The share in global income of the richest fifth of the world's people is 74 times that of the poorest fifth. (1999, p. 22)

This is not only a moral problem, but a practical one. History and social research demonstrate the connections between a society's wealth distribution and its propensity for social conflict and violence (Hoff, 1996; Wolpin, 1986). Conflict and violence not only squander vast quantities of financial resources, but inevitably, they also contribute to cultural instability and serious threats to the physical environment. Social work has always had a moral commitment to alleviating poverty. Social work's involvement in the planning and advocacy to develop economic opportunities for disadvantaged populations can contribute to social peace and thus promote cultural and environmental sustainability.

People are investments. People are viewed as investments, not costs. In the United States and elsewhere, some economic policy proponents tend to see social welfare expenditures (for health, housing, child care, etc.) as costs that drain the economy of needed resources for production. International lending agencies, such as the International Monetary Fund, also reflect this bias; under structural adjustment programs, poor nations are frequently forced to cut back on basic social expenditures for health and education to qualify for loans. Sustainable social development practice seeks to demonstrate that societies prosper economically when basic human needs are met, including improvements in the education and skill levels of people. The story of Ganados del Valle (Pulido, 1996) clearly illustrates this process.

Case Example 4

Ganados del Valle (Flocks in the Valley): Restoring a Rural Culture

In northern New Mexico, the Tierra Wools cooperative business is an economic development project in which men and women (descendants of the first Spanish settlers in the area) work together to sustain an ancient breed of

Churro sheep, introduced by the Spanish and valued for their distinctive wool. The project has enabled local *Hispano* (descendants of original Spanish settlers) women to learn traditional weaving and modern marketing skills for wool products. Members of the cooperative are deeply committed to land preservation, recognizing its importance in sustaining both their culture and their livelihoods. This project received assistance from churches and private foundations, as well as a university-based expert on sheep. Ganados del Valle is an excellent case example of integration of cultural, economic, and environmental goals, using both traditional skills and new knowledge and technology, including business management techniques (Pulido, 1996).

Locally based sustainable development initiatives will be characterized by explicit goals to foster the achievement of full human potential for every individual, as outlined in the Orange County vision statement. Social workers only need to act on the values expressed in their Code of Ethics (NASW, 1996) to move toward recognition of and commitment to the principle that investments in people are investments in the future of any community.

Reduction of violence. There is nothing as destructive to human development and environmental protection as violence (Hoff, 1986). As described by Van Soest (1997), violence is a global affliction. It can be evidenced in threats to personal security such as deprivation or oppression; as a part of state-sanctioned violence, such as torture, police brutality, or official neglect; as war, colonization, gang warfare, ethnic discrimination, and genocide; as domestic violence, rape, child abuse, and slavery; and even as self-inflicted violence, such as suicide and substance abuse (Van Soest, 1997). Individuals or groups who seek control over others through violence can make no progress toward sustainable development. Individuals and groups who are victims of any form of violence cannot devote their full capacity and resources to development or to the protection of their environment. The very concern that deprivation of the poorest individuals often promotes environmental destruction prompted the convening of the World Commission on Environment and Development. From their work with refugees; victims of partner abuse, child abuse, poverty, alcoholism and drug abuse, and racism; and youth at risk, social workers have the extensive knowledge and experience to understand the importance of reducing violence on whatever scale it occurs. Work toward the prevention of violence should be a central aspect of work toward sustainable community development.

Conclusions

The preceding set of concepts and skills are basic for anyone working in community building and community practice. They are especially basic for social workers who will work in sustainable community practice. Social work practitioners embracing sustainability will also need to gain greater familiarity with current research on ecological concerns, such as the effects of toxic chemicals and environmental degradation on child development (Rogge, 1994, 2001) or the connection between our fossil fuel–based economy and the consequences for global warming (see, for example, Union of Concerned Scientists, 2000; NASA's [2002] Global Change Master Directory, updated daily). The precautionary principle suggests a conservative approach to use of environmental resources, until research is more conclusive about the long-term effects of any given approach (Hardy & Lloyd, 1994). However, sophisticated practitioners will also recognize that political conservatives frequently use conflicting scientific opinions as an excuse for not being environmentally conservative. Calls for more study of an issue, such as the recovery of the salmon population in the Pacific Northwest, may be a cover for inaction and refusal to move toward more sustainable economic production practice.

The opportunity for social workers to work in sustainable community development will expand in the next half-century. Citizens faced with choosing among competing values and development approaches at the community level need the assistance of skilled facilitators and mediators. The contests for aggressive development at the local level can only be mediated by bringing together a diverse group of community members to engage in civil dialogue to establish common values and a redefinition of progress that is based on sustainability. These local efforts must be matched by equally energetic activity at the national and international levels to prevent the global destruction of air and water quality and the potentially serious results of global warming. As Estes described, the work of sustainable development is "political, social, and moral in nature" (1993, p. 15). We can work at the individual, community, regional, or global levels to make progress toward sustainable development.

References

Aspen Institute. (1996). *Measuring community capacity building: A workbook-in-progress for rural communities.* Queenstown, MD: Author.

Bernard, T., & Young, J. (1997). *The ecology of hope: Communities collaborate for sustainability.* Gabriola Island, Canada: New Society.

Berry, T. (1988). *The dream of the Earth.* San Francisco: Sierra Club.

Betancur, J. J., Bennett, D. E., & Wright, P. A. (1991). Effective strategies for community economic development. In P. W. Nyden & W. Wiewel (Eds.), *Challenging uneven development: An urban agenda for the 1990s* (pp. 198–224). New Brunswick, NJ: Rutgers University Press.

Breton, M. J. (1998). *Women pioneers for the environment.* Boston: Northeastern University Press.

Bryant, B., & Mohai, P. (1992). *Race and the incidence of environmental hazards.* Boulder, CO: Westview.

Bullard, R. D. (1990). *Dumping in Dixie: Race, class and environmental quality.* Boulder, CO: Westview.

Burbidge, J. (Ed.). (1998). *Beyond prince and merchant: Citizen participation and the rise of civil society.* New York: Pact.

Carson, R. (1962). *Silent spring.* Greenwich, CT: Fawcett.

Castelloe, P. (1999). *Community change and community practice: An organic model of community practice.* Unpublished doctoral dissertation, School of Social Work, University of North Carolina at Chapel Hill.

Castelloe, P., & Watson, T. (1999). Participatory education as a community practice method: A case example from a comprehensive Head Start program. *Journal of Community Practice, 6*(1), 71–89.

Chambers, R. (1997). *Whose reality counts? Putting the first last.* London: Intermediate Technology.

Cobb, J. B., Jr. (1992). *Sustainability: Economics, ecology and justice.* Maryknoll, NY: Orbis.

Costanza, R. (1991). *Ecological economics.* New York: Columbia University Press.

Daly, H. E. (1996). *Beyond growth: The economics of sustainable development.* Boston: Beacon.

Daly, H. E., & Cobb, J. B., Jr. (1994). *For the common good: Redirecting the economy toward community, the environment, and a sustainable future* (rev. ed.). Boston: Beacon.

Delbecq, A. L., Van de Ven, A. H., & Gustafson, D. H. (1975). *Group techniques for program planning.* Glenview, IL: Scott Foresman.

Dickens, P. (1992). *Society and nature: Towards a green social theory.* Philadelphia: Temple University Press.

Earth Pulse: We leave more than footprints. (2001, July). *National Geographic, 200*(1), vii.

Estes, R. J. (1993). Toward sustainable development: From theory to praxis. *Social Development Issues, 15*(3), 1–29.

Falk, R. (1972). *This endangered planet: Prospects and proposals for human survival.* New York: Vintage.

Freire, P. (1970). *Pedagogy of the oppressed.* New York: Continuum.

Freire, P. (1998). *Teachers as cultural workers: Letters to those who dare teach.* Boulder, CO: Westview.

Gamble, D. N., & Varma, S. (1999). International women doing development work define needed skills for sustainable development. *Social Development Issues, 21*(1), 47–56.

Gittell, R. (1990). Managing the development process: Community strategies in economic revitalization. *Journal of Policy Analysis and Management, 9*(4), 507–531.

Gubbels, P., & Koss, C. (2000). *From the roots up: Strengthening organizational capacity through guided self-assessment.* Oklahoma City, OK: World Neighbors.

Gunn, C., & Gunn, H. D. (1991). *Reclaiming capital: Democratic initiatives and community development.* Ithaca, NY: Cornell University Press.

Guyette, S. (1996). *Planning for balanced development: A guide for Native American and rural communities.* Santa Fe, NM: Clear Light.

Hallman, D. G. (Ed.). (1994). *Ecotheology: Voices from south and north.* Maryknoll, NY: Orbis.

Harcourt, W. (Ed.). (1994). *Feminist perspectives on sustainable development.* London: Zed Books.

Hardy, S., & Lloyd, G. (1994). An impossible dream? Sustainable regional economic and environmental development. *Regional Studies, 28*(8), 773–780.

Hart, M. (1999). *Guide to sustainable community indicators* (2nd ed.). North Andover, MA: Hart Environmental Data.

Harvey, D. (1996). *Justice, nature, and the geography of difference.* Malden and Oxford, UK: Blackwell.

Hawken, P. (1993). *The ecology of commerce: A declaration of sustainability.* New York: Harper Business.

Hawken, P., Lovins, A., & Lovins, L. H. (1999). *Natural capitalism: Creating the next industrial revolution.* Boston: Little, Brown.

Henderson, H. (1996). *Building a win-win world: Life beyond global economic warfare.* San Francisco: Berrett-Koehler.

Hoff, M. D. (1996). Poverty, environmental decline and intergroup violence: An exploration of the linkages. In J. S. Ismael (Ed.), *International social welfare in a changing world* (pp. 167–183). Calgary, Canada: Detselig.

Hoff, M. D. (1998). The Willapa Alliance: The role of a voluntary organization in fostering regional action for sustainability. In M. D. Hoff (Ed.), *Sustainable community development: Studies in economic, environmental, and cultural revitalization* (pp. 177–192). Boca Raton, FL: CRC/Lewis.

Hoff, M. D. (2002). Knowledge for sustainable development: An insight into the effects of global warming on human cultural diversity. In *Encyclopedia of life support systems.* Available from http://www.eolss.net.

Hoff, M. D., & McNutt, J. G. (Eds.). (1994). *The global environmental crisis: Implications for social welfare and social work.* Aldershot, UK: Avebury Books/Ashgate.

Intergovernmental Panel on Climate Change. (1996). *Climate change 1995: Economic and social dimensions of climate change.* Cambridge, UK: Cambridge University Press.

Korten, D. C. (1995). *When corporations rule the world.* West Hartford, CT: Kumarian & San Francisco, CA: Berrett-Koehler.

Livermore, M., & Midgley, J. (1998). The contributions of universities to building sustainable communities: The Community University Partnership. In M. D. Hoff (Ed.), *Sustainable community development: Studies in economic, environmental, and cultural revitalization* (pp. 123–138). Boca Raton, FL: CRC/Lewis.

Lusk, M. W., & Hoff, M. D. (1994). Sustainable social development. *Social Development Issues, 16*(3), 20–31.

Lutz, M. E., & Lux, K. (1988). *Humanistic economics: The new challenge.* New York: Bootstrap Press.

Matsuoka, J. K., & McGregor, D. P. (1994). Endangered culture: Hawaiians, nature and economic development. In M. D. Hoff & J. G. McNutt (Eds.), *The global environmental crisis: Implications for social welfare and social work* (pp. 100–116). Aldershot, UK: Avebury Books/Ashgate.

Mbogori, E. (Ed.). (1999). *Civil society at the millennium.* West Hartford, CT: Kumarian.

Merchant, C. (1980). *The death of nature: Women, ecology and the scientific revolution.* New York: HarperCollins.

Merchant, C. (1992). Radical ecology: The search for a livable world. New York: Routledge.

Midgley, J. (1995). *Social development: The developmental perspective in social welfare.* Thousand Oaks, CA: Sage.

Midgley, J., &. Livermore, M. (1997). The developmental model in social work: Implications for a new century. *Journal of Social Work Education, 33*(3), 573–585.

Midgley, J., &. Livermore, M. (1998). Social capital and local economic development: Implications for community social work practice. *Journal of Community Practice, 5*(1/2), 29–40.

National Aeronautic and Space Administration. (2002). *Global Change Master Directory: A directory of Earth science information.* Retrieved July 17, 2002, from http://gcmd.gsfc.nasa.gov

National Association of Social Workers. (1996). Code of ethics, National Association of Social Workers. Washington, DC: NASW.

National Association of Social Workers. (1999). *Environmental policy: Social work speaks.* Washington, DC: NASW Press.

Nussbaum, M., & Glover, J. (Eds.) (1995). *Women, culture and development: A study of human capabilities.* New York: Oxford University Press.

Orange County, NC. (2000). *Shaping Orange County's future.* Hillsborough, NC: Orange County Commissioners.

Partridge, E. (Ed.). (1981). *Responsibilities to future generations: Environmental ethics.* Buffalo, NY: Prometheus.

Pimentel, D., Westra, L., & Noss, R. F. (2000). *Ecological integrity: Integrating environment, conservation and health.* Washington, DC: Island Press.

Pulido, L. (1996). *Environmentalism and social justice: Two Chicano struggles in the Southwest.* Tucson: University of Arizona Press.

Putnam, R. (1993). *Making democracy work: Civic traditions in modern Italy*. Princeton, NJ: Princeton University Press.

Ralston, H., III. (1986). *Philosophy gone wild: Essays in environmental ethics*. Buffalo, NY: Prometheus.

Rao, A., Stuart, R., & Kelleher, D. (1999). *Gender at work: Organizational change for equality*. West Hartford, CT: Kumarian.

Redefining progress. (n.d.). Retrieved August 7, 2002, from http://www.rprogress.org.

Rogge, M. E. (1994). Environmental injustice: Social welfare and toxic waste. In M. D. Hoff & J. G. McNutt (Eds.), *The global environmental crisis: Implications for social welfare and social work* (pp. 53–74). Aldershot, UK: Avebury Books/Ashgate.

Rogge, M. E. (2001). Children, poverty, and environmental degradation: Protecting current and future generations. *Social Development Issues, 22*(2/3), 46–53.

Rothman, J. (2001). Approaches to community intervention. In J. Rothman, J. L. Erlich, & J. E. Tropman (Eds.), *Strategies of community intervention* (6th ed., pp. 27–64). Itasca, IL: F. E. Peacock.

Sale, K. (1985). *Dwellers in the land: The bioregional vision*. San Francisco: Sierra Club.

Scherch, J. (1998). Eco-village development: A report from southern Appalachia. In M. D. Hoff (Ed.), *Sustainable community development: Studies in economic, environmental, and cultural revitalization* (pp. 85–102). Boca Raton, FL: CRC/Lewis.

Schnurr, J., & Holtz, S. (Eds.). (1998). *The cornerstone of development: Integrating environmental, social, and economic policies*. Boca Raton, FL: CRC/Lewis.

Schumacher, E. F. (1973). *Small is beautiful: A study of economics as if people mattered*. London: Blond Briggs.

Shiva, V. (1993). Colonialism and the evolution of masculinist forestry. In S. Harding (Ed.), *The "racial" economy of science: Toward a democratic future* (pp. 303–314). Bloomington: Indiana University Press.

Stoesz, D., Guzzetta, C., & Lusk, M. (1999). *International development*. Boston: Allyn & Bacon.

Swimme, B., & Berry, T. (1994). *The universe story: From the primordial flaring forth to the Ecozoic Era, a celebration of the unfolding of the cosmos*. New York: HarperCollins.

Union of Concerned Scientists. (2000). *Global warning: Early warning signs*. Retrieved July 17, 2002, from http://www.climatehotmap.org

United Nations Development Program. (1990). *Human development report*. New York: Oxford University Press.

United Nations Development Program. (1992). *Human development report*. New York: Oxford University Press.

United Nations Development Program. (1995). *Human development report*. New York: Oxford University Press.

United Nations Development Program. (1996). *Human development report*. New York: Oxford University Press.

United Nations Development Program. (1997). *Human development report*. New York: Oxford University Press.

United Nations Development Program. (1999). *Human development report*. New York: Oxford University Press.

United Nations Development Program. (2000). *Human development report*. New York: Oxford University Press.

United Nations Development Program. (2002). *Human development report*. New York: Oxford University Press.

Van Soest, D. (1997). *The global crisis of violence: Common problems, universal causes, shared solutions*. Washington, DC: NASW Press.

Wachtel, P. L. (1989). *The poverty of affluence: A psychological portrait of the American way of life*. Philadelphia: New Society.

Weil, M., & Gamble, D. N. (1995). Community practice models. In R. L. Edwards (Ed.), *Encyclopedia of social work* (19th ed., pp. 577–594). Washington, DC: NASW Press.

Weil, M., Gamble, D. N., & Williams, E. S. (1998). Women, community, and development. In J. Figueira-McDonough, F. E. Netting, & A. Nichols-Casebolt (Eds.), *The role of gender in practice knowledge: Claiming half the human experience* (pp. 241–286). New York: Garland.

Wilson, E. O. (1988). *Biodiversity*. Washington, DC: National Academy Press.

Wolpin, M. D. (1986). *Militarization, internal repression and social welfare in the Third World*. London: Croom Helm.

World Commission on Environment and Development. (1987). *Our common future*. Oxford, UK: Oxford University Press.

CHAPTER 9

The Practice of Community Organizing

Herbert J. Rubin

Irene S. Rubin

C ommunity organizing is about people coming together to fight shared problems. Organizing efforts vary from a single concerned parent going door to door to unite neighbors to fight for a needed stop sign to massive social movements. People organize to protect civil liberties, combat ethnic prejudices, battle homophobia, or preserve freedom of speech. Sometimes organizing efforts start with a limited geographic focus and gradually expand to include the broader societal conditions that created the initial problems. Other times, organizing unites people who share problems, regardless of where they live, as when people with disabilities from across the country join together to fight for equal access and fair treatment. Organizing is also motivated by economic concerns, as when workers fight a plant closing or broad coalitions of activists join together to fight for a living wage.

Organizers follow numerous models in bringing people together. Marie Weil and Dorothy Gamble (1995) listed eight approaches ranging from confrontational social movements to accommodative social planning. The approach chosen depends on its social acceptability and its match to the problem at hand (Weil, 1996). Jacqueline Mondros and Scott Wilson (1994) portrayed organizing as the work done to build social action groups that create power for ordinary people, while Mark Hanna and Buddy Robinson (1994) emphasized that organizing also involves transforming individual and collective values to build support for social justice and social equity. For us, organizing is the process of helping people understand the shared problems they face while encouraging them to join together to fight back. Organizing builds on the social linkages and networks that bring people together to create firm bonds for collective action. It creates a durable capacity to bring about change. The process of building that capacity is called *development.*

Development is the ongoing creation of personal and collective resources that enable people to fight back and take charge. Development includes building organizations that have the knowledge to help those in need, creating the bonds of trust among people that constitute community, sharing technical skills, and gaining ownership of material wealth in ways that improve the lives of those in need.

Development is about empowerment. Empowerment occurs when groups of people with a shared mission act collectively to control decisions, projects, programs, and politics that affect them as a community (Rubin & Rubin, 2001, p. 6).

The choice of strategies and tactics depends on the climate of the times. In a conservative era, organizers might emphasize small-scale lobbying, while during more progressive times, they might encourage people to engage in dramatic confrontations that challenge the status quo and threaten the powerful. Today, some activists rely on confrontations to exert pressure for racial, gender, or economic justice, while others work to establish community-controlled organizations that provide social services, housing, and economic development (Fisher, 1994, 1996; Rubin, 2000).

People are mobilized—that is, come together for action—in a number of ways, through door-knocking campaigns; by building coalitions among existing religious, social, and work groups; or through electronic contacts through the Internet. Some organizations emerge in neighborhoods after angry community members persuade their neighbors to join together to combat an immediate problem such as polluted water supplies or drug dealers. Other community organizations get under way because of the work done by professional organizers from such national networks as the Association of Community Organizations for Reform Now (ACORN), National Peoples' Action, the Industrial Areas Foundation (IAF), the Pacific Institute for Community Organizing (PICO), Direct Action Research and Training Center, or the Gamaliel Foundation. Individuals who share a belief about a specific issue may join social movement organizations that focus on poverty, racism, gender equality, sexual orientation, pollution, ethnic heritage, or a variety of other shared concerns (Freeman & Johnson, 1999; Tarrow, 1994).

Community groups pursue an array of strategies ranging from disruptive protests to accommodationist approaches. Disruptive approaches include sit-ins, picketing, boycotts, and even sabotage (Cloward & Piven, 2000). In accommodationist approaches, organizers bring together community members, government, and business to work in partnerships on shared projects (Eichler, 1995).

Historically, organizers who advocate the *social action model,* which includes confrontations and aggressive lobbying against the establishment, have disagreed with those who support the *social production* or *development model,* in which people come together to work with the establishment to set up neighborhood businesses, provide social services, and build housing (Rubin & Rubin, 2001). Increasingly, however, activists are recognizing that social action and social production approaches complement one another (Anner & Vogel, 1997). By "rowing with two oars" (Callahan, Mayer, Kris, & Ferlazzo, 1999) social action groups can pressure governments and businesses to provide the resources needed by social production organizations to improve the economic and social lot of those in need.

Organizing is learned through experiences and by hearing narratives about past successes that convey what should and can be done now. Learning has been formalized in training academies, such as the Organizer Training Center and the National Training and Information Center, which offer weekend to several-weeks-long instruction in organizing tactics. National networks such as the IAF and PICO offer extensive training followed by supervised internships for future professional organizers. In another approach, support organizations such as the Center for Community Change send out experts to mentor community groups. Basic community courses are also offered in schools of social work; some have specializations in community organization and others in organizing and development. Most programs, however, emphasize learning about community services and management of social services programs, rather than organizing for direct action.

Stages of Community Organizing and Social Mobilization

Community organizing is a process that accomplishes three linked goals:

- solving the problems that people face individually and collectively;
- building permanent, democratically controlled organizations that provide an ongoing capacity for problem solving; and
- empowering individuals and the communities or neighborhoods to which they belong.

Organizing efforts are motivated by the issues that need to be confronted. People come together to work out goals, strategies, and tactics. Goals are the desired outcomes. Strategies involve the overall approach in solving the problem, and tactics detail the specific steps to be taken, such as circulating a petition, soliciting funding, or getting a newspaper story printed about a project. The skills that organizers learn are summarized in Chart 9.1 and elaborated in the rest of this chapter (based on Rubin & Rubin, 2001).

Chart 9.1   The Skills of Community Organizing and Social Mobilization

Understanding the values of a democratic empowerment model

Learning about problems and issues

Mastering tactics of political and social mobilization

Becoming an organizer

Building and sustaining the organization

Learning the tactics of social action

Learning the tactics of social production

Seeking external support

Undertaking reflection

Each skill relies on specific techniques and background knowledge that can be learned in ways that empower individuals and expand democratic involvement. Although experts might originally teach others how to run a demonstration or set up a budget, the goal is to empower community members by helping them master such technical knowledge. Let us sketch what goes on as people master the separate skills of organizing.

Understanding the Values of a Democratic Empowerment Model

Organizing empowers individuals, expands democratic involvement, and builds the capacity to fight back, while enlarging the sense of community that people share. People organize to combat the helplessness they feel when faced with domineering businesses, government, or social prejudice. By joining with others, people empower themselves and their communities. "Empowerment is a psychological feeling that individuals have when they believe they can accomplish chosen goals; it is also political organizational strength that enables people to collectively carry out their will" (Rubin & Rubin, 2001, p. 77). People are empowered as they gain a sense of personal efficacy through accomplishing their shared goals or by being treated with respect, regardless of their race, ethnicity, gender, or sexual orientation. Empowered neighborhoods receive their fair share of public resources, and empowered organizations gain a respectful hearing from those in public office.

Empowerment begins when people begin to challenge the assumption that current beliefs must be maintained or that those who are in office or who are rich must be right, and hence must be obeyed. *Consciousness raising,* in which people share stories and discover that what happened to them is part of a larger pattern, helps challenge the assumptions that keep people passive. People learn to frame the agenda so that the oppressed and the broader society understand that wrongs have been committed and need to be rectified. Empowerment grows as people see they can succeed, and it is institutionalized through building lasting neighborhood and social change organizations that concentrate knowledge needed to battle those in power. Empowerment is further increased when community organizations are run in a democratic fashion, soliciting opinions from group members and building consensus about goals and strategies.

Learning About Problems and Issues

Individuals are aware that they are ill housed, underpaid, or discriminated against, and they recognize traffic congestion, acrid or dirty air, and racist or sexist behavior. *What they learn through organizing is that such individual problems are structurally caused and can be collectively resolved.* Collectively people work to *reframe*—create a new collective definition—of the problem that makes clear its structural nature. Such reframings communicate that those who suffer are not to blame for the difficulties they collectively face and that by working together, people can solve problems.

The mass media might argue that the homeless and the extremely poor are too lazy to work to provide their own housing. Activist groups counter this framing by showing that when community groups receive a small amount of financial assistance, this money can be combined with the volunteer labor of poor people to build new homes that house those who have contributed "sweat equity." Once housed in property they own, individuals are conscientious in repaying their mortgage debt and are willing to work together to continue to improve their neighborhoods. Blaming the victim has been reframed to demonstrating hope and possibility.

Activists keep informed on the background of issues by chatting with peers, attending national meetings of alliances, subscribing to Internet lists on social problems and solutions, and participating in educational workshops. Specialized publications help keep people up-to-date; for example, for those involved in issues of affordable housing, the magazine *Shelterforce* is a must. The Web abounds in self-help information sites, such as the material put out by the Kensington Welfare Rights Union on how the poor can learn the skills needed to organize themselves (Baptist, 1999).

Political and Social Mobilization

Mobilizing means getting people involved in social actions. More precisely, "mobilization is the process of moving personal grievances to the realm of collective, organized, social action" (Rubin & Rubin, 2001, p. 140). Mobilization efforts are guided by understanding why people do and do not join collective activities.

In general, people are slowly mobilized, with often no more than 5% of those affected joining the group. People of higher educational and socioeconomic status are more likely to become active, but poor people, especially those of color, are willing participants in actions that affect their own communities. People can be mobilized by a dramatic event—a sexist ruling by a court or the discovery of toxic waste under a park. More often, however, mobilization takes time and background work, such as the months and years of preparation that were required for the successful civil rights efforts of the 1960s (Payne, 1995).

A few principles guide social mobilization strategies. First, because people are mostly aware of problems that cause them concern, mobilization is about showing it is possible to do something about those problems. Next, successful mobilization requires a personal touch—people are more likely to become active if an organizer or their friends and neighbors approach them individually.

Third, for mobilization to last, people must gain the emotional satisfaction that comes from successful actions. A visible victory—obtaining a stop sign, building a new home, getting a politician to attend a neighborhood meeting—strengthens people's willingness to participate by showing success is possible. Membership meetings help expand the commitment to the group as people share the stories of progress and past successes and see the potential power of the group through the large number of people attending.

Other rewards for participation include the satisfaction of battling an injustice and the personal growth that comes from such involvement. Teske found that

> many activists spoke of an increased personal confidence, a new willingness to speak in public forums, a greater desire to follow public affairs, a greater intro-spectiveness, a greater attentiveness to various social ills and evils that they had previously ignored, and most generically an ability to grow as a person. (1997, p. 122)

Becoming an Organizer

Organizers are employees of the organization, carrying out the collective's will by bringing people together and doing the mundane tasks of the group. Organizers provide technical information and guidance while helping community members become empowered. Organizers encourage people to fight back, teach group members needed skills, and manage much of the routine work of running the group, such as fundraising, bill paying, and circulating agendas for meetings. In their linking roles, organizers help their group work with other social change organizations. Crucial to the role of the organizer is the ability to put forth a "change vision" that offers a message of hope and possibility to those in the group (Mondros & Wilson, 1994, pp. 19–27).

Some organizers, such as Dr. Martin Luther King, Jr., or César Chávez, become symbolic leaders, representing their organization's cause to the public. Through their oratory and their personal actions—being jailed or killed—such symbolic organizers make clear to the public the need for change. For group members, these "symbolic leaders give voice and image where there was noise; they define humiliation as a collective experience and transform that experience into political energy for change" (Rubin & Rubin, 2001, p. 131).

The work life of an organizer is not easy—the hours are long and the pay modest. Organizers need to be good at a variety of technical tasks and have an engaging personality. They need patience, because the oppressed are often afraid to fight back, and battling those with more resources can be frustrating. Organizing is more than a job; it is a kind of calling for people who are deeply troubled by pervasive injustices and feel the need to help people help themselves.

Building and Sustaining the Organization

To sustain social change efforts, activists build permanent organizations. An established organization focuses the power of large numbers of people and warns the targets that actions can be sustained. People who work for the organization develop expertise in areas ranging from lobbying to housing construction.

To provide a permanent structure, social change organizations incorporate as nonprofits, either under Title 501(c)3, which allows groups to receive charitable donations but limits their ability to lobby, or under Title 501(c)4, which allows them to lobby but not to receive tax-deductible donations. Ongoing organizations are governed by a board of directors that sets overall policies but ought to be responsive to the broader membership.

Community organizations must handle administrative and financial tasks, assign and coordinate needed work among its members, and evaluate what is being accomplished. To pay for the efforts, organizations seek out campaign funds to cover specific activities such as busing people to a demonstration, capital funds to build community facilities such as affordable homes or stores, and operating or core funds for expenses such as rent or the salaries of employees. Funds are obtained by collecting dues; running special events like bingo nights; and applying for grants from governments, foundations, churches, and charities. When community organizations ask for money from other groups, the community group needs to ensure that its agenda prevails, rather than that of the funders. To ensure that money is effectively used, organizations establish budgeting procedures (to allocate money carefully) and accounting and auditing procedures (to document how money has been spent). Community organizations need to be efficient in business matters yet still be run democratically, with overall goals set either through meetings of the membership or by a board that is dominated by community members.

Learning the Tactics of Social Action

Through action campaigns, people "define or frame a problem, document its extent, target those who can effect a solution, use direct pressures on the target and work to ensure the implementation of promised changes" (Rubin & Rubin, 2001, p. 237). Direct actions have motivated major changes in civil rights and promoted feminism, environmentalism, AIDS treatment, and policies toward the disabled, as well as diverse neighborhood issues (Freeman & Johnson, 1999). The publicity given to action campaigns frames—gives definition to—problems, showing that the problems are socially caused and can be solved by government or business. However, activists must consider ethical issues when planning action campaigns. What means are legitimate to accomplish which ends? Is full democratic discussion needed before each tactic is chosen? Is violence ever acceptable? If so, under what circumstances and what actions constitute violence?

Analyzing tactics. In working out strategies for an action campaign, groups figure out what power they have and what power the opposition is willing to use. Are prayer vigils going to be more effective than direct confrontations? Can the opposition be persuaded by presentation of the facts, or must pressure be applied before they will pay attention? To what sorts of tactics is the opposition vulnerable— economic, political, or bad publicity? Does the broader society accept the legitimacy of the grievances of the group and the tactics followed? Are campaigns about gaining redress for an immediate problem, or are they about creating broader and lasting changes in the society? How quickly can such changes be brought about? Is the social action organization able to withstand the pressure if those in power use the police or economic sanctions to fight back? Finally, even when a group appears to have won an immediate campaign, are the mechanisms in place—new laws, for instance—that ensure that the status quo will not be reinstated?

Conventional political tactics. Action campaigns may include a variety of tactics ranging from conventional political lobbying to potentially violent direct confrontations. The least aggressive tactic is to lobby individuals, agencies, or committees in government to change policies in ways desired by those in the action organization. Lobbying involves providing information to likely supporters, informing them of what constituents want, and suggesting wording of laws and regulations.

Experienced lobbyists recognize how far they can push and what issues are not worth fighting because of the low probability of success. Lobbyists work with the professional staff of government agencies and legislative committees, master the legislative process in detail, and understand the constraints politicians face. Lobbying is more likely to succeed when those in office know, from letter-writing campaigns or from mass demonstrations, that the lobbyists represent a sizable block of voters.

Community groups sometimes play a direct role in electoral politics, but such involvement can distract from the activist organization's mission. Community groups can sponsor members who serve on neighborhood and city-wide boards, but they should do so only if these boards actually have final say in financial, redevelopment, or zoning matters that affect a neighborhood. Community groups can work with other social change organizations to put referenda on the ballot or to gain community approval of specific policies, but this strategy is time-consuming and may not work if it mobilizes a powerful opposition group. Finally, people from activist organizations can run for office. Having supporters in office is helpful to community change organizations, but the effort involved in getting them elected can be immense.

Legal tactics. If lobbying fails, social change organizations may wish to use legal tactics to force concessions from a target. With legal actions, activists claim that those in power are violating their own rules, and the organization seeks court orders to force the target to change its behaviors. Litigation, however, can be expensive, is almost always time-consuming, and requires employing lawyers, rather than creating the empowering experiences in which group members take actions on their own.

Direct actions. In contrast, through a series of direct actions, members of community and social change organizations directly confront those in power, putting their own bodies on the line, seeking to persuade by inconveniencing or embarrassing the targets of a campaign. Examples of direct actions include offering teach-ins, in which many are informed about a problem; filing complaints; staging attention-getting media events, such as mock funerals, that garner media attention; holding prayer vigils; organizing marches, rallies, and demonstrations; and even engaging in various forms of sabotage. Massive marches and rallies publicize injustices and hint at the number who are willing to fight to end the problem, while economic boycotts and rent strikes hurt the target financially.

Direct actions must gain the support of, rather than alienate, the larger public, so tactics must resonate with what the public will accept. A prayer vigil or a fast can garner sympathy in campaigns to battle homelessness, hunger, or racial discrimination; massive picketing that is an acceptable response to police brutality might be totally inappropriate for a cause that might be better served by less conflictual methods.

A direct action that is not sufficiently planned and controlled can lead to riots, unnecessary arrests, and a negative image of the group. Detailed planning is required that might include finding out about the security in a building in which a sit-down demonstration will be held, ensuring access to toilets, or assigning marshals to signal when particular rows of participants are to stand and leave. Participants may need to be trained in nonviolent responses to police provocations and taught how to deal with an arrest.

In direct action campaigns, the more people who are involved, the greater the chance that the press and the target will pay attention. Consequently, many direct action campaigns are undertaken by coalitions of different organizations that come together after finding common ground. Similarly, direct actions are more effective when activists learn how to work with the mass media to ensure that the images that the activist groups want to portray are the ones presented in newspapers and on television.

Direct actions provide the lever that encourages the enemy to treat the action organization with respect and engage in negotiations. Organizers must learn how to bargain, so as not to lose in the negotiations what seemed to have been gained through direct actions.

Learning the Tactics of Social Production

Social production is an important strategy in the community organizing model, but because the tactics involved are complex and are discussed in detail elsewhere in this volume, here we only briefly describe the approach.

The social production model complements the direct action approach by enabling community members to control the gains achieved through previous action campaigns. Through social production work, community organizations provide their membership and neighborhoods with needed services and material goods or help bring about physical repair. Social production organizations undertake projects such as setting up shelters for battered women, providing day care for seniors or disabled adults and children, offering peer counseling to substance abusers, building affordable homes and apartments, or helping a neighborhood renew itself economically. Those working in social production organizations master conventional social service and business skills, including how to put together financing packages or manage property.

However, social production is not simply about building homes or opening new stores. Rather, it is about community empowerment and capacity building. A community that has stable housing is empowered through the lasting concerns of the more permanent residents. Neighborhoods that have new stores have the capacity to better socialize the young by providing job opportunities that offer alternatives to gang life.

Seeking External Support

To learn needed skills, gain economic resources, and expand their power to pressure business and government, social change organizations work with coalitions, technical assistance providers, trainers, and an array of funders. Many of these support organizations have been established by community activists who recognize the importance of teaching and empowering other groups.

Both social production and direct action organizations join activist coalitions that lobby for the cause, provide technical assistance to individual organizations, and run conferences and training sessions at which activists can learn from one another. Organizing networks such as IAF help communities set up neighborhood groups. Technical assistance and training academies such as the Center for Community Change (Washington, DC) or the National Technical Information Center (Chicago) teach the tools of street-level organizing, while organizations such as the Development Training Institute (Baltimore, MD) help those involved in community economic development work learn how to proceed. Consultants, most of whom began their careers in community work, can be hired to help with such tasks as filling out a grant application or eliminating environmental hazards from a redevelopment site. Trade associations, such as the National Congress for Community Economic Development (Washington, DC), for those who build homes and do economic development, or the National Organizers Alliance (Washington, DC), for those involved in direct action work, hold conferences and provide literature through which activists share information. Many of these organizations publish handbooks and technical documents on how to do numerous tasks, such as packaging funding from several sources or writing an effective press release.

Updates on community actions and technologies can be found electronically from comm-org (http://comm-org.utoledo.edu/mailman/listinfo/colist); by subscribing to Handsnet (http://www.handsnet.org), an information service for those in community work and the social services; or from an array of specialized lists and e-mail bulletins. The Center on Budget and Policy Priorities (http://www.cbpp.org/) keeps track of the budget proposals that can harm social programs, while activist coalitions such as the National Community Reinvestment Coalition (Washington, DC) closely monitor attempts to weaken the Community Reinvestment Act.

Support organizations help in the difficult tasks of finding the funds to pay for operating expenses and capital projects. Local churches and religious charities such as the Campaign for Human Development can provide financial support, and a handful of small foundations such as the Haymarket Foundation in Boston are willing to fund social change organizations (Ostrander, 1995). Several financial intermediaries, such as the Local Initiative Support Corporation, help package investment money from banks and corporations to provide the equity for renewal projects. Major foundations support community development and social production work and historically have been instrumental in helping groups that work for social justice causes. Foundations, however, are more likely to support projects that provide tangible outcomes—homes built or individuals placed in jobs—than they are to provide direct operating costs of a community group. Organizers study books on fundraising and proposal writing (Klein, 1996), but success is most likely to occur after an iterative process in which ideas are tested with the funders, proposals written, and, if turned down, rewritten after further talk with the funder.

Undertaking Reflection

Those involved in community action need time to question how much progress they have made and whether they have remained faithful to the values that motivated action in the first place. Immediately after a campaign or a project is finished, those involved should think about what went wrong, what went right, and what they can do better. Should different politicians be targeted the next time? Should homes be built for seniors or for larger poor families?

Organization members also need to reflect on whether the organization is staying true to its initial purposes or whether its purposes need to be changed. Has the organization become so concerned with efficiently managing apartments that it forgets that it was established to help the poor find housing? Has victory become so important that the professional organizer negotiates behind the scenes with the target, leaving out the organization members?

Reflection is vital for future successes. Often, foundations and government funders require project evaluations. Community groups set up retreats, especially for board members, to reflect on where the organization is going and why. Organizers at coalition and trade association meetings and even at training sessions often challenge each other on the meaning of what their organizations do.

Common Processes

Some common themes cut across the stages of the organizing process. First, organizations are built step by step, following a bootstrapping process. Prior successes generate the confidence, willingness, and ability to take the next step. People may be hesitant when they first join a group, but the excitement and fun of participation in collective actions increase their enthusiasm and willingness to try another activity. Furthermore, opponents are more likely to treat respectfully a group that has succeeded in the past. Reputation bootstraps.

A second cross-cutting theme is that organizing involves issue framing—forging an understanding that members, targets, and the broader public accept about why problems occur and the possibilities for their solution. Issue framing works to increase the legitimacy of the proposed solutions. As part of mobilization, activists help people frame problems so they understand that their problems are widespread and structural. By sharing narratives of success and of suffering, those in a movement create a sense of shared past and common goals. Campaigns are about framing issues so government and the broader public come to accept that something must be done and can be done.

The third cross-cutting theme is the need for empowerment. It is not only the results of campaigns which are empowering, but also the decision making and work processes in community organizations. The direction of activist groups should be set through democratic means. Decisions should be carried out in ways that reflect the egalitarian, consensual models that underlie contemporary feminism.

Finally, although organizing often begins in response to a specific problem, activists rapidly discover that problems compound and solutions overlap. The homeless are more likely than others to have medical concerns, poor neighborhoods are more likely to have higher crime rates, and high crime rates make it more expensive to open new businesses that can employ local residents (W. J. Wilson, 1996). Sometimes several problems need to be attacked simultaneously to break out of a negative cycle. Neighborhood groups might demand more resources for housing from city hall, develop the housing themselves, and work with new tenants and owners to teach them needed skills for home maintenance (Rubin, 1997).

Problems and Tensions in Organizing

Organizing confronts many problems that slow the rate of progress. The first set of issues emerges from the environment in which community groups work; the second comes from disagreements and tensions among activists themselves.

Environmental Problems Facing Community Organizations

Funders are willing to provide money for visible projects, but they see little glory in paying for routine operating expenses. This lack of core funding requires that activists spend much time soliciting small contributions or running events rather than concentrating on core problems. Some organizations, especially developmental groups, pay so much attention to the bottom line of projects they run that they forget to be responsive to their communities. Historically, this lack of money has kept down salaries in the organizing field, although the situation is improving.

Another problem occurs because community groups have to work closely with government and business. Such partnerships provide needed resources but can lead to situations in which the values of government or business displace those of community work. Similarly, the financial dependence of community groups on government and major foundations can cause them to accommodate the priorities of those with money rather than the needs of those whom they represent.

Divisive Tensions in the Community Movement

Sometimes those in the community movement spend time fighting one another rather than working as allies. An unfortunate tension exists between activists who work in social production organizations and those who spend their time in direct action work. Street-level activists accuse those involved in economic or housing development of fearing to press for fundamental change, whereas developmental activists accuse those involved in direct action of being out for the glory of the moment. Fortunately, cooperation is improving, as those engaged in protest and pressure tactics realize that without social production organizations, the gains they win at the bargaining table would be lost (Peirce & Steinbach, 1987).

Other problems in organizing are also moving toward resolution. As organizers cope with an increasingly bureaucratic and financially complicated world, a gap grows between the need to work to master technical issues and the goal of increasing member participation and empowerment. Can a group be about empowerment if its members have to develop the detailed technical expertise to understand the tax credits that help pay for affordable housing? A balance between technical knowledge and democratic involvement comes about when the group hires technicians to provide such information but sets the agenda through participatory, democratic processes. For instance, in partnering with community groups in technical projects, evaluation experts from colleges accept that their agendas will be set by those in the community groups and also that their responsibility is to teach community members how to do the work on their own (Nyden, Figer, Shibleyh, & Burrows, 1997).

Future Directions in the World of Organizing

There is no simple way of predicting what specific issues community and social change organizations will face in the future, but some patterns are beginning to emerge. First, rather than the case-by-case actions of the past, organizing will increasingly be guided by underlying ideologies. Particularly important will be the feminist emphasis on achieving consensus, as well as the value-based ideologies that support preserving neighborhoods and community support systems. Second, neighborhood organizing will increasingly blur into issue organizing. For example, community groups may join with a resurrected union movement as both recognize that work in poorer neighborhoods is about empowering newer immigrant groups and the older minority groups that now live in areas that the broader economy has left behind (Bronfenbrenner, Friedman, Hurd, Oswald, & Seeber, 1998; Dreier, 2000). Third, in inner-city neighborhoods and in the older suburbs, different ethnic groups, some quite new to the American scene, share a common territory and face similar problems, so organizing will have to take on a much more multicultural face (Anner, 1996).

Successful organizing will increasingly require networking skills. Organizers will spend relatively more time building and working in coalitions to increase the numbers that can pressure a target and provide complementary perspectives. For example, environmentalists will work with neighborhood organizations in minority communities to ensure that economic changes are both environmentally sound and benefit those from previously exploited groups (Roberts-DeGennaro, 1997). Similarly, organizers will need to learn how to work with local, state, and national support groups to gain funding and technical expertise.

Conclusions

Although less media attention is paid to community and social activism now than it was during the dramatic 1960s, social activism is thriving (Beckwith, 1998). Activists in community and social change organizations have gained skills and confidence, and an expanding knowledge base of what to do, when, and why has been made more accessible through the Internet. National coalitions are actively involved in the policy process in Washington, DC, and in many, if not all, localities, community groups are treated by government as expected and accepted players in defining social issues and development work (Imbroscio, 1997; Mott, 1997; R. Wilson, 1997).

At the same time, however, many schools of social work have been neglecting social activism as part of their mission (Specht & Courtney, 1994), creating a "challenge to the profession . . . to expand the scope and recognition of CO [community organizing], while maintaining its integrity and contribution to the philosophical core of social work practice" (Starr, Mizrahi, & Gurzinsky, 1999, p. 46). Community organizing is thriving, and schools of social work should be at the forefront of training to provide nuts-and-bolts mechanics and the historical context of activism. Social work curricula can deal with some of the most pressing upcoming issues for organizing, including how to weave together people from different ethnic and religious backgrounds (Hardina, 2000; Reisch & Lowe, 2000), how to balance the increasing professionalization of organizing and development with the need to maintain fervor for change among activists, and how to respond to the increasing ideological hostility of many in government toward those who are promoting social change.

References

Anner, J. (Ed.). (1996). *Beyond identity politics: Emerging social justice movements in communities of color.* Boston: South End.

Anner, J., & Vogel, C. (1997). Getting it together. *Neighborhood Works, 20*(2), 3.

Baptist, W. (1999). *On the poor organizing the poor: The experience of Kensington.* Available from http://www.libertynet.org/knwru/educat/orgmod2.html

Beckwith, D. (1998, September/October). Organizing today: Ten reasons to cheer! *Shelterforce, 23*(8), 37.

Bronfenbrenner, K., Friedman, S., Hurd, R., Oswald, R. A., & Seeber, R. (1998). Introduction. In K. Bronfenbrenner, S. Friedman, R. Hurd, R. A. Oswald, & R. Seeber (Eds.), *Organizing to win: New research on union strategies* (pp. 1–15). Ithaca, NY: ILR/Cornell University Press.

Callahan, S., Mayer, N., Kris, P., & Ferlazzo, L. (1999). *Rowing the boat with two oars.* Retrieved December 20, 2002, from http://comm-org.utoledo.edu/papers99/callahan.htm

Cloward, R. A., & Piven, F. F. (2000). Disruptive dissensus: People and power in the industrial age. In J. Rothman (Ed.), *Reflections on community organization* (pp. 165–193). Itasca, IL: F. E. Peacock.

Dreier, P. (2000). Renewing bonds: Why the housing movement and organized labor need each other. *Shelterforce, 22*(3), 8–11, 29.

Eichler, M. (1995). Consensus organizing: Sharing power to gain power. *National Civic Review, 84*(3), 256–261.

Fisher, R. (1994). *Let the people decide: Neighborhood organizing in America* (rev. ed.). New York: MacMillan/Twayne.

Fisher, R. (1996). Neighborhood organizing: The importance of historic context. In W. D. Keating, N. Krumholz, & P. Star (Eds.), *Revitalizing urban neighborhoods* (pp. 39–49). Lawrence: University of Kansas Press.

Freeman, J., & Johnson, V. (Eds.). (1999). *Waves of protest: Social movements since the sixties.* Lanham, MD: Rowman & Littlefield.

Hanna, M. G., & Robinson, B. (1994). *Strategies for community empowerment: Direct-action and transformative approaches to social change practice.* Lewiston, NY: Edwin Mellen.

Hardina, D. (2000). Models and tactics taught in community organization courses: Findings from a survey of practice instructors. *Journal of Community Practice, 7*(1), 5–18.

Imbroscio, D. L. (1997). *Reconstructing city politics: Alternative economic development and urban regimes.* Thousand Oaks, CA: Sage.

Klein, K. (1996). *Fundraising for social change* (3rd ed.). Berkeley, CA: Chardon.

Mondros, J. B., & Wilson, S. M. (1994). *Organizing for power and empowerment.* New York: Columbia University Press.

Mott, A. H. (1997). *Building systems of support for neighborhood change.* Washington, DC: Center for Community Change.

Nyden, P., Figer, A., Shibleyh, M., & Burrows, D. (1997). *Building community: Social science in action.* Thousand Oaks, CA: Pine Forge.

Ostrander, S. A. (1995). *Money for change: Social movement philanthropy at Haymarket People's Fund.* Philadelphia: Temple University Press.

Payne, C. M. (1995). *I've got the light of freedom: The organizing tradition and the Mississippi freedom struggle.* Berkeley: University of California Press.

Peirce, N. R., & Steinbach, C. F. (1987). *Corrective capitalism: The rise of America's community development corporations.* New York: Ford Foundation.

Reisch, M., & Lowe, J. I. (2000). "Of Means and Ends" revisited: Teaching ethical community organizing in an unethical society. *Journal of Community Practice, 7*(1), 19–38.

Roberts-DeGennaro, M. (1997). Conceptual framework of coalitions in an organizational context. In Marie Weil (Ed.), *Community practice: Models in action* (pp. 91–108). New York: Haworth Press.

Rubin, H. J. (1997). Being a conscience and a carpenter: Interpretations of the community based development model. *Journal of Community Practice, 4*(1), 57–90.

Rubin, H. J. (2000). *Renewing hope within neighborhoods of despair: The community-based development model.* Albany, NY: SUNY Press.

Rubin, H. J., & Rubin, I. S. (2001). *Community organizing and development* (3rd ed.). Boston: Allyn & Bacon.

Specht, H., & Courtney, M. E. (1994). *Unfaithful angels: How social work has abandoned its mission.* New York: Free Press.

Starr, R., Mizrahi, T., & Gurzinsky, E. (1999). Where have all the organizers gone? The career paths of community organizing social work alumni. *Journal of Community Practice, 6*(3), 23–48.

Tarrow, S. (1994). *Power in movement: Social movements, collective action and politics.* New York: Cambridge University Press.

Teske, N. (1997). *Political activists in America: The identity construction model of political participation.* Cambridge, UK: Cambridge University Press.

Weil, M. (1996). Model development in community practice: An historical perspective. *Journal of Community Practice, 3*(3/4), 5–68.

Weil, M., & Gamble, D. N. (1995). Community practice models. In R. L. Edwards (Ed.), *Encyclopedia of social work* (19th ed., pp. 577–594). Washington, DC: NASW Press.

Wilson, R. (Ed.). (1997). *Public policy and community: Activism and governance in Texas.* Austin: University of Texas Press.

Wilson, W. J. (1996). *When work disappears: The world of the new urban poor.* New York: Alfred A. Knopf.

CHAPTER 10

Which Side Are You On?

Social Work, Community Organizing, and the Labor Movement

Steve Burghardt

Michael Fabricant

An analysis of social work and its professionals' labor activism has its own contradictions and dilemmas that make its labor movement activity distinct from that of traditional manufacturing industries like garment and apparel, mining, or automotive. Perhaps the following three scenarios, each having its own distinct context and demands, capture the variability in the social work field.

The March 2000 announcement in Honolulu, Hawaii, was the culmination of a worldwide effort to end sweatshops around the world. Led by two international human rights organizations, Global Exchange and Sweatshop Watch; a legal advocacy and civil rights group; the Asian Law caucus; and UNITE!, the labor union that represents many U.S. garment workers, a coalition forced Calvin Klein, Inc.; Jones Apparel, Inc.; Liz Claiborne, Inc.; and 17 other retailers to greatly alter their labor practices in the Western Pacific Island of Saipan. "These settlements will dramatically improve the lives of thousands of garment workers on Saipan," said Jay Mazur, President of UNITE! (www.globalexchange.org). The retailers paid $8 million, promising to maintain strict employment standards, including overtime pay for overtime work; provide safe food and drinking water; and honor employees' basic human rights. Social workers could be found actively supporting this struggle from its inception.

In New York State, a historic agreement 3 years in the making was reached between the state and New York City chapters of the National Association of Social

Workers (NASW) and Local 1199 of the Service Employees International Union (SEIU), the powerful union of drug, hospital, and health care employees. Initiated and developed by Robert Schachter, executive director of the National Association of Social Workers' New York City chapter, and Dennis Rivera, the president of 1199/SEIU, the carefully crafted agreement stated the pact would last for 2 years and focus on improving benefits, licensing, and other legislative items of common interest. Some social work activists were thrilled by the alliance; others have continued to voice their reservations.

A recent study of social workers offering clinical services to downsized workers showed that when they, in turn, were faced with their own work-related threats from managed care, they tended to define clients' responses to economic contraction in terms of personal pathology but framed their own conditions in terms of "victimization" (Rosenberg, 1999). Almost none of the social workers saw collective struggle through unionization as one of their options.

These three scenarios suggest the breadth of social work mobilization, community organizing, and the labor movement. They also capture the contradictory tensions and dilemmas of social workers' labor activism in the 21st century: There is almost an inverse relationship between social worker/community organizing and labor and the increasingly degraded concrete conditions of social work practice itself. In short, the more global the cause, the higher the level of widespread social worker activism; the more focused on social work agency life, the less likely workers' response will be grounded in solidarity with labor. This chapter explores why in the social services field, "think globally, act locally" often has been turned on its head by social work practitioners.

Globalization: Finance Capital, the Rise of Social and Economic Inequality, and the Internationalization of Jacob Riis

As practitioners confronted with the cost containment demands of managed care and organizers struggling with the neoliberal agendas of both Democratic and Republican parties now recognize, the political landscape since the 1980s has greatly shifted away from the pro–welfare state policies of the past. Indeed, we now see that the globalization of the world's economies, with the ensuing rise in the power of finance capital to dominate economic and social relations, has greatly increased both economic instability and social inequality. As Prigoff (1999) pointed out, the unprecedented expansion of greater and greater wealth for a narrower and narrower sector of the economic elite has simultaneously led to the worldwide reemergence of catastrophic working conditions and economic exploitation: children as young as four forced to work in the rug factories of Pakistan; men and women in the Philippines and across the Western Pacific forced to work 14-hour days making college sweatshirts in cramped, windowless, polluted factories; and the surge in selling children into prostitution in Thailand, to name just three examples. Although some sectors of the world—the United States and Western Europe especially—reaped the benefits of worldwide economic growth throughout the late 20th century, others were far less fortunate: 840 million people are still illiterate; 1.2 billion do not have access to clean water; 160 million children under the age of 5 are malnourished; and in industrial countries alone, 100 million people live below the poverty line (Prigoff, 1999).

These grievous economic conditions were being propelled by the fluctuations in finance capital, an especially unstable form of advanced capital formation (Soros, 1998). Governments, historically slower to respond to capital movement, began attempting to enforce certain trade and labor agreements among countries so that longer-term economic interests could be maintained or stabilized. Furthermore, they attempted to improve coordination of existing economic lending institutions such as the World Bank (WB) and the International Monetary Fund (IMF) and worked to ensure that national economies would be held to the specific financial provisions of intact trade agreements such as the North American Free Trade Agreement. Attempting both to support rapid capital formation and to moderate the extremes of economic dislocation, the World Trade Organization (WTO) was formed in 1995.

Established among 134 nations to oversee international trade agreements and with the power to enforce specific rules through trade sanctions, the WTO has served as broker for the IMF and WB. It has substantially increased its own influence, as well as that of the other two institutions, over various nations' economies and their leaders' decision making (see in particular, reports on Ecuador, Brazil, and the Philippines through www.globalexchange.org, which provides up-to-date information on particular countries and the WTO). As a recent AFL-CIO report stated, "International trade negotiators have grown increasingly ambitious, and world trading rules have begun to encroach on areas considered the domain of national governments, such as environmental and public health regulations . . . seen as 'barriers to trade'" (2002, p. 1). Although examples of increasing economic inequality and deepening poverty may be found worldwide, we need look no further than within the United States itself, where, as Doug Henwood said, "It was only under the reign of Clinton and Gore that the wealth of the top 1% came to exceed that of the bottom 90%" (2000, p. 26). Prigoff noted that "nearly one in three American children will be poor at least one year of their lives before turning 16" (1999, p. 163).

This mix of increasing economic impoverishment, rapid wealth accumulation, and widening global social injustice, much of it promulgated by worldwide organizations lacking national sanction or clearly defined auspices, has been the catalyst for a burgeoning social movement involving labor, environmentalists, social workers, and community organizers from across the world.

The presence of organized labor in environmental, social justice, and economic equality movements was, if not unprecedented, extraordinary to behold over the last decade. The election of the "New Voice" reformer John Sweeney as President of the AFL-CIO heralded this change most dramatically. As the former president of the fast-growing SEIU, he joined forces with Richard Trumka of the United Mine Workers in 1995 to push through a platform based on "a worker-based movement against greed, multi-national corporations, race-baiting, and labor-baiting politicians" (as cited in Brecher & Costello, 1996, p. 33).

Such movement-influenced rhetoric served to further embolden the already-activist grassroots and rank-and-file groups such as the Teamsters for a Democratic

Union, the Washington, DC–based national community-labor coalition of Jobs for Justice, and insurgent groups such as New Directions in the Transport Workers Union and the New Caucus of the Professional Staff Congress, a college faculty–staff union in New York City that is an affiliate of the American Federation of Teachers.

This current of labor and community organizations was rising in the early 1990s at the same time two other movements were growing across the world. The first was the environmental movement. From grassroots, militant Greenpeace to planning-focused Earth Watch to the electoralist-activist Green Parties in Western Europe and (to a much smaller but no less controversial degree) the United States, environmental organizations began to see the connections between environmental degradation and globalization, with its concomitant effect on specific local populations. As the 20th century drew to an end, it became easier and easier for activists to make connections between polluted rivers, unregulated toxic waste from multinational corporations, exploitation of workers, and the decline of ravaged communities. The ensuing political and economic analyses that emerged in these movements has begun to create an organizing framework of economic, environmental, and social coherency unseen since the 1930s. The leading exemplar of this synthesis is the protean Noam Chomsky, particularly as articulated in his 1998 work, *Profit Over People: Neoliberalism and Global Order.*

Perhaps nowhere has this sophisticated and energized analysis been more apparent than in the student-led, antisweatshop campaigns directed at the apparel industry. This emergent movement's leadership recognized student economic power as the primary market for such pervasive corporations as The Gap, Tommy Hilfiger, and Calvin Klein. Students also used their advanced understanding of the Internet to create a worldwide movement of support for a campaign that joined specific prongs of labor and economic boycott with environmental and social justice activist groups. Borrowing a page from Jacob Riis, the radical reformer of the Progressive Era who used his striking photographs of poverty, malnutrition, and illness among the residents of New York City's Lower East Side to fight for major social welfare reform, student activists created some of the first World Wide Web sites that showed the shocking conditions of 4-year-olds at work weaving rugs, 11-year-old prostitutes walking the streets of Bangkok, and starving families drinking water polluted by nearby toxic factories. (There are hundreds of Web sites on globalization and inequality.[1])

The ensuing activism these efforts unleashed on a cross-section of campuses helped contribute to the historic trade and labor agreements mentioned earlier. Their efforts are an exemplar of the burgeoning worldwide struggles against the WTO itself. Perhaps best-known for the storm of protest at the Seattle WTO meetings in 2000—at which AFL-CIO leaders, environmental activists, antisweatshop organizers, community activists, and anarchists marched arm-in-arm to protest a WTO meeting—this growing movement remains a fertile arena for labor and social activism. These protests vividly spotlighted the content and consequence of WTO policies. In addition, they were powerful enough to shut down the WTO's annual meeting. Among the ranks of the protesters were social workers committed to worldwide child welfare reform (whose campaign planks are remarkably similar to those of 19th-century reformers in the United States), women's rights activists, labor organizers, and community organizers who understand the linkage between runaway, unregulated economic globalization and their own communities' decline. Social workers' influence, joining grassroots activism, legislative advocacy, and the setting of international agendas through the mechanism of the Internet, has only begun to be felt, both in the field of social work and across the shrinking borders of the new world economy.

Pushing the Sisyphean Boulder: Trade Union–Social Work Alliances Begin to Form, Old Antagonisms Continue to Grow

Although the worldwide struggles related to free trade, economic exploitation and inequality, and environmental degradation are relatively straightforward in terms of group formation and social workers' activism, alliances between the social work profession and labor movement in the United States are less so. Of course, alliances between labor and the social work profession are hardly new forms of activism. From the social work Rank and File labor movement of the 1930s (J. Fisher, 1980; R. Fisher, 1998) to the National Welfare Rights Organization–American Federation of State County and Municipal Employees coalitions of the 1960s, to the anti-cutback coalitions of the 1970s, to the Jobs for Justice statewide campaigns of the late 1980s through the 1990s, activist alliances have emerged to fight for improved rights and conditions for social workers and the community.

Most present alliances between social work professionals and labor unions have focused on legislative agendas. Other, more formalized relationships have been drawn primarily from individual agencies and subcommittees of professional chapters known for their activist stance but lacking official sanction. The historical ambivalence of the profession to unionizing itself has limited formal alliances to electoral campaigns for particular political office (Alexander, 1980). Thus, the formal pact between the New York State and City Chapters of the NASW and Local 1199 of the Drug, Hospital, and Health Care Employees Union/SEIU was rightly hailed as a "historic breakthrough" when it occurred in late 2000. For one of the few times in the profession's history, NASW created a 2-year pilot project that transcended normal (and short-term) electoral/legislative alliances (Carten & Schachter, 2000). The groups found common identity on both the legislative agenda and the effect that managed care was having on the working conditions and professional autonomy of their joint memberships. For the first time in generations, the social work profession was aligning concern about both its own conditions—and its progressive causes—with those of a labor union's membership.

That it took NASW chapters' leadership years to convince the chapters' boards to create this alliance—and then only as a pilot project—is not difficult to understand. Among comparable professionals (teachers and nurses), 25% of social workers, as opposed to 40% of nurses and 75% of high school teachers, belong to labor unions (Karger, 1988). Indeed, if there had not been the surprising precedent of the Clinical Social Work Guild's alliance with the numerically small Podiatrists Union around conditions of managed care in the health care field, it is unlikely that this formal agreement between NASW and 1199/SEIU would have occurred at all.

This progressive alliance can be traced at least in part to the toll managed care has taken on all professionals and workers throughout the physical and mental health fields over the past 20 years. Social work professionals, allied health care professionals, and physicians have felt the constraints on their approach to their work through the imposition of Diagnostic Review Groups and Uniform Case Records. Such loss of professional autonomy and deteriorating working conditions are particular symptoms of cost containment and neoliberal attempts to diminish social welfare state expenditures. It may come as little surprise that these cost containment strategies are woven into the larger dynamic of globalization and worldwide economic competition now under way (Fabricant & Burghardt, 1993).

However, as significant as this alliance has been, there is a corresponding historic and contemporary tension between unionism and the professions. Like Sisyphus, the legendary king of Corinth doomed to push a boulder to the top of a mountain in Hades only to see it roll down again and again, those who work to unionize social work professionals face what sometimes seems like eternal frustration. Both in the unions, among social workers and administrators, and between the two groups, there are concrete dynamics that have restricted these alliances to the work of legislative coalitions.

For example, in social work, the boards of local, state, and national chapters of NASW are disproportionately represented by agency executives and managers with very different interests than those of a potential union member. The very cost containment issues affecting their nonprofit and public sector agencies—shrinking budgets and higher unit-of-service demands by managed care companies and other state funders—make union demands for higher wages and reduced caseload size anathema to a pragmatic administrator. Although some executives struggle with their staff to minimize these problems, others are as bureaucratic and centralized in their response as traditional managers of the corporate sector (Fabricant & Fisher, 2002).

As social workers address broad issues of social justice and international struggles for workers' rights, their contradictory class location (Wright, 1996) creates an internal divisiveness not easily bridged. Social workers are executives handling multimillion-dollar budgets, caseworkers overloaded with too many clients to visit and too much paperwork to do, managers forced to juggle multiple programs, and clinicians frequently interested in how object relations theory enhances their diagnostic skills. The cacophony of interests combined with the varying levels of power, influence, and responsibility that exist across the ranks of the social work profession does not lend itself to the common collective response demanded by a labor union.

The mirror image of this professional dilemma lies in today's trade unionism. Although the topic is too broad to cover in this chapter, the historic break by the labor movement in the 1940s from its earlier social agenda of community mobilization and support for the unorganized has led to a narrowing of vision and interests that finds little resonance among many community activists, especially people of color long denied access to craft unions or union leadership (Boyer & Morais, 1990; Draper, 1992). Although Sweeney, Trumka, and numerous local affiliates have made significant gains over the past 10 years in re-creating a more progressive voice in the ranks of labor, the overwhelming focus of trade union leadership has been toward the narrowest of interpretations of union activity. This "look at the contract" approach is often antithetical to social work values of engagement, participation, and extended protections for clients, as well as the provision of quality services.

Labor's Sisyphean boulder in the field of social services is its unwillingness to view a practitioner's response to clients' needs in anything other than the prescribed terms of workers' contractual rights and obligations. By joining the provisions of contracts to civil service regulations, many public-sector social service unions have been a significant brake on progressive reforms that might benefit social work clients. For example, in New York City, the major child welfare reform effort undertaken by the Administration for Children's Services (ACS) Commissioner, Nicholas Scoppetta, was consistently slowed by trade unionists battling to hold on to old contractual agreements that protected even those workers who consistently failed to go into the field to visit children at risk. In another example of union efforts in direct conflict with clients' interests, local union leadership in ACS voted to oppose the Title Series Plan, which would have resulted in salary increases of 15% to 25% for its membership as supervisory staff were reorganized onto two new tiers of accountability. The agency executives then were forced to fight the union grievance for months and months, thus diminishing the momentum for other reforms. Meanwhile, the individual leaders of the union local behind the scenes were applying for the raises the plan proposed—while continuing to fight against its acceptance!

Such individual maneuvering, combined with a narrow contractual interpretation of everything from worker-client relationships to job descriptions of tasks and functions, is the kind of "business union" framework that causes many social workers to be profoundly skeptical of trade unions' openness to their labor-intensive work that often focuses on building interpersonal relations, community, and social capital. Relationships in social work between staff members and clients, community members, and agency representatives cannot be built in a rigid, formalistic manner specified by job title and prescribed hourly quotas. It is therefore highly unlikely that major movement toward either "labor solidarity" or "social capital creation" is likely to occur between the social work profession and trade union leadership in the near future. Social work managers and community builders will rightly remain skeptical of union's flexibility regarding the needs of clients and agencies. Labor union leaders will justly doubt that the social work profession's leadership embraces union members' financial interests.

These dilemmas of class and social interest make the alliances forged by NASW chapters and individual trade unions and progressive legislative coalitions all the more important to support as incubators of further experimentation. It is perhaps here that the cross-fertilization of ideas and opportunities for joint ventures in community/labor solidarity will grow, but activists must recognize the historical conditions and causes of the present impasse if movement is to occur.

Which Side Are You On?
Methodological Choices in Relationship Building
and the Creation of Social and Class Consciousness

The first section of this chapter examined the shifting relationship between global economies and the social dislocations of millions of people around the world. The second briefly explored the changing relationship and ongoing strains in the formal relationship between the social work profession and the labor movement. This is perhaps no accident; after all, the enhancement of relationship, both collective and individual, worldwide and in the community, is one of the primary reasons why we engage in organizing in the first place.

That said, one of the continuing dilemmas we face in building mass social movements capable of countering the neoliberal agenda is that the vast majority of social workers (as well as many others) do not interpret their objective conditions as warranting a change in how they relate to their work, their clients, or their communities. As more than one analyst has noted, if objective conditions were sufficient for massive struggle, the left would have won the battle for social and economic democracy a long time ago (Heilbroner, 1980).

In surveying globalization, economic and social dislocation, and the still-sporadic level of organizing and mobilization in social work and the labor movement, it is clear that the famous axiom on the development of consciousness is only partially accurate:

> In the social production of their existence, people inevitably enter into definite relations, which are independent of them, namely relations of production appropriate to a given stage in the development of their material forces of production. The totality of these relations of production constitutes the economic structure of society, the real foundation, on which arises a legal and political superstructure and to which correspond definite forms of social consciousness. The mode of production of material life conditions the general process of social, political, and intellectual life. *It is not the consciousness of people that determines their existence, but their social existence that determines their consciousness.* (Marx, 1992, p. 287, emphasis added.)

In short, people of the 21st century may not think and act like those at the dawn of the 20th—we all have so much more information to digest, so much more open sexuality to consider, so much less time to grow vegetables or bake a cake from scratch. The material conditions of our lives make that inevitable.

These material conditions do not, however, translate into the inevitability of social struggle just because the conditions of our lives are more stress-filled and social inequality is greater. Why? What happens in the profession itself that might diminish a more collectivist response? This discussion is as old as the decline of Eugene Debs's presidential campaign right before World War I in 1912, and the debate ranges over such topics as the emergence of a nonfeudal working class, the lack of an aristocracy, and the social and economic escape valve of frontier expansion available to white working-class men and their families (Gorz, 1990; Sombart, 1976). For purposes of brevity, we will look at a select few of the dynamics of professionalization in this essay.

We believe that a significant part of the answer as to why social workers do not respond collectively to the material conditions encroaching on their professional lives can be found in Rosenberg's (1999) data. His study focused on social workers treating clients who had been downsized or had lost their jobs. The vast majority—92%—categorized downsizing as "a metaphor for 'traumatic loss.'" Rosenberg pointed out that this traumatic loss metaphor, with all its pathological implications, fits in Erikson's (1994) Life Cycle framework for understanding human behavior, which is commonly taught in schools of social work. Rosenberg further suggested that "by introducing the unpredictable social or personal effects of variables such as class, race, gender, and age into the highly volatile world created by occupational restructuring and globalization, the usefulness of the life cycle categories diminishes terribly" (p. 133). Rosenberg further argued that equating the traumatic loss of aging, death, or injury with the upheavals wrought by job loss is to vitiate the social content of the experience—for worker and client alike.

In short, diagnosing or telescoping a client's condition through the life cycle alters the relationship between worker and client to that of "worker/helper–client/ victim"—that is, individualized and particularistic to the conditions, concerns, and capacities of the client and worker alone. This narrow form of diagnosis models an individuated and inherently paternalistic approach to intervention that is at the heart of Paulo Freire's methodological critique of the "banking system of education," which structures most helping professions' approach to work with the oppressed (2002; see especially Chapters 1–3).

As Freire makes clear, this dynamic fostered between worker and client is critical, because any intervention's methodology, by definition, fosters a two-way relationship—not only worker to client, but client to worker. Understanding this explains Rosenberg's (1999) finding that social workers defined their own job-related problems in terms of individualized victimization. Social workers

> interact . . . in a *helping role* . . . which [orients] them to apply trauma, loss and pathology to those who seek help . . . [so that later] when thinking of themselves as individuals or members of a professional group, they are more apt to apply depoliticized explanations when conceptualizing their personal response to downsizing. (Rosenberg, 1999, p. 129)

In short, a professional relationship based on helping and individuation with clients socially reproduces the same narrow, nonsocially based interpretation to the professionals' own conditions. Collective struggle will not be part of this kind of interpretation.

The process of social reproduction is embedded in all spheres of economic and personal life. As Gorz wrote:

> Capitalism, as a complex social formation, does not exist in some massive and static reality, but is in the constant process of renewing conditions for its continued existence through all aspects of life. The concept of social reproduction explains not only that workers have to be fed, sheltered and kept healthy if they are to return each day to the work place . . . but they need their "own" ideas and attitudes, those which ultimately maintain them within the social hierarchy and which keep them subservient to routines of daily lifer under the domination of capitalism. (Gorz, 1977, p. 108)

Those routines obviously include social work processes as well.

Rosenberg's (1999) findings illuminate a central flaw in the strengths-based, "person-in-environment" framework common to most social workers' methodological choices: Solutions to problems, for worker and client alike, are rooted solely in the strengths, abilities, and resources of the clients and workers themselves. Reproduced over time, the relationship itself stands as the problem-solving incubator for change—an internally directed focus that vitiates attention to outside, external forces that constrain and moderate individual effectiveness. Profitt's brilliant analysis (2000) of woman abuse, feminist intervention, and collective action makes a similar point at the conclusion of her description of how battered women moved from individualized, blame-riddled interpretations of their condition to a socially charged and collectivist response to abuse: Although Profitt found that survivors can and did benefit from individual counseling and therapy, they also benefited from feminist social spaces that encouraged a critical exploration and analysis of their experience, emotions, and social world. Identifying our emotions and feelings and understanding them involves putting a name to the feeling, situating it in the social world, joining feeling and behavior in a meaningful way, and noting a purposeful pattern.

Explaining how such social spaces can be created by practitioners committed to a socially charged practice, Profitt adds a cautionary note from her clinical experience:

> We . . . need to challenge the appropriation of the language of feminism and activism by mental health, professional, and recovery discourses. . . . This situation has fostered the cleaving of the personal from the political and the conflation of the personal with the political. . . . We need to develop new modes of working together with survivors that would respect them and their experience, and refuse to define them in terms of their victimization. . . . The fact that survivors can be witnesses and experts, reporters and theorists of their experience, *will alter existing subjectivities.* (Profitt, 2000, p. 93, emphasis added)

Profitt (2000) and Rosenberg (1999) both make clear that the struggle in social work for the kind of collective response needed for building broad-scale labor and social movements will require as much commitment as engagement with antisweatshop and child protection campaigns around the world. Social workers, whether organizers or clinicians, will focus as much on socially changing their daily practice as in responding to the social conditions that drive managed care. Such a task may seem daunting and even unfair, given so much else that activists seek to do in today's globalized and increasingly inequitable marketplace. However, perhaps by seeing the connections in relationship building between client and worker, worker and agency, and agency and community as more socially charged than before, we can take the needed steps that make global and local action more closely linked than ever.

Note

1. For up-to-date information on particular countries and the World Trade Organization, see www.globalexchange. On globalization and inequality, see, for example, www.globalpolicy. org, on the effect of neoliberalism on social and economic inequality; www.panix.com for analyses of wealth, income, and wage distribution; and www.globalwatch.com for graphic description of social conditions around the world.

References

AFL-CIO. (2002). *What is the WTO?* Retrieved July 22, 2002, from www.aflcio.org/globaleconomy/whatiswto.htm

Alexander, L. (1980). Professionalization and unionization: Compatible after all? *Social Work, 25*, 341–351.

Boyer, R., & Morais, H. (1990). *Labor's untold story.* New York: United Electrical Radio & Machine Workers Union.

Brecher, J., & Costello, T. (1996, April). A new labor movement in the shell of the old? *Z Magazine, 14,* 28–36.

Carten, A., & Schachter, R. (2000, September). *Open letter to members of NASW.* New York: Currents of the New York City Chapter, National Association of Social Workers.

Chomsky, N. (1998). *Profit over people: Neo-liberalism and global order.* Boston: Seven Stories.

Draper, H. (1992). *Socialism from below.* (E. Haberkern, Ed.). New York: Brill.

Erikson, E. (1994). *Identity and the life cycle.* New York: International Universities Press.

Fabricant, M., & Burghardt, S. (1993). *The welfare state crisis and the transformation of social work.* Armonk, NY: M. E. Sharpe.

Fabricant, M., & Fisher, R. (2002). *Settlements houses under siege: The struggle to sustain community organizations in New York City.* New York: Columbia University Press.

Fisher, J. (1980). *The response of social work to the Depression.* Cambridge, MA: Schenkman.

Fisher, R. (1998). *Let the people decide.* Boston: Twayne.

Freire, P. (2002). *Pedagogy of the oppressed.* New York: Seabury.

Gorz, A. (1977). *Strategy for labor.* Boston: Beacon.

Gorz, A. (1990). *Farewell to the working class.* Boston: South End.

Heilbroner, R. (1980). *Marxism: For and against.* New York: Norton.

Henwood, D. (2000, May). Wealth news. *Left Business News, 94,* 22–29.

Karger, H. (1988). *Social workers and labor unions.* Westport, CT: Greenwood.

Marx, K. (1992). *Das capital* (Vol. 1). New York: Monthly Review Press.

Prigoff, A. (1999). *Economics for social workers: Social outcomes of economic globalization with strategies for social action.* Stamford, CT: Brooks/Cole.

Profitt, N. J. (2000). Survivors of woman abuse: Compassionate fires inspire collective action for social change. *Journal of Progressive Human Services, 11*(2), 73–96.

Rosenberg, S. (1999). Social work and downsizing: Theoretical implications and strategic responses. *Journal of Sociology and Social Welfare, 26*(2), 121–136.

Sombart, W. (1976). *Why is there no socialism in the United States?* (P. M. Hocking & C. T. Husbands, Trans.). Armonk, NY: M. E. Sharpe.

Soros, G. (1998, January). Toward a global society. *Atlantic Monthly, 281,* pp. 20–24.

Wright, E. O. (1996). *Class, crisis and the state.* Boston: Verso.

CHAPTER 11

Social Planning With Communities

Theory and Practice

Marie Weil

In seeking to manage our environment and shape our futures and the future of communities, humans plan. At its simplest, planning can be interpreted as the ability to envision a future that is better than the present. These visions, however, are largely shaped within a framework of competing values, different interests, political and social ideologies, and visions of "the good" (Blackburn, 2001; Edwards, Austin, & Altpeter, 1998; Friedmann, 1979; Quinn, 1988). In community practice, one major goal is to promote and facilitate citizen participation—especially that of low-income or marginalized groups—so that citizens' views of what is good for their communities is articulated and carried out. "Citizen-initiated groups that work voluntarily on complex social problems are the heart of a democratic, pluralistic society. They are also the means through which oppressed groups, which are often marginalized by government structures, can effect positive change in their communities" (Gamble & Weil, 1995, p. 483). Engaging with community members in participatory planning for neighborhoods and services is a strategy that can build depth in community connections (social capital) and breadth in physical, economic, environmental, and social neighborhood improvements.

This chapter focuses on a form of planning that has its roots in the settlement movement and that in new forms is experiencing a worldwide resurgence in the 21st century (Mayadas, Watts, & Elliott, 1997). Although several approaches to planning in communities have been used, what is needed now is a combination of economic, social, and physical planning at the community level as well as planning for needed services, community amenities, and facilities that promote community interaction and empowerment. Most critically needed are methods of carrying out planning with communities through a strongly participatory process to promote social and economic development and create neighborhood supports that can improve quality of life.

Fisher and Karger (1997) have documented the increasing segregation by income in housing in the United States, as illustrated by the contrasts among struggling working-class neighborhoods, under-resourced inner city areas, and the increase in gated communities as sites for middle- and upper-income housing. Two decades of studies have documented the increase in persistent poverty in the United States (see Padilla & Sherraden, this volume), disinvestment in inner-city communities (Halpern, 1995), and the economic decline in rural communities. Carlton-LaNey, Murty, and Morris (Chapter 22, this volume), Halpern (1995), Wilson (1987), and others have documented the damage to people caused by poverty in urban and rural areas and the disadvantages and dangers of living in very low-income areas.

However, there are telling examples of low-income communities that have reversed this downward spiral and reclaimed community structures, institutions, and facilities; and created opportunities for interaction and recreation to build or rebuild competent communities (Chaskin, 2001; Chaskin, Brown, Venkatesh, & Vidal, 2001; Fellin, 2001; Figueira-McDonough, 2001; Halpern, 1995; Medoff & Sklar, 1994), reversing the effects of decline.

Given the pressures on American communities, whether from the loss of jobs and places of employment or other vicissitudes, the time seems critical for community practitioners to reinvest in community building and to work with members of communities to promote positive change, interconnections among people, development of human and social capital, and creation of supportive environments.

Planning with communities is an approach that can increase the chances of reviving a sense of neighborhood as well as promoting community building, physical improvements, and economic development. This approach to community revitalization focuses on mutual work with members of communities. While planning is an initial and central focus, methods of both community organizing and development are employed. Planning provides the guidance for all three methods; successful organizing can bring people together and build political influence. Community development methods are used throughout the implementation of a neighborhood plan, and its results can in part be measured by the quality of the plan and the planning process. The organizing rubric is to encourage activities and processes to increase participation in planning and change. Midgley and Sherraden (2000), Noponen (2001, 2002), and others have discussed aspects of this focus as operating from a developmentalist perspective—and particularly for social work, focusing not just on the creation and operation of services, but also on opportunities for skills and economic development. This perspective seeks to create ongoing processes of positive community change that can build infrastructure and support opportunities for children, youth, and adults.

Early Development of Planning With Communities

Two major branches of planning within social work have existed from earliest professional development to the present (Betten & Austin, 1990; Weil & Gamble, 1995).

Both branches have rich literatures and specialized practice strategies. The Charity Organization Societies were highly involved in the planning and rationalization of services to fulfill goals related to both charity and social control (Betten & Austin, 1990; Gurteen, 1894). The Settlement Movement focused much more intensively on grassroots approaches, with many settlements engaged in neighborhood planning and community assessments, and some also engaged in surveys of public health problems as well as environmental planning for neighborhood improvement (Davis, 1971; Deegan, 1988; *Hull-House Maps and Papers*, 1895). Settlements also promoted the development of community-based services and citizens' organizations and action groups. In the early 1920s, a planning and organizing effort, the Cincinnati Social Unit Experiment, sought to establish participatory democracy in a large and complex urban community. The idea behind this social development project was to build supportive community units block by block. Planners and engaged residents hoped over time to expand the block-level development strategy to a larger scale for broad-based neighborhood improvement (Gurin, 1970).

Over the past half-century, scholars have presented a range of approaches to planning—from elitist to participatory. In the 1950s, Murray Ross articulated a very participatory model and in fact viewed larger or more centralized social planning as useful for social welfare and program development, but not as a direct community practice approach (Ross, 1955, 1958). Ross sharply separated planning done for neighborhoods or communities by governments or professional experts from efforts undertaken with communities and saw the "with" process as an essential component of community planning practice. He specified planning and development methods for work with community groups that focused primarily on developing local leadership and building strongly participatory processes—efforts that might now be called "community driven."

Scope of Planning With Communities

Throughout the literature on community practice, planning is described as a method in itself and also as a process that is integral to most community practice activities—in organizing, in community development and social change activities, and as a component of program design. Within social work, planning is typically viewed in four ways:

1. as broad-based community planning, typically including federated fundraising as carried out by United Ways and Planning Councils (see Brilliant, Chapter 12, this volume);

2. as sectorial planning, which focuses on planning services for particular populations such as for the aged or for children with disabilities (see Cross & Friesen, Chapter 24, and also Scheyett & Drinnin, Chapter 23, this volume);

3. as efforts to accomplish physical or infrastructure change in neighborhoods and regions, such as building new schools, creating a new water supply, and so forth; or

4. as neighborhood or community planning that is carried forward through participatory processes in which residents are leaders and direction setters for plan design and implementation, while planners provide consultation, technical support, and facilitation.

This chapter examines participatory planning with communities and provides four examples: an inner-city revitalization project, a small town's planning for service development, a country-wide Ethiopian planning process for youth-led AIDS prevention programs, and a rural Appalachian planning and community development project.

With the development of social planning—especially its evolution in the profession of social work—a greater concern for the needs and life opportunities of the poor and oppressed has obtained than in larger-scale city and regional planning. As social work developed, especially in its grassroots aspects, central questions with regard to planning have been and remain "Who plans for whom?" and "Who benefits and who suffers from public policies and decisions?" (Drake, 2001). These questions ground the rationale for planning with communities. When decisions are made centrally, low-income communities typically lose—suffering negative consequences of freeways that cut through and destroy business districts or divide ethnic communities, and experiencing loss of economic base, toxic waste, and other major physical and environmental problems that more powerful communities are able to fend off (Hall, 1988). In many instances, these governmental or corporate plans operate as environmental racism (see Bankhead & Erlich, Chapter 3, this volume; Hall, 1988). All too often, the "greater good" signals a major loss for poor and marginalized communities and neighborhoods.

Community-led planning can help to reverse these negative impacts and, over time, build both social and political power in communities. In this way, participatory community planning is one measure of the engagement of citizens in a democratic society. In a global analysis of social change, Zakaria (2003) commented:

> We live in a democratic age. . . . From its Greek root, "democracy" means "the rule of the people." And everywhere we are witnessing the shift of power downward. I call this "democratization" even though it goes far beyond politics, because the process is similar: hierarchies are breaking down, closed systems are opening up, and pressures from the masses are now the primary engine of social change. Democracy has gone from being a form of government to a way of life. (pp. 13–14)

Given the press for increased democratic participation in many parts of the world and the challenges that communities face as the effects of the global economy increase, participatory planning can be an antidote, acting to preserve human and social capital in marginalized communities and promoting a sustainable economic base to build civil society and create a "new localism" better prepared to be proactive in rapidly changing times (Figueira-McDonough, 2001).

In this book, *planning with communities* is defined as *the processes of social, economic, and physical planning engaged in by citizens and community practitioners to design services, community infrastructure, and neighborhood revitalization plans that are appropriate to given communities—urban or rural.* Local planning, therefore, can focus on service design to meet needs of specific populations or to build an appropriate service and support system in neighborhoods, or on broader-based community revitalization, taking into account community functions, infrastructure, institutions, environment, and quality of life. Many community development corporations (CDCs) engage in physical and social planning in communities—typically focused on housing, with differential attention also to creation of new community services and infrastructure—from day care services for children and seniors, to planning for housing and physical environment improvement, to development of cultural institutions, as is evident in CDCs such as Bethel New Life in Chicago and Chicanos por la Causa in Phoenix (National Congress for Community Economic Development, 1990). Comprehensive community initiatives (CCIs) are broader-based efforts to integrate this process, combining social, organizational, institutional, and physical development foci—developing services, housing, parks and recreation, and centers for community interaction; increasing public safety; and promoting economic development and community governance (Brisson, 2003; Halpern, 1995; Medoff & Sklar, 1994; see also Mulroy, Nelson, & Gour, Chapter 25, this volume).

Roles and Skills for Engagement in Community-based Planning

Although planners focused on community-level work may come from a variety of professional disciplines or may rise through the ranks in grassroots projects, the distinctions for social work community practice arise from social work's values, ethical principles, and strong commitment to plan with rather than for people in communities.

In this context, community practitioners engaged in planning will first be involved in establishing a relationship of trust with members of a community and with exploration of roles in the planning process as well as goals. Ross (1967) articulated several principles for this form of community work. In contrast with those who see planning primarily as research, setting priorities, and the production of a planning document, Ross held that planning "represents the whole act from the stirring of consciousness about a problem to the action taken to resolve that problem" (1958, p. 136). Planning processes and methods of work with community members must fit the specific context and work toward resolution of a particular problem or set of issues in a specific milieu and also initiate action to implement the proposed solutions. Within this perspective, planning that is community led has also been described as *participatory* or *action planning* (see Castelloe & Gamble, Chapter 13, this volume).

Planners need interpersonal and facilitation skills along with technical and analytic skills to work with community members on establishing the planning process and carrying out specific efforts (Brager & Specht, 1973; Ecklein & Lauffer, 1972). Although a city planner's role may most often be that of the technical expert, a community practitioner working with members of a community to plan for neighborhood or service improvement must first of all have excellent skills in facilitation—in bringing people together and developing a process through which they can lay out their ideas and transform them into a working plan (Gamble & Weil, 1995). In this situation then, skills in relationship building, interpreting and reframing ideas, and facilitating discussions, meetings, and tasks are primary requisites. Facilitation is indeed the central task in participatory planning.

Planners also need good skills in writing, strong skills in methods for conducting participatory needs and strengths assessments, and research on community infrastructure and social conditions such as poverty (see Chow & Crowe, Chapter 33, this volume). It is increasingly important to use mapping not only through resident engagement in making maps, photographs, and renderings, but also employing census data and geographic information system methods to map infrastructure, services, transportation, and other community variables. Planners also need skills in budgeting and proposal writing, and increasingly in fundraising and marketing skills—all of which the planner committed to work with communities will teach and coach residents to use as needed. Planners also greatly need political skills to work not only with community groups but also with the range of nonprofit and governmental organizations with which they and neighborhood committees will need to engage and negotiate agreements. Indeed, because of the complexity of tasks called for in planning with communities, planners need competence in almost all the skills for community practice presented in the *Handbook* Introduction.

The desire to plan within a community typically arises from dissatisfaction or concern about neighborhood conditions or problems, or lack of needed services, opportunities, or facilities. For community members to invest time and energy to develop a plan and find means to carry it forward, there must be sufficient concern for change to maintain momentum in action. Planning takes time, as does implementation, and a community-based planner will need to invest in leadership training to build community capacity and carry interest forward so that community members can direct different aspects of the process. Because planning and implementation involve an extended time frame, small gains—such as the clearing of a vacant lot—should be celebrated (Medoff & Sklar, 1994; Melaville & Blank, 1993). Overall, the planner needs skills in communication, research and data analysis, problem solving, and mediating to work with core leaders, community members, and community organizations to maintain commitment, carry out tasks, assess progress, and maintain morale during planning and project implementation.

Recent Evolution of Planning With Communities

In 1965, Stumpf presented a wide-ranging article on community planning and development considering the era following World War II up until the 1960s. He viewed community-based planning as on the rise and as greatly needed. He said, "Community planning is based on research and is the process by which citizens strive to achieve consensus about a desirable environment in which to live and then to move toward providing it" (Stumpf, 1965, pp. 192). This statement is still quite useful, as it emphasizes the importance of assessment and documentation of community conditions, and collection of information to assist in decision making as well as the critical process of consensus building necessary for community-led planning and development. Planning is most frequently described through a set of logical steps that guide those engaged from their initial identification of concern to outlines of how to achieve desired goals. The degree of focus on citizen participation and citizen leadership is often apparent through the selection of steps. The degree of focus on community-based participatory planning has shifted several times in the ensuing years in response to citizen action (mobilization), policy changes, and shifts in resources.

Community planning and development (Stumpf, 1965) received increased attention and expanded rapidly in the 1960s; there was much change in community planning and development in response to new needs, opportunities, and settings for practice. In 1963, the National Association of Social Workers Board of Directors changed the name of the field from "community welfare planning" to "community planning and development," a move which Stumpf said increased focus on "broader approaches and uses of social work to effect community changes beyond the technical scope of social welfare services and problems. Thus social action-oriented community planning and development is the emerging pervasive attitude of this field of social work" (1965, p. 190). According to Stumpf, by the mid-1960s, new forms of community planning and development included the following components:

> the human components of physical planning, urban renewal, adequate housing, the social and economic development of lesser developed communities; improvement of interracial and intercultural relationships and integration; the development of social and employment opportunities for vulnerable groupings; development of natural resources for human purposes; the improvement of community educational resources for the general population and training programs for specific groupings; the development of social correctives and rehabilitative resources for the diseased, disabled, delinquent, disadvantaged, or demoralized; and other programs of significance to human well-being and social advance. (p. 191)

Community-Based Planning: Steps and Processes

Participatory planning, like other planning strategies, is typically described as being composed of a set of steps to specify and effect desired changes. Stumpf (1965, p. 191) proposed the following steps in community planning and development:

1. Defining and describing current social conditions or problems

2. Formulating and "adopting higher goals and standards of social well-being" for the next level of social development in a community

3. "Developing community and organizational policies and strategies" that translate into operational stages, designated programs, and development or identification of auspices

(Continued)

(Continued)

4. Concerted action to develop needed resources (human and material)—development of a program (and administration)

5. "Assessing and re-assessing the program and its consequences in the community and cultural context," followed by modification, dissolution, or other change

6. Developing community leaders "and officials," both voluntary and professional—through participation in community problem solving—for social change and social advancement

Stumpf (1965, p. 197) held that "social values and conscious goals are the primary guides to the whole process of community planning and development" underlining the value base and approaches to work needed in community-based planning.

In recent years, there has been a resurgence in social planning with communities, although in the United States, there has been less funding from the federal government and more funding through foundations and through entrepreneurial efforts of CDCs. Through review of more recent literature and Web sites, it becomes abundantly clear that participatory community planning is increasing throughout the world. Acceptance and use of Freire's popular education approach has increased worldwide, along with participatory appraisal methods to increase the ability of people with low or no literacy to actively engage in planning and implementation processes (see Castelloe & Gamble Chapter 13, and Pennell, Noponen, & Weil, Chapter 34, this volume). This growing application of participatory planning methodology signals a need to consider the progression of work, the basic steps, and the means to ensure that participation is active and real rather than a form of tokenism.

Planning for neighborhood or community change with residents involves several basic activities (Gamble & Weil, 1995; Kretzmann & McKnight, 1993; Ross, 1967). These stages are not strictly linear. They will overlap and be recursive, relying on reflection, action, reflection, and further action—that is, on *praxis.*

As Table 11.1 indicates, planning with communities involves a multiple focus on processes, tasks, and stages of work with community members to build solid processes of interaction and widening circles of participation to carry out the assessment, decision making, and implementation of desired changes. The planner needs to employ both technical skills and political savvy.

In contrast to Stumpf and Ross, a number of scholars writing about planning in the 1970s—including Brager and Specht (1973), Gurin (1970), Kahn (1969), and Perlman (1971)—have described planning as a more elitist process primarily relying on the technical expertise and judgment of the planner and formal community leaders. These writers viewed planning as operating within a purely rational process. Indeed, rationality is viewed as the central criterion for the work. They correctly identified the complex technical skills needed for effective planning; however, this strand of planning placed little emphasis on working with neighborhood residents. As Brager and Specht (1973) explained, major tension can arise between values of expert planning and participation. If expertise resides only with the planner, the

Table 11.1   Processes and Stages in Planning With Communities

Processes	Stages
Continuous Processes of Relationship Building	Establishing credibility with community groups; building connections across groups
Continuous Work to Strengthen Community Connections	Facilitating relationships among community members, organizations and institutions; developing bonding social capital and determining needs for task groups and committees
Continuous Process of Leadership Development	Identifying current, emerging and nascent leaders; providing coaching, training and external connections
Preparing Residents for Engagement in Strengths/Needs Assessments and Community Research Processes	Identification of concerns and priorities; training, coaching, and implementation of community and asset mapping, community analysis methods, and determination of ongoing research needs with diverse groups
Negotiating and Consensus Building Within Community—Processes repeated with new stages of planning and development	Engaging residents in environmental scanning; use of focus groups and meetings to update central concerns and priorities; coaching in decision-making and conflict resolution processes
Collaborative Planning; Setting Priorities and Stages of Action	Compiling research and community information; presenting findings to groups and engaging groups and residents in planning process, priorities, decisions, and actions
Writing Community Development Plan and Implementing Plan in Stages— Later re-visioning and rewriting as needed	Dissemination and review of plan; implementation of priorities in social, physical, economic, environmental, and political change strategies
Building Horizontal and Vertical Linkages to Assist in Implementation; Building Political and Social Influence	Strengthening bonding social capital and building bridging social capital to accomplish plan; rehearsal and use of advocacy and action strategies
Continued Implementation and Monitoring of Plan	Garnering resources, technical expertise, and increasing neighborhood engagement in implementation; training in monitoring; feedback to community
Continuing Revitalization, and Development of Sustainable Community—Social, Environmental, and Economic	Continued leadership development; building human and social capital and strategies for sustainable community development

risk of elitism and removal from community concerns is high. However, Ecklein and Lauffer (1972), after intensive case studies of work with community-based planners, sought to reclaim the importance of process with community residents. Use of logical processes is of course a major component of planning—making issues and decision processes clear. In contrast to more elitist approaches, Ecklein and Lauffer and later community-based planners also focused on use of Delphi techniques and other participatory means that can be used to maintain a level playing field, ensure that all voices are heard, and build consensus for planning and neighborhood improvement.

There is need for greater focus on this kind of planning to revitalize and renew infrastructure for neighborhoods that have been largely abandoned to build social and human capital and engage in economic development, including microfinance programs and CDCs. Larger-scale efforts possible in CCIs not only can make physical and housing improvements, but also can work toward environmental and economic sustainability for communities within the current context of globalization and increasingly multicultural communities (see Gamble & Hoff, Chapter 8, this volume). The pressures of the global economy, along with political and economic pressures, illustrate the need for setting longer sights in community-based planning and the need to consider the interaction of environments and people—the connections of physical and social issues. Current problems are such that finding ways to reclaim and rebuild community and to work toward sustainability of environments, people, and economies is an essential issue.

Planning With Communities for Positive Change

Approaches to planning with communities relate to Rothman's (1968, 1979) model of locality development, his 2001 refinement (Rothman, 2001) of a mixed type of "planning/development," Weil and Gamble's model of social and economic development (see Weil & Gamble, Chapter 6, this volume), and the developmentalist perspective (Midgley & Livermore, Chapter 7, this volume). These models all are grounded in direct work with community members and a focus on planning as the precursor and concomitant guide for social and economic development. These models are not simply academic conceptions, but are evidenced in much past and current community planning and development efforts (Rothman, 2001; Rothman, Erlich, & Tropman, 2001; Weil & Gamble, 1995).

Given the changing contexts of rural and urban communities in the 21st century, there is a great need to refine and test a range of strategies that can improve both the physical conditions for living and working and the opportunities for positive civic and social engagement among residents. This chapter urges the combination of these strategies through a model of participatory planning for social and economic development that can strengthen civil society at the local level and increase community influence on external forces.

Much of this planning work calls for increased attention to leadership development in communities and an increased focus on mutual learning (between professionals and residents). Most particularly, specific work on coaching, mutual learning, teaching community assessment, community research approaches, and program evaluation methods is needed. Joint work by community members and practitioners is also needed to broaden and deepen citizen participation to (a) increase local skills, (b) improve neighborhood connections, and (c) strengthen civil society. Recently, there have been solid advances in community research methodology, continued development of knowledge, and increased recognition of exemplary communities that have successfully carried forward efforts for revitalization (for example, the Dudley Street Neighborhood Initiative and the Bethel New Life Community Development Corporation). These initiatives provide knowledge, new methods, and viable examples for positive planning and implementation of community change that is resident led. In such efforts, professionals have worked mutually with residents and have provided support and as needed provided facilitation and coaching in technical and change process skills. Current needs and the strengths of developing methodologies call for community practitioners to re-engage seriously, seek support, and work with communities to carry forward such change. Although there is currently decreased federal emphasis on support for community building, that can change. Over time, Friedmann (1962/1992), Khinduka (1971), Lauffer (1978), Mayadas and Elliott (1997), Midgley and Sherraden (2000), Ross (1955, 1967), Stumpf (1965), and many others have contributed careful thought to these kinds of efforts. More recently, work such as that by Castelloe (1999), Chaskin (2001), Checkoway (1995), Figueira-McDonough (2001), and Noponen (2002), among others, have provided useful guidance for community-based planning and change.

Planning and implementing community change with residents can combat negative forces affecting communities: cuts in state and local funding for human services, decreasing federal investment in communities, the dismantling of the federal safety net, disinvestment in low-income communities, and a backlash against the poor (Weil, 1997). Resource development and increasing local influence present major challenges; however, many CDCs have been able to build funding even with negative economic conditions. There is increasing recognition of the centrality of community practice to effect positive change in the face of combined negative forces (Ewalt, 1997; Figueira-McDonough, 2001; Naperstak & Dooley, 1997). Castelloe (1999) has made a significant contribution to the recent literature in developing an integrated model of community change.

Change is defined by Castelloe (1997, p. 1) as "the process by which the social, economic, political, or physical characteristics of communities are altered over time, whether for the benefit or harm of its people and environment." His model is particularly useful because it depicts a range of positive factors that can help to maintain or revitalize a community as well as negative factors that in combination are a recipe for decline. Castelloe's integrated model is constructed from analyses of rural practice studies and of two explanatory theories of community change constructed by Temkin and Rohe (1996, 1997): (1) a synthetic model, and (2) a model for development of social capital. Their initial model (1996) combined political-economic forces; the actions of local institutional actors, who have differing levels of influence over resources and services; and the "social fabric" of the neighborhood. In creating a synthesis of these factors, they argued that community members might or might not be socially cohesive and that the institutional actors could either support or work against the interests of neighborhood groups, and that the tensions and interactions between these two group processes affect the direction of neighborhood change.

A range of scholars including Chaskin (2001), Portes (1998), and Putnam (2002) now identify the development of social and human capital and community capacity as essential elements of community health or competence. The concept of social capital itself is elaborated in the literatures on economic development, social work community practice, and city and regional planning (Brisson, 2003). All three fields see the construction of social capital as an essential component of neighborhood-based development. This approach, unlike much earlier planning literature, is strengths based—recognizing and engaging connections among neighbors to build community capacity. *Human capital*—the development of skills, knowledge, and capacities—in combination with *social capital*—connections within and external to a neighborhood—can assist individuals and families in moving off the welfare rolls and out of poverty. Friedmann (1992) described the actions needed to move households out of poverty as the creation and use of paths to bases of social power, such as education or employment, which are likely to be located outside a very low-income neighborhood. This conceptualization makes explicit connections between personal development and group development within and across neighborhoods to increase connections, strengthen local bonding, and bridge to resources and people who can assist in creation of opportunities (Brisson, 2003; Friedmann, 1992; Portes, 1998; Putnam, 2002). Friedmann (1992) views participation of the state in development as a central responsibility of government to its more vulnerable citizens.

In the current economic and political climate, building trust in disadvantaged communities can be difficult; likewise, with political disinvestment in low-wealth communities and greater emphasis on taking American enterprise off-shore for cheaper labor, the likelihood of obtaining federal support for community investment is presently limited. However, countervailing forces offer approaches that can still be carried out despite these considerable risks. A number of nationally focused foundations—the Kellogg, Ford, Rockefeller, and Annie E. Casey Foundations, to name a few—recently have engaged in major efforts to strengthen institutions and opportunities in low-income communities. State-focused foundations, others that support development work in rural areas, and indeed smaller community foundations have also increased their focus and investment in integrated efforts to support positive community change. Foundations, of course, cannot take on the full-scale costs for revitalization of American communities—but they can help to make change, provide resources, and provide models for change processes that can be supported in other ways as well.

Figueira-McDonough (2001) describes the need for a "new localism" and a focus on building civil society as the central issue that can promote community revitalization. Her concept of new localism focuses on development within and by community members, as does much of the literature on positive community change drawn from examples in the developing world (Hokenstad & Midgley, 1997; Mayadas et al., 1997; Noponen, 2003; Ramanathan & Link, 1999; M. Wilson & Whitmore, 2000; among others). The understanding and knowledge of positive effects created by building social and human capital and focusing on a developmentalist perspective are increasing.

Temkin and Rohe's (1997) model for development of social capital in the inner cities of large metropolitan areas focuses on the political and economic forces that affect resources, the social structure, and the employment base of a community, as well as the social capital that already exists. Temkin and Rohe defined social capital as being composed of the combination of institutional infrastructure and the sociocultural milieu of the community—connections, interactions, patterns of relationships, neighborhood identity, and connections external to the community. Sociocultural connections also include recreation and amenities, cultural linkages and traditions, and perceived opportunities (Temkin & Rohe, 1997). The community infrastructure connotes "the level and quality of the organizational ability of the neighborhood" (Temkin & Rohe, 1997, p. 10). In their major quantitative study of neighborhoods in Pittsburgh, Temkin and Rohe's findings indicate that "neighborhoods with relatively large amounts of social capital are less likely to decline when other factors are held constant" (1997, p. 26). These neighborhoods had strong community-based organizations able to carry forward two important functions: They had the strength and support to act on behalf of residents, and they had earned respect from institutional actors within and external to their communities (Temkin & Rohe, 1997, pp. 21–26). The revitalization of the Dudley Street neighborhood in Boston and the examples that follow demonstrate the power of positive change through participatory planning.

Real-Life Stories: Examples of Participatory Change

Dudley Street Neighborhood Initiative

Dudley Street is a multicultural Boston neighborhood with history of high levels of poverty and neighborhood deterioration. The story of the Dudley Street Neighborhood Initiative (DSNI) is clearly recounted in *Streets of Hope: The Fall and Rise of an Urban Neighborhood* (Medoff & Sklar, 1994). The neighborhood was plagued with illegal waste dumping, arson perpetrated by slumlords in empty and occupied housing, drug traffic/substance abuse, and hundreds of abandoned cars. While a number of service agencies worked well with the neighborhood and several religious congregations were concerned about neighborhood issues, there had not been for years the kind of social cohesion and neighborhood mobilization to counter these serious problems. The Riley Foundation, seeking to promote better conditions, held meetings with representatives of about thirty community agencies to discuss possibilities for neighborhood revitalization in 1984. The agencies and Riley representatives developed such a plan and then called a community meeting. The meeting was large and residents were understandably unappreciative to have outsiders presume to plan for them; the plan was rejected in part because neighbors had not been part of the process (Medoff & Sklar, 1994).

With careful facilitation and willingness to work together on both sides, a collaborative was formed that included residents, businesspeople, agency staff, and staff from religious organizations. A new effort was set in motion that involved residents in the planning process, and the DSNI was born. Their governing board included representatives from two CDCs, representatives of the diverse ethnic groups in the neighborhood—African American, Hispanic, Cape Verdean, and White—service agency staff, and religious and business organizations. With Riley funding, DSNI was able to hire staff. Many residents were involved in a survey of neighborhood issues. After considerable work and pressure on the city, DSNI was able to get the abandoned cars towed, get illegal dumps and illegal trash transfer sites closed, and obtain new street lights and eventually get a rail stop to downtown Boston. Success in these engagements brought more and more residents into the revitalization work—building both bonding and bridging social capital.

In 1987, DSNI completed its plan for the area, *The Dudley Street Neighborhood Initiative Revitalization Plan: A Comprehensive Community Controlled Strategy,* with the intention of creating an urban village with good housing, shops, recreation, and improved quality of life for residents. The plan included the following 13 major strategies.

Summary of DSNI Master Plan

Development. Creation of an entity "to plan, finance, market and manage development projects."

Financing. Pursuit of both public and private financing. Establishment of a land trust. Development of alternative ownership through cooperatives and sweat equity.

Antidisplacement measures. Information and assistance to residents to stay in the neighborhood.

Qualification for financing and subsidized rental. Community action to curtail speculation.

Marketing research approach. Use of focus groups to determine community priorities.

Community review. "Increased local control of human service program priorities and resource allocations" and promotion of collaboration.

"The Force." Promotion of "pride dignity, energy and self help." Mobilization of volunteers, communicators, and role models in efforts to fight crime and drugs and to encourage job development and other projects.

Strengthening racial, ethnic, and cultural identity and diversity. Assistance to Cape Verdean community for human services and encouragement of interagency collaboration regarding diversity.

Child care. Establishment of a neighborhood registry for providers and consumers. Advocacy for additional child care services and youth programs.

Recreation and athletics (R&A). Establishment of a resident planning committee for R&A. Development of a master plan for R&A to present to city Department of Parks and Recreation.

Orchard Park planning process. Assistance to Tenants Association to fund and develop a comprehensive plan.

Employment and training advocacy. Inventory residents' employment needs, aspirations, and skills. Identify support services and tap existing programs.

Earning/learning project. "Work with public and private agencies to develop a comprehensive program of individual training"—providing child care and other appropriate support services.

Neighborhood-based business development and training. Work with government, agencies, and business schools to "provide entrepreneurial training and support" to residents. (from Medoff & Sklar, 1994, pp. 109–110)

> DSNI continues its work with considerable evidence of neighborhood improvement in regard to housing and neighborhood amenities. The central aspects of the master plan have not been changed, however, as is expected in any community development project, it has often taken longer to complete projects than was initially thought. DSNI's first executive director, Peter Medoff, said, "Deep, grounded community development takes time. . . . You have to have patience and you have to have faith in the people who live in the neighborhood" (Boston Foundation, 1992, p. 3).

As has been noted elsewhere in this volume (Carlton-LaNey, Murty, & Morris, Chapter 22), rural communities typically have received less attention in the practice literature. However, Castelloe (1999) identified three practice models that offer direction for revitalization, preservation, and planning with rural communities. The first model was developed by MDC, the second is a grassroots rural Appalachian model documented by Helen Lewis (1999), and the third is the Rural Economic Policy Program of the Aspen Institute (1996). A long-established nonprofit focused on rural development, MDC (1991) connects the ascendancy of the global economy, increased competition in production, technological advances, the decline of manufacturing and industrial production in the United States, and the rise of a service economy as structural changes that have been ruinous in many rural communities, particularly in the South. Given these major structural changes, MDC's report concludes that focus needs to move from "smokestack chasing" industrial planning and development to locally based community planning and development. Their recommended building blocks to stabilize rural communities are

1. local business development;

2. workforce development—from shifts in public education curricula to retraining for adults;

3. sound infrastructure—water, roads, transportation, and so forth;

4. strengthening social infrastructure, such as child care facilities, cultural and recreational opportunities, health care, and housing;

5. strengthening the culture for civic decision making; and

6. increasing focus on preservation of physical and social heritage. (MDC, 1991)

Helen Lewis (1999) of the Highlander Center in Newmarket, Tennessee, added interesting elements for planning to revitalize rural communities. Social capital is an important aspect of her model for positive community change; however, she emphasized the importance of women and the major role that women's community-based organizations have in rebuilding rural communities. She held that women tend to emphasize a holistic approach to development that, in addition to standard components, includes education, culture, creativity, and a positive focus on individual dignity as well as broad-based participation. In ways reminiscent of Freire, Lewis also stressed the importance of economic literacy and people's abilities to analyze their experience and economic context to assist in planning and implementing local development. The following vignette presents part of the planning and development work done by the group Federation of Communities in Service (FOCIS) with communities in Appalachia.

FOCIS: Rural Community Planning and Development

FOCIS was initially formed by a group of Catholic nuns who, after working with Appalachian people in the mountains and in Appalachian ghettos of Chicago and Cincinnati, left the Church and formed an organization that for more than 40 years has done planning and community development with residents in rural communities in the region. Over that period of time, they have worked with members of communities to plan and develop health clinics, arts programs, cooperatives, legal services, educational programs, and CDCs (Lewis & Appleby, 2003). Their work has been committed to social justice, and their philosophy is expressed in the title of their book *It Comes From the People* (Hinsdale, Lewis, & Waller, 1995), which denotes their popular education and empowerment approaches to planning and development. When FOCIS was formed, many Appalachian communities—which for generations had relied on mining, farming, or manufacturing—had lost their economic base. As an early response, FOCIS members worked with local women organizers to plan adult education programs. The first programs taught literacy and prepared students for the GED. Later, collaborative education plans were worked out with the outreach programs of local community colleges. These women organizers were not only planners but also the first students for a number of these programs. The old depots, abandoned schools, and company stores gradually became community learning centers. These centers

> provided a place for community discussions, a space where residents could come together to analyze their region's problems and plan and strategize ways of improving the quality of life in the community. Since many of the students were women, the centers provided a women's support service along with leadership development training. (Lewis & Appleby, 2003, p. 162)

As the economic decline worsened, unemployment skyrocketed. Many young people left the mountains, and job opportunities were greatly needed. FOCIS members joined with citizens' groups to work for feasible economic alternatives. As community members developed skills through learning center programs and, equally importantly, "gained confidence to try to rebuild and revitalize their communities." They planned and created "new approaches to economic development, concentrating particularly on ways to develop human capital, services to meet the needs of families in the community, and home-grown industries" (Lewis & Appleby, 2003, p. 178). As work progressed, community leaders and FOCIS members planned and developed a range of CDCs in the region. The CDCs helped to provide infrastructure, jobs in planning and development, community services, housing, and a sewing factory, among other projects. As their work progressed, FOCIS and community members recognized the success of their service and educational programs. However, as they experienced continuing difficultly in accessing capital for the needed level of economic development, they began to challenge development policies and funding priorities.

> Although they did not change the economic system, they made a difference in the quality of life in the community: houses were repaired and built, water systems were developed, health care and education were improved, recreation programs were started, some home-grown businesses provided jobs, and community spirit was revived. (Lewis & Appleby, 2003, p. 178)

Guidance for further developing local participatory planning and development has been provided by the Rural Economic Policy Program of the Aspen Institute (1996). To expand community capacity, it recommends (a) major work to expand citizen participation, (b) enlarging the leadership base, (c) building individual skills (human capital), (d) creating a shared vision of community change, (e) developing a strategic plan for development, (f) finding ways to move forward with progressive steps, (g) strengthening community organizations and community institutions, and (h) finding more efficient ways to use available resources (Aspen Institute, 1996). Castelloe (1999) pointed out that these steps are intended to expand local entrepreneurship along with community stewardship to promote sustainability.

This chapter has noted a number of current contextual factors that may well have deleterious effects on urban areas, towns, or rural communities. Castelloe (1999) identified four factors that he saw as potentially producing negative effects on communities—two from outside the community that can propel negative change: (a) the global economy and (b) broad-scale sociocultural prejudices engrained in national policies; and two that can eat away community cohesion from the inside: (c) local institutional discrimination and (d) exclusion from local decision-making processes.

The global economy can cause loss of industries and produce large-scale unemployment. On a societal level, sociocultural prejudices and stereotypes about ethnic or racial groups or prejudice against the poor (Fraser & Gordon, 1994; Mead, 1994; Schram, 1995) can engender intergroup problems or exacerbate disparagement of low-income families by encouraging the public to view them as lazy or unwilling to work. The national policy change from Aid to Families with Dependent Children to the more punitive current policy of Temporary Assistance for Needy Families, Castelloe held, can be viewed as an example of this negative effect of external sociocultural stereotyping (1999).

Within a community, institutionalized discrimination can be very damaging to outgroups. For example, remaining institutional discrimination against African Americans, particularly in the South, can be recognized as a holdover from the long period of legalized segregation (and historically as a legacy of the oppression and denial of human rights during slavery). Exclusion of groups from full civic participation and particularly from local decision-making processes produces a range of unhealthy conditions, and in extreme form, such as during the apartheid regime in South Africa, propels social unrest and social movements to right unjust political structures (Oberschall, 1993; Tilly, 1978, 1998; Weil & Gamble, 1995). Even in much less severe form, exclusion of some citizens from the polity is a negative force in any community (Castelloe, 1999).

The four social forces named previously, and a number of others, can effect severely negative changes in a community. Castelloe identified six factors that form the basis of a community's infrastructure: physical, economic, educational, social, civic, and organizational (1999). The specific combinations of positive and negative internal and external forces within a community affect both social ties and infrastructure and form the context in which a community's capacity (Chaskin et al., 2001; Fellin, 2001; Ross, 1958) and social capital are located—whether those "stores" of such capital are low, moderate, or high. The strength or weakness of social capital and community competence will significantly shape a community's responses to internal and external threats.

Three potential outcomes are predictable given the status of infrastructure and threats to any given community (Castelloe, 1999):

1. If a community has high social capital and community capacity, it is likely to be able to meet external challenges and exercise collective efficacy for positive community change.

2. If a community has moderate social capital and community competence, it has the potential to respond to internal and external threats.

3. If a community has low competency and low social capital, community deterioriation is likely to result from external and internal threats.

In the first condition, the community is likely to have collective efficacy and be able to mobilize and plan for community action, act to strengthen horizontal and vertical linkages to aid in improving community infrastructure, and preserve social and cultural heritage that over time can lead to strengthening ties. In the third instance, low community competency and low social capital leave a community much more vulnerable to internal and external threats. Social capital and community competency are components of collective efficacy (Bandura, 1997), and without this sense of shared efficacy, community deterioration over time is the most likely, but not inevitable outcome. Effective community building occurs that can support planning and action and also build collective efficacy.

In the second or intermediate situation, popular education (see Gamble & Castelloe, this volume), empowerment research (see Pennell et al., Chapter 34, this volume), and strategies for planning with communities and community development (see Rubin & Sherraden, Chapter 26, this volume) can be employed to build collective efficacy and develop skills, organization, and action to greatly increase the likelihood that positive social and economic community development—that also preserves culture and heritage—can prevail. Even from the low social capital and competency example, positive outcomes are also possible if precursors to effective community planning and action are enacted. An adapted and abbreviated version of Castelloe's model illustrates this process (see Figure 11.1).

The precursors to community action ground planning with communities in popular education tactics to assist community members in analyzing their community—scrutinizing the factors affecting it physically, socially, and economically. The following

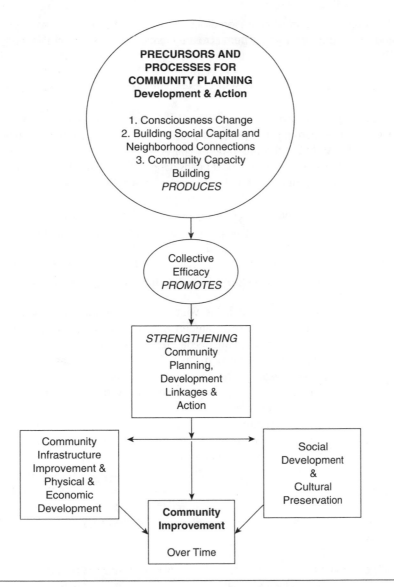

Figure 11.1   Precursors and Processes for Community Planning

Source: Adapted from Castelloe, 1999.

case example of youth engagement in nationwide HIV/AIDS education in Ethiopia provides an interesting example of development of social capital, consciousness change, and community capacity building that has many ripple effects.

Ethiopian Youth: Planning
for HIV/AIDS Prevention Education

A recent report from Ethiopia provides heartening news that the rate of HIV prevalence is dropping among pregnant teenagers (see http://www. globalhealth.org/reports/report.php3?id=88). This positive change has followed the development and implementation of an educational intervention plan designed and carried out by 51 youth from across the nation following intensive training. The National Ministry of Health adopted participatory learning and action (PLA) methods in an effort to be more effective in HIV/AIDS prevention and to increase understanding among young men and women regarding sexual and reproductive health.

Building on the work of Paulo Freire (1970), youth from across the country engaged in a learning and planning process. Following their training related to HIV/AIDS and PLA, the young people participated in planning an assessment of HIV/AIDS prevention educational needs. One exercise was "body mapping," with each participant illustrating their knowledge of anatomy and human reproductive systems. In a culture that discourages discussion of sexual functioning, the exercise made it possible for young women and men to talk more freely and address issues about sexuality and HIV/AIDS. One young man attested "[Before the training,] I was totally afraid and ashamed to talk about sex in my prevention activities. I don't know how I have been doing HIV prevention without being able to discuss openly sexual practices and the risks they entail" (*Ethiopian Youths*, n.d.).

Following their own training, the youth leaders designed and then "conducted participatory assessments among youth and adult stakeholders in both rural and urban settings nationwide" (*Ethiopian Youths*, n.d.) in a workshop format employing the body mapping and other exercises to heighten awareness and assess learning needs among youth and local HIV prevention program staff. The same strategies were then employed in a nationwide campaign built from local experiences.

After conducting assessments, the youth leaders learned to analyze their data employing written summaries, photo journals, and poster presentations. Although they received training in analysis from adult leaders, the youth completed the analysis themselves. They presented findings in workshops for Ministry staff, who were highly responsive and approved continued planning. The youth leaders were able to validate the earlier findings through regional consultations with a broader representation of youth from across the country.

> They brought their results to the first National Youth Consultation on Sexual and Reproductive Health and HIV/AIDS in Addis Ababa, Ethiopia. They developed their national youth charter and action plan at the Consultation, outlining specific recommendations to the Ethiopian government on creating a sustainable environment conducive to sexual and reproductive health. (*Ethiopian Youths*, n.d.)

Information from these various sources, as well as their own experience in conducting HIV prevention, were used to plan further training. "Since community appreciation for the true value of the data collection is key to successful participatory research, the training resulted not only in youths realizing their individual benefit, but also in positive changes experienced by their families and communities" (*Ethiopian Youths*, n.d.).

As illustrated in this example, assessments, analyses, and discussions build collective understanding, and as analysis proceeds to planning, the process helps members to develop a vision for community that will encompass development of human capital (skills and abilities) and social capital (positive connections among community members). In addition, engagement with significant people or organizations external to the community can open doors to new expertise and resources. The development of community capacity is also an essential element for positive change. Castelloe conceptualized *community capacity* as constituted by the Aspen Institute's building blocks: broad participation, leadership building, skills development, vision for community, a strategic agenda, measurable progress, stronger community organizations, and better resource utilization. The process of organization building "refers to the development and support of grassroots organizations that are accountable and responsive to community members" (Castelloe, 1999, p. 11). The development of a specialized program to serve people living with HIV/AIDS in small towns in western North Carolina provides a telling example of this kind of organization building and community planning.

The Hospice Program and People Living With HIV

This example was presented by a master's in social work (MSW) student who had worked out an excellent solution to a complex service problem in a western North Carolina town. Kevin Branch had been a member of the staff of a local hospice (which was the only hospice in a three-county area) in western North Carolina since he received his bachelor's in social work degree. After entering a part-time MSW program, he continued to work with Hospice as his field placement. When he had first started to work at Hospice, he had been aware of a number of people being referred who were dying of AIDS. In earlier years, it had not been uncommon for young gay men from rural western North Carolina to move to larger cities for work and partly to avoid the stigma evident in their home communities. Years later, following the epidemic-level progression of HIV, a considerable number of these men had "come home to die," and for many of them, to find reconciliation with their families—although not necessarily with their communities. The Hospice program began to provide services for a number of these men who had chosen to die at home with their families and for some who were hospitalized.

Several years later, staff found that health clinics and other service providers in surrounding counties were continuing to refer everyone with HIV/AIDS to Hospice. However, these new clients were not dying of AIDS; due to new medications and improvement in treatment, they were living with HIV/AIDS. It rather quickly became clear to Kevin that Hospice services—focused on helping people have a good death—were not really appropriate for these HIV/AIDS survivors. He began to talk with the men who had been referred regarding their real needs for support and services, documented their responses, and proceeded to meet with other human service providers, citizens' groups, and hospital and health care leaders about the good news of much better survival rates and the service needs that the men had reported for themselves and their families. Slowly, a coalition began to develop that included members who were living with HIV/AIDS, family members, physicians and other health care providers, heads of citizens groups and civic organizations, and representatives from a number of human service agencies.

The group undertook efforts to further identify people living with HIV/AIDS in the town and surrounding areas and did brief service assessments with them. Because other people with HIV/AIDS were conducting the interviews, potential respondents were not fearful about sharing their concerns. This assessment process and interviews with health providers revealed a much larger population of persons living with HIV/AIDS than had been referred to Hospice, and the informal coalition recognized that they had documented a major unmet need for support, services, and care. After widening their circle of concerned citizens and professionals, the group asked for a meeting with city and county councils to discuss this need; they also approached small community foundations to seek support for development of appropriate services. Rather unexpectedly, several councils showed more positive concern than had been anticipated, and although some were opposed to any public involvement in the issue, the positive responses began to reveal that the toll of AIDS deaths had already affected many families in the area.

Kevin and the coalition group were asked by three council groups to develop a specific plan documenting need and designing appropriate services. In this planning process, they again sought information and counsel from the community of HIV/AIDS survivors and their families, from a larger number of health care providers, and from civic leaders. The plan was completed with a full report of the needs assessment, program and service design, and budget for 4 years of operation of an HIV/AIDS support and service program that would work with people living with HIV/AIDS to provide needed services, handle referrals, and provide support groups for survivors and family members. Over the 3-year period that Kevin was in the MSW program, he and members of the coalition were able to obtain funding from three of the five local governmental councils and two small foundations. Kevin and another Hospice staff member became the director and program manager of the new nonprofit, Western North Carolina Action, and began to implement the program with the help of an advisory board, and a number of community volunteers. In the third year of operation, the new organization was recognized by the regional United Way and gained more sustainable funding.

New Localism, Participatory Planning and Thoughts for the Future

The heart of planning with communities is encompassed in the processes of working through Castelloe's precursors to community improvement with residents. These processes will likely be present in both community building activities and in community development efforts. The stages of planning, reassessment, and replanning indicate that the processes and praxis of planning are at the center of these efforts.

Development of resources for social and community development and securing resources and expertise from internal and external resources can set in motion a longer-term process to move community members from poverty to economic sustainability. Connecting community members with each other through horizontal linkages and using vertical linkages to increase access to bases of social power, such as education or job opportunities, can build capacity and aid in initiating economic development programs and diverse educational opportunities (Friedmann, 1992).

The risks discussed by Brager and Specht in *Community Organizing* (1973) bear reconsideration in light of the current context of practice. They noted that historically, although the programs of the New Deal had "aided the stable working class . . . they had failed to cope with the impact of major social problems of poverty, dependency, discrimination, and unemployment on many population groups" (Brager & Specht, 1973, p. 10). Likewise, the major push for urban redevelopment beginning in the 1940s produced unanticipated consequences—particularly the creation of larger-scale neighborhoods that were engulfed in poverty.

Maximum feasible participation was the clarion call of the antipoverty programs of the 1960s and 1970s; however, the Model Cities program (Halpern, 1995) was the triumph of mayors seeking to reassert municipal (and their own) power over planning and community investment processes. Subsequent federal administrations have not pressed such far-reaching programs related to community revitalization and certainly have not as strongly promoted greater citizen participation as did the philosophy and efforts of the War on Poverty.

More recent studies of poverty-stricken neighborhoods have documented the disinvestment of government, and authors have written more frequently about a "permanent" underclass (Halpern, 1995; W. J. Wilson, 1987). Certainly the problems Brager and Specht (1973) documented have not disappeared—some, indeed, seem more entrenched. However, there are also newer approaches to social planning with communities that offer promise for longer-term improvement in quality of life and community infrastructure in lower-wealth urban areas, towns, and rural communities.

Certainly municipal power holds sway, and there still are likely to be tensions between official expertise and broad-based participation; however, approaches to planning now also operate on the basis of investment in human capital, social capital, and development of community capacity (Chaskin et al., 2001). In some ways, these terms may be more capitalist-friendly versions of older concepts, but they resonate and receive increasing attention in a range of disciplines and professions—city and regional planning, economic development, urban studies, public policy and public affairs, as well as in social work community practice (Brisson, 2003). These concepts and strategies, especially as played out in the work of CDCs and CCIs, also do seem to make sense to governmental bodies, progressive business leaders, and other policy and community decision makers. Approaches based on assessment and utilization of community assets (Kretzmann & McKnight, 1993) and social investment based on asset-building approaches (Midgley & Sherraden, 2000) can also garner larger professional, governmental, and public appeal. Although some have criticized assets development as being overly "individualistic," this strategy does not exclude more community- and cooperative-based approaches operating conjointly (Association for Community Organization and Social Administration, 1998). As Friedmann (1992) described, the means of moving households out of absolute poverty requires connections to bases of social power in and external to their communities. Kretzmann and McKnight (1993), Portes (1998), and others emphasize the assets of communities and individuals and how they can be marshaled to create bonds and build opportunities. Gun and Gun (1991) held that true development occurs only in combination with efforts to broaden the practices of democracy, and like Friedmann (1992), they saw a necessary role for the state in this development process. Figueira-McDonough (2001) argues for the possibility of local regulations from stronger communities being able to limit corporate exploitation. Furthermore, she posits:

> As the nation state declines, the local community becomes the focus of hope for collective power to maintain everyday life. The potential strengths of communities as important units in the democratization of economic strategy derives from the evidence that the economic and political development of communities is closely interwoven. (p. 166)

Figueira-McDonough argues that community activism did not die with the demise of the War on Poverty. Rather, agreeing with Flacks (1995) and Anner (1996), she states that this pessimistic view is more the result of poor reporting than of actual decline in communities' efforts to win a larger voice in policies and decisions affecting their future (Figueira-McDonough, 2001). Community organizing initiatives, she notes, "reinforce the importance of democratic involvement for economically vulnerable communities and the potential of this involvement for generating political energy" (p. 166). The key to such combined planning and development lies in finding and maintaining the ability to obtain "external resources while maintaining local control over their use" (Figueira-McDonough, 2001, p. 166). Along with presenting sophisticated models for assessing communities to ascertain appropriate approaches for local development, she argues for and presents examples of synergy in the creation and cooperation of private, local, and governmental partnerships for planning and development. The new localism that Figueira-McDonough (2001) argues for does not assume self-sufficiency in communities, rather, it recognizes the importance of interdependence and cooperation within and between communities. Although CDCs offer considerable opportunity for economic development, they can become problematic and separated from the community if they do not attend to social development, continued community interaction, and community norms and level of cohesion (Matsuoka, 1997; Twelvetrees, 1989). The Comprehensive Community Revitalization Program (CCRP) of the South Bronx presents a strong and continuing model of multi-community collaboration to provide not only safe housing but also intensive work to address serious problems—such as drug abuse and health care—with strategies that include local government and planners working cooperatively and mutually with the CCRP. In the late 1990s, the CCRP had already taken on at least 12 projects in physical planning to improve quality of life (Schorr, 1997). Local CDCs have also continued housing and economic development projects, and taken on a range of collaborative social support projects including development of Family Support Centers, expansion of Head Start programs, creating locally sponsored welfare-to-work training, established home-based literacy and education programs for preschool children—which are often also of significant help to parents—and creation of domestic abuse support groups (Schorr, 1997). It is both interesting and important to take notice of the services and supports actually wanted by residents as compared to those services often presumed by governmental or nonprofit programs to be needed in low-income communities.

Strategies for planning with communities can be drawn from earlier analyses by Ecklein and Lauffer (1972), Lauffer (1978), Friedmann (1992), Kramer and Specht (1975), Ross (1967), and Stumpf (1965), and from more recent works by Figueira-McDonough (2001), Kretzmann and McKnight (1993), Rothman (2001), Rothman et al. (2001), Aspen Institute (1996), Castelloe (1999), Chaskin et al. (2001), Checkoway (1995), and Holmberg (1992), and can be adapted considering local contexts and needs. Strategies can usefully be built on the seminal guidance of Ross (1967, 1955), who strongly emphasized planning with rather than for communities. Castelloe's (1999) proposal to combine efforts to develop social capital and community competence to construct and enlarge collective efficacy for community revitalization can also be combined with Lauffer's earlier recommendations for community planning (1978). Lauffer supported the position of the community social work planner as an advocate for the community and stressed the importance of citizen participation in planning processes. Although almost all texts on planning emphasize a rational process with specific and logical steps from problem identification through evaluation of efforts, planning processes are equally if not more dependent on development and maintenance of relationships and good communication—with community groups, with agencies, and with governmental bodies.

Technical expertise (Kahn, 1969) is typically seen as a central characteristic of the planner's role. However, in planning with communities, the need and expectation is for the community practitioner not only to have a wide range of technical skills, but equally, to bear responsibility to teach and coach community residents in the understanding and use of assessment; planning and evaluation tools; community research methods; and negotiating skills for use with a range of organizations including funders, governmental bodies, human service organizations, and other community groups. Process and task skills, and relationship as well as technical skills, are equally needed for the complex work that community practitioners do— if they are to take up the important challenges to: (a) work with communities to plan for strengthening community social and physical infrastructure, (b) engage in mutual work and learning with community members, (c) develop supportive services, (d) establish sustainable social and economic development programs, and (e) promote strong and broad participation to develop resources and improve the quality of local community life.

References

Anner, J. (1996). Introduction. In J. Anner (Ed.), *Beyond identity politics: Emerging social justice movements in communities* (pp. 5–13). Boston: South End Press.

Aspen Institute. (1996). *Measuring community capacity building: A workbook in progress for rural communities.* Washington, DC: Aspen Institute.

Association for Community Organization and Social Administration, Membership Meeting— Discussion of assets-based strategies. (1998, February). ACOSA Symposium held in conjunction with Council on Social Work Education Annual Program Meeting, Washington DC.

Bandura, A. (1997). *Self-efficacy: The exercise of control.* New York: W.H. Freeman.

Betten, N., & Austin, M. (Eds.). (1990). *The roots of community organization, 1917–1939.* Philadelphia: Temple University Press.

Blackburn, S. (2001). *Being good: A short introduction to ethics.* London, UK: Oxford University Press.

Boston Foundation. (1992, Summer). *Building the Dudley Street Neighborhood.* Boston Foundation Report, pp. 1–3.

Brager, G., & Specht, H. (1973). *Community organizing.* New York: Columbia University Press.

Brisson, D. (2003). *Neighborhood comprehensive community initiatives and social capital: How they work together for low-income households.* Unpublished paper, School of Social Work, University of North Carolina, Chapel Hill.

Castelloe, P. (1999). Community change: An integrated model. In P. Castelloe, *Community change and community practice: An organic model of community practice.* Unpublished doctoral dissertation, School of Social Work, University of North Carolina at Chapel Hill.

Chaskin, R. J. (2001). Building community capacity. A definitional framework and case studies from a comprehensive community initiative. *Urban Affairs Review, 36*(3), 291–323.

Chaskin, R. J., Brown, P., Venkatesh, S., & Vidal, A. (2001). *Building community capacity.* New York: Aldine.

Checkoway, B. (1995). Two types of planning in neighborhoods. In J. Rothman, J. L. Erlich, & J. E. Tropman (Eds.), *Strategies of community intervention* (5th ed., pp. 314–326). Itasca, IL: F.E. Peacock.

Davis, A. F. (1971). Settlements: History. In R. Morris (Ed.), *Encyclopedia of social work* (16th ed., pp. 1175–1180). New York: NASW.

Deegan, M. J. (1988). *Jane Addams and the men of the Chicago School, 1892–1918.* New Brunswick, NJ: Transaction Books.

Drake, R. F. (2001). *The principles of social policy.* New York: Palgrave Macmillan.

Dudley Street Neighborhood Initiative Revitalization Plan: A Comprehensive Community Controlled Strategy. (1987, September). DAC International.

Ecklein, J., & Lauffer, A. A. (1972). *Community organizers and social planners.* New York: John Wiley & Sons.

Edwards, R. L., Austin, D. M., & Altpeter, M. A. (1998). Managing effectively in an environment of competing values. In R. L. Edwards, J. A. Yankey, & M. A. Altpeter (Eds.), *Skills for effective management of nonprofit organizations* (pp. 5–21). Washington, DC: NASW Press.

Ethiopian youths participate in HIV/AIDS policy. (n.d.). Global Health Council. Retrieved August 5, 2003, from http:www.globalhealth.org.reports/report.php3?id=88.

Ewalt, P. L. (1997). Social work in an era of diminishing federal responsibility: Setting the practice, policy and research agenda. In P. L. Ewalt, E. M. Freeman, S. A. Kirk, & D. L. Poole (Eds.), *Social policy: Reform, research and practice* (pp. 1–7). Washington, DC: NASW Press.

Fellin, P. A. (2001). *The community and the social worker* (3rd ed.). Itasca, IL: F.E. Peacock.

Figueira-McDonough, J. (2001). *Community analysis and praxis.* Philadelphia: Brunner-Routledge.

Fisher, R., & Karger, H. J. (1997). *Social work and community in a private world: Getting out in public.* New York: Longman.

Flacks, R. (1995). Think globally, act politically: Some notes toward new movement strategy. In M. Darnovsky, B. Epstein, & R. Flacks (Eds.), *Cultural politics and social movements* (pp. 251–363). Philadelphia: Temple University Press.

Fraser, N., & Gordon, L. (1994). A genealogy of dependency: Tracing a keyword of the U.S. welfare state. *Signs: Journal of Women in Culture and Society, 19*(21), 309–336.

Freire, P. (1970). Pedagogy of the oppressed. New York: Seabury Press.

Friedmann, J. (1979). *The good society.* Cambridge, MA: MIT Press.

Friedmann, J. (1992). *Empowerment: The politics of alternative development* (2nd ed.). Oxford: Blackwell. (Original work published 1962)

Gamble, D., & Weil, M. (1995). Citizen participation. In R. L. Edwards (Ed.), *Encyclopedia of social work* (19th ed., pp. 483–494). Washington, DC: NASW Press.

Gun, C., & Gun, H. D. (1991). *Reclaiming capital: Democratic initiatives and community development.* Ithaca, NY: Cornell University Press.

Gurin, A. (1970). *Community organization curriculum in graduate social work education: Report and recommendations.* New York: CSWE.

Gurteen, S. H. (1894, November). Beginning of charity organization in America. *Lend a Hand, 13,* 355–361.

Hall, B. (Ed.). (1988). *Environmental politics: Lessons from the grassroots.* Durham, NC: Institute for Southern Studies.

Halpern, R. (1995). *Rebuilding the inner city.* New York: Columbia University Press.

Hinsdale, M. A., Lewis, H. M., & Waller, M. S. (1995). *It comes from the people: Community development and local theology.* Philadelphia: Temple University Press.

Hokenstad, M.C., & Midgley, J. (Eds.). (1997). *Issues in international social work: Global challenges for a new century.* Washington, DC: NASW Press.

Holmberg, J. (1992). *Making development sustainable.* Washington, DC: Island Press.

Hull-House maps and papers, by residents of Hull-House, a social settlement, a presentation of nationalities and wages in a congested district of Chicago, Together with comments and essays on problems growing out of social conditions. (1895). New York: Crowell.

Kahn, A. J. (1969). *Theory and practice of social planning.* New York: Russell Sage Foundation.

Khinduka, S. K. (1971). Social planning and community organization: Community development. In R. Morris (Ed.), *Encyclopedia of social work* (16th ed., pp. 1345–1351). New York: NASW.

Kramer, R. M., & Specht, H. (1975). *Readings in community organization practice* (2nd ed.).Englewood Cliffs, NJ: Prentice-Hall.

Kretzmann, J. P., & McKnight, J. L. (1993). *Building communities from the inside out.* Evanston, IL: Northwestern University, Center for Urban Affairs.

Lauffer, A. (1978). *Social planning at the community level.* Englewood Cliffs, NJ: Prentice-Hall.

Lewis, H. (1999). Rebuilding communities: A 12-step model. In S. E. Keefe (Ed.), *Culturally relevant practice in Appalachia.* Manuscript submitted for publication.

Lewis, H., & Appleby, M. (2003). *Mountain sisters: From convent to community in Appalachia.* Lexington, KY: University Press of Kentucky.

Matsuoka, J. K. (1997). *Economic change and mental health of Lana'i: A longitudinal analysis. Report to the National Institute of Mental Health.* Honolulu, HI: University of Hawaii, School of Social Work.

Mayadas, N. S., & Elliott, D. (1997). Lessons from international social work policies and practices. In M. Reisch & E. Gambrill (Eds.), *Social work in the 21st century* (pp. 175–185). Thousand Oaks, CA: Pine Forge Press.

Mayadas, N. S., Watts, T., & Elliott, D. (1997). *International handbook of social work theory and practice* (2nd ed.). Westport, CT: Greenwood Press.

MDC. (1991). *Building blocks of rural development: An MDC discussion paper.* Chapel Hill, NC: MDC, Inc.

Mead, L. M. (1994, September). Poverty: How little we know. *Social Services Review, 68,* 322–349.

Medoff, P., & Sklar, H. (1994). *Streets of hope: The fall and rise of an urban neighborhood.* Boston: South End Press.

Melaville, A., & Blank, M. (1993). *Together we can: A guide for crafting a profamily system of education and human services.* Washington, DC: U.S. Government Printing Office.

Midgley, J., & Sherraden, M. (2000). The social development perspective in social policy. In J. Midgley, M. B. Tracy, & M. Livermore (Eds.), *The handbook of social policy* (pp. 435–446). Thousand Oaks, CA: Sage.

Naperstak, A. J., & Dooley, D. (1997). Countering urban disinvestments through community-building initiatives. *Social Work, 42*(5), 506–514.

National Congress for Community Economic Development. (1990). *Human investment: Community profits. Report and recommendations of the Social Services and Economic Development Task Force.* Washington, DC: Author.

Noponen, H. (2001). The Internal Learning System for participatory assessment of microfinance. *Small Enterprise Development, 12*(4), 45–53.

Noponen, H. (2002). The Internal Learning System: A tool for participant and program learning in microfinance and livelihoods interventions. *Development Bulletin, 57*(1), 106–110.

Noponen, H. (2003). The Internal Learning System: Impact assessment versus empowerment? In L. Mayoux (Ed.), *Sustainable learning for women's empowerment: Ways forward in microfinance.* New Delhi, India: Samskriti.

Oberschall, A. (1993). *Social movements: Ideologies, interests, and identities.* New Brunswick, NJ: Transaction.

Perlman, R. (1971). Social planning and community organization. In R. Morris (Ed.), *Encyclopedia of social work* (16th ed., pp. 1324–1345). New York: NASW.

Portes, A. (1998). Social capital: Its origins and applications in modern sociology. *Annual Review of Sociology, 24,* 1–24.

Putnam, R. D. (2002). *Democracies in flux: The evolution of social capital in contemporary society.* Oxford, UK: Oxford University Press.

Quinn, R. E. (1988). *Beyond rational management: Mastering the paradoxes and competing demands of high performance.* San Francisco: Jossey-Bass.

Ramanathan, C. S., & Link, R. J. (1999). *All our futures: Principles and resources for social work practice in a global era.* Belmont, CA: Wadsworth.

Ross, M. G. (1955). *Case histories in community organization.* New York: Harper & Row.

Ross, M. G. (1958). *Community organization: Theory, principles, and practice.* New York: Harper & Row.

Ross, M. G. (1967). *Community organization: Theory, principles, and practice* (2nd ed.). New York: Harper & Row.

Rothman, J. (1968). Three models of community organization. In *Social Work Practice. Proceedings of the 95th Annual Forum of the National Conference on Social Welfare* (pp. 39–54). New York: Columbia University Press.

Rothman, J. (1979). Three models of community organization practice: Their mixing and phasing. In F. Cox, J. L. Erlich, J. Rothman, & J. E. Tropman (Eds.), *Strategies of community organization* (4th ed., pp. 25–45). Itasca: IL: F.E. Peacock.

Rothman, J., Erlich, J. L., & Tropman, J. E. (Eds.). (2001). *Strategies of community intervention* (6th ed.). Itasca, IL: F.E. Peacock.

Rothman, J. (2001). Approaches to community intervention. In J. Rothman, J. L., Erlich, & J. E. Tropman (Eds.), *Strategies of community intervention* (6th ed., pp. 27–64). Itasca, IL: F.E. Peacock.

Schorr, L. (1997). *Common purpose: Strengthening families and neighborhoods to rebuild America.* New York: Anchor Books.

Schram, S.F. (1995). *Words of welfare: The poverty of social science and the social science of poverty.* Minneapolis: University of Minnesota Press.

Sherraden, M. S., & Ninacs, W. A. (Eds.). (1998). *Community economic development and social work.* New York: Haworth Press

Stumpf, J. (1965). Community planning and development. In H. L. Lurie, (Ed.), *Encyclopedia of social work* (15th ed., pp. 190–207). New York: NASW.

Temkin, K., & Rohe, W. (1996). Neighborhood change and urban policy. *Journal of Planning Education and Research, 15*(3), 101–112.

Temkin, K., & Rohe, W. (1997, February). *Social capital and neighborhood stability: An empirical investigation*. Paper presented at the 1997 Fannie Mae Foundation's Annual Housing Conference, San Francisco.

Tilly, C. (1978). *From mobilization to revolution*. Reading, MA: Addison-Wesley.

Tilly, C. (1998). *Durable inequality*. Berkeley, CA: University of California Press.

Twelvetrees, A. (1989). *Organizing for neighborhood development*. Brookfield, VT: Avebury.

Weil, M. O. (1997). Community building: Building community practice. In P. L. Ewalt, E. M. Freeman, S. A. Kirk, & D. L. Poole (Eds.), *Social policy: Reform, research and practice* (pp. 35–61). Washington, DC: NASW Press.

Weil, M. O., & Gamble, D. N. (1995). Community practice models. In R. L. Edwards (Ed.), *Encyclopedia of social work* (19th ed., pp. 577–594). Washington DC: NASW Press.

Weil, M., & Gamble D. (2001) Community practice models for the 21st century. In A. R. Roberts, & G. J. Greene (Eds,), *Social workers' desk reference* (pp. 525–534). New York: Oxford University Press.

Wilson, W. J. (1987). *The truly disadvantaged*. Chicago: University of Chicago Press.

Wilson, M., & Whitmore, E. (2000). *Seeds of fire: Social development in an era of globalism*. New York: Apex.

Zakaria, F. (2003). *The future of freedom*. New York: W.W. Norton.

CHAPTER 12

From Community Planning to Changing Communities

Fund raising and Fund Allocation for Human Services

Eleanor L. Brilliant

n the 19th edition of the *Encyclopedia of Social Work* (Edwards, 1995), there is no entry for community planning, although there are entries for social planning, community development, and even needs assessment. Does the absence of a substantive entry mean that community planning no longer exists, or that social workers no longer value or practice it? Or have we merely adopted new names for community planning while we continue to do it? Are community development, social planning, community problem solving, and other related terms merely new wrappings for the same bundle of activities? In this chapter, I argue that community planning has become less visible and more problematic, but may still remain a viable, even essential, construct for human service provision.

I start by reviewing three earlier models of allocation of resources for human needs in the community before addressing current approaches and issues in the United States today. My assumption in this discussion is that planning in the community, or *community-based social planning*, must be connected with resources, and is rational in the sense of being information based (Gummer, 1995). I begin, then, with the model for such planning that emerged at the turn of the 20th century; second, I consider the dominant model promulgated by federated funding organizations and schools of social work before and after World War II; and third, I discuss changes of the 1960s and 1970s before analyzing the present paradigm and emerging critical issues of the 21st century.

Councils of Social Agencies, Associated Charities, and Community Chests: Early Models

From the end of the 19th century and into the early 20th, nongovernmental, voluntary associations proliferated throughout the United States (Axinn & Stern, 2000; Skocpol, 1999). Although Skocpol (1999) has argued that many voluntary associations in this period existed at several levels—local, state, and national—most social service agencies, such as the YMCA or family-serving agencies, were squarely local, and place and identity had a definite primacy for their service function. Such organizations occupied particular physical spaces, served people in the community, and solicited financial support for their activities at the local level. Thus, businesses and community leaders in localities containing large numbers of social agencies received a constant clamoring of appeals for support. In an effort to eliminate such duplicative requests, a group of "associated charities" came together in 1887 for a unified fundraising campaign in Denver, Colorado (Watson, 1922). Although the Denver federation later encountered difficulties, a new direction had been signaled. In these years, groups of associated charities took several forms. The first was the Charity Organization Society (COS) model, which was concerned with efficient provision of service for the urban poor (Axinn & Stern, 2000; Lubove, 1969); many of these organizations evolved into today's family service agencies. But parallel efforts also existed, which developed into community-based financial federations (related to the Denver concept) or grew into councils of social agencies with broader approaches to meeting community welfare needs.

In 1908, the Central Council of Associated Charities in Pittsburgh, with funding from the Russell Sage Foundation, carried out a survey documenting social conditions in Pittsburgh. Scientific research was added to the COS concept of scientific charity, reinforcing the idea that research could result in more effective and efficient charitable praxis. Around this time, the Cleveland Chamber of Commerce amassed a group of leading citizens, businessmen, and government officials to organize combined fundraising and fund allocation for a group of "member agencies." In 1913, they formed the Cleveland Federation of Charities and Philanthropies, which is generally considered the first modern federated fundraising organization. Four years later, that federation merged with the Welfare Federation of Cleveland, a co-ordinating and planning organization. As a result of World War I, federations spread throughout the United States,[1] and in 1918, many of these federated funds and councils formed a national organization (Brilliant, 1990; Lubove, 1969). By 1939, the national organization of Community Chests and Councils (CCC) reported that there were "306 Councils of Social Agencies or similar federations with a different name . . . listed in the directory of Community Councils, Inc." Although apparently many were not active, the CCC publication, "What Councils Do" stated that "every city of over 500,000 is organized and councils are to be found in 68 of the 80 cities between 100,000 and 500,000 population." Their programs varied but included community planning, coordination, and research (Community Chests and Councils, 1939).

That national publication, "What Councils Do" like others later, did not specify how many councils were free-standing organizations. However, councils were usually connected to local community chests, and often they were combined into one organization. In either case, early councils dominated social welfare planning in the community and tended to work closely with local public officials. Underlying their activities was the belief that human service professionals and local leaders represented the community, and a consensus model prevailed in community planning as it did in American society generally. The fact that the consensus was based on a selected segment of the population and on elite community leadership was hardly recognized.

A new model developed after World War II in which both councils and federated fundraising organizations (called *chests*) were energized. Chests morphed into United Funds, which in practice meant more emphasis on workplace campaigns and inclusion of some health agencies in their package of social agencies, usually the local chapter of the American Red Cross (Brilliant, 1990).[2] Many community councils took the name "Health and Welfare Council" to signify their inclusion of health concerns and health agencies in their planning and coordinating activities. More professional staff members of councils and federated fundraising organizations staffed growing numbers of trained social workers. Indeed, a community organization text used in schools of social work in the late 1950s and early 1960s (Harper & Dunham, 1959) gave considerable space to federated fundraising and welfare councils. During these years, some schools (e.g., Ohio State University) had programs dedicated solely to training students for fund and council work (Brilliant, 1990).

In this period, the work of planning councils was defined comprehensively, almost with glowing romanticism. In "Community Planning for Social Welfare—A Policy Statement," the United Funds and Councils of America (1959) described planning this way:

> Sound community planning encompasses the whole range of welfare needs and considers all available resources—governmental and voluntary, local, state, and national—for serving those needs. (p. 363)

As conceptualized, community planning involved both research and activities coordination. Councils convened meetings of human service professionals from government and volunteer-run agencies with local leaders (including women's organizations and businesses) to achieve more effective matching of resources with community welfare needs. However, readings in the same text (Harper & Dunham, 1959, pp. 369–407) suggest that this view of community planning was not fully compatible with the agency mix and fundraising goals of United Funds. One telling quote of the time stated, "There is an incongruity in combining responsibility for overall planning with that of financing a small minority of health and welfare services" (Citizen's Study Committee, as cited in Pfeiffer, 1959, p. 405). In any case, planning was local and involved convening community groups and local leaders; such community planning was an ideal type (in the Weberian sense). Nevertheless, whether as part of one organization or separate, community councils depended on United Funds for financial support and, to an extent, for status with key social agencies and legitimacy with business and government.

Turbulent Times: New Models of the 1960s and 1970s

In the exciting, if turbulent, period of the 1960s, old notions of institutional permanence and elite leadership were challenged by emerging groups whose voices had not previously been heard. Social work education and models of practice were not immune. More static views of community organization and community planning lost their constituency; professional hegemony was also challenged. A new focus on the civil rights of oppressed groups, concern about issues of welfare and poverty, and the escalating war in Vietnam made it clear that the concept and practice of community organization had to change. Community organization effectively became community organizing for social change, and promoting leadership roles for women and people of color became salient social justice issues (Brilliant, 1986).

In a related but separate trend, there were now also echoes of international influence defining community work and planning. After World War II, the United Nations helped disseminate the practice of community development in less industrial or poorer nations around the world. By the late 1970s, community development in the United States often took the form of economic development corporations (Twelvetrees, 1989). Meanwhile, in other industrialized nations, such as Great Britain, France, and Sweden, as well as in communist countries, the concept of indicative or goal-oriented industrial planning also spread—and in some countries spilled over—to social planning under government auspices.

In the 1960s and 1970s, federal services legislation and regulations in the United States, such as the legislation that created the Office of Economic Opportunity and other programs related to the War on Poverty, incorporated new planning requirements for human service agencies. The new regulations also sought to enact the maxim of "maximum feasible participation" by mandating that agencies serving the poor and other vulnerable populations must include citizens in their planning processes at the local and state levels. Examples abound; among the first were the Community Action Agencies in the War on Poverty (1965) and Citizen Planning Councils under Model Cities (1966). By the 1970s, the concept of social indicators had high salience. In 1974, Title XX of the Social Security Act emphasized participatory state and local planning in social services, and health systems agencies established multilevel planning organizations dealing with targeted, health-related service needs at regional and state levels (Brilliant, 1990).[3]

Although scholars recognized limitations to comprehensive planning (Etzioni, 1968) and rational decision making (Cohen, March, & Olsen, 1972; Lindblom, 1959; Simon, 1957/1997), rational planning was proposed as a model by leading experts in social welfare (Kahn, 1969). Urban planning also flourished and began to include social planning; by then, there were almost 500 planning councils. Meanwhile, the growth spurt of new nonprofit organizations in this period (Weisbrod, 1988), together with a poor economic climate, greatly weakened the United Way's primacy in the human services. At the same time, federal requirements for human service planning undercut the coordinating and planning role of community councils as well as local United Ways.

Nonetheless, some councils were entrepreneurial in contracting with the government. More than 30 councils assumed the role of Community Action Agencies in their communities, and many took on new roles as providers of services such as information and referral (Brilliant, 1986; Tropman & Tropman, 1977). Unfortunately, these struggles by community planning councils to find a center and by United Ways to find new sources of income and use existing resources more effectively in the weakened economy of the mid-1970s engendered other consequences, as well. First, United Ways increasingly used planning councils in controversial efforts to establish community-wide priorities across the human services; in some cases, this contributed to what became an accelerated move to defund community councils or absorb them into local United Way organizations. By the mid-1980s, few autonomous councils remained.[4] By then it was evident that corporations were more interested in campaign-related activities than in the fate of planning councils.

Not surprisingly, as practice changed, so did the conceptualization of practice. In an influential article, community practice scholar Jack Rothman redefined community practice into three models: locality development, social action, and social planning (Rothman, 1979), thus downplaying the term *community planning*. Although Rothman recognized that social planning could take place in the community in general and in Health and Welfare Councils specifically, his use of the term *social planning* emphasized the connotation of sectoral, technical, or specialized planning, such as health or mental health planning, and was also related to multilevel state or national planning. In any case, less focus was given to community-wide participation in planning. Social action received new legitimacy, and a less determinate idea of locality development, around community integration, was promulgated. Fundraising and fund allocation essentially disappeared as elements in Rothman's models, and reflecting the changing mood of social work leadership, social change emerged as an overriding goal. In the spirit of the times, Rothman concluded that all three models, not just social action, could be "applied in such a way as to foster and support social change" (1979, p. 45).

In 1980, however, Ronald Reagan won the presidential election, and a dismal period began for the human services. Funding for human services was reduced in the 1981 Omnibus Budget and Reconciliation Act (Bawden, 1984; Crimmins & Keil, 1983; Salamon, 1993), and block grants to the states for the human services lessened federal oversight of how funds were used (Peterson, 1982). Still, new and emerging subgroups in our society continued their development, and now they challenged the closed system of United Way fundraising and allocations. The Combined Federal Campaign (CFC) for federal employees was attacked in Congress and in the courts as unduly restrictive and controlled by United Way. By 1986, the CFC was greatly expanded, with rules that allowed for widespread participation by activists and newly emergent groups, such as women's funds, environmental groups, and Black United Funds (Brilliant, 1990; National Committee for Responsive Philanthropy, 1987). State employee campaigns were also challenged successfully, although the private world of the corporations remained resistant. Still, the CEO of the United Way of America, William Aramony, was sufficiently shaken by the events of the early 1980s to suggest (without success) that United Ways might broaden their package of human service agencies to include arts and other causes. During the next decade, the alternative fund movement gained strength, although amounts raised remained only a small percentage of all charitable contributions.

In this conservative period, a business ethos prevailed in the country and in the human services. Strategic planning texts were now used in social work schools and other professional programs (Bryson, 1988; Migliore, Stevens, Loudon, & Williamson, 1995). Pressured by reductions in federal funding, agencies, particularly those that were not receiving mandated Medicare and Medicaid funds, were forced to search for new ways to support their services (Crimmins & Keil, 1983; Salamon, 1993). Although many charities became more successful in fundraising,[5] individual contributions and foundation grants were not sufficient to bridge the gap between federal aid and needed resources. Thus, the voluntary nonprofit sector became more entrepreneurial, more businesslike, and indeed added to their revenues by increasing fees and sales of products (Salamon, 1993, 1999; Skloot, 1987; Weisbrod, 1998). United Ways hired more professionals with business and marketing training (Brilliant, 1990), while communicating a double message of social work values with a business gloss. Planning councils also began hiring from other disciplines, including urban planning and public administration.

In another trend that was to continue through the 1990s and into the 21st century, the idea of common community and public interest lost credibility as commercialization in the human services spread. Marketing strategies accelerated in the difficult financial years of the early 1990s, and a competitive paradigm continued into the prosperous end of the decade, when contributions to charities rose along with personal wealth (Kaplan, 2000).[6] Meanwhile, with donor choice, United Ways were supporting a smaller percentage of total expenses for more agencies, so their "member" agencies were also forced to develop entrepreneurial activities.

Changing Perspectives: Pluralism and the Marketplace

A growing voluntary sector. At the beginning of the new millennium, the terrain of the human services and the voluntary sector is larger and more variegated than ever before in American history. Thus, if there is planning, it is taking place in a more multicentered and complex environment. One sign of this is the Master File of the Internal Revenue Service (IRS), which in 2002 listed more than 1.44 million tax-exempt 501(c) organizations, of which the most important for our purposes are 909,574 charitable 501(c)(3) organizations and the 137,526 closely allied 501(c)(4) social welfare and advocacy organizations (IRS, 2002).[7] It should be noted that the 501(c)(3) category includes both organizations needing resources and those allocating resources; that is, it encompasses foundations and fundraising organizations as well as recipient organizations like museums, universities, and human service organizations that compete for these funds.

Changes in the locus and amount of public support. Although federal funding cuts during the mid-1990s were less draconian then originally proposed, the reductions still caused problems for social service agencies. Devolution of responsibility to the states changed the rules of the game and made the role of the states and localities more significant, but did not replace federal support (Boris & Steurle, 1999; Salamon, 1999). Thus entrepreneurial survival strategies accelerated, along with competition for private gifts and public and private grants.

In the mid-1990s, government contracting expanded in new directions. Charitable choice was incorporated in the Personal Responsibility and Work Opportunity Reconciliation Act of 1996, promoting use of federal funds for non-profit faith-based services (those with sectarian, church auspices). The numbers involved early on were probably small (specifics are undetermined) (Chaves, 1999; Cnaan, 1999; Farnsley, 2001), although the Bush administration in 2001 urged broader use of faith-based services. Ideological and political factors have delayed full implementation of this effort (De Vita & Wilson, 2001; Kennedy & Bielefeld, 2002), but these sectarian group interests have added to the complexity of the human service marketplace, placing further strain on limited resources.[8]

Multiple perspectives in pluralism in the marketplace. By the 21st century, American society had become more markedly diverse; Latinos, African Americans, and Asians were growing in numbers and in some areas replacing populations of European origin (Schmidt, 2001). Organizations, particularly those in the human services and social welfare fields, have also become visibly multicolored and multiethnic and are characterized by more varied interests than before. Philanthropy is now giving more attention to resources in communities of color, including African Americans, Latinos, Native Americans, and South Asian–Pacific Islanders (Campoamor, Diaz, & Ramos, 1999; Carson, 1991; Rogers, 2001). Women's organizations and cause-related groups such as environmental foundations are also raising funds for issues that previously had not received consistent support from mainstream funders.

Members of the Women's Funding Network (Brilliant, 2000) provide an example of the growth in identity-driven, social change-oriented funding. Created in 1985 with a small group of funds, by spring 2002, the network included 90 member funds and foundations (Women's Funding Network, 2002) and was still growing. These members' resources were also increasing: Contributions tracked for a specific group of 37 established funds rose 38% between 1999 and 2001 (Brilliant & de Vries, 2003). Women's funds often serve as "regranting" intermediaries between funders and grassroots groups, to whom they pass funds received.

The idea of alternative workplace fundraising was spreading, albeit slowly, from public campaigns (e.g., CFC and state employee campaigns) to business workplaces. In 2003, the National Alliance for Choice in Giving (NACG) included 52 workplace federations in 34 states; like locally based Community Shares and the environmental funds, all were dedicated to social change. Three women's workplace federations were also members (NACG, 2003). In a similar trend, the nation's "alternative funds," a larger, all-encompassing group that includes 18 Black United Funds, raised more than $222 million in their 2001 campaigns (National Committee for Responsive Philanthropy, 2003). Alternative funds include social change groups as well as more traditional groups like community health appeals. These alternative fund campaigns were not large compared with United Way totals of $3.95 billion, even allowing for the fact that United Way figures include funds designated to alternative groups, but as more resources began going to new and emerging groups, the United Way's hegemony of the workplace was threatened (United Way of America, 2001). Indeed, by the 21st century, formerly marginal groups were becoming more mainstream, even as they were still struggling for social justice and reallocation of resources. This has created a paradox: The necessity to recognize the value and celebrate the fact of diversity makes the idea of community more elusive and raises questions about commitment to any sense of public interest or unifying identity.

Donor choice and donor-driven philanthropy. Another factor contributes to difficulties in reaching community consensus about allocation of resources—the phenomenon of donor-controlled funding. Donor control has increased in a number of ways: First, a group of new billionaires, including Microsoft's Bill Gates, financier and philanthropist George Soros, and others, have become major forces in the disposition of enormous personal resources in line with their own personal interests. Although it is hard to criticize the worthiness of their charity, these billionaires are playing outside the traditional foundation world, spreading large amounts of money as they wish for university-based projects, human services, or the arts in the United States or elsewhere. For example, in 1997, Soros gave $500 million to be spent in the Ukraine, Gates gave $20 million to Cambridge University in the United Kingdom, and media mogul Ted Turner pledged $1 billion to the United Nations. In the late 1990s, the grant-making capacity of large elite foundations increased along with their assets. Because government funds were reduced, such grants would be likely to have more influence.

Of course, donor-driven philanthropy has been a major factor in local United Way campaigns since the 1980s. Although United Way reported the process to be slowing down (Blum, 1999), donor choice continues to channel funds outside of United Way's allocation system, in the CFC and in other campaigns. Donor control, in the form of donor-advised funds, has also been an important factor in the mounting assets of community foundations. By 1999, there were about 600 community foundations across the United States with a total of $25 billion in assets, a large portion of which came from donor-advised funds (Lenkowsky, 2002).

Organization-centered planning. In the new market paradigm, organization-centered strategic planning assumed center stage in the human services as it has in business (Yankey, 1995). In this paradigm, planning by human service agencies frequently begins with questions such as "What is the nature of our organization?" "What are our needs?" and "What strategies would enable our organization to survive in a turbulent, highly competitive, and constantly changing environment?" Under these conditions, program planning begins in the center of one organization; at best, it may later lead to collaboration or partnership with other organizations.

Worsening Conditions and Vulnerable People

From the end of the 20th century into the 21st century, the gap between rich and poor increased (Burtless, 1999; Sanders, 2003; U.S. House of Representatives, 1998). Competitive allocation, diversification of resources, and decreased federal involvement apparently did not improve the well-being of everyone. Intractable problems such as AIDS, domestic violence, and childhood poverty require the kind of combined effort that organizations acting alone cannot develop (Austin, 2000; Mulroy & Shay, 1997; Rosenthal & Mizrahi, 1993). In addition, despite reports of positive results from the "welfare reform" of 1996, community needs did not diminish. A pattern of corporate downsizing, with worker layoffs and dislocations, began in the prosperous years of the late 1990s and continued through the period of the market downturn that followed (Hilsenrath, 2003). Even before the end of the stock market bubble, foundations and nonprofit agencies were pressured to develop community partnerships and promote leveraging of funds (Brilliant, 2000; Philanthropic Initiative, 1997; W. K. Kellogg Foundation, 2000); this pressure remains. In short, despite strong support for entrepreneurialism in the human services, funders and recipients perceive limits to the competitive model of resource allocation.

Community Planning and Community Building in a Multicentered Society

In the mid-1980s, it seemed possible to conceptualize a few primary models that essentially covered the terrain of human service planning (Brilliant, 1986). However, in the far more complex and variegated situation of the 21st century, this appears less plausible. Under the entrepreneurship paradigm, flexibility and partializing have become successful strategies, and groups concerned with human service needs have pragmatically tailored efforts to specific definitions of community. Like the omnipresent power described by Foucault (1977), adaptive solutions directed at changing resource allocation and attitudes appear ubiquitous; they are practiced by small groups as well as large institutions, including foundations. Indeed in this new paradigm, multicentered efforts for social change demonstrate great variety in forms of coordination, partnerships, collaborations, coalitions, contracts, and networking, and they also suggest minimal overall coherence.[9] The following examples of such activities will help to indicate their diversity and range.

To begin with, partnerships and collaborations around particular themes have been viewed as effective strategies for leveraging resources for programs facilitating social change goals. Thus, in the late 1990s, the Los Angeles Women's Foundation strategically developed the Economic Justice Initiative to serve girls ages 11 to 18 and also launched a community-wide Women's Health Initiative. In New York, the Ms. Foundation took the lead in developing the Collaborative Fund for Women's Economic Development, involving private and corporate foundations, and giving technical assistance to grassroots organizations. Not surprisingly, United Ways also have been practicing similar strategies under the rubric of community building or community impact initiatives, and in many communities, collaborative efforts have involved partnerships between corporations and nonprofit organizations (Austin, 2000). In one notable example, United Way received a 5-year, $50 million grant from Bank of America for "Success by Six," a program focused on needs of young children in selected communities (Sorenson, 2000; United Way of America, 2003). In many communities, United Ways now highlight a few priority areas for funding, such as children and youth activities or teen pregnancy prevention (Billiteri, 2000), while promoting a message of community building.

Across the country, there are other positive examples of partnerships centered on revitalization of communities in a holistic sense. Minneapolis-St. Paul, which can be considered one of the most hospitable climates for activities in the public interest, is the site of our next example, the Neighborhood Planning for Central Revitalization (NPCR) effort. There, private agencies, universities, and federal agencies such as the U.S. Department of Housing and Urban Development and the U.S. Department of Education have undertaken extensive community-building initiatives based on the concept of community development, in ways that affect schools, families, and community groups (NPCR, 2000). Unfortunately, this model does not appear to have been replicated widely beyond the Twin Cities—perhaps because of the effort required to sustain it.

In general, social and economic development activities involving for-profit and nonprofit organizations have become key aspects of the privatization paradigm at the community level. Among these, the leader has probably been the Local Initiatives Support Corporation (LISC), a 1990s spin-off of the Ford Foundation in the 1990s. At the beginning of the 21st century, LISC reported affiliated community development corporations operating in 38 locations across the United States. Aside from private funds and profit-making activities, the community development model is also supported by federal legislation, grants, and a variety of tax incentives, and is found in numerous communities across the country (Twelvetrees, 1989; Vidal, 2002).

Coalitions, which focus attention and combined action of autonomous groups around particular issues of community concern, have a long history in the human services and continue to evolve today (Dluhy & Kravitz, 1990; Weil & Gamble, 1995; see also DeGennaro & Mizrahi, Chapter 16, this volume). Coalitions vary in scope and longevity. In addition to such tight-knit coalitions as the Twin Cities' NPCR, other looser types of coalitions also abound. A somewhat newer form is the network, which has experienced huge proliferation in recent years. Networks vary greatly—they may be loosely structured, such as those that are created on the Internet, or they may adopt more permanent structural forms, similar to those of federations. The Women's Funding Network is one example of this second type of structure. In the related looser form, policy networks have developed to allow active communication among people with common concerns; their work may lead to legislative change (see Jansson, Dempsey, McCroskey, & Schneider, Chapter 17, this volume). In today's high-tech age, policy networks may exist through Internet discussion groups and Web sites, allowing quick and easy communication without the delays and loss of momentum common to groups that must wait for face-to-face meetings (see Lohmann & McNutt, Chapter 35, this volume).

Planning Councils and Community and Social Planning

At the beginning of the 21st century, the arena of the human services was market oriented and driven by entrepreneurship, and seemed to lack the cohesiveness that it appeared to have, however imperfectly, 50 years before. Earlier models of comprehensive planning, community priority setting and allocations in the public interest have been upstaged by a variety of partialized solutions to human service needs, including the use of economically oriented community development organizations, segmented community projects, and donor-driven resource allocations. In this environment, both planning councils and their sometimes-allied United Ways unavoidably face questions about the perceived "value added" by community-wide planning. Nevertheless, despite the apparent demise of community planning, the roots survive, and the need for some rationality in a complex world does not go away. Indeed, some signs of reawakening have already emerged.

First, community-building and community-impact initiatives are increasing, and they echo, at least in part, older concepts of priority setting in allocation of resources. Moreover, such initiatives often encompass traditional activities of research and coordinating, suggesting that new names are, in fact, being given to traditional planning activities. These new names are used by local United Ways, many of the surviving planning councils, and some of the new players, including the expanding community foundations across the country. Indeed, perusal of *The Chronicle of Philanthropy* reveals that language in employment advertisements for executives of many of these organizations is characterized by similar concepts and terminology concerning community roles. In addition, there are some spotty but significant government-sponsored efforts to continue older notions of cross-cutting city or regional planning, such as that of government in Tulsa, Oklahoma, in which their local planning council has been involved (Dessauer, 2001). A tighter economy may foster such developments.

Second, as already suggested, planning councils have not disappeared. Even if greatly diminished in number, many of the survivors have expanded their budgets through entrepreneurial activities. Like other human service organizations, successful councils tend to be project driven, to form partnerships with other groups (often city, county, or state agencies, and sometimes business), to be active in pursuit of specific contracts and consultantships for fees—and to achieve their goals. Like other groups, including United Ways, successful planning councils determine their scope and territory in a variety of pragmatic ways. For example, what was once the planning council of San Francisco is now delineated as the Northern California Council for the Community, and the planning council in Albany, New York, has expanded statewide. The former Community Council of Kanawha Valley (Charleston, West Virginia) recently merged with a United Way and, under the new name LifeBridges, now covers several counties. Only a few councils, such as the Federation for Community Planning in Cleveland, seem to connect their identity to a specific city—and even the Cleveland organization aims to cover a broader metro area.[10]

Third, in 1992, a group of planning councils formed an official national coordinating group, the National Association of Planning Councils (NAPC). Most planning councils are now believed to be members, although some—such as those in Camden, New Jersey, and Yonkers, New York—are not. NAPC has a small budget and only a part-time executive director, but it holds annual conferences and enables considerable communication about major social welfare issues and best planning practices among its approximately 28 member councils. Planning councils tend to be located in midsized cities such as Jacksonville, Florida, or Tulsa, Oklahoma, although Cleveland and San Francisco are notable exceptions. Large cities such as New York and Boston no longer have planning councils.

Fourth, at the end of the 20th century, the idea of social indicators, so popular in the 1970s, showed signs of revitalization (Miringoff, 1999; Zapf, 2000). In annual conferences between 2000 and 2003, members of NAPC discussed indicators as a tool, recognizing that indicators by themselves do not signify planning but might be a powerful tool for planners in the human services. Some planning councils use social indicators in work with their communities, and at its 2003 annual conference, NAPC voted to become a national partner in a newly established social indicators consortium. NAPC also intends to place its own "defined set of social indicators" on a Web site linked to its members (Sharon Clark, personal communication, May 16, 2003). Indeed, councils see social indicators as a way to direct their work toward social change goals.[11] Furthermore, at a time when accountability in the nonprofit sector is becoming an increasing public issue (U.S. General Accounting Office, 2002), social indicators might be used to help in measuring outcomes. In fact, the demand for greater nonprofit accountability could be another factor in enhancing awareness of the value of community planning.

Finally, planning councils are concerned about the need to train future community planners. More interns are needed to ensure a flow of young people into a planning system that is clearly showing signs of aging. Development of a national internship program with the National Association of Schools of Public Affairs and Administration (NASPAA) was discussed at the 2001 NAPC Conference but lapsed when the leadership of that organization changed. NASPAA's members include public policy programs, public affairs programs, nonprofit management programs, and schools of public administration. It was not certain at the time whether social work could be involved or whether social work schools wanted such involvement.

Concluding Thoughts

In this chapter, we have examined the paradoxical nature of community planning at the beginning of the 21st century. Notably, as human resource allocation has become partialized and more entrepreneurial, the concept of community has become more elusive, even while it is redefined to be more inclusive. Meanwhile, earlier ideas of information-based allocations of resources, cooperation, and collaboration have been elaborated into community partnerships and community building efforts, which may involve corporations, United Ways, governmental agencies, foundations, and other nonprofit organizations, including planning councils. These activities are now multicentered and generally more targeted toward groups that formerly fell outside the traditional funding and allocation activities of governments and United Ways. Still, the problem remains that they are often splintered or partial efforts lacking integration in a systematic effort to ensure that resources are allocated more effectively over time.

In the end, we may need to reinvent a community planning paradigm that recognizes that planning is a vulnerable activity requiring strong allies and a solid financial base to survive. Although there are some funds available for this purpose from grants and collaborative activities, the fact is that human service planning has often been a stepchild in relation to the United Way and in the corporate context. At the dawn of the 21st century, this condition needs reassessment. Perhaps even in the past, community planning was project oriented and promised more than it could deliver. However, our sluggish economy and heightening social concerns have placed pressure on foundations, United Ways, and corporate givers to ensure more effective use of resources. These conditions could lead to renewed interest in some form of planning. Contextual factors of increased competition and ambiguity about levels of intervention add to the complexity of the task, however. As states have become more important in human service funding and metropolitan areas continue to sprawl, planning councils also expand their boundaries; thus, community is more problematic.

In conclusion, if community-based planning exists, it exists on a continuum from partnerships and project orientations on one end to broader-based social planning and policy analysis on the other. Because planning councils do not have their own resources to allocate, they require connections to and support from organizations—such as the United Way, government agencies, and businesses—that do. Planning also requires an infusion of new views and younger professionals, who can come from internship programs with schools of social work. Indeed, in a conservative climate, social work values are critical in informing the process of allocating resources for community welfare and social justice. In sum, social workers should be more engaged in community work and resource provision, in planning councils, as well as in funding organizations such as United Way, alternative funds, and foundations. In the interconnected world of today, high-tech capacity must be joined with political skills in advocating for social change. Planning councils provide one prime location for such practice. And wherever resources are at issue, social workers should be there, helping to assess needs and use community resources for social transformation.

Notes

1. Many communities formed war chests for raising money to help "the cause," and health-related fundraising accelerated. This became the basis for more permanent federated fundraising organizations (see also Brilliant, 1990, pp. 22–24).

2. Nomenclature in this period becomes more confusing. Some federated funds retained the name Community Chest, whereas others switched to United Fund. Some locations (e.g., Toledo, Ohio) had a structure that included both names. Councils of social agencies (many of whom had created their local funds) also began switching names to community welfare council, planning council, and other variants.

3. It should be noted that the federal government had mandated service planning on previous occasions (e.g., with the enactment of the Social Security Act of 1935, which required state plans for many services, like Aid to Dependent Children, later called Aid to Families with Dependent Children); however, the scale of such planning and the mandate for public involvement was greatly enhanced after the 1960s.

4. One of those surviving autonomous councils was the Federation for Community Planning in Cleveland. Among the reasons for its survival was the fact that it had a substantial endowment.

5. The use of the term *charities* follows common usage in reference to those organizations that have a double benefit under the tax code (they are exempt from some local, state, and federal taxes, and donors receive a tax deduction). Under this 501 (c) (3) category, nonprofit organizations such as hospitals, museums, educational institutions, and others are defined as "charitable" because they provide for the common good and do not distribute profits to owners (Salamon, 1999).

6. Because foundations are required to pay out at least an amount equal to 5% of assets under the tax law, as the value of stocks increases, the mandated payout also goes up.

7. Figures from the Master List are the basis for most counts of the size of this sector, but these figures, or the method of gathering them, need to be adjusted, because they undercount religious groups (e.g., churches, mosques, and synagogues) and small organizations that do not have to register. Adding to the inaccuracy is the fact that organizations are not always removed from the list when they cease to exist.

8. Of course, sectarian agencies were used long before this time, but the use was more delimited and required to be more definitively separated from religious functions of the organization.

9. In-depth discussion of differences between these various kinds of activity is beyond the scope of this chapter. See Weil and Gamble (1995) for consideration of some of these differences.

10. I would like to acknowledge the invaluable assistance that I have received from Sharon Clark, the executive director of the National Association of Planning Councils (NAPC), and from other planning council staff and volunteer leaders. Most of the information in this section comes from NAPC; some of it is available from the NAPC Web site.

11. The author was fortunate to attend a National Association of Planning Councils conference in Charleston, West Virginia, in April 2001, to hear planning council leaders discuss use of social indicators.

References

Austin, J. E. (2000). Strategic collaboration between nonprofits and business. *Nonprofit and Voluntary Sector Quarterly, 29*(Suppl. 1), 69–97.

Axinn, J., & Stern, M. J. (2000). *Social welfare: A history of the American response to need* (5th ed.). Boston: Allyn & Bacon.

Bawden, D. L. (Ed.). (1984). *The social contract revisited: Aims and outcomes of President Reagan's social welfare policy.* Washington, DC: Urban Institute Press.

Billiteri, T. J. (2000, March 9). United Ways seek a new identity. *The Chronicle of Philanthropy,* p. 1.

Blum, D. E. (1999, October 7). Moving away from donor designation. *The Chronicle of Philanthropy,* p. 3.

Boris, E. T., & Steurle, C. E. (1999). *Nonprofits and government: Collaboration and conflict.* Washington, DC: Urban Institute Press.

Brilliant, E., & de Vries, J. (2003, April 2). *Comparison of numbers compiled for 2001 by the WFN and for 1999.* Unpublished manuscript.

Brilliant, E. L. (1986). Community planning and community problem solving: Past, present and future. *Social Service Review, 17*(4), 568–589.

Brilliant, E. L. (1990). *The United Way: Dilemmas of organized charity.* New York: Columbia University Press.

Brilliant, E. L. (2000). Women's gain: Fund-raising and fund allocation as an evolving social movement. *Nonprofit and Voluntary Sector Quarterly, 29*(4), 554–570.

Bryson, J. M. (1988). *Strategic planning for public and nonprofit organizations: A guide to strengthening and sustaining organizational achievement.* San Francisco: Jossey-Bass.

Burtless, G. (1999). Growing American inequality: Sources and remedies. In H. J. Aaron & R. D. Reischauer (Eds.), *Setting national priorities: The 2000 election and beyond* (pp. 137–165). Washington, DC: Brookings Institution Press.

Campoamor, D., Diaz, W. A., & Ramos, H. A. J. (Eds.). (1999). *Nuevos seneros: Reflections on Hispanics and philanthropy.* Houston, TX: Arte Publico Press.

Carson, E. D. (1991). Contemporary trends in black philanthropy: Challenging the myths. In D. F. Burlingame & L. J. Hulse (Eds.), *Taking fund-raising seriously: Advancing the profession and practice of raising money* (pp. 219–238). San Francisco: Jossey-Bass.

Chaves, M. (1999). Congregations and welfare reform: Who will take care of "charitable choice"? *American Sociological Review, 64*(6), 836–846.

Cnaan, R. (with Wineburg, R. J., & Boddie, S. C.). (1999). *The newer deal: Social work and religion in partnership.* New York: Columbia University Press.

Cohen, M., March, J. G., & Olsen, J. P. (1972). A garbage can model of organizational choice. *Administrative Science Quarterly, 17,* 1–25.

Community Chests and Councils of America. (1939). *What councils do.* New York: Author.

Crimmins, J. C., & Keil, M. (1983). *Enterprise in the nonprofit sector.* New York: Partners for Livable Places and the Rockefeller Brothers Fund.

Dessauer, P. (2001, February 26). Telephone interview with the author.

De Vita, C. J., & Wilson, S. (2001, July 1). *Faith-based initiatives: Sacred deeds and secular dollars.* Retrieved March 5, 2004, from www.urban.org/url.cfm?ID=310351.

Dluhy, M. J., & Kravitz, S. L. (1990). *Building coalitions in the human services.* Newbury Park, CA: Sage.

Edwards, R. (Ed.). (1995). *Encyclopedia of social work* (19th ed.). Washington, DC: NASW Press.

Etzioni, A. (1968). *The active society: A theory of societal and political processes.* New York: Free Press.

Farnsley, A. E., II. (2001). Can faith-based organizations compete? *Nonprofit and Voluntary Sector Quarterly, 30*(1), 99–111.

Foucault, M. (1977). *Discipline and punish.* New York: Pantheon.

Gummer, B. (1995). Social planning. In R. Edwards (Ed.), *Encyclopedia of social work* (19th ed., pp. 2180–2186). Washington, DC: NASW Press.

Harper, E. B., & Dunham, A. (1959). *Community organization in action: Basic literature and critical comments.* New York: Association Press.

Hilsenrath, J. E. (2003, May 29). Left behind: Casualties of a changing job market. *The Wall Street Journal,* A1.

Internal Revenue Service. (2002). Types of tax-exempt organizations by Internal Revenue Code Section. In *Data Book 2002.* Washington, DC: U.S. Government Printing Office.

Kahn, A. J. (1969). *Theory and practice of social planning.* New York: Russell Sage Foundation.

Kaplan, A. E. (Ed.). (2000). *Giving USA 2000: The annual report on philanthropy for the year 1999.* New York: AAFRC Trust for Philanthropy.

Kennedy, S. S., & Bielefeld, W. (2002). Government shekels without government shackles? The administrative challenges of charitable choice. *Public Administration Review 62*(1), 4–11.

Lenkowsky, L. (2002). Foundations and corporate philanthropy. In L. M. Salamon (Ed.), *The state of non-profit America* (pp. 355–386). Washington, DC: Brookings Institution.

Lindblom, C. E. (1959). The "science" of muddling through. *Public Administration Review, 19,* 79–88.

Lubove, R. L. (1969). *The professional altruist: The emergence of social work as a career 1889–1930.* New York: Atheneum Press.

Migliore, R. H., Stevens, R. E., Loudon, D. L., & Williamson, S. (1995). *Strategic planning for not-for-profit organizations.* New York: Haworth.

Miringoff, M. (1999). *The social health of the nation: How America is really doing.* New York: Oxford University Press.

Mulroy, E. A., & Shay, S. (1997). Nonprofit organizations and innovation: A model of neighborhood based collaboration to prevent child maltreatment. *Social Work, 42*(5), 515–624.

National Alliance for Choice in Giving. (2003, January). *Appendix A, NACG: A Brief History, and attached documents, including Chronology of Workplace Giving Federation and Fund Development, 1971–2001.* Portland, ME: National Alliance for Choice in Giving.

National Committee for Responsive Philanthropy. (1987). *The workplace giving revolution: A special report.* Washington, DC: Author.

National Committee for Responsive Philanthropy. (2003). *Charts with data on amounts raised by non-United Way, alternative funds and federations.* Washington, DC: Author.

Neighborhood Planning for Community Revitalization (2000). *NPCR Building Community: The first five years of NPCR.* Retrieved from http://www.npcr.org/index.html

Peterson, G. E. (1982). The state and local sector. In J. L. Palmer & I. V. Sawhill (Eds.), *The Reagan experiment* (pp. 157–217). Washington, DC: Urban Institute Press.

Pfeiffer, C. W. (1959). Chest and council relations: The case for separate councils. In E. B. Harper and A. Dunham (Eds.), *Community organization in action: Basic literature and critical comments* (pp. 402–407). New York: Association Press.

Philanthropic Initiative. (1997). *Promoting philanthropy: The experience and the potential of collaborative efforts.* Boston, MA: Author.

Rogers, P. C. (Ed.). (2001). *Philanthropy in communities of color.* Indianapolis, IN: Association for Research on Nonprofit Organizations and Voluntary Action Occasional Papers Series.

Rosenthal, B., & Mizrahi, T. (1993). Advantages of building coalitions. In M. Austin & J. I. Lowe (Eds.), *Controversial issues in communities and organizations* (pp. 9–22). Needham Heights, MA: Allyn & Bacon.

Rothman, J. (1979). Three models of community organization practice: Their mixing and phasing. In F. M. Cox, J. L. Ehrlich, J. Rothman, & J. E. Tropman (Eds.), *Strategies of community organization: A book of readings* (3rd ed., pp. 26–45). Itasca, IL: F. E. Peacock.

Salamon, L. M. (1993). The marketization of welfare: Changing nonprofit and for-profit roles in the American welfare state. *Social Service Review, 67,* 17–39.

Salamon, L. M. (1999). *America's nonprofit sector: A primer* (2nd ed.). New York: Foundation Center.

Sanders, B. (2003, March 13). *The very rich are getting even richer. But what's happening to the middle class?* Retrieved May 27, 2003, from http://bernie.house.gov/documents/opeds/20030313163427.asp.

Schmidt, E. (2001, April 30). Whites in minority in largest cities, census shows. *The New York Times,* A1.

Simon, H. A. (1997). *Administrative behavior: A study of decision-making processes in administrative organizations* (4th ed.). New York: Free Press. (Original work published 1957)

Skloot, E. (1987). Enterprise and commerce in nonprofit organizations. In W. W. Powell (Ed.), *The nonprofit sector: A research handbook* (pp. 380–393). New Haven, CT: Yale University Press.

Skocpol, T. (with Ganz, M., Munson, Z., Camp, B., Swers, M., & Oser, J.). (1999). How Americans became civic. In T. Skocpol & M. P. Fiorina (Eds.), *Civic engagement in American democracy* (pp. 27–71). Washington, DC: Brookings Institute.

Sorenson, R. (2000). Early childhood initiatives: Building communities with the youngest in mind. *Community, 3*(1), 1–7.

Tropman, E., & Tropman, J. (1977). Community welfare councils. In J. Turner (Ed.), *Encyclopedia of social work* (17th ed., pp. 187–192). Washington, DC: National Association of Social Workers.

Twelvetrees, A. (1989). *Organizing for neighborhood development.* Brookfield, VT: Gower.

United Funds and Councils of America. (1959).Community planning for social welfare: A policy statement. In E. B. Harper & A. Dunham (Eds.), *Community organization in action: Basic literature and critical comments* (pp. 361–368). New York: Association Press.

United Way of America. (2001, May 3). *Task force on strengthening the United Way System. The case for action* (draft report). Unpublished manuscript.

United Way of America. (2003). *Bank of America awards final $10 million of landmark $50 million grant to the United Way Success by 6 Initiative.* Retrieved May 27, 2003, from http://www.prnewswire.com.

U.S. General Accounting Office. (2002). *Report to the Chairman and Ranking Member, Committee on Finance, U.S. Senate. Tax-exempt organizations: Improvements possible in public, IRS, and state oversight of charities* (GAO-02–536). Washington, DC: Author.

U.S. House of Representatives. Committee on Ways and Means. (1998). *1998 Green Book.* Washington, DC: U.S. Government Printing Office.

Vidal, A. C. (2002). Housing and community development. In L. M. Salamon (Ed.), *The state of nonprofit America* (pp. 219–239). Washington, DC: Brookings Institute Press.

Watson, F. D. (1922). *The charity organization movement in the United States.* New York: MacMillan.

Weil, M. O., & Gamble, D. M. (1995). Community practice models. In R. Edwards (Ed.), *Encyclopedia of social work* (19th ed., pp. 577–594). Washington, DC: NASW Press.

Weisbrod, B. A. (1988). *The nonprofit economy.* Cambridge, MA: Harvard University Press.

Weisbrod, B. A. (Ed.). (1998). *To profit or not to profit: The commercialization of the nonprofit sector.* New York: Cambridge University Press.

W. K. Kellogg Foundation. (2000). *Women's philanthropy: Untapped resources, untapped potential.* Battle Creek, MI: Author.

Women's Funding Network. (2002). *Women's Funding Network Membership Directory, April 2002.* Retrieved at http://www.wfnet.org.

Yankey, J. A. (1995). Strategic planning. In R. Edwards (Ed.), *Encyclopedia of social work* (19th ed., pp. 2231–2237). Washington, DC: NASW Press.

Zapf, W. (2000). Social reporting in the 1980s and the 1990s. *Social Indicators Research, 51,* 1–15.

CHAPTER 13

Participatory Methods in Community Practice

Popular Education and Participatory Rural Appraisal

Paul Castelloe

Dorothy N. Gamble

n its 10th *Human Development Report*, the United Nations Development Programme (UNDP, 2000) focused on human development and human rights, describing seven basic freedoms necessary for human development:

1. Freedom from discrimination by gender, race, ethnicity, national origin or religion

2. Freedom from want, to enjoy a decent standard of living

3. Freedom to develop and realize one's human potential

4. Freedom from fear of threats to personal security, from torture, arbitrary arrest and other violent acts

5. Freedom from injustice and violations of the rule of law

6. Freedom of thought and speech and to participate in decision-making and form associations

7. Freedom for decent work without exploitation (UNDP, 2000, p. 1)

Although all these freedoms are important to community practice, this chapter will focus on the sixth freedom. The freedom to think and speak and participate in decision making is a basic right of any democracy, but it is easily eroded, even in nations believed to be mature democracies. In the United States, for instance, citizens easily fall into assumptions that only a select few should speak and participate in most decisions. In a society that places such a high value on formal education, we often dismiss those who have little formal education as having no knowledge. Even as professionals in community practice, we often believe that by demonstrating our personal expertise in problem assessment and problem resolution, we are more useful than if we help other people discover and solve their own problems.

Paulo Freire, a Brazilian educator, always asked the teachers he was training to lead literacy programs, "What is: 'to know'?" (Vella, 1989, p. 37). How do we know something ourselves, and how do we know what others know? This chapter focuses on how we help others to uncover and make use of the knowledge they have acquired through living and becoming adults—how we help others (re)discover, validate, and use what they already know. It also connects the practice of knowing and learning from life experiences to group- and community-level participation and action.

This chapter introduces two participatory methods that can be used in community practice: popular education and Participatory Rural Appraisal. We outline the ideas behind each method, describe the "how to" or practice of each method, and provide a concrete example of each method's use. The goal of this chapter is to enable community practitioners to become more participatory and empowering in their work, and thus more firmly rooted in the hopes and dreams of the communities they serve.

Popular Education

Popular education is a participatory method that is particularly useful for drawing forth the wisdom, knowledge, and skills that people have gained from their everyday life experiences—and for using that experiential wisdom to begin to look more critically at the systems in which they live their lives. Popular education, which usually occurs outside of formal educational institutions, is education for collective action and social change (Arnold, Burke, James, Martin, & Thomas, 1991; Castelloe & Watson, 1999; Freire, 1970; Nadeau, 1996). This method is most often associated with the work of Paulo Freire in the Global South (Freire, 1970, 1996) and Myles Horton of the Highlander Research and Education Center in the United States (Glen, 1996; Horton & Freire, 1990; Horton, Kohl, & Kohl, 1990).

To develop a working definition from the works just mentioned, a popular educator can be considered someone who helps groups of people in low-wealth and marginalized communities learn to use reflections on their daily experiences to analyze the social, political, and economic systems in which their communities are embedded. Popular educators also assume that the skills and knowledge that people have gained through their life experiences can provide the foundation for creating significant community change. The work of a popular educator is to facilitate people's expression of their experiential wisdom, help make connections among the skills and knowledge of group members, and help harness those skills and knowledge for community change.

Paulo Freire: Critiquing Conventional Education Practice

Much of the theory and practice of popular education is associated with the life and work of Paulo Freire. Freire was a Brazilian educator who worked throughout the 1960s, 1970s, and 1980s to link the practice of education with collective action and social change (Freire, 1970, 1974, 1996; Horton & Freire, 1990; McLaren & Lankshear, 1994; McLaren & Leonard, 1993; Taylor, 1993). Freire (1970) called his approach *dialogic education*. He emphasized that popular education is based on small-group dialogue, a form of interaction between educator and participants in which both are cospeakers, colearners, and coactors. He contrasted his approach to what he called *banking education,* the traditional approach in which directive teachers stand before passive learners and make deposits of prepackaged knowledge (Freire, 1970, 1974; Hope & Timmel, 1995). Some of the contrasts between dialogic education and banking education are outlined in Table 13.1 (see also Castelloe & Watson, 1999; Hope & Timmel, 1995).

One key concept in Freire's writings on popular education is *learning from experience,* the idea that people learn best when they ground their learning in their everyday experiences. This idea has a rich history in both education and social work. In education, learning from experience is associated with the seminal work of John Dewey (1916, 1938). In social work, experiential learning has been a core component of community practice since its inception. Indeed, one of the books that served as a foundation for Freire's approach to popular education, *The*

Table 13.1   Comparing Traditional and Freireian Approaches to Education

Traditional Banking Approach	*Freire's Dialogic Approach*
• Students are seen as "empty vessels" which the teacher must fill with knowledge.	• Students are seen as potential agents or actors, people who can re-create the world.
• The teacher has all the necessary information, which is passed on to students.	• Facilitator and participants are active and creative co-investigators/co-learners.
• The teacher talks and students listen and absorb—passively and meekly.	• As a group, participants dialogue, analyze, brainstorm, plan, decide, and act.
• The teacher chooses the content, and the students (who are not consulted) adapt to it.	• The content is chosen by participants—participatory curriculum development.
• Knowledge is seen as objective, as a collection of impersonal, technical "facts" that have little to do with everyday life.	• Knowledge is subjectively, personally, and socially constructed. Knowledge emerges from everyday experiences.
• The teacher is neutral, objective, distanced from social conflict.	• The facilitator refuses neutrality; he or she is openly committed to marginalized groups.
• The purpose of education is to directly transmit cultural knowledge and cultural values to students.	• The purpose of education is to help participants learn from their experiences, develop analyses of society, and plan for collective action.

Meaning of Adult Education (1926), was written by Eduard Lindeman, a professor at the Columbia University School of Social Work. Lindeman (1926) viewed adult education as a democratic and informal practice taking place in small groups where adult learners began their education from their own experiences. He believed that dialogues drawing from groups members' experiences could spur social action. "Every social action group should at the same time be an adult education group," Lindeman wrote, "and I go even so far as to believe that all successful adult education groups sooner or later become social action groups" (1945, p. 12). Other social workers echo this emphasis on experiential learning, including Jane Addams and the community social workers involved in the education programs at Hull-House in Chicago (Addams, 1910, 1930; Deegan, 1990); Mary Parker Follett, in her work with Boston neighborhoods and northeastern industrial relations organizations (1924); and Murray Ross, a founder of community organizing and development theory (Ross, 1955, 1958). Freire's emphasis on experiential learning springs from this rich history within education and social work.

According to Freire, the practice of popular education results in two major outcomes: critical consciousness and collective action (Freire, 1970, 1974, 1996; Horton & Freire, 1990; Taylor, 1993). In Freire's (1970) model, popular educators bring groups of people together to reflect on questions related to *generative themes,* that is, high-priority community concerns such as job losses or environmental degradation. This process of using questions to reflect on generative themes sparks grassroots groups' active involvement in using their everyday experiences to understand more critically the political, economic, and social systems in which group members live. Freire (1970, 1974) called this the process of *conscientization,* or the development of critical consciousness. As they develop critical consciousness, group members are able to break through their lack of self-confidence, their apathy, and their inaction to plan and carry out collective action to improve their communities. Thus, there is a cycle of reflection using questions to reflect on key community issues and the larger systems in which those issues are embedded, alternating with taking collective action to improve the community. Freire (1970) used the term *praxis* to describe this continual cycle of reflection and action.

Freire's code-centered model of popular education. The concepts outlined previously are useful for understanding popular education, yet they provide little guidance for the practice of popular education. A community practitioner might be left to ask, How do I *do* popular education? How do I work with a group using a popular education approach? How do I work dialogically? How do I facilitate learning from experience, the development of critical consciousness, and collective action for social change? Answers to such questions can be found in several handbooks on the practice of popular education (Arnold et al., 1991; Hope & Timmel, 1995; Lee & Balkwill, 1996; Lewis & Gaventa, 1988; Nadeau, 1996; VeneKlasen & Miller, 2002). These handbooks provide a collection of participatory small group exercises used by popular educators; they also provide practice models for popular education work.

One such practice model is Freire's code-centered model (1970, 1974). Freire conceptualized five steps in his model. First, popular educators immerse themselves in the community in which they will be working—they spend time there, talk with grassroots leaders and listen to their stories, and simply be with them as they live their daily lives. Second, they listen actively for generative themes—for pressing issues that community members mention and discuss (e.g., environmental degradation). Third, they create *codes*—pictures, drawings, or some other representation of a generative theme—that serve to represent a familiar issue from community members' everyday reality (e.g., a drawing of a pipe spewing waste into the local river). In the fourth step, the symbolic drawings (codes) are shared with community members, who gather as a group to label the parts of the drawing and discuss their meanings. Popular educators lead the group through a process of *decoding,* a process of discussion to analyze critically the meaning of the group's "lived experience." Decoding is based on such questions as: "What do you see (when you look at these codes/pictures)? How is this similar or different from what you experience? How has this come about? What are the consequences? Who benefits? How could we change this?" By struggling through dialogue with these questions, the group comes to a more critical understanding of their situation. With this new understanding, they move to the fifth step—a plan for collective action. This might mean joining with other groups in addressing environmental degradation; it might mean working to create alternative, community-driven, ecologically friendly economic structures.

As is true in any of the participatory methods, popular educators themselves must be grounded in ethical values similar to those of social work, which emphasize helping people in need, challenging social injustice, respecting the worth of persons, recognizing the importance of human relationships, behaving in a trustworthy manner, and practicing in one's area of competence (NASW, 1996, pp. 5–6). Freire described the relationship between the educator and learner when he said:

> Another testimony that should not be missing from our relationship with students is the testimony of our constant commitment to justice, liberty, and individual rights, of our dedication to defending the weakest when they are subjected to the exploitation of the strongest. (1998, p. 56)

The Spiral Model of Popular Education

Arnold and colleagues (1991), working with popular educators in Latin America and South Africa, have developed the spiral model of popular education, which builds on Freire's model but is applicable to a broader range of situations and is in some ways easier to apply. The spiral model is outlined in Figure 13.1.

As Figure 13.1 indicates, the spiral model has five steps:

1. Start by asking group members to talk about experiences in their everyday lives (i.e., learning begins with group members' experiences).

2. Deepen the analysis by working with group members to make connections among their experiences (i.e., group members look for commonalities and differences in their experiences).

3. When appropriate, add or create new information to supplement members' existing knowledge.

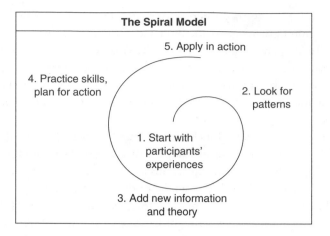

Figure 13.1   The Spiral Model of Popular Education

SOURCE: Arnold et al., 1991.

4. Practice skills and plan for action (i.e., group members try out what they have learned and plan for collective action).

5. Take action, and return again to reflection.

A concrete example. The collaborative work of Helen Lewis and the Ivanhoe Civic League in Virginia illustrates the use of popular education methods in community practice; this work provides a thoroughly documented example of popular education practice (Hinsdale, Lewis, & Waller, 1995). At the time of this work (the 1980s), Lewis was a popular educator at the Highlander Research and Education Center. She was invited by the Ivanhoe Civic League, a community-based organization, to help them develop a response to economic downturn. Ivanhoe had been a coal-mining town for most of the 20th century, but in 1981, the last major mine closed down. The Ivanhoe Civic League formed in 1986 to retain some of the former mining property, which the county was trying to sell, and bring industry back to the town.

In early 1987, Maxine Waller, a principal leader in the Ivanhoe Civic League, took part in Highlander's Southern and Appalachian Leadership Training (SALT) program, a popular education program designed to build the capacities of grass-roots leaders. The SALT program provided a space for Waller and other Civic League members to meet other grassroots leaders from community-based organizations throughout Appalachia and the South. They visited other communities and learned about their efforts to start community-based, community-driven economic development efforts. League members began to see the possibility of creating something similar in their own community and began to shift their focus from externally controlled industrial development to locally based development (a community-based tourism enterprise); they also began to focus on social development as much as economic development. The Civic League saw a need to reflect on this new direction for the community and plan it out carefully. Later in 1987, they asked Helen Lewis to come to Ivanhoe to facilitate a series of popular education sessions focusing on community-based economic development. Through these sessions, community members evaluated their past work and explored and planned possibilities for the future. This work led to many projects over the next few years, including general equivalency diploma classes; a youth group; plans for a community-based tourism facility; an oral history project that eventually resulted in two published books; a theater project; a series of Bible study discussion groups; and a series of cultural activities such as parades, potlucks, and performances by bluegrass bands, cloggers, and choirs. These activities helped local community leaders develop their capacities to plan and implement projects focused on community resources and strengths. This kind of social development is a necessary step toward helping communities develop their own small businesses, build community resources that would have value for new outside investors, and critically assess the value of externally controlled industries seeking to locate in their area.

Participatory Rural Appraisal (PRA)

It is perhaps not surprising that many ideas and methods relating to participatory community work come from the developing world. In the southern hemisphere, often identified as the Global South, great differences exist between the relatively small number of people who are wealthy and formally educated and vast groups of people who are poor and lack formal education (yet have a wealth of life experiences). In the developing world, many efforts have been introduced in the past 50 years to improve the condition of people who are poor and marginalized. These efforts have been generated primarily by Western countries, whose development experts have introduced technologies for food crop growth. They have also made huge investments in such infrastructure as hydroelectric dams, and their organizations deployed thousands of development experts who worked with local government bureaucracies and engaged with grassroots citizens and organizations (McKay, 1990; Weaver, Rock, & Kusterer, 1997). Among those development experts engaged with grassroots field workers were some who began to listen more closely to what local people knew and had to say about their conditions. One of these was Robert Chambers of Sussex University in the United Kingdom.

Robert Chambers: Critiquing conventional development practice. Robert Chambers, a scholar and practitioner of international development, has written two influential books critiquing development work and posing challenging perspectives and methods to overcome the mistakes of development: *Rural Development: Putting the Last First* (1983) and *Whose Reality Counts? Putting the First Last* (1997). Both summarize the efforts of participatory development practitioners across the globe, and both highlight the emphasis these practitioners place on the ability of local, often nonliterate, people to make observations and collect information related to their condition, analyze and interpret that information, and plan for improvements in their own communities.

Chambers's (1983, 1997) work is an implicit (and often explicit) critique of the status quo in international development. The foundation of his critique is that many of the mistakes in international development are the result of development professionals' tendency to base decisions on abstract, decontextualized information— usually from secondary data or survey questionnaires. Chambers (1997) contrasted this traditional assessment and research process with Participatory Rural Appraisal

(PRA), a method that is grounded in the voices, wisdom, and experiences of people living in low-wealth and marginalized communities. Chambers argued that PRA methods are more quickly carried out than traditional community assessment and planning methods (e.g., survey questionnaires), that they are more cost-effective, and most important, that they are more reliable (1997, pp. 122–125). When properly used, PRA methods inform not only the outside facilitator but the local participants, who become empowered to take action based on a better understanding of their situation.

While Chambers was making these practice-focused critiques of international development, more theoretical critiques were being leveled at Western-originated development efforts, whether they resulted from Euro-American capitalism or from the centralized planning approach of the Soviet Union and its allies (Brohman, 1996; Escobar, 1995; Rahnema, 1997; Sachs, 1990; Schuurman, 1993). Furthermore, the plight of many of the world's poor has steadily worsened. Although the proportion of the world's poor living in extreme poverty decreased slightly (from 29% to 23%) in the 1990s, it actually increased in sub-Saharan Africa (UNDP, 2002, p. 10). At the current rate of development, it would take more than 130 years to eliminate hunger in the world (UNDP, 2002, p. 11). According to a UNDP *Human Development Report* (1999, p. 2), "Competitive markets may be the best guarantee of efficiency, but not necessarily of equity." In spite of more than 50 years of development efforts, at the end of the past century, the top fifth of people in the world who had the highest incomes controlled 86% of the world gross domestic product, and more than 80 countries had per capita incomes lower than they had been a decade or more previously (UNDP, 1999). More specifically, worldwide development lags as more than 30,000 children every day die from preventable diseases; 113 million school-age children, the majority of whom are girls, are not in school; and 500,000 women die each year from complications of pregnancy and childbirth (UNDP, 2002, p. 11). It is within this larger context—declining well-being among most of the world's poor—that PRA has emerged as a practice method.

PRA. In *Whose Reality Counts?*, Chambers (1997) compared Rapid Rural Appraisal (RRA), a participatory method developed in the 1980s that grew out of work in universities in Thailand, the United Kingdom, and Australia, with PRA, a related method that emerged from the work of participatory development practitioners throughout the Global South (particularly South Asia and Sub-Saharan Africa) in the late 1980s and 1990s (see Pennell, Noponen, & Weil, Chapter 34, this volume). In comparing these two approaches, Chambers (1997) noted that although RRA does draw on people's local knowledge, the collection of data is done by outsiders for the purpose of taking away this knowledge and applying it to plans, publications, and projects developed by people outside the local community. Although PRA also seeks to discover local knowledge by engaging with local people, its purpose is to draw on people's wisdom in ways that strengthen their capabilities and empower them to take local, self-determined, community-driven action; to use their own skills to monitor and evaluate the action they take; and to build locally owned institutions that can become self-sustaining.

Attitudes and behaviors in PRA. The first steps in the PRA process require that a trained participatory practitioner or facilitator be invited into a community.

Engagement between the facilitator and local community members could be the result of development efforts initiated at the national, regional, or local level. Of primary importance in training the facilitator is the development of particular attitudes and behaviors. According to Chambers (1997), facilitators need to behave in ways that represent trustworthiness and relevance: "Trustworthiness is the quality of being believable as a representation of reality; relevance refers to practical utility for learning and action" (Chambers, 1997, p. 158).

Practitioners have realized that PRA is more than a set of exercises; it is a set of attitudes and behaviors that outsiders use when engaging local people (Aaker & Schumaker, 1996; Chambers, 1997; Keough, 1998). Most basic is the attitude based on beginning community work from a perspective of sharing and partnership, which means that everything is done in an open, welcoming, and nonpossessive spirit. According to Chambers (1997), other principles used in PRA are the following:

1. *Hand over the stick.* When the facilitator hands over the "stick, chalk, or pen" to local people, this act enables local people to be the analysts, mappers, diagrammers, observers, researchers, historians, planners, actors, and presenters of their analysis; eventually they become the facilitators (p. 117).

2. *Locals are the experts.* "The roles of expertise are reversed, with local people as experts and teachers and outside facilitators as novices," regarding local problems, culture, economic conditions, climatic conditions, health, and well-being (p. 117).

3. *Respect local knowledge.* Poor people's realities will always be local, complex, diverse, dynamic, and unpredictable. No one can know that reality as well as the people on the ground, the people who are living it. This principle builds on the critical idea developed for popular education of learning from experience.

4. *Be inclusive.* Be inclusive in gathering participants to impart and analyze local knowledge. It is not enough to simply hear from key informants and identified gatekeepers of knowledge. Many realities emerge when a range of people are involved. These should be people from all age, racial, income, and gender groups— including all marginalized people.

5. *Believe in local capacity.* Facilitators help most when they can introduce methods to allow knowledge, analysis, plans, and action to emerge from local people's knowledge. Facilitators help least when they frame the realities from their own observations and produce the analysis and project plans from their own expertise.

6. *The people create the data.* Diagramming and visual sharing are the best ways to help groups develop valid and reliable data. When using such methods, errors are more easily corrected, more complete information is generated, and the visual sharing is "the flowering of group-visual synergy" (Chambers, 1997, p. 207). In PRA, even nonliterate groups can do very complex analyses using diagrams and present the meaning of their analyses in sophisticated discourse.

7. *Behave in ways that may be contrary to formal training.* The best facilitator does not lecture, follow a blueprint, interrupt, or suggest solutions. Rather, the best facilitator establishes rapport, sits down, listens and learns, is patient and respectful, and knows when not to speak and when not to be present (Chambers, 1997, pp. 102–187).

PRA exercises. PRA has as its foundation a vast and ever-expanding set of participatory exercises developed by participatory development practitioners in the Global South that facilitators can use with grassroots groups (Archer & Cottingham, 1996; Gubbels & Koss, 2000; Leurs, 1996; Pretty, Guijt, Scoones, & Thompson, 1995; Theis & Grady, 1991; Thomas-Slayter, Polestico, Esser, Taylor, & Mutua, 1995; VeneKlasen & Miller, 2002). Chambers has described in more detail the methods and approaches of PRA in his book *Participatory Workshops: A Sourcebook of 21 Sets of Ideas and Activities* (2002). Practitioners have used these exercises in work related to management of natural resources, agricultural development, livelihood issues, health and nutrition, urban and rural poverty, violence reduction, housing issues, children and educational issues, crisis and refugee situations, and organizational analysis (Chambers, 1997). In *Whose Reality Counts?* Chambers (1997, pp. 118–119) outlined some of the participatory methods and approaches employed by PRA practitioners to elicit data collection and issue focus. The facilitator helps groups actively participate in these exercises and develops the questions that will help the group members analyze what they have represented. Examples of exercises and processes follow:

1. Mapping and modeling: People draw and color—using chalks, sticks, seeds, powders, or pens—making social, health, or demographic maps; resource maps; thematic maps; or topic maps (e.g., on issues such as water, trees, education, health and transportation resources, dangers, housing conditions, and access to things that fulfill their basic human needs).

2. Timelines and trend analysis: People chart, on paper or on the ground, chronologies of events, people's accounts of the past, or a picture of how things have changed for a given place, so that an analysis of the causes of change and trends can be discussed.

3. Seasonal calendars: People develop a seasonal calendar, often by month, to show the impact of specific things such as rainfall and crop cycles for agricultural communities; a tourism industry; production cycles; illness patterns; fuel needs; migration and population patterns; work for women, men, and children; and so forth.

4. Institutional or Venn diagramming: People draw the critical relationships that exist in a community, identifying individuals and institutions important in and for a community or group; they then analyze the relationships and the meaning of those relationships.

5. Well-being (or wealth) grouping: People identify individuals or groups of individuals on cards and organize a "card sort" into groups of people who are most well-off and those most deprived, with a discussion of the key indicators of well-being (monetary and nonmonetary). This can lead to a discussion of people who are poor and marginalized and how they cope with these conditions.

6. Analysis of difference: People identify different groups, especially by gender, social group, occupation, age, sexual orientation, race, and cultural identity; this is followed by discussions of problems and preferences of the groups (Chambers, 1997, pp. 117–119).

The initial participatory exercises in PRA focus on data collection, such as those outlined previously. The next steps are often participatory exercises focusing on group analysis—exercises such as matrix scoring and ranking to express preferences; presenting maps, models, and diagrams to check and correct the perspectives; developing plans, budgets, and implementation and monitoring schedules; developing a drama or video that expresses the project and its purpose; and generating reports immediately after activities are completed (Chambers, 1997, chap. 6). These group activities help to deepen the learning of both the local participants and the outside facilitators. They also build the capacity of people to use similar methods for different community problems and empower the community when a planned change results from their efforts.

PRA: A concrete example. There are several books that present case studies of the use of PRA methods in various contexts and settings (Blackburn & Holland, 1998; Guijt & Shah, 1998; Holland & Blackburn, 1998; Johnson, Ivan-Smith, Gordon, Pridmore, & Scott, 1998; Nelson & Wright, 1995). Among the hundreds of case examples presented in these books, we summarize one to provide a concrete sense of how PRA is used in everyday participatory development practice.

James Mascarenhas (1998), an Indian PRA practitioner with a nongovernmental organization called OUTREACH, outlined the use of PRA methods in watershed development in South India. OUTREACH worked in semi-arid and drought-prone areas in South India (parts of Karnataka, Andhra Pradesh, and Tamil Nadu) to help local people learn to manage their natural resources and environment in a way that would suit their needs. Mascarenhas outlined four stages that OUTREACH used when working with local communities. First, the OUTREACH staff worked to strengthen grassroots "self-help groups." The focus here was on increasing community participation, starting and building self-help groups, establishing savings and credit programs, and raising awareness about issues affecting the environment and watershed. Second, the staff used PRA methods to delineate the local watershed, then to create a watershed management plan. The end result of this process was a complex set of plans—a watershed treatment plan, a financial plan, a timeline, an implementation plan, and a management plan—all of which were generated by local people and built on their experiences. Third, the staff supported the local community through the stage of implementing its plan (often involving ongoing PRA exercises that assess and monitor progress). Fourth, the staff continually worked to help local groups become increasingly independent—that is, the OUTREACH staff laid the groundwork for withdrawing from the project by constantly stressing the strength and responsibility of the local group.

Application to Social Work Practice

As described in the beginning of this chapter, participatory methods were a part of early approaches to social work (Addams, 1910; Follett, 1924; Lindeman, 1945; Ross, 1955, 1958). In more recent years, models of community organization and community practice have focused on the skills and knowledge of the practitioner as well as on building skills among citizen groups. Rothman (2001), for example, described the basic change strategy for locality development as "involving a broad cross section of people in determining and solving their own problems" and described their role as "participants in an interactional problem-solving process" (p. 45). Six of the eight models of community practice described by Weil and Gamble (1995) have outcomes focused on developing capacity to organize, organizing for social justice, or initiating grassroots development. The methodological objectives are described as developing skills and abilities of citizens and citizen groups, making social planning more accessible and inclusive, connecting social and economic investments to grassroots community groups, advocating for broad coalitions, and infusing social planning with a concern for social justice (Weil & Gamble, 1995, p. 577). In his development of six models of community work practice in the United Kingdom, Popple (1996) also had a primary focus on the engagement role and skills of the worker. His description of the community education model developed critical perspectives for the worker derived from the experiences and writings of Paulo Freire. Perhaps there is no better prescription for social workers to learn participatory methods than to follow the principles of Freire himself for engaging with groups to identify and analyze their reality, planning and taking action based on that understanding, and reflecting on the participatory action taken. Community practitioners will find the roots of participatory methods, as well as the values, concepts, models, and skills for community engagement, throughout the history of social work literature.

Practitioners can continue to build a knowledge base by combining the historical roots of community practice, their own experience, and the directive found in the Code of Ethics developed by the National Association of Social Workers: to embrace "ethical responsibilities to the broader society," particularly to "facilitate informed participation by the public in shaping policies and institutions" (1996, pp. 26–27). The development and testing of participatory methods will provide more knowledge about the synergy that takes place between community members and workers. The two participatory methods described in this chapter should be part of community social workers' repertoire that ensures the active participation of grassroots representatives so that the local community can be both the author and owner of effective social and economic problem solving.

Conclusion

Understanding the application of participatory methods moves the community practitioner to an increasingly inclusive and empowering practice. Effectively using participatory methods such as popular education and PRA requires practice and a strong commitment to democratic principles. Community practitioners must be able to give up the "expert" role to become a partner in learning with community members. They must be able to pose the questions that stimulate analysis by community members of their local conditions in relation to regional, national, and global contexts. They must act on the understanding that local people have the capacity to identify complex conditions, analyze all aspects of conditions that prevent them from developing to their optimum potential, plan solutions to problems, develop resources and take action, and create and employ monitoring and evaluation techniques for the action taken.

Participatory methods facilitate the involvement of many people who may not have had the opportunity to engage in local planning and action strategies. They also create the potential for developing new and lasting democratic institutions. This chapter began with the UN Development Programme's (2000) list of freedoms necessary for human development—with its focus on the freedom of thought and speech, participation in decision making, and freedom to form associations. These are the freedoms that popular education and PRA can most directly affect. By using these participatory methods, community practitioners can ensure that their work is as democratic and empowering as possible.

References

Aaker, J., & Schumaker, J. (1996). *The Cornerstones Model: Values-based planning and management.* Little Rock, AK: Heifer Project International.

Addams, J. (1910). *Twenty years at Hull-House.* New York: MacMillan.

Addams, J. (1930). *The second twenty years at Hull-House.* New York: MacMillan.

Archer, D., & Cottingham, S. (1996). *REFLECT mother manual: Regenerated Freirean literacy through empowering community techniques.* London: ActionAid.

Arnold, R., Burke, B., James, C., Martin, D., & Thomas, B. (1991). *Educating for a change.* Toronto, Ontario, Canada: Between the Lines/Doris Marshall Institute for Education and Action.

Blackburn, J., & Holland, J. (Eds.). (1998). *Who changes? Institutionalizing participation in development.* London: Intermediate Technologies.

Brohman, J. (1996). *Popular development: Rethinking the theory and practice of development.* Oxford, UK: Blackwell.

Castelloe, P., & Watson, T. (1999). Participatory education as a community practice method: A case example from a comprehensive Head Start program. *Journal of Community Practice, 6*(1), 71–90.

Chambers, R. (1983). *Rural development: Putting the last first.* Harlow, UK: Longman.

Chambers, R. (1997). *Whose reality counts? Putting the first last.* London: Intermediate Technology.

Chambers, R. (2002). *Participatory workshops: A sourcebook of 21 sets of ideas and activities.* London: Earthscan.

Deegan, M. J. (1990). *Jane Addams and the men of the Chicago School, 1892–1918.* New Brunswick, NJ: Transaction Books.

Dewey, J. (1916). *Democracy and education: An introduction to the philosophy of education.* New York: Free Press.

Dewey, J. (1938). *Experience and education.* New York: Collier.

Escobar, A. (1995). *Encountering development: The making and unmaking of the Third World.* Princeton, NJ: Princeton University Press.

Follett, M. P. (1924). *Creative experience.* New York: Longmans, Green.

Freire, P. (1970). *Pedagogy of the oppressed.* New York: Continuum.

Freire, P. (1974). *Education for critical consciousness.* New York: Continuum.

Freire, P. (1996). *Pedagogy of hope: Reliving pedagogy of the oppressed.* New York: Continuum.

Freire, P. (1998). *Teachers as cultural workers: Letters to those who dare teach.* Boulder, CO: Westview Press.

Glen, J. M. (1996). *Highlander: No ordinary school* (2nd ed.). Knoxville: University of Tennessee Press.

Gubbels, P., & Koss, C. (2000). *From the roots up: Strengthening organizational capacity through guided self-assessment.* Oklahoma City, OK: World Neighbors.

Guijt, I., & Shah, M. K. (Eds.). (1998). *The myth of community: Gender issues in participatory development*. London: Intermediate Technology.

Hinsdale, M. A., Lewis, H. M., & Waller, M. (1995). *It comes from the people: Community development and local theology*. Philadelphia: Temple University Press.

Holland, J., & Blackburn J. (Eds.). (1998). *Whose voice? Participatory research and policy change*. London: Intermediate Technologies.

Hope, A., & Timmel, S. (1995). *Training for transformation: A handbook for community workers* (Rev. ed., Books 1–3). Gweru, Zimbabwe: Mambo Press.

Horton, M., & Freire, P. (1990). *We make the road by walking: Conversations on education and social change* (B. Bell, J. Gaventa, & J. Peters, Eds.). Philadelphia: Temple University Press.

Horton, M., Kohl, J., & Kohl, H. (1990). *The long haul: An autobiography*. New York: Doubleday.

Johnson, V., Ivan-Smith, E., Gordon, G., Pridmore, P., & Scott, P. (Eds.). (1998). *Stepping forward: Children and young people's participation in the development process*. London: Intermediate Technology.

Keough, N. (1998). Participatory development principles and practices: Reflections of a Western development worker. *Community Development Journal, 33*(3), 187–196.

Lee, B., & Balkwill, M. (1996). *Participatory planning for action: Popular education techniques to assist community groups to plan and act*. Toronto: CommonAct Press.

Leurs, R. (1996). *A resource guide for trainers and facilitators of participatory learning and action (PLA)*. Birmingham, UK: University of Birmingham Development Administration Group.

Lewis, H., & Gaventa, J. (1988). *The Jellico handbook: A teachers guide to community-based economics* (Working Paper Series No. 8, The Economics Education Project). New Market, TN: Highlander Center.

Lindeman, E. (1926). *The meaning of adult education*. New York: New Republic.

Lindeman, E. (1945). The sociology of adult education. *Journal of Educational Sociology, 19,* 4–13.

Mascarenhas, J. (1998). The participatory watershed development implementation process: Some practical tips drawn from OUTREACH in South India. In J. Blackburn & J. Holland (Eds.), *Who changes: Institutionalizing participation in development* (pp. 69–75). London: Intermediate Technology.

McKay, J. (1990). The development model. *Development, Journal of SID, 3/4,* 55–59.

McLaren, P. L., & Lankshear, C. (Eds.). (1994). *Politics of liberation: Paths from Freire*. New York: Routledge.

McLaren, P. L., & Leonard, P. (Eds.). (1993). *Paulo Freire: A critical encounter*. New York: Routledge.

Nadeau, D. (1996). *Counting our victories: Popular education and organizing*. New Westminster, Canada: Repeal the Deal.

National Association of Social Workers. (1996). *Code of ethics*. Washington, DC: NASW Press.

Nelson, N., & Wright, S. (1995). *Power and participatory development: Theory and practice*. London: Intermediate Technology.

Popple, K. (1996). Community work: British models. *Journal of Community Practice, 3*(3/4), 147–180.

Pretty, J., Guijt, I., Scoones, I., & Thompson, J. (1995). *A trainer's guide for participatory learning and action*. London: International Institute for Environment and Development.

Rahnema, M. (1997). *The post-development reader*. London: Zed Books.

Ross, M. G. (1955). *Community organization: Theory and principles*. New York: Harper.

Ross, M. G. (1958). *Case histories in community organization*. New York: Harper & Row.

Rothman, J. (2001). Approaches to community intervention. In J. Rothman, J. L. Erlich, & J. E. Tropman, *Strategies of community intervention* (6th ed., pp. 27–64). Itasca, IL: Peacock.

Sachs, W. (Ed.). (1990). *The development dictionary.* London: Zed Books.

Schuurman, F. J. (Ed.). (1993). *Beyond the impasse: New directions in development theory.* London: Zed Books.

Taylor, P. V. (1993). *The texts of Paulo Freire.* Buckingham, UK: Open University Press.

Theis, J., & Grady, H. M. (1991). *Participatory rapid appraisal for community development: A training manual based on experiences in the Middle East and North Africa.* London: Save the Children and International Institute for Environment and Development.

Thomas-Slayter, B., Polestico, R., Esser, A. L., Taylor, O., & Mutua, E. (1995). *A manual for socioeconomic and gender analysis: Responding to the development challenge.* Worcester, MA: Egogen.

United Nations Development Programme. (1999). *Human Development Report, 1999.* New York: Oxford University Press.

United Nations Development Programme. (2000). *Human Development Report, 2000.* New York: Oxford University Press.

United Nations Development Programme. (2002). *Human Development Report, 2002.* New York: Oxford University Press.

Vella, J. (1989). *Learning to teach: Training of trainers for community development.* Washington, DC: Save the Children.

VeneKlasen, L., & Miller, V. (2002). *A new weave of power, people, and politics: The action guide for advocacy and citizen participation.* Oklahoma City, OK: World Neighbors; San Francisco, CA: Asia Foundation.

Weaver, J. H., Rock, M. T., & Kusterer, K. (1997). *Achieving broad-based sustainable development.* West Hartford, CT: Kumarian Press.

Weil, M. O., & Gamble, D. N. (1995). Models of community practice. In R. L. Edwards (Ed.), *The encyclopedia of social work* (19th ed., pp. 577–593). Washington, DC: NASW Press.

CHAPTER 14

Political, Social, and Legislative Action

Jacqueline Mondros

S ocial, legislative, and political action are the processes, methods, and practice skills of pursuing social change. The pursuit of change has been included, if not embraced, within the profession since its earliest days (Austin & Betten, 1990; Weil, 1996). Virtually all the typologies of community practice (Checkoway, 1995; Rothman, 1964, 1996; Weil, 1996) have encompassed various social action approaches as legitimate methods of practice. Some frameworks (Fisher & Kling, 1990; Grosser & Mondros, 1985; Mondros & Wilson, 1994; Rubin & Rubin, 2001) have sought to further clarify the distinctions among each action approach. Hyde (1996) found aspects of social action in almost all organizations operating out of a feminist framework, and Rivera and Erlich (1995) described a variety of racial and ethnic communities using different approaches to social change. There are differences about what constitutes social action and the characteristics that best describe it, but there is consensus that this particular form of practice is a legitimate social work activity animated by our professional imperative for social justice.

This chapter first defines social, legislative, and political action and lists the activities associated with each of these approaches. As in many other works on the subject, the argument here is that it is more efficacious for organizers and organizations to consider these approaches not as distinct ways of operating, but as strategies to deploy based on an assessment of the change actors and the environmental context for change. Based on Hoefer's (2000) notion of "insider versus outsider" strategies, this chapter delineates a streamlined assessment and action process to be employed by social action organizations, and ends by considering the characteristics of today's environmental context and what they imply for the prospect of social change.

Three Approaches to Social Change

1. Social Action

Social action strategies are used by groups that organize to attain power to change conditions that are injurious to them (Mondros & Wilson, 1994) or to correct inequalities they experience (Rubin & Rubin, 2001). People who suffer from the adverse condition come together to pursue change. The targets of the change are those who have formal responsibility for the problem. Through meetings, confrontation, and direct negotiations, members of the social action organization attempt to pressure the targets into an agreement that will correct the condition. Most social action strategies are confrontational, based on the idea that this is the most effective means to resolution (Alinsky, 1971; Mondros & Wilson, 1994). Some recent literature, however, argues that conciliatory approaches to corporations and public officials and collaboration with decision makers are a more effective social action strategy (Eichler, 1995; Kretzmann & McKnight, 1993).

Social action includes eliciting people's experience, helping them to choose a problem on which to work, building wide awareness of the problem, recruiting people as leaders and activists, researching the problem and its ramifications, identifying targets for change, holding meetings with the target to demand accountability, publicizing the cause to the broader community through the media, and monitoring progress and modifying strategies accordingly. Social action organizations often escalate their confrontation when decision makers resist their demands.

2. Legislative Action

Legislative action attempts to influence legislators and other elected officials (including their staff members) to pass legislation that will provide rights and protections. Commonly, collaborative and persuasive means are used. Because politicians need to be convinced that a large number of voters support a proposed law, legislative action often requires a broad coalition of organizations. Persuading public officials to enact a bill is a long, often tedious process of monitoring the bill as it moves through government, and it generally requires a good deal of legislative acumen. Consequently, legislative action is frequently carried out by expert lobbyists on behalf of an organization or group of people pursuing a change. Legislative action includes meeting with elected officials and their staff members, writing legislation and securing legislative sponsors, issuing reports and data on issues that can be used to formulate policy, educating and persuading the majority party to support the legislation, obtaining the support of the executive branch and related agencies, testifying at hearings in support of the bill, and using amendments to promote favorable outcomes (Dear & Patti, 1981; Hardcastle, Wenocur, & Powers, 1997; Haynes & Mickleson, 1997).

3. Political Action

Political action is aimed at electing a person to public office to pursue change. It assumes that the newcomer will advance the group's issues and needs. In this model, activists contribute to campaign chests and work to get out the vote on election day. Political action can also include mounting citizen initiatives or working to include referenda on election ballots. Political action requires building support and persuading voters of the merits of voting for the organization's issue or candidate. Electoral campaigns are increasingly costly, and organizations with scarce resources are often discouraged from taking political action. In addition, the tax laws restrict the direct political activity of nonprofit organizations. Consequently, political action is most often carried out by political action committees, which are "organizations designed to collect and disburse voluntary contributions for political purposes from members of a special interest group. In order to meet state and federal regulations, they must be independently organized and funded" (Haynes & Mickleson, 1997, p. 142).

Political action typically includes identifying candidates who support the organization's agenda, making public the endorsement of candidates, informing members about the endorsement, canvassing for support of selected candidates, making and encouraging financial contributions, offering electoral training, and associating with other groups and political parties (Colby & Buffum, 1998; Haynes & Mickleson, 1997).

The three types of action have much in common. First, all have a commitment to transfer power and resources and improve conditions for a group of people. The differences are only in what is viewed as the most effective means to bring about change. Second, all these approaches also assume the existence of an organization that pursues the change. Social change requires persistent and continuous efforts that only a disciplined organization can provide, and there are organizational precursors for even such change activities as civil rights and gay and lesbian actions that appear to have arisen precipitously (Morris, 1984; Poindexter, 1997). Third, change actors differ solely in role (e.g., activist, petitioner, voter), and all actors have determined some interest (instrumental or altruistic) in pursuit of these changes. Change actors may also be working at any level (neighborhood, municipal, state, or national) in pursuit of the desired result. Although the degree to which activists are purposefully empowered by their activity may differ from organization to organization, there is nothing in any of the approaches that militates against such a process. Most organizations value and welcome the psychological growth and political sophistication of their members.

Furthermore, it does not appear that much is gained by treating these approaches as separate models. The reality seems to suggest that the practice of a pure approach is rare (Mizrahi & Rosenthal, 1998; Simmons, 2000; Soifer, 1998; Soifer & Singer, 1999). Hyde (1996) remarked on her struggle to place examples of feminist organizations within any single approach. The typologies note the overlapping of approaches (Weil, 1996). Even Rothman's (1996) latest formulation is an attempt to recognize the prevalence of blended approaches, noting that the distinction between radical and normative goals is seldom obvious.

Pragmatism also argues for diversity of approach. Current literature urges activists to "vary their strategic hands" by using "whatever works" to promote change (Mondros & Wilson, 1994). Rubin and Rubin (2001) made the point that most problems today are the responsibility of several levels of government, and therefore require simultaneous activities. Si Kahn wrote simply, "You need to know who the tactic is aimed at and what is likely to influence them" (1991, p. 167). For all these reasons, we agree with Hardina (1997), who used strategies as a way of discussing distinctions among social action organizations, and activists are encouraged to deploy them depending on the circumstances.

As social, legislative, and political action are treated as various strategies that can be potentially deployed by all organizations pursuing change, practitioners will need to think broadly about how they will react at any given moment. It is important for them to have some guidance about what might be most effective in each circumstance. I will suggest an assessment and action process that is streamlined and straightforward to guide a multistrategic approach to social change.

Assessment: Change Actors and Environment for Change

A basic and yet comprehensive assessment of amenability to change involves the examination of two factors: the activists who will pursue the change (the change actors) and the receptivity of the environment in which the change goal will be introduced. Each is briefly described below.

Change Actors

Perhaps the most important factor is the status or position of the people who will pursue the desired change, particularly their access to those who will make the critical decisions about the proposed change. How much contact have the activists had with decision makers? Are they known and respected by them? Are the activists viewed by the decision makers as people who require a response, or are they seen as people who can be ignored? Conversely, how do the activists view themselves? Do they see themselves as a group that is respected or ignored? The personal influence strategies of legislative and political action are more available to change actors with status and access. People with limited access need to find other avenues for influence and create the access they do not yet have.

The relative importance of the goal of empowerment for the organization and its members is also a critical consideration. Many organizations composed of people with low status have explicit goals for increasing the confidence and collective strength of their membership and at the same time raising the consciousness of decision makers and gaining their respect. If collective action as a means of empowerment is an explicit goal, then social action strategies that bring members into direct contact and negotiation with decision makers are more important.

Another question is the degree to which change actors have the time, knowledge, and resources to apply to the change effort. Legislative action is labor-intensive, requiring persistent contact with public officials and their staff. Lobbyists need to be quite knowledgeable about the intricacies of both the legislation and the legislative process. Political action usually requires intense periods of activity around election time and contributions to support candidates. In both legislative and political action, the timetable for work is not controlled by the social change organization, but prescribed by legislative and electoral calendars. With protest and direct action, activists can establish their own timetables, acquiring new activists, alliances, and information over the life of a campaign. Social action is also usually less costly than political or legislative activity.

Some change actors, then, have less status relative to other groups, that is, they have limited access, time, knowledge, and resources. Others have more status, with relatively available access, time, knowledge, and resources. Their status makes a difference in strategic selection.

In which group do social workers and their clients belong? When our clients are the change actors, the answer is clear: The poor, immigrants, people of color, and other groups with limited power belong to low-status groups. Social workers have had a hard time deciding "which side they are on" (Specht & Courtney, 1994). Although they work with the poor and vulnerable, they are educated and mostly middle class. During various historical periods, social workers have identified themselves differently, at times with the powerless and at times with the power holders (Fabricant & Burghardt, 1998). How they see themselves often determines the strategies they choose.

The Environment for Change

The study of social movements in the United States has emphasized the amenability of the environment for public protest and social change (Piven & Cloward, 1977). Relative deprivation, rising aspirations, and political realignments have afforded organizations opportunities for change that activists have seized. Conversely, events can radically alter the odds for a change effort. The September 11th attacks on the World Trade Center and the Pentagon, for example, fundamentally changed how many Americans view policies regarding privacy and civil rights. Consequently, an assessment of the environment is a critical factor in the practitioners' selection of issues and strategy.

The demographics of the population in a geographic area or domain for change are important factors to assess. Decision makers must respond to large constituencies and attend to emerging groups. In today's political environment, most politicians and decision makers must at least appear to be interested in the needs of minority groups, if only to gain the support of moderate white voters. Many politicians today include Spanish phrases in their speeches to appeal to the growing Latino populations in the country. An assessment of how one's group members fit within the population of the total community and how their issue may attract or discourage alliances is critical.

The political acceptability of the group's issue is a related variable. Older adults are widely considered a potent political force, and their issues are instantly recognized. Gay and lesbian issues, once anathema to most public officials, have increasingly gained attention. Regrettably, today the public and most decision makers seem uncomfortable with issues framed in terms of social class, making it difficult to get support for problems that affect the poor. Issues that are framed as basic rights and that concern a large majority of Americans are preferable.

It is critical to track major events, the public's reactions to those events, and trends that suggest opportunities or arguments for action. For example, widely publicized shootings at suburban schools fueled concern about gun control. Energy crises in Western states will likely have the same effect. Both events affected diverse communities and increased the likelihood of broad support among a wide range of constituencies. Organizers and activists have always scanned multiple newspapers and journals to keep abreast of happenings; editorial pages are of particular interest when gauging public reaction. The Internet has increased the accessibility of information, and information about opinion polls and focus groups is now even more readily available.

What is known about the personal histories, backgrounds, alliances, associations, and positions of change targets is also important in the selection of strategies. These factors enable an organization to determine more accurately where decision makers stand in relation to the issue, if they can be influenced, by whom, and what arguments will be most effective.

An assessment of current demographics, events, public opinion, and decision makers can suggest whether the environmental context is favorable or unfavorable for social change. Taken together, the environmental context and the social position of the change actors suggest whether, in Hoefer's terms, an insider or outsider approach is warranted: "An inside strategy tries to influence policy by 'working through the system' and approaching legislative and executive branch decision-makers directly. An outside strategy tries to influence . . . by indirect means, including litigation and protest" (2000, p. 87).

Insider strategies, that is, legislative and political action, are appropriate when change actors have access to and the respect of decision makers; when they have time, knowledge, and resources; and when the environment suggests that the public will be a receptive audience and decision makers will be amenable to the actors' ideas. Insider strategies are successful by virtue of the fact that both the petition and the petitioner are attractive, a situation that affords special entrée.

Outsider strategies, that is, social action and protest, are thought to be more effective for groups that are easily ignored or dismissed by the decision makers and that therefore have restricted and infrequent access to them. Outside strategies are also warranted when there is limited time and knowledge, few resources, and when the environment is less auspicious for change and decision makers are indifferent to the group's interests and arguments. In these cases, conflict and protest are necessary to bring attention to the cause. These groups must grab attention through means other than access.

At most times, groups with limited power will face conditions that indicate the utility of outsider strategies. Thus, it is not surprising that most of our client groups—welfare recipients, African Americans and Latinos, the mentally ill, and other members of low-status groups—are most likely to meet with success when they use outsider strategies. On the other hand, because social workers identify themselves as both low and high status, they have supported both insider and outsider strategies at various times (Colby & Buffum, 1998; Hoefer, 2000; Hyde, 1996), sometimes using both at once and sometimes "borrowing on" the status of other groups by joining with either lower-status client groups or higher-status public interest groups.

Many campaigns—perhaps even most—face situations in which the two factors of change, actor and environment, are not consistently either encouraging or adverse. For example, low-status change actors can be effective using insider strategies, as long as the environment is sufficiently favorable for the change. Beginning in the 1960s, political conditions were so favorable that older people could seek and gain access to decision makers, resulting in policy changes that are today accepted and supported by most. In fact, seniors have become such insiders that their power is assumed.

The obverse is also true; high-status actors may fail with an insider strategy during unfavorable times. For example, celebrities such as Rosie O'Donnell and James Brady were unable to make gun control a significant national issue during the 2000 election, despite the heightened visibility of the problem after several horrifying school shootings.

Groups of lower status should seek access to decision makers to assess the environmental climate. Groups must test whether decision makers' receptivity to their issue will allow them a hearing. If access is granted and decision makers are responsive, legislative and political action should be continued. If, on the other hand, the group is ignored and access denied, the group can organize an outsider strategy of protest and social action. This escalation of tactics is used by many grassroots organizations. They politely seek redress in the first round, and "up the ante" when their demands are denied (Hanna & Robinson, 1994; Mondros & Wilson, 1994).

High-status actors should always first attempt to talk with decision makers and test their access, even if the environment seems unfavorable. If nothing else, such discussions will tell them more about their opposition and the difficulties they will face in pursuing the change. Ultimately, an unfavorable environment will require even high-status actors to bring attention to the issue through public exposure or protest. High-status actors sometimes fear they will lose their access to decision makers if they participate in public protest (Ehrenrich, 1990). In these cases, coalitions are helpful. Outsider strategies can be carried out by low-status groups, while the high-status group continues to press for change using insider means. The campaign to halt military bombing at Vieques in Puerto Rico is an example of such an approach, which resulted in a compromise that could be claimed as a victory. Such coalitions and combinations of strategies have often been encouraged by the literature (Hoefer, 2000; Mizrahi & Rosenthal, 1998; Mondros & Wilson, 1994; Soifer, 1998). Table 14.1 shows the preferred strategies with the relevant variables.

Table 14.1   Conditions for Insider and Outsider Strategies

	Low-Status Actors	*High-Status Actors*
Favorable Environment	Escalation	Insider Strategies
Unfavorable Environment	Outsider Strategies	Coalitions

Ultimately, to accomplish their goals, social change organizations must move from outsiders to insiders. Even the most low-status social change organizations using the most disruptive strategies ultimately seek to come to the negotiating table with decision makers and receive the acclaim of the public. Organizations with explicit goals for empowerment of members use their newly established access as evidence that members are receiving the respect and recognition they deserve. It is a measure of how far they have come.

When the environment is unfavorable to change, low-status groups using outsider strategies introduce new ideas into the public consciousness and discussion. Over time, the views of the organization become more acceptable, and the opposition weakens. Such was the case with Act Up and Greenpeace, organizations that were at first vilified for their activity and then praised for their foresight on treatment for AIDS sufferers and safeguarding the environment.

Prospects for Social Change

The early years of the 21st century suggest conditions that are both encouraging and ominous for the prospect of social change. The 2000 Census documented the growth of the minority population, especially those of Hispanic origin, and this development is encouraging (Albacete, 2001; Schmitt, 2001a, 2001b, 2001c). Minority populations will account for nearly 90% of all population growth in the United States from 1995 to 2050, and they will likely be the majority population by the end of the next century (U.S. Department of Commerce, 1999). Such trends bode well for a variety of change goals. Although the political leanings of new Americans, especially those who arrive from repressive leftist regimes, are not totally clear, they are potential supporters of progressive issues and possible constituencies for social action organizations. Because most social change strategies rely on either numbers of activists (social action) or broad support (lobbying and electoral politics), these demographic trends are extremely good news.

Another trend is the increasingly common practice of polling citizens on a range of domestic and foreign issues and the reliance of politicians on polls and focus groups to frame their positions. Although there is concern about the fluidity of candidates' positions, it does mean that public opinion has influence on what public officials will support (Mitchell, 2000). This influence has at least the potential to balance campaign contributions and lobbying by moneyed interests. If activists can persuade the public of their positions, legislative action is possible.

The trend for issues to be decided at the state rather than the federal level, as we see it, raises both opportunities and difficulties for change. The shift means that targets for influence will devolve from Washington to state capitals. State capitals provide many more target points for activists, and states can be influenced by each other, as they were with antismoking legislation and as seems to be happening regarding the death penalty. State capitals should be more accessible to activists, especially in the smaller states, and state legislators and governors depend more on smaller segments of voters to be elected. Traditionally, however, the federal government has been more protective of rights and more generous with assistance than states, especially in the South and Southwest. For example, welfare benefits are typically lower in these states, and right-to-work laws diminish federal protections for unions to pursue collective bargaining. This may result once again in unfortunate regional differences. Finally, the focus on statewide rather than national campaigns will likely mean less attention to coalition building and collaboration among groups at the national level.

Other trends seem inauspicious for the prospect of social change. Overall, data appear to show that people are less likely to join together in civic groups (Putnam, 2000). Other data indicate that people, especially those of low and moderate income, have less time to engage in social action than once was the case (U.S. Bureau of the Census, 1995). Although the aftermath of the September 11th attacks and their affect on civic participation is not yet clear, in other historical periods of heightened patriotism and nationalism, and constrained civil liberties, organizing activity was understandably muted, especially among new Americans. Ethnic and racial groups, according to Rivera and Erlich (1995), understand issues of race and culture as more urgent than problems associated with class. This trend, too, has the potential to limit coalition building and cooperation with regard to common concerns. At one time, human service agencies were the breeding ground for new activism. Social agencies that once supported social change efforts have been increasingly defunded, privatized, restricted from political activity, and otherwise drained of energy (Fabricant & Burghardt, 1998).

Together, these trends suggest that there are many possible activists from ethnic communities who have the potential for greater influence than in the previous three decades. Demographics shifts portend a more favorable environment for low-status groups. However, given the other constraints, especially the suspiciousness and reticence that are likely to continue in the years immediately following the September 11th attack, the recruitment of new activists and the emergence of social, legislative, and political activity may be both more difficult and more important. In this climate, social change activity has the greatest chance of success if it takes advantage of the clustering of low-income and minority groups and targets issues that are also of concern to working-class and middle-income Americans in general. Neighborhood-based social action and electoral activities capitalize on the aspirations and political yearnings of new Americans who, by moving into middle-income communities, have the potential for political influence. By focusing on issues such as school reform and environmental justice, these groups can build common cause with their neighbors. In these ways, social change can be kept alive even during inauspicious historical periods.

References

Albacete, L. (2001, June 19). America's Hispanic future. *New York Times,* p. 1.

Alinsky, S. (1971). *Rules for radicals.* New York: Vintage.

Austin, M. J., & Betten, N. (1990). *The roots of community organizing, 1917–1939.* Philadelphia: Temple University Press.

Checkoway, B. (1995). Six strategies of community change. *Community Development Journal 30*(1), 2–20.

Colby, I., & Buffum, B. (1998). Social workers and PACs: An examination of National Association of Social Workers P.A.C.E. committees. *Journal of Community Practice, 5*(4), 87–103.

Dear, R., & Patti, R. (1981). Legislative advocacy: Seven effective tactics. *Social Work, 26,* 289–296.

Ehrenreich, B. (1990). *Fear of falling*. New York: Harper Perennial.

Eichler, M. (1995, Summer/Fall). Consensus organizing. *National Civic Review*, 256–261.

Fabricant, M., & Burghardt, S. (1998). Rising from the ashes of cutback: Political warfare and degraded services: Strategic considerations for community building: An editorial essay. *Journal of Community Practice, 5*(4), 53–65.

Fisher, R., & Kling, J. (1990). Leading the people: Two approaches to the role of ideology in community organizing. In J. Kling & P. Posner (Eds.), *Dilemmas of activism: Class, community, and the politics of local mobilization* (pp. 71–90). Philadelphia: Temple University Press.

Grosser, C., & Mondros, J. (1985). Pluralism and participation: The political action approach. In S. Taylor & R. Roberts (Eds.), *Theory and practice of community social work* (pp. 154–178). New York: Columbia University Press.

Hanna, M., & Robinson, B. (1994). *Strategies for community empowerment: Direct-action and transformative approaches to social change practice*. New York: Edwin Mellen.

Hardcastle, D., Wenocur, S., & Powers, P. (1997). *Community practice: Theories and skills for social workers*. New York: Oxford University Press.

Hardina, D. (1997). Empowering students for community organization practice: Teaching confrontation tactics. *Journal of Community Practice, 4*(2), 51–63.

Haynes, K., & Mickelson, J. (1997). *Affecting change: Social workers in the political arena* (4th ed.). Boston: Allyn & Bacon.

Hoefer, R. (2000). Human services interest groups in four states: Lessons for effective advocacy. *Journal of Community Practice, 7*(4), 77–94.

Hyde, C. (1996). A feminist response to Rothman's "The interweaving of community intervention approaches." *Journal of Community Practice, 3*(3/4), 127–145.

Kahn, S. (1991). *Organizing: A guide for grassroots leaders*. Silver Springs, MD: NASW Press.

Kretzmann, J. P., & McKnight, J. L. (1993). *Building communities from the inside out: A path toward finding and mobilizing a community's assets*. Chicago: ACTA.

Mitchell, A. (2000, October 8). The nation: A modest poll proposal. *New York Times*, 5.

Mizrahi, T., & Rosenthal, B. (1998). A whole lot of organizing going on: The status and needs of organizers in community-based organizations. *Journal of Community Practice, 5*(4), 1–24.

Mondros, J., & Wilson, S. (1994). *Organizing for power and empowerment*. New York: Columbia University Press.

Morris, A. D. (1984). *The origins of the civil rights movement*. New York: Free Press.

Piven, F., & Cloward, R. (1977). *Poor people's movements*. New York: Pantheon.

Poindexter, C. C. (1997). Sociopolitical antecedents to Stonewall: Analysis of the origins of the gay rights movement in the United States. *Social Work, 42*(6), 607–615.

Putnam, R. (2000). *Bowling alone: The collapse and revival of American community*. New York: Simon and Schuster.

Rivera, F. G., & Erlich, J. L. (Eds.). (1995). *Community organizing in a diverse society* (2nd ed.). Boston: Allyn & Bacon.

Rothman, J. (1964). An analysis of goals and roles in community organization practice. *Social Work, 9*(2), 24–31.

Rothman, J. (1996). The interweaving of community intervention approaches. *Journal of Community Practice, 5*(4), 69–99.

Rubin H. J., & Rubin, I. S. (2001). *Community organizing and development* (3rd ed.). Needham Heights, MA: Allyn & Bacon.

Schmitt, E. (2001a, April 30). Whites in minority in largest cities, the census shows. *New York Times*, p. 1.

Schmitt, E. (2001b, March 8). New census shows Hispanics are even with Blacks in U.S. *New York Times*, p. 1.

Schmitt, E. (2001c, May 30). To fill gaps, cities seek wave of immigrants. *New York Times,* p. 1.

Simmons, L. (2000). High-stakes casinos and controversies. *Journal of Community Practice,* 7(2), 47–62.

Soifer, S. (1998). Mobile home park lot "rent control": A successful rural legislative campaign. *Journal of Community Practice,* 5(4), 25–37.

Soifer, S., & Singer, J. (1999). The campaign to restore the disability assistance and loan program in the state of Maryland. *Journal of Community Practice,* 6(2), 1–10.

Specht, H., & Courtney, M. (1994). *Unfaithful angels.* New York: Free Press.

U.S. Bureau of the Census. (1995). *Money income in the United States* (Current Population Reports 60–193). Washington, DC: U.S. Government Printing Office.

U.S. Department of Commerce (1999). *The emerging minority marketplace: Minority population growth 1995–2050.* Available from www.mbda.gov/documents/mbdacolor.pdf.

Weil, M. (1996). Model development in community practice: An historical perspective. *Journal of Community Practice,* 3(3/4), 5–67.

CHAPTER 15

Radical Community Organizing

Michael Reisch

The Meaning of Radical Community Organizing

In a society in which acquiescence to the status quo is treated as a virtue, and in which the individual, rather than the community, is celebrated, it could be argued that any form of community organizing is radical. Yet collective mobilization to address common problems, to seek the redress of grievances, or to advocate for a redistribution of power, resources, status, and opportunities has a long and glorious history in the United States (Bystydzienski & Schacht, 2001; Fisher, 1994; Myers, 1989; Pardun, 2001). What, then, distinguishes radical community organizing from other forms of community organizing? In particular, what are the distinctions among radical community organizing and other methods of progressive organizing, such as feminist organizing, multicultural organizing, and class-based or labor organizing?

In this chapter, radical community organizing encompasses a dynamic set of theories, goals, ideologies, values, and practices that are focused on the attainment of social justice and fundamental structural and institutional changes in communities and society. Radical community organizing pursues these goals through a combination of analysis of the root causes of existing societal conditions; the development of alternative economic, political, social, and ideological systems; and the use

Author's Note: The author wishes to thank Professors Marti Bombyk of Eastern Michigan University and Cheryl Hyde of the University of Maryland for their assistance with an early draft of this chapter.

of nontraditional strategies and tactics. A structural theoretical approach underlies both the analysis and the development of practice strategies, with an emphasis on the replacement of oppressive institutions, conditions, systems, and practices with ones that reflect principles of justice, equity, and respect for human diversity.

As in other branches of social work, the concept of radical community organizing has been defined differently inside and outside the profession. Like other social work radicals, radical community organizers focus on "first causes of oppression or injustice" (De Maria, 1992, p. 237) and broad egalitarian goals. Radical views of organizing, however, may be less clearly articulated than those of organizers with other ideological perspectives or those that focus on pragmatic, less clearly ideological objectives. In general, radical organizing regards the market economy as the primary source of individual and social problems and favors both a major redistribution of resources and a fundamental restructuring of institutions to prevent or correct them.

Not all organizers who are labeled "radical," however, support socialist solutions, especially those that require the creation of large, state-run industries. In fact, some radicals of an anarchist or quasi-anarchist inclination share the suspicions of conservatives about the role of government; others regard the state as the primary arena of political struggle and the primary instrument of social progress. Some radical organizers adhere to Marxist or neo-Marxist analyses and have been associated with communist or socialist parties. Others do not identify with a particular ideology or political organization—in fact, they often deliberately downplay their ideology—yet they share many of the causal explanations and goals of those groups on the political left (Aronowitz, 1996; Buhle, 1998; Cantor, 1978; Rorty, 1998; Rubin & Rubin, 2001; Stephens, 1998; Wood, 1997).

The Evolution of Radical Community Organizing in the United States

Organizing for radical causes has existed in the United States since the colonial period. Throughout the 18th and 19th centuries, radical groups attempted to mobilize support around such issues as slavery, women's suffrage, the rights of workers, and the dangers of excessive government interference in people's lives (Foner, 1976; Shor, 1997; Wood, 1997; Young, 1993). After the Civil War, radical organizing often took on a more explicitly anticapitalist tone. The tumultuous environment of the late 19th century had a significant influence on the emergence and initial development of social work (Fisher, 1994; Kraditor, 1981; Shor, 1997).

Prior to World War I, radical community organizing within the field took several forms. Radical social workers developed a multifaceted analysis of socioeconomic inequality and the ways in which industrialization was contributing to the breakdown of community in the United States. Radical organizers like Florence Kelley and Lillian Wald drew attention to the root causes of poverty, promoted alternative policies at the state and municipal levels, and created new community institutions. By speaking out in favor of new roles for women, workers' rights, and racial justice, and by opposing militarism and imperialism, radical community organizers effectively linked people's problems with broader systemic changes in the political-economic context (Reisch & Andrews, 2001). Although radical community organizing during this period was distinguished more by its perspective and goals than its methods, radical organizers were more likely to employ such tactics as strikes and boycotts and even to advocate the use of force when circumstances required (Bombyk, 1995; Fisher, 1994).

During the Depression and through World War II, the principal proponents of radical community organizing were communists, socialists, and independent radicals like Saul Alinsky. Adopting a militant, neighborhood-based approach, they focused their efforts on developing councils of the unemployed in major cities, organizing tenants' unions, promoting interracial cooperation, and protesting against the inequities and inadequacies of New Deal legislation (Betten & Austin, 1990; Fisher, 1994; Rubin & Rubin, 2001). Radical organizers played a key role in the burgeoning rank and file movement within social work, particularly in developing strategies that stressed the mutuality of worker-client concerns (Reisch & Andrews, 2001; Wagner, 1989; Wenocur & Reisch, 1989). By the outbreak of World War II, the impact of the Rank and File movement on community organizing within social work had all but disappeared, as a consequence of internal factional disputes and growing efforts to professionalize community organization practice (Reisch & Wenocur, 1986). However, the work of Alinsky, begun in the Back of the Yards movement, remains influential today.

During the postwar Red Scare, radical organizers were often persecuted, and the radical community organizations they created were replaced by conservative groups, particularly at the neighborhood level. Although their opponents often blurred the distinctions between them, radical organizing differed from reformist organizing in its fundamental antipathy toward the capitalist system, its willingness to form alliances with the Communist and Socialist Parties, and its goals of structural change. Most of the radical or reformist-oriented organizing that occurred between 1945 and the early 1960s, such as the work of the Industrial Areas Foundation created by Alinsky, occurred at the neighborhood level and addressed somewhat parochial concerns such as housing and adequate services. Broader social movements, such as the civil rights movement, emerged from sources with few or no direct connections to social work (Hamilton & Hamilton, 1997; Meier & Rudwick, 1975; Morris, 1984; Sitkoff, 1981).

Radical organizing remained a marginal activity within the social work field until the resurgence of social action in the 1960s and early 1970s. Inspired by developments in the civil rights movement and the fusion of radical social action and community change created by groups like the Black Panthers and Students for a Democratic Society, and encouraged by the infusion of federal dollars through local community action programs, neighborhood organizations with a distinctly radical focus reemerged at the grassroots level. They pushed for the expansion of welfare rights and greater political participation by community residents with low incomes (Abramovitz, 1996; Bailis, 1974; Clark & Hopkins, 1969; Jackson, 1974; Piven & Cloward, 1979; Pope, 1989; Rose, 1972; West, 1981). For a time, this upheaval was so extensive—Harry Boyte (1980) later called it the "backyard revolution"—that it threatened to overturn traditional balances of political power in urban communities (Rose, 1972).

Although the recessions and government cutbacks of the 1970s and 1980s diminished the role of radical community organizing, groups with a distinctly radical or social justice approach continue to exist. Some, like the Industrial Areas Foundation, the Association of Community Organizations for Reform Now (ACORN), and the Center for Third World Organizing (CTWO), have clear political goals, a well-tuned model of organizing, and a national network of community-based affiliates. Others, like the AIDS Coalition to Unleash Power (better known as ACT-UP), have applied a radical analysis and radical tactics to the needs of gays and lesbians and people living with HIV/AIDS, although there is less connection among the local branches of the organization. Many groups have radical perspectives but limit their efforts to small-scale changes at the local level. Finally, some groups, such as the Kensington Welfare Rights Organization based in Philadelphia, employ a radical analysis with both national and local implications and have successfully used radical tactics, yet appear to lack a clear set of policy goals.

Distinguishing Characteristics of Radical Community Organizing

Radical community organizing can be distinguished from other forms of organizing by its analysis of structural arrangements and institutions; the issues it identifies as worthy of attention and action; the economic, political, and social goals it establishes; and the strategies and tactics it employs. Domhoff (1967) characterized this approach as encompassing "the 3 As": analysis (the development of a comprehensive explanation for social problems), alternatives (the formulation of goals and objectives that would involve structural or systemic change), and action (the creation and implementation of strategies and tactics to achieve these goals and objectives).

Analysis

Radical community organizing requires an analysis of the root causes of inequality, injustice, and oppression, with a particular emphasis on examining the fundamental distribution of resources and power. Radical organizing applies, therefore, a political-economic perspective to its analysis of community problems and issues, and it focuses on power dynamics within communities and among communities and the external forces with which they interact. It regards capitalism and its consequences as antithetical to the goals of social justice and empowerment, and it attributes people's problems not to their own failings but to the fundamental operations of the market system (Blee, 1998; Galper, 1980; Hanna, 1994; Knoche, 1987; Rubin & Rubin, 2001; Shaw, 1996).

Alternatives

Focus on basic institutions. Radical community organizing is distinguished from other types of organizing in its core focus on economic issues, especially on how capitalism affects the ability of community members to gain access to the basic necessities: employment, food, shelter, health care, housing, education, and social services. Radical community organizers are also concerned with issues of political participation, especially at the local level, with a particular emphasis on how such participation or nonparticipation influences the distribution of goods, services, status, and opportunities. Although they promote greater democracy, they are skeptical about the ability of existing political institutions to ameliorate the effects of capitalism. In addition, in recent years, radical organizers have also infused into social work a concern over how dominant ideologies affect the distribution of resources and power, particularly through the presence or absence of cultural institutions in communities (Rivera & Erlich, 1998).

Action

Promoting fundamental structural and institutional change. Unlike organizers who focus on maintaining or reforming the status quo, radical organizers promote a redistribution of resources and power at the community and societal level (Gorz, 1977). This involves the restructuring of existing institutions, the reformulation of social goals, and the reordering of policy priorities—for example, away from militarism and toward greater investment in human and social capital (Prigoff, 2001; Van Soest, 1997). Some radical organizers also work on the creation of alternative institutions, such as producer-consumer cooperatives, ecovillages, and local neighborhood governments (Furlough & Strikwerda, 1999; Holmstrom, 1993; Kasmir, 1996; Silver, 1980). Underlying this work is the promotion of an alternative vision of society, often based on socialist or collectivist principles, and a value system that is juxtaposed to the individualistically oriented, materialistic culture that pervades much of U.S. society.

Theoretical Foundations of Radical Community Organizing

The Nature of Social Change

Radical community organizing is founded on a view of social change that emphasizes the basic humanity and equality of all people (Gil, 1998). It largely rejects the conservative view of society as the aggregation of individual self-interests, as well as pluralist theories of politics and social change (Bellah, Madsen, Sullivan, Swidler, & Tipton, 1996; Cohen, 2002; Trotman, 2002). By viewing people instead as social beings, radical community organizers regard the community's "well-being as a more complex construct made up of not only the aggregate of its members but the relationships among them as well" (Mullaly, 1997, p. 32).

The intellectual roots of radical community organizing are found in diverse sources. These include the secular and religious utopian ideas of the 19th and early 20th centuries, such as Marxism, non-Marxian (or evolutionary) socialism, the Social Gospel movement, radical trade unionism, anarchism, and "first wave" feminism. More recent influences include modern interpretations of social justice, such as that of John Rawls (1971); a variety of anti-oppression philosophies from around the world, including *conscientization* and *animation*; various theories of human liberation, both secular and religious; and Gandhian principles of non-violence (Ackerman, 2000; Bruyn & Rayman, 1979; Epstein, 1991; Freire, 1971; Sharp, 1973). Among contemporary theories that most influence radical community organizing in the United States are neo-Marxism, structural theory, radical feminism, empowerment theory, and adaptations of conscientization, particularly as developed by Freire (1971) and applied first in Latin and Central America and later in Europe and North America.

Neo-Marxism. Neo-Marxists, whom George and Wilding (1994) divided into three groups (post-Marxists, analytical Marxists, and new structural Marxists), have modified classical Marxist theory in several important ways. Post-Marxists repudiate the notion that class divisions alone are central to social struggle and replace it with a model that combines "a multitude of interests emanating from various strata, groups, and social movements" (Chilcote & Chilcote, 1992, p. 90). This perspective suits those radical community practitioners who are seeking ways to build coalitions that transcend traditional boundaries marked by racial, ethnic, religious, or cultural identity.

Analytical Marxists maintain a materialist conception of history, although they largely eschew the Marxist formulation of class structure under capitalism and the idea of class consciousness. They define class action as the aggregation of self-interested, rational, individual choices—a perspective that is eerily similar to classic liberal and current neoliberal theories. By contrast, new structural Marxists accept many of the premises of classic Marxism, particularly the role of the environment in shaping human behavior. Like post-Marxists, however, they attempt to expand the traditional Marxist notion of social struggle beyond the parameters of class to encompass issues of gender, race, and ecology as coequal forces underlying political and social conflict (George & Wilding, 1994).

Structural theory. Structural theory, best articulated in recent years by Canadian scholars such as Carniol (1992), Moreau (1990), and Mullaly (1997), integrates into its conceptual framework elements of socialist ideology, critical social theory, conflict perspectives, dialectical analysis, a focus on all forms of oppression, and an emphasis on social transformation and emancipation (Mullaly, 1997, p. 99). It assumes that in spite of the contradictory position in which radical organizers find themselves, their values and goals are more consistent with those of socialism than of capitalism. Structural theory and critical theory, along with other aspects of radical community organizing, propose action to effect emancipating changes in society, particularly among marginalized populations (Leonard, 1990). Like conflict theorists since Marx, proponents of structural theory reject the status quo and desire radical change. By analyzing community issues from a conflict perspective, radical organizers can clarify the relationship between current institutional arrangements and the distribution of resources and power. Based on this perspective, they focus their work on the attainment of greater democracy and equality through the transformation of the structures that create inequality and oppression and on helping people overcome the damage produced by alienation and exploitation (Mullaly, 1997).

Radical feminism. Radical feminism emphasizes the critical role of gender in maintaining patriarchal institutions and cultural norms that oppress women. Although radical feminists acknowledge the impact of class and race, they assert that patriarchy, rather than capitalism per se, is primarily responsible for the persistence of social inequality. The major contributions of radical feminists to radical community organizing have been their elucidation of the dynamics of patriarchy, their emphasis on women's issues (such as reproductive rights, protection from violence, and workplace inequalities), their attention to process in community work, and their focus on the need for consciousness raising and nonhierarchical processes of decision making within community organizations (Blee, 1998; Crow, 2000; Gutiérrez & Lewis, 1998; Naples, 1998; Thompson, 2001; Ziarek, 2001). Radical feminism is linked to other aspects of radical organizing theory in its emphasis on the relationship between the personal and the political and through transformational politics, which "seeks individual liberation through collective activity [and] . . . the dismantling of all permanent power hierarchies" (Morell, 1987, pp. 147–148).

Empowerment theory. Although the concept of empowerment has deep roots within the fields of social work and radical community organizing, it was not until the 1970s—through the influence of the feminist and civil rights movements—that the term was first used in the social work field (Simon, 1994; Solomon, 1976). For organizers, empowerment theory focuses on the integration of a community's material, emotional, and psychological needs by fusing political-economic and psychosocial perspectives (Reisch, Wenocur, & Sherman, 1981). It provides a means for people to develop an awareness of their own capacities to change their environments as they address their basic needs. In sum, empowerment theory is "the tool through which ordinary people collectively combat the *mobilization of bias*" (Rubin & Rubin, 2001, p. 77).

Empowerment theory is closely related to several other key features of radical community organizing. As a process that emphasizes mutuality among people and between organizers and the community, it reflects the tradition of self-help and mutual aid that dates back to the 19th century (Goldman, 1910; Kropotkin, 1960). By focusing on the political-economic context of communities, it is consistent with classical and contemporary Marxism and both critical and structural theory (Delgado & Stefanic, 2000). Through the integration of people's material and psychosocial needs, it underscores the relationship between the personal and the political. Finally, like conscientization and radical feminism, it stresses the importance of consciousness raising in change-inducing and change-sustaining processes.

Conscientization. Conscientization is a version of consciousness raising developed by the Brazilian educator Paulo Freire and subsequently applied in educational and service settings by Latin American, European, and North American social workers. Its theories resemble the idea of radical praxis first articulated by Marx, the focus on the role of intragroup dialogue that emerged with the modern feminist movement, and the goals of liberation theology. Freire's (1971) model assumes that the environment is not a fixed reality but represents, instead, a problem to be defined, worked on, and solved collectively through critical thinking and action. It also focuses on creating community among organizers and the people by engaging in a process of demythologizing reality as a first step toward concerted political action. For community practitioners, conscientization provides a theoretical basis "for professional commitment to radical social change through a process that promotes self-awareness of the deprived, that fosters their appreciation of their oppressed state and evidences a willingness to join with them in their revolutionary struggle for self-realization" (Lewis, 1973, p. 32).

Transformative Dynamics: Underlying Principles of Radical Organizing

In addition to an emphasis on the structural causes of injustice and oppression, radical community organizing is also informed by several overarching principles. One, derived from the feminist movement, is the linkage of the personal with the political. For radical community organizers, this now-popular adage goes beyond the liberal approach of connecting private troubles with public issues to an examination of how oppression and privilege are manifest in all societal institutions and in all aspects of social interaction. It reflects a structural analysis of society as well as a conflict orientation, and it attempts to help "people . . . relate their personal experience with oppression to a broader political understanding" (Mullaly, 1997, p. 115).

A second principle of radical community organizing is the importance of self-help and mutual aid as integral aspects of community development and change. The theoretical and historical roots of this principle can be found in anarchist and anarcho-syndicalist philosophy; the cooperative movement of the late 19th and early 20th centuries; radical trade unionism; feminist and empowerment theory; and the experiences of such marginalized groups as people of color, immigrants, and refugees. Perhaps the best articulation of the principles of mutual aid in social work can be found in the writings of Bertha Reynolds (1951), whose ideas have found a receptive audience among radical community organizers.

A third principle involves the redefinition of the relationship between the individual and the community, the society, and the state. Radical organizers consider the community critical in the development of self-identity and group solidarity and in the formulation of efforts to resist external domination and oppression (Mullaly, 1997). Strongly influenced in recent years by radical feminists and organizers from communities of color and the gay and lesbian community, they view group specificity as of equal importance to the promotion of the idea of a universal humanity (Rivera & Erlich, 1998). Recognizing the significance of difference in people's lives helps organizers "encourage and support group-specific organizations and groups or the establishment of new ones" (Mullaly, 1997, p. 159). Although many radical community organizers echo Marx in their view of the state as an instrument of the ruling class (or as a manifestation of patriarchy or white supremacy), they also acknowledge the importance of organizers becoming involved inside the political system (Brecher & Costello, 1990; Naples, 1998; Russell, 1990). Increasingly linked to new social movement theory, this aspect of radical community organizing regards the state, however flawed, as an appropriate arena for political struggle (Fisher & Karger, 1997).

Radical Strategies

The strategies of radical community organizers differ from their nonradical counterparts in several ways. First, although like other organizers they use a community's definition of its problems as a point of departure, they seek to link these problems throughout the organizing process with a structural analysis of their origins. The goals of radical organizing, therefore, are not merely the amelioration or even the elimination of specific community problems. Instead, radical organizers focus on the redistribution of power and resources, the dismantling of oppressive systems, and the creation of viable alternative institutional arrangements. Although most radical organizers profess revolutionary goals, they remain cognizant of the limited potential of revolutionary activism in the United States. Even as they filter their radical agenda through a reformist lens, they distinguish between what Gorz termed "reformist reform" and "non-reformist reform" (1977).

Radical Tactics

The definition of radical organizing tactics constantly evolves in response to changes in the political and cultural context. At one time, strikes, boycotts, and sit-ins were regarded as radical tactics. Now they are accepted tools in political struggle by groups at all points on the ideological spectrum. As a result, they have frequently lost the critical element of surprise that originally made them effective. Radical organizers, therefore, are always searching for ways to push the edges of the tactical envelope by going outside the experiences and expectations of their opponents (Alinsky, 1971). In general, although radical organizers do not eschew the use of consensus tactics, they are more comfortable using conflict strategies in their work. One of the most effective groups in this regard in recent years has been ACT-UP, whose members risked alienating potential supporters in their use of tactics (such as blocking traffic on key arteries during rush hour) that brought the group's issues public exposure that less radical tactics may have failed to do. The worldwide protests against the World Trade Organization (WTO) are another example of the use of conflict-laden radical organizing tactics.

Significant differences exist among radical community organizers, however, about which tactics are appropriate and effective in the current political context. To some extent, these differences revolve around the classic "means/ends" debate presented so vividly by Alinsky (1971). The most salient areas of disagreement involve the following issues:

Whether an organizer's values should be imposed on the community, particularly in regard to the degree that community residents might be put at risk.

Whether organizers should focus their efforts inside or outside of existing (i.e., legitimate) political channels. On the one side are "radical pragmatists" who maintain that abandoning mainstream politics merely creates a political vacuum that more conservative forces will fill. They argue that the gains of social movements over the past century have resulted from the use of a combination of organizing tactics, particularly those which are deemed "acceptable" within the political culture of the period (Gamson, 1975). In this view, participation in electoral politics, for example, does not preclude the use of more radical, nonmainstream tactics as part of an "inside/outside" approach. On the other side are those radicals who warn that participation inside the political system inevitably leads to co-optation because of the intrinsically corrupt nature of democracy under capitalism. They assert that it is only by pushing on the margins of the system that the political center moves in the direction of progressive solutions to society's problems (Blee, 1998; Bystydzienski & Schacht, 2001; Knoche, 1987; Oberschall, 1993).

Whether violence is an acceptable tactic. Although nearly all radical organizers support the occasional use of illegal tactics such as nonviolent civil disobedience, the majority reject the use of violent tactics including the destruction of property (Ackerman, 2000; Bruyn & Rayman, 1979; Epstein, 1991; Sharp, 1973). Some radicals, like Gil (1998), argue that the use of violence effectively undermines the values and goals radicals profess. Others distinguish between the use of force—for example, in self-defense—and the deliberate, unprovoked use of violence, particularly against other people (Mooney, 1995; Shaw, 1996; Stock, 1996). In the absence of a genuinely revolutionary situation in the United States, these arguments have been largely confined to armchair debates, although recently they have surfaced over the anti-WTO protests and in the aftermath of terrorist attacks (Prigoff, 2001).

Ethical and Legal Issues

In addition to such ongoing value conflicts, ethical dilemmas for radical community organizers can emerge from several sources. As for other community practitioners, they appear when ethical principles come into conflict or when the factors that shape a particular situation are unclear or lack sufficient time to be analyzed and resolved (Reamer, 1999). Given the focus of radical community organizing, ethical dilemmas often arise when community groups are faced with a compulsory choice between equally unsatisfactory alternatives. A primary example of such a situation occurs when decisions have to be made about the allocation of scarce resources. Because of the strategies and tactics used by radical organizers, conflicts sometimes arise between the maintenance of ethical principles and the satisfaction of legal mandates. Radical community organizers, in particular, have to ask themselves "under what conditions should [they] separate themselves from unethical working arrangements or [from institutions] whose ideology and values differ markedly from their own? " (Reisch & Lowe, 2000, p. 31).

For example, radical community organizers confronting seemingly intractable power imbalances in their work, such as those that occur in protests against major utilities or other large multinational corporations, may be tempted to abandon the ethics of truth telling or confidentiality in pursuit of a higher purpose, such as the attainment of a redistributive goal. The constant pressures of community work and the desire to work for social justice may tempt radical community organizers to adopt paternalistic postures in their work with low-income and low-power communities and implicitly deny constituents their right to self-determination (Reisch & Rivera, 1999). Perhaps the classic ethical dilemma for radical organizers is the enduring conflict between means and ends, best articulated by Alinsky in *Rules for Radicals* (1971). The marginal status of radicals in U.S. society further exacerbates these ethical dilemmas.

Case Examples

Radical Organizing Successes

Most examples of successful radical organizing in the United States have occurred outside the social work field and have generally been linked to long-term social movements (Buhle, 1998; Fisher, 1994; Oberschall, 1993; Shor, 1997; Young, 1993). However, owing to the conservative nature of U.S. politics and culture, radical goals have often been diluted in the interest of pragmatic compromise. Although the victories of radical organizers in such areas as suffrage, reproductive choice, and labor rights have improved the lives of people, they have largely failed to alter the fundamental structure of U.S. capitalism and have made only modest changes in societal patterns of institutional racism and sexism.

Although modest in scope and limited in impact because of the overarching power of national and international political-economic forces, radical organizing in the United States has probably been more effective at the local level. Radical organizers in urban areas have enabled communities to acquire greater control over their schools, health care, and social services. They have helped community residents resist the encroachment of unchecked development and enhanced the power of constituents in local institutions. Groups like CTWO have attacked the sources of environmental racism, and living wage campaigns have attempted to address the growing disparity in income levels among U.S. workers. In rural areas, radical organizers have mobilized farm communities against power companies and the takeover of family farms by powerful agribusinesses (Mooney, 1995; Stock, 1996; Wellstone, 1978). It is often difficult, however, to distinguish radical and reformist organizing efforts at the neighborhood level (Medoff & Sklar, 1994; Rubin & Rubin, 2001).

Probably the best examples of radical organizing in the late 20th century have occurred outside the United States and were associated with radical or revolutionary movements in the developing world. These include the work of the Sandinistas in Nicaragua, the Frente Farabundo Marti Para La Liberacion Nacional in El Salvador, the African National Congress in South Africa, and Hamas in the West Bank and Gaza. On a smaller scale, successful radical organizing has occurred among women in the barrios of Lima, Peru, and Santiago, Chile; among the landless indigenous people of Chiapas, Mexico; and in the formation of producer-consumer cooperatives in the Basque region of Spain (Campfens, 1988; Finn, 1999; Kasmir, 1996).

Failures and Limitations of Radical Community Organizing

Radical community organizing in the United States is severely constrained by a number of structural and cultural factors. One major barrier is the absence of broad-based social movements or political institutions (e.g., parties) that could supply the resources and legitimacy for radical organizing. Another serious impediment is the ahistorical popular and political culture within the United States regarding perspectives on social policy and the lack of a systematic critique of the structural causes of inequality and injustice. These are most dramatically demonstrated by the nature of public discourse in the media and political arenas. Another barrier is the persistence of an individualistically oriented, materialistic culture (Bellah et al., 1996; Epstein, 1991). Finally, the sectarian schisms among radical groups and radical intellectuals in the United States undermine efforts to forge a unified radical perspective that could become the basis for local and national action.

Implications of Radical Community Organizing for 21st-Century Social Work

Practice and Research

Throughout its history, "not charity, but justice" has been the clarion call of radical community organizers in the United States. The revised *Code of Ethics* of the National Association of Social Workers (1996) makes the pursuit of social justice an ethical imperative for all social workers, and the latest *Curriculum Policy Statement* of the Council on Social Work Education (2001) requires all social work students to be taught how to work for social and economic justice. Nevertheless, there are few extant examples of radical community organizing practice in the United States today. There are several striking reasons why this is so.

First, since the collapse of the Soviet Union in the early 1990s, socialist ideology has been widely discredited as an alternative paradigm. Second, it is difficult to translate the ideal of social justice into specific goals and objectives, particularly when there is little immediate likelihood of transforming the basic economic and political structure of society. In addition, policy devolution, political decentralization, and the fragmentation of social movements have promoted the rise of narrow local organizing efforts that have limited potential for effecting changes in the institutional framework of society.

To overcome these formidable obstacles, radical community organizers might consider the following steps:

- Emphasize the educational function of organizing to create greater awareness of the relationship between local issues and their structural causes and to forge connections among groups that have common purposes but currently disparate agendas (Gutiérrez, 1997).
- Emphasize praxis in their training and community development efforts (i.e., ongoing reflection on the dynamic relationship between theory and action).
- Develop creative approaches to stimulate the involvement and mobilization of groups—particularly young people—that are often excluded from the organizing process. The Minority Apprenticeship Program run by CTWO is an excellent example of such efforts. More extensive application of interactive technologies through the Internet and the use of cultural activities as vehicles for community development and change are just two other tactical steps that radical organizers could adopt (Reisch & Jarman-Rohde, 1999).
- Engage in the difficult but essential task of forging and sustaining multiracial and multicultural coalitions at the local level (Chesler, 2001). This would

require outreach to neighborhood groups, such as churches, whose ideology and style might be difficult for some radical organizers to accept (Cnaan, Wineburg, & Boddie, 1999).

- Establish small-scale, community-based action research projects that would analyze community problems within a structural framework and generate ideas for local solutions. Such projects would help bring down the artificial separation of practice and research and provide the basis for greater collaboration between organizers and constituents (Coulton, 1995).

- Create ongoing mechanisms of support—formal and informal—to enable radical organizers to maintain the stamina necessary for long-term, often arduous work.

Education and Training

Radical organizing skills are infrequently taught in schools of social work today, although many schools identify social justice and empowerment as part of their educational missions (Hardina, 1997). If social work is to retain its longstanding commitment to social justice and the elimination of oppression, the social workers of the future will have to be prepared to work in communities whose economic plight and social tensions will be exacerbated by changes in national and international economics and politics. Minimally, to educate students for community practice in this environment, social work educators need to take the following steps:

- Provide students with a basic understanding of microeconomics and macroeconomics, with a particular emphasis on how the global economy affects the daily lives and self-concepts of the community residents with whom they work.

- Emphasize the growing, yet often overlooked significance of social class, without being drawn into divisive debates over which form of oppression is paramount in our society.

- Pay more attention to the changing nature of work and the socioeconomic, psychological, and cultural effects of this change at the community level.

- Stress the significance of the political-economic context in the development of new conceptual frameworks and intervention strategies.

- Make explicit the connections between politics and social work, particularly as they are manifested at the community level.

- Teach skills in community-based action research, coalition building, and advocacy to all students.

- Consider rethinking what constitutes a suitable field placement so that students may have the opportunity to work with groups that reflect radical organizing principles and methods.

- Use field instructors who are committed to radical goals and models of field supervision that recognize the different realities of organizations that use radical strategies and tactics.

Finally, one of the key features of radical community organizing is the conscious integration of values into the process of community change (Graf, 1979). Social work educators need to incorporate an ongoing discussion of the ethics of radical organizing in their classes and informal contacts with students. They will also have to examine the meaning of social justice and empowerment carefully in a rapidly changing, multicultural environment. This will involve framing new inquiries about the function of community organizing in a context "that increasingly restricts the choices available to people in need and those who work with them" (Reisch & Rivera, 1999, p. 53).

The Future of Radical Community Organizing

Given the pervasive influence of capitalist values in U.S. society and the ongoing pressure on social workers to retain their precarious professional status, it is unlikely that radical community organizing will acquire dramatically increased prominence among social workers in the foreseeable future. The adoption of the theories and methods that underlie radical organizing would require a transformation in which few social workers would be willing or able to engage. Nevertheless, there are substantial numbers of students and practitioners who are receptive to radical theoretical perspectives and to the application of a critical analysis of capitalism in their community work (Andrews & Reisch, 2002). The development of collaborative, community-based research and training projects that link faculty, students, practitioners, and community residents may be one means of promoting a radical vision of community organizing in the future (Delgado, 1994; Wenocur & Soifer, 1997). As socioeconomic inequality increases and social tensions intensify, such collaborative relationships could provide a small-scale model of the type that radical community organizers have been seeking to create for over a century.

References

Abramovitz, M. (1996). *Under attack, fighting back: Women and welfare in the United States.* New York: Monthly Review Press.

Ackerman, P. (2000). *A force more powerful: A century of non-violent conflict.* New York: St. Martin's Press.

Alinsky, S. (1971). *Rules for radicals.* New York: Vintage.

Andrews, J., & Reisch, M. (2002). The radical voices of social workers: Some lessons for the future. *Journal of Progressive Human Services, 13*(1), 5–30.

Aronowitz, S. (1996). *The death and rebirth of American radicalism.* New York: Routledge.

Bailis, L. N. (1974). *Bread or justice: Grassroots organizing in the welfare rights movement.* Boston: Lexington Books.

Bellah, R., Madsen, R., Sullivan, W. M., Swindler, A., & Tipton, S. M. (1996). *Habits of the heart: Individualism and commitment in American life* (rev. ed.). Berkeley: University of California Press.

Betten, N., & Austin, M. (1990). *The roots of community organization, 1917–1939.* Philadelphia: Temple University Press.

Blee, K. M. (1998). *No middle ground: Women and radical protest.* New York: New York University Press.

Bombyk, M. (1995). Progressive social work. In R. L. Edwards (Ed.), *Encyclopedia of social work* (19th ed., pp. 1933–1942), Washington, DC: NASW Press.

Boyte, H. C. (1980). *The backyard revolution: Understanding the new citizens movement.* Philadelphia: Temple University Press.

Brecher, J., & Costello, T. (Eds.). (1990). *Building bridges: The emerging grassroots coalition of labor and community.* New York: Monthly Review Press.

Bruyn, S. T. & Rayman, P. M. (1979). *Nonviolent action and social change.* New York: Irvington.

Buhle, P. (1998). *Images of American radicals.* Hanover, MA: Christopher.

Bystydzienski, J. M., & Schacht, S. P. (Eds.). (2001). *Forging radical alliances across difference: Coalition politics for the new millennium.* New York: Rowman and Littlefield.

Campfens, H. (1988). On the move: Women organize in Lima's shanty towns. *Women and Environments, 10,* 4–7.

Cantor, M. (1978). *The divided left: American radicals, 1900–1975.* New York: Hill and Wang.

Carniol, B. (1992). Structural social work: Maurice Moreau's challenge to social work practice. *Journal of Progressive Human Services, 3*(1), 1–20.

Chesler, M. (2001). The charge to the white male brigade. *Journal of Applied Behavioral Sciences 31*(3), 292–304.

Chilcote, E., & Chilcote, C. (1992). The crisis of Marxism. *Rethinking Marxism 5*(2), 84–107.

Clark, K. B., & Hopkins, J. (Eds.). (1969). *A relevant war against poverty: A study of CAPS and observable social change.* New York: Harper and Row.

Cnaan, R., Wineburg, R., & Boddie, S. (1999). *The newer deal: Social work and religion in partnership.* New York: Columbia University Press.

Cohen, N. (2002). *The reconstruction of American liberalism, 1865–1914.* Chapel Hill: University of North Carolina Press.

Coulton, C. J. (1995). Poverty, work, and community: A research agenda for an era of diminishing federal responsibility. *Social Work, 40,* 437–439.

Council on Social Work Education. (2001). *Curriculum policy statement* (Rev. ed.). Alexandria, VA: Author.

Crow, B. A. (2000). *Radical feminism: A documentary reader.* New York: New York University Press.

Delgado, G. (1994). *Beyond the politics of place: New directions in community organizing in the 1990s.* Oakland, CA: Applied Research Center.

Delgado, R., & Stefanic, J. (Eds.). (2000). *Critical race theory: The cutting edge* (2nd ed.). Philadelphia: Temple University Press.

De Maria, W. (1992). On the trail of a radical pedagogy for social work education. *British Journal of Social Work, 22*(3), 231–252.

Domhoff, G. W. (1967). *Who rules America?* Englewood Cliffs, NJ: Prentice Hall.

Epstein, B. (1991). *Political protest and cultural revolution: Nonviolent direct action in the 1970s and 1980s.* Berkeley: University of California Press.

Finn, J. L. (1999). *Tracing the veins: Of copper, culture, and community from Butte to Chuquicamada.* Berkeley: University of California Press.

Fisher, R. (1994). *Let the people decide: A history of neighborhood organizing in America* (rev. ed.). New York: Twayne.

Fisher, R., & Karger, H. J. (1997). *Social work and community in a private world: Getting out in public.* White Plains, NY: Longman.

Foner, P. S. (1976). *We, the other people: Alternative declarations of independence by labor groups, farmers, workers' rights advocates, socialists, and blacks, 1829–1975.* Urbana: University of Illinois Press.

Freire, P. (1971). *Pedagogy of the oppressed.* New York: Seabury.

Furlough, E., & Strikwerda, C. (1999). *Consumers against capitalism? Consumer cooperation in Europe, North America, and Japan, 1840–1990.* Lanham, MD: Rowman and Littlefield.

Galper, J. (1980). *Social work practice: A radical perspective.* Englewood Cliffs, NJ: Prentice Hall.

Gamson, W. (1975). *The strategy of social protest.* Homewood, IL: Dorsey Press.

George, V., & Wilding, P. (1994). *Welfare and ideology.* New York: Harvester/Wheatsheaf.

Gil, D. (1998). *Confronting injustice and oppression: Concepts and strategies for social workers.* New York: Columbia University Press.

Goldman, E. (1910). *Anarchism and other essays.* New York: Mother Earth Press.

Gorz, A. (1977). *Strategy for labor.* Boston: Beacon Press.

Graf, A. (1979). *Integrating the discussion of values into the organizing process.* Baltimore, MD: Industrial Areas Foundation.

Gutiérrez, L. (1997). Multicultural community organizing. In M. Reisch & E. Gambrill (Eds.), *Social work in the 21st century* (pp. 249–259). Thousand Oaks, CA: Pine Forge.

Gutiérrez, L., & Lewis, E. (1998). A feminist perspective on organizing with women of color. In F. Rivera & J. Erlich (Eds.), *Community organizing in a diverse society* (3rd ed., pp. 97–116). Needham Heights, MA: Allyn & Bacon.

Hamilton, D. C., & Hamilton, C. V. (1997). *The dual agenda: The African-American struggle for civil and economic equality.* New York: Columbia University Press.

Hanna, M. G. (1994). *Strategies for community empowerment: Direct action and transformative approaches to social change practice.* Lewiston, NY: Mellen.

Hardina, D. (1997). Empowering students for community organization practice: Teaching confrontation tactics. *Journal of Community Practice, 4*(2), 51–63.

Holmstrom, M. (1993). *Spain's new social economy: Workers' self-management in Catalonia.* Oxford, UK, and Providence, RI: Berg.

Jackson, L. R. (1974). *Protest by the poor: The welfare rights movement in New York City.* Boston: Lexington.

Kasmir, S. (1996). *The myth of Mondragon: Cooperatives, politics and working class life in a Basque town.* Albany, NY: SUNY Press.

Knoche, T. (1987). *Organizing communities: Building anarchist grassroots movements.* Anti-Authoritarian Network of Community Organizers.

Kraditor, A. S. (1981). *The radical persuasion, 1890–1917: Aspects of the intellectual history and the historiography of three American radical organizations.* Baton Rouge: Louisiana State University Press.

Kropotkin, P. (1960). *Anarchism and revolution.* London: Freedom Press.

Leonard, P. (1990). Contesting the welfare state in a neo-conservative era. *Journal of Progressive Human Services, 1*(1), 1–25.

Lewis, H. (1973, Fall). Agology, animation, conscientization: Implications for social work education in the USA. *Journal of Education for Social Work, 9,* 31–38.

Medoff, P., & Sklar, H. (1994). *Streets of hope: The fall and rise of an urban neighborhood.* Boston: South End Press.

Meier, A., & Rudwick, E. (1975). *CORE: A study in the civil rights movement.* Urbana: University of Illinois Press.

Mooney, P. M. (1995). *Farmers' and farmworkers' movements: Social protest in American agriculture.* New York: Twayne.

Moreau, M. (1990). Empowerment through advocacy and consciousness-raising: Implications of a structural approach to social work. *Journal of Sociology and Social Welfare, 17*(2), 53–67.

Morell, C. (1987). Cause is function: Toward a feminist model of integration for social work. *Social Service Review, 61*(1), 144–155.

Morris, A. (1984). *The origins of the civil rights movement.* New York: Free Press.

Mullaly, R. (1997). *Structural social work* (2nd ed.). New York: Oxford University Press.

Myers, R. D. (Ed.). (1989). *Toward a history of the new left: Essays from within the movement.* Brooklyn, NY: Carlson.

Naples, N. A. (Ed.). (1998). *Community activism and feminist politics: Organizing across race, class and gender.* New York: Routledge.

National Association of Social Workers. (1996). *Code of ethics* (Rev. ed.). Washington, DC: Author.

Oberschall, A. (1993). *Social movements: Ideologies, interests, and identities.* New Brunswick, NJ: Transaction.

Pardun, R. (2001). *Prairie radical: A journey through the sixties.* Los Gatos, CA: Shire Press.

Piven, F. F., & Cloward, R. (1979). *Poor people's movements: How they succeed, why they fail.* New York: Vintage Press.

Pope, J. (1989). *Biting the hand that feeds them: Organizing women on welfare at the grassroots level.* New York: Praeger.

Prigoff, A. (2001). *Economics for social workers.* Belmont, CA: Brooks/Cole.

Rawls, J. (1971). *A theory of justice.* Cambridge, MA: Harvard University Press.

Reamer, F. G. (1999). *Social work values and ethics* (2nd ed.). New York: Columbia University Press.

Reisch, M., & Andrews, J. (2001). *The road not taken: A history of radical social work in the United States.* Philadelphia: Brunner-Routledge.

Reisch, M., & Jarman-Rohde, L. (1999, November). *Strengthening community advocacy through cultural activities and political action.* Paper presented at the annual conference of the Association for Research on Nonprofit Organizations and Voluntary Action, Seattle, WA.

Reisch, M., & Lowe, J. I. (2000). "Of means and ends" revisited: Teaching ethical community organizing in an unethical society. *Journal of Community Practice, 7*(1), 19–38.

Reisch, M., & Rivera, F. (1999). Ethical and racial conflicts in urban-based action research. *Journal of Community Practice, 6*(2), 49–62.

Reisch, M., & Wenocur, S. (1986). The future of community organization in social work: Social activism and the politics of profession building. *Social Service Review, 60*(1), 70–91.

Reisch, M., Wenocur, S., & Sherman, W. (1981). Empowerment, conscientization and animation as core social work skills. *Social Development Issues, 5*(2–3), 108–120.

Reynolds, B. C. (1951). *Social work and social living.* New York: Citadel Press.

Rivera, F., & Erlich, J. (1998). *Community organizing in a diverse society* (3rd ed.). Boston: Allyn and Bacon.

Rorty, R. (1998). *Achieving our country: Left thought in 20th century America.* Cambridge, MA: Harvard University Press.

Rose, S. (1972). *The betrayal of the poor: The transformation of community action.* Cambridge, MA: Schenkman.

Rubin, H., & Rubin, I. S. (2001). *Community organizing and development* (3rd ed.). Boston: Allyn & Bacon.

Russell, D. M. (1990). *Political organizing in grassroots politics.* Lanham, MD: University Press of America.

Sharp, G. (1973). *The politics of nonviolent action.* Boston: P. Sargent.

Shaw, R. (1996). *The activist's handbook: A primer for the 1990s and beyond.* Berkeley: University of California Press.

Shor, F. R. (1997). *Utopianism and radicalism in a reforming America, 1888–1918.* Westport, CT: Greenwood Press.

Silver, M. (1980). *Social infrastructure organizing technology.* Baltimore: University of Maryland School of Social Work and Community Planning.

Simon, B. L. (1994). *The empowerment tradition in American social work.* New York: Columbia University Press.

Sitkoff, H. (1981). *The struggle for black equality, 1954–1980.* New York: Hill and Wang.

Solomon, B. (1986). *Black empowerment: Social work in oppressed communities.* New York: Columbia University Press.

Stephens, J. (1998). *Anti-disciplinary protest: Sixties radicalism and postmodernism*. New York: Cambridge.

Stock, C. M. (1996). *Rural radicals: Righteous rage in the American grain*. Ithaca, NY: Cornell University Press.

Thompson, D. (2001). *Radical feminism today*. London: Sage.

Trotman, C. J. (Ed.). (2002). *Multiculturalism: Roots and realities*. Bloomington: Indiana University Press.

Van Soest, D. (1997). *The global crisis of violence: Common problems, universal causes, shared solutions*. Washington, DC: NASW Press.

Wagner, D. (1989). Radical movements in the social services: A theoretical framework. *Social Service Review, 63*(2), 264–284.

Wellstone, P. (1978). *How the rural poor got power: Narrative of a grassroots organizer*. Amherst: University of Massachusetts Press.

Wenocur, S., & Reisch, M. (1989). *From charity to enterprise: The development of American social work in a market economy*. Urbana: University of Illinois Press.

Wenocur, S., & Soifer, S. (1997). Prospects for community organization. In M. Reisch & E. Gambrill (Eds.), *Social work in the 21st century* (pp. 198–208). Thousand Oaks, CA: Pine Forge.

West, G. (1981). *The national welfare rights organization: The social protest of poor women*. New York: Praeger.

Wood, G. S. (1997). *The radicalism of the American revolution*. New York: Alfred A. Knopf.

Young, A. F. (Ed.). (1993). *Beyond the American revolution: Explorations in the history of American radicals*. Dekalb: Northern Illinois University Press.

Ziarek, E. P. (2001). *An ethic of dissensus: Postmodernity, feminism, and the politics of radical democracy*. Palo Alto, CA: Stanford University Press.

CHAPTER 16

Coalitions as Social Change Agents

Maria Roberts-DeGennaro

Terry Mizrahi

Central to community practice is a fundamental understanding of social change and the strategies relevant to effecting change (Meenaghan & Gibbons, 2000). Coalition building is a strategy for social action that can bring together diverse organizations to advocate for reform in the structural arrangements for delivering and accessing health care, education, social welfare, and other human services. In addition, coalitions can influence political, social, and economic forces that affect the development of policies and services. In advocating for social change, coalitions orchestrate a diverse range of tactics and techniques from consensus to conflict.

In this chapter, the concept of social change is viewed from the perspective of a progressive agenda, in which change is directed at achieving social and economic justice that fosters the humanistic values of equity and fairness. The authors make several assumptions regarding the outcomes of coalition building. First, coalitions engage people in identifying common concerns. Second, coalitions collectively build a shared sense of public activism and challenge the structures that oppress and disempower communities. Third, this social change orientation emphasizes a commitment not only to changing the structure of health and human services, but also to the values of mutual responsibility, diversity, and democratic decision making. Finally, as social change agents, coalitions strive to improve the condition of the oppressed and the disadvantaged, as well as advocate for social and economic justice (Mizrahi & Rosenthal, 2001; Roberts-DeGennaro, 2001a).

Changing culturally entrenched structures of prejudice and discrimination is a paramount focus in social change activities. The success of a coalition to effect broad change depends to a great extent on its efforts to break down these barriers. For example, coalitions that were formed to address the burning of churches document the importance of speaking out against hate crimes and making an ethical commitment to respecting human equality and diversity (Carter, 2000).

A variety of religious, economic, and political strategies are used by coalitions to advocate for social justice. Single community-based efforts often are not large enough to challenge the enormous power of corporate capital or centralized government (Fisher, 1995). Thus, coalitions need to support and mobilize diverse elements in their communities and strengthen the belief in their own efficacy to advocate successfully for improving social, economic, and community conditions.

This chapter focuses on the definition, activities, roles, and components of organizational coalitions as successful change agents. To further our understanding of coalition behavior, we suggest action theory as a useful approach for examining the development of the roles and activities of a coalition, as it engages in social action and social change (Parsons, 1951; Parsons & Shils, 1951). Along with this theoretical perspective, four components of social action coalitions are presented to provide a conceptual framework for analyzing interorganizational dynamics.

The primary assumption in this chapter is that coalitions can advocate for structural changes in the social system as well as promote values that support community involvement in the planning and delivery of equitable and comprehensive services. As coalitions engage in social action in the new millennium, technology will become an increasingly important tool in designing and implementing change tactics (see also Hillier & Culhane, Chapter 36, and Lohmann & McNutt, Chapter 35, in this volume).

The Nature of Organizational Coalitions

A coalitions is defined as an interacting group of organizational actors who (a) agree to pursue a common goal, (b) coordinate their resources in attempting to achieve this goal, and (c) adopt a common strategy in pursuing it (Roberts-DeGennaro, 1997, p. 92). Similarly, Rosenthal and Mizrahi (1994b, p. 7) defined a coalition as an organization of independent organizations that share a common goal for social change and join forces to influence external institutions while maintaining their autonomy. Both of these conceptual definitions support the organizing ideology of coalition building, which promotes mutual responsibility and social justice while recognizing that coalitions are complex interorganizational mechanisms with inherent tensions that need managing over time (Alicea, 1978; Gamson, 1961; Miller & Tomaskovic-Devey, 1983; Whitaker, 1982; Zeitz, 1980).

Three concepts of organizational theory are useful in understanding the behavior of a coalition: *cooperation, coordination,* and *collaboration.* Although these terms have frequently been used interchangeably, Harbin and Terry (1991) suggested they constitute a hierarchy or continuum of interorganizational relationships ranging from the simplest to the most complex. Peterson (1991) suggested that at one end of the continuum, for example, agencies within a coalition cooperate with one another by offering general support, sharing information, or providing endorsements for each other's programs. Their decisions are autonomous, and each agency pursues its own goals within the coalition.

In the middle of this continuum, coordination occurs when organizations within a coalition synchronize their activities to promote compatible schedules, events, services, or other kinds of work that contribute to the achievement of the goals of both the agencies and the coalition. However, the coalition members remain autonomous.

At the other end of the continuum, collaboration is guided by a common plan and set of strategies designed and approved by all participating organizations. Some autonomy is relinquished by each agency in the interest of accomplishing identified common goals. Gray suggested that "cooperation and coordination often occur as part of the process of collaborating" (1989, p. 15).

Other authors view coalitions as one type of interorganizational relationship within a broader framework of collaborations (Schopler, 1994). Rosenthal and Mizrahi (1994b) distinguish collaborations—which are agency based and task focused—from coalitions, which are more community based and variable in terms of auspices, specificity of goals, and longevity.

Regardless of how the interorganizational behavior of a coalition is defined, coalitions engage in a pattern of interactions within a larger social system. From within this system, a coalition generates values and perspectives about the problem areas it seeks to address. The impact and magnitude of these actions can influence the value orientation of the entire system because values are promoted by a coalition while its members advocate for social change. Depending on the level of resistance to change owing to the value base and structural complexity of the larger system, the coalition acts to reshape the value orientation of the larger system as well as to achieve specific change goals. Thus, the efforts to bring about change require the ability to think critically and learn about the positions and the "stakes" of those who control the major institutions of the social system, the agency staff that manages those institutions, and those who receive the services (Gottschalk, Frumkin, & Kaufman, 1984).

Beyond the ability to influence a larger social change agenda, Roberts-DeGennaro (1997, pp. 92–93) suggested that there are many advantages for organizations when they join a coalition. First, political and economic events are rearranging boundaries, structures, and assumptions regarding the delivery of health and human services. Through coalition building, organizations can influence the design and implementation of these arrangements. Second, as organizational representatives interact within a coalition, they are introduced to new ideas, perspectives, and technologies for solving problems. (The use of electronic communications is presented later as an example of new learning within a coalition.) Third, through the coalition, a more extensive channel of internal communication is created within the member organizations. Thus, organizations can nurture their own information networks, which encourages awareness and activism among staff members around social change strategies.

Although there are advantages to coalition building, there are also obstacles and constraints. In cost-cutting and competitive political and economic environments, agencies are challenged to develop resources for emergent needs. This puts a great deal of pressure on most agencies to minimize service duplication and maximize delivery using the fewest possible staff and financial resources to provide the largest

er of client contacts. Consequently, organizational actors often
whether it is economical to join forces with other agencies, given
volved in coalition interactions versus the possibility of increased
ources within the coalition. Sometimes it is not economical to
oalition's activities because they require too much staff time and
expended for the cooperative action are greater than the resources
individual coalition organizations (Roberts-DeGennaro, 1986b).

wide range of issues usually affects most client populations and communities.
This poses a challenge to coalitions attempting to organize joint activities that
truly meet the needs of their members' client populations or constituencies.
In addition, the cultural and ethnic diversity within most communities requires a
well-orchestrated strategy by a coalition to facilitate joint activities, overcome distrust or ignorance, and create a common agenda (Chesler, 1996; Powell et al., 1999;
Reisch & Rivera, 1999). Trust and respect are always key elements in building successful coalitions, especially ones that seek to include diverse community groups.

Acion Theory: Interaction
of a Coalition in a Social System

Action theory provides a useful approach for understanding the roles and behavior
of coalitions, particularly as they engage in advocacy activities in a social system.
Parsons defined the social system as one of several possible types:

> The social system consists of a plurality of interacting persons motivated in
> terms of a tendency to the "optimization of gratification" and whose relation
> to their situations, including each other, is defined and mediated in terms of a
> system of culturally structured and shared symbols. (1952, pp. 5–6)

The fundamental units that make up this social system are activities, roles, and
collectivities (Parsons, 1951, 1952, 1961). McLeish (1969) portrayed a social system
as being made up of organizations that, in turn, are made up of roles generated
from actions. Thus, activities originate within a coalition as key organizational
actors pursue particular goals that are expected to satisfy specific needs of the constituents served by their organizations. These organizational actors then persuade
others to perform these activities together by joining a coalition.

To promote support for continued membership in the coalition, the organizational actors evaluate their joint activity and plan future behavior on the basis of
what they have learned through their social change activities. This evaluation is
basically a determination of whether an optimal level of gratification was accrued
as a result of the cooperative action. In other words, did coalition members achieve
their own particular goals while engaging in this joint performance?

Within the coalition, a set of mutual expectations evolves among the organizational members, and a set of reciprocal expectations is established on the basis of
the initial and continuing interactions. Thus, from the continued interactions and
from their reciprocal expectations, roles come to be differentiated among coalition
members. A role can be defined as a coalition member's participation that is

structured, normative, and regulated as it interacts with other members of the coalition. This habitual interaction begets a system of rules that defines permissible and anticipated behavior patterns, both within the coalition and across the organizational membership of the coalition. These rules develop from the necessity of ensuring optimal gratification of emergent needs as perceived by the coalition members (McLeish, 1969, p. 57).

A complementary system of rights and duties attaches itself to the differentiated roles within a coalition. These special elements are summed up in norms or rules. The rules perform several functions for the coalition. First, they define the limits of action for the coalition members; second, they specify rules of performance; third, they state the sanctions and rewards attached to the performance of a role; and finally, they specify the particular situations or environments in which a role is acted out. Thus a collectivity such as a coalition evolves through this plurality of organizational actors who operate according to an agreed-on set of rules that have the sanction of a system of social values. In turn, these values legitimize the activities of the entire social system (McLeish, 1969, p. 57; Parsons, 1952, 1961).

The coalition's value orientation is a significant factor that affects the magnitude of the social change it can achieve. The exchanges among the member organizations reflect an underlying set of ethics and values that influence the direction of social action effort (Roberts-DeGennaro, 1986a, 1987). This value orientation focuses on a more responsive social system with an emphasis on the values of mutual responsibility and social justice. Such a system promotes the principle of human equality, requiring the equal distribution of civil, human, and material rights and the equal allocation of responsibilities among all citizens (Tawney, 1964). Coalitions need to identify and agree on a set of value assumptions as well as establish a division of labor and accountability that is fair and reflects those values.

As change agents, coalitions assume specific roles in working to reform policies and procedures that ensure access to high-quality, comprehensive services and benefits. Coalitions seek to implement a humanistic value perspective in the delivery of services throughout a system. Of particular importance to successful coalitions are the key organizational actors, who form the leadership core of the coalition and who define and are committed to the values that legitimize the activities of the coalition. Coalition leaders also must manage the inherent tensions among the coalition members: (a) between the unity needed to influence the target of social change and the diversity needed for power and legitimacy, (b) between accountability to member organizations and autonomy to make decisions and take action in a timely fashion, (c) between those who view the coalition as a means to achieve a specific social change goal and those who perceive it as a model of intergroup relations, and (d) between their commitment to the coalition's agenda and their loyalty to the organizations they are representing (Mizrahi & Rosenthal, 1993).

Components of Successful Coalitions as Change Agents

Mizrahi and Rosenthal's (2001) study of 40 coalitions identified four components that appear to be important in developing successful interorganizational working relationships: conditions, commitment, competence, and contributions. These components provide a conceptual framework for understanding the dynamics of the interorganizational behavior within the coalition as it operates in a social action system. Each of these components will be briefly described.

The significance of the issue and whether the timing is right to address it are important conditions in determining whether to form and develop a coalition. Also, the climate within the community must support using tactics and techniques that support consensus building and negotiation. Other conditions that affect coalition formation and development are

- the type and level of resources possessed by the member organizations,
- prior working experiences among and between the member organizations,
- the salience and urgency of the social change goal,
- agreement on which social change targets to influence, and
- the feasibility of "winning."

Political and economic realities have a major impact on the coalition's success. Organizations join coalitions in response to their own needs and the needs of their clients as they seek resources from their political and economic environment (Benson, 1975; Galaskiewicz, 1985; Grusky, 1992; Levine & White, 1961; Roberts-DeGennaro, 1987). The alignment of political and economic forces affects the level of competition for fiscal resources and the decision-making structure used to distribute resources and power in a community.

Organizers need to assess whether conditions exist that will stimulate both an interest in and a response from organizations and groups in building a coalition. If the conditions do not exist, organizers should determine whether it is possible and desirable to create the conditions under which a coalition becomes possible. In some instances, it might not be realistic to pursue the development of a coalition; in such cases, efforts might be focused on increasing public awareness, creating informal networks, and developing support for social action.

Second, there must be a core group of people representing different organizations with a commitment to work toward achieving social change and to developing and maintaining the coalition. However, over time, coalition members might have different levels of commitment toward the coalition and its goals (Frey, 1974).

Organizational theory suggests that the basis of an organization's commitment to a coalition is a balance between pragmatism and ideology (Bacharach & Lawler, 1980). The pragmatic reasons for coalition formation are usually categorized as a quest for resources and power based on self-interest. The ideological bases underlying the decision to form or join a coalition include some specific value-based commitment to a cause or to a general concept of the "common good." This more general altruism is crucial to maintaining a climate conducive to working toward a shared goal.

In the extreme, actions based on organizational self-interest, an inevitable factor in coalition formation, might be interpreted as self-centeredness, competition, calculation, or having a hidden agenda. Conversely, other-directedness and altruism might be seen by other coalition members as naïve or disingenuous. These seemingly contradictory motivations may be reframed as the need to identify mutual or collective self-interest among all of the members, with cost/benefit ratios calculated and rewards or benefits for participation identified. This information allows coalition leaders to use tactics of tradeoffs, negotiation, and bargaining in obtaining and maintaining commitment. Mizrahi and Rosenthal (1993) defined this inevitable tension as "mixed loyalties." That is, the member organizations participate in a coalition because of the resources, status, and power they gain and because they want to be identified with a successful coalition in accomplishing some greater good for their constituency or community.

Member organizations must contribute in a variety of ways to the formation and maintenance of the coalition. These contributions vary according to the stage of the coalition's development, and they must be maintained or replenished over time. If contributions are not optimum, a coalition might have to modify its goal, alter its timeline, revise its plan of action, and replace or recruit additional members. Contributions fall into three major categories: resources, ideology, and power.

The contribution of resources goes beyond the tangible issues of staffing and funding (Brown, 1984; Dluhy, 1990; Mattessich & Monsey, 1992). Resources also include such intangibles as expertise, legitimacy, information, contacts, and access to a constituency. As coalitions grow, their need for various resources changes. At the same time, the incorporation of new and different resources might alter the pattern of interactions within a coalition and its relationship with other organizations and groups. Most coalitions seek members with a variety of attributes and assets, because diversity strengthens the coalition's power base.

Organizations that have a mission and purpose sanctioned by the community and that have produced measurable outcomes can make a significant contribution through their reputation for procuring resources and making rational decisions. Organizations that are perceived to express ideologically extreme positions (e.g., groups on either side of the debate about abortion) can also contribute to the social change activities of a coalition because of their steadfastness, loyalty, and determination. However, the mission and purpose of these types of organizations should be considered before accepting contributions from them or their sponsors (Brown, 1984; Dluhy, 1981). Organizations whose ideology supports equitable decision making, mutual trust, and shared responsibility are important to the success of a coalition (Mizrahi & Rosenthal, 2001).

Coalitions form to attain the collective power necessary to influence an external target and achieve a common goal. Coalitions need some autonomy to take independent action, but by definition they must be accountable to the member organizations (Mizrahi & Rosenthal, 1993). The actual power of a coalition resides with the collective power derived from the member organizations and their clients and constituencies. From the perspective of social movements, power is wielded by the coalition because the member organizations representing a collective have given or delegated some of their power to the coalition (Mauss, 1975). The challenge for coalition leaders is to identify and use power from various sources—for example, from economic and political sources—and then balance different amounts of actual and perceived power.

Finally, a coalition must have the competence to move toward the social change goal, maintain the coalition leadership core, and sustain its membership base. Leadership is a critical factor in determining whether a coalition will be successful.

Kaufman (2001) contended that the core leadership group should consist of a few representatives from the member organizations who can maintain a high level of activity and commitment to the coalition.

Competent leaders must have analytical and interactional skills to make a coalition work—they must be able to establish agreement about coalition goals, tactics, and techniques; division of labor; the structure and process for decision making; and an implementation and evaluation plan.

Rosenthal and Mizrahi (1994b) suggested that the complexity of leading a social change coalition is based on the simultaneous management of three critical operational levels. First, leaders must sustain movement toward the external social change goals by influencing social change targets. They must also maintain internal relations among the core leadership of organizational members. Finally, they must develop trust with, accountability to, and contributions from the coalition membership base. Successful methods of handling difficulties or conflicts within the coalition include knowledge of, skill in, and commitment to conflict management, negotiation, and compromise (Wilford & Annison, 1995). Thus, leaders need to possess a range of process (relationship), strategic-political, and administrative (technical) skills.

In Mizrahi and Rosenthal's study (2001), certain components were consistently found to have a major impact on the success of coalitions, regardless of how success was defined. Commitment to the coalition's goal and competent leadership were the top two components, followed by commitment to the unity and work of the coalition, an equitable decision-making structure and process, and mutual respect and tolerance. In terms of what sustained a member organization's involvement over time, commitment to the goal exceeded other identified incentives such as opportunities to obtain additional resources, power, credibility, information, or contacts, or even to obtain particular services or advantages for its constituency.

Other important elements related to the success of coalitions were maintaining a broad-based constituency, achieving interim victories, continued contributions of member organizations, and sharing of responsibility and ownership. Contributions, defined broadly as resources, ideology, and power, were critical elements in the success of coalitions as social change agents. The continuation of these contributions depends on reciprocity—that is, successful coalitions emphasize to their members the value of giving in order to receive. The concept of exchange is important in maintaining coalitions (Roberts-DeGennaro, 1987). However, coalitions engaged in complex, long-term social change activities also need interim victories and secondary goals to sustain involvement (Gamson, 1975; Mizrahi & Rosenthal, 2001; Mondros & Wilson, 1994).

The Use of Technology in Promoting Social Change

To support advocacy efforts, it has become increasingly critical for community organizers to use the Internet to obtain information about other coalitions working on similar issues, model community organization programs, community-based research, and electronic databases. The rapid growth in the transfer of technology and information to and from sites around the world has the potential to link coalitions and strengthen efforts to achieve social and economic justice at home and internationally.

Community activists are using technology to create innovative tactics and techniques for promoting social change. Community computer networks are designed to ensure access to technology and the Internet, create community free space for public debate and discussion, provide public information, and facilitate community building (Downing et al., 1991; McNutt, 2000; Nartz & Schoech, 2000).

These community computer networks are often referred to as "electronic greenbelts," in which one or more computers are used to gain access to those services and to each other (Cisler, 1993; Schuler, 1996). Greenbelts form a bond between coalitions that are not located in the same city or community but that share a common interest or mutual concern. Coalitions can participate in these greenbelts by connecting with other coalitions in other parts of the country that are advocating for the same target population or addressing the same community issue.

One of the more important missions of community computer networks is to reach people with low incomes and provide them with access to information technology. This can include training in the use of computers as well as access to computers via public terminals in libraries, community centers, social agencies, and kiosks (Fitzgerald & McNutt, 1999). Thus, computer networks can provide citizens access to electronic mail and the Internet, information related to government and private-sector services, and opportunities to participate in public debates about proposed legislation and social policies (Roberts-DeGennaro, 2001b, 2002).

A case study of the Public Electronic Network program documented the activities of an advocacy program for the homeless. Users from social groups worked together to create changes in the way that homeless people were treated and to develop a transitional center (Wittig & Schmitz, 1996). Likewise, coalitions could participate in similar electronic communications and link people, resources, and ideas. Community practice in cyberspace might shift the balance of power so that it is shared between those in the established power structure and the disenfranchised, especially as grassroots groups seek and enlist allies and experts from around the world (Blundo, Mele, Hairston, & Watson, 1999).

Web sites are a strategy for disseminating information and raising awareness. Most of the sites dedicated to fighting poverty are intended to educate the public on issues ranging from hunger relief to low-income housing, and many provide information for those who need or want help. A coalition could develop both a webpage and a listserv to provide information to individuals and to other listservs requesting support while attracting media attention to the social justice issue it has been formed to address. For example, the New York–based Welfare Law Center (2004) has a Web site that serves grassroots groups across the country. This site helps community-based groups keep informed about programs for low-income people.

The use of technology can expand and revitalize opportunities for community-based social action practice. This will enhance a coalition's efforts to achieve outcomes that support social justice in the face of well-funded opposition to change entrenched in social structural frameworks. The Internet and other telecommunications allow less hierarchical, place- and space-based interorganizational structures to emerge (Klein, 2000). Successful coalitions will increasingly incorporate the use of electronic communications as the context and structure for decision making.

Caveats and Conclusions for Building Coalitions as Change Agents

Coalitions use social change strategies to address issues and facilitate collaborative processes that reflect the needs of diverse groups. The range of expertise and resources within a coalition provides a valuable mechanism to advocate for social change. Moreover, the success of a coalition can result in the construction of a unified community better able to respond to local needs in a timely manner.

If the progressive social planning and community organizing frameworks from the 1960s and 1970s are to be reflected in the coalition-building efforts of the 2lst century, several assumptions underlying these interorganizational agendas must be examined. As indicated in the social action theory presented earlier, previous assumptions cannot be taken for granted. First, organizational actors do not always represent or understand the real needs of client or constituency groups. To accurately represent or advocate for constituencies, organizations must assess client needs from the clients' perspective, rather than presuming automatic understanding from the viewpoint of formal organizations.

Second, definitions of the problems and solutions posed by the various constituent groups—the viewpoints, for example, of members of the business community as compared with those of religious institutions—may not easily be reconciled. To the contrary, ideologies shape those perspectives and create value dissension and discord as often as they produce consensus. Thus, consensus-building techniques must be part of the learning environment in the coalition (Beck & Eichler, 2000).

Third, various sectors of the larger social system often have different degrees of influence in decision-making processes and structures. To be sure, a grassroots organization frequently will have to struggle to have as much clout as the local chamber of commerce, even if both groups have equal votes in a coalition. Thus, coalitions that include groups such as neighborhood and parent associations and civic organizations must acknowledge and attempt to minimize internal power differences to build a strong and inclusive power base.

Fourth, in a large and complex coalition that attempts to unite many diverse groups, it will take more skill and time to orchestrate roles and activities. Efforts to reconcile differences in power, resources, and values among member organizations take time, energy, skill, and additional resources. Building large coalitions may be more effective in the long run, but in the short run, the assessment of resources needed to create them should be weighed against the benefits of forming a smaller, more easily unified coalition.

Fifth, many coalition-building initiatives aim to reorganize or coordinate existing services rather than create or expand services. Thus, if resources are scarce to begin with, a coalition's efforts to support sharing of resources among its member organizations might not be enough to effect major social change. Two or more weak organizations coming together does not automatically create a stronger, more efficient coalition (Rosenthal & Mizrahi, 1994a; Sampson, 1994). This reality should be acknowledged to promote a positive, supportive environment that encourages continued resource acquisition for the coalition as well as for its member organizations.

Sixth, measures for determining successful outcomes are often not apparent or agreed on by the member organizations. At the very least, it is important to recognize the effect of differences in ideology, power, and resources on setting goals and establishing criteria by which to evaluate them before beginning the process of developing standards to measure outcomes.

Finally, given this country's history of ambivalence toward social welfare, it is important to note that reactionary and protectionist politics could result from increased community and grassroots involvement to change the social system. The frequent backlash of NIMBY ("not in my backyard") responses to the establishment of social programs provides clear evidence of this problem. Although democratic participation at the community level should be inclusive and reflect the community's racial, ethnic, and economic composition, coalition builders need to be keenly aware of the divergent approaches and means of problem solving likely to exist in multicultural and economically diverse communities. Indeed, the major initial work of coalition leaders and members may be to negotiate shared strategies and means of achieving goals to create a community with stronger bonds and commitments across cultural, racial, and economic differences.

As social change agents, coalitions can create a learning environment in which organizations and groups work together to achieve common goals. This process requires competent leaders who understand and identify what the member organizations want and receive from participating, as well as what they can contribute to the coalition and to changing the social system. There will always be different types and levels of commitment and contributions, so a range of expectations for participation should be identified and accepted.

Coalitions should focus on the commonalities while acknowledging the differences between and among member organizations. Otherwise, these differences can keep members apart rather than uniting them to effect major social change. Effective leaders of coalitions need skills in reframing issues and redefining goals and priorities to strengthen and promote participation from all members. Coalitions should strive to achieve a balance between commonalities and differences to create a shared ideology and promote social change.

Encouraging racially and ethnically diverse groups to coalesce is an especially difficult task given the extent of bias and prejudice in this country. Such coalitions will not be built unless there is a conscious, deliberate, unified effort to acknowledge this social fact. The leadership within a coalition needs to assess which groups are already committed to working together and then recognize that it will require time, energy, and resources to bring these and more resistant groups together. Leaders must also make clear the motivation for uniting, especially when groups have been isolated from, in competition with, and even in conflict with each other in the past. Appeals to collective self-interest and reciprocity may bring these divergent groups to the table. The ability to negotiate and compromise in a spirit of trust and openness is what will keep them working together over time.

Committed and competent professional practitioners grounded in the theory, practice, and value of coalitions as social change mechanisms understand that coalitions can be the important and necessary link between individual organizations and social movements, as well as the vehicles for making substantial structural changes in the social system.

References

Alicea, V. G. (1978). *Community participation, planning influence: Toward a conceptual model of coalition planning.* Doctoral dissertation, Columbia University, New York.

Bacharach, S. B., & Lawler, E. J. (1980). *Power and politics in organizations.* San Francisco: Jossey-Bass.

Beck, E., & Eichler, M. (2000). Consensus organizing: A practice model for community building. *Journal of Community Practice, 8,* 87–102.

Benson, K. (1975). The interorganizational network as a political economy. *Administrative Science Quarterly, 20,* 229–249.

Blundo, R. G., Mele, C., Hairston, R., & Watson, J. (1999). The Internet and demystifying power differentials: A few women on-line and the housing authority. *Journal of Community Practice, 6,* 11–26.

Brown, C. R. (1984). *The art of coalition building: A guide for community leaders.* New York: American Jewish Committee.

Carter, C. (2000). Church burning: Using a contemporary issue to teach community organization. *Journal of Social Work Education, 36,* 79–88.

Chesler, M. (1996). White men's roles in multicultural coalitions. In B. Bowser & R. Hunt (Eds.), *Impact of racism on white Americans* (pp. 202–229). Thousand Oaks, CA: Sage.

Cisler, S. (1993). *Community computer networks: Building electronic greenbelts.* Retrieved July 2, 2002, from http://www.cpsr.org/dox/program/community-nets/building_ electronic_ greenbelts.html.

Dluhy, M. (1981). *Changing the system: Political advocacy for disadvantaged groups.* Beverly Hills, CA: Sage.

Dluhy, M. (1990). *Building coalitions in the human services.* Newbury Park, CA: Sage.

Downing, J., Fasano, R., Friedland, P. A., McCullough, M. F., Mizrahi, T., & Shapiro, J. (1991). *Computers for social change and community organizing.* Binghamton, NY: Haworth.

Fisher, R. (1995). Social action community organization: Proliferation, persistence, roots, and prospects. In J. Rothman, J. Erlich, & J. Tropman (Eds.), *Strategies of community intervention* (pp. 327–340). Itasca, IL: F. E. Peacock.

Fitzgerald, E., & McNutt, J. (1999). Electronic advocacy in policy practice: A framework for teaching technologically based practice. *Journal of Social Work Education, 35,* 331–341.

Frey, G. (1974). *Coalitions in community planning.* Doctoral dissertation, Brandeis University, Waltham, MA.

Galaskiewicz, J. (1985). Interorganizational relations. *American Sociological Review, 11,* 281–304.

Gamson, W. (1961). A theory of coalition formation. *American Sociological Review, 226,* 373–382.

Gamson, W. (1975). *The strategy of social protest.* Homewood, IL: Dorsey.

Gottschalk, S., Frumkin, M., & Kaufman, A. (1984). Social work intervention with the aged: Toward a change in the institutionalized thought structure. *Journal of Sociology and Social Welfare, 11,* 24–55.

Gray, B. (1989). *Collaborating: Finding common ground for multiparty problems.* San Francisco: Jossey-Bass.

Grusky, O. (1992). Intergroup and interorganizational relations. In E. F. Borgatta & M. L. Borgatta (Eds.), *Encyclopedia of sociology* (Vol. 2, pp. 962–968). New York: Macmillan.

Harbin, G., & Terry, D. (1991). *Interagency service coordination: Initial findings from six states* (ED357581). Chapel Hill, NC: Carolina Policy Studies Program, University of North Carolina.

Kaufman, R. (2001). Coalition activity of social change organizations in a public campaign: The influence of motives, resources and processes on levels of activity. *Journal of Community Practice, 9,* 21–42.

Klein, N. (2000, July 10). The vision thing. *Nation, 271,* 18–21.

Levine, S., & White, P. (1961). Exchange as a conceptual framework for the study of interorganizational relationships. *Administrative Science Quarterly, 5,* 583–601.

Mattessich, P., & Monsey, B. (1992). *Collaboration: What makes it work: A review of research literature on factors influencing successful collaboration.* St. Paul, MN: Amherst H. Wilder Foundation.

Mauss, A. (1975). *Social problems as social movements.* Philadelphia: Lippincott.

McLeish, J. (1969). *The theory of social change.* New York: Schocken.

McNutt, J. (2000). Organizing cyberspace: Strategies for teaching about community practice and technology. *Journal of Community Practice, 7,* 95–109.

Meenaghan, T., & Gibbons, W. E. (2000). *Generalist practice in larger settings.* Chicago: Lyceum.

Miller, S. M., & Tomaskovic-Devey, D. (1983). A framework for new progressive coalitions. *Social Policy, 13,* 8–14.

Mizrahi, T., & Rosenthal, B. (1993). Managing dynamic tensions in social change coalitions. In T. Mizrahi & J. Morrison (Eds.), *Community organization and social administration: Advances, trends, and emerging principles* (pp. 11–40). New York: Haworth.

Mizrahi, T., & Rosenthal, B. (2001). Complexities of effective coalition building: A study of leaders' strategies, struggles, and solutions. *Social Work, 46,* 63–78.

Mondros, J., & Wilson, S. (1994). *Organizing for power and empowerment.* New York: Columbia University Press.

Nartz, M., & Schoech, D. (2000). Use of the Internet for community practice: A Delphi study. *Journal of Community Practice, 8,* 37–59.

Parsons, T. (1951). *The social system.* Glencoe, IL: Free Press.

Parsons, T. (Ed.). (1961). *Theories of society.* New York: Free Press of Glencoe.

Parsons, T., & Shils, E. (Eds.). (1951). *Toward a general theory of action.* Cambridge, MA: Harvard University Press.

Peterson, N. (1991). Interagency collaboration under Part H: The key to comprehensive, multidisciplinary, coordinated infant/toddler intervention services. *Journal of Early Intervention, 15,* 89–105.

Powell, J., Dosser, D., Handron, D., McCammon, S., Temkin, M. E., & Kaufman, M. (1999). Challenges of interdisciplinary collaboration: A faculty consortium's initial attempts to model collaboration. *Journal of Community Practice, 6,* 27–48.

Reisch, M., & Rivera, F. (1999). Ethical and racial conflicts in urban-based action research. *Journal of Community Practice, 6,* 49–62.

Roberts-DeGennaro, M. (1986a). Building coalitions for political advocacy efforts in the human services. *Social Work, 31,* 308–311.

Roberts-DeGennaro, M. (1986b). Factors contributing to coalition maintenance. *Journal of Sociology and Social Welfare, 13,* 248–264.

Roberts-DeGennaro, M. (1987). Patterns of exchange relationships in building a coalition. *Administration in Social Work, 11,* 59–67.

Roberts-DeGennaro, M. (1997). Conceptual framework of coalitions in an organizational context. *Journal of Community Practice, 4,* 91–107.

Roberts-DeGennaro, M. (2001a). Conceptual framework of coalitions in an organizational context. In J. Tropman, J. Erlich, & J. Rothman (Eds.), *Tactics and techniques of community intervention* (pp. 130–140). Itasca, IL: F. E. Peacock.

Roberts-DeGennaro, M. (2001b, March). *Using Blackboard.com in teaching an online social policy course.* Media technology presentation at the 2001 Annual Program Meeting of the Council on Social Work Education, Dallas, TX.

Roberts-DeGennaro, M. (2002). Constructing and implementing a Web-based graduate social policy course: A pilot test in cyberspace. *Social Policy Journal, 1*(2) 73–90.

Rosenthal, B., & Mizrahi, T. (1994a). Should community-based organizations give priority to building coalitions rather than building their own membership? Point. In M. Austin & J. I. Lowe (Eds.), *Controversial issues in communities and organizations* (pp. 9–15). Needham Heights, MA: Allyn & Bacon.

Rosenthal, B., & Mizrahi, T. (1994b). *Strategic partnerships: How to create and maintain interorganizational collaborations and coalitions.* New York: Hunter College School of Social Work, Education Center for Community Organizing.

Sampson, T. (1994). Should community-based organizations give priority to building coalitions rather than building their own membership? Counterpoint. In M. Austin & J. I. Lowe (Eds.), *Controversial issues in communities and organizations* (pp. 16–22). Needham Heights, MA: Allyn & Bacon.

Schopler, J. H. (1994). Interorganizational groups in human services: Environmental and interpersonal relationships. *Journal of Community Practice, 1*, 7–28.

Schuler, D. (1996). *New community networks: Wired for change.* Reading, MA: Addison-Wesley.

Tawney, R. W. (1964). *Equality.* London: George Allen and Unwin.

Welfare Law Center. (2004). *Mission.* Retrieved February 10, 2004. from http://www.welfarelaw.org/who_wlc.htm#mission.

Whitaker, W. H. (1982). Organizing social action coalitions. In M. Mahaffey & J. W. Hanks (Eds.), *Practical politics and political responsibility* (pp. 136–160). Washington, DC: National Association of Social Workers.

Wilford, D. S., & Annison, M. H. (1995, November/December). The competitive collaborators. *Healthcare Forum Journal,* 28–31.

Wittig, M., & Schmitz, J. (1996). Electronic grassroots organizing. *Journal of Social Issues, 52,* 53–69.

Zeitz, G. (1980). Interorganizational dialectics. *Administrative Science Quarterly, 25,* 72–88.

CHAPTER 17

Four Models of Policy Practice

Local, State, and National Arenas

Bruce S. Jansson

David Dempsey

Jacquelyn McCroskey

Robert Schneider

I t was axiomatic to Jane Addams and many other founders of the social work profession that its members would prioritize policy-changing work, whether by electing progressive candidates, lobbying legislators, monitoring the implementation of existing policies, or obtaining data about social problems (Schneider & Netting, 1999; Wenocur & Reisch, 1989). Yet many social workers have not—and do not—follow Addams's vision, preferring Mary Richmond's emphasis on services to individuals. Nor have agencies and universities that employ social work practitioners and academics consistently supported policy-reforming work. Some social workers have believed, moreover, that it is unethical for professionals to participate in the political process. Even on the so-called macro side of the profession, many policy theorists have emphasized analytic, historical, and philosophical themes with scant reference to politics, power, policy implementation, lobbying, interest groups, or campaigns (see, for example, Weissman, 1959).

Considerable progress has been made during the past three decades, however, toward reconceptualizing policy as an interventive discipline under the rubric of *policy practice*, a term that first appeared in policy literature in 1984. Policy practice draws on the work of many theorists, including those who discuss ways in which social workers can influence legislation or participate in political campaigns (Dear & Patti, 1981; Haynes & Mikelson, 2003; Mahaffey & Hanks, 1982); strategies for changing agency policies (Brager & Holloway, 1978); and skills, styles, and tasks that are needed in policy reform work (Flynn, 1985; Jansson, 1997, 2000, 2003; Pierce, 1984).

Several developments in the profession have provided a favorable context for policy practice. In 1975, the National Association of Social Workers (NASW) established Political Action for Candidate Election, thus committing itself to social reforms within the political process. Robert Schneider organized the formation of Influencing State Policy, a national organization developed in 1997 to foster involvement by social work educators and students in the legislative process (Influencing State Policy, n.d.). The Social Welfare Policy and Policy Practice Group, which was formed in 1993 to place policy-practice papers on programs of annual meetings of the Council on Social Work Education, developed the idea to provide an academic forum for policy-practice theory and research. Policy practice includes efforts to

- analyze social problems, fashion policy proposals, place policies on decision makers' agendas, enact (or block) policies, shape implementation of policies, and evaluate policies;
- change the cast of decision makers who make policies in the first instance;
- influence how resources are allocated in the human services;
- change formal (written) policies such as legislation, court rulings, administrative regulations, mission statements, and budgets; and
- change informal (unwritten) policies that influence policy formulation and implementation, including the beliefs, prejudices, definitions, and perceptions of decision makers and policy implementers. Examples include legislators' or administrators' negative stereotypes of welfare recipients, views of line staff that make them insensitive to specific populations, and administrators' proclivity to create turf boundaries when clients need coordinated services.

Policy practitioners work in many arenas, including national, state, and local legislatures; public (service-delivery) agencies; public planning agencies; public administrative or oversight agencies (such as a state's department of children's services); nongovernmental agencies (both nonprofit and for-profit); think tanks; special boards or commissions appointed by public officials; and academic settings. They engage in policy practice as solo advocates, members of a group of advocates (such as children's advocates in a specific jurisdiction), members or staff of a community-based group or agency, members or staff of a time-limited or long-standing coalition, staff or volunteers for a political campaign, or participants in such legal actions as class-action suits. (Policy practitioners typically work closely with organizations, advocacy groups, or coalitions as staff or volunteers because these organizations provide resources, clout, and ideas not available to a freelance advocate.) They can engage in time-limited projects, such as a campaign to enact a specific law, or they can engage in long-term undertakings, such as advocating for children's issues over a period of many years in a specific jurisdiction. They can work on issues that affect the entire population—or they can focus on issues particularly germane to low-income or oppressed populations, which Jansson (2003) called "policy advocacy."

Policy practitioners need an array of skills (Jansson, 2003; McInnis-Dittrich, 1994; Pierce, 1984, 2000; Schneider & Lester, 2001). They need to be able to develop and use power, develop political strategy, and manage conflict, because policy reform and implementation can be associated with conflict between or among contending factions, particularly when the factions possess divergent values and interests. They need to be able to make effective presentations, work with task-focused groups, analyze problems and issues, develop proposals, collect data, identify policy alternatives, and foster collaboration and compromise. Policy practice links concepts and skills drawn from community organization, policy analysis, administration, political science or applied politics, and program evaluation and research.

Four Models of Policy Practice

We discuss four models of policy practice in this chapter: ballot-based advocacy, legislative advocacy, analytic-based advocacy, and implementation advocacy models (see Table 17.1).

Of course, the four models overlap. Political candidates often seek to reform the implementation of specific programs such as early childhood education. People who try to change legislation often support candidates for office who favor specific legislative proposals. Policy practitioners who aim to reform the implementation of specific policies sometimes seek changes in budgets or legislation—or support political candidates who agree with their perspectives.

Ballot-Based Advocacy

Governments are a powerful source of a large number and array of policies. Legislative branches, whether they are city or county councils, state legislatures, or the U.S. Congress, can originate, modify, or revise policies at will. Government officials can implement policies or regulate how policies are enforced, whether they are civil servants, mayors, county executives, governors, or presidents. Judges and courts have the authority to enforce, sanction, or nullify policies in all courts.

A distinction between electoral politics and government relations is useful. *Electoral politics* are the formal and informal systems by which citizens and groups in a democracy contest for the power to run government (Plano & Greenburg, 1989). *Government relations* (called the *legislative advocacy model* in this chapter) are the active interventions of citizens and groups to influence the formal decision making of government officials (Ornstein & Elder, 1978).

When a policy practitioner decides that legislative advocacy is futile without people with different perspectives to occupy the executive or legislative offices or be

Table 17.1 Four Models of Policy Practice

Variable	Ballot-Based Advocacy	Legislative Advocacy	Analytic Advocacy	Implementation Advocacy
Goal	To change the composition of governments	To secure enactment of or to block specific legislative proposals	To make policy choices that are based on hard data and structured analysis.	To increase effectiveness of operating programs and ensure integration among local jurisdictions
Pivotal organizations to which policy practitioners are linked	Campaign organizations, political action committees, electoral coalitions, and political parties	Interest groups, community-based organizations, and professional associations	Think tanks, academic centers, government agencies, and funders	Planning groups required for specific programs, planning groups that mix insiders with outsiders, legal teams concerned with monitoring programs for compliance, and consumer-based organizations and community groups
Levels of conflict	High conflict between contending campaigns and candidates in win-lose contests	Variable conflict, but usually moderate to high conflict	Conflict between stakeholders about technical issues and interpretive issues	Conflict often moderated by desire to develop collaborative solutions to implementation problems and issues
Pivotal skills of policy practitioners	Performing force-field analysis, developing campaign organizations, raising funds, developing presentations, developing media relations, developing grassroots support, researching issues, conducting and using polls, surveys, and focus groups	Performing policy analysis, developing strategy and tactics during an extended campaign for legislative proposals, developing coalitions inside and outside the legislative arena, and deciding when to compromise	Research and analytic skills, obtaining and processing data, and making technical presentations	Obtaining data for planning and performance measurement, monitoring compliance, trouble shooting operating programs, developing collaborative solutions, developing consensus between program insiders and outsiders, and engaging community groups in government processes

appointed to specific administrative departments, then electoral politics offers a way out of an impasse. It is axiomatic that to change a policy, you sometimes must change who runs a government. When this moment of recognition occurs, policy practitioners can turn to electoral politics.

Electoral politics is a ubiquitous, accessible, and durable tool that social workers often neglect and ignore or misunderstand and fear. Social workers frequently approach electoral politics with great caution because of its potential for divisiveness. The major cause for division occurs around the concepts of partisanship and political parties. *Political parties* are voluntary groups of voters with some shared ideology who organize to try to win elections, control government, and influence public policy. (A person who holds firmly to a party or its cause is a *partisan,* hence the term *partisan politics.*) American politics are partisan and focused on candidates. Parties and candidates dominate ballots, but ballots sometimes contain initiatives (proposed legislation or constitutional amendments placed on a ballot by petitions signed by a required number of voters), a referendum that allows voters to "veto" a bill passed by the legislature, or a recall that provides voters an opportunity to oust a public official from office (Plano & Greenberg, 1989). Social workers can move adeptly between politics and government. The ability to perform in each realm boosts a practitioner's credibility in both places. Social workers can navigate the shoals of partisan electoral politics in constructive and civil ways. Partisan politics need not necessarily alienate powerful people. Once people demonstrate political power, they establish themselves as a force to contend with, either to cultivate or counter.

Transition refers to the time between election to an office and the assumption of the office. Although legislative and executive transitions differ, policy practitioners should strive to be members of transition groups or teams, because these groups make important decisions about staffing, budgets, appointments, and policies. Being included on a transition team is clear acknowledgment that a policy practitioner's campaign activities were visible and valuable to a candidate. Participation on a transition team amplifies a group's political influence in both politics and government.

Sound electoral strategies depend mainly on what kind of power a group or groups can muster to compete in campaigns and elections (DiClerico, 2000; Johnson-Cartee & Copeland, 1997; Thompson & Moncrief, 1998). The most important components of power are people and money (Dempsey, 1998). Massive amounts of money are unnecessary but it is very difficult to achieve electoral success with only person power. Modern mass communication techniques, including print and electronic media as well as direct mail, phone banking, polling, and focus groups, cost money. They also improve a candidate's or party's chance of winning. Although campaigns and elections remain more art than science, political professionals (often called consultants) are knowledgeable about their craft and can provide valuable strategic advice, but their services, too, cost money (Thurber, Nelson, & Dulio, 2000).

The executive and legislative branches of government, from local to federal, provide many opportunities for change. American elections are frequent and regular, allowing time for planning, gathering resources, building coalitions, educating voters, and mobilizing supporters. The most promising position to campaign for is what is called an "open seat," that is, a legislative or executive position for which no incumbent officeholder is seeking re-election. Because incumbency is normally a big advantage, challengers should look for open-seat opportunities, which are more competitive and require fewer resources (DiClerico, 2000). The best prospects for challenging incumbents normally occur in primary elections, which usually take place within a political party and with a smaller voter turnout than in general elections, where greater resources are needed by candidates (Jacobson, 1997).

One can develop many strategies to try to change a legislative body, depending on one's objective. In a state legislature, one aim might be to work in an election to defeat a difficult committee chair. This is a high-stakes, high-risk strategy that sends a powerful message, if successful, but which can carry a devastating price if unsuccessful. Or, policy practitioners may try to switch control of a legislative chamber from one party to another by defeating large numbers of incumbents with suitable challenger candidates. This is a desirable strategy in situations in which a chamber is almost equally divided along partisan lines.

Social workers can work with other groups to build electoral coalitions to elect desirable candidates (Scher, 1997). Coalitions are an effective way to share information and resources. Electoral coalitions mobilize the community to vote for specific candidates. Potential election coalition partners can include organizations from the civil and women's rights movements, as well as those advocating for fair labor practices, sound environmental policy, consumer protection, and welfare reform. Some groups also marry community organization to electoral politics, particularly at local levels (Kahn, 1991; Bobo, Kendall, & Max, 1991). Such successful candidates as the late Senator Paul Wellstone (D-Minn.) and Senator Barbara Mikulski (D-Md.) have skillfully linked their statewide campaigns with grassroots organizations.

Social workers make wonderful political candidates and elected officials. (People often move between elective office and governmental positions.) The NASW Web site (2003) identifies almost 170 social workers serving in offices from school board to U.S. Congress, including 4 social workers in the House, 2 in the Senate, and more than 60 in state legislatures. Fourteen social workers sought national Congressional seats in 2000, 12 in the House and 2 in the Senate ("Social workers out to expand," 2000).

Ballot-based advocacy can be used by social workers to achieve their social justice goals as well as their professional needs. The profession champions a long list of social justice policies, from child welfare, civil and human rights, economic security, and education issues, to protection for victims of HIV/AIDS, better physical and mental health care for the poor, reproductive rights, and welfare reform, that often are vital issues in campaigns and elections. A clear perspective on how electoral politics affect social work's professional interests has been offered by U.S. Representative Debbie Stabenow, who has a master's of social work (D-Mich.):

> Many social work jobs are publicly funded, and the fate of those jobs is decided by people like me—elected officials. It is easier to spend a few months and some money electing the right people than to spend years and a lot of money trying to get the wrong people to do the right things. (Hiratsuka, 1992)

At the same time, however, the election process is not always responsive to social needs, because poor people tend not to vote (Piven & Cloward, 2000) and because corporate political action committees and wealthy individuals possess greater resources than reform groups (Biersack, Herrnson, & Wilcox, 1999).

In coming years, the Internet will allow new electoral strategies (Davis, 1999). Campaigns will make even greater use of Web sites to communicate with voters, to disseminate information to specific groups, to conduct polls, to find volunteers, and to raise funds.

The Legislative Advocacy Model

The NASW (1996) Code of Ethics states that "social workers should be aware of the impact of the political arena on practice and advocate for changes in policy and legislation to improve social conditions in order to meet human needs and promote social justice" ([604][a]). Social workers who are policy practitioners are prepared to represent their clients and causes in the legislative arenas and to influence the decision makers who formulate policies and laws at the local, state, and federal levels (Dluhy, 1981). Some social work advocates empower their clients to plead their own cases and stand up effectively for their rights (Butler, 2002; Schneider & Lester, 2001; Schneider & Netting, 1999).

State legislatures, municipal and county governments, and Congress are forums in which laws are proposed and passed. (See the Web site of the Influencing State Policy organization at www.statepolicy.org for advocacy and legislative resources.) These laws affect all citizens and social work clients because they stipulate what benefits are provided by law, who is eligible, how much money will be spent, and who will provide the services. To change laws or to introduce new ones, social workers must organize clients and allies. It must be noted, however, that there is not an equal playing field in legislative deliberations, as some lobbyists possess extraordinary resources and connections that allow them to wine and dine legislators, to make large campaign contributions, and to fund expensive media projects to put public pressure on legislators (Birnbaum, 2000; West & Loomis, 1999).

Policy practitioners should plan their strategies and tactics before taking action (Ezell, 2001; Schneider & Lester, 2001). Decisions about an overall plan or a broad blueprint (strategy) must be debated, followed by the selection of the day-to-day, nitty-gritty actions (tactics) that are designed to carry out the strategy. Choosing a strategy is based on assumptions about human behavior and why people actually modify or change their minds on an issue. This requires community practitioners to learn what legislators who may oppose their legislative proposal are like. Are they hostile, indifferent, friendly, favorable, or ignorant toward a proposed change in a law? The crucial decision for the policy practitioner is analyzing the opposition and determining an approach that will have the best chance of persuading them to change their opinions. The following are three strategies and accompanying tactics that form an action framework for community social workers to use in attempting to influence legislative decision makers. Before proceeding further, however, it is important to note that one must first determine what one's opponents are like, because the choice of strategy depends largely on this judgment.

Analysis of the mindsets of possible opponents, as well as their resources and skills, is particularly important. If likely opponents are highly motivated and well organized, for example, proponents must invest considerable resources in their attempt to soften or allay their opposition and to mobilize allies into an effective group. Advocates usually need to organize a coalition or work with an established advocacy group that possesses leadership, resources, and sophisticated strategy (Berry, 1977; Hula, 1999).

Policy practitioners need knowledge of the procedures and protocols of legislative bodies. They must be aware of the likely route that their proposal will follow in the legislative body, as well as key influential persons who preside over committees and deliberations at pivotal points (Oleszek, 2001). They need to be familiar with time constraints and other complications—realizing, for example, that they must get hearings on a legislative proposal relatively early in a session to be successful (DeKieffer, 1997). They must understand how legislative offices are organized and how policy practitioners gain access to legislators (DeKieffer, 1997).

The Internet will assume an increasing role in lobbying in coming decades (Davis, 1999). Advocates use the Web to locate information about pending legislation and to track it through the legislative process, to convey constituents' views to legislators, and to attract support for legislative measures from citizens.

1. Collaborative Strategies and Tactics

When a legislator is perceived to share many of the basic values of the advocate and has cooperated previously on similar issues, but seems to be uninformed or simply need more information, a collaborative strategy is usually appropriate. The policy practitioner must remember to provide an adequate rationale and political cover for the legislator in seeking his or her support of the proposed bill. A collaborative strategy can be carried out by using the following tactics.

Meet with legislator and staff. Personal meetings with a legislator and staff are common practice for advocacy groups (Rickards, 1992). These meetings should be well planned and viewed as a means of presenting information to the legislator or staff member. Policy practitioners should identify themselves as constituents whenever possible and politely present a position on an issue with accompanying personal or client anecdotes. The meeting should be brief, concise, friendly, and informative. Leave a fact sheet and business card, and send a thank-you note.

Provide information. Legislators are faced with hundreds, even thousands, of complicated bills and gain a substantial understanding of only a few of them. They are forced to rely on staff, colleagues, and advocates for information. Lack of information is often an obstacle that can be overcome by providing facts and researching issues for legislators. Smith (1979) noted that the most important factor determining a group's influence was the capacity of the group to provide lawmakers with technical and political information. This information should be timely and available when it is needed; it should be balanced and credible, aimed at solving problems, and not propagandistic and narrow; and it should provide the basis for alternative proposals and feasible options (Patti & Dear, 1975).

Provide fiscal impact data. Perhaps the most significant information advocates can provide to decision makers is cost-related. Legislators will want to know how much a new or modified policy will cost, pure and simple. Careful fiscal analysis by the advocates is required, including startup costs, first-year costs, and ongoing costs such as staff, overhead, or special equipment. Human costs can also be calculated, including what it would cost if the proposed bill were not passed or how much human suffering would continue (Haynes & Mickelson, 2003).

Use a supportive legislator to introduce a bill. It is important to obtain as many sponsors of proposed legislation as possible because it will increase the likelihood of passage. Knowledge of the interests, values, and voting records of legislators will help advocates determine who to ask to introduce a bill and lead the fight during the legislative session. In addition to sympathetic legislators, advocates should also try to enlist bipartisan support, leaders of the majority party, and key powerful legislators who are respected among their colleagues (Kirst-Ashman & Hull, 1993).

Draft legislation jointly. The most hazardous segment of the policy process is often the most overlooked. Drafting a bill means choosing the language and inserting the dimensions of the solution that translate the policy practitioner's preferences into tangible and verbal form (Jansson, 2003; Martineau, 1991). This is a very important task, and advocates should attempt to participate fully in finalizing the wording of the proposed legislation.

Conduct a legislative workshop. Advocates heighten awareness, educate participants, and decide on future actions by bringing together various groups, legislators, experts, community leaders, clients, and constituents. Advocates may want to organize a workshop around their highest-priority issue and devote time to discussing and analyzing it to learn which proposal or option would be likely to pass. Supporters of a bill can also be identified based on their participation in the workshop.

2. Campaign Strategies and Tactics

When a legislator is perceived to be neutral, indifferent, or apathetic about a proposed initiative, policy practitioners can consider a campaign strategy. These legislators share fewer values, have different attitudes than social policy advocates, and have little invested in the outcome of the legislation. The legislators' behavior toward social workers may be cool and distant, especially if this encounter marks the first time they have worked side by side with social work advocates. The legislator may have a "show-me" attitude, compelling the advocate to use persuasive skills effectively. A campaign strategy can be carried out by using the following tactics.

Lobby legislators one-on-one. Smith (1979) cited studies pointing to the importance of interaction between legislators and advocates, indicating that greater frequency of contact between them led to more change in the legislators' opinions. Richan (1996) and Melton (1983) stated that the most direct way of influencing a legislator is by talking with him or her in person. Lobbying can also be thought of as an exchange in which the policy practitioner wants action on a bill and the legislator wants to be re-elected (Richan, 1996).

Educate the public. It is not at all surprising that citizens are often unaware of complex policy and political issues, because even lobbyists find it difficult to keep up on proposed bills or amendments. Advocates must try to demonstrate to potentially supportive groups and to the general public how their own interests are tied to the well-being of often marginal groups.

Use the media. Elected officials pay attention to media coverage and respond to the views of the general public (Morgan, 1983). Advocates gain power by having access to the media (Amidei, 1982; Segal & Brzruzy, 1998). Dorn, Teitelbaum, and Cortez (1998) recommended integrating a media plan with lobbying efforts.

The aim is to raise the visibility of an issue and help shape the terms of the debate. Among the media methods are press releases to local, daily, and weekly newspapers and TV and radio news programs; letters to the editor and op-ed pieces; fliers, handouts, and posters; newsletters; interviews on the radio and TV; postings on online news message boards; news conferences; solicitation of coverage by well-known columnists; pitching of feature stories with a human interest focus; publication of articles in journals and magazines; and paid advertisements. The media must, of course, be used with care to be certain that coverage emphasizes themes and arguments that help the advocates' cause. The timing of coverage must be integrated, as well, with advocates' strategy so that it comes at critical junctures.

Organize letter-writing campaigns and phone calls. A 1977 study by Jeffrey Berry discovered that nearly half of responding lobbyists perceived letter-writing campaigns as effective. Segal and Brzruzy (1998) stated that congressional staff listed spontaneous constituent mail as important. The most effective letters are clear, personal, hand-written, and not mass produced. Letters should be no longer than one page, be positive and courteous, be explicit about the issue, offer personal points of view, be factual, and provide alternatives. Request a written response and include your name and address. The same guidelines apply to making a telephone call or sending an e-mail message.

Use "power people." Affiliation with people within the "establishment" or power structures of a state or community can increase the leverage that policy practitioners can apply. These individuals usually know legislators and the legislative process, and their opinions are typically respected (Segal & Brzruzy, 1998). Policy advocates must carefully determine how best to interest these influential citizens in a specific campaign, such as by finding people who can best approach them and by developing effective arguments. Power people can be engaged in behind-the-scenes advocacy, or they can make public presentations to the media and to legislative committees. Such leaders must be recruited with care, however, because they need to agree with the basic goals and values of persons who are organizing a campaign.

Refer to precedents. Decision makers often are willing to support a policy if it has been tried before (Eriksen, 1997). Initiating a brand new, never-been-tried-before idea is something that makes many legislators nervous. Hence, advocates should strive to illustrate how the policy has worked elsewhere, what the cost savings have been, what outcomes and impact there were, and how it will assist a given client group now.

Take the high moral ground. To overcome apathy or indifference among legislators, advocates can often take the high moral ground. It places the decision makers in a moral context that is usually had to reject or dismiss (Kaminski & Walmsley, 1995). Legislators will need to declare their positions on an issue of justice, poverty, or fairness to ensure they will not appear too detached from citizens' lives and problems. By framing proposals as measures that will advance equity, fairness, and equality and will redress important social problems, advocates may make it more difficult for legislators to oppose them (Kaminski & Walmsley, 1995).

Monitor the legislative process carefully. To keep track of the progress of a bill and to prevent obstacles from developing, advocates frequently use individuals to monitor a piece of legislation on a regular basis at legislative meetings, hearings, and floor debates. These people must be patient, often wait long hours, and keep records of voting patterns. A monitor will also be able to alert others to crises, get help in responding to word changes or amendments, note absent committee members, provide information, and alert the media to key developments.

3. Contest Strategies and Tactics

When a legislator is perceived to be hostile to the policy advocacy group's position, be unwilling to listen, be unsupportive of a bill, and share few, if any values, in common with them, policy practitioners usually can employ a contest strategy. There may be open conflict between the advocate and the legislator. Distrust is high, as is disagreement about the importance of outcomes of the legislation. Here, advocates might be lucky to change behaviors, but not beliefs or values. The question of degree of conflict is important to consider because advocates must weigh carefully whether to burn bridges and heighten conflict to intense levels. Today's opponents could be tomorrow's allies. There undoubtedly will be more issues in the future, and alienation of legislators is a risk that must be weighed very carefully.

Different confrontational tactics exist. Advocates may mobilize pressure against opponents, such as bombarding them with mail and seeking media coverage that highlights their opposition. They can threaten to target opponents in forthcoming elections, or they can develop protests and demonstrations in strategic locations such as outside a legislative hearing or a legislative chamber.

In such situations, policy practitioners must carefully weigh their options. They can employ highly confrontational tactics, but such tactics may antagonize legislators who might otherwise support the policy practitioner's legislative proposals in future years. Even when engaging in confrontational tactics, policy practitioners should focus on substantive issues rather than personal matters, and they should never engage in behavior that is contrary to the NASW Code of Ethics.

Schlozman and Tierney (1986) found that legislative advocacy groups ranked protests and demonstrations as the lowest means of influence. Patti and Dear (1975) advised advocates to realize that, under most circumstances, heavy-handed, coercive, and confrontational tactics are usually counterproductive. Advocates must try not to tarnish the public image of the legislator unnecessarily. Making a legislator look bad is risky, as it may undermine his or her image with constituents back home. Using threats is also risky because it creates antagonism and removes policy advocates' future access to the legislator involved. In fact, a demonstration may well mobilize the opposition into devoting even greater resources to defeating a measure—or will harden them so that they will not support even a diluted legislative proposal.

If advocates have already tried a collaborative or campaign approach as described previously and made little or no progress, they can consider a contest strategy. Jansson (2003) and Melton (1983) suggested that protests or demonstrations can be used when a group does not have access to decision makers, an issue or bill has not reached a significant level of public consciousness, considerable conflict is necessary to secure enactment of a controversial bill, or legislators continue to ignore an important issue. In these circumstances, to advance a proposed bill or issue, advocates need to organize their actions carefully to maximize effect and minimize alienation or loss of goodwill from supporters.

Legislative advocates who lead demonstrations must cope with these tensions simultaneously by nurturing and sustaining their own organization, choosing tactics that maximize exposure to the media, influencing legislators capable of approving a bill, and influencing others with greater resources and influence to team up with them (Lipsky, 1969). A protest can also motivate members, attract new members, increase solidarity, and gain credibility for a group (Eriksen, 1997). However, long-term success nearly always includes other policy strategies in addition to protest activities.

The Analytic-Based Advocacy Model

Policy selection lies at the heart of the policy-making process. Policy practitioners often must identify policy alternatives and then select a preferred one, often in a deliberative process that makes extensive use of research and data. This rational approach to policy analysis came of age in the 1960s as economists and systems analysts assumed major roles in policy selection and finds expression in the research and data often collected and analyzed in think tanks and academic settings (Jansson, 2000).

An extensive body of literature discusses various research and data analysis tools relied on by many policy analysts (Patton & Sawicki, 1993; Weimer & Vinning, 1992). Other policy analysts discuss analysis as an art rather than a science, noting that value assumptions, power realities, and other irrational considerations often intrude (Bardach, 1996; Heineman, Bluhm, Peterson, & Kearny, 1997). A vast research literature now exists on virtually any social problem or issue that can be accessed from governmental and academic sources.

Analysis-based advocacy seeks data that support the need for social reforms. It includes data about the extent and distribution of social problems like poverty, mental illness, and malnutrition. It includes information about the effectiveness of alternative remedies to specific social problems, such as different approaches to getting people who are eligible for food stamps to actually receive them. It includes data about demonstration or pilot projects that offer promising policy options.

It includes outcome studies, such as ones that examine the effectiveness, cost-effectiveness, and cost-benefit of specific policy options.

Policy analysis is often coupled with other models of policy practice. People engaged in legislative advocacy often engage in policy analysis before and during their advocacy so that legislators will take their recommendations seriously. Ballot-based advocates often seek data that support specific positions that candidates take, as well as data that demonstrate that political opponents have made ill-considered policy choices.

Because policy analysis has been discussed at considerable length in a companion publication to this *Handbook of Community Practice,* we refer readers to it (Jansson, 2000).

The Implementation Advocacy Model

When social workers try to change rules, procedures, program strategies, budgets, informal belief systems, and interorganizational relations that guide the implementation of policies, they engage in policy practice (Nakamura & Smallwood, 1980). As with other kinds of policy practice, social workers seek to influence implementation processes to improve the well-being of consumers of service, whose needs and interests often are not adequately addressed by existing social programs or by those charged with implementing new programs.

We live in an "administrative state" in which "administrative regulations and administrative adjudications dwarf, both in number and in practical effect, the legislative output of the Congress and the decisions of the courts" (Mashaw, 1997, p. 106). Because implementation decisions are made at many levels, policy practitioners correspondingly must work at each of these levels, including in federal, state, county, and city governments; school districts; local communities; and other specialized agencies. Depending on the issue, work may focus on one or many of these levels. Indeed, policy practitioners often determine where to focus their energies by analyzing the flow of money and policy through the implementation system. For example, Head Start advocates focus most of their activity at the federal level because Head Start money flows directly from the federal government to local grantees. However, this process may be converted to state grants by the incumbent federal administration. If this change is made, Head Start advocates will have to compete for funds with many other state and local early education programs. Money for child welfare services flows from federal to state governments, and in some states from state to county governments, an arrangement that requires coordinated action and monitoring at multiple levels. Funding for some services (such as education or juvenile justice) comes primarily from local revenues. Many nonprofit agencies raise much of their operating revenue locally through charitable donations, participation as a member agency in United Way, or from government grants and contracts.

Many approaches to policy practice exist when using the implementation model. Sometimes, organizations led by clients and their community-based advocates seek specific changes in specific programs, as was illustrated by the work of the local chapters of the National Welfare Rights Organization in the 1960s and 1970s. Others, such as the Western Center on Law and Poverty initiate class action or other suits to promote compliance with enacted policies or with legal principles (Mashaw, 1997). Some social workers engage in policy practice "from the trenches," that is, from line and supervisory positions where they advocate for their clients, aiming to improve implementation processes from the inside out (Scheirer, 1981). Still others influence policy from positions in unions of human services workers. Some policy practitioners aim to change administrative regulations established by agencies in the executive branches of state and federal governments (Mashaw, 1997). Or they may focus on budget-making processes of governments to modify public priorities (Wildavsky, 1988).

The Los Angeles Roundtable for Children and the Children's Planning Council

This discussion of the implementation advocacy model focuses on the role of policy practitioners at the local level, because that is where most social programs are implemented. To illustrate the multiple strategies that are used by policy practitioners, we highlight the work of the Los Angeles Roundtable for Children and the work of a group of advocates dedicated to improving the lives of children and families in Los Angeles County over the past 20 years.

Budget Analysis

The Los Angeles Roundtable for Children began an intensive 2-year study of county expenditures on behalf of children and families in 1984. The roundtable, a volunteer organization founded by Celeste Kaplan (a social worker who had recently retired as executive director of a local nonprofit agency), included key leaders from public and private agencies, universities, and civic groups concerned about children. Its 1986 report, which analyzed cross-departmental expenditures for children, documented that about one third of the county's budget ($1.5 of $4 billion in 1980–1981) was spent on services for children and families provided by 90 programs in 17 county departments. A 1999 update documented an increase to about 200 such programs in 24 departments that expend $3.8 of the county's total budget of $14 billion (McCroskey & Yoo, 1999). The genesis of the roundtable's work on the children's budget was recognition of the need for more information about the distribution of funds, the sources of these funds, and changes in funding patterns over time:

> The Roundtable believes that a crucial step in improving County government's service provision capabilities is the development of widespread understanding of the fiscal realities which constrain and enable county decision-makers. Effective collaboration for children requires the talents of budget and program experts, public and private agencies, professionals and civic leaders. (Los Angeles Roundtable for Children, 1986, pp. i–ii)

Collaborative Planning

The County Board of Supervisors accepted the roundtable's report and ordered its chief administrative officer (CAO) to work with the group to improve cross-departmental coordination, improve budget practices, and develop a "practical mechanism" for planning across public and private sectors. These efforts eventually led to the formation in 1991 of the Los Angeles County Children's Planning Council (CPC). The CPC, created by the board to serve as its principal planning body for children and families, works to improve conditions and services through integration, coordination, and increased community access to health and human services. Its primary task is to develop and periodically refine a strategic plan that could end the unfocused use of resources. Without better planning, coordination, and tracking, the board recognized that county efforts had little promise of improving results for disadvantaged children and their families.

The CPC, a public-private partnership of decision makers, includes directors of the six key child-serving county departments and representatives of cities and school districts, business, philanthropy, and the United Way and nonprofit agencies, as well as representatives of the ethnic and geographic communities of Los Angeles county. Its work—carried out primarily by volunteers with funding support from public and private sectors—has laid a shared groundwork for change and has helped steer a culture shift within county government. Through this policy and advocacy work, the county's service culture has begun to move from a climate of chaos and blame to a shared focus on results and accountability in the design, funding, and implementation of services for children and families in Los Angeles. In addition, the CPC has devised a regional infrastructure that was previously missing due to the sheer size and scope of the largest county in the nation, as well as to the fragmentation of services endemic to the field of child and family services. The geographic service planning areas (SPAs) recommended by the CPC and adopted by the board of supervisors connect countywide and neighborhood planning efforts, helping to engage citizens in planning across the eight large regions and hundreds of smaller geographic and ethnic communities that make up Los Angeles county.

Key accomplishments of the CPC include

1. developing and convincing others to adopt a shared vision for children and families,

2. developing agreement on five major outcome areas and corresponding indicators to measure results for children and families,

3. producing a regular Children's Score Card for the county in partnership with United Way of Greater Los Angeles,

4. developing a widely accepted geographic structure (the eight SPAs and a ninth American Indian Children's Council [AICC]) for planning and information sharing, and

5. developing and nurturing community partnerships throughout this SPA/AICC structure.

Data-Based Planning and Accountability

One of the continuing key issues for child and family advocates had to do with the lamentable state of knowledge on what was happening to and for children in Los Angeles County. Advocates continue to work on ways to better integrate data from many different data sources to produce timely and strategic information, to support proactive planning for children and families, and to track accountability for outcomes. The concerns raised in a 1988 report from the county's CAO (written in collaboration with the Roundtable) sound very current:

> To begin with, decision makers need to know how many children are being served, for what reason, through what programs and by what funding. They also need to know where there are serious gaps in service as well as where overlap exists. They should have estimates of trends in service needs, as well as the needs that can realistically be met by County departments, and those for which mobilization of additional resources will be needed. Such information would help decision makers prepare for legislative changes or for community-wide resource mobilization. (Children's Budget Implementation Coordination Committee, 1988, pp. 22–23)

The group that wrote this report in 1988 had just identified 50 different information systems dealing with children's services in county government (some computerized and some manual). A count of information systems in county government dealing with children's and family services today would undoubtedly find many more than 50 such systems. The difficulties of integrating information from so many different sources to inform proactive planning continues to be one of the key roadblocks to effective and efficient management of individual programs, integration of services across key institutions (i.e., county, cities, school districts, and nonprofit agencies), and community engagement in local planning process (McCroskey, in press). One of the authors, who has worked on this issue in Los Angeles for the past decade, is now helping to develop a shared countywide information resource, tentatively called the Los Angeles County Data Partnership for Children Center, that may solve some of our most pressing data problems.

The activities of these advocates in Los Angeles fall under the rubric of policy practice—not research, analysis, or organizing—because they were designed to influence elected officials and the administrators of the many hundreds of organizations concerned with children and families in Los Angeles County. Advocates strive to remain focused on results for children, rather than on organizational needs, political rivalries, or funding streams, because they believe that the fragmented, categorical nature of service provision hurts families and children. Improving results for children in any community is a very big job requiring the efforts of many groups, including professional social workers who can assume leadership roles by becoming policy practitioners. Community practitioners who engage in the implementation model of policy practice need organizing skills required to develop and sustain groups with cross-cutting membership, data collection and analysis skills, skills in developing collaborative solutions to implementation problems, negotiating skills, and budgeting skills.

Conclusion

Policy practice is an intervention that seeks to influence and reform policies in electoral, legislative, and implementation venues. It allows social workers to impact the well-being of citizens and consumers of services by influencing not just the rules, regulations, resources, and operating procedures of programs, but the legislative statutes and administrative regulations that establish them in the first place. Moreover, policy practitioners influence the content of these policies by shaping the composition of governments through electoral politics.

Our discussion illustrates that different models of policy practice exist. It also suggests that permutations exist within the four models. Further theoretical and empirical work is needed to validate the models and to analyze different approaches used by policy practitioners within each of them.

Our discussion argues that policy practice should suffuse social work curricula, as well as in-service training of practicing social workers. Policy practitioners need specific skills to implement each of the models effectively. A major challenge confronting the social work profession is not only to familiarize social workers with the four models, but to ground them in the skills needed to implement them, whether in class, field, or continuing education courses. Policy increasingly must be viewed as an intervention that lies at the heart of the mission of social work. Then, and only then, will the cadre of committed policy practitioners expand to include most practicing social workers who will aim to be not merely foot soldiers but shapers of governments, policies, and operating programs (Sunley, 1970).

References

Amidei, N. (1982). How to be an advocate in bad times. *Public Welfare, 40,* 37–42.

Bardach, E. (1996). *The eight-step path of policy analysis: A handbook for practice.* Berkeley, CA: Berkeley Academic Press.

Berry, J. (1977). *Lobbying for the people.* Princeton, NJ: Princeton University Press.

Biersack, R., Herrnson, P., & Wilcox, C. (1999). *After the revolution: PACs, lobbies, and the Republican Congress.* Boston: Allyn & Bacon.

Birnbaum, J. (2000). *The money men: The real story of fund-raising's influence on political power in America.* New York: Crown.

Bobo, K., Kendall, J., & Max, S. (1991). *Organizing for social change: A manual for activists in the 1990s.* Arlington, VA: Seven Locks Press.

Brager, G., & Holloway, S. (1978). *Changing human service organizations.* New York: Free Press.

Butler, S. S. (2002). Advocacy with rural elders. *Aging (NASW Section on Aging), 4*(2), 8–10.

Children's Budget Implementation Coordination Committee. (1988). *Investing in our children: A priority for Los Angeles County Government* (Vol. 2, Subcommittee Reports). Los Angeles, CA: County Chief Administrative Office.

Davis, R. (1999). *The web of politics: The Internet's impact on the American political system.* New York: Oxford University Press.

Dear, R., & Patti, R. (1981). Legislative advocacy: Seven effective tactics. *Social Work, 26,* 289–297.

DeKieffer, D. (1997). *The citizen's guide to lobbying Congress.* Chicago: Chicago Review Press.

Dempsey, D. (1998, August). *Social policy and social change.* Paper presented at the annual Policy Practice Conference, Charleston, SC.

DiClerico, R. (2000). *Political parties, campaigns, and elections.* Upper Saddle River, NJ: Prentice Hall.

Dluhy, M. J. (1981). *Changing the system: Political advocacy for disadvantaged groups.* Beverly Hills, CA: Sage.

Dorn, S., Teitelbaum, M., & Cortez, C. (1998). *Advocate's tool kit.* Washington, DC: Children's Defense Fund.

Eriksen, K. (1997). *Making an impact: A handbook on counselor advocacy.* Washington, DC: Accelerated Development.

Ezell, M. (2001). *Advocacy in the human services.* Belmont, CA: Brooks/Cole Wadsworth.

Flynn, J. (1985). *Social agency policy: Analysis and presentation for community practice.* Chicago: Nelson-Hall.

Haynes, K. S., & Mickelson, J. S. (2003). *Affecting change: Social workers in the political arena* (5th ed.). New York: Longman.

Heineman, R., Bluhm, W., Peterson, S., & Kearny, E. (1997). *The world of the policy analyst.* Chatham, NJ: Chatham House.

Hiratsuka, J. (1992, January). Active role in '92 elections urged. *NASW News,* p. 1.

Hula, K. (1999). *Lobbying together: Interest group coalitions in legislative politics.* Washington, DC: Georgetown University Press.

Influencing State Policy. (n.d.). *Influencing State Policy.* Retrieved at www.statepolicy.org/.

Jacobson, G. (1997). *The politics of Congressional elections* (4th ed.). New York: Longman.

Jansson, B. S. (1997). *Social welfare policy: From theory to practice* (3rd ed.). Belmont, CA: Wadsworth.

Jansson, B. S. (2000). Policy analysis. In J. Midgley, M. Tracy, & M. Livermore (Eds.), *The handbook of social policy* (pp. 41–52). Thousand Oaks, CA: Sage.

Jansson, B. S. (2003). *Becoming an effective policy advocate: From policy practice to social justice* (4th ed.). Pacific Grove, CA: Brooks/Cole.

Johnson-Cartee, K., & Copeland, G. (1997). *Inside political campaigns.* Westport, CT: Praeger.

Kahn, S. (1991). *Organizing: A guide for grassroots leaders.* Silver Spring, MD: NASW Press.

Kaminski, L., & Walmsley, C. (1995). The advocacy brief: A guide for social workers. *Social Worker, 63,* 53–58.

Kirst-Ashman, K., & Hull, G. H. (1993). *Understanding generalist practice.* Chicago: Nelson-Hall.

Lipsky, M. (1969). *Protest in city politics: Rent strikes, housing, and the power of the poor.* Chicago: Rand McNally.

Los Angeles Roundtable for Children. (1986). *The children's budget of Los Angeles county government.* Los Angeles, CA: Author.

Mahaffey, M., & Hanks, J. (Eds.). (1982). *Practical politics: Social work and political responsibility.* Silver Spring, MD: NASW Press.

Martineau, R. (1991). *Drafting legislation and rules in plain English.* New York: West.

Mashaw, J. (1997). *Greed, chaos, and governance.* New Haven, CT: Yale University Press.

McCroskey, J. (in press). *Walking the collaboration talk: Ten lessons learned from the Los Angeles County Children's Planning Council.* Los Angeles, CA: Los Angeles County Children's Planning Council.

McCroskey, J., & Yoo, J. (1999). *The children's budget of Los Angeles County Government, 1980–1999.* Los Angeles, CA: Los Angeles County Children's Planning Council.

McInnis-Dittrich, K. (1994). *Integrating social welfare policy and social work practice.* Pacific Grove, CA: Brooks/Cole.

Melton, G. B. (1983). *Child advocacy: Psychological issues and interventions.* New York: Plenum Press.

Morgan, G. G. (1983). Practical techniques for change. *Journal of Children in Contemporary Society, 15*(4), 91–102.

Nakamura, R., & Smallwood, F. (1980). *The politics of policy implementation.* New York: St. Martin's Press.

National Association of Social Workers. (1996). *Code of ethics.* Washington, DC: NASW Press.

National Association of Social Workers. (2003). *National Association of Social Workers.* Retrieved from http://socialworkers.org/pace/state.asp.

Oleszek, W. (2001). *Congressional procedures and the policy process.* Washington, DC: Congressional Quarterly Press.

Ornstein, N., & Elder, S. (1978). *Interest groups, lobbying, and policymaking.* Washington, DC: Congressional Quarterly Press.

Patti, R. J., & Dear, R. B. (1975). Legislative advocacy: One path to social change. *Social Work, 20,* 108–114.

Patton, C., & Sawicki, D. (1993). *Basic methods of policy analysis and planning.* Englewood Cliffs, NJ: Prentice Hall.

Pierce, D. (1984). *Policy for the social work practitioner.* New York: Longman.

Pierce, D. (2000). Policy practice. In J. Midgley, M. B. Tracy, & M. Livermore (Eds.), *Handbook of social welfare policy* (pp. 53–63). Thousand Oaks, CA: Sage.

Piven, F., & Cloward, R. (2000). *Why Americans still don't vote and why politicians want it that way.* Boston: Beacon Press.

Plano, J. C., & Greenberg, M. (1989). *The American political dictionary* (8th ed.). Fort Worth, TX: Holt, Rhinehart, & Winston.

Richan, W. C. (1996). *Lobbying for social change* (2nd ed.). Binghamton, NY: Haworth Press.

Rickards, L. D. (1992). Professional and organized provider associations. *Administration and Policy in Mental Health, 20,* 11–25.

Scheirer, M. A. (1981). *Program implementation: The organizational context.* Beverly Hills, CA: Sage.

Scher, R. (1997). *The modern political campaign.* Armonk, NY: M. E. Sharpe.

Schlozman, K. W., & Tierney, J. T. (1986). *Organized interests and American democracy.* New York: Harper Collins.

Schneider, R. L., & Lester, L. (2001). *Social work advocacy: A new framework for action.* Belmont, CA: Brooks/Cole Wadsworth.

Schneider, R. L., & Netting, F. E. (1999). Influencing state policy in a time of devolution: Upholding social work's great tradition. *Social Work, 44,* 349–357.

Segal, E. A., & Brzuzy, S. (1998). *Social welfare policy, programs and practice.* Itasca, IL: F. E. Peacock.

Smith, V. W. (1979). How interest groups influence legislators. *Social Work, 24,* 234–239.

Social workers out to expand presence in Congress. (2000). *NASW News, 45*(9), 5.

Sunley, R. (1970). Family advocacy: From case to cause. *Social Casework, 51*(6), 347–357.

Thompson, J., & Moncrief, G. (1998). *Campaign finance in state legislative elections.* Washington, DC: Congressional Quarterly Press.

Thurber, J., Nelson, C., & Dulio, D. (Eds.). (2000). *Crowded airwaves: Campaign advertising in elections.* Washington, DC: Brookings Institution.

Weimer, D., & Vinning, A. (1992). *Policy analysis: Concepts and practice.* Englewood Cliffs, NJ: Prentice Hall.

Weissman, I. (1959). *Social welfare policy and services in social work education.* New York: Council on Social Work Education.

Wenocur, S., & Reisch, M. (1989). *From charity to enterprise: The development of American social policy in a market economy.* Urbana, IL: University of Illinois.

West, D., & Loomis, B. (1999). *The sound of money: How political interests get what they want done.* New York: W.W. Norton.

Wildavsky, A. (1988). *The new politics of the budgetary process.* Glenview, IL: Scott, Foresman.

PART III

Issues, Areas, and Fields of Community Practice

Part III of the Handbook—"Issues, Areas, and Fields of Community Practice"—provides in-depth coverage of a range of particular and important arenas of community practice. Section A begins with a central issue for America's future, "Multicultural Community Practice Strategies and Inter-group Empowerment," by Lorraine Gutierréz, Edith Lewis, Biren (Ratnesh) Nagda, Laura Wernick, and Nancy Shore. This chapter discusses two approaches to making intergroup dialogue possible and a major part of community building. Cheryl Hyde analyzes feminist community practice and illustrates feminist approaches to all major community models. Women have always been the informal if not formal leaders in grassroots work—and had at least important if small representation early on in the movement to organize and coordinate services. If women are not at the table, they should be; the time is long past when a segment of society should consider itself competent to plan for gender or cultural groups who are not involved from the beginning. It is of major importance that feminist practice strategies be integrated within all aspects of community practice. In the chapter on faith-based community organizing, Ram Cnaan, Stephanie Brodie, and Gaynor Yancey encourage practitioners to understand the areas in which they can make common cause with neighborhood congregations for community improvement and highlight the range of community outreach and program activities carried out by religious congregations and interfaith groups. John Morrison provides a cogent discussion of current and emerging issues in service coordination that is useful for assessing needs and planning programs with community representatives and other agencies. Service coordination is a major means of responding to new social needs or intervening in recalcitrant problems with new strategies. The formation of community networks and coordinated services is becoming an increasingly important means of planning, building new programs, and promoting service integration.

Section B opens with a discussion of rural community practice, presenting characteristics of rural communities and the context for community practice. Iris Carlton-LaNey, Susan Murty, and Lynne Morris provide insightful examples of community practice in a wide range of rural communities. Increasingly, rural practitioners seek to connect services and encourage community development. Rural practice typically unites organizing, planning and development strategies seeking to strengthen communities and improve quality of life as rural areas face the economic challenges of the 21st century.

The health and mental health systems of the United States have been and seem to continue in a state of constant of change, if not chaos, in some areas of policy and service provision. In "Community Practice in Health and Mental Health Settings," Anna Scheyett and Erin Drinnin explain the progression of change in both systems, and the barriers to service posed by managed care and inadequate policies. People with health/mental health problems face increasing challenges to mount successful advocacy and system change efforts to humanize the system and engage client populations more successfully in organized efforts to secure their rights.

The child mental health system has undergone extraordinary practice advances in the past fifteen years, but the current economic climate will challenge gains made. Terry Cross and Barbara Friesen analyze the advances made in cultural competence areas and the development of family-centered practice in "Community Practice in Children's Mental Health" and document areas of best practice in these central components of developing a responsive system of care.

Another rapidly emerging arena is comprehensive community-based initiatives. This practice as discussed by Elizabeth Mulroy, Kristine Nelson, and Elizabeth Gour is grounded in community-building strategies. Collaboratives can create community-based means of working with communities and coordinating services in ways that engage consumers in planning, implementation, governance and evaluation of programs. In "Community Economic and Social Development," Herbert Rubin and Margaret Sherraden provide both information and insight into emerging modes of CED. They analyze the political/economic/policy context and provide examples of successful efforts which work to combine the building of human capital and strengthening economic structures in low-income areas. They present cogent arguments for social work community practitioners to fully engage with economic and social development—central ways to assist people in improving the physical and social settings of their communities as well as increase opportunities. Moving further with issues of social and human capital, and opportunity and asset development, Walter Farrell and James Johnson illustrate and challenge community practitioners to engage with inner-city youth in order to provide the skills that can help them seize and create opportunities for productive lives. Their chapter, "Investing in Socially and Economically Distressed Communities: Comprehensive Strategies for Inner-City Community and Youth Development," also encourages community practitioners to engage seriously in the work of connecting of social and human capital development to economic opportunity.

Section C presents the intersection of Global Approaches and Local Issues, leading off with Richard Estes's presentation of and argument for use of social indicators for analysis in all community practice. His chapter, "Global Change and Indicators of Social Development," furnishes both specific information and a method of using social indicators as a major means of analyzing national and international issues and social problems. Measurements of positive developments can become benchmarks for further planning and interventions. In "Community Practice Challenges in the Global Economy," Michael Reisch moves further into analysis of global shifts, demographic changes, and the challenges to move forward with participatory development in the face of the growing power of multinational corporations. Salome Raheim, Helzi Noponen, and Catherine Alter provide an exciting analysis of women and community economic development using examples of programs and efforts to improve women's social and economic status in the United States and in India. Common principles and similar strategies can be adapted in efforts to empower women in many areas of the world.

CHAPTER 18

Multicultural Community Practice Strategies and Intergroup Empowerment

Lorraine Gutiérrez

Edith A. Lewis

Biren (Ratnesh) A. Nagda

Laura Wernick

Nancy Shore

I n 1999, Peggye Dilworth-Anderson made a keynote address at the National Council on Family Relations Conference that helped set the stage for understanding the changes experienced by women of color, their families, and their communities over the last two decades. She asserted that our conceptualizations of families of color were based on outdated economic, political, and social analyses that were no longer relevant. This being the case, it follows that the practice methods based on these constructs are outdated as well. To address our current and emerging context, the following questions must be addressed:

- What types of political, social, and economic forces do communities of color face in this new millennium?
- Is there still a role for multicultural community practice strategies, or are those that have been developed for the entire population, irrespective of gender and race or ethnicity, sufficient?

- What role does interracial participation play in the ability of communities and groups to organize themselves and engage in empowering outcomes?
- Are the roles social workers played in community building in the past sufficient to meet the challenges communities of color face in the coming decades?
- What lessons have we learned, and how might we apply these to enhance intergroup empowerment?

These questions set the stage for challenges that face community organizers working with multicultural communities. We begin this chapter on multicultural community practice strategies and intergroup empowerment by outlining some of the economic, social, political, gender, and policy changes that have affected communities of color in the last two decades. We next address the historical bases of multicultural community building and organizing, social workers' roles in supporting the development of these models, and how this multicultural perspective can inform community-organizing strategies. Finally, we outline some of the principles we have learned about effective multicultural community practice. Two examples of ways in which these lessons have been implemented to build communities within and between communities of color and other communities will illuminate the move from theory to practice and application.

Our Current Context for Work With Diverse Communities

Over the past 30 years, the social work profession has paid increasing attention to issues of oppression, diversity, and social justice. This focus arose in relation to civil rights struggles and the development of community organization as a focus in schools of social work (Iglehart & Becerra, 1995; Rothman, 1999). This concern continues to be relevant because our social context is becoming increasingly multiracial, multicultural, and multiethnic, with growing economic inequality and stratification by gender, race, and ethnicity. Current social movements to eliminate affirmative action, eliminate universal income supports, and restrict immigration and benefits to immigrants and their children are just a few examples of issues related to multiculturalism that community organizers must address. Although community organizers are often at the forefront of dealing with issues of racism, ethnocentrism, and other inequities, methods for working from a multicultural perspective have only recently being documented and evaluated. It is impossible to be a social worker today without confronting and addressing issues of diversity and social justice. In our quest to develop culturally relevant or culturally competent programs and services, social workers at all levels have sometimes romanticized or idealized communities of color. Although we must understand and build on the strengths that exist in communities, we must not overlook the negative impacts of economic inequality, sexism, and racism. Romanticizing communities of color can lead to desensitization regarding the realities of current social and economic experiences in the United States.

The following are just some of the critical issues facing communities of color today that must be addressed by community workers.

Health Care

Although research in gerontology has identified a racial crossover effect that suggests that people of color who survive into old age are often healthier than other elders, the life expectancy of people of color still lags behind that of the general population. Life expectancy for African American males is 67.7 years, that for Latinos is 69.6 years, and for American Indian men, life expectancy is only 66.1 years. These figures constitute a major public health issue. AIDS is a major cause of early death for both Latinos and African American men between 25 and 44. A CDC report documents that in 1998, seven out of ten murder victims for that year were men of color. Maternal and infant mortality rates in communities of color have continued to rise. The infant mortality rates for African Americans in 2002 was 13.6 deaths per 1,000 and that of American Indians was 8.3 per 1,000, in comparison to a rate of only 5.7 deaths per 1,000 among non-Hispanic whites in the U.S. population (Annie E. Casey Foundation, 2003, p. 41.)

Children and Youth

The community and familial supports that were available to youth of color as recently as 20 years ago are almost nonexistent today. The networks that were once available through religious, spiritual, ethnic, and community organizations have weakened considerably, and adults in poor families of color have neither the resources nor the time to participate in those groups at the levels they did before 1980 (Ehrenrich, 2001). In addition, children of color are more likely than other children to attend poorly funded and overburdened public school systems (Dilworth-Anderson, 1999; Zippay, 2002). These factors have a direct effect on youth of color and diminish their ability to develop their own human capital and to become financially self-sufficient (Frazier-Kouassi, 2002; Soderberg, 2001; see also Padilla & Sherraden, Chapter 5, this volume).

Income and Employment

With the implementation of the Personal Responsibility and Welfare Reconciliation Act (1996), women of color are disproportionately pushed into marginal and low-paying employment with inadequate supports. These conditions lead to situations in which women with low incomes are forced to work without adequate child care, medical assistance, or other benefits. The degree to which our social services systems and private employers are required to provide these supports has not been clarified. This quandary is an example of why we must pay attention to how policy is implemented, given the economic, historical, and social situations of the populations affected by these policy changes.

Globalization and Transnationalism

Increased globalization requires us to think about the impact of policy decisions on people both inside and outside the United States. (In this volume, see

Gamble & Hoff, Chapter 8, and Estes, Chapter 28.) People of all income levels have transnational ties. For example, within immigrant communities, some families spend the year traveling between the United States and their home countries in search of economic security, while others send much of their income to members of extended families in their home countries. Neighborhood and community changes that affect families of color in the United States can have an impact on extended family members in other countries as well (see Reisch, Chapter 29, this volume). The globalization of media and access to satellite TV and the Internet in communities with even the lowest incomes have brought ethnic media from all over the world to U.S. communities of color. Because this information comes from a variety of locations, perspectives, and ideologies, people of color may be able to learn much more about both local and global economic and social problems.

To address these issues, community practitioners must integrate an understanding of the importance of culture and personal identity with practice approaches and methods that deal directly with issues of social justice and inequality. These multicultural methods would work toward the empowerment and economic development of disenfranchised groups while creating mechanisms for greater intergroup interaction and change toward greater inclusion in the society generally. A multicultural practice approach begins with a pluralistic foundation, but it goes beyond pluralism to recognize and work to eliminate social injustices and oppression based on group membership. It attempts to address ways in which we can respect diversity and reduce inequality while working toward a common good.

This perspective is in direct contrast to social work approaches that have been ethnocentric or culturally insensitive. Although social work has often promoted social justice and equality, some aspects of social work, such as those associated with the criminal justice system, have clearly functioned as tools of social control. Historically, social work has considered, either explicitly or implicitly, the norms, values, and needs of European American culture to be the most desirable. Social work has placed little or no value on the unique experiences of people of color and may view their traditions and practices as the basis of many of the problems these groups face (Gutiérrez & Lewis, 2000). Consequently, social workers have been involved in such activities as the removal of Native American children from their families, placing them in boarding schools or with White foster families; the "repatriation" of people of Mexican descent during the Depression; the "Americanization" efforts that led to the loss of language and culture of European immigrants; and the lack of attention to specific cultural groups such as the diverse range of Asian Americans (Gutiérrez, 1992).

This ethnocentric focus led many communities of color to develop their own agencies or institutions parallel or in opposition to those in the European American community (Iglehart & Becerra, 1995). Within all communities of color, there is a rich tradition and heritage of community organizing and organizational development aimed at addressing the lack of responsive human services programs and the need to mobilize for social justice (Anner, 1996; Rivera & Erlich, 1998). These organizing activities have built on the strengths and resources that exist in all communities of color (Delgado, 1999). These projects often incorporate cultural symbols, the arts, and spiritual beliefs and practices. For example, programs developed in Puerto Rican communities may enlist spiritualists and mediums to reach and involve community members (Hum-Delgado & Delgado, 1986. The methods developed and used by these indigenous organizations can provide insights into ways in which all social workers can work effectively with communities of color (Delgado, 1999; Iglehart & Becerra, 1995).

Although earlier practice models were often culturally insensitive (see Cross & Friesen, Chapter 24, this volume), multicultural educational and practice efforts have increased dramatically over the last decade. It should be noted, however, that social workers, particularly community and group workers, have frequently allied themselves with communities of color. For example, social group workers and community workers were instrumental in the development and implementation of Mobilization for Youth and other efforts in the 1950s and 1960s that worked toward the empowerment of communities of color in urban areas (Brager, 1999). Similarly, community organizers played a critical role in encouraging integration and racial stabilization in an effort to stem "White flight" in Cleveland in the 1950s (Turner, 1999). These comprehensive community development programs involved multi-ethnic and multiracial coalitions of community leaders, grassroots organizers, and social workers.

Principles for Multicultural Community Building and Organizing

During the last decade, significant attention has been paid to the issues of multiculturalism (Nagda & Gutiérrez, 2000), empowerment (Gutiérrez, 1992), and their specific combination in practice (Gutiérrez & Lewis, 2000; Ristock & Pennell, 1996). Theory development and its practical application have led to the distillation of several guiding principles for multicultural work (shown in Table 18.1), which can be used to develop intervention processes and determine desired outcomes. Community practitioners and researchers can use these principles to guide their practice as they seek to build empowerment in low-income communities and promote positive multicultural interactions both within and among diverse groups (Spencer, Lewis, & Gutiérrez, 2000).

These principles are based on an empowerment perspective that uses the strengths, perspectives, and interests of community members to work toward social justice. Practice methods derived from these principles become the "building blocks of empowerment"—developing consciousness, confidence, and connection (Gutiérrez & Lewis, 2000, p. 18).

Effective multicultural community work is grounded in consciousness-raising and requires social work practitioners and community members to develop both a complex understanding of situations and the skills necessary to gain power. Consciousness-raising on a community level can involve such activities as oral history projects or other activities that capture and tell the stories that are at the crux of understanding vital community issues. Such stories may include tales of exploitation and of resistance. Community members may also focus on why the conditions they are concerned about exist and who has the power to change them. The community members and practitioners can identify the skills and resources—including advocacy, community education, and even the use of street theater—that

Table 18.1   Principles of Multicultural Practice

- Multicultural practice needs to be flexible in addressing the dynamic changes and processes of the future.

- Multicultural practice requires self-reflection and practitioners' willingness to take action at all levels, from the interpersonal to the societal.

- Multicultural practice requires practitioners to be flexible and to understand theory and how it applies to practice at all levels of social intervention. It also demands an ability to combine practice modalities from different levels into consistent and coherent overall plans of intervention.

- Multicultural practice requires the ability to organize and facilitate groups to cause change.

- Multicultural practice depends on the inclusion of the community's perspective in assessing problems and resources.

- Multicultural practitioners must be aware of the historical context of the concepts and methods they use and how the suppositions underlying these concepts and methods may affect their appropriateness.

- Multicultural practice is enhanced by expanding the training of social work practitioners in conducting appropriate research and interpreting research findings.

- Multicultural practice recognizes the importance of language and concepts used in assessment instruments and intervention tools.

- Multicultural practice requires the consistent use and operationalization of constructs to further the knowledge base.

- Multicultural practice at all levels is enhanced by the involvement of community-based workers.

are necessary to make these changes. Strategies should focus on both immediate and long-range goals in conceptualization, design, and implementation. Participants should ask:

How can we make an immediate change in our community?

What are the consequences of this activity for our community 3, 5, or 9 years from now?

What benefits are we likely to miss if we use this plan?

To overcome the impact of powerlessness, individuals and groups must have confidence in their abilities and actions. Community members who feel powerless to influence their social and political environment may experience a sense of futility and feel despondent and anxious. Actions to increase confidence can help community members overcome these feelings and work more effectively (Bandura, 1982). Among the ways to enhance feelings of self-efficacy are personal mastery of a new activity, seeing a similar person master this activity, being told one is capable of mastering the activity, or experiencing manageable levels of anxiety while attempting the new activity. Both individual capacity and supportive social environments are necessary for confidence to develop (Bandura, 1982; Crosbie-Burnett & Lewis, 1993).

Confidence can be built by organizing activities intentionally focused on the development of new skills. This skill development can be fostered by mentoring and role modeling by other community members, encouragement, and time to process setbacks and difficulties. It is important that "failures" be understood as a normal and even expected part of the developmental process.

Activities focused on connection build on and strengthen the social capital in the community (Delgado, 1999). In multicultural work, asset-focused assessments that consider the importance of culture, family, and spirituality serve as resources for community engagement. Methods and strategies to build connections within and across communities recognize and build on the diversity that exists in all communities, embrace the conflicts in that diversity, and seek to bridge differences through recognition of similarities in social group memberships, values, and goals. Recognizing the significance of transnationalism, these connecting activities will build on relationships within the locality, the community, the nation and the world. For example, environmental and/or social justice coalitions can be developed among organizations both within and outside of the United States.

As social workers who are building partnerships with community-based organizations, it is also imperative that we recognize, understand, and take responsibility for our *positionality*—the place where we stand. Drawing further on Freire, "To understand one's positionality, we must articulate and take responsibility for our own historical and social identities," and we must "interrogate how [our identity and position] have helped shape our particular world views" (Reed, Newman, Suarez, & Lewis, 1997, p. 52). Because we are all implicated in and affected by racism, sexism, classism, heterosexism, ablism, and other forms of oppression, we must take responsibility for all our oppressed and privileged identities. The better we are able to understand the power relationships that exist within our work, the more effectively we will be able to work within diverse communities and in our mutual struggle for social justice.

The term *multicultural community organizing* has been used to describe many different activities. Research conducted with organizers in the field has found that there are real differences in how people define this work. One perspective is that multicultural organizing is a process to enhance the functioning of separate communities while finding strategies to build coalitions among equals; another is that constructive multicultural community building is a goal in and of itself (Gutiérrez & Rosegrant Alvarez, 2000). Both of these perspectives on multicultural organizing are reflected in current practice. The following two case examples reflect these differing but complementary perspectives on this work.

Community Voices Heard: A Participatory Research Project

Participatory research is an organizing strategy that has the potential to make a critical difference in the lives of disfranchised communities. Currently, almost all the research on issues affecting poor women is taking place within academic and policy institutions. It is quite rare that the people most affected by poverty, particularly poor women, participate directly in the design and implementation of research on their situation. Community-based research, on the other hand, places the community at the center of the research process, with its purpose, structure, and outcomes focusing on the community's strengths, resources, and needs (see Pennell, Noponen, & Weil, Chapter 34, this volume). Community-based research can be defined as research that is committed to working with individuals and communities, particularly those who are disenfranchised, to gain understanding, voice, and influence over issues affecting their lives (Rappaport, 1990). One form of community-based research, participatory action research (PAR), equally values community participation and the facilitation of action as a result of the knowledge gained (Nyden, Figert, Shibley, & Barrows, 1997; Stoecker, 1999; see also Castelloe & Gamble, Chapter 13, this volume). This approach seeks to increase community members' empowerment during the research process through the knowledge and the skills they gain by participating and the roles they take on to carry out the evaluation (Gutiérrez, Alvarez, Sakamoto, & Wernick, 2000). Moreover, PAR is committed to critical analysis and the responsible use of power (Ristock & Pennell, 1996).

In July 1998, Mayor Rudolph Giuliani pledged to end welfare and make New York City the "work capital of the country" (Topousis, 1998). Individuals participating in New York City's Family Assistance program (formerly Aid to Families with Dependent Children [AFDC]) then had a 5-year time limit on benefits and were required to participate in mandatory work activities, primarily Workfare. In addition, childless adults receiving assistance through the city's Safety Net program also were required to participate in work activities. New York City's Work Experience Program, which went into effect in 1995, was heralded as the centerpiece of Giuliani's efforts to move people off welfare and into jobs.

However, members of Community Voices Heard (CVH), an organization of people with low income who were receiving public assistance—mostly women of color with children—had not seen any positive change. "Workfare is phony and doesn't lead to real jobs," CVH member Chris Calafell exclaimed at a press conference in April 1997. Many CVH members echoed Calafell's concern.

CVH is one of the few membership organizations working on welfare issues in New York City that is led, directed, and run by low-income people themselves. Many members are formerly homeless and dependent on emergency services, with few ties to community and neighborhood institutions. CVH works to enable members and their low-income neighbors to acquire the experience, skills, and resources necessary to improve their neighborhoods and influence public policy while they work to improve the lives of their families and children. They aim to accomplish this through a multipronged strategy that includes educating the public, organizing the community, developing local leaders, training low-income people about their rights, educating them about the political process, engaging in advocacy for legislative change, and launching direct action campaigns.

The local perception of the lack of real jobs matched the Department of Labor's data, particularly in poor areas. For example, in January 1998, New York City's unemployment rate was at 9.1%, among the highest in the country. In the boroughs of

Brooklyn and the Bronx, unemployment rates were at 10.6% and 11.0%, respectively. Moreover, even with the national economy booming at that time, most newly created jobs that paid close to a living wage required job skills at a higher level than most Workfare participants had (McCall, 1998; Stettner, 1998; U.S. Conference of Mayors, 1998). Most jobs created were in the service industry, which pays very low wages.

Because it was clear that Workfare was not assisting people in moving out of poverty and finding jobs that paid a living wage, CVH decided to use participatory action research methods to draw on the knowledge within the community. Results of the PAR would then be used to outline an alternative program that CVH leaders believed would effectively move people out of poverty. CVH chose to use PAR for three main purposes. First, they recognized the need to document the reality and needs of people trying to move from welfare into work and out of poverty so they could make the case for a public job creation proposal for people on Workfare. They also wanted to evaluate whether current New York City welfare recipients had obtained or were likely to get jobs, assess the effectiveness of different welfare-to-work strategies, and assess barriers to employment. Second, they sought to use the participatory research process to empower CVH and other community members and to organize and build power for change. In doing so, they wanted to make sure that the CVH program proposal was informed and supported by people on welfare who were not CVH members. They sought to communicate the experiences and opinions of current welfare recipients, provide an opportunity for members to take ownership of the research process, and provide education, leadership training, and skills. Finally, a key reason for using PAR was to develop CVH membership and use the research process as an organizing and mobilizing tool for the creation of new jobs in the community.

Emerging out of their desire to work on a proactive solution, CVH members developed the CVH's Job Creation Policy Proposal (Community Voices Heard, 1997), which sought to:

- target welfare recipients and unemployed people with barriers to employment;
- educate and train participants so they could move to unsubsidized employment;
- provide participants with real living wages and health and child care benefits for 18 to 24 months;
- ensure that workers would receive cash wages so they could qualify for the federal and state earned income tax credit (ETIC);
- protect permanent employees from layoff and ensure workplace rights and make real improvements in communities.

While CVH members maintained leadership in developing and pushing this proposal through the state and city governments, they recognized the importance of working within a coalition of other antipoverty activists, policy analysts, lawyers, and legislators. The coalition supported this common effort with great enthusiasm and provided much-needed resources to bring this proposed legislation to fruition.

The PAR project developed by CVH consisted of a survey completed by participants in the Work Experience Program regarding the work they did, their attitudes toward work, and their goals for the future. The survey instrument specifically inquired about people's education, training, and work experiences. It asked what sorts of jobs were available in their communities, whether there were enough jobs in their communities, how much their last job paid, and how they were going about looking for work. It inquired about what sorts of barriers people faced, such as child care, discrimination, and lack of skills. Moreover, it asked whether current job programs were working. It also asked respondents to suggest what they felt was needed to assist them in moving from welfare to work and what components and aspects they believed were essential to carry out a successful jobs program. The survey concluded by asking people if they were interested in working with CVH to fight for a job program that met their needs; thus, the survey served as both an information-gathering and community-organizing tool.

The survey found that Workfare was not helping people move into jobs or increasing their skills and experience. At follow-up, only 4% of respondents had found jobs. Also, people on welfare wanted to work, and 70% were looking for work without help from the city. The survey found that 57.5% faced three or more personal obstacles that would have to be overcome to enable them to move from welfare to work. Moreover, welfare participants faced a labor market that had many more job seekers than available jobs. Finally, almost all those surveyed supported the call for public job creation and the CVH program proposal in particular.

In response, CVH members used these findings to build support for the CVH jobs campaign. Armed with their new knowledge, CVH members developed a network of supporters from a citywide coalition of antipoverty activists, policy analysts, social workers, lawyers, and legislators, and they worked with this new coalition to design legislation to pressure New York City to create jobs for those who could not find them. The CVH jobs program was designed to provide valuable work in the public and private sectors that paid $7.50 per hour and provided health and child care benefits. The program would also provide participants with the experience and training needed to obtain better jobs.

Beyond providing the much-needed data to confirm CVH organizers' experiences and to support their call for change, the survey raised significant community interest, prompting more than 50 additional people to join in CVH's actions, at least 25 of whom took on leadership roles. The PAR project strengthened CVH's reputation among legislators, reporters, funders, and the advocacy community. It helped to legitimize participatory action research within CVH and among other New York City community-based organizations, and it served as an important tool in gathering needed information, building power, organizing, and advocacy.

CVH worked with local policy analysts and lawyers to develop the job creation proposal (Community Voices Heard, 1997), which was informed by the survey, into the Empire State Jobs Bill (1999). Members used the findings in testimonies in front of state and local representatives. They released a report based on the research at a press conference, which CVH used successfully to pressure Roberto Ramirez, chair of the Social Services Committee in the New York State Assembly, to introduce the Empire State Jobs Bill, which was eventually included as a budget line item, with $13 million ($12 million for New York City) being appropriated to pilot the project. Finally, they were able to use the data to help push a similar bill successfully through the New York City Council.

In a subsequent PAR project, CVH documented that Workfare workers were performing work comparable to the work of paid municipal employees and therefore should be similarly compensated. Through this project, CVH has built more solid relationships with the unions in New York City in response to a shared need for this documentation. The unions recognized that CVH was in a much better position to collect this information because of the direct experience of their members and because Workfare participants might be more apt to be honest with those whom they see as representing their interests. In this project, CVH took increased ownership in all stages of the project and reduced their need for outside consulting and technical assistance.

These examples of the work of CVH demonstrate how an organization whose members had low incomes and relatively little formal education recognized their own hard-earned expertise and strengthened their voices and positions to gain a better understanding of and then document their struggle to move off welfare and into jobs that paid a living wage. This organization itself was diverse in respect to race, ethnicity, class, sexual orientation, and gender, and CVH built on the positive aspects of these differences to use the strengths inherent in diversity. Through the PAR process, CVH was able to use research to assess the social relations and structures affecting members' lives and then gain the influence to change these conditions.

Community Study Circles

Robert Putnam (2000) notes that the trend of declining civic involvement in neighborhoods and communities in the last few decades is similar to a trend at the beginning of the 20th century. The difference, however, is in the demographic context in which the decline is occurring, and that difference is manifested in the solutions attempted. In the late 1890s and early 1900s, for instance, civic isolation led to the creation of Rotary Clubs and other associations that brought together people who were largely similar in social backgrounds. With the increasing demographic diversity, the challenge at the beginning of the 21st century is to generate social bonds and social capital across differences of race, class, gender, and other social groups. The Study Circle Resource Center (SCRC) in Pomfret, Connecticut, responded to this challenge by promoting deliberative democracy among diverse community members (SCRC, n.d.).

Multicultural community-building and organizing principles shape the work of SCRC, which has developed a community-wide study circle program model based on principles of citizens' involvement. Study circles are dialogue groups that bring together community members to address public concerns. SCRC defines a study circle as

> a simple and powerful process for democratic discussion and community problem-solving. In these small-group, face-to-face settings, citizens address public concerns, bringing the wisdom of ordinary people to bear on complex issues. Cooperation and participation are emphasized so that the group can capitalize on the experience of all its members. (Campbell, 1998, p. 15)

To date, SCRC has supported more than 200 communities across the United States, which have used the study circle model to address such critical issues as violence, race relations, and neighborhood development.

Study Circles Resource Center (SCRC)

The origin of the study circle can be traced back to the social centers movement of the 1870s and New York's Chautauqua Assembly. Study circles were originally designed to provide an alternative opportunity for adult learners to continue their education and to discuss public issues. Building from this rich history, the SCRC was formed by the Topsfield Foundation in 1989. SCRC's goal was to promote "deliberative democracy," where citizens could engage in productive discussions of critical political and social issues. According to executive director Martha McCoy, the current study circles are similar to those of the 19th century. In both instances, the process is highly participatory and intended to extend beyond a single meeting. Furthermore, both the current and Chautauqua study circle models are "led by ordinary citizens who facilitate the discussion instead of 'teaching' the group" (Flavin-McDonald & Barrett, 1999, p. 29).

The SCRC provides resources to help communities create their own local study circle processes. Working in partnership with these communities, SCRC supports local organizers, through training and other technical assistance, to shape the program to fit the community's interests and needs. SCRC also facilitates dialogue among participating communities to exchange stories of their successes and challenges. Such a networking system provides support and inspiration, leading toward greater engagement of citizens in democratic civil society.

Community-Wide Organizing Model

SCRC has developed a flexible community-building model that can be adapted to the local context. Key features of the model, however, are consistent, and are as follows:

- The model calls for large-scale organizing that involves a broad-based coalition of community organizations to ensure that people from all sectors of the community are included. Coalition partners include grassroots organizations, religious or spiritual organizations, corporations, educational institutions, and others.
- Multiple study circles occurring in a single community during a specific time frame create inclusive and widespread involvement. Such extensive participation, as a model of deliberative democracy, helps to create a sense of community consciousness that builds a basis for problem solving and action.
- Study circles, which generally comprise two trained facilitators and 8 to 12 participants, meet regularly over a period of weeks or months to address critical public issues. Diversity among participants and facilitators is crucial. In general, study circles progress from a session on personal experiences

regarding the issue, to sessions providing multiple viewpoints, to a session to examine and discuss strategies for action. Topics range from racism and race relations to crime and violence, education reform, youth issues, and building strong neighborhoods.

- Study circles involve community members in creating change through the power of dialogue. As part of the dialogue process, participants are encouraged to connect the dialogue with action steps. Within the study circle, the facilitators guide the process and ensure that the group sets its own ground rules that allow for respectful, productive discussion. Consensus is not a requirement; rather, the focus is to uncover areas of agreement and common concern.

As a whole, this community-organizing and participatory education model seeks to build both personal and community connections and to bolster citizens' participation in public issues. Reported outcomes include changes on the individual, group, and community levels, which in some cases have also led to changes in public or institutional policy.

Stories From the Field

Experiences of study circles in Syracuse, New York, and New Castle County, Delaware, illustrate how effective they can be in community building and organizing. These two sites, selected from a broader study of 17 communities nationwide that engaged in study circles (Roberts, Houle, Kay, Nagda, & Elliott, 2000), demonstrate the possible role that study circles can play in the community change process.

Syracuse, New York: Community-wide dialogue on ending racism, improving race relations, and beginning racial healing. Building on earlier public conversations about "What kind of community do we want for our children, and how do we make it happen?" and the finding that racism was a major factor affecting the differential academic success of children in the community, the Inter-Religious Council in Syracuse provided leadership to organize study circles on race. Given the racial schisms within the community, which had become evident in the human services agencies, the organizers intentionally focused on building the program to model the types of interracial relationships and leadership roles they hoped would result from study circles. Following an intense, 6-month process concentrating on relationship building among participants and determining the focus of the study circles, organizers decided to explicitly address three aspects of race: ending racism, improving race relations, and beginning racial healing. By using this dialogic approach, organizers hoped to bring together group members' differing experiences and hopes for study circles on race.

The emphasis on positive interracial modeling and active participation was built into all aspects of the program. The first advisory board had two co-chairs, one African American and one European American. The primary responsibility of the board's 50 members was to recruit participants of all races to take part in the study circles. The circles were composed of almost equal numbers of white people and people of color, and each group was cofacilitated by an interracial team.

One of the primary ways the advisory board expanded its duties was through the creation of action task forces to address specific issues requiring institutional change. In response to complaints that people of color were being followed in shops at a major mall in Syracuse, one action task force worked successfully to improve their retail shopping experience. Another task force began tackling the problem of racial inequity in mortgage lending. In addition to these formal task forces, the advisory board initiated a Benchmark Report to serve as a baseline for examining racial and ethnic disparities in the community and to identify changes in the community that result from the study circles and other related activities to promote positive change.

New Castle County, Delaware: Study circles on racism and race relations. Wilmington, Delaware, is the site of the longest peacetime occupation by the National Guard, which was brought in for 9 months following the assassination of Martin Luther King, Jr., to contain the resulting racially motivated riots. The YWCA of New Castle County developed a study circle program in 1996 as a way to address the part of its mission that seeks to eliminate racism and to heal the racial wounds that have existed in the community for so many years. Given the racial fracturing of the community, the YWCA adopted a collaborative approach from the outset, and it engaged more than 100 community partners in the effort. Partners collaborated in a variety of ways, ranging from providing visibility in their program materials to volunteering for activities, to providing financial support. Examples of critical partnerships include cooperation and collaboration among the media, human service organizations, schools, and the state government. With assistance from the *Wilmington News Journal*, which helped cosponsor major speakers and publicized the study circle efforts, the YWCA joined with other like-minded organizations to host such high-profile speakers as Maya Angelou, Cornel West, and Bernice King at well-publicized kickoff events. These events often included a brief description and demonstration of the study circle process. One organizer reported that events such as these guaranteed about 100 registrations for community-wide study circles. Organizers also partnered with local private and public schools, where they worked with teachers and trained student leaders to serve as facilitators. In addition, the YWCA developed a fruitful partnership with retired citizens, who have served as facilitators and helped to produce a *Study Circle Action Guide*, which highlights volunteer opportunities in the community.

Yet another notable partnership has been with the state government. The YWCA collaborated with the State Department of Labor to offer workplace study circles. More than 400 employees took part in a 2½-day retreat based on the previous study circles about race. The retreat was considered quite successful, and state officials have planned additional study circles about gender for labor department employees. Workplace study circles are also expanding into other government agencies, including the Environmental Protection Agency of Delaware, and other workplaces have been considering conducting study circles on race.

As the core organizers, YWCA staff members report the beneficial impact of study circles on their own organization. For example, the YWCA board now uses dialogue as a tool at each meeting. The focus of the YWCA's programming has begun to shift from service-oriented to empowerment-oriented approaches. The organization has contributed to other community-building efforts by offering trained facilitators for different events. Finally, more African Americans and other people of color have begun to volunteer for the YWCA and are willing to serve on its board. As one staff member and study circle organizer said, "It has been incredibly enriching to our organization. This has allowed us to create a much broader bonding with a far broader community. We have only begun to see the power of that" (Roberts, Houle, Kay, Nagda, & Elliot, in press).

Critical Lessons for Community Change

The imperative to infuse and model diversity in every aspect of community-wide study circles may be obvious from these cases. From the initial preparation and generation of ideas, to coalition building, recruiting and training facilitators, and designing the groups, diversity is a critical factor that can enhance or detract from the experience of participants and efforts toward community change. In their book *Toward Competent Communities: Best Practices for Producing Community-Wide Study Circles,* Roberts and colleagues (2000) document a number of changes— from the individual to the community level—that have resulted from participation in study circles. Some of these are apparent from the case examples cited above, but it is worth elaborating here on the factors that appear to move circles and their participants from talk to action.

- Personal and individual change seems most influenced by the diversity of the group, the skills of the facilitator, and the explicitness of the topic.
- Organizational change is most influenced by the diversity and commitment of coalition partners and the clarity of roles.
- Institutional and community-level change is influenced by the careful selection of a topic that leads to the expectation of change in communities and institutions. Furthermore, partners in the strategic coalition can also accelerate changes at these levels. In addition to human services agencies, educational, corporate, and other partners can influence the visibility and impact of study circles in the community.

There is much discussion as to whether dialogue groups lead to action and whether dialogue itself is enough, and study circle practitioners note that the effectiveness of the small groups may be compromised if their dialogues are not linked to potential for change in the larger community. Conversely, large-scale action itself may be compromised without the trust, relationships, and commitment the circles can build among community members, who may not have other substantive relationships with each other (McCoy & McCormick, 2001). Communities continually innovate ways of linking dialogue to action. Roberts and colleagues (2000) found a number of ways in which dialogues are linked to action; these can be broadly divided between short-term and long-term approaches.

Short-term approaches focus on channeling citizens into existing community efforts that can benefit from their input and participation. These approaches focus on developing sound tools for initiating action. Written action guides that outline how participants can engage in action through volunteering are commonly used to link dialogue and action. Other methods include holding action forums that promote linkages with existing organizations and change efforts. Participants are also encouraged to make recommendations to government and decision-making bodies.

Long-term approaches involve working toward sustained change and involvement while remaining responsive to emerging issues in the community. Forming permanent task forces or work groups can help sustain action. Some communities have also hired program staff to support action efforts. These staff members are responsible for providing leadership, sustenance, and continuity for change efforts. A permanent staff can help provide legitimacy, time, and leadership resources that volunteer participants may not be able to sustain over the long term.

The number of communities using the community-wide study circles organizing model doubled from less than 100 in 1998 to more than 200 in 2001. Such growth testifies to ways in which the decline in civic involvement highlighted in Putnam's *Bowling Alone* (2000) can be countered through citizens' involvement in small groups focused on concerns for civil society. As Paul Aicher, founder of the Topsfield Foundation, states,

> We've always worked from the fundamental principle that the impact of the small group experience extends into other spheres of community and politics. That is, when people get together, delve into discussion about important issues, and begin to feel real ownership of them, they're more likely to go out and become engaged in other aspects of community life and politics. They are profoundly affected by their encounters with other participants and by seeing connections between their own experiences and big, sometimes abstract, public issues. (Flavin-McDonald & Barrett, 1999, p. 31)

To successfully fulfill the founding vision of study circles, community organizers and facilitators have concurred that the study circle cannot be viewed as merely a single, isolated event in people's lives. For sustainable change to occur, study circles must be linked to or followed up with other arenas of participation (Roberts et al., 2000).

Conclusion

In this chapter, we have focused on the important work that must be done if social workers and other community workers are to make an impact on issues of sexism, racism, classism, and other social inequities. This goal requires that our work with diverse communities reflect current and emerging trends in our society. Principles of multicultural practice, including self-awareness and mastery of empowerment practice methods, are imperative if our work is to make a critical difference. The two case examples cited present promising methods and roles for social workers doing multicultural community work. Methods for PAR can be used to engage community members in projects that investigate and seek to change the conditions that most concern them. As demonstrated in the case of CVH, a compelling community issue can be used to mobilize community members despite racial and cultural differences. In this way, multicultural work is more of a process to promote positive change and communication than a means to a specific end. Study circles and community dialogue projects are a very promising method of multicultural community building. Through deliberate engagement across differences, community members can be brought together to achieve greater unity.

These methods of multicultural organizing may call on social workers to extend their usual roles. They will need to be active in building coalitions and alliances that bridge traditional differences. They may need to take educational roles with community members and other professionals. This type of work also requires the ability to recognize and work with conflict and facilitate intergroup dialogue. Although this work can be daunting, it holds promise for addressing some of the most serious problems facing our society and world today.

References

Anner, J. (1996). *Beyond identity politics: Emerging social justice movements in communities of color.* Boston: South End Press.

Annie E. Casey Foundation. (2003). Kids Count. Baltimore, MD: Author. Retrieved June 13, 2004, from http://www.communityvoices.org/Uploads/31zt4iqkqymlsxrx2zobfgq4_20020730082713.pdf

Bandura, A. (1982). Self-efficacy mechanism in human agency. *American Psychologist, 37*(2), 122–147.

Brager, G. (1999). Agency under attack: The risks, demands, and rewards of community activism. In J. Rothman (Ed.), *Reflections on community organization: Enduring themes and critical issues* (pp. 57–76). Itasca, IL: F. E. Peacock.

Campbell, S. L. (1998). *A guide for training study circle facilitators.* Pomfret, CT: Topsfield Foundation.

Community Voices Heard. (1997). *CVH job creation policy proposal.* New York: Author.

Crosbie-Burnett, M., & Lewis, E. (1993). A social cognitive model of couples and families: An integration of contributions from psychological theories. In P. Boss, W. Doherty, R. LaRossa, W. Schumm, & S. Steinmetz (Eds.), *Sourcebook of family theories and methods: A contextual approach* (pp. 531–557). New York: Plenum.

Delgado, M. (1999). *Social work practice in non-traditional urban settings.* New York: Oxford University Press.

Dilworth-Anderson, P. (1999, November). *Shifting paradigms in the study of contemporary American families: Issues of race, culture, and ethnicity.* Paper presented at the annual conference of the National Council on Family Relations, San Diego, CA.

Dressel, P. (1994) . . . . and we keep on building prisons: Racism, poverty and challenges to the welfare state. *Journal of Sociology and Social Welfare, 21*(3), 7–30.

Ehrenreich, B. (2001). *Nickel and dimed.* New York: Henry Holt.

Empire State Jobs Bill. (1999). New York State Assembly Bill 7632.

Flavin-McDonald, C., & Barrett, M. H. (1999). The Topsfield Foundation: Fostering democratic community building through face-to-face dialogue. In P. J. Edelson & P. L. Malone (Eds.), *Enhancing creativity in adult and continuing education: Innovative approaches, methods, and ideas* (pp. 25–36). San Francisco: Jossey-Bass.

Frazier-Kouassi, S. (2002). Race and gender at the crossroads: African American females in schools. *Perspectives, 8*(1), 151–162.

Gutiérrez, L. (1992). Empowering ethnic minorities in the 21st century: The role of human service organizations. In Y. Hasenfeld (Ed.), *The organization of human services: Structure and processes* (pp. 320–338). Thousand Oaks, CA: Sage.

Gutiérrez, L., Alvarez, A., Sakamoto, I., & Wernick, L. (2000, January). *Interdisciplinary approaches to community-based research: Building practice knowledge through collaboration.* Paper presented at the Society for Social Work and Research (SSWR) conference, Charleston, SC.

Gutiérrez, L., & Lewis, E. (2000). *Empowering women of color.* New York: Columbia University Press.

Gutiérrez, L., & Rosegrant Alvarez, A. (2000). Educating students for multicultural community practice. *Journal of Community Practice, 7*(1), 39–56.

Harris, H. (2001) The power of the spirit. *Crisis Magazine,* 108(3) 42–45.

Hum-Delgado, D., & Delgado, M. (1986). Gaining community entree to assess service needs of Hispanics. *Social Casework, 67*(2), 80–89.

Iglehart, A., & Becerra, R. (1995). *Social services and the ethnic community.* Boston: Allyn & Bacon.

McCall, H. C. (1998, August 13). *New York City's economic and fiscal dependence on Wall Street* (Report 5–99). New York: Office of the State Comptroller for the City of New York.

McCoy, M., & McCormick, M. A. (2001). Engaging the whole community in dialogue and action: The Study Circles Resource Center. In D. Schoem & S. Hurtado (Eds.), *Intergroup dialogue: Deliberative democracy in school, college, community, and workplace* (pp. 137–150). Ann Arbor: University of Michigan Press.

Nagda, B., & Gutiérrez, L. (2000). A praxis and research agenda for multicultural human service organizations. *International Journal of Social Welfare, 9* (1), 43–52.

Nicolas, G., & Varzi, J. (2001). Experiences of women on public assistance. *Journal of Social Issues, 57*(2), 299–309.

Nyden, P., Figert, A., Shibley, M., & Barrows, D. (1997). *Building community: Social science in action.* Thousand Oaks, CA: Pine Forge.

Personal Responsibility and Work Opportunity Reconciliation Act (P.L. 104–19). (1996).

Putnam, R. D. (2000). *Bowling alone: The collapse and revival of American community.* New York: Simon & Schuster.

Rappaport, J. (1990). Research methods and the empowerment social agenda. In P. Tolan, C. Keys, F. Chertok, & L. Jason (Eds.), *Researching community psychology: Issues of theory and methods* (pp. 51–63). Washington, DC: American Psychological Association.

Reed, B. G., Newman, P. A., Suarez, Z., & Lewis, E. (1997). Interpersonal practice beyond diversity and towards social justice: The importance of critical consciousness. In C. Garvin & B. Seabury (Eds.), *Social work practice* (pp. 44–77). New York: Garland.

Ristock, J. L., & Pennell, J. (1996). *Community research as empowerment: Feminist links, postmodern interpretations.* Ontario, Canada: Oxford University Press.

Rivera, F., & Erlich, J. (1998). *Community organizing in a diverse society* (3rd ed.). Boston: Allyn & Bacon.

Roberts, R., Houle, K., Kay, S., Nagda, B. A., & Elliott, V. (2000). *Toward competent communities: Best practices for producing community-wide study circles.* Lexington, KY: Roberts & Kay.

Roberts, R., Houle, K., Kay, S., Nagda, B. A, & Elliott, V. (in press). *What works: Study circles in the real world.* Pomfret, CT: Topsfield Foundation.

Rothman, J. (Ed.). (1999). *Reflections on community organization: Enduring themes and critical issues.* Itasca, IL: F. E. Peacock.

Soderberg, A. K. (2001). Statewide testing: Problem or solution for failing schools? *Michigan Family Review,* 6(1), 55–66.

Spencer, M., Lewis, E., & Gutiérrez, L. (2000). Multicultural perspectives on direct practice in social work. In P. Allen-Meares & C. Garvin (Eds). *Handbook of direct practice in social work: Future directions* (pp. 131–149). Thousand Oaks, CA: Sage.

Stettner, A. (1998). *The welfare jobs gap in New York City.* New York: Ad-Hoc Coalition for Real Jobs.

Stoecker, R. (1999). Are academics irrelevant? Roles for scholars in participatory research. *American Behavioral Scientist, 42*(5), 840–854.

Study Circle Resource Center (SCRC). (n.d.). *Who we are.* Retrieved July 1, 2003, from http://www.studycircles.org.

Topousis, T. (1998, July 21). Rudy sounds death knell for welfare; wants everyone on dole to work by 2000. *The New York Post,* p. 4.

Turner, J. (1999). Neighborhood organization: How well does it work? In J. Rothman (Ed.), *Reflections on community organization: Enduring themes and critical issues* (pp. 91–105). Itasca, IL: F. E. Peacock.

U.S. Conference of Mayors. (1998). *The welfare challenge facing Americas cities: A 125-city survey.* Washington, DC: Author.

Zippay, A. (2002) Dynamics of income packaging: A 10-year longitudinal study. *Social Work, 47*(3), 291–300.

CHAPTER 19

Feminist Community Practice

Cheryl Hyde

Thirty years ago, the field of community practice essentially ignored the experiences of women and the insights of feminism. Since then, a proliferation of feminist scholarship and activism has changed the way theorists, educators, and practitioners approach the field. This chapter traces the development of feminist community practice and its influence on the field as a whole.

Why should feminist approaches be recognized by and incorporated into community practice? Community practice, regardless of type or model, is fundamentally concerned with building healthy communities in which families and individuals can thrive. Many issues that feminists champion directly relate to community well-being. Social problems such as sexual violence, pay inequity, a dearth of family support policies, and lack of affordable child care have detrimental effects on community life. Women who do not feel safe, nurtured, and rewarded will not fulfill their potential; consequently, communities suffer. To cultivate democratically based community practice, women need to feel recognized and have their issues validated. Moreover, feminist praxis offers principles and guidelines that enhance communication, participation, and long-term change processes.

This chapter will first consider what is meant by feminism and then proceed to examine why feminist perspectives are needed in community practice. Specific principles of feminist practice are delineated, focusing on how to infuse them into community practice. The chapter concludes with discussion as to the future directions of feminist community practice. Because of space limitations, much of this chapter is based on work of U.S. feminists. Feminism has a strong global presence, however, and international examples of feminist community practice abound (Harcourt, 1994; Hyde, 1996; Margolis, 1993; West & Blumberg, 1990).

Defining Feminism

There is considerable debate in feminist scholarship as to what constitutes feminism. Yet the common thread is the recognition that collectively women have been and continue to be denied power and privilege because of gender.

Feminism is (minimally) the recognition that women, compared to men, are an oppressed group and that women's problems are a result of discrimination. Women's status is shaped by processes of structural inequality, not individual actors or circumstances. Feminism is transformational because it involves a vision of a society that does not exist and sees social, political, and economic change as necessary for that vision to be realized (Martin, 1990, p. 184). Feminist activism, then, is concerned with "challenging women's subordinate (or disadvantaged) status in the society at large and in their own community" (Gluck, 1998, p. 34).

Feminism is not, however, a singular ideology, perspective, or movement. Following feminism's reemergence in the 1960s, several dominant ideological streams developed, including liberal, radical, socialist, and cultural perspectives. Within each of these frameworks, different visions, strategies, tactics, organizational types, and outcomes were articulated (Ferree & Martin, 1995; Hyde, 2001; Martin, 1990). Stemming from critiques that feminism was insufficiently attentive to racial oppression, a woman of color (also termed *womanist*) perspective evolved (Walker, 1983; Weil, 1996). More recently, feminist scholars and activists have advocated a multiracial or multicultural feminism in order to weave together gender, race, class, and sexual orientation (Gluck, 1998; Gutiérrez & Lewis, 1997, 1999; Naples, 1991, 1992, 1998b; Wolfe & Tucker, 1995; Zinn & Dill, 1996). Regardless of perspective, gender is a lens through which one's identity and experiences are understood, either exclusively or in combination with other dimensions of one's cultural identity (Lather, 1988).

Yet while feminism is pro-woman, it should not be seen solely as women working with other women on issues of concern to women. First, women-dominated ventures or activities are not feminist when they seek to impose or support patriarchal gender norms and values. For example, Phyllis Schlafly's Eagle Forum, a largely female organization, sought to defeat the Equal Rights Amendment and further institutionalize traditional male and female roles (Hyde, 1995a). Second, men as well as women can be proponents and beneficiaries of feminism (Ferree & Merrill, 2000; Hyde, 1996). New gender scholarship, influenced significantly by feminist theory, focuses on the constraints of stereotypic male roles and the high price that men pay when they step outside the confines of these expected roles (Connell, 1995; Edin, 1998). Finally, the issues that are addressed do not have to be quintessentially feminist ones (e.g., sexual violence, pay equity). Women have been and continue to be involved in social change campaigns that concern neighborhood safety, environmental racism, public education, and labor (for examples, see Naples, 1998a; West & Blumberg, 1990); it is the empowering aspects of such endeavors that render them feminist (Abrahams, 1996; Gluck, 1998; Naples, 1998b).

The Need for Feminist
Perspectives in Community Practice

"Official" histories of community practice are often dominated by the actions and ideas of men, despite the fact that women were substantially involved in historical projects (e.g., settlement houses) that led to community practice and were and are key actors in social change efforts (Weil 1986, 1996; Weil, Gamble, & Williams, 1998). Community practice literature and leadership developed primarily as a male preserve, largely ignoring the grassroots and social movement work of women in and outside the feminist movement (Fisher, 1994; Rubin & Rubin, 1992; Weil, 1986). Moreover, some male community practitioners (such as Saul Alinsky) assumed, at least into the 1970s, that women's capacities to organize were futile, pointless, and in some cases, ridiculous.

The social work profession, as a whole, did little to help correct these perceptions. Macro practice opportunities, specifically administration and community organizing, were used to entice men into the profession. With rare exceptions, social work colluded with the notion that the private sphere (e.g., personal and family caretaking) was for women and the public sphere (e.g., political arena) was for men. Community practice became the sanctioned male domain (Weil, 1986; Weil et al., 1998).

These views began to change largely because of the experiences that women gained in the social movements of the 1960s and 1970s, most notably feminism but also civil rights, labor, and antiwar efforts, and through encounters with discrimination and other forms of sexism in education and employment. In social work and the social sciences, there was a resulting boom of feminist scholarship in the 1980s, one that continues today. As part of this, feminists demanded the recognition and inclusion of women in community practice.

In the early 1980s, several works articulated feminist social work principles in general (Gottlieb, 1980; Norman & Mancuso, 1980; Weick & Vandiver, 1982) and feminist community practice in particular (Brandwein, 1981, 1982; Ellsworth, 1982; Masi, 1981). These writers provided rationales as to why feminism is important to macro practice and documented efforts by women as organizers, planners, and developers. They critiqued the often unacknowledged masculine bias within existing practice models and suggested ways in which feminist ideas could be infused into community practice. These works set the stage for the articulation of feminist models of macro practice (Hooyman & Cunningham, 1986; Hyde, 1989; Weil, 1986). Feminist researchers also began to illuminate the work done by women community activists in such arenas as the peace movement, education reform, and environmentalism (Cantarow, 1980; Garland, 1988; Hyde, 1986; Reinharz, 1983).

Throughout the 1980s and 1990s, primarily in sociology, there was increased attention to the rise and fall of social change campaigns. Feminist scholars contributed substantially to this area of inquiry with their work on feminist movements and feminist movement organizations (Ferree & Martin, 1995; Hyde, 1992, 1994, 1995a, 1995b, 2000; Martin, 1990; Riger, 1984, 1994). They documented the invisible leadership and activism of women in other social movements, most notably the civil rights movement (Irons, 1998; McNair Barnett, 1993; Robnett, 1997), and they explored the grassroots activism of women on the community or neighborhood level (Abrahams, 1996; Naples, 1991, 1992, 1998a, 1998b; West & Blumberg, 1990). More recently, civil society theorists have focused on the efforts of women in promoting civic health and on the role that gender plays in creating local democratic structures and processes (Figueira-McDonough, 2001; Gittell, Ortega-Bustamante, & Steffy, 2000; Miller, 2002; Paulsen & Bartkowski, 1997). Particular attention was and is paid to the intersections of race, class, and gender and how these intersections shape social change endeavors (Erbaugh, 2002; Naples, 1998a; Smith, 1995; Wolfe & Tucker, 1995). Feminist approaches were critiqued for race and class bias, and new frameworks that addressed the needs of women of color and working-class and poor women were proposed (Gutiérrez & Lewis, 1994, 1997, 1999; Smith, 1995; Zinn & Dill, 1996). Increasingly, efforts have been made to incorporate other identity dimensions within feminist analyses, such as religion/spirituality, disability, age, and sexual orientation (Davidman, 1991; Gibson, 1996; Jenness & Broad, 1994; Minkler, 1997; Morris, 1999; Rosenthal, 1996; Roth, 1998; Wendell, 1996).

Feminist approaches, however, do not remain within the usual confines of community practice models (e.g., locality development, social action, social planning). Feminist community practice blurs these models considerably. Feminists shift from one type of community practice to another, exhibiting fluidity in strategies and tactics (Ferree & Martin, 1995; Hyde, 1996; Irons, 1998). Feminist community practitioners explicitly link their work to organizational and group development. In addition to work on feminist approaches to administration and management (Chernesky, 1995), there is also a body of literature on developing and sustaining social change organizations using feminist principles (Ferree & Martin, 1995; Hyde, 1992, 1995a, 1995b, 2000, 2001; Martin, 1990; Riger, 1984, 1994). Many of these organizations (e.g., rape crisis centers, feminist health clinics) deliver services as a means of achieving social change. Similarly, attention has been paid to the ways in which gender influences group development, and feminist principles of groupwork have been articulated (Garvin & Reed, 1995; Gutiérrez, Reed, Ortega, & Lewis, 1998). Because groups are the building blocks of many macro interventions, this work contributes greatly to a more democratized community practice.

Feminist Principles for Practice

As is apparent from the summary above, a key theme within the feminist community practice literature is the documentation of women's activism. This involves the reclamation of historical groundbreakers, such as Jane Addams, Florence Kelly, sisters Edith and Grace Abbott, Judith Lathrop, Mary Richmond, and Bessie McClenahan (for a complete review, see Weil et al., 1998); recognition of current activists, including Gail Cincotta, Lois Gibbs, and Heather Booth; and revelation of the community work done by thousands of unrecognized women (Naples, 1998a; West & Blumberg, 1990). Culled from these accounts are a number of principles that are key to feminist community practice (for more complete overviews, see Gutiérrez & Lewis, 1994, 1997, 1999; Hyde, 1986, 1989, 1996; Weil, 1986, 1996; Weil et al., 1998).

The core principle of feminism is that of a *gendered lens,* that is, understanding societal dynamics by recognizing gendered roles and relations. With respect to feminist community practice, this means that gender, specifically the status and experiences of women, needs to be a factor in the identification and solution of problems and in the processes employed. Because feminism is also, by definition, transformational, this recognition of gender does not mean that women are merely included in status quo arrangements, which are then left unaltered. Rather, feminist community practice seeks basic structural and cultural changes in terms of gender roles, norms, and status.

Another principle, which serves as a foundation for the discovery and analysis of gendered processes and as a catalyst for action, is that the personal is political. Feminist politics are embedded in everyday enactments of gender. Only by deconstructing the seemingly mundane aspects of what it means to be female and male, and how these roles are socially reproduced, can fundamental change be achieved. In other words, what is experienced personally can and should be understood politically. One strategic implication of this is the demystification of knowledge: Women are experts in their own lives, and problem analysis is built on shared experiences. Consciousness raising is a key tactic in understanding and examining social concerns. Practice is built from the bottom up.

Closely related to the idea that *the personal is political* is the import of relational ties. Whereas men tend to engage in social change for more instrumental reasons, women become involved in activism because of an emotional connection, usually having to do with a threat to family or loved ones (Ferree & Merrill, 2000; Gittell et al., 2000; Miller, 2002). The context for feminist practice is social ties and networks. Women also tend to emphasize nurturing as part of their practice, a phenomenon referred to as *activist mothering* (Naples, 1992) or *bridge building* (Robnett, 1997). These terms capture the caretaking and maintenance of social ties that are essential to social change work and are usually performed by women. Feminist practice reorients the change process to include these private as well as public acts.

Parallel to facilitating more intimate social ties is emphasis on developing groups and organizations with democraticized processes and structures. Feminists are not solely concerned with achieving the stated goal or objective. Also important is how it is achieved. Attending to the process of practice, from a feminist perspective, means facilitating collaborative styles. Examples would include consensus decision making and delegation or rotation of tasks. Structures such as collectives or "flattened" hierarchies are put into place to support such cooperative processes. As part of democraticizing strategies, there is emphasis on inclusivity and diversity. Feminists are committed to the elimination of all forms of oppression and strive to enhance participation by bridging differences. This has meant working toward understanding social problems and solutions through perspectives other than those of White middle-class women. It also requires a close examination of the ways in which various forms of privilege are manifested in community practice efforts.

These principles are not easy to achieve and do not all fit together in a harmonious whole. It is, for example, difficult to always engage in consensus decision making when the task of organizing a rally is on the agenda. Also, many feminist efforts have unfortunately fallen short in addressing the goals of diversity. Nonetheless, these principles are exhibited in feminist community practice endeavors in and outside the women's movement. Even if ideal, these feminist practice principles suggest an egalitarian, nurturing, empowering, and holistic approach to community practice.

Integrating Feminism Into the Field of Community Practice

Despite the richness of the feminist community practice and social change literature, it remains underutilized in macro social work. Any gleaning of most texts or Web sites indicates that women as a constituency and as agents of social change, and feminism as a theory for practice, are underrepresented or missing entirely. To be sure, there are exceptions (see, e.g., Fisher, 1994; National Organizers Alliance Web site, www.noacentral.org; Rothman, 1996; Rubin & Rubin, 1992). But more common is just a mention of famous female activists or the existence of a "feminist model," with little comprehensive discussion.

It is not that the field is specifically hostile to feminist insights or interpretations. Rather, most work assumes (implicitly or explicitly) a gender-neutral or generic stance. The danger with such a position, however, is that the ways in which gender roles and status are reproduced are unacknowledged. Unless gender (and race, class, and sexual orientation) is explicitly addressed, then the scripts for who becomes a leader, who does "housekeeping" tasks, whose labor should be compensated, and so forth remain unaltered (Garvin & Reed, 1995). The supposedly universal notions of the politico, the organizer, the leader, or the practitioner are, in reality, gender-specific (Ferree & Merrill, 2000; Miller, 2002; Pateman, 1986). Community practice will remain a male domain until the gendered nature of how this work is understood and pursued is fully recognized (Brandwein, 1987; Weil, 1996; Weil et al., 1998).

Integration of feminism into community practice does not mean "add women and stir," as in the listing of a few famous women or the mere admonishment not to forget women as part of "the constituency." Nor does integration mean mentioning a feminist model as an interesting alternative to "real" community practice. Forcing feminism into existing models, but not fundamentally changing these models, leaves masculine biases within the field unaltered. Integration means fully incorporating feminist principles of practice and being explicit as to the gendered dynamics of this work, so that new models of community practice are developed.

Incorporating feminist principles would enhance the field of community practice in several important ways. One is the redefinition of community. Community practice primarily understands "the community" as a geographic concept (e.g., the neighborhood). Feminists broaden the notion of community to include communities of interest, which cut across geographic boundaries. In doing so, diversity is enhanced and broader networks established (Naples, 1992; Stall & Stoecker, 1998; Weil, 1986).

Another contribution is understanding organizations as avenues of social change. Perhaps the greatest legacy of feminism is the myriad organizations that continue to promote and shape feminist praxis. From a feminist perspective, the building and sustaining of organizations are strategic components of larger movement dynamics rather than signs of co-optation or conservatism. Alternative means of delivery of much-needed services, such as health care, reinforce feminist ideals of empowerment and nurturance (Ferree & Martin, 1995; Hyde, 1992, 1995a, 1995b; Martin, 1990; Riger, 1984, 1994).

Furthermore, feminism can address some critical gaps or omissions in community practice. One is the incorporation of ideology, which is largely absent from the community practice literature. Without ideology, there is no vision of what one is working toward or direction as to why problems exist. The many different feminist ideologies provide blueprints for social change and make explicit the dynamics of power (Gluck, 1998; Hyde, 1996; Pateman, 1986). Bringing in emotion corrects another gap. Community practice is often cast as a rational process, yet passion and emotion are key dynamics in any change effort. Feminism views emotion as a source of strength rather than an irrational weakness, as generic practice often views it. Emotions link people to a cause, help them assume risk, and sustain constituencies through difficult times. Yet, emotions are often viewed as the sole purview of women, rather than essential to everyone involved in change (Ferree & Merrill, 2000; Hyde, 1994, 2000).

Feminism also offers important strategies for democratizing social change efforts. The demystification of knowledge is one approach. Feminism is inherently anti-elitist. A key manifestation of this is the ways in which knowledge is developed and disseminated. Embedding practice in the feminist principle of linking personal struggles with political initiatives, specifically via consciousness raising, would cultivate greater involvement and ownership of the change process (Abrahams, 1996; Gutiérrez & Lewis, 1994; Weil, 1986). This connects with a larger contribution of feminism, that of enhancing participation. By building on the importance of emotions, demystifying knowledge, and ensuring inclusivity, feminists have demonstrated numerous innovations in recruitment and retention. Much of this emphasis is embedded in the bridge-building and "activist mothering" activities that solidify personal ties. Enhancement of participation and recognition of local knowledge also come from understanding which issues, specifically those having to do with family welfare, resonate with women (Abrahams, 1996; Naples, 1991, 1992, 1998b; Robnett, 1997; Stall & Stoecker, 1998).

Finally, feminism has demonstrated a remarkable resiliency, particularly during the 1980s when it was subjected to repeated, vociferous attacks from the New Right (Hyde, 1995a, 2000). Feminism's decentralized nature, strategic fluidity, cultivation of emotional bonds, diversification, and coalition building contributed to its continuance. Thus, the feminist movement provides critical lessons in surviving hostile times. Given the current conservative political climate, this could be the most important contribution that feminism makes to community practice.

Future Directions

In the nearly three decades since the re-emergence of feminism, feminists have generated important new insights into the ways community practice is conceptualized and accomplished. Feminists have rendered visible the often unacknowledged community and movement work of women. They have suggested different ways of recruiting, understanding, and developing leadership; framing issues; and securing victories. Principles of feminist practice call for an expansion of what is traditionally meant by "community" and for the inclusion of emotion, ideology, and diversity. Yet, in many ways, feminist community practice is still evolving.

Proponents of feminist community practice need to take a more analytical stance regarding the extent of empowerment that occurs when women organize other women (rather than assuming that empowerment always results). This, in part, means articulating feminism as a praxis that extends beyond the simplistic "women helping other women." The focus should be on the gendered nature of social change processes, which would incorporate the work of men as well as women (Ferree & Merrill, 2000). It also means posing difficult questions, such as: Under what scenarios do feminist approaches work best? and When should other approaches be used? Stall and Stoecker (1998) provide a thoughtful and provocative analysis along this line, comparing an Alinsky-style campaign with a women-centered endeavor. They make the argument that each approach has utility, albeit under different community conditions. This kind of analysis helps evaluate the strengths and weaknesses of feminist approaches.

More work needs to be done to specify how feminist agendas work within non–gender-specific groups or movements, such as feminists working within HIV/AIDS groups (Roth, 1998). Does marginalization or divisiveness occur, and if so, how are they addressed? Can women promote their concerns and, if so, through what tactics? Do feminists alter the culture of these organizations and, if so, in what ways and with what repercussions? With the exception of scholarship on women in the civil rights movement, most research on feminist practice has focused on endeavors organized primarily by women and for women (Gluck, 1998). This has limited the development of a critical understanding of the impact of feminism in various spheres.

More attention also needs to be paid within feminist community practice to the unique dynamics that result from the intersection of gender, race, class, sexual orientation, disability, and other social categories. Although feminists have engaged in considerable reflection and critique of the White, middle-class biases within the field, much more work needs to be done (Smith, 1995). Is an identity-specific model such as that articulated by Gutiérrez & Lewis (1994, 1997, 1999) needed, or can common ground be identified? Incorporating the feminist scholarship on social movements and social change would be particularly beneficial in understanding the dynamic interplay between privileged and subordinated status (specifically race and class) possessed by activists and members. Unfortunately, campaigns pertaining to age, sexual orientation, and disability are almost entirely absent from the feminist community practice literature (and are not well represented in the field as a whole). How applicable is a feminist macro practice model to the needs of elderly women or to those with disabilities? There are few empirically based answers.

In essence, feminist community practice faces three challenges. First, it must become more analytically robust. This means moving beyond descriptive modeling to critical self-reflection and evaluation. Second, it must become more multicultural, more able to analyze commonalities and differences across social classes, and more able and willing to bring forth leadership reflecting this broad diversity. Achieving this goal should not have to be the task solely of working-class women or women of color; all feminists need to embrace this task by documenting multicultural efforts and conceptualizing multicultural praxis frameworks. Third, feminist community practice must become more interdisciplinary. The feminist social science literature needs to be tapped more thoroughly; to do so would help attend to the analytical and multicultural challenges.

In turn, the broader field of community practice needs to recognize the wealth of insight, information, knowledge, and strategies that can be gained from feminist theorists and practitioners. Rather than viewing feminism as a model with some potential or as a framework that applies only to women, community practice proponents should understand that the integration of feminism in literature, practice, and praxis would greatly enhance the entire field. Feminist practice takes place within and across all community practice models (Hyde, 1996). The further integration and application of feminist praxis and theory called for here would result in more vibrant community practice frameworks.

References

Abrahams, N. (1996). Negotiating power, identity, family, and community: Women's community participation. *Gender & Society, 10*(6), 768–796.

Brandwein, R. (1981). Toward the feminization of community and organization practice. *Social Development Issues, 5*(2/3), 180–193.

Brandwein, R. (1982). Toward androgyny in community and organizational practice. In A. Weick & S. Vandiver (Eds.), *Women, power, and change* (pp. 158–170). Washington, DC: NASW Press.

Brandwein, R. (1987). Women and community organization. In D. S. Burden & N. Gottlieb (Eds.), *The woman client.* New York: Tavistock.

Cantarow, E. (1980). *Moving the mountain: Women working for social change.* Old Westbury, NY: Feminist Press.

Chernesky, R. (1995). Feminist administration: Style, structure, purpose. In N. Van Den Bergh (Ed.), *Feminist practice in the 21st century* (pp. 70–88). Washington, DC: NASW Press.

Connell, R. W. (1995). *Masculinities.* Los Angeles: University of California Press.

Davidman, L. (1991). *Tradition in a rootless world: Women turn to Orthodox Judaism.* Berkeley: University of California Press.

Edin, K. (1998, August). *"Single" mothers and "absent" fathers: Real-life families, work, and social welfare categories.* Paper presented at American Sociological Association Annual Meeting, San Francisco.

Ellsworth, C. (1982). Toward a feminist model for planning for and with women. In A. Weick & S. Vandiver (Eds.), *Women, power, and change.* Washington, DC: NASW Press.

Erbaugh, E. (2002). Women's community organizing and identity transformation. *Race, Gender, & Class, 9*(1), 8–32.

Ferree, M., & Martin, P. (Eds.). (1995). *Feminist organizations: Harvest of the new women's movement.* Philadelphia: Temple University Press.

Ferree, M., & Merrill, D. (2000). Hot movements, cold cognition: Thinking about social movements in gendered frames. *Contemporary Sociology, 29*(3), 454–462.

Figueira-McDonough, J. (2001). *Community analysis and praxis: Toward a grounded civil society.* Philadelphia: Taylor & Francis.

Fisher, R. (1994). *Let the people decide: Neighborhood organizing in America.* New York: Twayne.

Garland, A. W. (1988). *Women activists: Challenging the abuse of power.* New York: Feminist Press.

Garvin, C., & Reed, B. (1995). Sources and visions for feminist group work: Reflective processes, social justice, diversity, and connection. In N. Van Den Bergh (Ed.), *Feminist practice in the 21st century* (pp. 41–69). Washington, DC: NASW Press.

Gibson, D. (1996). Broken down by age and gender: "The problem of the old women" redefined. *Gender & Society, 10*(4), 433–448.

Gittell, M., Ortega-Bustamante, I., & Steffy, T. (2000). Social capital and social change: Women's community activism. *Urban Affairs Review, 36*(2), 123–147.

Gluck, S. (1998). Whose feminism, whose history? Reflections on excavating the history of (the) U.S. women's movement(s). In N. Naples (Ed.), *Community activism and feminist politics: Organizing across race, class, and gender* (pp. 31–56). New York: Routledge.

Gottlieb, N. (Ed.). (1980). *Alternative social services for women.* New York: Columbia University Press.

Gutiérrez, L., & Lewis, E. (1994). Community organizing with women of color: A feminist approach. *Journal of Community Practice, 1*(2), 23–44.

Gutiérrez, L., & Lewis, E. (1997). Education, participation, and capacity building in community organizing with women of color. In M. Minkler (Ed.), *Community organizing and community building for health* (pp. 216–229). New Brunswick, NJ: Rutgers University Press.

Gutiérrez, L., & Lewis, E. (1999). *Empowering women of color.* New York: Columbia University Press.

Gutiérrez, L., Reed, B., Ortega, R., & Lewis, E. (1998). Teaching about groups in a gendered world: Toward a curricular transformation in group work education. In J. Figueira-McDonough, F. E. Netting, & A. Nichols-Casebolt (Eds.), *The role of gender in practice knowledge: Claiming half the human experience* (pp. 169–204). New York: Garland.

Harcourt, W. (Ed.). (1994). *Feminist perspectives on sustainable development.* London: Zed Books.

Hooyman, N., & Cunningham, R. (1986). An alternative administrative style. In N. Van Den Bergh & L. B. Cooper (Eds.), *Feminist visions for social work* (pp. 163–186). Silver Spring, MD: NASW Press.

Hyde, C. (1986). Experiences of women activists: Implications for community organizing theory and practice. *Journal of Sociology and Social Welfare, 13*(3), 545–562.

Hyde, C. (1989). A feminist model for macro practice: Promises and problems. *Administration in Social Work, 13*(3/4), 145–181.

Hyde, C. (1992). The ideational system of social movement agencies: An examination of feminist health centers. In Y. Hasenfeld (Ed.), *Human services as complex organizations* (pp. 121–144). Thousand Oaks, CA: Sage.

Hyde, C. (1994). Commitment to social change: Voices from the feminist movement. *Journal of Community Practice, 1*(2), 45–64.

Hyde, C. (1995a). Feminist social movement organizations survive the New Right. In M. Ferree & P. Martin (Eds.), *Feminist organizations: Harvest of the new women's movement* (pp. 306–322). Philadelphia: Temple University Press.

Hyde, C. (1995b). The politics of authority. In N. Van Den Bergh (Ed.), *Feminist practice in the 21st century* (pp. 89–102). Washington, DC: NASW Press.

Hyde, C. (1996). A feminist response to Rothman's "The interweaving of community intervention approaches." *Journal of Community Practice, 3*(3/4), 127–145.

Hyde, C. (2000). Volunteerism in hostile times: An examination of feminist social movement organizations in the 1980s. *Journal of Voluntary Action, 2*(2), 27–43.

Hyde, C. (2001). The hybrid nonprofit: An examination of feminist social movement organizations. *Journal of Community Practice, 8*(4), 45–68.

Irons, J. (1998). The shaping of activist recruitment and participation: A study of women in the Mississippi civil rights movement. *Gender & Society, 12*(6), 692–709.

Jenness, V., & Broad, K. (1994). Antiviolence activism and the (in)visibility of gender in the gay/lesbian and women's movements. *Gender & Society, 8*(3), 402–423.

Lather, P. (1988). Feminist perspectives on empowering research methodologies. *Women's Studies International Forum, 11*(6), 569–581.

Margolis, D. (1993). Women's movements around the world: Cross-cultural comparisons. *Gender & Society, 7*(3), 379–399.

Martin, P. Y. (1990). Rethinking feminist organizations. *Gender & Society, 4*(2), 182–206.

Masi, D. (1981). *Organizing for women: Issues, strategies, and services.* Lexington, MA: Lexington Books.

McNair Barnett, B. (1993). Invisible southern black women leaders in the civil rights movement: The triple constraints of gender, race, and class. *Gender & Society, 7*(2), 162–182.

Miller, M. (2002). Male and female civility: Toward gender justice. *Sociological Inquiry, 72*(3), 456–466.

Minkler, M. (1997). Community organizing among the elderly poor in San Francisco's Tenderloin district. In M. Minkler (Ed.), *Community organizing and community building for health* (pp. 244–260). New Brunswick, NJ: Rutgers University Press.

Morris, J. (Ed.). (1999). *Encounters with strangers: Feminism and disability.* New York: Women's Press.

Naples, N. (1991). "Just what needed to be done": The political practice of women community workers in low-income neighborhoods. *Gender & Society, 5*(4), 478–494.

Naples, N. (1992). Activist mothering: Cross-generational continuity in the community work from low-income urban neighborhoods. *Gender & Society, 6*(3), 441–463.

Naples, N. (Ed). (1998a). *Community activism and feminist politics: Organizing across race, class, and gender.* New York: Routledge.

Naples, N. (1998b). Women's community activism: Exploring the dynamics of politicization and diversity. In N. Naples (Ed.), *Community activism and feminist politics: Organizing across race, class, and gender* (pp. 328–349). New York: Routledge.

Norman, E., & Mancuso, A. (Eds.). (1980). *Women's issues and social work practice.* Itasca, IL: F. E. Peacock.

Pateman, C. (1986). Introduction: The theoretical subversiveness of feminism. In C. Pateman & E. Gross (Eds.), *Feminist challenges: Social and political theory* (pp. 1–10). Boston: Northeastern University Press.

Paulsen, R., & Bartkowski, J. (1997). Gender and perceptions of success among neighborhood association activists. *Social Science Quarterly, 78*(1), 196–208.

Reinharz, S. (1983). Women as competent community builders: The other side of the coin. *Issues in Mental Health Nursing, 5,* 19–43.

Riger, S. (1984). Vehicles for empowerment: The case of feminist movement organizations. *Prevention in Human Services, 3*(2/3), 99–117.

Riger, S. (1994). Challenges of success: Stages of growth in feminist organizations. *Feminist Studies, 20*(2), 275–300.

Robnett, B. (1997). *How long? How long? African-American women in the struggle for civil rights.* New York: Oxford University Press.

Rosenthal, E. (Ed.). (1996). *Women, aging, and ageism.* New York: Harrington Park Press.

Roth, B. (1998). Feminist boundaries in the feminist-friendly organization: The women's caucus of ACT UP/LA. *Gender & Society, 12*(2), 129–145.

Rothman, J. (1996). The interweaving of community intervention approaches. *Journal of Community Practice, 3*(3/4), 69–99.

Rubin, H., & Rubin, I. (1992). *Community organizing and development* (2nd ed.). Boston: Allyn & Bacon.

Smith, B. (1995). Crossing the great divides: Race, class, and gender in southern women's organizing, 1979–1991. *Gender & Society, 9*(6), 680–696.

Stall, S., & Stoecker, R. (1998). Community organizing or organizing community? Gender and the crafts of empowerment. *Gender & Society, 12*(6), 729–756.

Walker, A. (1983). *In search of our mothers' gardens: Womanist prose.* New York: Harcourt Brace Jovanovich.

Weick, A., & Vandiver, S. (Eds.). (1982). *Women, power, and change.* Washington, DC: NASW Press.

Weil, M. (1986). Women, community and organizing. In N. Van Den Bergh & L. Cooper (Eds.), *Feminist visions for social work* (pp. 187–210). Silver Spring, MD: NASW Press.

Weil, M. (1996). Model development in community practice: An historical perspective. *Journal of Community Practice, 3*(3/4), 5–67.

Weil, M., Gamble, D., & Williams, E. (1998). Women, communities, and development. In J. Figueira-McDonough, F. E. Netting, & A. Nichols-Casebolt (Eds.), *The role of gender in practice knowledge: Claiming half the human experience* (pp. 241–286). New York: Garland Press.

Wendell, S. (1996). *The rejected body: Feminist philosophical reflection on disability.* New York: Routledge.

West, G., & Blumberg, R. (Eds.). (1990). *Women and social protest.* New York: Oxford University Press.

Wolfe, L., & Tucker, J. (1995). Feminism lives: Building a multicultural women's movement in the United States. In A. Basu (Ed.), *The challenge of local feminisms* (pp. 435–462). Boulder, CO: Westview.

Zinn, M., & Dill, B. (1996). Theorizing difference from multiracial feminism. *Feminist Studies, 22*(2), 321–331.

CHAPTER 20

Rise Up and Build the Cities

Faith-Based Community Organizing

Ram A. Cnaan

Stephanie C. Boddie

Gaynor I. Yancey

This chapter identifies a very active type of community organization that has too often been neglected in community practice literature and training, namely the local religious congregation. Based on the notion that mediating structures are the key sources of residents' sense of power and protection, we argue that religious congregations whose basic values are congruent with those of the profession and its *Code of Ethics* can be effective partners for various community-based initiatives. We demonstrate that congregations are the most frequently found local community organizations in the United States and that half the adult population holds membership in these face-to-face organizations. Highlighting the many assets that congregations bring with them for social and community endeavors, we also discuss the range of ways congregations are involved in community practice and encourage practitioners, educators, and policymakers to recognize the great potential for positive community engagement embedded in congregations. In conclusion, we suggest means for enhanced collaboration so as to advance the quality of life in communities and address large-scale social problems.

Ideologies differ widely when it comes to the nature of community organizing. The understanding of the power relationship between government and large businesses on one hand and community residents on the other has been central to understanding community practice, regardless of the preferred method or ideology. A pluralistic ideology, appropriate for a nation of great diversity, emphasizes the need for intermediary bodies that can serve as buffers between the individual and larger power structures. With the dismantling of the welfare state in the United States, government is less and less responsive to the needs of citizens of low wealth, those who live in impoverished communities or regions, and those who have little political influence. By its nature, government holds extraordinary power and all too often overrides the rights of citizens—particularly those with few resources and little political clout. Similarly, corporations may have great influence on government, hold great economic power, and frequently violate the rights of residents, thus causing serious social and environmental problems.

Berger and Neuhaus (1977) characterized mediating, voluntary associations as independent of the state and composed of citizens who are interested in protecting their shared interests vis-à-vis the power of the state. These associations, although not affiliated with the government, perform many essential societal tasks. Ideally, the government encourages the establishment of voluntary associations because these associations help the state to carry out its work and enlarge civil society.

Antonio Gramsci (1988) asserted that the state is destined to try to impose its ideology on society and that civil society (that is, intermediary organizations such as labor unions, political parties, and nonprofit organizations) is the only context in which the oppressed can defend themselves against this kind of dominance. From a Marxist point of view, Gramsci viewed civil society as the only instrument that can oppose capitalism. We define *civil society* as one of the three overlapping spheres of societal interaction, the other two being the economy and the state. Civil society includes the social institutions of the family and associations or voluntary organizations, as well as social movements and forums of direct public communication (Cohen & Arato, 1994). Civil society is a necessary foundation of democracy and is the basis for the formation of social capital (Coleman, 1990). Because government is constrained by the limits of the principle of the median voter (that is, it caters to the needs of most voters, who will then reelect these politicians, thus silencing the voices of small and minority groups) and businesses are concerned with maximizing profit, only community groups and associations can stand up for the varying and often unique interests of local residents.

In tandem with the pluralistic view of welfare and the importance of civil society for the preservation of democratic institutions, we need to consider the value that the vigorous operation of the nonprofit or voluntary sector in the United States adds to social and political functioning.

The nonprofit sector not only functions as a major arena for intermediary organizations that buffer the power of the state over its citizens, but also fosters the abilities of concerned citizens to organize themselves into groups that represent certain preferences or viewpoints. These groups greatly strengthen civic engagement and often work to educate the public about issues and also pressure politicians and other decision makers to support their agenda. Where these organizations represent human services or values consonant with democratic principles, they can add considerable strength to the causes and concerns of social work. At times, these groups also produce goods and services on their own, with the implicit or explicit approval of the state. Their existence helps to ensure that local viewpoints and preferences have a place at the decision-making table at local, state, and national levels.

No matter how one views community practice, some aspects of the pluralistic approach are essential. When we review the rich literature on community practice, we see approaches ranging from organizing residents to form a representative group, to collaborating with existing local and citywide nonprofit organizations. Yet, these discussions and practices often neglect to include local religious congregations and faith-based organizations as either the potential nuclei of neighborhood organizations or organizations with which to collaborate (Lugo, 1998).

It is our contention that congregations of multiple religious traditions and other faith-based organizations are a community-based power source with many tangible and symbolic assets. These entities are vital as organizational networks and as community resources. Faith-based organizations can effect change in communities and in concert can influence governmental bodies. Although people may see religious groups as oppressive and conservative, many progressive social change campaigns—from the civil rights movement to liberation theology—were, in fact, originated within religious groups (Cnaan, Wineburg, & Boddie, 1999). Similarly, major opposition to the 1996 Welfare Reform Bill came from religious circles and especially from religious coalitions such as Call for Renewal. Even after the bill was signed by President Clinton, Call for Renewal continued to lobby for the poor; on March 5, 1997, more than 300 Washington, D.C.-area homeless people and advocates met on the Capitol lawn for a meal, prayer service, and press conference led by Call to Renewal. Their message to Congress, the national religious community, and the American people was that the homeless and other marginalized people could not, in a good society, be written off or "discarded." As citizens of a democracy, people of faith should support democratic principles of civil rights, equality, and opportunity. The ethical principles of all of the world's major religions also support individual dignity and human rights and encourage taking on the responsibility for charity—providing support and care for the poor and dispossessed; indeed, the Greek root, *caritas,* denotes love of humanity. Members of religious communities that hold these traditions should, then, enact these principles both to serve and to witness for justice.

The lack of engagement of religious congregations and faith-based organizations in some forms of community practice is a tragedy when we study the ecology of face-to-face organizations to which local residents belong. Robert Putnam (1995) documented that although more and more Americans are becoming members of voluntary associations, today's citizens are more often "cardholders" than active participants. Putnam equated this decline in active participation with a decline in social capital and local vitality as well as political participation. However, there is more and more evidence that congregations and faith-based organizations fill the void of face-to-face local belonging (Cnaan, Boddie, & Diiulio, 2002).

It is well known that congregations are, at the core, based on values teaching and moral enhancement. People who join local religious congregations do so to find a venue in which to express religious beliefs and practice moral behavior within an agreed-upon theology. These people do not come together to be community activists or service providers; they come to worship as a group and to actualize their faith. In the process, however, a cohesive group is formed. This cohesive group is community based and community minded; thus, a nucleus of social strength is formed.

With the decline of governmental investment in human services and Americans' shrinking engagement in civic groups, congregations and faith-based organizations are increasingly providing social and community services (Yancey, 1998). Faith-based organizations have recently been recognized for their contribution to a variety of community-organizing approaches (Byrd, 1997; Cisneros, 1996; Wood, 1994, 1997). Although other mediating organizations serve similar functions, only local congregations and faith-based organizations are found in every neighborhood across the country, have reputations as trusted and stabilizing entities in residential areas, boast regular attendance of at least half the adult population, and have as an organizational norm an obligation to the advancement of humankind. The distinct contribution of congregations and faith-based organizations is linked to the translation of their religious values and beliefs into acts of service and advocacy that build the community.

How Central Are Congregations in the Community?

Estimates of the number of congregations in America vary widely, from 200,000 to a half million. A study by the philanthropy-focused coalition, Independent Sector, found an estimated 350,000 congregations in the United States (Hodgkinson, Weitzman, Kirsch, Noga, & Gorski, 1993). In a study of Philadelphia, a city of about 1.5 million, we documented just over 2,000 congregations, an average of one congregation for every 750 residents (Cnaan et al., 2002). Congregations vary greatly in size, of course; both studies documented congregations ranging from 25-member groups meeting in storefronts to 6,000-member mega-churches.

The United States is the most religious of all modern democracies. According to the World Value Survey conducted from 1990 to 1993, more people in the United States—82%—defined themselves as religious than did people in any other country ("The Counter-Attack of God," 1995). In a 1993 CNN/USA Today/Gallup poll, 71% of Americans reported membership in a church, synagogue, or mosque, and 41% reported attendance at such a place of worship in the 7 days prior to the poll (McAneny & Saad, 1993). In our study (Cnaan et al., 2002), we found that the average weekly attendance in a Philadelphia congregation is 350. When that number is multiplied by 2,000 congregations, we estimate that about half of all Philadelphia residents attend a worship service on an average weekend. These numbers imply that a large portion of Americans from all walks of life belong to religious congregations.

It is important to note, therefore, that members of religious congregations tend to contribute time, expertise, and money to benefit and empower their community; many studies have found that people who are active in their faith communities, more than any other demographic group, volunteer and donate money to all types of charities, secular and religious (Hoge, Zech, McNamara, & Donahue, 1998; Jackson, Bachmeier, Wood, & Craft, 1995). In our Philadelphia study, we found that religious congregations, on average, allocate 21.7% of their annual income to social causes (Cnaan et al., 2002). In other research, the *Yearbook of American and Canadian Churches* (Bedell, 1996) reported that American congregations direct 21% of their contributions toward benevolence. Elsewhere, it has been shown that congregations are keenly concerned with the welfare of others (Cnaan et al., 2002).

Religious congregations can be found in every community—metropolitan, suburban, and rural—in America. In a study of the institutional ecology of four Los Angeles neighborhoods, Orr found an average of 35 religious congregations and 12.5 religiously affiliated nonprofit corporations per square mile, "far more than the number of gasoline stations, liquor stores, and supermarkets combined" (1998, p. 3). Similarly, in our study of West Philadelphia, we found 321 places of worship in a territory between 6 and 9 square miles in size, about the same ratio of congregations per square mile as found by Orr in Los Angeles. In Philadelphia, we found that the longest distance one can walk from one congregational meeting place before encountering another is eight tenths of a mile. In most cases, the distance is far shorter.

Congregational Resources That Are Paramount for Community Practice

As society becomes increasingly transient and businesses move out of inner cities, congregations and faith-based organizations are becoming, for many communities, the last strongholds able to garner available resources to meet the needs of our most vulnerable populations. Kretzman and McKnight (1993) recognized that congregations have an abundance of resources that can be unleashed in creative ways to improve community relationships and conditions. Congregations command a wealth of resources, including people, space and facilities, materials and equipment, expertise, economic power, relationships, values, and political influence, and they can pool their resources and energies with those of other organizations to meet a variety of community needs (Wineburg, Ahmed, & Sills, 1997).

People who are active in their faith communities are not necessarily more moral or decent than their nonreligious counterparts. Although there is an ample literature to show that religious people are less prone to criminal activities, substance abuse, and vandalism (Ellis & Peterson, 1996; Ellison & Smith, 1991; Engs & Hanson, 1985; Gartner, Larson, & Allen, 1991), the mere fact that half the U.S. population is engaged in congregational activity suggests that not all congregation members are perfectly law-abiding. In fact, many congregants are people who in other contexts may be viewed as self-centered or even unethical. Regardless of personal traits, however, the key power of congregations and other faith-based organizations is their powerful group dynamics. People join congregations to be uplifted and feel spiritually and morally fulfilled. The interaction between members is enhanced by routine activities such as committee meetings, picnics, fellowship after worship services, and an array of communal social activities. People come to these venues to leave behind the pressures of daily living and choose to do so with people who share their belief and value systems. The end result can be a cohesive group of people who often engage as a collective unit in social events and in the provision of social services.

The correlation between volunteering and membership in an organized religious community suggests that people who worship together form a functional community and are more likely to volunteer with that community or as a representative of it. For example, in Council Grove, Kansas, each local congregation bands together once a month to provide the local thrift store with volunteers who sort, mend, and sew clothing, shelve items, and assist customers. Robert Wuthnow noted that religious organizations "tell people of opportunities to serve, both within and beyond the congregation itself, and provide personal contacts, committees, phone numbers, meeting space, transportation, or whatever it may take to help turn good intentions into action" (1994, pp. 242–243).

When churches and other religious institutions share congregational space with individuals and organizations from the community, it is much more than a simple real-estate transaction (Cnaan et al., 1999). When congregations open their facilities for public use, they communicate that faith communities are good neighbors who are generous with their assets and supportive of the common good. Congregational spaces—including not only meeting rooms but also kitchens, gymnasiums, classrooms, dormitories, and parking lots—often are the only spaces available for public use at minimal or no cost. In many communities, especially impoverished inner cities and isolated rural areas, churches may be the only available meeting space of any kind. Indeed, one third of American's day care centers are housed in congregational buildings; half of these are run by their host congregations. More than three quarters of Alcoholics Anonymous and other Twelve Step groups, and many scout troops, also meet on congregational premises. Use of these facilities saves money and decreases frustration when people are involved in organizing local campaigns or social activities on behalf of local residents. In many areas, congregational buildings have become de facto community meeting spaces where police host discussions with residents, city officials reveal plans, and neighborhood associations meet.

Many congregations also own or have access to computers, photocopiers, fax machines, musical instruments, sports equipment, and furniture that can be made available for community use and to promote community interests. When a group of community residents receives permission to use a congregational facility, they often are allowed free or low-cost use of its supplies and equipment. These facilities and equipment are especially helpful in educational programs for children and other community members.

Verba, Scholzman, and Brady (1995) found that congregations are important resources for the development of civic competence, especially for people with lower incomes. They defined civic competence in terms of concrete skills, specifically writing letters, taking part in decision-making meetings, planning and chairing meetings, and giving presentations or speeches in public forums. The authors found that religious communities are among the key places where people can acquire these civic skills (see also Ammerman, 1997). Often, it is within the context of religious organizations that women, people of color, and the poor are provided with the opportunities to acquire skills of political participation. The congregational member who learns to write letters to support religious activities or collects money to pay for holiday services can transfer those skills to civic, business, and political contexts. The authors concluded that religion is the predominant institution working against the class bias in American civic engagement (Verba et al., 1995).

The Russ Reid Company, in conjunction with the Barna Research Corporation, conducted a study of donors who had given money to a nonprofit organization other than a church or place of worship in the 12 months preceding the study. They found that the best predictor of people's giving behavior relates to religious involvement: 82% of the people who give to nonprofit organizations also give to churches or places of worship. They concluded that "no other characteristic is so predominant or defining [of donors] as religious giving" (Russ Reid Company, 1995, p. 3). Among the regular donors in the study, 60% had attended a church or other religious service in the previous month; 37% had volunteered at their place of worship during that time; and 84% agreed that religious faith was very important in their lives. Congregations, in turn, funnel a significant percentage of their budget to social causes: more than 20% on average (Cnaan et al., 2002). Hall estimated that "churches and church-based institutions currently command approximately 66 percent of all contributions, 34 percent of all volunteer work, and 10 percent of all wages and salaries in the nonprofit sector" (1990, p. 38). Obviously, congregations and their members and organizations command enormous economic power that can be mobilized to support worthy community and social causes.

Congregations are characterized by the network of relationships they maintain both inside and outside of their membership. Congregations can extend their reach by participating with any of the hundreds of "parachurch" organizations, from Habitat for Humanity and Call for Renewal to the Christian Coalition, denominational groups, or other organizations in the broader community with shared interests. As such, a congregation is an established and recognized institution that can be recruited not only for its individual members but also for its lateral and vertical connections. Most congregations are members of at least one local coalition; hence, collaborating with one congregation can open the door for interaction with other groups, providing local representation as well as access to constituents who otherwise would be unavailable. This type of organizing cuts across racial, ethnic, class, and political lines and can develop new channels of cooperation (Gittell & Vidal, 1998). By creating relationships with those outside the community, congregations are able to strengthen relationships within communities, creating *bonding social capital,* and between and among communities, known as *bridging social capital.*

Congregations also build on their tradition with rich scriptural texts, moral teachings, and values that encourage building strong communities and empowering individuals and families (Bakke, 1997; Dennison, 1999). People who join congregations do so to feel connected with a higher being who asks them, irrespective of their religion or denomination, to manifest honesty, humility, and care for others. Although not all people who are active in their faith communities meet these and other expectations, many congregations generally are viewed in a positive light. Organizations that work with religious groups may gain a sense of credibility among certain segments of the community. Furthermore, incorporating religious values and traditions changes the flavor of community organizing. This approach to community organizing is focused on a consensus approach with a priority on reconciliation.

In many communities, especially inner-city African American communities, clergy and congregational lay leaders are also community leaders. When racial or social unrest erupts, it is not uncommon for politicians to seek out the local clergy and ask for their support in restoring community peace (Orr, Miller, Roof, & Melton, 1994). Between the collective economic and social resources of their members and the clergy's status as community leaders and role models, religious congregations have a potential for significant political influence.

Congregations and faith-based organizations have resources that are highly relevant to community practice. As social institutions embedded in communities, congregations can be natural allies for community organizing. Congregations also are often a great stabilizing force in communities experiencing transition and decline.

The Ways Congregations Are Engaged in Community Practice

Congregations have been viewed as highly effective mediating bodies due to their ability to assess and meet the unique and ever-changing needs of their membership and the surrounding community. Although congregations in the United States operate independently from the government, they nonetheless interact in the public sphere as they invest in community goals and serve as a buffer between the power of the government and vulnerable populations (Berger & Neuhaus, 1977). Congregations also emphasize the importance of ritual and belonging as their members share history and a common direction (Kretzman & McKnight, 1993). Finally, congregations are known to be a potential source of political influence and power base, as was demonstrated by Saul Alinsky (1972).

The following cases illustrate the role of clergy and congregations in mediating between the government and local residents and impacting their quality of life. These include religious coalitions, faith-based organizations and public housing, capacity-enhancing faith-based initiatives, faith-based organizations and community development coalitions (CDCs), faith-based organizations and health initiatives, and campaigns for a living wage.

Religious Coalitions

The most frequently noted examples of faith-based community organizing efforts are by coalitions between urban congregations and community organizations. Under the auspices of four national federations—the Industrial Areas Foundation (IAF), the Pacific Institute for Community Organization, Direct Action and Research Training Centers, and Gamaliel—networks of urban community organizations have been developed. Most of the organizations participating in these coalitions are congregations. Each local federation is composed of 10 to 40 congregations or religious groups affiliated with and supported by the national organization (Wood, 1997). Organizers meet with individuals and small groups to identify problems and find strategies for addressing them. When a strategy is agreed upon, the group targets the appropriate person or group to make the change, be it City Hall, an individual politician, a utility company, transportation authority, or a private company. The large number of people participating in federations of religious congregations is a compelling reason for politicians and business owners to listen and attempt to cooperate.

IAF is the most prominent national organization committed to serving as a change agent at the local level. Founded by Saul Alinsky in 1940, IAF had its beginnings in Alinsky's Back of the Yards organization, a coalition between Catholic congregations and Labor/Communist Party organizers who sought to enhance the quality of life in some of Chicago's poorest neighborhoods (those just behind the stockyards) through advocacy and lobbying (Alinsky, 1972). Its current network of affiliates includes groups in New York, Connecticut, Illinois, Tennessee, Georgia, Texas, and California. IAF, which considers itself "an organization of organizations," provides professional organizers with expertise in the workings of metropolitan political economies as well as social movement dynamics. IAF does not determine political agendas at the local level but encourages local coalitions to determine their own courses of action.

Tie Nashville Together (TNT) is a religious coalition based in Nashville, Tennessee (Byrd, 1997). Started as a convention of congregations in 1993, it grew to become a large-scale community mobilization effort. In the months following the founding convention, TNT members visited schools, conducted public hearings regarding nursing homes, and held "accountability nights" for school board and local political candidates. Leaders also developed an after-school program for Grades K to 8 and a "strategy for labor force development and economic development," both of which were based on IAF initiatives in other communities. In addition, TNT members convinced the mayor's office to open and fund a Neighborhood Justice Center for mediating disputes without police intervention as a means of fostering a sense of community. By 1995, TNT included 43 congregations and associations representing 5,000 people.

Wood (1997) has argued that some of the most effective community organizing of residents in low-income inner cities has taken place through church-based coalitions. These efforts have significantly affected the residents' social, political, and economic environment. To build a strong church-based coalition over the long term, it is best to have the congregational members do most of the organizing.

Faith-Based Organizations and Public Housing

One of the greatest needs of people with low income and no political power is decent housing. In today's economy, even households with two wage-earners working full-time and earning minimum wage cannot expect to be able to rent, let alone own, a quality residence. One way to address this need is collaboration between faith-based organizations and people with expertise in construction. One such example is Habitat for Humanity. An international nonprofit organization dedicated to building homes with and for low-income families, Habitat for Humanity was founded in 1976 by Millard and Linda Fuller. "Habitat houses," financed by a revolving Fund for Humanity, are built with no profit added and no interest, terms based in biblical principles. Habitat for Humanity's faith-into-action ministry is based on the conviction that Christian ethics necessarily involve taking meaningful action to help the poor. Habitat founder and President Millard Fuller explained it this way: "We may disagree on all sorts of things . . . but we can agree . . . on the idea of building homes for God's people in need" (Habitat for Humanity, 1997; Vuyst, 1989).

The principle of Habitat for Humanity is relatively simple. Families purchase homes from Habitat after construction and after contributing several hundred hours of their own "sweat equity"—that is, the family that will own the house works with Habitat volunteers to build it. Sweat equity reduces the monetary cost of the house for its eventual owners, increases the personal stake of the family members in their house, and fosters the development of partnerships with others in the community. Volunteers from religious congregations, colleges, and the local community provide most of the labor. Funding comes from churches, foundations, businesses, and individuals. Habitat has built more than 60,000 houses around the world, providing more than 300,000 people with safe, decent, affordable shelter. There are now more than 1,300 U.S. affiliates; more than 250 international affiliates coordinate some 800 building projects in 57 other countries around the world.

Habitat for Humanity is only one religious organization that helps alleviate the pain of homelessness and low-quality housing. In New York, a coalition called East Brooklyn Churches (EBC) joined with IAF to redevelop deteriorating neighborhoods experiencing financial instability, a growing number of abandoned properties, and outmigration of most working-class families. To engender confidence, early campaigns were well organized and specifically chosen to ensure success. Street signs were replaced, food and sanitation in local supermarkets were improved, long-abandoned buildings were demolished, illegal narcotics markets were shut down, and a voter registration campaign recruited 10,000 new voters in 1984.

The coalition then tackled a much larger problem—housing. When EBC wanted to build 1,000 new homes, the estimated cost was $7.5 million. Support for this Nehemiah Project (such projects are dedicated to rebuilding inner-city neighborhoods) came from the Missouri Synod Lutherans ($1 million); the Roman Catholic bishop of New York, who became an avid supporter of the coalition ($2.5 million); and the Episcopalians of Long Island ($1 million). Pressured to support the project, the city of New York donated the land, paid for landfill removal, and provided $10,000 in interest-free loans to new home owners.

This successful organizing effort was truly local, with each congregation represented by its clergy and three to four lay leaders. EBC has no president, and decisions are made by consensus. In a review of EBC, Gittings states: "In an area bereft of banks, civic clubs, industry, and professionals, the churches were the only organizations—apart from the rackets—that remained alive amid the wreckage of the community" (1987, p. 10). For the projects to be successful, pastors of these churches were forced to become community entrepreneurs and subsequently spearheaded the civic organization that became the first Nehemiah Project. In the years since, Nehemiah Projects have formed in Philadelphia, Los Angeles, and several other large cities.

Capacity-Enhancing Faith-Based Initiatives

As is true for many small grassroots social service agencies, leaders of small faith-based organizations often have vision and compassion but lack business administration and management skills. At the same time, many successful businesspeople desire to express their faith by investing their marketplace-developed skills in faith-based social sector initiatives that mirror their values. The key community practice challenge is linking the people who have the necessary business skills with the faith-based service providers who need them to build community programs.

FaithWorks is an intermediary organization that links these two groups. Based on principles developed by Buford (1993), FaithWorks helps business professionals put their altruistic commitments and beliefs into action. Buford believes that many successful businesspeople may wish to take their services into a new arena. While still active in their businesses, they are encouraged by FaithWorks to seek an opportunity for meaningful and significant work, thus creating a parallel volunteer career in community service.

One partnership that FaithWorks assisted is a health clinic in Austin, Texas. This faith-based health clinic, which provides low-cost or free basic health services to the indigent, was seeing few patients and was facing closure until organizers developed a relationship with a local real estate executive through FaithWorks. Through his skills and contacts, the clinic was able to secure a new and much larger location and expand its services to meet the needs of many more clients. The clinic had served 8,000 people per year at the previous location; it now serves more than 50,000 people a year. Such partnerships are based on shared faith and a mission to serve others.

Faith-Based Organizations and CDCs

CDCs are considered one of the most effective tools to help people in impoverished and underserved communities to participate in the political and economic affairs of their neighborhoods (Clavel, Pitt, & Yin, 1997; Gittell & Vidal, 1998; Goetz, 1993; Harris, 1994). CDCs seek to become influential actors in local civic and economic arenas, to channel resources to the community, and to represent residents in decision-making processes (Thomas, 1997). They work to redistribute resources and provide needed services. CDCs are credited with successful rehabilitation and management of considerable housing stock in a number of cities. Some CDCs are also involved in building and running homes for older adults, managing rental properties, sponsoring adult education and voter registration, influencing local and state decision making, developing leadership, sponsoring community-wide events, and hiring community organizers. The more than 8,000 CDCs in the United States—two thirds of which are religiously based—are credited with reversing urban blight and preserving housing in many American cities while allowing more citizen representation than any other local institution (National Congress for Community Economic Development [NCCED], 1999).

CDCs usually come in two forms: freestanding and coalition-based. The freestanding CDC is a corporation owned by one organization that works to promote that organization's philosophy. For example, Bethel New Life's CDC in Chicago has developed a broad range of community programs including a small business center, employment skills training and employment services, individual development accounts, family support programs, and a Senior Services Division that provides services to about 700 people a year and has created more than 250 new jobs in community-based services (Bethel New Life, n.d.).

Coalition-based CDCs are owned and run by a group of organizations. Several smaller congregations, for example, may join forces and organize a coalition-based CDC. Coalition-based CDCs also can be owned by a combination of congregations and secular groups. They are rarely owned solely by secular groups (Clemeston & Coates, 1992; Owens, 1999). In both forms, the influence and contributions of religious groups and congregations are quite strong and serve as a means to mobilize minority residents to solve problems on their own using both public and private resources.

Congregations bring with them a wide array of resources that secular organizations do not. Their size alone (an average congregation has 350 members) makes congregations special partners in CDC development. Furthermore, many CDCs start with congregational funding and are housed on congregational properties. Only large and highly successful CDCs manage to acquire enough resources and staff to open an independent office located separately from their sponsoring churches (NCCED, 1999).

Faith-Based Organizations and Health Initiatives

It is no secret that more than 40 million Americans do not have health insurance—mostly the unemployed and the working poor, the most politically disempowered groups in our society. The uninsured can rarely pay for preventive medical care; they seek care only when a serious health problem erupts, and they usually go to hospital emergency rooms. They also are often uninformed about warning signs and symptoms of illness and rarely attend community-based health education programs. In response to the country's significant health needs, the Robert Wood Johnson Foundation sought to provide health education programs in places of worship (Robert Wood Johnson Foundation, n.d.).

The New Covenant Church of Philadelphia developed a Health Team Ministry to deliver basic medical assistance, educate the congregation about health and safety issues, and promote wellness. The ministry produces a quarterly newsletter featuring brief articles, written in layperson's terms, about such topics as over-the-counter medications, smoking cessation, and the connection between religion and health care. This newsletter is a major source of health education for many New Covenant members. Its editors are two medical doctors who are members of the congregation. The health team, composed of congregation members, provides assistance that complements formal health services, such as counseling and referrals for victims of domestic violence. Team members rely on the traditions and solidarity of the African American culture to tackle this and other problems to which the larger society has routinely turned a blind eye.

In 1993, a Methodist church in Indianapolis contracted with the nearby Indiana University School of Nursing to open a wellness center on the congregational site. The program helps people of all ages with both acute and chronic illnesses and serves more than 5,500 patients per year. The Shalom Health Care Center employs nurse practitioners, an outreach worker, a secretary, and a director; a general practitioner and a pediatrician are on call. The annual cost of running the center, which operates 2 days a week, is $82,000; funding is provided by private foundations and the Indiana State Department of Health. Fees are $2 to $5 per visit, but no one is turned away.

Helping in the Campaign for Living Wage

Not all faith-based coalitions are formed in the same manner. For example, the Clergy and Laity United for Economic Justice (CLUE) is a Los Angeles-based coalition of clergy whose congregants organized to assist and support the working poor. Their ongoing pressure was instrumental in promoting the city's 1997 living-wage law. In 1999, CLUE held a parade on Los Angeles's famous Rodeo Drive, giving the biblical gifts of milk and honey to hotels that had adopted the living wage and bitter herbs to those that had not. A few weeks later, the dissenting hotels signed new contracts that included living wages (Parker, 2000).

Summary and Conclusions

The theory of community participation and empowerment calls for the existence of intermediary organizations that buffer the power of the state and powerful corporations. One can argue that the key role of community practitioners is to organize collectives that diminish such authority and amplify the voice of citizens. However, as Robert Putnam (2000) argues, Americans' participation in face-to-face groups and organizations is in decline. The only community-based organization in which face-to-face interaction is the norm and which can be found in every community is the local religious congregation. It is our contention that many community practitioners would enhance their work and benefit the people and causes they serve if they were to link with congregations and other faith-based organizations in the types of community-based programs discussed here.

References

Alinsky, S. D. (1972). *Rules for radicals: A practical primer for realistic radicals.* New York: Vintage Books.

Ammerman, N. T. (1997). *Congregation and community.* New Brunswick, NJ: Rutgers University Press.

Bakke, R. (1997). *A theology as big as a city.* Downers Grove, IL: Inter-Varsity Press.

Bedell, K. B. (Ed.). (1996). *Yearbook of American and Canadian churches.* Nashville, TN: Abington.

Berger, P. L., & Neuhaus, R. J. (1977). *To empower people: The role of mediating structures in public policy.* Washington, DC: American Enterprise Institute for Public Policy Research.

Bethel New Life. (n.d.). *Our programs.* Retrieved July 15, 2003, from http://www.bethelnewlife.org/pgms.html

Buford, B. (1993). *Half time: Changing your game plan from success to significance.* Grand Rapids, MI: Zondervan.

Byrd, M. (1997). Determining frames of reference for religiously based organizations: A case of neo-Alinsky efforts to mobilize congregational resources. *Nonprofit and Voluntary Sector Quarterly, 26,* 122–138.

Cisneros, H. (1996). *Higher grounds: Faith communities and community building.* Washington, DC: U.S. Department of Housing and Urban Development.

Clavel, P., Pitt, J., & Yin, J. (1997). The community option in urban policy. *Urban Affairs Review, 32,* 435–458.

Clemeston, R., & Coates, R. (1992). *Restoring broken places and rebuilding communities: A casebook of African-American church involvement in community economic development.* Washington, DC: National Congress for Community Economic Development.

Cnaan, R. A., Boddie, S. C., & Diiulio, J. J. (2002). *The invisible caring hand: American congregations and the provision of welfare.* New York: New York University Press.

Cnaan, R. A., Wineburg, R. J., & Boddie, S. C. (1999). *The newer deal: Social work and religion in partnership.* New York: Columbia University Press.

Cohen, J. L., & Arato, A. (1994). *Civil society and political theory.* Cambridge: MIT Press.

Coleman, J. S. (1990). *Foundations of social theory.* Cambridge, MA: Harvard University Press.

The counter-attack of God. (1995, July 8). *The Economist,* pp. 19–21.

Dennison, J. (1999). *City reaching: On the road to community transformation.* Pasadena, CA: William Carey Library.

Ellis, L., & Peterson, J. (1996). Crime and religion: An international comparison among thirteen industrial nations. *Personality and Individual Differences, 20,* 761–768.

Ellison, C. W., & Smith, J. (1991). Toward an integrative measure of health and well-being. *Journal of Psychology and Theology, 19,* 35–48.

Engs, R. C., & Hanson, D. J. (1985). The drinking patterns and problems of college students: 1983. *Journal of Alcohol and Drug Education, 31,* 65–83.

Gartner, J., Larson, D. B., & Allen, G. (1991). Religious commitment and mental health: A review of the empirical literature. *Journal of Psychology and Theology, 19,* 6–25.

Gittell, R. J., & Vidal, A. (1998). *Community organizing: Building social capital as a development strategy.* Thousand Oaks, CA: Sage.

Gittings, J. (1987, February 2). East Brooklyn churches and the Nehemiah project: Churches in communities: A place to stand. *Christianity and Crisis,* pp. 5–11.

Goetz, E. (1993). *Shelter burden: Local politics and progressive housing policy.* Philadelphia: Temple University Press.

Gramsci, A. (1988). *An Antonio Gramsci reader: Selected writings, 1916–1935* (D. Forgacs, Ed.). New York: Schocken.

Habitat for Humanity (1997). *How it works: Habitat for Humanity fact sheet.* Retrieved July 15, 2002, from http://www.habitat.org/how/factsheet.htm

Hall, P. D. (1990). The history of religious philanthropy in America. In R. Wuthnow, V. A. Hodgkinson, and associates (Eds.), *Faith and philanthropy in America: Exploring the role of religion in America's voluntary sector* (pp. 38–62). San Francisco: Jossey-Bass.

Harris, F. C. (1994). Something within: Religion as a mobilizer of African-American political activism. *Journal of Politics, 56,* 42–68.

Hodgkinson, V. A., Weitzman, M. S., Kirsch, A. D., Noga, S. M., & Gorski, H. A. (1993). *From belief to commitment: The community service activities and finances of religious congregations in the United States, 1993 edition.* Washington, DC: Independent Sector.

Hoge, D. R., Zech, C., McNamara, P., & Donahue, M. J. (1998). The value of volunteers as resources for congregations. *Journal for the Scientific Study of Religion, 37,* 470–480.

Jackson, E. F., Bachmeier, M. D., Wood, J. R., & Craft, E. A. (1995). Volunteering and charitable giving: Do religious and associational ties promote helping behavior? *Nonprofit and Voluntary Sector Quarterly, 24,* 59–78.

Kretzman, J. P., & McKnight, J. L. (1993). *Building communities from the inside out: A path toward finding and mobilizing a community's assets.* Evanston, IL: Northwestern University, The Asset-Based Community Development Institute for Policy Research.

Lugo, L. (1998). *Equal partners: The welfare responsibility of governments and churches.* Washington, DC: The Center for Public Justice.

McAneny, L., & Saad, L. (1993, April). Strong ties between religious commitment and abortion views. *The Gallup Poll Monthly, 331,* 35–43.

National Congress for Community Economic Development (NCCED). (1999). *Community-based development organizations.* Washington, DC: Author.

Orr, J. B. (1998). *Los Angeles religion: A civic profile.* Los Angeles: University of Southern California, Center for Religion and Civic Culture.

Orr, J. B., Miller, D. E., Roof, W. C., & Melton, J. G. (1994). *Politics of the spirit: Religion and multi-ethnicity in Los Angeles.* Los Angeles: University of Southern California.

Owens, M. L. (1999, November 4–6). *The political potential of black church-based community development organizations.* Paper presented at the annual meeting of the Association for Research on Nonprofit Organizations and Voluntary Action, Arlington, VA.

Parker, R. (2000, January). Progressive politics and, uh . . . God. *The American Prospect, 11*(5), 32–37.

Putnam, R. D. (1995). Bowling alone: America's declining social capital. *Journal of Democracy, 6,* 65–78.

Putnam, R. D. (2000). *Bowling alone: The collapse and revival of American community.* New York: Simon & Schuster.

Robert Wood Johnson Foundation (n.d.). *Our programs.* Retrieved July 15, 2003, from http://www.rwjf.org/programs

Russ Reid Company. (1995). *The heart of the donor.* Pasadena, CA: Author.

Thomas, J. M. (1997). Rebuilding inner cities: Basic principles. In T. D. Boston & C. L. Ross (Eds.), *The inner city: Urban poverty and economic development in the next century* (pp. 67–74). New Brunswick, NJ: Transaction Books.

Verba, S., Scholzman, K. L., & Brady, H. E. (1995). *Voice and equality: Civic voluntarism in American politics.* Cambridge, MA: Harvard University Press.

Vuyst, A. (1989). Self-help for the homeless. *Humanist, 49*(3), 13–49.

Wineburg, R. J., Ahmed, F., & Sills, M. (1997). Local human service organizations and the local religious community during an era of change. *Journal of Applied Social Sciences, 21*(2), 93–98.

Wood, R. L. (1994). Faith in action: Religious resources for political success in three congregations. *Sociology of Religion, 55,* 397–417.

Wood, R. L. (1997). Social capital and political culture: God meets politics in the inner city. *American Behavioral Scientist, 40,* 595–605.

Wuthnow, R. (1994). *Producing the sacred: An essay on public religion.* Urbana: University of Illinois Press.

Yancey, G. I. (1998). *Congregations as social service providers: A picture of community involvement.* Unpublished doctoral dissertation, University of Pennsylvania.

CHAPTER 21

Service Coordination

Practical Concerns for Community Practitioners

John Morrison

S ocial workers have always understood that individuals, families, and communities often have multiple problems that require service from a variety of agencies and professionals. The complex nature of individual and social problems often means that a number of service systems must be involved to resolve problems because no single agency has the capabilities to meet all client needs. At times, a single referral will ensure the mobilization of all necessary client services. However, the complexity of many of today's problems, combined with agencies' funding and service limitations, often requires that social workers coordinate the efforts of a number of organizations to ensure their clients get the care they need.

Too often, social service agencies and funds are narrowly focused and highly specialized. Unfortunately, social problems are rarely that simple. People in need of services cannot be reduced to one-dimensional entities and expected to respond to one-size-fits-all services. Agencies are often set up to provide a specific set of services, however, and individuals and communities with complex needs are often expected to negotiate complicated systems and coordinate a maze of services for themselves.

A potential alternative to formal service coordination arrangements are market arrangements (Wallis, 1994), which might use vouchers or other payment arrangements and may be more subject to market forces in assessment and/or service planning. Although such arrangements might work for simple service needs, market arrangements also leave to clients the responsibility for coordinating complex service situations by themselves, and involved agencies may not see coordination with a service system as part of their mission. Experienced social workers know that for services to be effective, service coordination is needed. This holds true historically and currently.

Among the earliest attempts at service coordination were the charity organization societies, which sought to eliminate duplication of services among agencies and improve effectiveness and efficiency. Service coordination has continued to be an ongoing theme, with efforts of the United Way, other private entities, and government organizations being devoted to such efforts. A great deal of professional literature has discussed service coordination issues (Austin, 1997; Dill & Rochefort, 1989; Dunst & Bruder, 2002; Edelman, 2001; Goering & Rogers, 1986; Lehman, 1989; Meyers, 1993; Reitan, 1998; Rosenblatt, 1996). Variations of service coordination efforts may also be known as service integration, collaboration, community liaison networks, partnerships, or wraparound services.

Service Coordination as Compensation for a Fragmented Service System

The nature of current social service arrangements too often mitigates against easy problem resolution. Historically, many agencies were founded and developed independently of a clear and overall systematic plan for social services. Instead, charities were formed by individuals or groups in response to the funders' often narrow perception of what was needed in society. Funding was equally disjointed. Increases in government funding over time did not resolve such problems because funding often was provided in a way that focused on narrow problems or categorical definitions. Separate rules and regulations applied to each service system or domain, such as child welfare, mental health, and juvenile justice. Adelman and Taylor describe this phenomenon as "hardening of the categories" (1997, p. 415). Others have referred to these funding and planning domains as "smokestacks" or "silos" where there is little connection among service systems. Each service system too often operates within its own silo, independently of other systems. The problem, of course, is that individual, family, and community problems rarely fit neatly into the categories established by agencies; as a result, services remain uncoordinated and are thus not fully effective. Mitchell and Scott state that "the single most potent threat to successful interagency collaboration lies in the historical division of client needs into distinctive 'problems' that are seen as amenable to treatment by the application of a particular agency's staff energy and expertise" (1996, pp. 172).

Although government agencies are usually the largest ultimate source of funding for social programs, government agencies increasingly choose to contract with nongovernmental agencies to provide the actual services, which only adds to the complexity. Not surprisingly, the lack of central planning and funding and the entrepreneurial nature of social services have resulted in a multitude of agencies, which all too often operate without coordination or sometimes even at cross-purposes with each other (see Brilliant, Chapter 12, this volume).

At the agency level, eligibility, philosophy, and service methodology may reflect idiosyncratic decisions about what is good practice or simply convenient for the agency or its workers. Service decisions are often made without regard for overall policy needs or the needs of individual clients. In the Chicago area, for example, it is very hard to find shelter services for homeless families with adolescent sons because all relevant agencies have chosen not to serve this population.

Incentives

Beatrice (1990) identifies a range of reasons for agencies to engage in service coordination: (a) to better serve clients, (b) to provide a more integrated mix of services, (c) to improve program design and implementation, (d) to build consensus and support for all services, and (e) to gain access to additional clients. In reviewing the literature that discusses reasons that agencies enter into service coordination agreements, Miller, Scott, Stage, and Birkholt (1995) suggest that the need for resources, for accurate information about other organizations, and for increased efficiency, stability, and legitimacy are all motivating factors. Reisch and Sommerfeld (2003) suggest that in addition to service collaboration, agencies also work together on advocacy, training and technical assistance, and resource sharing. Mulroy and Shay identify, in addition to resource considerations, other motivators for agencies to become involved in service coordination, including "shared values, compatible service philosophies, and the opportunity to extend the mission and strategically meet organizational needs" (1998, p. 14; see also Mulroy, Nelson, & Gour, Chapter 25, this volume). Backer and Norman (1999, p. 40) identify leverage, capacity building, community building, and enhancement of grant-making ability as additional reasons.

Funding organizations and policymakers are increasingly recognizing that there is merit in service coordination and may even make funding contingent on the demonstration of such coordination or the development of "partnerships."

Disincentives

Despite the obvious advantages to an agency participating in service coordination efforts, there are also disincentives that must be considered. One is that such partnerships can interfere with the natural interests of individual agencies in maintaining their autonomy, mission, market, and ability to secure funding and maintain long-term survival. It may not always seem rational for agencies to pursue service coordination efforts in today's highly competitive service environment. Indeed, the saying that collaborations among agencies are "unnatural acts committed by unwilling partners" is often bandied about at conferences and seminars.

There are also issues of funding and focus. Many granting organizations target funds to narrowly focused, specialized programs with centrally determined funding arrangements. Such arrangements may provide few obvious or immediate incentives for collaboration and thus act as a deterrent for local service partnerships. For agencies to honestly participate in service coordination efforts, both the costs and benefits must be made explicit. Agencies that come to service coordination meetings simply because it is the "right thing to do" are unlikely to be reliable partners (see Roberts-DeGennaro & Mizrahi, Chapter 16, this volume).

The Limits of Service Coordination

Although there are obvious advantages to service coordination, it is often viewed uncritically by social workers as a valuable end in itself and, therefore, as something to be pursued without question by agencies and social workers. Service coordination efforts are common, but they are not always successful or long-lasting, often because they are initiated without sufficient thought or analysis. Service coordination in itself cannot make up for critical gaps in local service systems. It is not a panacea for complex problems. It will not compensate for a preexisting or collective lack of expertise or limitations in funding, and it won't overcome legal or political barriers.

Range of Service Coordination Efforts

A range of service coordination mechanisms can be identified, and a number of these are listed in Table 21.1. Three levels of service coordination are suggested: (a) state/federal-level mechanisms, (b) community-level mechanisms, and (c) case-level mechanisms. Mechanisms range from highly centralized system changes to much smaller individual worker initiatives that involve only a few colleagues. Service coordination efforts that are identified as the most "system oriented" (state/federal-level mechanisms) are probably the most difficult for social workers to influence and are likely to involve more focus on policy practice and system reform than on traditional community practice. At the other end of the spectrum are those efforts that are most "individual worker oriented" (case-level mechanisms), including referrals and case conferences, which are likely to be part of good and normal casework practice. Table 21.1 describes these three levels in more detail.

Middle-range activities such as core agency/single-entry point partnerships that are based on service to a specific client group or neighborhood and integrated core teams are those most within the domain of community practitioners. Therefore, service coordination partnerships are the focus of this chapter.

Inclusivity, Intensity, and Evaluation

Miller et al. (1995) discuss issues of inclusivity and intensity. Inclusivity describes the number of partners involved in service coordination efforts from dyads to networks, and intensity refers to the level of activity, ranging from mutual adjustment to corporate relationships. Intensity of the consortium or partnership can be measured in terms of how many meetings take place and whether any independent actions are taken beyond the member agencies such as making a joint funding proposal (Fleishman, Mor, Piette, & Allen, 1992).

Inclusivity and intensity form a basis for evaluation of service coordination efforts. In addition, whether service coordination efforts have been integrated into the day-to-day operation of participating agencies can be determined. The length

Table 21.1   Some Service Coordination Mechanisms: A Continuum

| *System Oriented*
(Power, funding,
and/or control are key) | ← —————————————— → | *Individual Worker Oriented*
(Attitude change, goodwill, and
personal relationships are key) |

[On this continuum, the balance of key elements changes, moving from left to right. For example, community-level approaches combine elements of power, funding, and control as well as attitude change, goodwill, and personal relationships to achieve results.]

State/federal mechanisms	*Community-level mechanisms*	*Case-level mechanisms*	*Individual-level mechanisms*
• Integrated entitlements (e.g., Medicare) • Sub-state or regional authorities (e.g., Mental Health, Inc., Rochester, New York) *These depend on clear, formal authority, usually from government (Lynn, 1976). See Lehman 1989, Dill & Rochefort 1989.* • Capitation payment systems • *Such mechanisms are like vouchers.*	• Intergovernmental/ interagency agreements *These typically would be fairly formal.* • Core agency *Single entry point for clients.* • Co-location *Several independent agencies are located at the same site.* • Service partnerships *Two or more agencies agree to collaborate around specific initiatives/issues. Such arrangements vary in formality. These include school-based partnerships, variously referred to as school-linked services, community schools, or full-service schools (Briar-Lawson et al., 1997).* • Integrated core team (community and institution) *In these arrangements the same team serves clients in an institution and in the community; deinstitutionalization can be expedited and maintained.*	• Multidisciplinary treatment teams *Agencies authorize a team to make collective decisions for a group of clients. See Bronstein (2003).* • Case conferences *Called for individual cases/families.* • Intensive case management *An individual worker takes the lead in decision making for client(s). See Farel & Rounds (1998).* • Individual worker as advocate and collaborator • Referral	• See Dill & Rochefort (1989), Lehman (1989), and Shern, Surles, & Waizer (1989) for further discussion.

of time that the service coordination effort has continued in operation is a good measure of future sustainability.

Kunz (2000) describes a range of mutual efforts related to service partnerships, from informal affiliation and separate accountability to formal affiliation and mutual accountability. In advancing degrees of formality in affiliation, these mutual efforts are: consensus groups, coalitions, collaboratives, cooperatives, partnerships, functional consolidations, joint ventures and, at the most formal level, mergers.

In their discussion of the organization of service coordination efforts, Fleishman et al. (1992) state that mediated structures, in which the lead agency is not a service provider, may have advantages over voluntary structures, in which the lead agency is also a service provider. The mediated structure may be more trusted by partners.

Key Factors in Service Coordination

Authority

Service coordination efforts often fail because there is no clear authority to mandate participation on the part of relevant individuals and agencies, and players do not see a payoff for voluntary participation in such efforts. As we have seen, a number of disincentives need to be overcome if such efforts are to be successful.

Clear policy to achieve service coordination coupled with significant authority for action can successfully bring about service coordination. The author observed an interesting example in Birmingham in the United Kingdom in the summer of 2000. The central government identified a national need for better coordination of services for youthful offenders. Local authorities (municipal governments) were mandated to develop "youth offending teams" to coordinate services. Independent agencies that had not closely coordinated their services in the past were brought together under the leadership of the Birmingham Department of Social Services, and a social worker was designated to be the team leader. Services included those provided by the Department of Social Services (which was responsible for both individual counseling and the operation of secure facilities), the local police, the National Health Service, the local education authority, and the Probation Service (part of the central government's Home Office). More than 50 staff members were part of the team, and most were posted full-time. A series of neighborhood offices with teams composed of representatives from various departments was developed to provide counseling, vocational, educational, and recreational services for juvenile offenders.

Several important factors contributed to the success of this effort. Most important was the national Labor government's newly developed philosophy of "joined-up thinking and action" related to social, health, and educational services, which recognized that coordination of services would result in better results for citizens and communities. British services are much more likely to be funded by central or local government than services in the United States, meaning that there are potentially fewer players to involve in coordination efforts. Much of the funding for local services comes directly from the central government to the local authority (municipality); there are no equivalents of U.S. states to modify or reinterpret clear national policy directives. Central policies must be taken even more seriously in Great Britain than in the United States. Finally, future funding for the local authorities is dependent on demonstrating to government officials compliance with national standards.

Relationships and Trust

Although the example cited above demonstrates that centralized authority can be helpful in achieving service coordination, it cannot be relied on by itself to achieve desired goals in most American contexts. Many service coordination arrangements are developed on a voluntary basis, and participants always have the option of ending their participation. In these situations, building strong relationships and trust between participants is important and can be seen as an alternative to authority.

Individual versus institutional focus. It has been said that ultimately, individuals rather than agencies enter into service coordination arrangements (Adler, 1994). Obviously, both individual and institutional needs must be taken into account when developing service coordination arrangements. "Relationships of trust and understanding among agency professionals can overcome organizational inertia. It is easier to build coordination on the basis of relationship than purely on organizational self-interest" (Beatrice, 1990, p. 57).

Process. Similarly, attention to process details is critical. There are numerous process issues that must be identified as the work of service coordination proceeds.

Product versus process. As in all community practice, a balance must be struck between achieving a "product" or outcome (in this case, service coordination) and spending enough time with "process" to ensure that all the actors (in this case, partner agencies) have bought into the planned change and are likely to want to sustain coordination work for the foreseeable future.

Steps in the process. O'Looney (1994, p. 67) outlines the following three-step process for service coordination:

1. problem setting,

2. direction setting, and

3. structuring.

Wallis (1994) suggests a similar four-phase process:

1. baseline analysis,

2. problem setting,

3. strategy setting, and

4. structuring.

Uncertainty needs to be tolerated in the developmental stages of building coordination strategies. It is important to understand that no one person can entirely control the development process; therefore, outcomes cannot be fully predicted or evaluated. Service coordination efforts may overlap, and some partners may participate in more than one partnership. Partnerships take time to build, often more than a year. Not all partners can be expected to participate equally (see Roberts-DeGennaro & Mizrahi, Chapter 16, this volume).

Exchange. One of the most helpful concepts for practitioners engaged in service coordination efforts is exchange. Exchange theory is an overall framework that is useful in analyzing what different actors give and get in partnership arrangements. It also serves as a way of thinking about what incentives might encourage the development and sustaining of partnerships (Schmidt & Kocan, 1977). Partnerships in which there is a clear and mutually beneficial exchange (e.g., clients, funding, service resources, or information) are likely to be successful. Partnerships that lack a balanced exchange are less likely to be successful (Wimpfheimer, Bloom, & Kramer, 1990).

Both commonalities and differences are required for an exchange to take place and for successful partnerships to be developed. Agencies that are very similar in terms of services and clients will probably have little incentive to coordinate because they are essentially only competitors. On the other hand, agencies that share almost nothing in terms of mission also have little to gain through coordination because there is little to be exchanged. Agencies that can benefit their own position by advocating for a common position, sharing resources, or making beneficial referrals have a strong incentive for coordination. It also should be recognized that in many instances, the same pair of agencies may operate as both collaborators and competitors at different times, depending on the particular client served or service provided. In such situations, emphasis needs to be placed on clearly identifying the areas of collaboration.

Improving the Success of Service Coordination Efforts

A series of steps can improve efforts of service coordination. Among the more important are the following:

- *Clarify agency interests.* Identify the incentives and disincentives for a particular agency to get involved in service coordination efforts.

- *Start with the most interested allies, who are likely to be able to produce the most impact.* Interest or commitment between potential partners is likely to vary, and realistically, some may be so resistant as to make their inclusion not worthwhile.

- *Start closest to home.* Similarly, it makes sense to initially involve potential partners with whom relationships have already been built.

- *Understand the history of relationships among potential actors and the history of prior service coordination efforts in that area or with a specific population.* Whether negative or positive, prior collaborative efforts should be analyzed and acknowledged as they may either support or hinder future efforts.

- *Be realistic about the scope of a particular service coordination effort.* Limiting the scope of a particular service coordination effort may be practical. Universal service coordination among all relevant agencies and services or among all the "silos" discussed above may be a generally positive goal, but it would be very difficult to achieve. Building the potential network of linkages needed to achieve a fully integrated system would be a monumental task, particularly in a large city. It is not unusual to have hundreds of agencies and services in a major metropolitan area. The potential relationships among sets of agencies could run into the thousands. The management of these relationships would be impossible even if there were a will to do so.

• *Determine a reasonable size.* The inclusion of too many participants in a coordination effort will be likely to make the partnership effort too unwieldy to sustain. On the other hand, having too few participants may limit the potential benefit.

• *Decide how comprehensive the coordination effort should be.* There are probably practical limits to how many domains can be successfully included in one partnership. More success may be achieved by focusing on discrete client groups or problems such as abused and neglected children, the aged, or the mentally ill. Although service partnerships within domains such as services for children and families or aging and adult mental illness may work, there may be too little in common between these two service population-oriented systems to promote reasons and practices to make them coordinate effectively with each other.

• *Focus on a limited geographic neighborhood.* In a dense urban community, this might be an area that could be reached within 10 minutes by foot or an area served by a neighborhood elementary or junior high school. This geographic compactness reduces some of the complexity of a service network.

• *Reach agreement about the intensity of the coordination effort.* Fleishman et al., in their review of the literature, recognized that coordination efforts differ by "the degree to which one entity can impose binding decisions on other agencies" (1992, p. 550). The same authors also discuss the advantages and disadvantages of whether a service provider or non-service provider should serve as the lead agency.

• *Realistically assess the costs and benefits.* Resources needed for partnerships include money, time, and people. It must be understood that service coordination requires professional resources to achieve success.

• *Don't shortcut process.* Crowson, Boyd, and Mawhinney (1996) discuss service coordination from a "new institutionalism" perspective which suggests that institutional stability is the paramount consideration for agencies and that unless service coordination efforts change the "core technology" of the agency, such efforts will be vulnerable and seen only as an expendable add-on to the core mission of the agency. They suggest the need to reach staff at all levels of an agency through "infection" of coordination perspectives.

• *Decide on how citizens or consumers can be involved.* Typically, service coordination efforts involve only agency representatives. Adelman and Taylor (1997) suggest that if nonagency forces can be involved, a more comprehensive effort can evolve, which can help to create an overall community development or community-building process. Similarly, Edelman (2001) discusses the benefits of community-based initiatives that involve service integration and community building.

Examples of Successful Partnerships

Two examples of successful partnerships will be presented, and the factors related to their effectiveness will be discussed. Both partnerships are middle-range, community-level service coordination efforts (see Table 21.1) that were developed in Aurora, Illinois, an old industrial city about 40 miles west of Chicago. This city of 150,000 is quite diverse; about 35% of its citizens are either Latino or African American.

School/Community Partnership

Our first example is a partnership that was established in a middle school in 1996. The school first approached the local university and a few agencies to help deal with problems manifested by students. What evolved was a partnership that now involves some 25 agencies that provide services in the school, including recreational/development type services, prevention services such as violence reduction classes, and services to deal with individual/family problems. A good deal of literature is related to community-school partnerships, sometimes called full-service schools or community schools (Boyd & Boyd 1996; Briar-Lawson, Lawson, Collier, & Joseph, 1997; Edelman, 2001; Smylie & Crowson, 1996). Details of the Aurora school-community partnership are discussed in Morrison et al. (1997).

Several issues had to be dealt with initially. The school wanted agencies to operate only as "helpers" under the direction of school personnel. This was, of course, unacceptable to the independent agencies, who demanded a degree of autonomy even when working in a school. It was determined that independent oversight of the partnership was needed, and this was assigned to the local affiliate of Communities in Schools, a national organization that provides liaison between schools and external organizations. A staff person was hired to develop coordination and provide case management.

A second problem involved the expectation by agencies that they would be allocated additional funds to provide services in the school. However, several funders represented in the partnership, including the local mental health board, insisted that agencies could provide services in the school by simply relocating some staff resources. The authority of the funders prevailed, with the agencies feeling some implied threat that regular funding might be jeopardized if they did not provide the school-based services without additional financial support.

The project operates under an advisory board that includes participating agencies, funders, the school principal, the school district superintendent, and a faculty member from the local university. Each year, several social work graduate students have their field placements in participating agencies. Although there was an almost-immediate dramatic reduction in school suspensions and an increase in parent participation following program implementation, school officials expressed considerable concern during the first few years of the project that academic performance had not significantly improved. However, research results most recently have shown that there is also an improvement in academic performance.

This partnership has now operated for 5 years, and agencies, schools, funders, and city leaders are strongly committed to continuing to operate in this coordinated and co-located manner. The program has now been extended to two additional schools, and additional funding has been secured. The project has received an award for Excellence in Community Collaborations for Children and Youth Program from the national Local Collaboration for Children and Youth, a group comprising six national organizations, including the U.S. Conference of Mayors and the National Association of School Administrators.

Factors Related to Success of the School-Community Partnership

- *Limited scope*—it was focused on a neighborhood-based school.
- *Support*—key funders were highly involved and supportive.
- *Clear leadership*—one relatively independent agency provided leadership and coordination of the collaborative effort.
- *Authority*—key community leaders (e.g., the school superintendent) wanted the project to be successful.
- *Balanced exchange*—agencies got clients; schools got needed services.
- *Formalization of agreements*—partnership agreements were formalized in a way that was acceptable to participating agencies.

This project represents a growing movement to coordinate social services and schools successfully in what variously have been described as community schools, full-service schools, or school-based or school-linked services (Adelman & Taylor, 1997).

The Drug Prevention Task Force

Our second partnership example deals with efforts to prevent and diminish substance abuse and violence among local youth. These are the major problems that were identified in surveys of local residents and community leaders conducted by the local university's school of social work under the sponsorship of United Way of the Aurora Area.

Sponsorship of the Red Ribbon Task Force was undertaken by the City of Aurora Youth Department, using funds from a federal drug prevention grant. Some 25 organizations are involved, including the Aurora Police Department, local school districts, the county health department, several direct-service agencies, and the local university. The focus of the task force is drug, alcohol, tobacco, and violence prevention. Monthly task force meetings involve information exchange among agencies as well as planning for a year-round series of prevention activities. Major events include a fall citywide campaign including a rally, an interdenominational prayer service, and a law enforcement recognition luncheon. An interesting activity is a calendar project through which students at public and private schools submit posters to a citywide competition. The 12 entries judged to be the best are included in a special annual calendar that features each month's scheduled prevention activities.

Factors Related to Success of the Task Force

- *Mandate*—a clear community need was addressed.
- *Critical leadership and support*—this was provided by city officials.

- *Clear exchange*—publicity for agency activities was provided; opportunities for agency involvement in a very public effort to deal with major community problems were expanded; and opportunities for groups such as schools to receive additional resources in the form of prevention programs were established.
- *Common purpose*—the realization that the drug and violence problems in the area could be dealt with most effectively on a citywide basis became the prevailing perspective.
- *Legitimacy*—the umbrella provided legitimacy, auspice, and institutional support for each agency's activities.

This program also parallels national efforts. The federal government has clearly identified partnerships or coalition building as a major strategy in drug prevention efforts. Some funding to communities has been made on a two-phase basis. An initial coalition building/planning phase requires that coalitions actually be formed and that joint planning efforts take place that result in proposals that involving cooperative efforts between partners. Failure to form a coalition or develop cooperative plans precludes the second stage of funding, which covers actual implementation. Such results-based funding is a fairly powerful incentive for cooperation.

General Principles Related to Success

These examples shared several commonalities. Each focused on issues of limited scope but dealt with problems that were of clear concern to the community. Because of the critical nature of the issues, all relevant agencies had an incentive to be involved in coordination. A clear exchange existed in which agencies both contributed to the collaboration and received benefits as well. In each case, there was a strong lead agency and at least one clearly defined individual leader who convened meetings.

There were also differences. The school partnership required more change in the way that partner agencies conducted their day-to-day work, and there was more resistance at some points in the process of development of the partnership. The drug prevention task force was a new initiative, so existing ways of working were less impacted. The drug prevention task force also was able to use new monies, so reallocation of resources was not an issue.

Wimpfheimer et al. (1990) identify both preconditions (mutuality, timing, authority/influence, and creativity) as well as conditions ("everyone's a winner," acknowledging responsibility, common risk, and acceptance of limits) that are associated with successful interagency collaboration efforts.

Factors that are critical for success are the following:

- Clear purpose
- Beneficial exchange
- Good leadership by a lead agency (or individual) with legitimacy or authority
- Manageable/limited scope

The Role of the Worker or Leadership Team

Beyond contextual factors, how the lead worker or team operates has a great deal to do with the ultimate success of service coordination efforts. The worker or team who is responsible for interagency coordination needs to keep in mind a number of suggestions related to the phases of intervention.

Initial Phase in Development of Service Coordination

- Identify the costs and benefits of service coordination for clients and the community.
- Prioritize the agencies and individuals that need to be involved in the service coordination effort.
- Assess the fit between and among agencies.
- Determine agency competencies and specializations, and identify common interests.
- Determine the costs and benefits of service coordination for agencies.
- Identify potential agency representatives. The ideal agency representative is someone in the agency who is both committed to service coordination and able to speak with authority on behalf of the agency.
- Begin to assess the scope of the service coordination effort. Which groups of clients are likely to need other services, and what are the types of services likely to be needed? Which services are in short supply? These types of questions can be addressed by reviewing current referral patterns, identifying areas in which referrals and available resources do not match, and determining which services are desired.
- Try to get buy-in from as high a level of administrative offices and community leaders as possible.

Ongoing Phase of Service Coordination Operation

- Meetings of the full partnership are only one part of the process. The lead worker or leadership team should maintain communication with individual members between meetings.
- Expectations must be communicated to all participants early in the process.
- Understandings, agreements, and major decisions can be recorded and used to sustain interest.
- Both persistence and flexibility are important for the worker and/or leadership team.
- Good communication, including honest and timely responses, is important. Good listening skills are important in being able to determine the attitudes of those who are involved in collaborative efforts.
- The key worker or leadership team will need to provide a clear summary of meetings and take good notes.
- Agreements between and among agencies should be committed to writing.

- Group dynamics within the partnership need to be continually reassessed, as they often determine ultimate success.
- Participants should strive for a sound balance between product and process.

Conclusion

Efforts to coordinate social services have been part of social work for more than a century. Social workers can improve the outcomes of such efforts through understanding basic theory related to interorganizational work and through developing clarity about the purpose and limits of an intended collaborative effort. Basic community practice skills are critical in achieving success.

References

Adelman, H. S., & Taylor, L. (1997). Addressing barriers to learning: Beyond school-linked services and full-service schools. *American Journal of Orthopsychiatry, 67*(3), 408–421.

Adler, L. (1994). Individual versus institutional factors. In L. Adler & S. Gardner (Eds.), *The politics of linking schools and social services: 1993 Yearbook of the Politics of Education Association* (pp. 1–18). Washington, DC: Falmer.

Austin, M. J. (Ed.). (1997). Human services integration. *Administration in Social Work, 21*(3/4), Special issue.

Backer, T. E., & Norman, A. J. (1999). Partnerships and community change. *California Politics and Policy, 5*(1), 39–44.

Beatrice, D. F. (1990). Inter-agency coordination: A practitioner's guide to a strategy for effective social policy. *Administration in Social Work, 14*(4), 45–60.

Boyd, R. L., & Boyd, W. L. (1996). Achieving coordinated school-linked services: Facilitating utilization of the emerging knowledge base. *Educational Policy, 10*(2), 140–179.

Briar-Lawson, K., Lawson, H. A., Collier, C., & Joseph, A. (1997). School-linked comprehensive services: Promising beginnings, lessons learned, and future challenges. *Social Work in Education, 19*(3), 137–148.

Bronstein, L. R. (2003). A model for interdisciplinary collaboration. *Social Work, 48*(3), 297–306.

Crowson, R. L., Boyd, W. L., & Mawhinney, H. M. (Eds.). (1996). Introduction and overview. In *The politics of education and the new institutionalism: Reinventing the American school: 1995 Yearbook of the Politics of Education Association* (pp. 1-7). Washington, DC: Falmer.

Dill, A. E. P., & Rochefort, D. A. (1989). Coordination, continuity, and centralized control: A policy perspective on service strategies for the chronic mentally ill. *Journal of Social Issues, 45*(3), 145–149.

Dunst, C. J., & Bruder, M. B. (2002). Valued outcomes of service coordination, early intervention, and natural environments. *Exceptional Children, 68*(3), 361–375.

Edelman, I. (2001). Participation and service integration in community-based initiatives. *Journal of Community Practice, 9*(1), 57–76.

Farel, A. M., & Rounds, K. A. (1998). Perceptions about the implementation of a statewide service coordination program for young children: Importance of organized context. *Families in Society: The Journal of Contemporary Human Services, 79*(6), 606–614.

Fleishman, J. A., Mor, V., Piette, J. D., & Allen, S. M. (1992). Organizing AIDS service consortia: Lead agency identity and consortium cohesion. *Social Service Review, 66*(4), 547–570.

Goering, P., & Rogers, J. (1986). A model for planning interagency coordination. *Canada's Mental Health, 34*(1), 5–8.

Kunz, C. (2000, December). *Effective collaboration.* Paper presented at the meeting for Center for Mental Health Services School and Community Action Grantees, Washington, DC.

Lehman, A. F. (1989). Strategies for improving services for the chronic mentally ill. *Hospital and Community Psychiatry, 40*(9), 917–920.

Lynn, L. E. (1976). Organizing human services in Florida. *Evaluation, 3*(1/2), 58–97.

Meyers, M. K. (1993). Organizational factors in the integration of services for children. *Social Service Review, 67*(4), 547–575.

Miller, K., Scott, C. R., Stage, C., & Birkholt, M. (1995). Communication and coordination in an inter-organizational system: Service provision for the urban homeless. *Communication Research, 22*(6), 679–699.

Mitchell, D. E., & Scott, L.D.. (1996). Institutional theory and the social structure of education. In R. L. Crowson, W. L. Boyd, & H. M. Mawhinney (Eds.), *The politics of education and the new institutionalism: Reinventing the American school: 1995 yearbook of the Politics of Education Association* (pp. 167–188). Washington, DC: Falmer.

Morrison, J. D., Howard, J., Johnson, C., Navarro, F. J., Plachetka, B., & Bell, T. (1997). Rebuilding and empowering neighborhoods by developing community networks. *Social Work, 42*(5), 527–534.

Mulroy, E. A., & Shay, S. (1998). Motivation and reward in nonprofit interorganizational collaboration in low-income neighborhoods. *Administration in Social Work, 22*(4), 1–17.

O'Looney, J. (1994). Modeling collaboration and social services integration: A single state's experience with developmental and non-developmental models. *Administration in Social Work, 11*(1), 61–86.

Reisch, M., & Sommerfeld, D. (2003). Interorganizational relationships among nonprofits in the aftermath of welfare reform. *Social Work, 48*(30), 307–329.

Reitan, T. C. (1998). Theories of interorganizational relations in the human services. *Social Services Review, 72*(3), 285–309.

Rosenblatt, A. (1996). Bows and ribbons, tape and twine: Wrapping the wraparound process for children with multi-system needs. *Journal of Child and Family Studies, 5*(1), 101–117.

Schmidt, S. M., & Kocan, T. A. (1977). Interorganizational relationships: Patterns and motivations. *Administrative Science Quarterly, 22*(2), 220–234.

Shern, D. L., Surles, R. C., & Waizer, J. (1989). Designing community treatment systems for the most seriously mentally ill: A state administrative perspective. *Journal of Social Issues, 45*(3), 101–117.

Smylie, M. A., & Crowson, R. L. (1996). Working with the scripts: Building institutional infrastructure for children's service coordination in schools. *Educational Policy, 10*(1), 3–21.

Wallis, A. D. (1994). *Networks, trust, and values: Improving local human services.* Denver, CO: National Civic League Press.

Wimpfheimer, R., Bloom, M., & Kramer, M. (1990). Inter-agency collaboration: Some working principles. *Administration in Social Work, 14*(4), 89–102.

CHAPTER 22

Rural Community Practice

Organizing, Planning, and Development

Iris Carlton-LaNey

Susan Murty

Lynne Clemmons Morris

The basic principles of community practice are as relevant in rural areas as they are in cities. The major models of community practice have been successfully applied in rural communities (Weil, 1996a, 1996b; Weil & Gamble, 1995). Indeed, a number of basic practices used throughout community practice were also evident in the earliest work in the Rural Development Movement in the United States (Christenson & Robinson, 1989; Weil, 1996b). There is a long tradition of rural community practice, and aspects of the rural locale give it a unique character. Historical forces that affected rural areas have, however, left their influence, creating specific challenges to effective practice. Community practice strategies have been applied in rural areas in ways that draw on the assets of rural communities while addressing the challenges these communities face. Rural life is distinctly different from life in more population-dense environments, however, and rural community practitioners must understand and appreciate these differences. The most successful practitioners will recognize and draw on the unique aspects of these tight-knit and often tradition-rich communities while building on current strengths, addressing current needs, and finding strategies to deal with specific economic, social, and political challenges that accompany rural life. For these reasons, a chapter focused on rural practice is included in this volume.

Identifying the Community

Residents of rural areas generally have a strong sense of place and/or belonging to a community. Early rural communities in the United States generally encompassed an area that was accessible on foot or by horse and buggy with a social and commercial hub comprising a general store, a school, at least one church, and perhaps a post office. Over the last 50 to 75 years, however, good "farm-to-market" roads, along with automobiles and trucks, have made it possible to travel considerable distance to transport crops or purchase needed products in a reasonable time frame. As a result, rural communities have become less isolated. As rural residents increasingly interact with city dwellers, or have to travel to towns or cities to find work, the time to invest in close "hometown" relations may diminish, and it becomes more difficult to maintain the expected level of interactions with family and friends. Local or small town stores in rural America are increasingly threatened by "Walmartization" and many local businesses have failed as a result of the growth of "big-box-low-price" stores. The political economies of rural areas of America have been greatly affected by these trends and by the rapid industrialization of farming, resulting in large agribusinesses squeezing out family farmers. Increased mobility, the necessity to commute to cities for jobs, and the incursions of strip malls have caused a blurring of community boundaries.

The increased economic pressure involved in living on the land or in rural townships has major effects on social and community life, and community practitioners may have to work harder in nourishing or rebuilding connections. Community practice in rural areas is based on involving local players and stakeholders as well as local formal and informal organizations in community services and development. Practitioners now often have to facilitate regeneration of local investment and commitment. Positive engagement with and acceptance by local informal networks is a necessary function for rural social workers.

In the past, many researchers have used geographic and administrative lines, such as county or township lines, to set the boundaries of rural communities. It is clear that such communities will vary in the amount of communication, exchange, and sense of identity they share. Because of improvements in transportation and communications and the increase in interaction between rural and urban areas, rural communities are becoming less and less self-contained and isolated (Carlton-LaNey, Edwards, & Reid, 1999). On the other hand, in most cases, a county is too large to be considered a single community. Counties usually contain numerous small towns, and their residents identify these towns as their communities. Frequently, school districts function as communities because children and parents share social activities and institutions. Rather than make assumptions, it is wise to allow rural residents to identify what they perceive as their community. Conversations with residents, attendance at local events and activities, church affiliations, local newspaper coverage, and school district boundaries all provide sources of information useful for identifying communities.

Communities of common interest must be distinguished from geographic communities. Within any particular geographic community, a variety of groups exist, and no one person can accurately claim to speak for the entire community. Because communities are made up of groups whose interests may conflict, it is often difficult to determine a community's choices or the degree to which its diverse residents participate in decision making.

Much research on rural areas has neglected the study of conflict and controversy in rural communities. Often, these communities are thought to be homogeneous when actually they are characterized by significant diversity. Like urban communities, rural ones have social divisions based on social class, race, ethnicity, and status as a "come here" or a "from here." A growing division in many areas relates to the in-migration of "snowbirds," "in-betweeners," and other relatively well-to-do people from urban areas, who are retiring to rural communities with results as varied as changes in types of restaurants and sharp increases in taxes. In addition, in rural communities, history is always present at the table, and whatever community discussions and decision processes take place, locals may well not only see the person at the table, but also envision his or her parents and even grandparents—remembering their positions on earlier community issues (Messinger, 1999). However, as in most other parts of the United States, race is likely to be the strongest force of division in rural communities.

The initial division by race in North America occurred when colonists forced forest, woodlands, plains, and mesa Indian tribes first off their lands and later onto reservations, which tend to be not only rural, but the poorest land in any given area. Most reservations are among the poorest communities in the nation, and few tribal groups have been able to maintain their traditional rural economic base (Snipp, 1996).

There are nearly 4 million African Americans in rural areas, 3.5 million of whom live in the South. In many Southwestern states, Mexican farmers and ranchers were established long before European farmers and ranchers settled there. Currently, a substantial migrant labor population, many of whom become permanent residents, has contributed to a new cultural diversity in many rural areas of the nation. The Hispanic population continues to grow rapidly in rural areas. For example, the first detailed U.S. Census Bureau estimates since the 2000 census indicate that the state of Georgia is estimated to have experienced a 17% increase in the Latino population between July 2000 and July 2002, to total 516,000 Latino residents (U.S. Census Bureau, 2000). North Carolina's growth is ranked second, with a 16% growth in the Latino population from July 2000 to July 2002, indicating a Latino population of about 444,463 (Armas, 2003). Of the 10 North Carolina counties with the largest percentage of Latinos, 8 are rural (Raynor & Reid, 2001). This demographic shift has caused considerable tensions and conflicts over housing, school, employment, and other services and resources (Johnson, Johnson-Webb, & Farrell, 1999). Although Americans may tend to romanticize rural communities, we also are inclined to ignore or minimize the racial tensions and the competition for scarce resources that are an enduring and growing aspect of these communities as well (Snipp, 1996).

Defining Rurality

Rural areas have been identified by a variety of characteristics, including small population size; low density of population; long distance from large population centers;

certain types of occupations and economic bases such as agriculture, mining, and fishing; and social factors such as primary relationships, traditional norms, and values. The categories *farm* and *nonfarm* have been used in much research in rural sociology, but because the number of farm owners living in rural areas has been steadily decreasing (Davenport & Davenport, 1995), using *farm* as a definition relates only to a limited sector of modern rural society and so is no longer particularly useful in discussions of rural communities.

Nonmetropolitan is a term used by the U.S. Bureau of the Census to categorize any area that is not included in a metropolitan statistical area of 50,000 people or more. *Rural* is used to categorize any place with a population of less than 2,500 people. These two categories are not mutually exclusive: There are rural areas within metropolitan areas, and many nonmetropolitan areas do not qualify as rural.

Essentially, the concept of rurality is relative, and any particular community can be located somewhere on a continuum from urban to rural. In fact, Davenport and Davenport (1995) suggest that a number of definitions of *rural* that are more liberal than the Census Bureau's indicate that the portion of the population in small towns and rural areas is much greater than the Census Bureau's estimate.

The discussion in this chapter is applicable to a wide range of communities, from those that are moderately rural to those that are extremely rural, very low in population, and isolated from urban areas. Because the unique characteristics of communities should always guide the community practitioner, those characteristics are much more important than some arbitrary definition of *rural.*

Whatever their definition, rural communities are changing. During the 1970s, the population increased more rapidly in rural areas than in urban areas (Beale, 1996). Although populations in suburban areas and communities within commuting distance of metropolitan areas are increasing, in many parts of the rural United States, populations are now decreasing. Rural communities continue to experience an exodus of young adults looking for education and employment opportunities in metropolitan areas. Indeed, in some areas of persistent poverty, such as Appalachia, those who can gain sufficient skills to leave often do so. "The rural poor in the Appalachian mountains live in concentrated poverty, much like those in the nation's troubled inner-cities"; however, these youth lack access to many programs and institutions that can be of assistance to urban youth (Duncan, 1992, p. 131).

> In the poor coal communities of Appalachia, these programs (e.g., job training, skill development, child-care) are part of a corrupt patronage system, and the poor have been assigned permanent places at the bottom of the social structure. The rigid stratification system, a small world of haves and have-nots, means that there is no public-sector investment that buffers the inequalities and offers opportunities for those who want to work hard and escape poverty. (Duncan, 1992, p. 131)

In addition, many rural areas in the South and Midwest continue to see rapid growth in the population of young immigrant or migrant families; many of their members are Latino, and almost all of them are seeking work—even very low-wage work. These families are subject to discrimination, at the least, and at worst to contemporary forms of indentured servitude.

Poverty

Poverty limits options for everyone, including residents of rural communities. On the average, rural households have lower incomes than those in urban areas; many rural households live at or below the poverty level, even when both parents work (Carlton-LaNey et al., 1999; Davenport & Davenport, 1995). Many rural communities also suffer from recurring farm crises (Jacobsen & Albertson, 1987). Unemployment and seasonal employment are common, and the jobs that are available are often low-paying and do not provide benefits (Besser, 1998). Employment opportunities are especially bleak for women in rural areas. In the South, the systemic oppression and the long-term connection between race and poverty continues and has particularly cruel effects on single-parent families. As Dill and Williams report,

> Low wages and seasonal employment, when combined with child-care burdens and other gender specific factors, tend to keep poor women poor. . . . Employment in these near-minimum wage jobs rarely provides for unemployment insurance, medical benefits, or retirement. Thus even those who acquire a decent living through work are vulnerable to poverty as periods of unemployment follow or are interspersed with periods of employment. (1992, p. 105)

In addition, rural elders are more than 50% more likely to be poor than their urban counterparts. Elders with multiple risk factors, such as being very old, widowed, grade school-educated, African American, and female, have the highest poverty rates of all (Glasgow & Brown, 1998).

Pockets of especially deep poverty coincide with the areas in which rural minority groups are concentrated: American Indian reservations, Latino *colonias* (settlements of Hispanic workers throughout the rural Southwest), and African American communities (Snipp, 1996). Over the years, tribal sovereignty has brought a modicum of self-sufficiency to American Indians who live on reserved lands; yet most American Indians on these reservations remain poor. Gaming has brought money and enhanced the tourism business in some of these areas, and for some tribes, this has meant a newfound wealth that has spilled outside the reservation to improve the economic situation of the surrounding small towns. Unlike American Indians who live on reservations or Hispanics who live in *colonias,* rural African Americans live in communities that often have no formal or specific name. Nonetheless, these areas are an easily identifiable section of the landscape in the South. Sometimes referred to as the "Black Belt," the "bottoms," or the "quarters," these communities are home to 90% of the African American population living in rural areas. However, these communities have not benefited from the southern economic boom of the 1970s and 1980s (Carlton-LaNey et al., 1999).

Wherever these rural communities of color are located and regardless of the ethnicity of the inhabitants, they suffer from a lack of public services and are subject to the whims of policymakers, as public opinion typically encourages the flow of funds to more urban areas (Duncan, 1992). Rural and poor African American, American Indian, and Latino communities share several characteristics, including the fact that they are usually poor and physically isolated from mainstream society.

Many rural residents are geographically isolated, living many miles from highways on dirt roads that may be seasonably impassable due to floods, mud, and snow. Many women, especially older ones, do not have driver's licenses or have decided to discontinue driving because of health-related problems. There is often no public transportation of any kind, and where it does exist, it is difficult to access. Many rural households still do not have telephone service, and even when they do, communicating by phone often involves expensive long-distance toll charges.

Characteristics of Rural Communities

Lack of Anonymity—Everyone Knows Everyone

Farley, Griffiths, Skidmore, and Thackeray (1982) describe the lack of anonymity as an *open communication system*. Within an open communication system, news and information travel fast, and people generally are aware of each other's comings and goings. Because of this system, rural life is sometimes described as a "fish bowl." An important aspect of communities with small populations is that the residents tend to be acquainted with each other in multiple ways and have very little privacy. Those who advocate the use of natural and informal support systems often claim that rural residents have stronger, more cohesive support systems than do residents of urban areas (Ginsberg, 1993; Martinez-Brawley, 1990). They argue that these advantages of rural areas are a direct result of the low density of population, the high density of social networks, and the high proportion of acquaintanceship, as well as the more traditional values and norms of behavior in rural areas.

While the close-knit community is in many ways a strength, lack of anonymity can create special problems with confidentiality (Johnson, 1998). Close rural social networks can either support or block effective social services (Ginsberg, 1993). A distrust of outsiders is another feature associated with the close-knit rural community. Individuals who have lived in a rural community for 10 years or more are still often considered newcomers by the long-term residents. Furthermore, there are frequently negative attitudes toward formal social services, especially when provided by "outsiders."

Local Power Structure and Denial of Conflict

The local power structures in rural communities often allow a few individuals to influence local services according to their personal values and interests. Although such "good old boy" or "best families" networks can exist in any community, evidence suggests that they are a more serious problem in rural areas. Where population size is small, opposing interest groups often do not have sufficient critical mass or sufficient access to decision making to challenge the local power structure successfully (Davenport & Davenport, 1995; Ginsberg, 1993). Because the "good old boy network" affords local power only to White men, and because members of the "best families," who in small communities have considerable control over social norms, usually are White and relatively well-to-do, populations of color are often excluded from the community power structure. Moreover, rural communities often ostracize or act with hostility toward those who do not acquiesce to the accepted community norms. The failure of outsiders to conform to specific community expectations for behavior contributes to an air of suspicion toward them.

Traditional Attitudes About Sources of Assistance and Human Services

Attitudes in rural communities also dictate some degree of suspicion of government interference and uneasiness with the growth of public services and welfare programs. Rural attitudes change gradually but lag behind urban attitudes. For example, in many rural communities, it is still often considered inappropriate to go to formal service providers for assistance. Rural people often value individualism and self-sufficiency, and "family problems" are expected to be kept within the family. Although shared traditional attitudes and values foster a *sense of community* (Farley et al., 1982), they may also deter rural families and individuals from availing themselves of public or nonprofit human services. The early rejection of the Head Start program by many rural poor White families is an example. Community compassion and concern are essential elements that encourage communities to take care of their own without outside intervention, but with changing times and worsening economic conditions, these networks of care and concern are now more strained.

Assets of Rural Communities

Although rural families may be slow to approach human service providers, the social workers and community practitioners in rural areas are usually closely connected. Indeed, interagency cooperation is a strong asset in many rural communities (Farley et al., 1982; Locke, Garrison, & Winship, 1998). The limited numbers of public agencies in these communities work cooperatively. Recognition of the shortage of services and programs encourages practitioners to collaborate and cooperate for the good of the community. Essentially, community practitioners involve and build on the assets of their communities. Effective rural practitioners must align themselves with the strong rural community traditions and primary social institutions within each community.

Churches are important organizations in rural communities. They provide social services that are generally provided by formal social agencies in more populated areas. For example, in West Liberty, Iowa, a rural community in the Midwest, the Ministerial Association organizes social and community events such as the ecumenical vacation Bible school in the summer and Bible study at the local nursing home. Churches also often provide child care or house Head Start programs and may have volunteers to provide food for people in emergency situations or to transport them to medical appointments. In one North Carolina county, a volunteer program was developed to train community members to be supportive friends to people with severe and persistent mental illnesses and to provide transportation for them (Gammonley, 1998).

There are also strong formal organizations in rural areas. The County Extension Service of the U.S. Department of Agriculture is an enduring example (Austin & Betten, 1990; Coward, Van Horn, & Jackson, 1986; Crawford, 1986). County Extension programs are designed to link experts from universities with local rural communities, and their directors are important contacts in many counties. Land grant university-based Cooperative Extension Departments offer a wide variety of programs and services designed to help individuals, families, and communities put research-based knowledge to work to improve their lives. Although in the past these programs have emphasized dissemination of information about agricultural techniques, they have more recently developed a variety of new programs. Some of these have been designed to respond to farmers devastated by the rural crisis (Crawford, 1986), but others focus on common family problems or on establishing family support programs. Still others provide information to help communities engage in employment training or economic development as well as strategic planning for decision making on environmental or economic development issues.

Other organizations with potential to assist rural social and health programs include agricultural conservation and stabilization programs, the Farmers' Home Administration, the U.S. Forest Service, and rural Job Corps programs. However, government programs that target rural areas have historically tended to exclude African Americans, resulting in years of unnecessary financial hardship, bankruptcies, and land loss. These years of systematic exclusion have resulted in a class action lawsuit. In 1999, the U.S. Department of Agriculture (USDA) agreed to compensate African American farmers who suffered discrimination in lending practices. Although this potential settlement acknowledges one problem, it does not solve the multiple and long-standing problems of discrimination against African American farmers in relation to the USDA and other federal agencies.

Essentially, successful service delivery in rural areas must include an array of services and must involve interagency and interprofessional collaboration, as well as coordination between public services and the voluntary and informal sectors. Service providers must also work actively to discard the entrenched tradition of racism while seeking to include and empower disfranchised groups. Successful interventions that focus on the well-being of rural communities require knowledge that goes beyond medical or social expertise; in addition, they must address the social, psychological, economic, and environmental issues that face rural communities. Goicoechea-Balbona (1997) indicates that the interagency or interdisciplinary team should reflect the ethnocultural makeup of the target community. If this is not possible, an intervention team should at least seek out and use the consultation services of indigenous providers from the targeted group or culture. Furthermore, rural community practice must include rural development and strategies for including previously excluded groups. Women, elders, and people of color represent three groups often excluded from planning for social service programs. The discussion below presents some unique aspects of the problems that these groups encounter.

Challenges in Rural Settings

Women and Rural Domestic Violence

Some challenges of rural community practice can be illustrated by a discussion of the situation of rural battered women. Although rural communities have many positive characteristics, they are not immune to family violence, which presents a major challenge to service providers. Rural women often have greater difficulty getting assistance from law enforcement. Owing to personal relationships, these women are often hesitant to call the police. The "good old boys network" operates to pressure officers who are relatives and acquaintances of abusers not to take the violence seriously and to avoid arresting perpetrators or filing criminal charges.

Rural women may be less likely to acknowledge domestic violence or to turn to others for support because of the lack of anonymity. They also may hesitate to seek help because of the reactions of acquaintances, neighbors, friends, and kin. They may be reluctant to go to the emergency room at the hospital because staff members may be acquaintances or relatives of the abuser (Mauney, Williams, & Weil, 1993). Frequently, when battered women seek help, they are viewed with suspicion by people who believe that the accused is not capable of committing violent acts or who believe that the woman is violating some code of silence by openly accusing her partner.

Traditional attitudes that permeate rural communities add to the problem. Rural community members are expected, as noted, to avoid conflict and to keep family problems private. Attitudes of rugged individualism are common, and rural residents are often hesitant to ask for help or admit that they have problems. Women are often still expected to submit to their husbands, and physical abuse is commonly considered necessary for discipline of children and sometimes even for women. Rural communities may engage in active denial of the abuse that occurs in families (Ray & Murty, 1990). The church is very important to many rural women, but this organization may not provide an open and approachable environment. Essentially, domestic violence is considered a private matter closed to intervention from outsiders.

In areas populated by recently arrived Latino families, immigrant status provides a further complication. When victims are fearful of deportation, they may believe they have no recourse against the violence. Weissman (2000) suggests that to provide protection to immigrant women, service providers must form an alliance. Domestic violence shelters, law enforcement agencies, and social service agencies need to work closely together to protect battered women. Weissman adds that for such an alliance to be successful, "education, cross-disciplinary training, and a commitment to provide culturally sensitive services to victims" is imperative (p. 18).

Elder African American Return Migrants

The population of African American elders who are moving into small towns and rural communities throughout the South is growing at such a rapid rate that the phenomenon has become grist for both scholarly (Stack, 1996) and popular literature (Campbell, 1998). North Carolina has in recent years become a preferred destination for streams of retirees. Several factors, including the state's attractive quality of life and the relationships that African American elders have maintained with their homes of origin throughout the years, help explain why they are returning. In their youth, these individuals moved to urban areas, usually in the Northeast, to pursue employment opportunities; on retiring, they are returning to their state of birth (Waites & Carlton-LaNey, 1999).

Many of these return migrants are bringing skills, resources, entrepreneurial spirit, and willingness to invest in the social fabric of their home communities, qualities that contribute to the area's economic development. Hass and Crandall (1988) found that physicians in two rural North Carolina mountain communities felt that retirement migrants' effect on rural health care systems had altered them in positive ways. Essentially, the health care community has grown and adjusted to accommodate the needs of this new group of residents. Still other return migrants are coming back to their places of birth with very few resources and are looking to the community to provide needed services.

In their study of return migrants' use of senior centers in two North Carolina communities, Waites and Carlton-LaNey (1999) found that the return migrant African American population can be almost invisible if the majority population is White; most rural communities have no way of documenting their presence. It is only through informal mechanisms that they can be identified. Whether or not small towns or rural communities are prepared for this population, these return migrants are "coming home," with or without resources, and they are bringing with them the normal problems and issues of aging. Retirement migration is a complicating factor in planning for rural elders because of the tremendous diversity of the group and because most communities have not identified them as a unique and growing feature of the rural landscape. As these migrants, whether new to the area or returning home, need community resources, rural communities must prepare themselves to provide services.

Economic Development

Employment opportunities and economic development are perennial problems in rural areas. Because rural areas have been closely associated with farming, community practitioners have long been involved in activist struggles to maintain or restore stability as the economic base of family farming has eroded. More recently, rural community practitioners have been involved in such rural activist groups as the Southern Tenant Farmers' Union, the United Farm Workers Union (Fisher, 1994; Mitchell, 1987), and Prairie Fire. In Appalachia and other areas, many generations of rural men have worked at coal mining and have been engaged in unions and union organizing for miners (Duncan, 1992). More recently, many residents of Appalachia have been deeply involved in seeking alternative development (Hinsdale, Lewis, & Maxine, 1995) following mine closings, whereas others have fought against environmental degradation, particularly through the Highlander Center (1982).

Manufacturing wages are lower in rural areas, and capital expenditures per worker have declined relative to urban areas. Now manufacturers tend to move even low-wage operations from rural communities to other countries to take advantage of labor available in the global economy that is cheaper still (Bernat, 1995).

Some rural communities have come up with innovative approaches to economic development: in some areas by drawing tourists with gaming, historic preservation, country music shows, outdoor dramas, and other attractions (Ackerman, 1996; Jansen, 1995); some market their communities as retirement/recreation centers (Siegel, Leuthold, & Stallman, 1995). At the other extreme, a number of rural communities across the nation have encouraged prisons to relocate there (Beale, 1996) or have agreed to accept large-scale waste transfer sites.

As an example of this first strategy, the small Midwestern town of West Liberty is working to restore the historic train depot as part of efforts by the Chamber of Commerce and Heritage Trust to promote the town's unique artistic and historic character. The town has also worked to attract industry and has worked with a local turkey farmers' cooperative to keep the turkey processing plant open.

West Liberty is also home of the Owl Glass Puppetry Center. Its puppet theater troupe performs at the center and on tour, providing various school programs. It has helped to stimulate the growth of a community arts council and is also working with the Chamber of Commerce and local Heritage Foundation. In addition, the puppetry center contributes to community events and provides an after-school program and summer camp for children. Guest puppeteers of renown from the United States and other countries also perform there. The puppetry center has embraced a holistic approach to the community and is currently developing a puppet-making project as an employment training opportunity for women with low incomes.

Preserving the Rural Environment

Economic development in rural areas, however, has sometimes come at a substantial cost to the environment and raised issues of social justice with regard to how that environment has been used. Organizations such as the Highlander Center in Tennessee have helped to train and mobilize many rural groups to combat social injustice in their home communities and more widely (Carawan & Carawan, 1990; Horton, 1992).

Serious problems of environmental racism and rural environmental pollution have forced a number of people who would never have envisioned themselves as activists to become organizers against toxic and nuclear waste dumps, as well as against water and air pollution and destruction of land. People of color, especially in rural areas, are disproportionately subjected to toxins in their land, air, and water (Hall, 1988). This environmental racism is often carried out in the name of progress, profit, or goodwill. Companies and government agencies have for decades located toxic waste sites near or in African American communities (Hall, 1988). Likewise, many Southwestern Indian and Latino communities have been threatened by nuclear testing and location of nuclear waste dumps, and grassroots organizers, like those trained at the Highlander Center, have emerged to protect their homes, families, and communities from the invasion of environmental toxins. The First National People of Color Environmental Leadership Summit, held in 1991 in Washington, D.C., was attended by more than 650 grassroots and national workers.

Environmentalist Connie Tucker, executive director of the Atlanta-based Southern Committee for Economic and Social Justice, believes strongly that African Americans have been targets of environmental racism. At the summit, she said that "for Black people, this is the worst attack we've had since the Middle Passage, because the chemicals that we're getting exposed to are causing long-term, multi-generation damage" (Robinson, 1995, p. 44). If recent trends around environmental racism persist and other problems continue to encroach on the health and safety of rural communities, there will be a call for more and more activists, both grassroots and professional, to take leadership roles in protecting homes and communities.

Crossing the Digital Divide

Advancing technology offers some exciting new approaches for rural communities. Rural women can be encouraged to develop the skills they need to contact other rural women by means of the Internet to share experiences and resources (Kelly & Lauderdale, 1996). Service providers can also benefit from these new methods to overcome isolation in rural communities. The new technology can be especially important for isolated rural families. Distance education using Internet and other advanced technologies is now making additional educational opportunities available to rural areas (Morris, 1995). To take advantage of these new opportunities, private and public funding must be used to make computers accessible to residents of rural communities; otherwise, they will be left behind in the technological revolution. Unfortunately, many rural communities have inadequate telephone and cable access and carrying capacity, and the Telecommunications Act of 1996 may have made the situation worse through deregulation (Enders & Seekins, 1999; Sell, Leistritz, & Allen, 1999). Local Internet service providers are often unavailable in rural communities, requiring users to pay long-distance charges for access. The telephone and cable infrastructure must be improved to handle the projected increased communication by means of the Internet from rural communities. One exciting effort in this direction is the Rural Internet Connection being developed by the North Carolina Rural Development Center, which seeks to make Internet connections available throughout rural communities (North Carolina Rural Economic Development Center, n.d.).

Regional Service Delivery Issues

Regional service delivery is becoming more and more common in the United States—that is, rural areas are being served by programs that cover two or more counties and are administered from an office located in a central county or in the closest metropolitan area. Although it may provide economies of scale for the organization, regionalization has three principal drawbacks for rural communities: (a) absorption of small local service delivery organizations, (b) wide spatial dispersion of recipients of services in relation to the main headquarters of the organization, and (c) reduced participation in decision making by citizens and recipients from areas remote from the main headquarters. The delivery of rural health care is an example of this trend and of its drawbacks. The closing of rural hospitals has resulted in a decrease of services and added to the shortage of rural health care professionals, as well as having a negative effect on local economies and communities (Doelker & Bedics, 1989; Krout, 1998). Many of the surviving rural hospitals have been purchased by large corporations or have become part of various regional multihospital systems. Local medical practices and nursing homes in rural areas may now be operated by a larger medical practice, health maintenance organization, teaching hospital, or corporation. Nursing homes in particular are frequently owned and controlled by large health care corporations that are located in distant metropolitan headquarters and are unfamiliar with the communities they serve. Home-based nursing care is another service frequently provided by agencies that serve multiple counties and sometimes even multiple states (Krout, 1998).

The same pattern is evident in the delivery of other types of health and social services. Rural mental health services are now often provided by a multicounty community mental health center or through a multistate behavioral health maintenance organization. With the system reforms being undertaken in many states, which focus on the state contracting out to private mental health service providers, it is likely that rural areas will have even greater difficulty securing mental health care (see Scheyett & Drinnin, Chapter 23, this volume).

Services for elders are delivered by area agencies on aging, which almost always cover multicounty service regions in rural areas (Krout, 1998). Public welfare services may be administered by offices covering multiple counties or from county offices that are administered by district offices. Special education services for children may be provided by area education agencies or collaboratives that serve multiple school districts. Services for adults with disabilities may be planned by case management programs that are administered from a state office or regional offices located in several sites in the state. Family preservation services may be contracted to a large corporation covering a region of the state or even many states. Economic development services may be provided from regional offices covering many counties. These are just a few examples of a general trend toward regionalization that has transformed the way rural services are organized.

Because of the continuing trends toward centralization, and because of reductions in funding for services and pressures to cut costs and reduce taxes, regionalization of service delivery is not likely to disappear from the rural United States in the 21st century. Instead, local services are likely to continue being absorbed into large regional service areas and owned and controlled from metropolitan and urban centers. Proponents of regionalization argue that it is the most rational and efficient way to deliver services and that it improves access to services and quality of care for a whole region. Nonetheless, it is reasonable to question whether these claims are justified. Certainly, these new mechanisms are unlikely to meet rural people's expectations that they will be acquainted with service providers and their hopes that services will be available locally.

In conclusion, rural communities will be more successful in coming decades if they develop their own programs and strategies to meet their needs rather than attempting to imitate programs designed for urban environments. Because they have fewer resources and formal service providers and need to cover large, sparsely settled areas, rural programs must be resourceful. They must be carefully and respectfully crafted, taking into consideration traditions, community diversity, and local history. Resourcefulness and creativity are some of the rewarding aspects of rural community practice. Collaboration with local leaders and community organizations can be very effective. It can also empower workers to master the skills needed to help to bring about change and to help communities develop much-needed resources.

References

Ackerman, W. V. (1996). Deadwood, South Dakota: Gambling, historic preservation, and economic revitalization. *Rural Development Perspectives, 11*(2), 18–24.

Armas, G. C. (September 18, 2003). United States Hispanic population continues surge after Census. *The* (Raleigh, NC) *News & Observer* [from the Associated Press], Section A, p. 5.

Austin, M. J., & Betten, N. (1990). Rural organizing and the agricultural extension service. In N. Betten & M. J. Austin (Eds.), *The roots of community organizing 1917–1939* (pp. 94–105). Philadelphia: Temple University Press.

Beale, C. (1996). Rural prisons: An update. *Rural Development Perspectives, 11*(2), 25–27.

Bernat, G. A. (1995). An update on rural manufacturing: Rural capital expenditures lagged urban in 1992. *Rural Development Perspectives, 10*(2), 15–19.

Besser, T. L. (1998). Employment in small towns: Microbusinesses, part-time work, and lack of benefits characterize Iowa firms. *Rural Development Perspectives, 13*(2), 31–39.

Campbell, B. M. (1998). *Singing in the comeback choir.* New York: Putnam.

Carawan, G., & Carawan, C. (1990). *Songs for freedom: The story of the civil rights movement through its songs.* Bethlehem, PA: Sing Out.

Carlton-LaNey, I., Edwards, R., & Reid, N. (1999). Small towns and rural communities: From romantic notions to harsh realities. In I. Carlton-LaNey, R. Edwards, & N. Reid (Eds.), *Preserving and strengthening small towns and rural communities* (pp. 5–12). Washington, DC: NASW Press.

Christenson, J. A., & Robinson, J. W., Jr. (1989). *Community development in perspective.* Ames: Iowa State University Press.

Coward, R. T., Van Horn, J. E., & Jackson, R. W. (1986). The Cooperative Extension Service: An underused resource for rural primary prevention. In J. D. Murray & P. A. Keller (Eds.), *Innovations in rural community mental health* (pp. 105–120). Mansfield, PA: Mansfield University, Rural Services Institute.

Crawford, C. (1986). Response to the rural crisis: Missouri Cooperative Extension Service. *Human Services in the Rural Environment, 10*(1), 33–35.

Davenport, J., & Davenport, J. (1995). Rural social work overview. In R. Edwards (Ed.), *Encyclopedia of social work* (19th ed., pp. 2076–2085). Washington, DC: NASW Press.

Dill, B. T., & Williams, B. B. (1992). Race, gender, and poverty in the rural South: African American single mothers. In C. M. Duncan (Ed.), *Rural poverty in America* (pp. 97–109). New York: Auburn House.

Doelker, R. E., & Bedics, B. C. (1989). Impact of rural hospital closings on the community. *Social Work, 34*(6), 541–543.

Duncan, C. M. (1992). Persistent poverty in Appalachia: Scarce work and rigid stratification. In C. M. Duncan (Ed.), *Rural poverty in America* (pp. 111–134). New York: Auburn House.

Enders, A., & Seekins, T. (1999). Telecommunications access for rural Americans with disabilities. *Rural Development Perspectives, 14*(3), 14–21.

Farley, W., Griffiths, K., Skidmore, R., & Thackeray, M. (1982). *Rural social work practice.* New York: Free Press.

Fisher, R. (1994). *Let the people decide: Neighborhood organizing in America.* New York: Twayne.

Gammonley, D. L. (1998). *Social support in a lay helper intervention for older adults with severe mental illness.* Doctoral dissertation, University of North Carolina, Chapel Hill. (UMI No. 9902464)

Ginsberg, L. (1993). Introduction: An overview of rural social work. In L. H. Ginsberg (Ed.), *Social work in rural communities* (2nd ed., pp. 2–17). New York: Council on Social Work Education.

Glasgow, N., & Brown, D. (1998). Older, rural, and poor. In R. Coward & J. Krout (Eds.), *Aging in rural settings: Life circumstances and distinctive features* (pp. 187–207). New York: Springer.

Goicoechea-Balbona, A. (1997). Culturally specific health care model for ensuring health care use by rural ethnically diverse families affected by HIV/AIDS. *Health & Social Work, 22,* 172–180.

Hall, B. (1988). *Environmental politics: Lessons from the grassroots.* Durham, NC: Institute for Southern Studies.

Hass, W., & Crandall, L. (1988). Physicians' views of retirement migrants' impact on rural medical practice. *Gerontologist, 28,* 663–666.

Highlander Center (Producer). (1982). *You gotta move* [Motion picture]. (Available from Highlander Center, 1959 Highlander Way, New Market, TN 37820)

Hinsdale, M. A., Lewis, H. M., & Maxine, S. M. (1995). *It comes from the people: Community development and local theology.* Philadelphia: Temple University Press.

Horton, M. (with Kohl, J., & Kohl, H.). (1992). *The long haul: An autobiography.* Garden City, NY: Doubleday.

Jacobsen, G. M., & Albertson, B. S. (1987). Social and economic change in rural Iowa: The development of rural ghettos. *Human Services in the Rural Environment, 10*(4)/*11*(1), 58–65.

Jansen, A. C. (1995). American Indian gaming operations and local development. *Rural Development Perspectives, 10*(2), 2–7.

Johnson, H. W. (1998). Newer approaches in social work practice: The generalist. In H. W. Johnson & contributors, *The social services: An introduction* (5th ed.). Itasca, IL: F. E. Peacock.

Johnson, J., Johnson-Webb, K., & Farrell, W. (1999). A profile of Hispanic newcomers to North Carolina. *Popular Government, 65,* 2–13.

Kelly, M. J., & Lauderdale, M. L. (1996) The Internet: Opportunities for rural outreach and resource development. *Human Services in the Rural Environment, 19*(4), 4–9.

Krout, J. A. (1998). Services and service delivery in rural environments. In R. T. Coward & J. A. Krout (Eds.), *Aging in rural settings: Life circumstances and distinctive features* (pp. 247–266). New York: Springer.

Locke, B., Garrison, R., & Winship, J. (1998). *Generalist social work practice: Context, story, and partnerships.* Pacific Grove, CA: Brooks/Cole.

Martinez-Brawley, E. E. (1990). *Perspectives on the small community: Humanistic views for practitioners.* Silver Spring, MD: NASW Press.

Mauney, R., Williams, E., & Weil, M. (1993). *Beyond crisis: Developing comprehensive services for battered women in North Carolina.* Winston-Salem, NC: Z. Smith Reynolds Foundation.

Messinger, L. (1999). *History at the table: Planning a comprehensive community initiative in the rural South.* Unpublished doctoral dissertation, University of North Carolina, Chapel Hill.

Mitchell, H. L. (1987). *Roll the union on: A pictorial history of the Southern Tenant Farmers' Union.* Chicago: Charles H. Kerr.

Morris, L. (1995). Rural poverty. In R. L. Edwards (Ed.), *Encyclopedia of social work* (19th ed., pp. 2068–2075). Washington, DC: NASW Press.

North Carolina Rural Economic Development Center. (n.d.). Rural Internet Access Authority. Retrieved August 12, 2003, from http://www.ncruralcenter.org/internet/

Ray, J., & Murty, S. A. (1990). Rural child sexual abuse prevention and treatment. *Human Services in the Rural Environment, 13*(4), 24–29.

Raynor, D., & Reid, L. (2001, March 22). North Carolina's uneven growth. *The* (Raleigh, NC) *News & Observer,* p. 14A.

Robinson, L. (1995). Fighting dirty. *Emerge, 6*(9), 42–47.

Sell, R. S., Leistritz, F. L., & Allen, J. C. (1999). Impact of the Telecommunications Act of 1996 for rural areas. *Rural Development Perspectives, 13*(3), 45–48.

Siegel, P. B., Leuthold, F. O., & Stallman, J. I. (1995). Planned retirement/recreation communities are among development strategies open to amenity-rich rural areas. *Rural Development Perspectives, 10*(2), 8–14.

Snipp, C. (1996). Understanding race and ethnicity in rural America. *Rural Sociology, 61*, 125–142.

Stack, C. (1996). *Call to home: African Americans reclaim the rural South.* New York: Basic Books.

U.S. Census Bureau. (2000). Profile of general demographic characteristics, 2000. Retrieved August 14, 2003, from http://factfinder.census.gov/servlet/BasicFactsTable?_lang=en &_vt_name=DEC_2000_ SF1_U_DP1&_geo_id=04000US37

Waites, C., & Carlton-LaNey, I. (1999). Returning to rural roots: African American return migrants' use of senior centers. In I. Carlton-LaNey, R. Edwards, & N. Reid (Eds.), *Preserving and strengthening small towns and rural communities* (pp. 236–248). Washington, DC: NASW Press.

Weil, M. (1996a). Community building: Building community practice. *Social Work, 41*(5), 481–499.

Weil, M. (1996b). Model development in community practice: An historical perspective. *Journal of Community Practice, 3*(3/4), 5–67.

Weil, M., & Gamble, D. N. (1995). Community practice models. In R. L. Edwards (Ed.), *Encyclopedia of social work* (19th ed., pp. 577–594). Washington, DC: NASW Press.

Weissman, D. (2000). Addressing domestic violence in immigrant communities. *Popular Government, 65*, 3–18.

CHAPTER 23

Community Practice in Adult Health and Mental Health Settings

Anna Scheyett

Erin Drinnin

The town of Gheel, Belgium, has been dedicated to the memory of St. Dympna, patron saint of people with mental illness, for more than 700 years. According to legend, Dympna was an Irish princess whose mother died when Dympna was a young woman. Her father, driven mad by the loss, searched the country for another woman who looked like his wife and, finding no one, determined his daughter should replace his wife and be his bride. Horrified, Dympna fled to Europe. Her father pursued her and, in the town of Gheel, captured and killed her. A shrine was later built in her memory, and miraculous healings of people with mental illness occurred there. As more and more mentally ill pilgrims came, the shrine could not house everyone. The people of Gheel, determined that these suffering pilgrims should not be rejected, discriminated against, or left home-less, agreed that each family should take in one person with mental illness, treat that person with kindness, and welcome him or her as a part of the community. To this day the citizens of Gheel, with the contemporary support of a few professionals, provide a welcoming, healing community for people with mental illness.

This story is a powerful example of community practice in health and mental health reversing the then-common oppression and exclusion of people with mental illness. Citizens banded together to create a new and kindly method of care and created a way to address a community problem and right a social wrong, developing a policy and system of care that has been effective for seven centuries (Earle, 1994).

Throughout history, there have been multiple examples of health and mental health care systems shaped by community practice, reformed and restructured to be more responsive to community needs, to promote social justice and protect people's rights, and to enhance citizen participation and partnership in the health care process. Community practitioners have worked to improve these systems through advocacy, activism, participation in social planning processes, and facilitation of consumer empowerment. In the United States, these actions have resulted in improved funding for health care through programs such as Medicaid, Medicare, community health centers, and community mental health centers (Schlesinger, 1997); increased rights for people with disabilities through legislation such as the Americans with Disabilities Act and court decisions such as *L. C. v. Olmstead* (Bazelon Center, 2000b); led to the establishment of powerful national advocacy organizations in the areas of health and mental health (e.g., National Alliance for the Mentally Ill [NAMI] and The Arc); and helped an increasing number of consumers become involved in shaping their own health care and that of their community (Mickelson, 1995).

Despite these improvements, contemporary health and mental health care systems are in crisis. A primary challenge is a lack of access to quality care for consumers, particularly for those who face economic hardship, discrimination, financial and structural barriers, and barriers based in discrimination and oppression. In addition, health and mental health systems are not integrated into holistic care for consumers (Bazelon Center, 2000a) or with other public systems such as criminal justice (Munetz, Grande, & Chambers, 2001). Perhaps most important, individuals with health and mental health disabilities are not well integrated into their communities, and the informal community helping networks that do welcome consumers are not integrated with formal helping systems. Finally, health and mental health systems face the challenge of true inclusion of consumer voice and self-determination in the creation of programs, provision of care, and decision-making processes around treatment.

The goals of this chapter are to explore the challenges outlined above, identify creative community practice strategies and responses where they exist, and identify future directions and actions for community practitioners.

Access to Care: Affordability and Financing Issues

Access to care is often conceptualized as having four primary dimensions: affordability, availability, accessibility, and acceptability (Donabedian, 1976). Affordability is a major barrier to health and mental health care for many Americans. Many individuals cannot afford health care because they are uninsured. Even those covered by government, employer-based, or other private insurance struggle to pay for health care.

The Uninsured

Lack of insurance leads to poor health, less prevention and treatment, and financial burden for individuals, and it overwhelms the financial and structural capacity of public hospitals and community providers (National Governors Association Center for Best Practices, n.d.). Uninsured families pay more than 40% of medical costs out-of-pocket, increasing their risks for poverty and bankruptcy. They often delay needed care and are more likely to be hospitalized when avoidable conditions become life-threatening (Kaiser Commission on Medicaid and the Uninsured, 2001).

The uninsured in the United States are overwhelmingly poor. The U.S. Census Bureau reported that almost one third of the poor, representing 10 million people, were uninsured in 2001, but because of very low Medicaid eligibility levels in many states, the majority of the poor are not covered by Medicaid (U.S. Census Bureau, 2001). Hispanics have the highest uninsured rate at 33.2%, followed by African Americans and Asians and Pacific Islanders at about 19% each; White non-Hispanics are least likely to be uninsured with a 10% uninsured rate (U.S. Census Bureau, 2001). Surprisingly, workers represent three quarters of the uninsured population (Bodenheimer & Grumbach, 2002). Other groups at high risk of lacking health insurance are those working in small firms (usually fewer than 50 employees), people with only a high school diploma, young adults, and men (U.S. Census Bureau, 2001). People belonging to two or more of these risk groups exhibit especially significant disparities in health care coverage (Bodenheimer & Grumbach 2002).

A number of innovative community interventions address this lack of insurance. Community practitioners have developed creative approaches to improve access, expand services and eligibility, and increase prevention efforts for the most vulnerable uninsured populations. Three major strategies are employed: political advocacy, use of expansion programs, and community-level strategies to strengthen a health care safety net.

Advocacy-initiated policy proposals often focus on national health care plans, tax credits, and mental health parity. Though many community practitioners have advocated and lobbied for the most comprehensive movement toward equality in coverage—national health care—this does not seem likely to occur in the near future because of political opposition and cost implications. Tax credit proposals, more likely to succeed in Congress, aim to relieve the financial burden of health insurance premiums for either individuals or employers. Political advocacy can also include pressure to use existing laws in ways that benefit the uninsured. In Massachusetts, for example, the Lynn Health Task Force advocated for the implementation of the Community Benefits law to increase services to the uninsured by requiring hospitals and health care providers to offer some free services to clients in their communities (Community Voices, n.d.). In Lynn, this advocacy resulted in hospital provision of $20 million in services for the indigent.

An important consideration when examining the issue of lack of insurance involves coverage for mental health services. Despite passage of the 1996 Mental Health Parity Act, a number of health plans do not cover these services (Centers for Medicare and Medicaid Services [CMMS], 2002a). Limited parity (often meaning coverage only offered to state employees or restricted to specific diagnoses) leaves out many adults with various conditions listed in the *Diagnostic and Statistical Manual of Mental Disorders (DSM-IV;* American Psychological Association, 1994;

National Mental Health Association, n.d.). As of this writing, comprehensive parity is available in only four states—Connecticut, Maryland, Minnesota, and Vermont (National Mental Health Association, n.d.). Nationally, advocacy efforts are focusing on strengthening community-based treatment for the mentally ill and establishing full parity for all insured Americans (NAMI, n.d.-b).

Several proposals advocate for populations vulnerable to program gaps, such as early retirees, displaced workers, the near-elderly (Kaiser Family Foundation, HRET & The Commonwealth Fund, 2002), and the increasing numbers of legal immigrants, who threaten to overwhelm safety net capacity (National Association of Public Hospitals and Health Systems, 2001).

Community-level practice interventions that have been used to address problems of the uninsured also include partnering with providers, community organizations, and schools to identify sources of indigent care and share this information with citizens; forming provider collaboratives; addressing language and cultural barriers; providing outreach; and increasing citizen knowledge through health care access projects (Silow-Carroll, Anthony, Sacks, & Meyer, 2002).

Technology has played a key role in developing innovative tools to address issues of eligibility and outreach. Shands Jacksonville in Florida uses a software program, developed with a Robert Wood Johnson Foundation Communities in Charge grant, to increase communication and collaboration among providers (Thrall, 2001).

Volunteers also play an effective role in increasing access to health care. Montgomery County, Ohio, designed a successful all-volunteer program through a Robert Wood Johnson Foundation grant that required the community to work closely with the medical society, the public health agency, and a local medical school to reach underserved populations (Ahmed & Maurana, 2000). Some of the most powerful resources, and many of the most effective and influential volunteers, are themselves recipients of services. People in recovery from mental illness can provide outreach services to mentally ill individuals not yet connected with care through homeless outreach programs and drop-in centers (Davidson et al., 1999).

Medicaid and Medicare

There are significant problems within Medicaid and Medicare that limit both affordability and availability of care, including eligibility definitions, service limits, and cost-containment strategies. Client access to Medicaid, which unlike Medicare is needs based, is a significant concern for community practitioners. Medicaid covers about 1 in 10 Americans and is the source of financial access to health and mental health care for about 24 million adults (Smith, Ellis, Gifford, Ramesh, & Wachino, 2002). To receive Medicaid, individuals must navigate Byzantine rules and requirements, fit into one of up to 60 eligibility categories, and meet variable state income and resource means tests (Perkins, 2002). As a result of this complex and time-consuming application process, it is estimated that up to 3 million adults eligible for Medicaid are not enrolled in the program (Silow-Carroll et al., 2002). Additional barriers to Medicaid enrollment include poor accessibility of enrollment sites, language barriers for those whose native language is not English, and lack of acceptability of the enrollment process to individuals with cultural differences.

A number of community practice initiatives, called Community Voices and supported by the Kellogg Foundation, have developed innovative programs and community partnerships to increase Medicaid enrollment. Outreach to potentially eligible individuals through stationing workers in libraries, churches, nursing homes, and other community locations has been successful in a West Virginia project, as has stationing workers in a local emergency room in Detroit (Silow-Carroll et al., 2002). The use of neighborhood Latina residents, called *promotoras*, who themselves receive Medicaid and can answer potential enrollees' questions, has been a successful enrollment strategy for New York's Alianza project (Silow-Carroll, et al., 2002).

One of the most egregious gaps is the lack of prescription medication coverage in Medicare. Given that individuals over age 65 fill an average of 20 prescriptions per year (Artz, Hadsall, & Schondelmeyer, 2002), this is a serious financial burden for older Americans. Older adults are more likely to curtail their use of essential medications if they have no prescription benefit, and minority elderly are at highest risk of doing so (Steinman, Sands, & Covinsky, 2001), resulting in the exacerbation of costly and often life-threatening health conditions.

Community practice efforts to address this problem have focused on both local and national efforts. In North Carolina, for example, many community mental health centers have a staff person dedicated to obtaining medications for clients without a prescription benefit through pharmaceutical company indigent medication programs, local donations, and other sources (M. Swartz, personal communication, May 13, 2002). At the national level, advocacy organizations for older adults and people with physical and mental disabilities have lobbied Congress, demanding a prescription benefit for Medicare recipients. This advocacy resulted in the Medicare Prescription Drug, Improvement and Modernization Act of 2003. This act, being implemented in 2004, allows eligible seniors to select a drug discount card from those offered by 70 different providers. The complex options are confusing to many seniors, and response to the program has been much lower than anticipated. Nevertheless, the federal government and drug companies maintain that this card will save beneficiaries between 10% and 25% on medication costs. Beginning in 2005, beneficiaries will be able to enroll in a prescription drug plan that will cover a portion of prescription costs (CMMS, 2004).

Finding a provider willing both to accept the state-set Medicaid reimbursement rate and to complete the complex paperwork is challenging at best and often impossible. It is estimated that less than one third of the nation's office-based physicians will accept new Medicaid patients (Rowland & Salganicoff, 1994). Prescriptions, though covered, require an onerous preapproval process, which is particularly problematic for adults with serious mental illnesses, who need expensive antipsychotic medications but rarely receive them (Bazelon Center, 2002).

Advocacy and legal action have been used effectively at the state level to address these service limitations. Nine years of advocacy and relationship-building efforts by speech-language pathologists in Ohio resulted in a significant increase in the reimbursement rates for these providers, who previously reported losing money each time they treated a Medicaid client (Moore, 2000). In *Antrican v. Hooker-Odum*, a private law firm in coalition with the National Health Law Program and the North Carolina Justice and Community Development Center (NCJCDC) successfully argued that Medicaid recipients had a right to sue their state if the state did not follow federal Medicaid law around accessible dental care (NCJCDC, 2002).

Managed Care

Managed care has developed as a response to the rising cost of health care. It uses a number of strategies to control costs, including price controls, utilization management, gatekeeping, selective contracting, and cost sharing (Bodenheimer & Grumbach, 2002). Although managed care has been used to pursue a number of other goals, including better service integration, it has created significant financial barriers to accessing quality health care (Forquer & Sabin, 2002). Some analysts have criticized managed care and argued that any reduced costs realized by managed care organizations (MCOs) are a result of recruiting healthier enrollees and/or denying reimbursement for needed care. Added to this criticism is the significant concern that the bottom line and profits for stockholders are guiding medical care (Kaiser Family Foundation, 1999b). The increase in for-profit MCOs is dramatic. By 1997, 62% of MCOs were for-profit, an increase from 12% in 1981 (Rodwin, 2000). Health care advocates have initiated a number of actions to combat the problems of managed care. Provider coalitions organized "Say No to Managed Care" initiatives to protest lower reimbursement and quality-of-care issues and develop ways to practice outside of managed care systems (Ackley, 1997). National advocacy efforts prompted a federal commission and a Consumer Bill of Rights and Responsibilities. The advocacy group Families USA, in a survey of all 50 states' managed care laws, found a lack of uniformity and extent of consumer protections that spurred both improvements in state laws and attempts to pass federal patients' bill of rights legislation (Families USA, 1998).

Both Medicare and Medicaid have moved to managed care models. Medicare's earliest attempt at managed cost control through diagnostic related groups (DRGs) has often been criticized as resulting in insufficient care and early hospital discharges (Moniz & Gorin, 2003). Medicare + Choice, established in 1997, allows individuals to choose among a number of managed care and related options, including HMOs, preferred provider organizations (PPOs), and medical savings accounts. However, a significant number of HMOs exited the Medicare + Choice program in January 2001, stating that the federal reimbursement levels did not keep up with medical inflation, high prescription drug costs, and the increasing utilization of health care by older adults ("What's behind the Medicare HMO woes?", 2000). The recent Medicare Modernization Act will replace Medicare + Choice with a regionalized HMO system, called Medicare Advantage, in 2006 (CMMS, 2004).

In 2001, more than 7 million Medicaid eligibles were enrolled in some form of managed care program, representing 58% of the total Medicaid population (CMMS, 2002b). Sixteen states are using comprehensive 1115 Medicaid waivers as a way to control increasing Medicaid costs (CMMS, 2002b). These programs, which allow certain federal Medicaid requirements such as freedom of choice to be waived, initially focused on healthier Medicaid populations such as recipients of Temporary Assistance to Needy Families (TANF) and children. More recently, states have expanded waivers to all Medicaid populations, including the chronically ill and disabled (Moniz & Gorin, 2003).

For both federal programs, community practitioners have a number of concerns regarding access to care: the complexity of these systems and the lack of education provided to Medicare and Medicaid recipients on their rights, ways to access reimbursable services, and ways to appeal service denials. For example, a study completed in New York after implementation of a mandatory Medicaid managed care system found that 40% of recipients report never being told they must use an in-network provider, and only 18% understood the restrictions on emergency room use (Mason & Nichols, 2000). A second concern involves the definition of *medical necessity*; too tightly defined criteria can result in limiting needed services for vulnerable patients and those with complex problems, as well as eliminating preventive care.

When Medicaid and Medicare dollars are siphoned from the existing public sector system to managed care networks, safety net providers are left with fewer funds while being forced to treat more uninsured and underinsured clients (Waitzkin et al., 2002). This excessive pressure can, in a few years, leave the safety net system in ruin (Chang et al., 1998).

In response to these challenges and barriers, community practice interventions have occurred on the local, state, and federal levels. To address the lack of education regarding managed care, the nonprofit group Community Social Services of New York offered 167 workshops across New York City, and partnered with the community media to sponsor a weekly radio show discussing health care access issues (Mason & Nichols, 2000). Local community action has also occurred in New Mexico to preserve the public safety net at the county level, with county leaders meeting to collaborate, share resources, and ensure the ongoing fiscal viability of programs (Waitzkin et al., 2002).

At the state level, advocates have been active in the ongoing monitoring of problems in managed care systems. In New Mexico, advocacy resulted in a temporary halt to the Medicaid waiver until the system could be restructured and improved. The Citizen's TennCare Review Commission was instrumental in revisions to the troubled Tennessee Medicaid waiver program (Waitzkin et al., 2002).

Federal actions have involved a number of lawsuits, including an ongoing lawsuit demanding a clear and accessible appeals process for Medicare recipients denied services (Duff, 2002). However, public sector problems are ongoing and unresolved. Continued action and advocacy by community practitioners is essential to protect consumer and community rights.

Managed Mental Health Care

Medicaid managed care has been a particular focus in the mental health system. In 2002, 37 states had some Medicaid managed mental health care benefit, usually operationalized in one of two ways: as a "carve-out," where mental health care funds are managed separately from physical health care funds, often by a separate behavioral health care management organization (BHMO); or as a "carve-in," where mental health care is part of the larger managed health care benefit (Forquer & Sabin, 2002). Problems with carve-ins include patients accessing mental health care through primary care physicians, whose knowledge may be less specialized; there is also the risk that fewer dollars will go to mental health care if all funds are blended into one capitation or case rate (Forquer & Sabin, 2002).

Advocates raise particular concern regarding access to care for people with severe and persistent mental illness (SPMI) under managed care. As a chronic population, adults with SPMI have needs that go far beyond a traditional medical model, including housing, supported employment, case management, and other psychosocial services, which have been reimbursed under traditional Medicaid. Unless definitions of medical necessity are carefully crafted, these services may no longer be available to them (Bazelon Center, 1999). In addition, MCOs may not be knowledgeable about best practices for this population, and they may develop and/or authorize treatment plans that are not appropriate to SPMI needs.

Incentives to undertreat and shift costs are prevalent in Medicaid managed care systems for people with SPMI. Shifting individuals from capitated community-based systems to state-funded psychiatric hospitals, safety net public sector providers, other social services, or the criminal justice system is a way to control costs and preserve profit, as is denying service or severely restricting access to high-cost intensive services. Morrissey, Stroup, Ellis, and Merwin (2002) found that capitation plans were associated with lowest use of high-cost services and also with poorer mental and physical health.

A final concern with Medicaid managed mental health care involves the problems of working with an underfunded system. Public mental health systems are woefully underfunded; managed care can help those funds go further, but it cannot solve the problem of insufficient funds (Bazelon Center, 2000a).

Access to Care: Structural and System Barriers

Capacity

Community capacity in health and mental health care refers to the ability of a community to meet the various health care needs of its members. In the United States, there is insufficient capacity in the public health and mental health care systems to provide screening and treatment of those who need it, particularly for those who are most vulnerable due to poverty, chronic illness, or minority status (Forrest & Whelan, 2000; Institute of Medicine, 2001a). More than one half of all people with diabetes are unaware that they have the disease and thus go untreated, leading to the more complicated conditions of heart disease and stroke (National Institute of Diabetes & Digestive & Kidney Disease, 2003). It is estimated that only one third of the 44 million people with a mental illness receive treatment (U.S. Department of Health and Human Services, 1999), and many public systems report long waiting lists and inadequate resources for services (Bazelon Center, 2001).

As a result of this insufficient capacity, the community safety net is the only source of care for many. It is estimated that 18% of those lacking access to a regular physician (Forrest & Whelan, 2000) and 10% of those who are uninsured (National Association of Community Health Centers, 2002) are served by community health centers. Others seek sporadic crisis care from public hospitals and community clinics as well as homeless shelters (National Council on Disability, 2002). Morrissey and Goldman (1984) point out that reform movements within the mental health system, from community to institution and back again, have led to an inadequate and disconnected patchwork of services that cannot meet consumer needs. Individuals who are untreated find themselves in other public systems, such as criminal justice and social services. As a result, these systems have become a de facto part of the mental health care safety net (Bazelon Center, 2001).

Current services often are not based in best practice models. According to the Institute of Medicine (2001a), the health care system is not equipped with the appropriate tools to translate scientifically based knowledge into practice, and huge gaps remain between effective treatment and the reality faced by many patients. Examples include the underutilization of preventive measures, including eye exams and hemoglobin monitoring, which can decrease health complications for diabetics, and inappropriate pain management for cancer patients (Institute of Medicine, 2001b). Similar patterns are seen in mental health care. In a study of treatment of individuals with schizophrenia, Lehman and Steinwachs (1998) estimated that best practices services were provided in less than 50% of cases. People with mental illnesses, addiction, and even physical health problems often must hit "rock bottom" before they are able to receive community supports, "creating dependency and perpetuating failure" (National Council on Disability, 2002, p. 4).

The reasons for the appalling lack of capacity in health care services are related to the lack of flexibility in service delivery as well as poor funding. Inflexible service schedules can result in a shift in service provision to jails, homeless shelters, and emergency rooms that are open 24 hours, 7 days a week. In mental health, despite increased knowledge of evidence-based practices that work for certain populations, Medicaid continues to support ineffective programs and services (Bazelon Center, 2001; President's New Freedom Commission on Mental Health, 2002).

The deinstitutionalization policies of the 1960s and 1970s did not allocate sufficient funding for community-based services; thus, community programs did not have the capacity to provide the services and supports for the influx of people with mental illnesses leaving the institutions (Morrissey & Goldman, 1984). Psychiatric hospitals continue to close and shift people into the community, but the necessary resources do not follow the individuals into the community (Bazelon Center, 2001).

System Fragmentation

Despite inadequate resources, health services are facing increased legislative, public, and consumer pressure to move toward full-service, integrated, community-based systems of care (Forquer & Sabin, 2002; National Council for Community Behavioral Healthcare, 2002). Advocacy and legislative action are especially significant for vulnerable populations with complex needs, including children, the elderly, ethnic minorities, Medicaid recipients, the uninsured, rural dwellers (Forrest & Whelan, 2000), inner-city residents, the dually diagnosed (those with mental health and substance use disorders), and people with mental illness or substance abuse in the criminal justice system (Forquer & Sabin, 2002). Many individuals have overlapping risk factors and compounding issues of poverty, cross-systems needs, and health problems, which could be significantly improved through an integrated focus on all psychosocial and medical needs (Forquer & Sabin, 2002).

Health and mental health care delivery systems are fragmented, and constant shifts of responsibility and accountability among federal, state, and local entities have only worsened the fragmentation that exists in the systems of public and private care (President's New Freedom Commission on Mental Health, 2002). Policymakers have failed to design and coordinate the comprehensive services necessary for populations with complex needs (Bazelon Center, 2001).

U.S. Department of Justice funding is supporting model community programs targeting unmet mental health needs in the criminal justice system, improving interactions between law enforcement and the mentally ill and preventing the incarceration of people with mental illnesses (National Governors Association Center for Best Practices, n.d.). One such community program, jail diversion, redirects low-level, nonviolent mentally ill individuals from jail into community-based treatment. This cross-discipline solution decreases money spent, reduces overcrowding in jails, and improves recovery chances for the mentally ill (Center on Crime, Communities, and Culture, 1996).

Access to Care: Discrimination, Disadvantage, and Health Disparities

Racial and Ethnic Minorities

The increase of racial and ethnic diversity in the changing U.S. population has created a growing demand that practitioners have an understanding of the complexities and interactions of race, ethnicity, culture, language, income, gender, age, education, occupation (National Institute on Aging, 2000), health insurance, and residency, as well as their impacts on health care service and delivery. "Failure to understand and manage social and cultural differences may have significant health consequences for minority groups in particular" (Betancourt, Green, & Carrillo, 2002, p. v). Community practitioners in the health and mental health fields must pay particular attention to issues specific to these populations to enable promotion of equality, social justice, and culturally competent care.

Disparities continue for African Americans, Hispanic Americans, Asians and Pacific Islanders, and American Indians and Alaska Natives (U.S. Department of Health and Human Services, 2002). Consistently, uninsured minorities report less frequent use of a regular physician and more difficulty accessing care than uninsured Whites (Hargraves, 2002). Minorities have worse health outcomes than Whites in several areas, even when adjusting for income differences, variations in health insurance, and type and severity of disease (Kaiser Family Foundation, 1999a). Total age-adjusted death rates are highest among non-Hispanic Blacks (Keppel, Pearcy, & Wagener, 2002), who are less likely to receive treatments and procedures that prolong life. One study showed that Blacks on Medicare were 60% less likely than Whites on Medicare to have heart bypass surgery (Kaiser Family Foundation, 1999a).

The fragmentation of health care service delivery and the increased use of a managed care financing structure contribute to the obstacles to minority access to care. Research by Cunningham and Trude (2001) has demonstrated that managed care may negatively affect a person's likelihood of receiving regular care from traditional providers familiar with the culture and language of the community.

Language barriers, fear, misunderstanding, and ineligibility, as well as distrust and poor cultural fit with providers, all lead to patient refusal of services, delays in seeking care, and poor treatment adherence (Institute of Medicine, 2002). A lack of interpreters for non-native English speakers is also a growing problem (Betancourt et al., 2002).

The general public and physicians agree that people "very or somewhat often" get treated unfairly based on whether they have insurance, but the public is more likely to say that how much money a person has is also a factor (71% of the public versus 47% of physicians), as is how well they speak English (58% versus 43%) (Kaiser Family Foundation, 2002). Research has proven that unconscious negative racial and ethnic stereotypes influence health care decisions, even among providers who are unaware of any personal biases (Institute of Medicine, 2002). When asked "How often do you think our health care system treats people unfairly based on what their race or ethnic background is?" White physicians answered *very often* or *somewhat often* only 25% of the time, whereas 77% of Black physicians selected one of those two responses (Kaiser Family Foundation, 2002). Low socioeconomic status (SES) is also "one of the most important predictors of adverse changes in health status," and it is significantly correlated with race (Jackson, Williams, & Torres, 1995, p. 2).

Since the beginning of the civil rights movement, activists have identified health disparities and discrimination as central issues to be addressed. Currently, the U.S. Department of Health and Human Services (2002) is engaged in several initiatives, including the Initiative to Eliminate Racial and Ethnic Disparities in Health (through the Office of Minority Health), Closing the Health Gap (focused on educating minorities on health issues), and the Healthy Communities Innovation Initiative (interdisciplinary initiative aimed at preventing specific conditions and eliminating racial and ethnic disparities in health).

Cultural competence can be achieved through increased education and awareness among health care providers and the community, increased financial incentives and recruitment of minority care providers (Institute of Medicine, 2002), and development of culturally competent programs and services that respect diversity. To better serve minority populations, traditional healing and cultural practices must be incorporated into health services by focusing on empowerment, education, and health management that incorporates traditional beliefs (Institute of Medicine, 2002). The Awakening the Spirit—Pathways to Diabetes Prevention and Control program, sponsored by the American Diabetes Association, targets American Indians and Alaska Natives with diabetes, promoting empowerment and wellness congruent with cultural beliefs and practices (Scott, 2002).

Geographic Disparities and Underserved Populations

Location of care is more of a concern in rural and inner-city areas than in large metropolitan areas with access and lack of infrastructure being the main difficulties (Best Practices in Rural Medicaid Managed Behavioral Health, 1998) as well as a lack of appropriate health and mental health services in these areas (President's New Freedom Commission on Mental Health, 2002). The struggles of rural and inner-city areas to retain providers is related to persistent poverty, a lack of conventional physical and cultural amenities, and populations with high percentages of ethnic or racial minorities (Council on Graduate Medical Education, 1998). Inner-city residents often experience poor health, poor economic conditions, high unemployment, poor housing, violence, and crime (Council on Graduate Medical Education, 1998), and similar difficulties are faced by rural populations, along with transportation problems (Pol, 2000). Rural residents are also more likely to be poor, to be old, and to rely on individual or small employer insurance coverage (Pol, 2000). Additional barriers to effective health care in underserved areas include issues of stigma, confidentiality, and culture (Waitzkin et al., 2002).

Geographic disparities in health care require unique solutions, including placing an emphasis on primary care (Geller, Beeson, & Rodenhiser, n.d.), developing prevention programs, and integrating and networking systems of care (Bazelon Center, 2000a; Geller et al., n.d.; National Institute of Mental Health, 2000), increasing the use of telecommunications technology (telemedicine) (Council on Graduate Medical Education, 1998), and increasing consumer involvement (Best Practices in Rural Medicaid Managed Behavioral Health, 1998; Geller et al., n.d.).

Integrating services in rural and inner-city areas by creating public-private partnerships and cross-system collaboration improves access, reduces costs, improves management, and reduces duplication (Council on Graduate Medical Education, 1998). Managed care plans with Medicaid recipients should forge contracts with already established community clinics and providers (Council on Graduate Medical Education, 1998; Scheyett & Fuhrman, 1999; Waitzkin et al., 2002). Programs of peer support, consumer education, volunteerism, and support groups serve to increase crisis support, provide transportation, involve consumers and families in planning and development, and increase community self-reliance (Best Practices in Rural Medicaid Managed Behavioral Health, 1998; Geller et al., n.d.).

Community Integration

Along with medical and mental health care, individuals need a place in the community, an identity and life beyond that of patient or ill person, for recovery to occur. This includes the opportunity to build relationships with others in the community who do not share their disorder, to live in a setting of their choosing, and to engage in meaningful work.

Stigma

For many individuals with health or mental health disorders, particularly those with chronic, potentially disabling disorders, one of the greatest barriers to community integration is stigma, which prevents the community from seeing the person with the disorder as "one of us" and encourages community rejection, segregation, and ostracism. Community practitioners have used a number of strategies to attack stigma and discrimination, including community education (Fraser, 1994), dialogue processes (Scheyett & Kim, in press), and legal protection through legislation and court action (Petrila & Brink, 2001).

One of the most powerful ways community practitioners facilitate community integration of individuals with health and mental health disorders is through linkage with informal associations and gatherings in the community. As noted by McKnight (1997), communities are strengthened by the informal associations within them, and full participation in these associations is both meaningful and protective for vulnerable individuals. In community practice, individuals with health and mental health disorders are helped to join with others in their community around common interests and concerns. An excellent example of this is found in strengths-based case management programs. In this model of practice, the community, not the formal service system, is seen as "an oasis of resources" that should be plumbed to meet the individual's needs and wants (Rapp, 1998). In the Dayton, Ohio, Veteran's Administration program, for example, individuals with substance abuse and mental disorders are linked with local employment resources, and other "real life" community connections are explored (Siegal et al., 1996). The Center for Psychiatric Rehabilitation of Boston University helps individuals with severe mental illness enroll in and succeed at college- and graduate-level courses, connecting with others with like interests and skills (Unger, Anthony, Sciarappa, & Rogers, 1991).

Employment and Disability

Although most people with disabilities wish to enter or rejoin the workforce, many report great concern about losing their disability-related health insurance if they do because employer-based insurance may not cover their preexisting condition. If they were to lose their employment for health or other reasons, it could take many months before disability benefits are reinstated (Key & DeNoon, 1997). Intensive advocacy efforts have decreased some of the barriers to employment for people with disabilities. Expanded support for disabled individuals wishing to return to work has been provided through the Ticket to Work and Self-Sufficiency Programs, P.L. 106–170 (Social Security Administration, n.d.), and President George W. Bush's New Freedom Commission on Mental Health Initiative (New Freedom Initiative, n.d.).

The Americans with Disabilities Act

Perhaps the most significant legislative action to protect the rights of individuals with physical and mental disorders to live and work in the community has been the Americans with Disabilities Act (ADA) of 1990. Passed after years of activism on the part of advocates, leaders in the disability community, health care professionals, and others, the ADA has the goal of assuring that people with disabilities have equality of opportunity for full community participation, independent living, and economic self-sufficiency. It places particular focus on access to public places, access to services, and prevention of discrimination in the workplace (Moss, Ullman, Starrett, Burris, & Johnsen, 1999).

Research on the effectiveness of Title I of the ADA (employment) has shown that the number of claims resulting in benefits to the individual making charges is low.

Moss and colleagues (1999) found that from 1992 to 1998, 16% of charges resulted in benefit to individuals with physical disabilities, and only 13.6% resulted in benefit to individuals with psychiatric disabilities. In addition, the median benefit was low, $3,500 for physical disability and $5,000 for psychiatric. Most disturbingly, Moss et al. found that charges filed after 1995 were less likely to result in benefits, and they speculate this could be a result of the narrowing interpretations of the ADA as well as changes in administrative processes.

Community advocates must be aware of the erosion of the breadth and effectiveness of the ADA and the impact this is having on individuals with disabilities. Social and political action is needed both to restore the ADA's scope and relevance and to ensure that existing protections under the ADA are operationalized to protect the rights of individuals with health and mental health disorders in the community.

Community Integration: Looking at Two Populations

Among the most stigmatized groups in our society are individuals who are HIV positive (HIV+) and individuals with severe and persistent mental illness (SPMI). The following discussion of community integration issues for these two populations illustrates challenges faced by many with health and mental health disorders.

HIV

Community responses to people with HIV/AIDS frequently include stigma, rejection, and fear (Valdiserri, 2002). People who are HIV+ struggle to maintain their employment and find safe and affordable places to live in the community. A 1999 survey of attitudes toward people with HIV showed that more than 20% reported being afraid of people with AIDS, and 48% stated that most people with AIDS are responsible for having their illness. The survey also showed that 30% reported discomfort with their child attending school with a child with AIDS, and 22% reported discomfort with the idea of having a coworker with AIDS (Herek, Capitanio, & Widaman, 2002). Even though attitudes and resultant behaviors toward people with HIV have improved over time, misinformation and discrimination still exists and is a target for ongoing social action. The International Red Cross, for example, has mounted a new campaign to combat AIDS/HIV stigma. With the slogan "Take a Look: Stigma Kills," the initiative plans to increase education, offer counseling, and encourage preventive behavior ("International Red Cross Launches," 2002).

Political and social action and program development activities have been effective in improving community integration for people with HIV. Early AIDS activists in organizations such as ACT UP combined aggressive public protest with dogged political action to keep the issue of HIV in the public eye and to ensure that both services and civil rights existed for people with HIV (Gierach, 2002). Over time, the impact of these grassroots efforts led to significant federal funding for treatment and ancillary services, such as housing. At the local level, grassroots organizing led to the development of AIDS service organizations across the country, which serve a variety of roles, including prevention education, social support, legal and disability entitlement information, and development of housing, case management, and other community-based programs for people with HIV (Somlai et al., 1999). However, with the development of more effective treatments for HIV, individuals may now have decades of productive life and wish to remain engaged in some meaningful and supporting work activity. Employer-based insurance is becoming essential for people who are HIV+, given the great expense of medications used to treat HIV.

AIDS activists have fought for the rights of HIV+ individuals around employment and other issues, often using the ADA in the courts to protect HIV+ individuals from discrimination. Several significant court decisions have impacted the application of sections of the ADA to people with HIV. In *Holiday v. City of Chattanooga,* a federal court determined that an HIV+ individual could not be disqualified for a particular job based solely on his or her diagnosis (ACLU, 2000). A Supreme Court ruling, *Bragdon v. Abbott,* determined that HIV+ individuals are covered under the ADA at every stage of the disease (Lazzarini, 1998). Ongoing aggressive advocacy is needed to protect the rights of HIV+ individuals to live and work in the community.

SPMI

People with SPMI have been stigmatized and segregated throughout history. Until late in the 20th century, the only place considered proper for individuals with mental illness was the asylum or psychiatric institution; only with significant advocacy and legal action did people with SPMI establish their right to live and work in the community. In addition to programs to integrate people with mental illness back into communities (Rapp, 1998), interventions aimed specifically at decreasing stigma and discrimination against people with SPMI have been initiated. The federal Center for Mental Health Services has launched an extensive national anti-stigma campaign with the slogan, "Know me as a person, *not* by my mental illness," and the National Alliance for the Mentally Ill (NAMI), an advocacy group made up primarily of family members, established StigmaBusters, which seeks to fight the inaccurate, stigmatizing representations of mental illness found in TV, film, print, or other media depictions (NAMI, n.d.-a).

Lack of employment is identified as one of the primary barriers to community integration for people with SPMI (Mallik, Reeves, & Dellario, 1998). As noted in the first report from the President's New Freedom Commission on Mental Health (2002), 90% of individuals with SPMI are unemployed, despite the fact that most state they want to work. Barriers to employment for people with SPMI include discrimination, disincentives in the disability system, and challenges posed by the mental disorders themselves (Drew et al., 2001; Henry & Lucca, 2002). However, exemplary programs have demonstrated that people with SPMI can be successful in the workplace. Supported employment programs such as Individual Placement and Support (IPS) programs, help individuals find work and provide on-site job support. This model has shown a 60% to 80% success rate (Dixon et al., 2002).

Another effective community practice intervention is the vocational component of psychosocial rehabilitation clubhouse programs (Blyler, 2003). People with SPMI who participate frequently in clubhouse programs have higher employment rates than those who do not (DiMasso, Avi-Itzhak, & Obler, 2001). In addition, many consumer self-help organizations provide support and advice as people look for employment and also provide employment.

People with SPMI have consistently expressed a desire for independent housing that is safe, comfortable, private, and convenient and that offers support services when needed (Massey & Wu, 1993). Community programs offering supported housing (housing of the individual's choosing combined with the supports and services needed for the person to live there) have been shown to be effective (Ridgeway & Zippie, 1990), but these are often in short supply. Project HOME, a supported housing program in Vermont, matched adults with mental illness or disabilities who were at risk of losing their homes due to lack of income or support services with "home seekers" (i.e., boarders), who provided companionship and daily task assistance in exchange for reduced rent. More than 4,000 people were served by Project HOME between 1982 and 1994 (Baker, 1994).

Consumer Voice, Empowerment, and Health and Mental Health Care Reform

A central tenet of community practice is empowerment of individuals and communities, that is, facilitating a process whereby people gain control over their lives and influence the organizational and societal structures in which they live (Segal, Silverman, & Temkin, 1995). In health and mental health care, this can happen when individuals and communities determine the type and amount of services, the manner in which services are provided, and define the delivery systems and delivery sites of services. For this to occur, recipients of services must attain meaningful participation and voice, the ability to express their views and preferences, make demands and protests, and exert political pressure to improve and reform the service system (Rodwin, 2000). Meaningful participation and voice require a number of things: consumers who are well-informed about health care, service systems, and reform processes; vehicles and venues for consumers to express their views; and systems that are open and responsive.

However, health care is not an economic market like any other but rather a combination of government-controlled and privately managed functions with complex and sometimes chaotic processes. For vulnerable and oppressed populations, market forces are ineffective tools for change, and even consumer voice, though strengthening over the past few decades, is still a minor force (Rodwin, 2000). Lack of consumer voice underpins many of the challenges in health and mental health care identified throughout this chapter. Vulnerable populations do not yet have the political clout to demand access to adequate and affordable care that addresses needs from a holistic, community-based perspective and is provided in a nondiscriminatory and culturally competent manner.

Consumer Voice and Its Challenges

Consumer voice can be defined on three levels. At one level, individual consumer voice is needed in the process of shaping a person's treatment within the health care system. Based on the principle of self-determination, individual consumer voice must be present if a truly healing partnership is to develop between consumer and care provider. Individual consumers must have the right to appeal treatment decisions, file grievances, and receive rapid and respectful responses (McCourt, 2000).

A second level of consumer voice is seen when consumers shape the creation and ongoing functioning of health care programs, and a third is seen when consumer voice impacts health care policy. Impact on both programs and policy requires individual consumer action plus representation, where consumers have an intermediary who effectively speaks for them in program and policy development (Rodwin, 2000). The National Health Law Project and the Bazelon Center for Mental Health Law are examples of institutional representation.

Consumer voice at the program level can occur through a number of means. At the most basic level, consumers can participate in opinion surveys and focus groups to identify needs and influence program development. Consumers may also serve on planning and operations committees for programs and agencies, on grievance and appeals committees, or on advisory and governance boards (Rodwin, 2000). At the policy level, consumer voice can be expressed through lobbying efforts to impact state and federal legislation; through participation on state and federal level planning, oversight, or investigative boards and committees; through consultation with state and federal policy-making bodies; and through court actions such as class action lawsuits (Rodwin, 2000). Consumer movements in health and mental health have resulted in significant advances in consumer voice at the individual, program, and policy levels.

Consumer voices shape programs and policy through a number of mechanisms—participation in focus groups, grievance and appeals committees, and oversight and operating boards, as well as participation in state and federal planning groups, lobbying activities, and legal action. One dramatic example of consumer voice at the program level involves consumer-directed programs and service provision in mental health (National Council on Disability, 2002). Peer-run services focus on mutual support and help, noncoerciveness, equality, and the provision of useful services (National Mental Health Consumers Self-Help Clearing House, n.d.). Programs like Incube, which helps mental health consumers start and run their own businesses (Bassman, 2001), and The Quad, a drop-in and resource center (McLean, 1995), were established and are run by people with mental illnesses dissatisfied with the services provided by the traditional system. At the policy level, a number of initiatives are increasing consumer voice. Examples include the Gay Men's Health Crisis initiative, which focuses on increasing the participation of HIV+ Medicaid consumers in the development, implementation, and monitoring of New York State's Medicaid managed care system (Chaney, 2002); and the Bazelon Center for Mental Health Law (2002), which has partnered advocates and mental health consumers to develop and promote laws providing rights to mental health services (Chaney, 2002).

The Future of Community Practice in Health and Mental Health Care

Strengthening the responsiveness of the health and mental health care systems requires community practice with a three-pronged focus: interventions aimed at national and systemic changes, interventions to develop and modify health care programs, and grassroots interventions to strengthen and empower communities and individuals. Next steps at all three levels are outlined below.

National and Systemic Changes

Using a political and social action model (Weil & Gamble, 1995), community practitioners must shape legislation, engage in litigation, and become involved in policy-making bodies to

- ensure that citizens have a right to effective treatment of their choice in health and mental health care.
- develop system structures that minimize financial and structural barriers to care, including investment of sufficient resources to ensure adequate health care capacity.
- protect citizens from coercive and abusive involuntary treatment.
- ensure that health and mental health care systems are integrated with other relevant systems, such as social services and criminal justice, and that the holistic health and mental health care needs of citizens can be addressed in a coordinated, seamless fashion.
- ensure that all citizens have equal access to the benefits of community life, irrespective of disability or disorder.

Program Interventions

Using a program development and community liaison model (Weil & Gamble, 1995), community practitioners in collaboration with consumers and providers must engage in interventions that

- create and maintain culturally competent programs sensitive to the needs and preferences of vulnerable and oppressed populations.
- support consumer-directed, peer-run, and peer support programs.
- embed programs within the larger context of the community in relevant relational ways, collaborating with natural supports and informal community resources.
- ensure that programs are accessible, affordable, available, and acceptable to citizens.
- create and maintain programs with a focus on the whole person in the context of their family, their community, and other significant relationships.

Grassroots Interventions

Using a community development model (Weil & Gamble, 1995), community practitioners must work to

- strengthen local communities' ability to develop and direct the provision of health care services in their area.
- increase community ability and willingness to include individuals with disabilities in meaningful participatory roles.

Using a functional community building model (Weil & Gamble, 1995), community practitioners must engage in interventions that

- establish and strengthen functional communities among mental health care consumers.
- increase community members' understanding of health care and health care systems.
- maximize community members' skills for participation in health care planning at the level of their own care as well as at program and policy levels.

Using a social movements model (Weil & Gamble, 1995), community practitioners must intervene to strengthen the health and mental health consumer movement, ensuring that our society recognizes the legitimacy of health and mental health care consumer rights. This focus interweaves all interventions discussed above—individual and community empowerment, self-determination in programs, and voice in policy development. Without a comprehensive social movement to establish this larger context, an ethical, effective, and just health and mental health care system cannot exist.

References

Ackley, D. (1997). *Break free from managed care.* New York: Guilford.

Ahmed, S. M. & Maurana, C. A. (2000). Reaching out to the underserved: a successful volunteer program. *American Journal of Public Health, 9*(3), pp. 439–440.

American Civil Liberties Union. (2000). *Federal court rejects HIV-based job discrimination, ties employment to individual capabilities, not biases.* Retrieved November 1, 2002, from http://www.aclu.org/news/NewsPrint.cfm?ID=7865&c=89

American Psychological Association. (1994). *Diagnostic and statistical manual of mental disorders* (4th ed.). Washington, DC: Author.

Artz, M., Hadsall R., & Schondelmeyer, S. (2002). Impact of generosity level of outpatient prescription drug events and expenditures among older persons. *American Journal of Public Health, 92*(8), 1257–1263.

Baker, D. (1994). Independent living in communities: The Vermont Independence Fund. *American Rehabilitation, 20*(1), 39–41.

Bassman, R. (2001). Whose reality is it anyway? Consumer/survivor/ex-patients can speak for themselves. *Journal of Humanistic Psychology, 41*(4), 11–35.

Bazelon Center. (1999). *Under court order.* Washington, DC: Author.

Bazelon Center. (2000a). *Effective public management of mental health care: Views from states on Medicaid reforms that enhance service integration and accountability.* Washington, DC: Author.

Bazelon Center. (2000b). *Olmstead v. L.C.* Retrieved December 11, 2001, from http://www.bazelon.org/olmstead.html

Bazelon Center. (2001). *Disintegrating system: The state of the states' public mental health systems.* Washington, DC: Author.

Bazelon Center. (2002). *An act providing a right to mental health services and supports.* Washington, DC: Author.

Best Practices in Rural Medicaid Managed Behavioral Health. (1998). *Research & policy brief.* Retrieved November 10, 2002, from http://www.muskie.usm.maine.edu/ihp/ruralhealth/pdf/policybriefs/Nov98.pdf

Betancourt, J., Green, A., & Carrillo, J. (2002). *Cultural competence in health care: Emerging frameworks and practical approaches.* New York: The Commonwealth Fund.

Blyler, C. (2003). Understanding the employment rate of people with schizophrenia: Different approaches lead to different implication for policy. In M. Lensenweger & J. Hooley (Eds.), *Principles of experimental psychopathology* (pp. 107–115). Washington, DC: American Psychological Association.

Bodenheimer, T. S., & Grumbach, K. (2002). *Understanding health policy.* New York: McGraw-Hill.

Center on Crime, Communities, and Culture. (1996). *Research brief: Occasional paper series no. 1.* Retrieved May 16, 2001, from http://www.soros.org/crime/research_brief_1.html

Centers for Medicare & Medicaid Services (CMMS). (2002a). *HHS issue final regulation on Medicare-endorsed prescription drug card initiative.* Retrieved September 20, 2002, from http://cms.hhs.gov/media/press/release.asp?Counter=486

Centers for Medicare & Medicaid Services (CMMS). (2002b). National summary of Medicaid managed care programs enrollment as of December 31, 2001. Retrieved September 19, 2002, from http://cms.hhs.gov/medocaod/1915b/default.asp

Centers for Medicare & Medicaid Services (CMMS). (2004). *The Medicare Prescription Drug, Improvement, and Modernization Act of 2003.* Retrieved March 29, 2004 from http://www.cms.hhs.gov/medicarereform/.

Chaney, R. (2002, April). The value of consumer involvement in Medicaid managed care. *CHCS Briefs.*

Chang, C., Kiser, L., Bailey, J. Martins, M., Gibson, W., Schaberg, K., Mirvis, D., Applegate, W. (1998). Tennessee's failed managed care program for mental health and substance abuse services. *JAMA, 279*(1), 864-869.

Community Voices. (n.d.). *Community benefits program.* Retrieved September 20, 2002, from http://www.communityvoices.org/Articles/Article.asp?ID=177

Council on Graduate Medical Education. (1998). *Physician distribution and health care challenges in rural and inner-city areas.* Rockville, MD: Author.

Cunningham, P., & Trude, S. (2001). Does managed care enable more low income persons to identify a usual source of care? *Medical Care, 39*(7), 716–726.

Davidson, L., Chinman, M., Kloos, B., Weingarten, R., Stayner, D., & Tebes, J. (1999). Peer support among individuals with severe mental illness: A review of the evidence. *Clinical Psychology: Science and Practice, 6*(2), 165–187.

DiMasso, J., Avi-Itzhak, T., & Obler, D. (2001). The clubhouse model: An outcome study on attendance, work attainment and status, and hospital recidivism. *Work: Journal of Prevention, Assessment, and Rehabilitation, 17*(1), 23–30.

Dixon, L., Hoch, J., Clark, R., Bebout, R., Drake, R., McHugo, G., et al. (2002). Cost-effectiveness of two vocational rehabilitation programs for persons with severe mental illness. *Psychiatric Services, 53*(9), 1118–1124.

Donabedian, A. (1976). Effects of Medicare and Medicaid on access to and quality of health care. *Public Health Reports, 91*(4), 322–331.

Drew, D., Drebing, C., Van Ormer, A., Losardo, M., Krebs, C., Penk, W., et al. (2001). Effects of disability compensation on participation and outcomes of vocational rehabilitation. *Psychiatric Services, 52*(11), 1479–1484.

Duff, S. (2002). Appealing problems. *Modern Healthcare, 32*(35), 12–13.

Earle, P. (1994). Gheel. *American Journal of Psychiatry, 151*(6), 16–19.

Families USA. (1998). *Hit and miss: State managed care laws.* Washington, DC: Author.

Forquer, S. & Sabin, J. (2002). *Medicaid behavioral managed care: What lies ahead.* Lawrenceville, NJ: Center for Health Care Strategies.

Forrest, C. & Whelan, E. (2000). Primary care safety-net delivery sites in the United States. *Journal of the American Medical Association, 284*(16), 2077–2083.

Fraser, M. (1994). Educating the public about mental illness: What will it take to get the job done? *Innovations & Research, 3,* 29–31.

Geller, J., Beeson, P. & Rodenhiser, R. (n.d.). *Frontier mental health strategies: Integrating, reaching out, building up, and connecting.* Retrieved September 30, 2002, from http://www.wiche.edu/MentalHealth/Frontier/letter6.html

Gierach, R. (2002). AIDS history project documents valuable lessons. *Lesbian News, 27*(1), 1–2.

Hargraves, L. (2002). *Tracking report: Results from the community tracking study No. 2.* Washington, DC: Center for Studying Health Systems Change.

Henry, A. & Lucca, A. (2002). Contextual factors and participation in employment for people with serious mental illness. *Occupational Therapy Journal of Research, 22*(Suppl.1), 83S–84S.

Herek, G., Capitanio, J., & Widaman, K. (2002). HIV-related stigma and knowledge in the United States: Prevalence and trends, 1991–1999. *American Journal of Public Health, 92*(3), 371–377.

Institute of Medicine. (2001a). *Crossing the quality chasm: A new health system for the 21st century.* Washington, DC: National Academy Press.

Institute of Medicine. (2001b). *Envisioning the national health care quality report.* Washington, DC: National Academy Press.

Institute of Medicine. (2002). *Unequal treatment: Confronting racial and ethnic disparities in health care.* Washington, DC: National Academy Press.

International Red Cross launches campaign against stigma of AIDS (2002, June 3). *AIDS Weekly,* p. 20.

Jackson, J., Williams, D., & Torres, M. (1995). Perceptions of discrimination, health and mental health: The social stress process. In *Socioeconomic conditions, stress, and mental disorders: Towards a new synthesis of research and public policy* (pp. 1–26). Retrieved November 15, 2002, from http://www.mhsip.org/nimhdoc/socioeconmh_home.htm

Kaiser Commission on Medicaid and the Uninsured. (2001). *The uninsured and their access to health care.* Washington, DC: Author.

Kaiser Family Foundation. (1999a). *Key facts: Race, ethnicity and medical care.* Washington, DC: Author.

Kaiser Family Foundation. (1999b). *Medicare managed care.* Washington, DC: Author.

Kaiser Family Foundation. (2002). *National survey of physicians part 1: Doctors on disparities in medical care.* Washington, DC: Author.

Kaiser Family Foundation, HRET, & The Commonwealth Fund. (2002). *Erosion of private health insurance coverage for retirees.* Washington, DC: Authors.

Keppel, K., Pearcy, J., & Wagener, D. (2002). *Trends in racial and ethnic-specific rates for the health status indicators: United States, 1990–1998* (Healthy People 2000 statistical notes, no. 23). Hyattsville, Maryland: National Center for Health Statistics.

Key, S., & DeNoon, D. (1997, September 8). AIDS patients living longer, facing new problems. *AIDS Weekly Plus,* pp. 23–24.

Lazzarini, Z. (1998). The Americans with Disabilities Act after *Bragdon v. Abbott:* HIV infection, other disabilities, and access to care. *Human Rights, 25*(4), 15–18.

Lehman, A., & Steinwachs, D. (1998). At issue: Translating research into practice: The schizophrenia patient outcomes research team (PORT) treatment recommendations. *Schizophrenia Bulletin, 24*(1), 1–10.

Mallik, K., Reeves, R., Dellario, D. (1998). Barriers to community integration for people with severe and persistent psychiatric disorders. *Psychiatric Services, 22*(2), 175–180.

Mason, D., & Nichols, T. (2000). Using public media to teach Medicaid recipients about managed care. *American Journal of Public Health, 90*(1), 34–36.

Massey, O., & Wu, L. (1993). Important characteristics of independent housing for people with mental illness: Perspectives of case managers and consumers. *Psychosocial Rehabilitation Journal, 17*(2), 81–92.

McCourt, C. (2000). Life after hospital closure: Users' views of living in residential "resettlement" projects. A case study in consumer-led research. *Health Expectations, 3,* 192–202.

McKnight, J. (1997, March/April). A 21st-century map for healthy communities and families. *Families in Society,* 143–153.

McLean, A. (1995). Empowerment and the psychiatric consumer/ex-patient movement in the United States: Contradictions, crisis, and change. *Social Sciences Medicine, 40*(8), 1053–1071.

Mickelson, J. (1995). Advocacy. In R. Edwards (Ed.), *Encyclopedia of social work* (19th ed., pp. 95-100). Washington, DC: NASW Press.

Moniz, C., & Gorin, S. (2003). *Health and health care policy: A social work perspective.* Boston: Allyn & Bacon.

Moore, M. (2000). Advocacy lifts the bottom line. *ASHA Leader, 5*(6), 6.

Morrissey, J., & Goldman, H. (1984). Cycles of reform in the care of the chronically mentally ill. *Hospital and Community Psychiatry, 35*(8), 785–793.

Morrissey, J., Stroup, T., Ellis, A., Merwin, E. (2002). Service use and health status of persons with severe mental illness in full-risk and no-risk Medicaid programs. *Psychiatric Services, 53*(3), 293–298.

Moss, K., Ullman, M., Starrett, B., Burris, S., Johnsen, M. (1999). Outcomes of employment discrimination charges filed under the Americans with Disabilities Act. *Psychiatric Services, 50*(8), 1028–1035.

Munetz, M., Grande, T., & Chambers, M. (2001). The incarceration of individuals with severe mental disorders. *Community Mental Health Journal, 37*(4), 361–372.

National Alliance for the Mentally Ill. (n.d.-a). *NAMI StigmaBusters.* Retrieved on October 21, 2002, from http://www.nami.org/campaign/stigmabust.html

National Alliance for the Mentally Ill. (n.d.-b). *Where we stand: parity in insurance coverage.* Retrieved October 6, 2002, from http://www.nami.org/update/unitedparity.html

National Association of Community Health Centers. (2002). *Issue Brief 1, Strategies for early network development.* Washington, DC: Author.

National Association of Public Hospitals and Health Systems. (2001). Coverage expansion proposals. Retrieved September 26, 2002, from http://www.naph.org/Content/Navigation Menu/Issues_Advocacy/Access_to_Care

National Council for Community Behavioral Healthcare. (2002, October). *National Council News, 35*(9), 1–10.

National Council on Disability. (2002). *The well-being of our nation: An intergenerational vision of effective mental health service and supports.* Washington, DC: Author.

National Governors Association Center for Best Practices. (n.d.). *Issue brief: Health insurance coverage and financing.* Retrieved September 25, 2002, from http://www.nga.org/center/topics/1,1188,D_355,00.html

National Institute of Diabetes & Digestive & Kidney Disease. (2003). *National diabetes statistics, general information and national estimates on diabetes in the United States, 2000.* Bethesda, MD: National Institutes of Health.

National Institute of Mental Health. (2000). *Mental health in rural America: How research is helping.* Retrieved September 24, 2002, from http://www.nimh.nih.gov/research/senatemhwg.cfm

National Institute on Aging. (2000). *Strategic plan to address health disparities, FY 2000–2005.* National Institutes of Health, Bethesda, Maryland.

National Mental Health Association. (n.d.). *It is time to pass comprehensive health insurance parity!* Retrieved September 26, 2002, from http://www.nmha.org/state/parity/ index.cfm

National Mental Health Consumers Self-Help Clearing House. (n.d.) *Consumer-run businesses and services.* Washington, DC: Author.

New Freedom Initiative. (n.d.). *Interim report to the president.* Retrieved November 1, 2002, from http://www.whitehouse.gov/news/freedominitiative/freedominitiative.html

North Carolina Justice and Community Development Center. (2002). *Low-income children and adults with Medicaid coverage win Fourth Circuit Appeal in dental lawsuit.* Retrieved on September 20, 2002, from http://www.ncjustice.org/health/Dent_PR_ May_02.htm

Perkins, J. (2002). Medicaid: Past successes and future challenges. *Health Matrix, 12*(1), 7–38.

Petrila, J., & Brink, T. (2001). Mental illness and changing definitions of disability under the Americans with Disabilities Act. *Psychiatric Services, 52*(5), 626–630.

Pol, L. (2000, August). Health insurance in rural America. *Rural Policy Brief, 5*(11), 1–10.

President's New Freedom Commission on Mental Health. (2002). *Interim report to the president, October 29, 2002.* Rockville, MD: Author.

Rapp, C. (1998). *The strengths model: Case management with people suffering from severe and persistent mental illness.* New York: Oxford University Press.

Ridgeway, P., & Zippie, A. (1990). The paradigm shift in residential services: From the linear continuum to supported housing approaches. *Psychosocial Rehabilitation Journal, 13*(4), 11–31.

Rodwin, M. (2000). *Promoting accountable managed health care: The potential role for consumer voice.* Indianapolis: Indiana University Law School, Center for Law and Health.

Rowland, D., & Salganicoff, A. (1994). Commentary: Lessons from Medicaid—improving access to office-based physician care for the low-income population. *American Journal of Public Health, 84*(4), 550–552.

Scheyett, A., & Fuhrman, T. (1999). Managed behavioral healthcare in a rural environment: Lessons learned from Carolina Alternatives. In I. Carleton-LeNay & R. L. Edwards (Eds.), *Small towns and rural communities* (pp. 119-133). Washington, DC: NASW Press.

Scheyett, A., & Kim, M. (in press). Can we talk? Using facilitated dialogue to positively change student attitudes towards people with mental illness. *Journal of Teaching in Social Work.*

Schlesinger, M. (1997). U.S. health policy. *Journal of Health Politics, Policy, and Law, 22*(4), 2–65.

Scott, B. S. (2002). *Using culture and tradition to fight diabetes: Closing the gap.* Washington, DC: U.S. Department of Health and Human Services, Office of Minority Health.

Segal, S., Silverman, C., & Temkin, T. (1995). Measuring empowerment in client-run self-help agencies. *Community Mental Health Journal, 31*(3), 215–227.

Siegal, H., Fisher, J., Rapp, C., Kelliher, C., Wagner, J., O'Brien, W., et al. (1996). Enhancing substance abuse treatment with case management: Its impact on employment. *Journal of Substance Abuse Treatment, 13*(2), 97–98.

Silow-Carroll, S., Anthony, S., Sacks, H., & Meyer, J. (2002). *Reaching out: Successful efforts to provide children and families with health care.* Battle Creek, MI: W. K. Kellogg Foundation.

Smith, V., Ellis, E., Gifford, K., Ramesh, R., & Wachino, V. (2002). *Medicaid spending growth: Results from a 2002 survey.* Menlo Park, CA: Kaiser Family Foundation.

Social Security Administration. (n.d.) *The Ticket to Work and self-sufficiency program: Final regulations.* Retrieved on November 4, 2002, from http://www.ssa.gov/work/Resources Toolkit/FinalRegs2002.html

Somlai, A., Kelly, J., Otto-Salaj, L., McAuliffe, T., Hackl, K., DiFranseisco, W., et al. (1999). Current HIV prevention activities for women and gay men among 77 ASOs. *Journal of Public Health Management Practice, 5*(5), 23–33.

Steinman, M., Sands, L., & Covinsky, K. (2001). Self-restriction of medication due to costs in seniors without prescription coverage: A national survey. *Journal of General Internal Medicine, 16*(12), 793–800.

Thrall, T. H. (2001). Communities take charge. *Hospitals & Health Networks, 75*(12), 52–54.

Unger, K., Anthony, W., Sciarappa. K., & Rogers, S. (1991). Supported education programs for young adults with long-term mental illness. *Hospital and Community Psychiatry, 42*(8), 179–183.

U.S. Census Bureau. (2001). *Health insurance coverage: 2001,* Table 1. Retrieved October 3, 2002, from http://www.census.gov/hhes/hlthins/hlthin01/hi01t1.html

U.S. Department of Health and Human Services. (1999). *Mental health: A report of the Surgeon General.* Washington DC: Author.

U.S. Department of Health and Human Services. (2002, September 24). *HHS fact sheet: Protecting the health of minority communities.* Washington, DC: Author.

Valdiserri, R. (2002). HIV/AIDS stigma: An impediment to public health. *American Journal of Public Health, 92*(3), 341–342.

Waitzkin, H., Williams, R., Bock, J., McCloskey, J., Willging, C., & Wagner, W. (2002). Safety-net institutions buffer the impact of Medicaid managed care: A multi-method assessment in a rural state. *American Journal of Public Health, 92*(4), 598–610.

Weil, M., & Gamble, D. (1995). Community practice models. In R. L. Edwards (Ed.), *Encyclopedia of social work* (19th ed., pp. 577–593). Washington, DC: NASW Press.

What's behind the Medicare HMO woes? (2000). *People's Medical Society Newsletter, 19*(6), p. 1.

CHAPTER 24

Community Practice in Children's Mental Health

Developing Cultural Competence and Family-Centered Services in Systems of Care Models

Terry L. Cross

Barbara J. Friesen

The mental health system is driven by the needs and preferences of the child and family, using a strengths-based perspective. Family involvement is integrated into all aspects of service planning and delivery. The locus and management of services are built on multi-agency collaboration and grounded in a strong community base. A broad array of services and supports are provided in an individualized, flexible, coordinated manner and emphasize treatment in the least restrictive, most appropriate setting. The services offered, the agencies participating, and the programs generated are responsive to the cultural context and characteristics of the populations that are served.

—Center for Mental Health Services, 1998, p. 3

For more than two decades, advocates for children's mental health, supported by the federal government, have pursued significant changes in service systems and delivery in a model referred to as *systems of care*. These changes arose in response to a fragmented system in which parents were frequently blamed for their children's mental health problems, where agencies that served children seldom talked with one another, and culturally based behaviors were often judged as one more sign of pathology. Prior to the systems of care movement, there were no federal policies to positively influence practice in children's mental health. Achieving needed changes took a movement comprising service providers who recognized the system problems, grassroots parent groups willing to fight for better services, and professionals and grassroots advocates of color, working to end discriminatory practices and to gain access to services for children of color. Together, they conducted research, sponsored public meetings, and rallied for the necessary legislation to bring the systems of care model to its current level.

A system of care is defined as a comprehensive spectrum of mental health and other necessary services that are organized into a coordinated network to meet the multiple and changing needs of children and adolescents with serious emotional disturbances and their families. According to Stroul and Friedman (1996), the core values of the systems of care model state that services must be

- Child centered and individualized
- Family focused, with families as full participants in the planning and implementation of formal and informal services and supports
- Community based (services, management, decision making, interagency collaboration, integrated services)
- Culturally competent

Planning and implementation of these systems of care is an exercise in community practice. Holding these principles in place, once gained, is proving to be equally as challenging, as budget cuts and privatization threaten the system of care ideals in many locations. However, when children end up in locked facilities because there are no community-based mental health services for them and when the demographics of those children include children of color at a rate 5 to 10 times their representation in the general population, community practice professionals cannot rest (Center for Mental Health Services, 200).

This chapter examines two of the core values of the systems of care model, cultural competence and family centeredness, and discusses community practice strategies for their implementation. As illustrated in Table 24.1, these two principles share many common values and should be pursued simultaneously. Working to bring each principle to reality, however, also involves giving attention to the unique history and circumstances associated with the call for cultural competence and for family-centered systems. For this reason, the two principles are discussed in separate sections of the chapter, noting overlap where it occurs.

Cultural Competence

The culturally competent system is defined as a congruent set of policies, structures, practices, and values that together empower service providers to deliver effective

Table 24.1   Comparing Elements of Culturally Competent and Family-Centered Systems

Element	Family-Centered System	Culturally Competent System
Respectful and inclusive	Acknowledges the expertise and wisdom of parents and other caregivers, using them as a resource for planning	Values diversity and embraces culture as a resource
Self-assessing	Engages in continuous quality improvement using feedback from families and youth	Is capable of cultural self-assessment
Knows dynamics of difference	Recognizes that families, service providers, and policymakers are likely to have different values and perspectives	Is conscious of the dynamics, risks, and potential conflicts inherent when different cultures intersect
Has knowledge of cultural issues	Is prepared to address the values, needs, and preferences of families from diverse backgrounds	Has institutionalized knowledge about various cultures and cultural issues
Has adapted services to culture, community	Individualizes services to meet the needs of each child and family	Has adapted services to fit the cultural diversity of the community served
Strengths based	Builds on the strengths and capacities of children and families	Views cultural strengths as a resource for help and change
Family focused	Is committed to keeping children with their families (and to using innovative strategies to accomplish this goal) Addresses the needs of the entire family (family defined broadly: family support, siblings, extended family)	Recognizes the family, as defined by culture, as the primary point of intervention
Participatory	Recognizes family members as full partners in the planning, implementation, and evaluation of services (at all levels)	Includes people of diverse cultures in the planning process, and sets goals of service that are consistent with goals of various groups
Broad definitions of "help"	Acknowledges the importance and power of informal as well as formal services and supports	Includes natural helpers and support networks as integral to the system of service delivery
Consumer-oriented	Views families and youth as customers Recognizes the importance of family-run organizations as a source of informal and formal support and as mechanisms through which participation in organizational and system-level planning can be realized	Recognizes the importance of culturally specific services and agencies

services to diverse populations. A culturally competent organization, according to Cross, Bazron, Dennis, and Isaacs (1989), should

- value diversity and embrace culture as a resource.
- be capable of cultural self-assessment.
- be conscious of the dynamics, risks, and potential conflicts inherent when different cultures intersect.
- have institutionalized knowledge about various cultures and cultural issues.
- have services that can be adapted to fit the culture of the community served.

Each of these five elements must function at every level of the system. Values, policies, infrastructure, and practices must all be congruent within all levels of the system (Cross et al., 1989). Practice must be based on accurate perceptions of client behavior; policies must be impartial; infrastructure must be responsive to diverse needs; and values must be unbiased. Unbiased does not mean being color- or culture-blind. It means recognizing, respecting, and valuing the differences of others.

Family-Centered Services

As noted in Table 24.1, community-based mental health and other services that are family centered must be

- respectful and inclusive.
- strengths based.
- family focused.
- participatory.
- consumer oriented.

A family-centered system can be compared to a program-centered system (Friesen & Huff, 1996). The family-centered system focuses on the family as a single unit, emphasizing its needs, strengths, and preferences, understanding that formal services usually are short-term and often occur during a transition period in the life of the family. From a family's perspective, a question might be, "What place do formal services have in our lives at this time?" Adequately addressing the needs of a family may require the resources and concerted efforts of a number of agencies. This can be contrasted with a program-centered model, in which each agency is focused on a single issue and the biggest concern appears to be, "How do this family's needs fit the services that we have to offer?" (Friesen & Huff, 1996). These two views are contrasting but not incompatible; community planners need to be able to hold both perspectives at the same time.

Respectful and Inclusive

This first element means that the philosophy, policies, structures, and practices of the system of care acknowledge the expertise and wisdom of parents and other caregivers and use them as a resource for planning.

Strengths Based

A central tenet of system of care principles is that services should build on the strengths and capacities of children and families (Stroul & Friedman, 1996). This principle is restated here, however, because of the legacy of family blaming that has characterized much of mental health theory and practice and continues to be taught in professional schools (Johnson, Renaud, Schmidt, & Stanek, 1998; Ruffolo, Sugamele, & Taylor-Brown, 1994). A strengths-based approach also includes a broad definition of *help* in recognition of the importance of informal relationships and supports. Many families use broad networks of informal supports (e.g., friends, relatives, church and social groups) instead of or as a complement to formal services. These informal networks will ultimately sustain them long after formal services have ended; thus, it is particularly important to acknowledge the wide variety of beliefs and preferences that characterize families across cultural backgrounds (Friesen & Koroloff, 1990).

Family Focused

The concept of family is broadly defined to include any blood or interpersonal ties that are important to the child and constitute strong and supportive bonds. Two important ideas should be emphasized here. First, the system of care must be committed to keeping children in their communities and with their families, and the system includes a willingness to use innovative strategies to accomplish this goal. Second, services must be designed to address the needs of the entire family—parents, brothers and sisters, grandparents, and other extended family members.

Participatory

Here, the system of care recognizes family members as full partners in the planning, implementation, and evaluation of services at all levels (individual—in this case, child and family—organizational, system, and policy). All families should be allowed and encouraged to participate in planning and reviewing services for their children. At the organizational and system level, family participation is best supported when there is a family-run advocacy organization represented in planning and evaluation processes.

Consumer Oriented

This principle is included to acknowledge that the system of care exists to serve the needs of children and youth who have emotional, behavioral, or mental problems and their families. Thus, children and their families are the customers; they should have full input about the type of services and manner of delivery involved in the assistance they receive. In addition, family-run organizations should be recognized as an important source of informal and formal services and supports and as a desirable mechanism through which participation in organizational and system-level planning can be realized.

Strategic Planning

Community practice has helped bring about and actualize cultural competency and family-centered practice in the system by strategically planning for their development and operation. This strategic approach requires assessing the environment for social, political, and economic conditions that present supporting resources or challenging barriers to systems change. Change is guided by a mission and vision that is shared among stakeholders and propelled by advocates developing support both internally and externally. Internally, change agents sensitize others and clarify goals to build a constituency with vision. Externally, advocates form alliances, empower and organize grassroots advocates, and promote role models to "give away the problem and share the vision" (Cross et al., 1989).

To achieve results, community practitioners must develop appropriate resources, which include people (parents, diverse professionals, community leaders), skills (in relationship building and articulating the problem), information (about situation, background, models, and progress), funding (existing, potential, opportunities, and barriers), and infrastructure (policies, procedures, and contracts).

Leadership development is key to the success of achieving a family-centered, culturally competent system of services. Leadership may be exercised through formal roles such as board membership, heading a department, or chairing a committee, or it may be evident in the informal roles taken on by advocates, elders, and parents. Action in the form of goals and objectives, work plans, and action steps followed up by evaluation help move ideas from concept to reality.

Planning for Cultural Competence

This section describes what a system of care might look like if it were designed to meet the cultural needs of all children with serious emotional disturbances and their families. This model represents an ideal toward which agencies can work and is intended for discussion and planning purposes. It includes suggestions for changes at the policy development and planning level, administrative level, and service delivery level. Implementation would require action at all levels to bring together a congruent set of attitudes, policies, structures, and practices called "cultural competence."

A culturally competent system is one that appreciates and values diversity, understands the cultural forces that impact programs as well as the dynamics that result from cultural differences, institutionalizes cultural knowledge, and adapts its services to fit the cultural context of the clients it serves. These elements are essential to ensure services are appropriately applied and scarce resources are not wasted. For example, American Indian children have historically been misdiagnosed and medicated needlessly due to misunderstood cultural behaviors. African American children have been channeled into the juvenile justice system for the same behaviors that send Caucasian children to be seen in mental health facilities. Latino children from Spanish-speaking families have historically been denied counseling due to language barriers, and Asian children, particularly children of refugee populations, have posttraumatic stress symptoms that often are unaddressed and passed off as cultural behavior.

Cultural competence is not an absolute; rather, it is assessed on a continuum ranging from culturally destructive to culturally proficient. Most agencies in the mental health field are somewhere between these two extremes (Cross et al., 1989). One of the first tasks of the model outlined below is to assess more clearly where an agency falls on this continuum and then develop a strategy for growth. Below is an outline of a model that ideally would promote such growth.

An Organizational Approach

To be effective, the development of cultural competence must be systematic and comprehensive. The system of care must institutionalize cultural competence at every level through the following:

- policies
- structures
- service design and practice approaches
- a value base

The following discussion offers some concrete actions for the improvement of services to people of diverse cultures. These actions are useful steps in the development of a true working partnership between people of diverse cultures and system planners and decision makers. Cooperative efforts, in turn, empower agencies and professionals as well as clients and communities in meeting their needs. The more an aggregate of such actions is developed, the further the system will move toward cultural competence. For example, many cultural groups have an extensive and a clearly defined extended family system. To achieve cultural competence, an agency would need to incorporate a flexible definition of family in its policies. Intake forms, client information systems, and consent forms would need to accommodate multiple caretakers of children. Family services would need to include extended kin in family group meetings, and the entire extended family would need to be assessed for its strengths and resources.

Policy and Planning

Cultural competence is developed over time through training, experience, guidance, and self-evaluation. Change occurs in a complex interplay between practice and policy set in the context of politics and the culture of the system. Cultural competence is not something that happens merely as a result of training or education; it is a process dependent on willingness to change and commitment to provide quality services for all. It can be accomplished only when policy, practice, and attitudes come together in a congruent service system.

At the policy level, policymakers can enhance the cultural competence of the agency by revising mission statements to address cultural issues. Setting minimum standards for services to children of diverse cultures, identifying client families' cultural identity, and teaching employees about needs of specific groups are essential. Personnel policies that require staff members to be culturally competent can become a solid foundation for holding a workforce accountable for competent services. Agency policies that require adequate identification of the cultural identity of families and data collection about needs of specific groups are essential.

Community Participation

An effective decision-making structure is one that listens to diverse voices and empowers the less powerful segments of communities. For example, one agency asked representatives of a targeted cultural community to conduct focus groups about service gaps, employed consultants from that community to analyze the results, and then contracted with grassroots providers from the community to fill the identified gaps. Empowerment, in this case, involved an exchange of resources between the system of care and the particular community of color, which enhanced or increased the functional capability of one or both.

Proper planning to bring together the system of care and groups from diverse cultures must be designed to respond simultaneously to various cultural norms and values (Gallegos, 1982). People of varying cultural viewpoints must be included in the planning process, and policies developed must be consistent with goals of all groups represented by the service program. To improve services to children of color, one state agency created a multicultural advisory group (see Gutiérrez, Lewis, Nagda, Wernick, & Shore, Chapter 18, this volume) and contracted with an ethnic-specific agency to conduct key informant research at the grassroots level. The agency published the findings and recommendations and sought comment from the communities to be served. Based on feedback and essential findings, the top recommendations to improve service to children of color were implemented.

Incorporating cultural competence into a 5-year plan is one way to break down the process into manageable parts with reasonable timelines. Planning steps include the development of a mission statement as well as the development of policies and procedures that enhance services.

The first step toward such a culturally competent policy-making process is recruiting community involvement (Brown, 1977; Higginbotham, 1987; VanDenBerg & Minton, 1987; Wilkinson, 1980). To do so, policymakers must establish linkages with existing networks in communities of color. Key individuals within each of these communities must serve on advisory bodies, task force groups, and/or evaluation teams. The skills needed to successfully bring diverse stakeholders to the table include such relationship-building and communications skills as genuine listening, humility, active engagement in work, or loan of resources in support of the causes of the target community. One private agency leader, after years of failed outreach attempts, began to volunteer at a community-based, culturally specific organization. His contacts at this organization led to an invitation to join a community task force, and within a year, his agency had secured board members, staff, and volunteers from that cultural community.

At the state or agency level, advisory groups have been effective in helping to develop and guide standards for cross-cultural services. Agencies that have committed the resources necessary to consult community cultural advisers and implement recommended policies have experienced the most success (Cameron & Talavera, 1976). Many agencies have discovered that community cultural advisers or consultants should be used on more than a critical-need-only basis. The development of ongoing relationships that have fostered mutual respect has enhanced the effectiveness of the consultation process.

Service Design

Culturally competent interventions incorporate the concept of equal and nondiscriminatory services; they also go beyond that to include the concept of services responsive to their particular client population. Planning for culturally competent services necessitates a careful assessment of the environment in which change is desired to identify barriers to and resources for change. Such an assessment is accomplished through the use of existing methods conducted in culturally sensitive ways or through the development of new methods. Appropriate assessment methods may be determined after gaining an understanding of the cultures represented in the community.

Locus of Intervention

A culturally competent system of care recognizes the family, as defined by culture, as the primary point of intervention. Service units are adapted to keep count and reimburse service providers equitably for services that are culturally tailored. Natural helpers and support networks are included in the system of service delivery as integral, legitimate service providers. Community practice engages these helpers as brokers linking a family to a helper. The successful community practice professional knows the cultural protocol for engaging and compensating the natural healer and assists the family in following protocol and offering the appropriate compensation. For example, in some Native American communities, helpers are engaged only after a designated number of exploratory conversations and an offering of tobacco. Relationship and trust are key elements that grow with exposure, sincerity, and positive experiences.

The grassroots community and its supports are mobilized through network building. Treatment plans consider the whole person and make available or help bring to bear those services and resources that help to right the balance of the individual and family.

Funding

In a culturally competent system of care, funding procedures and requirements become an incentive for developing cultural competence. Policies encouraging the improvement of services to diverse cultural groups have more influence when they are attached to funding. Funding agencies have the capacity to greatly influence the development of services by placing requirements on contract or grantee agencies.

Standards of service delivery that address cultural competence help make this possible (Center for Mental Health Services, 2001).

Funding mechanisms and paths can be adapted to improve service access for people of diverse cultures. For example, through the use of contracting, agencies can fund culture-specific service providers who might not otherwise be able to respond to community needs. Funding pilot or demonstration projects that symbolize efforts toward cultural competence not only provides working models, but also helps to increase the awareness of diverse community members. Successful projects are more likely to receive continued financial support.

Administrative and Management Structures

The administrative level of a service delivery system not only creates policy but also oversees its interpretation and implementation. At this stage in the process, commitment to cultural competence must be embraced and promoted.

When we use the term *structure,* we mean procedures, resources, forms, and any other administrative tools or processes that help the agency function. Some agencies find administrative structures helpful in enhancing agency cultural competence. Advisory committees or cultural consultants are helpful in keeping the organization in tune with events and needs in various communities. Agencies that use a team approach are finding that designating a member of the team as cultural coordinator helps the team keep the issue in focus. Other agencies work to enhance cultural competence by requiring that every child of color have a cultural plan. Such plans address identity enhancement, recognize group esteem as an element of self-esteem, and enhance the interdependence of extended families.

Self-Assessment

An administrator's primary role is to set the context for the development of cultural competence within the agency. Essential to this process is some form of self-assessment. First, the administrator must define the service population, determine the demographic characteristics of the agency's service area, and review policies and procedures to ensure that staff and governing boards are representative of this population. The degree to which services and programs are accessible, both physically and culturally, to all segments of the community and the compatibility of the agency's philosophical orientation with the belief systems of the community being served must also be assessed. Such a process addresses whether the system has the capacity to adapt its services to meet the needs of a diverse client population. There are now a number of formal tools designed to be used for self-assessment in organizations and communities (Goode, Jones, & Mason, 2002).

Preparing the Workforce

Staffing and training guidelines should be developed by agency administrators to ensure that all staff members are culturally competent and that people of diverse cultures are recruited and retained on the staff. It is essential that employees and volunteers alike have diverse perspectives and an understanding of behavioral health, including knowledge about the unique issues facing children of color with mental illness. When developing job descriptions, administrators should include cultural competence as a qualification. Performance criteria for cultural competence should be clearly communicated and incorporated into performance reviews. Both internal and external evaluations, including client surveys, should be conducted regularly. Career advancement can be made contingent, in part, on an employee's responsiveness to unique needs of clients in their culture; training can be implemented if necessary. Continuing education to improve cross-cultural understanding should be mandatory. Guidelines for culturally competent practice are provided by many organizations, including the Center for Mental Health Services (2001) within the federal government.

The recruiting and hiring processes of a culturally competent agency should remain flexible. A candidate's academic record is important, but it is only one of the many criteria that must be considered when judging ability to deliver competent services. For example, understanding cultural protocol for engaging natural helpers is usually not learned in school. Community recognition of a person as an effective helper should be another consideration. Paraprofessional positions can also be established to engage the services of helpers without formal credentials. It is important to remember, however, that cultural competence requires much more than hiring a token number of minorities. Administrators and supervisors must ask themselves if they are hiring people because of the color of their skin, yet expecting them to act congruently with mainstream (white middle-class) staff and "leave their own culture at the door," or because organizational leaders really are invested in creating diversity of thoughts, backgrounds, and viewpoints to enhance service delivery.

Administrators can ensure that appropriate resources and networks are established to support culture-specific service provisions—indeed, without administrative structures, workers are unable to carry out necessary culturally appropriate practices. Training and orientation to clients' cultures and communities must be routine, mandatory, and supported in the supervisory processes. A network of community experts may be used as a training source. For example, church elders or community health workers are excellent sources of information about community networks. Training should occur in both workshop settings and on-site in the communities served, and it should be both recurrent and comprehensive. Some agencies have found success when staff, community leaders, and cultural experts all participate in the selection and development of content for training.

Resources/Network Building

Administrators and supervisors should actively seek and secure the services of consultants versed in culturally competent practice and/or in the character of the specific cultures of the groups the agency serves. Consultants should be used to help build networks, select community advisors, develop helping approaches, and design and conduct culturally appropriate evaluations. Consultants or appropriately trained staff can act as brokers between the formal system and the helping networks within communities. Consultants and community advisors can also help determine the sites from which the agency can best reach targeted communities. As child mental health agencies contract with community-based programs and organizations, a more functional and responsive service network is formed. These efforts can foster and support the development of cultural community-designed and -operated programs. Increasingly, through more specific contracting regulations and requests for proposals, funders are requiring mainstream agencies to be culturally responsive in their contracting process for service provision.

Service Delivery and Practice

Culturally competent service delivery is dependent on both practice models and skills. Models designed to respond to the context of the targeted client population help ensure meaningful services. Cross-cultural practice skills (e.g., intervention, assessment, counseling, etc.) developed through training and supervision help ensure quality in service delivery.

Holistic/Context-Driven Approach

Culturally competent mental health providers view the client holistically in the context of culture, community, and family. All aspects of the individual (i.e., mental, physical, emotional, and spiritual) are in the realm of the practitioner's interventions as long as those interventions are guided by the context in which the client lives. Client self-determination should be ensured by the worker. Assimilation or adoption of mainstream cultural values is not the focus of treatment; however, adaptation and adjustment are subjects of discussion, as are identity and self-concept, and each client has a cultural plan as part of his or her service plan.

Outreach and Community-Based Models

Service providers work in the homes and communities of their clients. They seek out key individuals in each community with whom they work to educate community members about available services. Workers become identified as part of the community and become, in some instances, informal extended family members or recognized natural helpers. Service model designs emanate from the community through a task force approach, and service models are tested and adapted for specific concerns, interests, or needs of various communities.

Use of Natural Helpers

The caseworker or a consultant acts as a cultural broker to facilitate the client's or family's access to natural helpers and natural support networks. Practitioners learn about the roles of natural helpers and the character of functional support networks (i.e., extended family, churches, neighbors, and clans). When natural resources exist, the professional helps the client use them more effectively and, when unavailable, the caseworker helps the client develop resources.

Planning for a Family-Centered System of Care

State or system-level policies can do much to promote culturally competent, family-centered services. For example, Washington State has developed standards for children's mental health services and cultural competence that providers must meet to be certified. Full family participation and the participation of representatives of cultural groups, including the voices of youth, is crucial at this level because it is here that decisions are made and standards are set about service definitions, priorities, resource allocation, provider qualifications, and a myriad of other important issues. However, it is at this level that family members are often least prepared to participate because they lack experience at the system level, information about how the system operates, and an understanding of political considerations on decisions. Building credibility for family input constitutes a particular challenge at this level.

Koroloff, Hunter, and Gordon (1995) discuss four major barriers identified by family members and professionals regarding family participation in policy-making bodies, including (a) parental barriers such as lack of time and energy, family crises, and child care and supervision responsibilities, disruption in home life, blame and stigma, and a sense of vulnerability about speaking up, including fear of losing services; (b) structural and procedural barriers created by the policy-making body, including inconvenient meeting times and locations, refusal to reimburse families for expenses, lack of representation or tokenism, and lack of appreciation for cultural differences, including language barriers; (c) professionals' attitudes and behaviors, including lack of support for parental input, lack of respect for families' perspectives, and the pervasiveness of professional subcultures or "in groups"; and (d) impediments related to the service system, such as the slow rate of change that characterizes most bureaucracies and the lack of available services.

One important consideration with regard to family participation at the policy level is that family input is probably most effective when family members are representatives of a family advocacy and support organization rather than simply representing themselves and their own family's concerns. This approach accomplishes several things. First, family members who represent a constituency of members of a family organization gain credibility because they are seen as speaking for a larger group of families. This strategy is especially effective when the family organization has regular policy forums or other mechanisms to present issues and solicit feedback from family members who serve on a variety of decision-making bodies, as well as from its membership at large. Family members who represent such a constituency thus have support and a sounding board for their ideas. In addition, creating policy teams provides backup for individual family members serving on a given committee, so that others can fill in when family or employment demands interfere with the ability to attend meetings.

Family advocacy and support organizations focused on children's mental health have members successfully serving on a number of state-level boards, committees, and task forces such as state mental health planning councils, health and child welfare advisory groups, and interagency planning councils, among others. Family organizations have also been successful at initiating policy change (Briggs, Koroloff, & Carrock, 1994). For example, in Oregon, family members worked with state agencies and other advocacy groups to pass legislation prohibiting the child welfare system from requiring that families give up legal custody of their children in order to gain access to needed out-of-home services (Blankenship, Pullmann, & Friesen, 1999; Friesen, Giliberti, Katz-Leavy, Osher, & Pullmann, 2003; McManus, Reilly, Rinkin, & Wrigley, 1993). Representatives of family organizations also served on an advisory committee for an evaluation of the implementation of this policy (Blankenship, Pullmann, & Friesen, 1999). Their input was crucial in identifying the details of implementation problems and strategies for improvement. In Georgia, the Georgia Parent Support Network took leadership in designing a comprehensive, family-centered system of care. The Georgia Parent Support Network (2004) now operates the system of care for children with mental health problems and their families, in collaboration with other mental health, health, and social service organizations.

Organizational/Agency Level

Those seeking to move toward a culturally competent, family-centered system of care will also want to examine policies, administrative structures, and practice within agencies or other organizations that constitute the community's provider network. Families, of course, should be fully involved in this process; administrative staff can model commitment to family participation by inviting family members to serve on review teams, evaluation groups, and/or boards of directors. Family members also can serve important roles as employees of the system, either directly or through contracts with family organizations. A full discussion of the various service delivery and support roles that family members occupy in systems of care is beyond the scope of this chapter, but common functions include helping families through the intake process; preparing for service and/or educational planning meetings; and serving as system guides to help families negotiate complicated access, eligibility, and service requirements (Friesen & Stephens, 1998; Koroloff, Friesen, Reilly, & Rinkin, 1996). Recently published guidelines for hiring consumers and family members provide a potential policy framework for this aspect of practice (Consortium for the Employment of Parent Representatives, 2002).

Conducting a review at the agency or organizational level will often begin with the agency mission statement, asking simply whether it adequately reflects the goals that the organization is trying to achieve and the organization's intentions with regard to family and cultural issues. This process provides an opportunity for all staff to reflect on the organization's mission and reflect about how well its policies, structures, and practices are aligned with that mission.

Personnel policies are one area that may be strategically leveraged to promote desired change. Incorporating goals of cultural competence and family-centered service into personnel policies provides an excellent opportunity to promote accountability on the part of individual workers. Likewise, skills in areas such as cultural competency and family-centered practice can be incorporated into job descriptions. In California, a consortium of counties has adopted a framework for a family/professional development plan, which each participating county can tailor to fits its specific needs. The Sonoma County plan calls for family participation in all levels of policy making, the grievance structure, evaluation of services, and staff hiring and performance review (Simpson, Koroloff, Friesen, & Gac, 1999). In addition, the plan states that job descriptions and performance expectations for staff are reviewed to ensure that they reflect family/professional partnership advocacy.

Another area for review is the service process, from intake to termination. Because it is the first contact that families have with the agency or system, the intake process often makes a lasting impression on children and their families. Family members who serve as part of this review will be able to identify points at which to repair the process. Important points to consider include the following:

Do we engage in any intake practices that may be interpreted by families as blaming? Many agencies still gather extensive social and psychological history at the first meeting. Although not intended to communicate blame, questions about whether a pregnancy was planned or whether breast-feeding occurred may suggest or reinforce a parent's fears that the child's problems are a result of their attitudes, behaviors, or experiences.

Does our intake procedure routinely identify child and family strengths as well as problems? A strengths-oriented intake procedure helps families enter the helping process with a sense of hope and possibility.

Do we allow families to tell their stories and ask for their input about what help is most needed? Can we understand the family in the context of its community, its culture, and its unique situation? The process of defining needs and making decisions about services is an area where the family-centered nature of services becomes most apparent. The mental health field has largely moved beyond the point where asking for concrete services (e.g., food, housing, child care) is interpreted as denial or resistance of psychological issues or mental health needs, but many agencies, especially mental health organizations, are not equipped to provide comprehensive services. That is usually accomplished through referral to other agencies or through contractual arrangements with a consortium of services. Here, it is very important to make sure that the services that families need are actually available and accessible, so that families don't get the "community runaround."

Family members are also essential partners in the evaluation process (Jivanjee, Schutte, & Robinson, 2004; Vander Stoep, Green, Williams, Jones, & Trupin, 2000). Turnbull, Friesen, and Ramirez (1998) propose a continuum of family participation in research and evaluation that ranges from being research subjects, on one end of the spectrum, to becoming designers and principal investigators of studies, assisted by people with research and evaluation expertise. The Federation of Families for Children's Mental Health, a national family support and advocacy organization, has developed an evaluation training curriculum that reflects a similar approach (Federation of Families for Children's Mental Health, 2000). Family members play a variety of roles in evaluation, helping to design studies (Vander Stoep et al., 2000), collect data, interpret findings, and consult about or participate in dissemination.

With regard to services for their own children, parents and other caregivers often are in the best position to take the lead in evaluating how well interventions are working. DeChillo, Koren, and Schultze (1994) reported that responsiveness to feedback about the evaluation of services on the part of service providers was one of four factors that characterized collaborative practice.

Summary

This chapter has briefly outlined some of the issues that community practitioners should consider as they work toward a family-centered and culturally competent child mental health system of care. Please note that it only scratches the surface of the many possibilities for planning and policy development. It is advisable to take a long-range approach in such work and to implement changes in a well-planned, progressive manner to ensure that all communities and cultural groups receive the best representation and services.

References

Blankenship, K., Pullmann, M., & Friesen, B. J. (1999). *Keeping families together: Implementation of an Oregon law abolishing the custody relinquishment requirement.* Portland, OR: Portland State University, Research and Training Center on Family Support and Children's Mental Health.

Briggs, H. E., Koroloff, N. M., & Carrock, S. (1994). *The driving force: The influence of statewide family networks on family support and systems of care. Statewide family advocacy organization demonstration project, 10/90–9/93. Final Report.* Portland, OR: Portland State University, Research and Training Center on Family Support and Children's Mental Health.

Brown, E. F. (1977) Self-determination for Indian communities: A dilemma for social work education and practice. In F. J. Pierce (Ed.), *Mental health services and social work education with Native Americans.* Norman: University of Oklahoma.

Cameron, J. D., & Talavera, E. (1976). An advocacy program for Spanish-speaking people. *Social Casework, 57,* 417–431.

Center for Mental Health Services (CMHS). (1998). *Annual report to Congress on the evaluation of the Comprehensive Community Mental Health Services for Children and Their Families Program.* Rockville, MD: Author.

Center for Mental Health Services (CMHS). (2001). *Cultural competence standards for managed care mental health services: Four underserved/underrepresented racial/ethnic groups.* Rockville, MD: Author.

Consortium for the Employment of Parent Representatives. (2002). *Guidelines.* Gainesville, FL: Institute for Child Health Policy.

Cross, T. L., Bazron, B. J., Dennis, K. W., & Isaacs, M. R. (1989). *Towards a culturally competent system of care: A monograph on effective services for minority children who are severely emotionally disturbed.* Washington, DC: Georgetown University Child Development Center.

DeChillo, N., Koren, P. E., & Schultze, K. (1994). From paternalism to partnership: Family/professional collaboration in children's mental health. *American Journal of Orthopsychiatry, 64*(4), 564–576.

Federation of Families for Children's Mental Health. (2000). *The world of evaluation: A training curriculum.* Retrieved November 24, 2003, from http://www.ffcmh.org/WorldOfEval.htm

Friesen, B. J., Giliberti, M., Katz-Leavy, J., Osher, T., & Pullmann, M. (2003). Research in the service of policy change: The "custody problem." *Journal of Emotional and Behavioral Disorders, 11*(1), 39–47.

Friesen, B. J., & Huff, B. (1996). Family perspectives on systems of care. In B. A. Stroul (Ed.), *Children's mental health: Creating systems of care in a changing society* (pp. 41–67). Baltimore: Paul H. Brookes.

Friesen, B. J., & Koroloff, N. M. (1990). Family-centered services: Implications for mental health administration and research. *Journal of Mental Health Administration, 17,* 13–25.

Friesen, B. J., & Stephens, B. (1998). Expanding family roles in the system of care: Research and practice. In M. H. Epstein, K. Kutash, & A. Duchnowski (Eds.), *Outcomes for children and youth with emotional and behavioral disorders and their families* (pp. 231–259). Austin, TX: Pro-Ed.

Gallegos, J. (1982). Planning and administering services for minority groups. In J. Austin & W. Hershey (Eds.), *Handbook on mental health administration: The middle manager's perspective* (pp. 87–105). San Francisco: Jossey-Bass.

Georgia Parent Support Network. (2004). *What we do.* Retrieved April 4, 2004, from www.gpsn.org

Goode, T., Jones, W., & Mason, J. (2002). *A guide to planning and implementing cultural competence organization self-assessment.* Washington, DC: National Center for Cultural Competence, Georgetown University Child Development Center.

Higginbotham, H. N. (1987). The culture accommodation and mental health services for native Hawaiians. In A. B. Robillard & A. J. Marsella (Eds.), *Contemporary issues in mental health research in the Pacific islands* (pp. 94–126). Honolulu: University of Hawaii Press.

Jivanjee, P., Schutte, K., & Robinson, A. (2004). *Families as evaluators: Annotated bibliography of resources in print.* Portland, OR: Portland State University, Research and Training Center on Family Support and Children's Mental Health.

Johnson, H. C., Renaud, E. F., Schmidt, D. T., & Stanek, E. J. (1998). Social workers' views of parents of children with mental and emotional disabilities. *Families in Society, 79*(2), 173–187.

Koroloff, N. M., Friesen, B. J., Reilly, L., & Rinkin, J. (1996). The role of family members in systems of care. In B. A. Stroul (Ed.), *Children's mental health: Creating systems of care in a changing society* (pp. 409–426). Baltimore, MD: Paul H. Brookes.

Koroloff, N. M., Hunter, R., & Gordon, L. (1995). *Family involvement in policy-making: A final report on the Families in Action Project.* Portland, OR: Portland State University, Research and Training Center on Family Support and Children's Mental Health.

McManus, M., Reilly, L., Rinkin, J., & Wrigley, J. (1993). *An advocate's approach to abolishing custody relinquishment requirements for families whose children have disabilities: The Oregon experience.* Salem: The Oregon Family Support Network.

Ruffolo, M. C., Sugamele, M., & Taylor-Brown, S. (1994). Scapegoating of mothers: A study of mother-blaming in case studies included in core foundation social work practice textbooks. *Journal of Teaching in Social Work, 10*(1/2), 117–127.

Simpson, J. S., Koroloff, N. M., Friesen, B. J., & Gac, J. (1999). *Promising practices in family-provider collaboration.* Washington, DC: American Institutes for Research, Center for Effective Collaboration and Practice.

Stroul, B. A., & Friedman, R. M. (1996). The system of care concept and philosophy. In B. A. Stroul (Ed.), *Children's mental health: Creating systems of care in a changing society* (pp. 115–130). Baltimore, MD: Paul H. Brookes.

Turnbull, A. P, Friesen, B. J., & Ramirez, C. (1998). Participatory action research as a model for conducting family research. *Journal of the Association for the Severely Handicapped, 23*(3), 178–188.

VanDenBerg, J., & Minton, B. A. (1987). Alaska native youth: A new approach to serving emotionally disturbed children and youth. *Children Today, 13,* 1615–1618.

Vander Stoep, A., Green, L., Williams, M., Jones, R., & Trupin, E. (2000). Parents as evaluators: King County Blended Funding Project evaluation pilot results. In C. Liberton, C. Newman, K. Kutash, & R. Friedman (Eds.), *12th annual research conference proceedings. A system of care for children's mental health: Expanding the research base* (pp. 149–153). Tampa: University of South Florida, Research and Training Center for Children's Mental Health.

Wilkinson, G. T. (1980). On assisting Indian people. *Social Casework, 61,* 451–454.

CHAPTER 25

Community Building and Family-Centered Service Collaboratives

Elizabeth A. Mulroy

Kristine E. Nelson

Denise Gour

Momentum is growing for the creation of comprehensive, community-based approaches to rebuild disinvested communities to better serve families and children. The principal assumption is that improving the quality of communities and neighborhoods through economic and social development will improve the quality of life for the children and families who live there (Burns & Spilka, 1997; Ife, 1995; Sherraden & Ninacs, 1998; see also Rubin & Sherraden, Chapter 26, this volume). The goal is systems change—a mandate that requires public and nonprofit organizations serving children and families, as well as a host of related institutions, to work together in new and different ways—primarily in cooperative interorganizational collaborations—to build healthy communities (Benson, 1997; Mulroy & Lauber, 2002; Schorr, 1997a).

The National Community Building Network states that its purpose is

> to reduce poverty and pursue social and economic equity for all communities by advancing community-building principles—in practice and in policy. . . . There is an intense passion for changing communities, rebuilding fractured lives and creating economic opportunities for people who are trying to swim in America's mainstream. (Berry, 2000)

The community-building movement was started by a diverse group of grassroots organizers, public housing activists, funders, providers of technical assistance, and local residents. One characteristic of the movement is its comprehensiveness; it strives to go beyond fixing people's individual problems one at a time. Rather, advocates acknowledge that the well-being of children, families, and communities cannot be separated (Connell, Kubisch, Schorr, & Weiss, 1995; Mulroy & Shay, 1997; Schorr, 1997b). A number of community-building endeavors have been implemented in urban and rural areas across the country, and in the process, these advocates are challenging the traditional ways of operating both public and nonprofit institutions, delivering services, and practicing social work (Chaskin, Joseph, & Chipenda-Dansokho, 1997; Kretzman & McKnight, 1993; McKnight, 1995; Mulroy & Matsuoka, 2000; Naparstek & Dooley, 1997b; Richman, Brown, & Venkatesh, 1996; Sherraden & Ninacs, 1998).

By examining these trends through the lens of a multifocused model, we can look at the implications for community practice. The model presented here is grounded in the community-building ethic (Ife, 1995). It is intended to (a) respond proactively to increased environmental complexity; (b) improve the way local services for children, families, and seniors are conceived, constructed, and delivered; and (c) remain grounded in and committed to empowerment and social justice for local residents. The case of GEARS (Gaining Empowerment, Access, Responsibility, Support), located in outer southeast Portland, Oregon, is presented as an example of how multifocused community practice works.

Systems Change

Community Building

In many ways, community building is an attitude or perspective—a fresh way of viewing the world at this particular time (Mulroy & Lauber, 2002; Schorr, 1997b). It operates in defined geographic areas in face-to-face relationships with neighborhood residents to build social and human capital (Fellin, 1998; Naparstek & Dooley, 1997a). Community building is not new. Community-based interventions have roots in the utopian and Settlement Movements of the 19th century and extend to the War on Poverty programs and theories of community organizing from the 1960s and community development projects of the mid-1970s (Naparstek & Dooley, 1997a; O'Connor, 1995; Rothman, 1996; Rubin & Rubin, 1992; Weil, 1996, 1997). However, the confluence of several forces in the 1980s and 1990s helped to spur the reemergence of comprehensive community interventions. First came rapid changes in the nature of federal policy dismantling the social safety net, the restrictive categorical nature of programs, and the reduced federal role in fields affecting children and families: health, education, income security, affordable housing, and child welfare (Fisher, 1995; Naparstek & Dooley, 1997b; Weil, 1997, 2000).

Second was the shift to privatization of services from the public sector to the for-profit and nonprofit sectors. This increased reliance on the private sector to achieve public purposes resulted in a purchase-of-service relationship among the sectors and the emergence of a new culture of competitive contracting, which has had adverse impacts on community-based social service organizations (Fabricant & Fisher, 2002; Mulroy & Shay, 1998; Nelson, 2001; Smith & Lipsky, 1993).

Third has been the push from public and philanthropic funders for multidisciplinary collaboration and multisector relationships among organizations, as well as partnerships both in the provision of community-based services and in community problem solving (Potapchuck, 1999). This was motivated in part by Wilson's (1991) research, which linked persistent poverty to intergenerational transmission in neighborhoods of concentrated poverty. Such neighborhoods were found to be without a strong social infrastructure, supportive neighborhood networks, or accessible services (Naparstek & Dooley, 1997a; Wilson, 1991).

Finally, devolution—the downward push of decision making from the federal to the state and local levels of government—was expected to generate more innovative, community-based solutions to complex social problems, particularly those experienced by children and families in their respective localities (Burns & Spilka, 1997; Schorr, 1997a; Weil, 1997). Thus, the community or neighborhood again became the unit of analysis through which to target more comprehensive strategies for much-needed systems change.

Characteristics and implications. A key characteristic of community building is that it merges what is often called "place-based" investment in physical infrastructure such as streets and buildings with "people-based" investment in social infrastructure (Naparstek & Dooley, 1997b; Sviridoff & Ryan, 1996; see also Weil, Chapter 11, this volume). Typically, there are two effects. First, this merging brings together professionals from divergent fields—urban planners, public administrators, nurses, politicians, social workers, and developers—who usually know little of each other's capabilities, potential contributions, or purposes. Second, these professionals work side by side with community residents and other key community actors as equal partners. Tensions may exist on both sides of the decision table until professionals used to working in a top-down, expert-client relationship, each with his or her respective professional "lingo," learn new, egalitarian ways of relating and communicating with residents in a community setting and develop an appreciation of local knowledge (Cohen & Lavach, 1995; Mulroy, 1997; Smale, 1995; see also Castelloe & Gamble, Chapter 13, this volume).

Goal: healthy communities. Comprehensive community interventions are not needed in neighborhoods and communities that are already healthy. According to Bruner, by focusing on solutions rather than problems, the community-building approach first identifies the conditions considered minimal for the success of children in healthy communities:

- economic and physical security
- environmental and public safety
- a nurturing and stable family environment
- adult role models and mentors in the community
- positive peer activities
- opportunities to exert effort and achieve success
- health care for medical needs

- decent schools and schooling
- access to professional services to treat conditions or needs that may require professional care (Bruner, 1998, pp. 6–11)

These conditions then become the community indicators for disinvested neighborhoods or rural areas. However, achieving the goal of true and lasting systems change—not just tinkering at the margins of discrete systems—also requires an understanding of the underlying causes of poverty among the specific populations in a locale (Wilson, 1991), as well as a clear understanding of the reasons for disinvestment in these neighborhoods. Only after these key concerns have been addressed can a set of comprehensive strategic responses be developed (Bruner, 1998). The strategic responses typically adhere to four essential principles:

1. They are comprehensive and integrative.

2. They leverage new forms of partnerships and collaboration (Hendrickson & Omer, 1995).

3. They view the neighborhood as the unit of analysis for the purpose of enhancing residents' participation.

4. They build on neighborhood assets, resources from residents, and existing institutions (Naparstek & Dooley, 1997a).

Three Directions for Practice

As the community-building movement continues to expand, three themes emerge that are important for social work practice: the need for strong community-based organizations (CBOs), a single continuum of care for family-centered services, and new community-based interorganizational collaborations.

Strong Community-Based Organizations

Community building relies on the existence of strong CBOs, usually small nonprofit agencies that offer programs tailored to local residents' needs, provide opportunities for civic participation, and have long-term financial sustainability (DeVita, Manjarrez, & Twombly, 2000). This organizational capacity has been threatened by the effects of privatization and devolution, resulting in the closing or merging of many smaller CBOs in very low-income neighborhoods. While collaborations, mergers, acquisitions, and closures may be seen by some as examples of market alignment and needed restructuring, the need to build organizational capacity to sustain small, nonprofit CBOs in very low-income neighborhoods is of central concern to the future of community building.

A Continuum of Family-Centered, Community-Based Services

When conceptualized as a continuum, the field of child and family services becomes a seamless, noncategorical way to distribute "caring energy" (Martinez-Brawley &

Delevan, 1993) across a wide spectrum of family realities that reflect distinct strengths, needs, and problems over time (Weil, 2000). A similar continuum exists for community engagement with and care for seniors. The reality of many families is that the middle generation provides caregiving and much caring energy for both parents and children. Enormous caring energy and resources are wasted when people fight over the efficacy of prevention versus intervention programs. The continuum, as conceived by Weil (2000), is comprehensive and community based. It acknowledges that all forms of service, starting with informal developmental and support programs designed to promote healthful families and prevent problems through formal interventions such as child welfare services, have a needed and respected place on the continuum. The major service areas include family support, family preservation, family group conferencing, and child welfare. Service continuums for addressing the needs of adults with disabilities and seniors focus primarily on the setting for service delivery. The classic article on a continuum of care for frail older adults is Kane and Kane (1980). For a more recent review of the issue, see Palley and Van Hollen (2000) and Jome's response (2000).

Family support services are particularly compatible with community building. The family support movement contends that "all families have strengths and assets, are viewed as partners, deserve support, [and] need comprehensive services and opportunities to develop their capacities" (Resource Coalition of America, 1995). People-based activities such as educational programs, volunteerism, recreation, leadership development, job-readiness training, and civic pride events fold into place-based community economic development activities and are mutually reinforcing as community economic and social development (Harris, 1997; Ife, 1995; Sherraden & Ninacs, 1998; see also in this volume, Midgley & Livermore, Chapter 7, and Rubin & Sherraden, Chapter 26).

Despite the organizational complexity and multisector nature of all child, family, and senior services today, viewing such services as a multisystemic continuum of care offers social workers and their community partners a holistic conceptual framework from which to develop and select a range of options appropriate for specific families in their respective communities at a given point in time.

Interorganizational Collaboration as Process

Interorganizational collaboration is the means to an end within the community-building movement. It is the process through which community-building goals can be achieved, not an end in itself (in this volume, see Roberts-DeGennaro & Mizrahi, Chapter 16, and Morrison Chapter 21). Therefore, most social workers engaged in child and family services will be community practitioners, and a major focus of their work will be the development and sustainability of complex interorganizational partnerships and collaborations.

Social workers may be skilled in participating in and facilitating interdisciplinary collaborative teams for case conferences, but this work is different. The task is to work across organizational boundaries to create new interorganizational forms and structures. This boundary-spanning work involves a high degree of uncertainty because the needed alliances have yet to be identified or constructed.

Research on community-based collaborations is limited, but a number of phases of interorganizational development have been identified: assembling/sponsorship, planning, initiation, institutionalization, stabilization, and termination (Alter, 2000; Bailey & Koney, 1995; Mulroy, 2001; Vosburgh & Perlmutter, 1984). The point of entry and form of assembly/sponsorship is key to how the process will unfold, who claims ownership of it, who funds it, and who controls it. The community approach to economic and social development begins inside the targeted geographic community with a visioning process conducted by and for local residents and community stakeholders (Benson, 1997). This "inside out" approach (Kretzmann & McKnight, 1993) is grounded in assets accumulation and the development of indigenous leadership (Ife, 1995; Ramanathan & Link, 1999). CBOs in particular have local legitimacy to lead this phase, as they usually have established authority to invite nonlocal but like-minded organizations to become partners.

Conversely, conventional wisdom among planners of comprehensive community initiatives and demonstration projects is to assemble a large, multisector audience to include all organizational stakeholders at the outset. The rationale is that many are needed to solve problems that are complex and multidimensional (Chaskin et al., 1997; Naparstek & Dooley, 1997b). However, starting small and growing incrementally has also been found to offer benefits, particularly in the sustainability of a collaboration (Benson, 1997; Mulroy, 2001). For example, incremental growth allows time to build new interpersonal relationships that lead to new interorganizational relationships. It facilitates learning how to share power, negotiate and resolve conflicts, communicate effectively, build mutual trust, and develop a common theory for the innovation, what Alter calls a "common cognitive structure" (2000, p. 293), which provides a similar definition of the problem and agreement on the solution and how to achieve it. This becomes the shared vision—the compelling motivation to participate and to stay involved. In sum, the interorganizational form will become a viable structure for the next several decades, and social workers can expect not only to work in many variant forms at the same time but to help in the design and implementation of them.

Multifocused Practice

Family-centered initiatives require thinking about and across multiple systems and having the ability to see that the problems of children, families, seniors, and their communities are inextricably intertwined. Alter (2000) suggests that for this work, skills are needed in all areas of traditionally defined social work practice: management, program planning, direct service, and community organizing and development.

- Executive managers need to build and maintain strong community-based organizations capable of providing the added value that arises from and is needed for participation in collaborations. They must be risk takers with leadership skills who are ready to leap into yet-unformed interorganizational arrangements and help mold them into partnerships, alliances, or networks.

- Program-level planners and managers provide relationship-building skills. They must have knowledge about and appreciation for potential multidisciplinary, multisector, multiorganizational contributions. They need to work across organizational boundaries to create new program entities, and they need to use technical skills to design management information systems and evaluation procedures capable of measuring the results and outcomes of the interorganizational endeavor.
- Strong direct practice skills are needed in natural settings. Street corners, laundry rooms in public housing complexes, and other informal settings provide community-based locations to engage residents as partners.
- Community organizers are needed to facilitate grassroots organizing and development and to defend nonprofits against co-optation. Community-based nonprofits that collaborate with public-sector partners that may also be their funders may be intimidated by the power differential and lose their motivation to advocate on behalf of the poor.

However, skills alone are not enough. Equally important are values, attitudes, and work style. What is needed is an overarching commitment to social justice as a core principle; a participatory, culturally sensitive concept of community; an adherence to the shared vision; cooperative behavior and preference for teamwork; an acceptance of multiple and fluid staff roles; and skill sharing among coworkers and residents (Alter, 2000; Ife, 1995; Nelson & Allen, 1995; Weil, 2000). The case of GEARS provides an example of a family-centered service collaborative.

The Case of MFS-GEARS

In Portland, Oregon, Metropolitan Family Services (MFS), a social services agency, collaborated with GEARS (Gaining Empowerment, Access, Responsibility, Support) to form MFS-GEARS, a multifaceted community-based program with a multilingual team of neighborhood leaders and social workers who help community members access social services, education, and health care. Located in the outer southeast part of the city, an area with few resources and many needs, MFS-GEARS works to create a sense of community and self-sufficiency. In 2000, 178 volunteers provided more than 2,000 hours of service as parent helpers, bilingual assistants (in Spanish, Russian, and Arabic), group facilitators, office assistants, classroom aides, and neighborhood cleanup volunteers (see the MFS-GEARS website for additional details). The founding and development of MFS-GEARS offer examples of the multifocused practice skills necessary to establish and sustain comprehensive community-based initiatives that include management, program development, direct service, and community organizing.

Management

MFS-GEARS is the result of a combination of vision, leadership, and supportive community organizations dedicated to empowering and improving the lives of neighborhood residents and the community as a whole. A social work intern with training in community-based approaches, as well as organizational leadership skills and the courage and willingness to innovate, along with a preexisting network of community agencies, were the underpinnings of a new approach to supporting family, neighborhood, and economic development. The social work intern applied community organizing methods such as organizing focus groups, facilitating community resource mapping, and recruiting natural leaders as paid staff. MFS provided training and ongoing consultation to the social work intern in staff development, strategic planning, and marketing. The worker's outreach to other neighborhood organizations revealed their common interest in broader community strategic planning. As funding opportunities arose, it was apparent to everyone that a collaborative application for larger grant awards would be more advantageous than competing against one another for smaller grants and narrowly focused programs.

Strong Community-Based Organizations

At the time of MFS-GEARS's inception, MFS had recently reinvented itself as a multifaceted, community-based social service agency. Although mental health services had been a large part of its 50-year history, the agency could no longer sustain these services in a fiercely competitive managed-care environment. Instead, the agency decided to focus on and expand its diverse offerings of community-based services, which included in-home health care for disabled and frail older adults, a foster grandparent program, and senior volunteers working with elementary school children to improve academic performance, social interaction, and parental involvement. In these programs, MFS was already committed to strengthening and preserving the quality of community life and enhancing residents' participation. Most of the programs employed natural helpers or volunteers from the community, offering stipends to senior volunteers and providing wages and benefits comparable to those of other health organizations and above minimum-wage salaries for certified nursing assistants.

For several years, MFS had been part of a diverse range of collaborators from local agencies who had been meeting as the Outer Southeast Caring Community to discuss common concerns. The participants included publicly funded agencies such as county-sponsored family centers; private, nonprofit social service agencies such as MFS and a neighborhood health clinic; and a grassroots organization—the Neighborhood Pride Team, founded and staffed by local residents. This network provided information and support essential to the development of the GEARS program, including identification of needs and community resources and help in recruiting the original staff from the neighborhood.

Using unexpended grant and United Way funds from a discontinued project, the MFS-GEARS coordinator hired the first coaches, neighborhood residents with life experiences similar to those of the community residents expected to participate in the program. To complete the original resource base, the principal of the neighborhood middle school, who was committed to school-based services, provided office space for the program.

Knowledge of Local Strengths and Needs

With the help of an advocate in county government who had knowledge of the neighborhood, community organizations, and funding sources, MFS-GEARS worked with eight other collaborators to apply for welfare reinvestment funds made available through the county from the Temporary Assistance to Needy Families (TANF) program. All nine organizations had staff members working in the neighborhood within blocks of each other, or they agreed to place staff members in the neighborhood. For the grant application, they developed an assets map of the strengths, needs, and resources of the community and a coordinated plan for responding to the identified needs. In addition, a recently published statistical profile from the county health department documented two specific targets for community intervention: high rates of infant mortality and of recidivism among people released from prison. Other needs included an underdeveloped public infrastructure (dirt roads and lack of a central sewage system) in this community, which was annexed by the city of Portland in 1990.

Risk Taking

Although MFS had a 50-year history as a multiservice agency with United Way funding and extensive fund-raising and grant-writing capacity, MFS-GEARS was different from the other programs offered by the agency because it did not provide service directly but instead linked participants to other resources while building community involvement. Aspects of the program that may have appeared risky to other organizations, such as using community residents as line staff members and providing services in natural settings, were already part of other programs in the agency. Indeed, some of the collaborators in the original grant expressed concern about employing neighborhood residents without professional education or training. This was a liability risk that MFS was willing to assume, given its previous experience.

Still, starting with only a coordinator, one half-time and three full-time coaches, and a program assistant, and proposing to organize and link services in an impoverished area of the city, was a risky proposition. Not only MFS but the county advocate who had assisted the new collaborative to obtain more than a million dollars in county money for an untried program accepted this challenge.

Multiple Coalitions, Partnerships, and Networks

From the original Caring Community and nine collaborators on the county grant, MFS-GEARS's partnerships expanded via funding from a local foundation for health care outreach; county Community and Family Services funds to replace the welfare reinvestment grant; and small local grants and contracts, including a grant from a local health maintenance organization for outreach to Russian- and Spanish-speaking residents eligible for state medical benefits. In addition, the local bureau of housing and community development provided funding for office space for coaches in outposts that came to be called connection sites. In a partnership with private business, Bank of America enabled MFS-GEARS to start the first Families and Schools Together (FAST) program in Portland, in partnership with Portland Parks and Recreation. Finally, a contract from the state department of human services allowed MFS-GEARS to place coaches in public assistance offices, completing a continuum of partnerships from natural support networks through local family support programs to statewide public services.

Program Skills

Relationship building. Relationship-building skills were required on several levels. First, skills in collaborating with other organizations were vital in obtaining grant funding. This included navigating some turf issues about providing services to families, using an unfamiliar program model. Both clarifying the model and establishing relationships with line workers in other agencies were accomplished by placing part-time MFS-GEARS coaches in connection sites in schools, a nonprofit employment development organization, and later in public assistance offices. After it became clear that the other organizations did not understand the service-linking role played by the coaches, MFS-GEARS developed written agreements delineating roles and responsibilities.

The MFS-GEARS model is based on empowering relationships with both coaches and participants. From the outset, policy has been set democratically, with coaches and professional staff members taking responsibility for its development. Coaches, for example, played a key part in creating the MFS-GEARS mission statement. Also, from the beginning, collaborative goal-setting between participants and coaches included an agreement that participants would reciprocate by helping out as volunteers in some capacity.

Working with multiple organizations. After the feasibility of the program model was established in the first 18 months, the focus of the MFS-GEARS staff became sustainability. To enhance its ability to obtain grants and contracts, MFS-GEARS hired an evaluation consultant to assist in designing user-friendly assessment and evaluation forms to collect data on services and outcomes. Key outcome measures, achievement of goals, and completion of tasks were integrated into the goal-setting process with each participant. The evaluation data gathered in the early years of the program provided the basis for obtaining further grants and contracts from multiple sources.

Direct Service Skills

Natural settings. Using coaches from the community provided a basis for less formal relationships with participants, but it required clear goals, boundaries, and mentoring by professionals. Coordinators accompanied new coaches on their first visits with participants. Weekly team meetings, group supervision, and individual supervision constituted ongoing staff training efforts and facilitated implementation of policies and procedures developed collaboratively with the coaches. Experienced coaches became mentors for new coaches. Professional staff members modeled collaborative relationships with coaches, who are expected to work collaboratively with participants. To develop these skills at the beginning of the program, professional staff members received supervision and support from a mental health professional experienced in group process.

Despite the advantages of working with natural helpers in the community, several obstacles had to be overcome. The coaches, who had either a high school or general education degree, did not understand the responsibilities of the professional coordinating team (for example, fund-raising) and questioned the pay differential between the two groups. Partly to overcome this differential, career development for coaches to further their education and move them into higher-paying jobs became a critical part of building and maintaining staff morale.

Clients as partners. At MFS-GEARS, community residents taking part in the program are called participants, not clients. They are expected to share responsibility for reaching goals and for reciprocating by donating their time or sharing their skills with other participants or the community. After an initial period of providing in-home services, MFS-GEARS began to encourage participants to come in to connection sites to reduce their isolation and increase their self-confidence in reaching out to community resources. Large numbers of participants and other community volunteers take part in community-building events sponsored by MFS-GEARS, including clothing exchanges, school events, and activities in the larger neighborhood. Success in integrating participants into the community is validated when they are hired as staff by MFS-GEARS or other community organizations.

Community Organizing Skills

Grassroots advocacy. While MFS-GEARS does not advocate directly, it collaborates with grassroots advocacy organizations including local welfare rights organizations. Participants and coaches also testify at the city, county, and state levels to support needed programs and press for policy changes. In addition, participants learn self-advocacy to enhance their self-determination and ability to access resources.

Co-optation. In its development, MFS-GEARS faced several challenges resulting from its collaboration with public and private agencies, challenges that could have undermined the program model. For example, in the welfare reinvestment grant, the county originally wanted MFS-GEARS staff to record participants' social security numbers, a request likely to be greeted with suspicion in an immigrant population. A different kind of co-optation was avoided in working with the health maintenance organization. In Oregon, children and families with low incomes are eligible for free health insurance through the Oregon Health Plan (OHP). HMOs receive funds from the state to provide services to people eligible for OHP, but they are subject to losing this funding if they do not serve such clients. Many people who are not accustomed to having health insurance use emergency rooms as their primary care provider, a very costly service to HMOs and the OHP. This HMO contracted with MSF-GEARS to provide staff to encourage new low-income members to make their first appointment with a primary care provider and to identify people with serious untreated health risks (e.g., diabetes). The HMO originally wanted MFS-GEARS to contact new members by telephone to make appointments and administer a health-risk questionnaire. The HMO was not aware of the significant barriers their new members faced, including language differences, lack of transportation, and unfamiliarity with health care systems. Although home visits are more costly than telephone calls, MFS-GEARS successfully advocated for face-to-face, personal visits with new members. Demonstrated outcomes soon justified the costs.

One of the most recent concerns has been maintaining the program's integrity in school-based programs, which must meet statewide academic standards to justify their funding. This places tremendous pressure on schools to show academic success, measured by benchmark testing. These test scores fail to take into account the impact that socioeconomic, language, and cultural challenges have on a child's ability to learn. MFS-GEARS services, along with other MFS school-based social service programs, are often seen as ancillary (at best) to academic achievement and are consistently challenged to demonstrate the connection between systemic social service support and student academic success. MFS-GEARS has successfully negotiated all these challenges by standing its ground and maintaining the original program model.

Conclusion

The emergence of comprehensive community-based approaches to rebuilding neighborhoods and improving the lives of children and families has stimulated many innovations in social services organizations and in social work practice. Going beyond fixing individual problems one at a time requires systemic change at the community level, collaboration among different disciplines and organizations, and empowerment of community residents. Characteristically, the resulting strategic responses are comprehensive and integrative, leverage new types of partnerships and collaborations, enhance resident participation, and build on neighborhood assets and resources.

Strong community-based organizations, usually small nonprofit agencies, can establish a continuum of family-centered, community-based services through collaboration. The development and sustenance of complex interorganizational partnerships is an integral part of social work in child, family, and senior services. Social workers must be able to span professional boundaries, tolerate the uncertainty of new organizational entities, help create a local vision, and develop indigenous leadership. Starting small and growing incrementally allows time to build these new relationships.

Fostering multifocused practice across multiple systems requires strong leadership and risk taking from executive managers, relationship-building and evaluation skills in program planners and managers, strong direct practice skills in line staff members, and community organization skills to guard against co-optation by public sector partners. MFS-GEARS and many other successful community-based programs demonstrate the feasibility and effectiveness of community-building approaches in addressing problems of poverty, neighborhood disintegration, and lack of access to services and resources while they empower local residents and secure greater social justice for disenfranchised and oppressed neighborhoods.

References

Alter, C. (2000). Interorganizational collaboration in the task environment. In R. Patti (Ed.), *The handbook of social welfare management* (pp. 283–302). Thousand Oaks, CA: Sage.

Bailey, D., & Koney, K. (1995). Developing community-based consortia: One model for creation and development. *Journal of Community Practice, 2*(1), 21–42.

Benson, P. (1996). Beyond the "village" rhetoric. *Assets Magazine,* Autumn, 3–4.

Benson, P. (1997, Autumn). The seasons of growing a healthy community. *Assets Magazine,* pp. 3–5.

Berry, S. (2000, Spring). NCBN from my perspective. *Community Vision, 7*(3). Retrieved July 31, 2002, from http://www.ncbn.org

Bruner, C. (1998). A vision for children, families, and neighborhoods. *The case for kids: Community strategies for children and families—promoting positive outcomes.* Atlanta, GA: The Carter Center, pp. 6–11.

Burns, T., & Spilka, G. (1997). *Assessment report: The planning phase of the Rebuilding Communities initiative.* Baltimore, MD: Annie E. Casey Foundation.

Chaskin, R., Joseph, M., & Chipenda-Dansokho, S. (1997). Implementing comprehensive community development: Possibilities and limitations. *Social Work, 42*(5), 435–444.

Cohen, R., & Lavach, C. (1995). Strengthening partnerships between families and service providers. In P. Adams & K. Nelson (Eds.), *Reinventing human services: Community and family-centered practice* (pp. 261–277). Hawthorne, NY: Aldine de Gruyter.

Connell, J., Kubisch, A., Schorr, L., & Weiss, C. (1995). *New approaches to evaluating community initiatives.* Washington, DC: The Aspen Institute.

DeVita, C., Manjarrez, C., & Twombly, E. (2000). *Organizations and neighborhood networks that strengthen families in the District of Columbia.* Washington, DC: Center on Nonprofits and Philanthropy, The Urban Institute.

Fabricant, M., & Fisher, R. (2002). *Settlement houses under siege: The struggle to sustain community organizations in New York City.* New York: Columbia University Press.

Fellin, P. (1998). Development of capital in poor, inner-city neighborhoods. *Journal of Community Practice, 5*(3), 87–98.

Fisher, P. S. (1995). The economic context of community-centered practice: Markets, communities, and social policy. In P. Adams & K. Nelson (Eds.), *Reinventing human services: Community and family-centered practice* (pp. 41–58). Hawthorne, NY: Aldine de Gruyter.

Gaining Empowerment, Access, Responsibility, Support (GEARS). (n.d.) Retrieved July 30, 2002, from http://www.metfamily.org.

Harris, K. (1997). Integrating community development and family support—The practice, the challenge, the possibilities. *Family Resource Coalition of America Report, 16*(3), 4–5.

Hendrickson, J. M., & Omer, D. (1995). School-based comprehensive services: An example of interagency collaboration. In P. Adams & K. Nelson (Eds.), *Reinventing human services: Community and family-centered practice* (pp. 145–162). Hawthorne, NY: Aldine de Gruyter.

Ife, J. (1995). *Community development: Creating community alternatives—vision, analysis, and practice.* Melbourne, Australia: Longman.

Jome, M. M. (2000). Long-term care for people with developmental disabilities [Letter to the editor]. *Health and Social Work, 25*(4), 283–284.

Kane, R. L., & Kane, R. A. (1980). Alternatives to institutional care of the elderly: Beyond the dichotomy. *Gerontologist, 20,* 249–259.

Kretzman, J., & McKnight, J. (1993). *Building communities from the inside out.* Evanston, IL: Northwestern University, Center for Urban Affairs and Policy Research.

Martinez-Brawley, E., & Delevan, S. A. (Eds.). (1993). *Transferring technology in the personal social services.* Washington, DC: NASW Press.

McKnight, J. (1995). *The careless society: Community and its counterfeits.* New York: Basic Books.

Mulroy, E. (1997). Building a neighborhood network: Interorganizational collaboration to prevent child abuse and neglect. *Social Work, 42*(3), 255–264.

Mulroy, E. (2001, November). *Transforming community-based collaboration: Planning the pace of development.* Paper presented at the Association for Research on Nonprofit Organizations and Voluntary Action (ARNOVA), Miami, FL.

Mulroy, E., & Lauber, H. (2002). Community building in hard times: A post-welfare view from the streets. *Journal of Community Practice, 10*(1) 1–16.

Mulroy, E., & Matsuoka, J. (2000). The Native Hawaiian Children's Center: Changing methods from casework to community building. In E. Netting, D. Fauri, & S. Wernet (Eds.), *Cases in macro practice* (pp. 228–242). Belmont, CA: Brooks/Cole.

Mulroy, E., & Shay, S. (1997). Nonprofit organizations and innovation: A model of neighborhood-based collaboration to prevent child maltreatment. *Social Work, 42*(5), 515–526.

Mulroy, E., & Shay, S. (1998). Motivation and reward in nonprofit interorganizational collaboration in low-income neighborhoods. *Administration in Social Work, 22*(4), 1–18.

Naparstek, A., & Dooley, D. (1997a). Community building. In R. L. Edwards (Ed.), *Encyclopedia of social work* (Supplement 1997, pp. 77–90). Washington, DC: NASW Press.

Naparstek, A., & Dooley, D. (1997b). Countering urban disinvestment through community building initiatives. *Social Work, 42*(5), 506–514.

Nelson, K. (2001). Shaping the future of family-centered services: Competition or collaboration. In E. Walton, P. Sandau Beckler, & M. Mannes (Eds.), *Balancing family-centered services and child well-being* (pp. 359–376). New York: Columbia University Press.

Nelson, K., & Allen, M. (1995). Family-centered social services: Moving toward systems change. In P. Adams & K. Nelson (Eds.), *Reinventing human services: Community and family-centered practice* (pp. 109–126) Hawthorne, NY: Aldine de Gruyter.

O'Connor, A. (1995). Evaluating comprehensive initiatives: A view from history. In J. Connell, A. Kubisch, L. Schorr, & C. Weiss (Eds.), *New approaches to evaluating community initiatives* (pp. 23–63) Washington, DC: The Aspen Institute.

Palley, H. A., & Van Hollen, V. (2000). Long-term care for people with developmental disabilities: A critical analysis. *Health and Social Work, 25*(3), 181–189.

Potapchuk, W. (1999). Building an infrastructure of community collaboration. *National Civic Review, 88*(3), 165–169.

Ramanathan, C., & Link, R. (1999). *All our futures: Principles and resources for social work practice in a global era.* Belmont, CA: Brooks/Cole.

Resource Coalition of America. (1995). *Guidelines for family support practice.* Chicago: Author.

Richman, H., Brown, P., & Venkatesh, S. (1996). The community base for new service delivery strategies. In A. Kahn & S. Kamerman (Eds.), *Children and their families in big cities* (pp. 151–162). New York: Columbia University, Cross-National Studies Research Program.

Rothman, J. (1996). The interweaving of community intervention approaches (with personal preface by the author). *Journal of Community Practice, 3*(3/4), 69–100.

Rubin, H., & Rubin, I. (1992). *Community organization and development.* New York: MacMillan.

Schorr, L. (1997a). *Common purpose: Strengthening families and neighborhoods to rebuild America.* New York: Archer.

Schorr, L. (1997b, Fall). Community rebuilding: Something important is happening. *Family Resource Coalition of America Report,* pp. 27–29.

Sherraden, M., & Ninacs, W. (1998). Introduction: Community economic development and social work. [Special Issue on Community Economic Development]. *Journal of Community Practice, 5*(1/2), 1–10.

Smale, G. (1995). Integrating community and individual practice: A new paradigm for practice. In P. Adams & K. Nelson (Eds.), *Reinventing human services: Community and family-centered practice* (pp. 59–80). Hawthorne, NY: Aldine de Gruyter.

Smith, S., & Lipsky, M. (1993). *Nonprofits for hire: The welfare state in the age of contracting.* Cambridge, MA: Harvard University Press.

Sviridoff, M., & Ryan, W. (1996). *Investing in community: Lessons and implications of the comprehensive community revitalization program.* New York: Comprehensive Community Revitalization Program.

Vosburgh, W., & Perlmutter, F. D. (1984). The demonstration project: Politics amid professionalism. In F. D. Perlmutter (Ed.), *Human services at risk* (pp. 109–125). Lexington, MA: Lexington Books.

Weil, M. (1996). Model development in community practice: An historic perspective. *Journal of Community Practice, 3*(3/4), 5–68.

Weil, M. (1997). Community building: Building community practice. In P. Ewalt, E. Freeman, S. Kirk, & D. Poole (Eds.), *Social policy: Reform, research, and practice* (pp. 35–61). Washington, DC: NASW Press.

Weil, M. (2000). Services for families and children: The changing context and new challenges. In R. Patti (Ed.), *The handbook of social welfare management* (pp. 481–510). Thousand Oaks, CA: Sage.

Wilson, W. J. (1991). Public policy research and the truly disadvantaged. In C. Jenks & P. Peterson (Eds.), *The urban underclass* (pp. 460–482). Washington, DC: Brookings Institution.

CHAPTER 26

Community Economic and Social Development

Herbert J. Rubin

Margaret Sherrard Sherraden

E ven though many neighborhoods, especially inner-city communities of color, confront severe economic and social problems, the public sector ignores their needs, instead continuing to subsidize economic development for the better off. This chapter suggests an alternative model for community renewal, one of humane capitalism, which combines economic and social development in ways that build capacity, increase assets, improve life chances, and empower low-income and low-wealth communities (see also Sherraden & Ninacs, 1998).

The holistic approach we term *humane capitalism* begins by redirecting conventional development to benefit poor neighborhoods instead of just middle- and upper-class communities. For instance, rather than subsidize business development in the downtowns or suburbs, government incentives can be focused on projects built in poor neighborhoods. Humane capitalism also can be accomplished through innovative techniques that go beyond mainstream economic development models. Programs such as Individual Development Accounts (IDAs; see also Padilla & Sherraden, Chapter 5, this volume) help families accumulate assets for long-term investment and development, while land trusts and cooperatives preserve and enhance community assets. Business incubators help would-be entrepreneurs find the economic and social resources to enter the market economy. Social service efforts improve the human capital needed for economic change, while social service agencies provide training and jobs to community members. Advocacy groups work to bring about a humane capitalism through pressuring government to support set-aside jobs for the poor, fund guaranteed loan programs for community enterprises, redirect capital budgets for infrastructure repairs to poor communities, and provide contracts to firms that guarantee "living wages" that enable people to live above the poverty level.

In this chapter, we sketch out the possibilities and challenges for a humane, progressive approach to community economic and social development (CESD). We begin by exploring the philosophy that guides humane capitalism, then highlight a variety of strategies used by community-based organizations to guide these efforts. We briefly examine the technical skills that social workers and other practitioners must master and discuss their role in CESD (Midgley, 1995; see also Midgley & Livermore, Chapter 7, this volume). After identifying dilemmas faced by those involved, we conclude with a challenge to social work education.

Philosophy and Aims

CESD reflects a set of goals that distinguish it from corporate-centered redevelopment. CESD simultaneously addresses social and economic needs of those within the nation's poorest communities. It is inspired by a moral mission to help the poor by fighting systemic economic injustice, recognizing that just as poverty comes about through human neglect, intervention by human agency can reverse the process. In a practical vein, CESD works to provide the poor with the very assets that enable them to escape from cycles of poverty (Edin, 2001).

First, CESD is part of a broader holistic package of community renewal strategies that recognize the need to integrate social and economic development (Midgley, 1995), encourage social change, and strengthen families (Wilson, 1996). Second, CESD involves building capacity by creating institutional structures that facilitate and encourage sustained renewal among people who live within neighborhoods of poverty (Beverly & Sherraden, 1997). Third, CESD builds assets and expands social capital, paving the way for continued development. Asset building provides long-term resources to provide economic stability, to continue economic and social improvement, to increase hope for the future, and to enhance intergenerational welfare (Page-Adams & Sherraden, 1997; Sherraden, 1991, p. 148). By expanding social capital, defined as the "resources embedded in social relations among persons and organizations that facilitate cooperation and collaboration in communities" (Committee for Economic Development, 1995, p. 12; Putnam, 1993), CESD builds capacity for subsequent development (Woolcock, 1998). Social capital not only allows individuals themselves to obtain needed resources but can create an image among business and government that a neighborhood has the capacity to absorb new resources (Gittell & Thompson, 2001).

Fourth, CESD is a catalyst for continued development. In other words, it focuses on projects that not only help the original beneficiary but also generate other neighborhood improvements. For instance, a community-based housing organization that builds an affordable quality housing cooperative may encourage subsequent neighborhood improvement. Or, as Briggs, Mueller, and Sullivan (1997) find, people living in housing cooperatives are more likely to be socially and politically active and show concern about the neighborhood than those renting homes.

Finally, CESD is not simply about an expanded pocketbook, but instead, it aims to enhance personal and community empowerment. Partnerships built among community stakeholders, including public, private, and nonprofit organizations already present within poor neighborhoods, increase capacity for further change (Hirschman, 1988). Networks set up to lure new stores are born anew as they move to fight crime or lobby city hall for a fair share of public improvements.

Approaches to Community-Based Economic and Social Development

The possibility for bringing about a humane capitalism is demonstrated by the wide variety of already successful efforts, such as the examples presented in Table 26.1. Such endeavors range from friends growing their own produce in community gardens (Delgado, 2000) to the multitude of tasks performed by the large Newark-based New Communities Corporation, a virtual nonprofit conglomerate that owns and manages several thousand apartments; provides day care, job training, nursing, and food services; and is a partner in a large supermarket (Rubin & Rubin, 2001).

Housing

Thousands of community groups are involved in building and renovating affordable housing, an important social service that has profound economic consequences. Overall in the last decade, community nonprofits have built more than "550,000 units of affordable rental and ownership housing . . . nearly 40% of which has been completed in the last four years" (National Congress for Community Economic Development [NCCED], 1999, p. 3). Housing does more than shelter people. Neighborhood-led housing construction helps community members gain skills in construction and management while increasing levels of homeownership, which in turn contributes to family stability and low school transfer rates. Communities with higher levels of homeownership, including cooperative ownership, show reduced crime rates and higher political participation (Rohe & Stegman, 1994a, 1994b; Scanlon, 1998).

Commercial and Industrial Development

CESD often includes various forms of commercial and industrial development, including creation of revolving loan funds, startup and expansion of local businesses, assistance to microentrepreneurs from poor communities, and industrial development.

Startup firms, especially those owned by minorities and women, often lack access to the capital needed to see them through the first critical years of operation, while banks are unwilling to provide what they consider risky loans. To encourage

Table 26.1 Examples of Effects of Development Projects at Household and Neighborhood Levels

	Effect on	
	Economic Development	*Social Development*
Individual and household level		
Housing construction and repair	Increase in household assets New jobs in housing construction and repair	Fewer school transfers
Commercial development	More accessible goods and services New jobs in construction and retail	Locally provided goods and services encourage network building
Community social services	Training and job opportunities for local residents Social services (e.g., safe child and eldercare) facilitate employment and household economic development	More social support for residents
Neighborhood level		
Housing construction and repair	Reverses economic deterioration Increases local tax base (more community services and improved schools)	Improves community safety (e.g., neighborhood watch) Increases community participation and political participation Builds local pride and cooperative efforts
Commercial development	Encourages economic investment by local entrepreneurs Increases local tax base allowing for more community services and improved schools	Encourages social investments by local entrepreneurs Street crime reduced with increased foot traffic
Community social services	Develops local expertise and involvement in social services	Improved formal and informal systems of social support

business starts, government agencies, foundations, and sometimes banks make available a lump sum loan or grant to a community group, which sets up a revolving loan fund; the community group can more easily check the credit-worthiness of loan recipients (Rubin & Rubin, 2001).

Some of these startup firms are small businesses—microenterprises—that are either family run or sole proprietorships with few or no employees. CESD organizations provide microenterprises with business training, mentoring, technical assistance, and supportive social services. Because so many microentrepreneurs cannot obtain money from traditional lending institutions, CESDs provide them with access to business loans of a few hundred to a few thousand dollars. Some funding programs follow a method developed in overseas microenterprise programs called *lending circles,* in which entrepreneurs work out business plans in consultation with group members, who then oversee lending and repayment (Counts, 1996; see also Raheim, Noponen, & Alter, Chapter 30, this volume). Members meet at fixed intervals and provide business advice and support to each other (Balkin, 1989). Despite the challenges of replicating strategies developed in other countries (Carr & Tong, 2002), by 1997, there were 283 microenterprise assistance programs in the United States, assisting a total of 57,125 individuals in 24,145 businesses, including 6,300 startups (Langer, Orwick, & Kays, 1999). This included 6,153 people who received loans totaling $33.3 million and 50,972 who received training or technical assistance.

Research suggests that microenterprise increases income and assets in poor households (Clark & Kays, 1999; Raheim & Alter, 1998; Servon, 1999). Even when income gains are negligible or modest, microenterprise has important noneconomic benefits, providing opportunity for personal growth and learning, flexibility for family responsibilities, empowerment, and a positive influence on children (Novogratz, 1992; Raheim & Alter, 1998; Sanders & Sherraden, 1999; Straatmann & Sherraden, 2001). However, microenterprise in the United States seems to attract and work best with those who are not the poorest of the poor (Schreiner, 1999).

Community development organizations may also create and operate their own businesses. In San Francisco, Asian Neighborhood Design's custom furniture store trains its own labor force. In Milwaukee, Wisconsin, Esperanza Unida's auto repair and job training complex has trained hundreds of mechanics and, over time, has spun off day care services, housing, and commercial development, as well as an asbestos removal company (Rubin, 2000). These types of social enterprises may operate independently in the open market, have special contracts or connections with nonprofit agencies, be associated with a national franchise, or form cooperatives, all with varying rates of success (Emerson & Twersky, 1996).

Business incubators are another enterprise development tool used by community development groups. By providing inexpensive business spaces for small startup firms, incubators help small businesses reduce expenses by providing shared photocopy machines, Internet connections, support staff, and other necessities. Some incubator programs teach new entrepreneurs how to develop business plans and learn management and marketing skills. Incubators have been successful in creating jobs that employ community members. For instance, the business center/incubator, the Brewery, created by the Jamaica Plain (Massachusetts) Neighborhood Development Corporation, brings jobs back into the neighborhood. A recent survey indicates that 20% of all employees live within five blocks of the Brewery, another 20% in the Jamaica Plain neighborhood, and another 40% in Boston; only 20% live outside city boundaries (NCCED, 1997, pp. 88–89). Another example, the Appalachian Center for Economic Network (ACEnet), operates specialty food businesses using a community kitchen incubator that acts as a hub for networking as well as a place to produce and package products (ACEnet, 2000).

Community development organizations also partner with traditional entrepreneurs to build shopping centers, restaurants, and malls to serve and employ community members (NCCED, 1997, pp. 88–89). Over the last several decades, CESD organizations have built more than 71.4 million square feet of commercial and industrial property (NCCED, 1999), while encouraging successful entrepreneurs to reinvest in the poor neighborhoods where they grew up. Some community businesses supply ethnic goods and services, such as Hispanic or Asian grocery stores

(Light & Gold, 2000) that appeal to a niche market, while others capitalize on tourists brought into poor communities to visit cultural attractions set up by partnerships between city and community groups. For instance, new stores have been set up in the Kansas City neighborhood that is now home to museums that celebrate the birth of jazz and the Negro Baseball League.

Social Services

Social services are an essential component for CESD. To provide needed services, community groups encourage the expansion of social and health agencies within poor communities while persuading these services to employ community members. In Indianapolis, for instance, a community group refurbished an abandoned school as a Medicaid facility for seniors and worked with other organizations that helped to train community members as care providers (Rubin, 2000). Other efforts provide child day care, community-based medical services, youth programs, and education and job training programs, which offer both needed services and support while training community members as service providers.

Job Creation, Training, and Placement

Job creation, training, and placement have become increasingly important in CESD efforts because the 1996 Temporary Assistance to Needy Families (TANF) program (Personal Responsibility and Work Opportunity Reconciliation Act of 1996) requires that welfare recipients find stable jobs within a limited amount of time. Many states encourage community-based organizations to take on this difficult task (Greenberg, 1999). Community development groups join in employment training networks that bring together a variety of separate organizations to recruit eligible participants, help them acquire job skills, make up for educational deficiencies, and then link them to available jobs (Harrison & Weiss, 1998). Other CESD organizations concentrate on placing those with checkered employment histories or confounding problems in temporary positions to help them gain the skills needed for full-time employment (Molina, 1998).

Some CESD programs create their own businesses and train community members both as their own employees and as workers in comparable firms (Emerson & Twersky, 1996). In addition to Esperanza Unida, discussed above, Bethel New Life in Chicago trains people to work in its home health care facilities and then to move on to other health care jobs. New Communities Corporation (NCC) of Newark, New Jersey, manages apartments, restaurants, food preparation businesses, child care services, and health care facilities. At the same time, it contracts as a job trainer to prepare community health care workers, food workers, and others to work for NCC or find jobs in other firms. The goal is to provide job training that catalyzes other efforts; for instance, NCC restaurant trainees have built careers as independent caterers (Harrison & Weiss, 1998, p. 80).

More specialized employment programs are run by other organizations. In the Chicago area, for instance, Suburban Job Link provides van transportation for inner-city residents to reach suburban jobs (Giloth, 1998, pp. 56–57). In Portland, Oregon; Minneapolis, Minnesota; and elsewhere, government agencies work with community development organizations to establish job nets that publicize employers' job needs; then community groups seek out, and if needed, train potential employees (Molina, 1998). In addition, numerous advocacy efforts in support of living wages have enabled those employed in new jobs to afford both housing and medical insurance (Reynolds, 2002).

Savings

Economic advancement requires building on social and financial assets that the poor often lack. Individual Development Accounts (IDAs) help low- and moderate-income households save. With IDAs, individuals put aside money from earnings, which is then matched at varying rates with public and private funds. The goal is to enable families to accumulate assets for long-term personal and economic development, including education, job training, home ownership, small business (including microenterprise), and retirement. More than 350 community-based IDA programs are operating, and at least 100 more are in the planning stages (Dailey, 2001). At the federal level, legislation for IDA demonstrations passed in 1998 (Sherraden, 2001). At the state level, 22 states have passed IDA legislation and are operating matched saving programs. Welfare policy changes in 1996 included IDAs as state options, and 19 states now use TANF or welfare-to-work funds to offer IDAs to families with very low incomes (Edwards, 2000). Preliminary findings from a nationwide demonstration of IDAs suggest that the working poor can and do save when incentives and financial training are present (Schreiner et al., 2001).

Organizational Forms and Funding

Many, but not all, CESD organizations (CESDOs) are set up in ways that are quite familiar to social workers. Social workers have long worked in community-focused service agencies, as well as for groups that provide housing services; each of these usually has a familiar board-staff nonprofit structure. However, other CESD efforts are run through housing or producer cooperatives in which control is exercised by the tenants or the workers rather than by outside investors or an external board. In cooperatives, each family or worker is a coequal owner/director, setting overall direction and taking shared responsibility.

A less familiar type of CESDO, but one that is increasingly involved in handling the physical work of community-based renewal, is a community development corporation (CDC). CDCs are hybrid organizations that take on characteristics of both nonprofits and for-profits (Peirce & Steinbach, 1987, Stoutland, 1999). As nonprofits incorporated as 501(c)3 organizations, CDCs are eligible for grants from foundations and government and can receive free land donated by government, but unlike most nonprofits, CDCs are legally permitted to make capital investments in property, become stockholders or partners in commercial ventures, provide capital for business ventures, acquire equity debt, and maintain earnings from profits so long as the earnings are used for community betterment. Tax law provides for-profit firms significant financial advantages if they partner with CDCs in projects to benefit poor neighborhoods. CDCs try to blend social and economic missions, but because they are at financial risk if projects fail, they have to make sure that what they attempt is economically viable (Rubin, 2000). CDCs can employ the experts needed to understand the complicated federal programs, such as the New Markets Tax Credit, that provide some funding for community-based economic development programs.

Capital for community reinvestment comes from conventional sources, as well as from public and foundation grants. Increasingly, banks are willing to support community redevelopment initiatives to satisfy Community Reinvestment Act (CRA) obligations (Haag, 2000; Joint Center for Housing Studies, 2002). (The CRA requires banks and thrifts to provide credit and financial services to low-income and minority communities.) Funds for capital projects also come from community-focused nonprofit financial intermediary organizations such as the Local Initiatives Support Corporation (LISC) or Enterprise Foundation (Gittell & Vidal, 1998; Rubin, 2000). Intermediaries also provide technical assistance and act as brokers bringing together for-profit firms, financial institutions, and nonprofit community organizations.

In addition to receiving grants from the public sector or qualifying for conventional bank loans, CESDOs work with and sometimes help to create community development financial institutions (CDFIs) (McLenighan & Tholin, 1997). Community development credit unions (CDCUs) offer credit and financial services to individuals and businesses within low-income and minority communities lacking access to traditional financial services (Tholin & Pogge, 1991; Williams, 1999). Community development banks act like conventional banks in maintaining fully insured deposits and issuing mortgages and conventional loans, but they do so in ways that help rebuild poor neighborhoods (Rubin & Rubin, 2001). The best-known development bank is the Shorebank in Chicago, which has invested tens of millions of dollars in housing, commercial, and industrial development in the South Shore and West Chicago; funds neighborhood renewal projects in Michigan, Missouri, and Ohio; and provides advice to development banks throughout the nation (Taub, 1994). While the CRA has likely increased lending in low-income and minority communities (Haag, 2000), relatively few CDFIs have been created and even fewer of the very poor have benefited from these structures (Balkenhol, 1999).

Skills for Community Social and Economic Development

Clearly, no single profession can adequately prepare people for CESD work, which requires a variety of business, advocacy, and communication skills as well as a great deal of practical experience. Social workers who study social service administration or community practice learn many of these skills as they study planning and project implementation, as well as financing and financial management. However, as

Table 26.2   Skills Needed by Practitioners in Community Economic and Social Development (CESD)

Skills	Description/Additional Problems Faced in CESD Work
Planning	Anticipating and accounting for contingencies that occur as projects proceed
	Planning efforts must overcome past deprivations, while symbolizing hope for the future
Implementation and management	Multidisciplinary team of social and economic development experts and residents work together to bring projects to fruition
	CESD is often undertaken in neighborhoods that others have abandoned and that face numerous historic disadvantages
Financial and financial management	Obtaining and managing the needed capital and operating funds
	CESD projects are often economically marginal and require coordination of numerous and separate forms of financing
Political and interorganizational	Ways of working with other organizations, especially those in the political realm
	Many CESD projects can only be accomplished through elaborate partnerships, while obtaining support for the projects requires political actions, including advocacy

shown in Table 26.2, such skills take on a slightly different slant for those engaged in CESD work.

Planning Skills

Planning means anticipating what will happen as development work proceeds. Planning highlights the interdependence of tasks while determining how specific steps lead to the accomplishment of an overall goal. Successfully planned CESD projects tend to follow a set of guidelines (Rubin & Rubin, 2001). First, the projects that are planned make up for what is missing economically and socially in the community. For instance, affordable day care provides jobs, frees others for employment, and is often in short supply in poor communities. Next, projects are worked out in ways that stimulate further improvements. A CESDO might refurbish a transportation node and by doing so encourage private sector business investment. Third, projects are planned to be as visible as possible, serving as a public symbol that the community is being revitalized. New stores without the metal bars or blockades so often found in poor neighborhoods show that the neighborhood is gaining in confidence. Fourth, projects build on resources already in the community. Local ethnic bakeries are expanded and begin to market their product to upscale specialty stores in wealthier neighborhoods. Finally, with careful planning, projects can be designed to accomplish several goals at once. Rather than just building an apartment house, for example, the ground floor can be left open for enterprises that the neighborhood also needs, such as a coin-operated laundry, a convenience food store, a recreation center, or a police substation.

Implementation and Management Skills

Despite the promise of CESD, implementing programs and projects is difficult and expensive. CESDOs typically work in communities that government, business, and social services have abandoned; that suffer numerous social problems; and in which infrastructure is old and dilapidated. For example, clearing out property for new business or housing can be complicated by the presence of lead paint and asbestos or the presence of the narcotics trade. To give another example, microentrepreneurs often face security problems when they develop businesses in a community without access to nearby banks.

By attempting to accomplish both economic and social goals, CESD costs more. Employing and training community members takes longer and uses more resources than hiring those already prepared. Managing an affordable rental property is expensive because residents may be inexperienced in maintaining their own places and because families may take in relatives or friends who need housing, resulting in severe overcrowding. Running an IDA program requires developing ancillary services for credit repair, financial management, and access to banking. Bratt, Keyes, Schwartz, & Vidal (1994, p. 3) suggest that in these cases, management confronts a "double bottom line" between the CESDO's social mission and its need for economic survival.

Some CSEDOs find that their budgets and staff are insufficient. For example, Bethel New Life, an exemplary community-based CDC, set up a home health care service, but eventually had to withdraw from the effort. This occurred because

> Bethel New Life is a community-based organization and not a medical institution. [I]t was difficult and more costly than they anticipated to build the infrastructure to deliver health care services. Specifically, the start-up costs associated with the program prior to the delivery of services were not covered. In addition, administering such a complex and large program required Bethel New Life to establish procedures and hire staff for a much different program than had previously existed within the organization. (Community Information Exchange, 1995, p. 14)

In addition to acquiring adequate funding, CSEDOs must be sure that they have staff members with appropriate skills. Projects typically require a multidisciplinary team because of the combined social and economic goals of the work. Depending on the focus of the project, the team might include a social worker, as well as people with experience in construction and other trades, building design, security, financing and financial management, and development law, in addition to members of the community who have the day-to-day experience of living and working in the community.

Financing and Financial Management Skills

Financing is rarely available from a single source, thereby requiring mastery of skills and knowledge on how to piece together many separate funding sources.

Local resources and sweat equity provide a beginning (Kretzman & McKnight, 1993), but CESDOs must also generate new resources from outside. As Halpern points out, it is neither reasonable nor fair-minded to rely solely on local community resources:

> Neglected and depleted local communities . . . are created largely by the decisions of others not to invest in, insure, support, or interact with those communities and their residents. . . . It is problematic to then turn around and encourage these same communities to draw on the very types of resources that have been depleted to renew themselves. (1993, p.113)

The complexity of project funding is illustrated in one CESD project to convert an abandoned school to a community office center. The established CESDO invested $167,000 of its own money toward the $2.2 million cost, acquired $1.1 million from conventional loans, another $250,000 from tax syndication proceeds, and $47,000 from local intermediaries. Another 23 grants were obtained, including $300,000 from the Office of Community Services, $50,000 from Housing and Urban Development, $37,500 from the National Trust for Historic Preservation, and grants ranging from $150 to $50,000 from numerous small foundations and businesses (Rubin, 2000, p. 167). Once the money is raised, managing this portfolio requires staff members with adequate financial management skills.

For-profit entrepreneurs rely on money made in previous projects to pay for the predevelopment expenses of future projects—testing the market, doing preliminary engineering work, or hiring an architect. Lacking profit from previous work, CESDOs need to scrounge for money for predevelopment expenses. If they are lucky, they obtain these funds from LISC, a funding intermediary, or from federal Community Development Block Grant (CDBG) funds. CESD practitioners have to know the funding terrain and master skills in leveraging funds—that is, soliciting and using smaller amounts of money to obtain larger investments, as well as piecing together multiple small sources to fund projects.

Political and Interorganizational Skills

In addition to these technical skills in project development, CESD work involves both political skills and knowledge of interorganizational relations. Resources for CESD work come about only through effective advocacy with federal, state, and local governments; private foundations; churches and religious groups; corporations, banks, and local businesses; and private individuals (Rubin, 2000, pp. 171–175). Fortunately, advocacy campaigns have succeeded in making funds available for economic development, infrastructure repair, and housing programs in poor communities (Rubin, 2000, pp. 237–260). For example, a coalition of social workers and their partners convinced the Missouri legislature to provide $4 million a year in tax credits (leveraging a possible additional $8 million in private sector funds) for IDA programs in Missouri (Sherraden, Slosar, & Sherraden, 2002). CESDOs and advocacy groups helped persuade Congress to pass the bill supporting CDFIs and helped thwart efforts to repeal the CRA. Moreover, as a result of advocacy campaigns, federal and municipal legislation often mandates that a minimum percentage of government redevelopment funds be spent through community groups, as occurred in the federal HOME program (Cranston-Gonzales National Affordable Housing Act of 1990).

In addition, skills in networking, partnering, and interorganizational coordination are also vital in CESD work. Partnerships can be frustrating, especially when the partners have different historical roles and professional and practical orientations. CESDOs often have to pressure for-profit partners to make sure that community members rather than outsiders are hired. When working with local government, normal bureaucratic inefficiencies that delay the receipt of funds can be maddening. Conversing with bankers and intermediaries can be problematic because financiers are most concerned about producing countable, visible projects, while CESD groups also focus on the social impacts of their work. Social service funders, such as United Way, do not always understand why a CESDO that owns a $6 million business needs a $50,000 grant for operating expenses (because the business is not making a profit and the CESDO has no way of paying its core expenses). Ironically, when working with neighborhood associations or conventional social service groups, CESDOs are often seen as too concerned with the product and not enough with the social processes.

CESD practitioners must master an array of interorganizational skills to work within such a complicated environment, but doing so can pay off. For instance, the Center for Employment Training is quite effective as a community training program, placing 75% of the people it serves in jobs. Its success comes about because the center is able to work closely with private sector employers, while gaining needed political strength through its association with the activists who formed the United Farm Workers of America (Harrison & Weiss, 1998, pp. 51–53, 57).

Challenges to Community Economic and Social Development

Many of the challenges facing CESD work are obvious enough. CESDOs are often undercapitalized, lacking the reserves needed for startup and long-term survival. The very mission of CESDOs creates fiscal stress. Unlike for-profit businesses, which choose to work where profits are highest, CESDOs work in the nation's poorest neighborhoods, with the highest crime rates, in areas that others have abandoned (Vidal, 1992, p. 81). Special grants must be sought to pay for the costs of alleviating social problems. When grants are insufficient, socially committed development activists end up relying on the limited overhead monies meant to keep the CESDO afloat, further stressing a budget that is already too small. A CESDO that fails to undertake a social mission is little better than a for-profit firm, but a CESDO that is so concerned with handling social problems that it goes bankrupt also accomplishes little.

At times, value conflicts and misunderstandings threaten CESD work. Because CESD work is often undertaken through partnerships that cross boundaries among nonprofit, for-profit, and governmental sectors, organizational cultures can clash. For-profit organizations may be chiefly concerned about running in the black, whereas nonprofits are more concerned about benefiting and empowering poor communities. To resolve such conflicts, these partnerships often end up being managed by separate for-profit subsidiaries of a CESDO that run the newly formed business.

Misunderstandings can also occur between neighborhood associations and CESDOs. Research indicates how the ideals and hopes of neighborhood associations can exceed the limits of economic realities (Rubin, 2000). A neighborhood might want (and deserve) a quality mall, but all the market will support is a basic shopping strip with a grocery store, drug store, and hardware store. Neighborhood association members may be disappointed at the limited scope of the final project.

More generally, concerns exist about whether a focus on economic development distracts from goals for social welfare and social justice (Rubin & Rubin, 2001). Opponents of CESDOs claim that as CESD workers develop technical expertise, master spreadsheets, and pay close attention to the bottom line, they may lose their focus on social justice and become too capitalist. Observers worry that CESD projects are fixing buildings and not taking care of people or changing the broader social structure (Yeoman, 1998). Others are concerned that CESD encourages compromise and collaboration with the power structure when confrontation is required (Fisher & Shragge, 2002).

Direct action and social production may not be easily combined, but they do complement each other. For example, housing production organizations have joined with housing advocacy groups to pressure cities to set up housing trust funds, attack banks that ignore the CRA, and demand more federal funds for affordable housing (Goetz, 1993, 1996; Rubin, 2000). In Illinois, the Chicago Rehab Network, a coalition of housing developers, contracted with an Alinsky-style organizer to coordinate a nonviolent, direct action campaign that secured hundreds of millions of dollars for affordable housing (Ervin, 1994). In numerous efforts, direct action advocates have fought with government to make sure that all contractors who receive public funds and all businesses that receive subsidies are required to hire workers at livable wages—wages above the poverty level—and to provide health benefits (Reynolds, 2002). Community activists need to row the boat with the two oars of direct action and community development by "increasingly using these two strategies, and their related tactics, in complementary ways" (Callahan, Mayer, Palmer, & Ferlazzo, 1999, Introduction).

Another challenge for CESD is the pressure felt by development practitioners to comply with the funders' priorities rather than the local community's priorities. Studies suggest that when partnering with the city to obtain funds, neighborhood groups tend to lose their community focus (Jezierski, 1990). Development activists report "mission drift," the propensity of nonprofits to follow the priorities of the granting agency (Rubin, 2000), and communities resent this lack of "voice" (Sherraden, Slosar, Chastain, & Squillace, 2003).

But even when funds are controlled by a community group, the expertise needed to carry out a project may distance the CESDO from the community. Histories of CDCs show that many begin with volunteer boards and staffs, but after a short time, volunteers can no longer afford the time required to master the technical details, and the organizations become more and more dependent on professional staff (Rubin, 2000). There are no simple solutions to these inherent tensions. One approach is to accept the need for permanent professional staff but then assure that a strong supervisory board is composed of community members. Experts on the staff thus become the hired laborers whose job it is to achieve what the members of the organization want to do. A longer-term approach is to develop local talent through educational and work opportunities for residents who may continue working in local CESD efforts.

CESDOs also have to be clear about whom they are serving. They already help the poor, enabling people with very low incomes to obtain jobs and assisting people with poverty-level incomes to acquire quality homes. Nevertheless, the poorest are still not reached by the community development movement because the deep subsidies needed are simply not available. In addition, CESDO staff members may not have the full range of skills needed to work effectively with members of the community who individually have suffered multiple types of vicitimication. Also, CESDOs must decide how much they will focus on improving the physical attributes of neighborhoods compared to how much emphasis they will place on helping poor individuals directly. Job training programs, especially those involving suburban links, improve the economic outlook of individuals mired in poverty at the risk that successful participants will sooner or later leave the neighborhood, creating a tension between success for the individual and for the community as a whole. Programs to reduce crime or improve the physical infrastructure benefit the neighborhood as a whole, setting up a base for renewal, but they can backfire as wealthier people move in, displacing the resident poor.

Finally, because CESD has been led by community activists and professionals in the field, the focus has been on developing new approaches and identifying best practices. Not unlike community development as a whole, relatively little rigorous research and evaluation has taken place. Despite some exceptions, such as the IDA demonstration (Schreiner et al., 2001), the field would benefit from more research and evaluation that addresses theoretical and practical issues in community social and economic development.

Conclusions

Community economic and social development is about improving economic and social well-being of poor individuals and families and enhancing the capacity within poor neighborhoods for economic rejuvenation. Through entrepreneurial efforts, people learn new jobs and start new businesses. Homeownership and rehabilitation programs provide not only a place to live but also an economic platform for family stability and future investments in family welfare. IDAs enable the poor to accumulate assets to invest in their family's economic well-being. Community organizing and advocacy for livable wages, more jobs, or community services improve the social and economic infrastructure within neighborhoods of need. CESD is a capitalism of renewal and of economic and social uplift that can bring about individual and community empowerment.

Undertaking CESD, however, requires a wide array of skills, tempered by belief in the possibility of social betterment. Practitioners of CESD need to be creative, entrepreneurial, and daring enough to attempt solutions to problems that have perplexed both conventional capitalists and government alike. To be successful, CESD practitioners must master business skills such as financial management, project management, infrastructure development, construction, personnel management, and planning and development. At the same time, they must know how to stimulate people to take charge of their community's development. They must know how to nurture partnerships, build coalitions, and not lose sight that the ultimate goal is social improvement and empowerment. Having this wealth of skills, who would want to work for a nonprofit in the community movement when these very skills can lead to remunerative employment in for-profit firms?

Fortunately, many individuals with backgrounds in social work, planning, public administration, and even business administration are choosing the path of CESD (Brophy & Shabecoff, 2001). The satisfaction of doing good by empowering people and communities makes up for lower income. Many professionals have moved from conventional jobs to join CESD efforts, and at the same time, new graduates from a variety of professional schools are choosing this path. Membership in organizations that support CESD (e.g., National Congress for Community Economic Development, Association for Enterprise Opportunity, the IDA network, the National Community Capital Association) is steadily increasing. Numerous mid-career training programs and online resources help activists gain tools needed for CESD work (Brophy & Shabecoff, 2001).

Academic programs, including schools of social work, are moving in the direction of teaching future CESD workers, albeit not fast enough to meet the need for technically trained and socially responsible leaders in the field. Universities such as Southern New Hampshire University (formerly New Hampshire College), the Pratt Institute, the New School for Social Research, and Spertus College offer focused programs in CESD. In social work, a number of schools are expanding their curricula in social and economic development. These courses are taught in community practice, management, and social development specializations. In others, certificate programs and joint degrees in nonprofit management and leadership, urban planning, and public policy have been developed that include CESD.

Nonetheless, the curricular offerings in CESD should be expanded to prepare new leadership capable of organizing poor communities and administering community-focused development organizations in ways that enable the poor to take ownership of their neighborhoods and control of their own economic fate. As John M. Perkins, the founder of the Christian Community Development Association, said,

> The motto of community development in the 1960s could have been this: "Give people a fish and they'll eat for a day." The 1970s motto could have been: "Teach people to fish and they'll eat for a lifetime." The 1990s (and beyond) approach to development needs to ask the question: "Who owns the pond?" (Perkins, 1993, p. 119)

Social work courses can teach future social workers how to work with community members to help them "fish in ponds that they own." Students should be introduced early in their training to the field of community economic development through field visits, volunteer experiences, and books (Brophy & Shabecoff, 2001; Green & Haines, 2001; Rubin, 2000). These activities can provide factual background on CESD and indicate numerous career paths that can be followed to bring about community renewal. Thereafter, course work can balance technical content with content on social advocacy, coalition building, and organizing. The curricula should expose social work students to other disciplines and future partners in community development work. The content of programs should be shaped in part by discussions about certification in CESD, which are now under way in organizations such as the National Consortium for Community University Partnerships. The curricular goal should be to provide sufficient technical expertise so that the future community developer can help bring about successful CESD projects. At the same time, the curricula should reinforce core values and beliefs about empowering and building capacity within poor communities, not simply providing communities with completed projects.

References

Appalachian Center for Economic Networks (ACEnet). (2000). *About ACEnet.* Retrieved August 24, 2000, from http://www.acenetworks.org/frames/framesabout.htm

Balkenhol, B. (Ed.). (1999). *Credit unions and the poverty challenge: Extending outreach, enhancing sustainability.* Geneva, Switzerland: International Labour Office.

Balkin, S. (1989). *Self-employment for low-income people.* New York: Praeger.

Beverly, S. G., & Sherraden, M. (1997). Investment in human development as a social development strategy. *Social Development Issues, 19*(1), 1–18.

Bratt, R. G., Keyes, L. C., Schwartz, A., & Vidal, A. C. (1994). *Confronting the management challenge: Affordable housing in the nonprofit sector.* New York: New School for Social Research, Graduate School of Management and Urban Policy, Community Development Research Center.

Briggs, X. d. S., Mueller, E. J., & Sullivan, M. (1997). *From neighborhood to community: Evidence on the social effects of community development.* New York: New School for Social Research, Community Development Research Center.

Brophy, P. C., & Shabecoff, A. (2001). *A guide to careers in community development.* Washington, DC: Island Press.

Callahan, S., Mayer, N., Palmer, K., & Ferlazzo, L. (1999). *Rowing the boat with two oars.* Paper presented on COMM-ORG: The On-Line Conference on Community Organizing and Development. Retrieved August 7, 2002, from http://comm-org.utoledo.edu/papers99/callahan.htm.

Carr, J. H., & Tong, Z. Y. (Eds.). (2002). *Replicating microfinance in the United States.* Washington, DC: Woodrow Wilson Center Press.

Clark, P., & Kays, A. (with Zandniapour, L., Soto, E., & Doyle, K.). (1999). *Microenterprise and the poor.* Washington, DC: Aspen Institute, Economic Opportunities Program.

Committee for Economic Development. (1995). *Rebuilding inner-city communities: A new approach to the nation's urban crisis.* New York: Author.

Community Information Exchange. (1995). *Case studies on economic revitalization and health care.* Washington, DC: Author.

Community Reinvestment Act. (1977). Public Law No. 95–128.

Counts, A. (1996). *Give us credit.* New York: Times Books.

Cranston-Gonzales National Affordable Housing Act of 1990. (1990). Public Law No. 101–625.

Dailey, C. (2001). IDA Practice. In R. Boshara, (Ed.), *Building assets: A report on the asset-development and IDA field.* Washington, DC: Corporation for Enterprise Development.

Delgado, M. (2000). *Community social work practice in an urban context.* New York: Oxford University Press.

Edin, K. (2001). More than money: The role of assets in the survival strategies and material well-being of the poor. In T. Shapiro & E. Wolff (Eds.), *Assets for the poor: The benefits of spreading asset ownership* (pp. 206–231). New York: Russell Sage Foundation.

Edwards, K. (2000). *State IDA policy profiles.* Center for Social Development, St. Louis, MO. Retrieved June 17, 2002, from http://gwbweb.wustl.edu/csd/statepolicy/

Emerson, J., & Twersky, F. (1996). *New social entrepreneurs: The success, challenge, and lessons of nonprofit enterprise creation.* San Francisco: Homeless Development Fund.

Ervin, M. (1994). Building blocks: A step-by-step organizing campaign leads to new funding for housing. *The Neighborhood Works, 17*(1), 7–10.

Fisher, R., & Shragge, E. (2002). Challenging community organizing: Facing the 21st century. *Journal of Community Practice, 8*(3), 1–19.

Giloth, R. (Ed.). (1998). *Jobs and economic development: Strategies and practices.* Thousand Oaks, CA: Sage.

Gittell, R., & Thompson, J. P. (2001). Making social capital work: Social capital and community economic development. In S. Saegert, J. P. Thompson, & M. R. Warren (Eds.), *Social capital and poor communities* (pp. 115–135). New York: Russell Sage Foundation.

Gittell, R., & Vidal, A. (1998).*Community organizing: Building social capital as a development strategy.* Thousand Oaks, CA: Sage.

Goetz, E. G. (1993). *Shelter burden: Local politics and progressive housing policy.* Philadelphia: Temple University Press.

Goetz, E. G. (1996). The community-based housing movement and progressive local politics. In W. D. Keating, N. Krumholz, & P. Star (Eds.), *Revitalizing urban neighborhoods* (pp. 164–178). Lawrence: University Press of Kansas.

Green, P. G., & Haines, A. (2001). *Asset building and community development.* Thousand Oaks, CA: Sage.

Greenberg, M. (1999). *Developing policies to support microenterprise in the TANF structure: A guide to the law.* Washington, DC: Aspen Institute.

Haag, S. W. (2000). *Community reinvestment and cities: A literature review of CRA's impact and future* (Discussion paper). Washington, DC: Brookings Institution, Center on Urban and Metropolitan Studies.

Halpern, R. (1993). Neighborhood initiative to address poverty: Lessons from experience. *Journal of Sociology and Social Welfare, 20*(4), 111–135.

Harrison, B., & Weiss, M. (1998). *Workforce development networks: Community-based organizations and regional alliances.* Thousand Oaks, CA: Sage.

Hirschman, A. O. (1988). The principle of conservation and mutation of social energy. In S. Annis & P. Hakem (Eds.), *Direct to the poor: Grassroots development in Latin America* (pp. 7–10). Boulder & London: Lynne Reinner.

Jezierski, L. (1990). Neighborhoods and public-private partnerships in Pittsburgh. *Urban Affairs Quarterly, 26*(2), 217–249.

Joint Center for Housing Studies (2002). *The 25th anniversary of the community reinvestment act: Access to capital in an evolving financial services system.* Cambridge, MA: Harvard University, Joint Center for Housing Studies.

Kretzman, J. P., & McKnight, J. L. (1993). *Building communities from the inside out: A path toward finding and mobilizing a community's assets.* Chicago: Northwestern University, Center for Urban Affairs and Policy Research, Neighborhood Innovations Network.

Langer, J. A., Orwick, J. A., & Kays, A. J. (1999.) *1999 Directory of U.S. microenterprise programs.* Washington, DC: Aspen Institute, Microenterprise Fund for Innovation, Effectiveness, Learning and Dissemination (FIELD).

Light, I., & Gold, S. J. (2000). *Ethnic economies.* San Diego: Academic Press.

McLenighan, V., & Tholin, K. (1997). *Partners in community building: Mainstream and community development financial institutions.* Chicago: Woodstock Institute.

Midgley, J. (1995). *Social development: The development perspective in social welfare.* Thousand Oaks, CA: Sage.

Molina, F. (1998). *Making connections: A study of employment linkage programs.* Washington, DC: Center for Community Change.

National Congress for Community Economic Development (NCCED). (1997). *Jobs for communities: Case studies of successful community economic development programs.* Washington, DC: Author.

National Congress for Community Economic Development (NCCED). (1999). *Coming of age: Trends and achievements of community-based development organizations.* Washington, DC: Author.

Novogratz, J. (1992). *Hopeful change: The potential of microenterprise programs as a community revitalization intervention.* New York: Rockefeller Foundation.

Page-Adams, D., & Sherraden, M. (1997). Asset building as a community revitalization strategy. *Social Work, 42,* 423–434.

Peirce, N. R., & Steinbach, C. F. (1987). *Corrective capitalism: The rise of America's community development corporations.* New York: Ford Foundation.

Perkins, J. M. (1993). *Beyond charity: The call to Christian community development.* Grand Rapids, MI: Baker Books

Personal Responsibility and Work Opportunity Reconciliation Act of 1996. (1996). Public Law No. 104–193.

Putnam, R. D. (1993). The prosperous community: Social capital and public life. *American Prospect, 13,* 35–42.

Raheim, S., & Alter, C. F. (1998). Self-employment as a social and economic development intervention for recipients of AFDC. *Journal of Community Practice: Organizing, Planning & Change, 5*(1/2), 41–61.

Reynolds, D. B. (2002). *Taking the high road: Communities organize for economic change.* Armonk, NY: M. E. Sharp.

Rohe, W. M., & Stegman, M. (1994a). The effects of homeownership on the self-esteem, perceived control, and life satisfaction of low-income people. *Journal of the American Planning Association, 60*(2), 173–184.

Rohe, W. M., & Stegman, M. (1994b). The impact of homeownership on the social and political involvement of low-income people. *Urban Affairs Quarterly, 30*(1), 152–172.

Rubin, H. (2000). *Renewing hope within neighborhoods of despair: The community-based development model.* Albany: SUNY Press.

Rubin, H. J., & Rubin, I. S. (2001). *Community organizing and development* (3rd ed.). Boston: Allyn & Bacon.

Sanders, C. K., & Sherraden, M. S. (1999). Women, microenterprise and family: Promises and prospects. *Women and Work, 1,* 113–140.

Scanlon, E. (1998). Low-income homeownership policy as a community development strategy. In M. S. Sherraden & W. A. Ninacs (Eds.), *Community economic development and social work* (pp. 137–154). New York: Haworth.

Schreiner, M. (1999). Self-employment, microenterprise, and the poorest of the poor in the United States. *Social Service Review, 73*(4), 496–523.

Schreiner, M., Sherraden, M., Clancy, M., Johnson, L., Curley, J., Grinstein-Weiss, M., Zhan, M., & Beverly, S. (2001). *Savings and asset accumulation in individual development accounts.* St. Louis, MO: Washington University, Center for Social Development.

Servon, L. (1999). *Bootstrap capital: Microenterprises and the American poor.* New York: Brookings Institution.

Sherraden, M. (1991). *Assets and the poor: A new American welfare policy.* Armonk, NY: M. E. Sharpe.

Sherraden, M. (2001). Asset-building policy and programs for the poor. In T. Shapiro & E. Wolff (Eds.), *Assets for the poor: The benefits of spreading asset ownership* (pp. 302–323). New York: Russell Sage Foundation.

Sherraden, M. S., & Ninacs, W. A. (1998). Introduction: Community economic development and social work. In M. S. Sherraden & W. A. Ninacs (Eds.), *Community economic development and social work* (pp. 1–10). New York: Haworth Press.

Sherraden, M. S., Slosar, B., Chastain, A., & Squillace, J. (2003). "Human-sized" economic development: Innovations in Missouri. *Journal of Social Thought, 22*(2/3), 97–117.

Sherraden, M. S., Slosar, B., & Sherraden, M. (2002). Innovation in social policy: Researcher, practitioner, advocate, and student collaboration. *Social Work, 47*(3), 209–224.

Stoutland, S. E. (1999). Community development corporations: Mission, strategy, and accomplishments. In R. Ferguson & W. Dickens (Eds.), *Urban problems and community development* (pp. 193–240). Washington, DC: Brookings Institution Press.

Straatmann, S., & Sherraden, M. S. (2001). Welfare to self-employment: A case study of the First Step Fund. *Journal of Community Practice, 9*(3), 73–94.

Taub, R. P. (1994). *Community capitalism* (2nd ed.). Boston: Harvard Business School Press.

Tholin, K., & Pogge, J. (1991). *Banking on the poor.* Chicago: Woodstock Institute.

Vidal, A. C. (1992). *Rebuilding communities: A national study of urban community development corporations.* New York: New School for Social Research, Graduate School of Management and Urban Policy, Community Development Research Center.

Williams, M. (1999). *Building the savings and assets of lower-income consumers: Examples from community development credit unions.* Chicago: Woodstock Institute.

Wilson, W. J. (1996). *When work disappears: The world of the new urban poor.* New York: Vintage.

Woolcock, M. (1998). Social capital and economic development: Toward a theoretical synthesis and policy framework. *Theory and Society, 27*(2), 151–208.

Yeoman, B. (1998). Left behind in Sandtown: The Enterprise Foundation led a $60 million effort to repair a broken Baltimore neighborhood. All it fixed was the buildings. *City Limits, 23*(1), 25–29.

CHAPTER 27

Investing in Socially and Economically Distressed Communities

Comprehensive Strategies for Inner-City Community and Youth Development

Walter C. Farrell, Jr.

James H. Johnson, Jr.

Over the last two decades, poverty in socially and economically distressed communities has escalated exponentially, becoming a seemingly intractable problem. Past experiences with single-service community and personal development strategies have revealed that they alone cannot reverse the unemployment, youth and adult crime, and deteriorating public education in such impacted and underresourced neighborhoods (Johnson, 1997). This chapter will present comprehensive strategies for community and youth development that are designed to change conditions and improve the overall opportunities and quality of life for such communities in general, and youth in particular.

To contextualize the problems confronting today's inner-city communities, we first examine the causes and consequences of income inequality in American society. We focus specifically on the impact of policies enacted in four domains: (a) business, immigration, and local economic development; (b) employment and training; (c) education; and (d) crime and criminal justice. We then offer strategies for community development to foster competitiveness for job creation and poverty alleviation, reconnect disadvantaged youth and adults to mainstream society, and facilitate civic entrepreneurship.

Income Inequality

Business Policy, Immigration, and Economic Development

It is generally agreed that policy-driven changes on both the demand side and the supply side of the U.S. labor market have contributed to growing income inequality in American society over the past two decades (Freeman, 1996a; Johnson, Oliver, & Bobo, 1994). These factors undergird major structural changes in the American economy.

A key contributing factor on the demand side, according to Grant and Johnson, was the Reagan administration's efforts during the 1980s to "create a deregulated business environment in order to enable U.S. firms to be competitive in the global marketplace" (1995, p. 135). This business policy, the authors observed, altered the structure of economic opportunity by (a) accelerating the decline of unionized, high-wage, central-city manufacturing employment (Bluestone & Harrison, 1982; Kasarda, 1992) and (b) fostering high-tech production methods in the manufacturing and craft specialty industries, which also resulted in a significant loss of jobs (Scott, 1988).

This shift "has resulted in the emergence of new industrial spaces on the U.S. landscape—most often in places where there are few Blacks and other minorities in the local labor market and few within reasonable commuting distance" (Grant & Johnson, 1996, p. 135–136). Although some of these new industrial spaces are in older metropolitan regions, such as New York and Boston, others have emerged in communities that historically were on the geographic margins of the U.S. manufacturing core: the high-technology centers in the Sun Belt cities of Albuquerque, New Mexico; Austin, Texas; and Boulder and Colorado Springs, Colorado; and the suburban complexes in Silicon Valley and Orange County, California (Grant & Johnson, 1996). While employers have been developing new industrial spaces throughout the United States, especially in the Southern states, the evidence indicates that, in an effort to lure international capital to cities, local officials have been pursuing, consciously and aggressively, a strategy of downtown redevelopment at the expense of the poorer residential neighborhoods nearby. As a consequence of this redevelopment strategy, many large U.S. cities have become transactional centers, housing the headquarters of multinational corporations that offer few employment opportunities to the poor and low skilled (Johnson, 1997).

The primary employment opportunities that exist in these downtown redevelopment zones are low-level service and custodial jobs, which typically are filled by newly arrived immigrants and which pay, at best, minimum wage (Johnson & Farrell, 1998). Thus, these downtown business development policies have substantially contributed to the polarization of urban labor markets into high-wage and low-wage sectors— the latter being where ethnic minority groups tend to be concentrated—and, by extension, growing income inequality in U.S. society (D'Amico & Maxwell, 1995). With respect to changes on the supply side of the U.S. labor market, income inequality also reflects the growing presence of women in the U.S. labor market since World War II and the failure of U.S. businesses to develop family-friendly policies to accommodate them (Johnson, Bienenstock, & Farrell, 2000).

In addition, U.S. immigration reforms have played a major role in the income disparities in contemporary American society, beginning with the Hart-Cellar Act of 1965 and continuing with the Immigration Reform and Control Act of 1986 and the Immigration Act of 1990. Between 1961 and 1992, legal immigration to the United States averaged 561,000 people per year, compared with an average of 206,000 per year between 1921 and 1960 (Johnson, Farrell, & Guinn, 1997). Along with those entering by means of the hemispheric quota and family/occupation preference provisions established in the Hart-Cellar Act of 1965, the new arrivals have also included a significant number of refugees, parolees, and asylum seekers fleeing political persecution in their home countries and a substantial number of illegal immigrants searching for jobs and an improved quality of life.

About 400,000 undocumented immigrants also have entered the United States each year during the past 20 years. However, the actual number of those who have settled permanently in the United States remains unknown, partly because their illegal status makes it difficult to enumerate them. Many undocumented workers move through the migrant labor corridors in the East, Midwest, and West below the official radar screen and out of the public eye. In addition, it is not feasible to keep track of the multitude of day laborers, who enter and exit the United States frequently (Johnson & Oliver, 1996). Any undocumented immigrant who could demonstrate that he or she had lived in the United States before 1982 was eligible to apply for citizenship under the Immigration Control and Reform Act of 1986; 3 million people took advantage of this opportunity to become U.S. citizens (Lowell & Jing, 1994). It was believed that if amnesty were granted to such a large number of people who were residing in the United States illegally, these new legal workers would saturate domestic labor demand and thereby stem the flow of undocumented immigrants. In an effort to reduce undocumented immigration further, the Act also introduced sanctions designed to prohibit employers from hiring undocumented or unauthorized workers, and it allocated additional resources to enhance control of the U.S.-Mexico border. However, both of these provisions have proven largely ineffective (Andreas, 1994; Lowell & Jing, 1994; Tichenor, 1994).

Reforms implemented by the Immigration Act of 1990 have been similarly counterproductive. In the 1990 Act, conservatives were successful in winning stays of deportation for family members of immigrants legalized under the 1986 Act, which heightened the flow of legal immigrants to the United States under the family preference provision. And liberals succeeded in getting the cap raised on legal immigration by increasing the number of employer-sponsored and skilled-worker visas (Tichenor, 1994). These reforms were also implemented precisely when the U.S. economy was experiencing a major downturn, characterized by massive layoffs, increasing job insecurity, and sharply declining wages—all of which figure heavily in the recent increase in opposition among native-born Americans to current U.S. immigration policy (Johnson, Farrell, & Guinn, 1997). This opposition has been further exacerbated by the events of September 11, 2001 (Davis, 2002;

Martinez, 2002). In addition, the large-scale influx of immigrants, both legal and illegal, over the past four decades has created labor-surplus environments in which there are far more job seekers than available jobs (Freeman, 1991). Employers tend to favor both low- and high-skilled immigrant workers because they are able to pay them lower wages than their American counterparts at either level, and immigrants tend to be compliant with the ways in which employers organize their workplaces (Kirschenman & Neckerman, 1991; Neckerman & Kirschenman, 1990; Turner, Fix, & Struyk, 1991).

Employment and Training Policy

Employment and training policy has also played a role in income inequality. During the past 20 years, many individuals and groups have been constrained from gaining the skills that would qualify them for well-paying jobs in the high-growth sectors of the U.S. economy by the employment and job training assistance policies enacted in the 1980s. The Job Training and Partnership Act of 1981 (JTPA), which replaced the Comprehensive Employment and Training Act of 1973 (CETA), represented the Reagan administration's programmatic response to the growing mismatch between skills and jobs in the U.S. economy.

Fitzgerald and McGregor (1993) observed that the JTPA program contributed to income inequality in American society during the 1980s by placing applicants without respect to quality of employment, emphasizing job placement over training because placement was quicker and cheaper than training, creaming off the most employable individuals, and channeling White males into on-the-job training opportunities that allowed them to progress in the workforce, while minorities and women were more likely to receive classroom training with little guarantee of employment on completion. More specifically, the latter groups were more likely to be directed into general equivalency diploma (GED) programs (Heckman, 1994). Commenting on the labor market experiences of these individuals, Fitzgerald and McGregor concluded that "there is no demand for their newly acquired skills in the local labor market," a finding supported by other research that documents the modest economic returns to securing a GED (1993, p. 171). In addition to the discrimination inherent in program implementation, Grant and Johnson (1996) point out that the Reagan administration substantially cut the federal budget for job training and employment assistance. Fitzgerald and McGregor estimated that "real per capita funding for federal employment and job training programs declined by nearly 80 percent between 1979 and 1986" (1993, p. 171).

Education Policy

Several studies note that the growing income inequality in American society is also related to recently implemented policies designed to remedy what is increasingly being perceived as a failing public education system. In dissecting and challenging the crisis in American public education, researchers contend that analysts and policymakers have instituted a series of "get-tough" education policies—such as tracking by ability, grade retention, increasing reliance on standardized tests as the ultimate arbiter of educational success, and extreme disciplinary sanctions—that have disenfranchised large numbers of Black and other minority youth (Oliver & Johnson, 1988; Orfield & Ashkanize, 1991).

With respect to tracking, Oliver and Johnson (1988) cite data indicating that Black youth are underrepresented in the gifted and talented or college-bound tracks and overrepresented in the vocational, general education, and special education or non-college-bound tracks. Moreover, they note that individuals who have little or no training in child and adolescent development often do this tracking. Pursuant to the adverse effects of tracking, they also show how school officials have tightened requirements for both high school graduation and college admission without paying proper attention to whether qualified teachers and the necessary facilities are available at the primary and secondary school levels. These developments, they contend, have been especially problematic for urban ethnic minorities from impoverished backgrounds who attend economically and educationally inferior schools.

Oliver and Johnson (1988) also cite the educational system's dramatically increased reliance on standardized general and subject-specific tests, despite abundant evidence that these tests contain biases against Black and other minority students and inaccurately predict their future academic success in higher education. Finally, they draw attention to research showing that Blacks generally, and Black males specifically, are more likely than their White counterparts to be subjected to extreme disciplinary sanctions, including permanent expulsion from school. A number of studies confirm that these and related get-tough education policies are directly responsible for the recent rise in the dropout rate and the decrease in the college attendance rate of Black youth, especially Black males. They also argue that because many of those who drop out of high school or fail to qualify for admission to a college or university do not possess the skills to compete effectively for jobs in the rapidly growing high-wage sectors of the U.S. economy, these policies have further exacerbated joblessness and eroded the earning power of young Black males.

Crime Policy and Criminal Justice

State governments' anticrime policies also have contributed to growing income inequality in American society. For nearly three decades, states have pursued a policy of resolving the problems of the inner city through the criminal justice system (Farrell & Johnson, 1996b; Petersilia, 1992). California, once a leader in the rehabilitation of criminals, epitomizes this shift in anticrime policy. Describing this shift, Petersilia states,

> In 1977 the California legislature enacted the Determinant Sentence Law, which, among other things, embraced punishment (and, explicitly, not rehabilitation) as the purpose of prison, required mandatory prison sentences for many offenses formerly eligible for probation, and dramatically increased the rate at which probation and parole violators were returned to prison. (1992, p. 176)

This law was followed in 1994 by Proposition 184, "Three Strikes and You're Out," which stimulated explosive growth in California's prison population, sending repeat violators to prison for life on conviction for a third felony (Gibbs & Bankhead, 2001). As a consequence of this determinant sentencing law, "the California prison population skyrocketed from 22,000 to 106,000 between 1980 and 1992, an increase of more than 400 percent" (Petersilia, 1992, p. 176), and has increased in double-digit percentages on an annual basis since the implementation of Proposition 184 (Gibbs & Bankhead, 2001).

Following California's lead, a number of other states have enacted determinant sentence laws and also have gone on a prison construction binge to accommodate the resulting increase in their prison populations. Freeman (1996b) found that as a consequence of this "lock them up and throw away the key" approach to the crime problem, state spending on criminal justice has far outstripped total spending on education. According to Petersilia (1992), over a 5-year period, spending on the criminal justice system jumped by 70% in California, an increase rate about four times greater than that of total state spending, whereas state spending on education increased by only 10%. Minorities, especially Black and Hispanic males, have been affected disproportionately by these get-tough-on-crime policies (Miller, 1996). In California and several other states, Blacks and Hispanics make up the overwhelming majority of the prison population (Farrell & Johnson, 1996b). Freeman estimates,

> In 1993, about 7 percent of Black men over 18 were incarcerated [nationally]. One Black man was in prison for every 11 Black men in the workforce; and approximately one was under the supervision of the criminal justice system for every three to four Black men in the workforce. Combine race and age and you find that 23 percent of Black men age 25–34 were incarcerated. (1996b, p. 26)

What are the prospects of landing a job in general, and a good job in particular, if you have a criminal record? As Johnson and Oliver (1992) stated, for the African American male, "incarceration breeds despair and hopelessness, and in the employment arena, it is the 'Scarlet Letter' of unemployability" (p. 144). Thus, racial disparities in income are related, at least in part, to state-level anticrime policies that have been implemented over the past three decades. In light of this problem, we now turn to strategies for inner-city community development.

Strategies for Inner-City Community Development

Fostering Competitiveness for Job Creation and Poverty Alleviation

Strategies for urban job creation and poverty alleviation must be based on a deep and comprehensive understanding of the forces driving economic development in metropolitan areas. Driven increasingly by global economic forces, the primary engine of regional development in the United States is shifting from mass-production industries and low-skilled service jobs to a more sophisticated technology- and knowledge-based system of production and services. This shift is providing jobs and higher incomes to those workers who have the skills and knowledge to participate effectively in the new urban economy, while leaving behind those who do not—a disproportionate number of whom are African Americans and other minority youth and adults. Increasing evidence suggests that those cities that can develop a comparative advantage in responding to the needs of businesses involved in international commerce will prosper while those that cannot are likely to decline. In the emerging global economy of the 21st century, export-based manufacturing and service industries will be key drivers of metropolitan growth and crucial sources of local jobs and wealth (Johnson & Farrell, 1999, 2000).

Rapidly expanding global markets will provide metropolitan areas and their residents with immense opportunities to prosper, but only to the extent that their businesses and workers are prepared to respond to new global challenges. Although large firms in America's major cities have always been engaged in international trade, in recent years, a growing number of smaller enterprises in small- and medium-size cities have also become more heavily involved. The U.S. Department of Commerce reports that in 1995, firms in 253 U.S. metropolitan statistical areas had export sales totaling more than $467 billion, an increase of nearly 13% over the previous year. About 85% of these metropolitan areas recorded export increases. Moreover, cities are now competing for foreign direct investment by European, Asian, and Latin American firms whose mergers, acquisitions, and new plant locations bring with them capital, technology, and jobs (Johnson & Farrell, 1999, 2000).

Preparing the urban workforce, and especially the inner-city poor, to attain skills and professional jobs in businesses involved in global trade will be a key to urban poverty alleviation in the 21st century, and it will require new and more creative programs of human resource development and urban investment than American cities have used in the past (Johnson & Farrell, 1999, 2000). If the United States is to compete effectively in the 21st-century world economy, strategies must be developed to reverse economic decay, rebuild human capital, and reduce debilitating social problems such as poverty, crime, drug abuse, and school failure in our inner cities. To effectively address these challenges, it is imperative that the following initiatives be implemented.

First and foremost is private-sector job creation. There is an urgent need to pursue inner-city employment anchors or job generators that are linked to the growth sectors of the economy. In contrast to the enterprise-zone concept of attracting companies back to central cities, however, these employment anchors must be fostered from within the community. Aspiring entrepreneurs must be encouraged and assisted in the development of businesses that employ substantial numbers of inner-city workers and that also pay family-supporting wages. Without such employment anchors, the general retail and low-level service establishments that remain in depressed urban neighborhoods likely will continue as marginal enterprises. On the other hand, with a stable supply of better-paying jobs generated by anchor businesses, these retail and other establishments are more likely to prosper and grow as workers have more discretionary income to purchase non-basic items. These new anchor businesses will provide opportunities for minority youth and adults to access the labor market via on-the-job training and special internship and training programs (Farrell & Johnson, 1997b).

Second, recruitment and training of workers must be tied directly to specific job opportunities. Research shows that generic education and training programs (i.e., those not connected to specific job placement) have not succeeded in the past, especially for the inner-city poor, and they are unlikely to succeed in the future. Customized training programs, on the other hand, have proven to be a highly effective economic development tool. Studies show that such programs are most effective when they are offered at no cost to prospective employers as part of a location incentive package. These training programs have been instrumental in luring major job generators to selected, formerly economically distressed areas (Farrell & Johnson, 1997b).

Third, if we are to revitalize our central cities, the aforementioned economic development strategies must be undertaken in conjunction with efforts to mend the social fabric of these communities. A widely held view is that a decline in individual responsibility and family values and morals has contributed to rising rates of poverty, joblessness, family disruption, out-of-wedlock births, and gang- and drug-related violence in our cities and throughout the nation. Based on this interpretation of the underlying causes of problems plaguing inner cities, policymakers have instituted a series of punitive policies designed to reduce the level of violence and to foster normative behavior among the poor. But there is growing evidence that these policies may not yield the desired results. It is clear, for example, that the "get tough on crime" policies enacted by a number of states during the 1980s have not significantly reduced the incidence of illegal and violent criminal activities in economically distressed communities (Farrell & Johnson, 1997b).

All of the nation's assets, including the resources of the government, the business sector, community-based organizations, the philanthropic community, and especially our colleges and universities, must be mobilized if we are to successfully revitalize inner-city communities. What is needed to deal with heretofore intractable problems of the inner city are institutions capable of designing and implementing cooperative, collaborative, and coordinated strategies that draw on and fully use the complete range of community assets (Farrell & Johnson, 1997b). One of the most important of these community assets is our youth.

Reconnecting Disadvantaged Youth and Adults to Mainstream Society

In developing strategies to reconnect disadvantaged youth and adults to mainstream society, we draw on several field-based techniques. Each is discussed in turn.

At the outset, increased literacy is a must in the radically restructured and continuously restructuring national and global economy. There is a widespread view among today's employers, based on experience, that a substantial number of inner-city workers of all ages are deficient in the necessary hard skills—reading, basic mathematical competency, computer literacy, and the ability to critically assess technical information. These skills are in decline at the precise time that they are in increased demand in the workplace of the new economy. Even those employers who are willing to provide on-the-job training for their entry-level employees complain that they frequently lack the basics of reading, writing, and arithmetic that would enable them to take full advantage of this educational opportunity (Farrell & Johnson, 1997c). Moreover, a growing number of high-tech business owners believe that it is not cost-effective to take on the complex educational needs of today's low-income workers who need significant training, even with government subsidies. Thus, it is urgent that those engaged in youth and adult literacy and numeracy programs build these realities into their program development.

Next, youth and adult literacy programs must use teaching strategies and techniques that provide learners with a sense of self-efficacy—the belief that they can master the appropriate reading materials. In addition, the program materials must be respectful of the chronological ages of the participants. Books and reading aids for children are inappropriate for inner-city youth and adults. Inner-city residents often tell us that they know they have a reading problem but that they do not wish to be treated like children (Farrell & Johnson, 1997c).

Equally important is that as more jobs in the U.S. economy require direct interface with the public, African American and other minority youth and adults in socially and economically distressed inner-city environments must be taught to *code switch* if they are to succeed in the 21st-century employment arena. They must be able to respond to changing conditions and relations as they move from one situational context to the next. Most of the research on code switching treats it primarily as a linguistic phenomenon: the ability to shift between Black English and Standard English. However, code switching is a far more complex and multifaceted skill. As more jobs in the U.S. economy require direct interface with the public, it is an increasingly applicable skill in a range of employment situations as well as in other areas of life (Farrell & Johnson, 1997a).

Owing to their racial isolation from the mainstream, most inner-city youth have not acquired the ability to code switch. If they are to compete successfully, they will have to develop *bicultural competence*—that is, the ability to function in their families and neighborhoods, on the one hand, and in school, the broader community, and beyond on the other. Inner-city minority youth who demonstrate the ability to adapt their style and manner of presentation to a range of situations will be more likely to succeed academically and in other aspects of life than will their counterparts who do not. Furthermore, inner-city youths' ability to successfully navigate the multiple worlds of family, school, neighborhood, and community (i.e., to code switch) will depend, primarily, on the complement of *cultural capital* and *social capital* resources that they have at their disposal (Boys & Girls Clubs of America, 2001; Farrell & Johnson, 1997a, 1997c).

Morals, values, and attitudes, especially toward literacy, are typically included under the heading *cultural capital,* whereas the individuals and institutions through which citizens maintain their social identity and through which they receive emotional support, material aid and services, information, and new social contacts constitute *social capital.* Those individuals who are embedded in less-than-ideal community, neighborhood, and family contexts may very well experience successful literacy outcomes if they possess the appropriate set of cultural capital attributes and if they are surrounded by a dense network of social capital resources that serve as bridges to the mainstream (Farrell & Johnson, 1997c). Such bridging resources will enable them to overcome the negative forces they encounter in each of their multiple worlds. Thus, linking youth and adults to supportive programs—for example, veterans' services, counseling services, and training programs that teach soft skills such as human relations, friendliness, and positive social interaction as well as hard skills (i.e., task-oriented and technical competancies)—will facilitate their success in their literacy and skill development programs (Hartmann, Watson, & Kantorek, 2001).

During our work in an inner-city literacy program in Lansing, Michigan, we routinely received students from the General Motors Oldsmobile plant. When teaching the company's line workers who were aspiring to become foremen, we regularly employed reading materials that were job related. These materials were age- and experience-appropriate, provided real-world incentives that encouraged students to commit to the necessary study to master them, and had an adult context. For those adults who are unemployed during the period of literacy training, a real-world connection of reading to potential employment, such as the review of job applications, will enhance their motivation to become more literate. Most important, adults in literacy programs must be advised that the quest for literacy is ongoing. Even those of us who read must read regularly to refine the skill. Adults must be told that literacy in today's rapidly changing employment environment is a lifelong undertaking. It is important not only to be able to read but also to be able to read with increased understanding of the subtleties and nuances of words. Literacy also means a basic understanding of the technology in one's workplace. Adults need to be made aware that in today's workplace, literacy has an academic, social, and personal meaning (Farrell & Johnson, 1997c).

All three of the aforementioned strategies have to be combined: the academic context for reading comprehension and understanding; the social context for the ability to fit into the workplace via attitudes, dress, and communication skills; and the personal context for the ability to get along with one's coworkers. If we can teach these lessons to today's youth and adults who struggle with literacy, they will possess the necessary hard and soft skills to acquire and retain jobs and thus cross the employment bridge into the 21st century. Using this comprehensive approach, we all will be on the path toward building better communities for our cities, our states, and our nation.

Civic Entrepreneurship

There is an urgent need to mobilize the requisite resources to narrow the gap between the haves and the have-nots in our nation's inner cities. But the challenge is to figure out the most efficient way to do this. We suggest that any strategy, to be effective, must be anchored in what we term the four Cs: cooperation, collaboration, coordination, and capital. We use the term *capital* to include the social and cultural as well as the financial capital resources of government, business, philanthropy, community-based organizations (including churches), and the higher education system. The plan should also create and promote "win-win" strategies for all community stakeholders. To maintain interest and a high level of participation in the plan, community stakeholders, especially representatives from the private sector, must recognize that it is in their best interest to become actively involved in the process of eliminating geographical and socioeconomic disparities in the inner city. What this means is that the plan must be anchored in a business-oriented rather than a social welfare–oriented model of community development (Farrell & Johnson, 1996c; Johnson & Kasarda, 2001).

Nonprofits can leverage the dollars they currently spend with private sector companies. It has been estimated that federal, state, and local governments buy some $1.2 trillion in goods and services from profit-seeking businesses each year. But in contrast to their private sector counterparts, public sector entities rarely negotiate a return on their investment in the private sector companies with whom they do business (Johnson, Rees, & Horton, 1999). If a nonprofit organization is a major customer of a local paint company or distributor, for example, it is not at all unreasonable for the nonprofit to insist or require that the company, as part of the business relationship, hire a specific number of inner-city residents or contribute financially or otherwise to the resolution or amelioration of the social and economic problems that plague the economically distressed community that it serves. If the company balks at such a request, then perhaps the nonprofit could find another paint company—one that is more socially responsible—with which to do business. What is being suggested here is neither unethical nor illegal; it is standard practice among private sector companies and is viewed simply as the "price of doing business" in the highly competitive marketplace. Public sector and other nonprofit institutions need to learn how to leverage their resources, for it is a form of enlightened self-interest that can significantly contribute to the revitalization of economically distressed communities (Farrell & Johnson, 1996a, 1996c; Johnson & Kasarda, 2001; Johnson, Rees, & Horton, 1999).

Cause-related marketing alliances with private sector companies are another way that nonprofit, community-based organizations can generate revenue. Research shows that companies trying to differentiate themselves in highly competitive markets, or attempting to launch a new product or service, can substantially benefit—in terms of profits and public image—when aligning themselves with social causes. When a corporation and a nonprofit organization enter a cause-related marketing alliance, the corporation agrees to undertake a series of actions that will benefit both the nonprofit and the company. Transaction-based promotions are the most common types of cause-based marketing alliances. Corporations donate a specific amount of cash, food, or equipment in direct proportion to sales revenue—often up to a set amount—to one or more nonprofits. To motivate people to use their credit card, American Express launched a Charge Against Hunger Promotion in 1993, which netted a nonprofit organization several million dollars (Farrell & Johnson, 1996c; Johnson & Kasarda, 2001; Johnson, Rees, & Horton, 1999).

How does one go about developing cause-related marketing alliances? Nonprofit managers who want partners from the for-profit world must go out and find those partners instead of waiting for corporations to find them. They must become as proficient at marketing their organization as corporations are at marketing their products and services. In short, they must be able to demonstrate all the ways in which a nonprofit can add value to a potential corporate partner. To eliminate inner-city disparities, a comprehensive plan must be developed to build the necessary capacity among inner-city residents to allow them to engage in community development. That is, through using a set of formal education and training programs, community practitioners must equip the residents of these neighborhoods with the skills and know-how to take control of their own lives and the destiny of their communities as opposed to relying solely on the government to assist them in trying to overcome their plight (Farrell & Johnson, 1996a).

It is not enough to proverbially teach a man how to fish. Consistent with a business-oriented approach to community development, there is a need to "teach the urban disadvantaged the entre prenvrial skills required to develop resources so that they can eventually buy the pond. Building on this notion nonprofit organizations can launch a set of training and technical assistance programs designed to achieve three objectives: (a) to upgrade the technical and managerial skills of existing community development specialists, including the employees of community development corporations, other nonprofit community-based organizations, and government agencies; (b) to provide aspiring inner-city entrepreneurs with assistance in the "nuts and bolts" of sound business practices; and (c) to recruit and train the next generation of community development practitioners.

Nonprofit agencies and organizations in our nation's inner cities can provide the necessary leadership for improving the quality of life for citizens in social and economic distress (Farrell & Johnson, 1996a, 1996c; Johnson & Kasarda, 2001). Finally, we are recommending that social workers use the previously noted private sector strategies in their management and community practice initiatives. By doing so, they will remain true to social work's *Code of Ethics* and its commitment to racial and cultural diversity in terms of advocating for and facilitating the social and economic development of the poor and oppressed (National Association of Social Workers [NASW] National Committee on Racial and Ethnic Diversity, 2001; NASW, 1996). The changing local, state, and federal government priorities in serving the poor and disadvantaged demand that we be creative and innovative in securing the necessary resources for low-income citizens in the 21st century. By engaging in entrepreneurial activities via nonprofit organizations, social workers will be able to make a difference in the communities in which they work and improve the public perception of the profession (Bent-Goodley, 2002).

References

Andreas, P. (1994). Border troubles: Free trade, immigration, and cheap labor. *The Ecologist, 24,* 230–234.

Bent-Goodley, T. B. (2002). Defining and conceptualizing social work entrepreneurship. *Journal of Social Work Education, 38*(2), 291–302.

Bluestone, B., & Harrison, B. (1982). *The deindustrialization of America.* New York: Basic Books.

Boys & Girls Clubs of America. (2001). *Tools for inspiring and enabling young people to realize their full potential.* Atlanta, GA: Author.

D'Amico, R., & Maxwell, N. L. (1995). The continuing significance of race in minority male joblessness. *Social Forces, 73*(3), 969–991.

Davis, A. (2002, March 12). Firms dig into worker's pasts amid post–Sept. 11 security anxiety. *Wall Street Journal,* p. 1.

Farrell, W. C., Jr., & Johnson, J. H., Jr. (1996a, December 14). Building blocks of community development. *The Milwaukee Courier,* p. 4.

Farrell, W. C., Jr., & Johnson, J. H., Jr. (1996b, July 21). Current crime policy is wrong-headed. *Wisconsin Review,* p. 14.

Farrell, W. C., Jr., & Johnson, J. H., Jr. (1996c, December 7). Mobilizing inner city investment. *The Milwaukee Courier,* p. 4.

Farrell, W. C., Jr., & Johnson, J. H., Jr. (1997a, January 11). Code switching and inner-city youth. *The Milwaukee Courier,* p. 4.

Farrell, W. C., Jr., & Johnson, J. H., Jr. (1997b, March 22). Enhancing "hard" and "soft" adult literacy skills. *The Milwaukee Courier,* p. 4.

Farrell, W. C., Jr., & Johnson, J. H., Jr. (1997c, February 15). Towards comprehensive inner city revival. *The Milwaukee Courier,* p. 4.

Fitzgerald, J., & McGregor, A. (1993). Labor community initiatives in worker training. *Economic Development Quarterly, 7,* 160–171.

Freeman, R. B. (1991). Employment and earnings of disadvantaged young men in a labor shortage economy. In C. Jencks & P. Peterson (Eds.), *The urban underclass* (pp. 103–121). Washington, DC: Brookings Institution.

Freeman, R. B. (1996a, September-October). Toward an apartheid economy? *Harvard Business Review,* pp. 114–121.

Freeman, R. B. (1996b). Why so many young American men commit crimes and what we might do about it. *Journal of Economic Perspectives, 10,* 25–42.

Gibbs, J. T., & Bankhead, T. (2001). *Preserving privilege: California politics, propositions, and people of color.* Westport, CT: Prager.

Grant, D., & Johnson, J. H., Jr. (1996). Conservative policymaking and growing urban inequality in the 1980s. In R. Ratcliff, M. L. Oliver, & T. Shapiro (Eds.), *Research in politics and society* (pp. 127–160). Greenwich, CT: JAI Press.

Hartmann, T., Watson, B. H., & Kantorek, B. (2001). *Community change for youth development in Kansas City.* Philadelphia: Public/Private Ventures.

Heckman, J. (1994, Spring). Is job training oversold? *The Public Interest,* pp. 91–115.

Johnson, J. H., Jr. (1997). Unraveling the paradox of deepening urban inequality: Theoretical underpinnings, research design, and preliminary findings from a multi-city study. In T. D. Boston (Ed.), *A different vision: Race and public policy* (pp. 77–89). London: Routledge.

Johnson, J. H., Jr., Bienenstock, E. J., & Farrell, W. C., Jr. (2000). Bridging social networks and female laborforce participation in a multi-ethnic metropolis. In L. D. Bobo, M. L. Oliver, J. H. Johnson, Jr., & A. Valenzuela (Eds.), *Prismatic metropolis: Inequality in Los Angeles* (pp. 383–416). New York: Russell Sage.

Johnson, J. H., Jr., & Farrell, W. C., Jr. (1998). Growing income inequality in American society: A political economy perspective. In J. A. Auerbach & R. S. Belous (Eds.), *The inequality paradox: Growth of income disparity* (pp. 133–180). Washington, DC: National Policy Association.

Johnson, J. H., Jr., & Farrell, W. C., Jr. (1999). *Creating jobs and alleviating poverty in Gary, Indiana: An action agenda.* Chapel Hill: University of North Carolina at Chapel Hill, Frank Hawkins Kenan Institute of Private Enterprise.

Johnson, J. H., Jr., & Farrell, W. C., Jr. (2000). *Strategies for engaging the private sector in inner city job creation and poverty alleviation: An overview of proposed initiatives.* Chapel Hill, NC: University of North Carolina at Chapel Hill, Frank Hawkins Kenan Institute of Private Enterprise.

Johnson, J. H., Jr., Farrell, W. C., Jr., & Guinn, C. (1997). Immigration reform and the browning of America: Tensions, conflicts, and community instability. In C. Hirschman, P. Kasinitz, & J. DeWind (Eds.), *The handbook of international migration: The American experience* (pp. 390–411). New York: Russell Sage Foundation.

Johnson, J. H., Jr., & Kasarda, J. D. (2001, July 29). *The Charlotte Observer,* p. 3D.

Johnson, J. H., Jr., & Oliver, M. L. (1992). Structural changes in the economy and Black male joblessness: A reassessment. In G. E. Peterson & W. Vroman (Eds.), *Urban labor markets and job opportunity* (pp. 113–147). Washington, DC: Urban Institute Press.

Johnson, J. H., Jr., & Oliver, M. L. (1996). Interethnic minority conflict in urban America: The effects of economic and social dislocations. *Urban Geography, 10,* 449–463.

Johnson, J. H., Jr., Oliver, M. L., & Bobo, L. D. (1994). Understanding the contours of deepening urban inequality. *Urban Geography, 15,* 77–89.

Johnson, J. H., Jr., Rees, J., & Horton, W. (1999). *Social capital, nonprofit organizations, and regional potential in the Piedmont Triad.* Chapel Hill: University of North Carolina at Chapel Hill, Frank Hawkins Kenan Institute of Private Enterprise.

Kasarda, J. D. (1992). *The severely distressed in economically transforming cities.* Chapel Hill: University of North Carolina at Chapel Hill, Frank Hawkins Kenan Institute of Private Enterprise.

Kirschenman, J., & Neckerman, K. (1991). "We'd love to hire them but . . .": The meaning of race for employers. In C. Jencks & P. E. Peterson (Eds.), *The urban underclass,* (pp. 203–232). Washington, DC: The Brookings Institution.

Lowell, B. L., & Jing, Z. (1994). Unauthorized workers and immigration reform: What can we ascertain from employers? *International Migration Review, 28,* 427–448.

Martinez, R. (2002, April 10). Our future with immigrants. *The* (Raleigh, NC) *News & Observer,* p. 22.

Miller, J. (1996). *Search and destroy: African American males and the U.S. criminal justice system.* New York: Cambridge University Press.

National Association of Social Workers [NASW]. (1996). *Code of ethics.* Washington, DC: Author.

National Association of Social Workers, National Committee on Racial and Ethnic Diversity. (2001, June 23). *NASW standards for cultural competence in social work practice.* Washington, DC: NASW.

Neckerman, K., & Kirschenman, J. (1990). Hiring strategies, racial bias and inner city workers. *Social Problems, 38,* 433–447.

Oliver, M. L., & Johnson, J. H., Jr. (1988). The challenge of diversity in higher education. *The Urban Review, 20,* 139–145.

Orfield, G., & Ashkanize, C. (1991). *The closing door: Conservative policy and black opportunity.* Chicago: University of Chicago Press.

Petersilia, J. (1992). Crime and punishment in California: Full cells, empty pockets, and questionable benefits. In J. Steinberg, D. Lyon, & N. Vaiaina (Eds.), *Urban America: Policy choices for Los Angeles and the nation.* Santa Monica: Rand Corp. (Reprinted by the California Policy Seminar as a CPS Brief)

Scott, A. J. (1988). Flexible production systems and regional development: The rise of new industrial spaces in North America and Western Europe. *International Journal of Urban and Regional Research, 12,* 171–186.

Tichenor, D. J. (1994). Immigration and political community in the United States. *Responsive Community, 4,* 16–28.

Turner, M., Fix, M., & Struyk, R. J. (1991). *Opportunities denied, opportunities diminished: Racial discrimination in hiring* (Report No. 91–9). Washington, DC: Urban Institute Press.

CHAPTER 28

Global Change and Indicators of Social Development

Richard J. Estes

K nowledge-based intervention has been a hallmark of community practice since the turn of the 19th century. Indeed, the social survey movement of the 1900s was a direct outgrowth of efforts on the part of community practitioners to systematically (a) identify the nature, extent, and severity of new and emerging social needs in their communities; (b) organize people and institutions to respond more effectively to those needs; and (c) establish baseline measures against which intervention successes and failures could be assessed (Zimbalist, 1977). Even the renaming of one of the profession's leading journals of the day, from *Charities and Commons* to *The Survey*, illustrates the importance that practitioners assigned to the role of scientific inquiry for advancing practice. Mary Richmond's *Social Diagnosis* (1917) offered further reinforcement of the powerful relationship that practitioners recognized to exist between knowledge-based intervention and the realization of more effective outcomes. Today, of course, community practitioners all over the world seek to incorporate rigorous approaches to needs assessment, planning, and program development and evaluation in their work with communities and other social collectivities (Andrews, 1996; Balaswamy & Dabelko, 2002; Chow & Coulton, 1996; Conner, Tanjasiri, & Easterling, 1999; Drummond, 1995; Johnson, 2002; Sawicki & Flynn, 1996; Schultz et al., 2000; Telfair & Mulvihill, 2000; Wong & Hillier, 2001; Zachary, 1995).

This chapter discusses the contribution of social indicators, social reporting, and social indexes to community practice. The chapter is divided into two sections: Part I discusses the development of social indicators, social reporting, and social index construction from a historical perspective; Part II discusses the contribution of these innovations in community-focused social measurement from a contemporary perspective. The concepts discussed in both parts of the chapter are illustrated with examples drawn from community practice in the United States and other countries. The chapter also contains links for practitioners to some of the most important sources of local, national, and international social indicator data.

Part I

Social Indicators and Social Reporting in Historical Perspective

Social indicators, social reporting, and the development of composite measures of social progress have a long history in American social science. Indeed, the earliest efforts in all three of these fields began in the United States—initially as part of the work of the Hoover Committee on Social Trends, but subsequently, as part of the country's assessment of the impact of its space program on American life. President Johnson's Great Society program of the 1960s, with its emphasis on the attainment of five national goals, reinvigorated the social indicators effort and, in turn, forcefully linked the goals and processes of development to specific measurable outcomes.

One of the earliest contributions toward the development of a coherent conceptual framework for the emerging social indicator, social reporting, and social indexing movements was made by Raymond Bauer (1966). In his edited volume, *Social Indicators,* Bauer offered a comprehensive framework for integrating analyses which, until that time, largely had been undertaken independently of one another: for example, trend analyses of changes over time in the health, education, transportation, housing, labor, urban development, and other sectors of public activity. Simultaneously, Daniel Bell (1966) published *Toward a Social Report,* in which he laid out the conceptual framework for undertaking and reporting to policymakers and the general public analyses of critical national trends. Wilbur Cohen (1968) subsequently applied the analytical principles specified by Bauer and Bell to the work of the U.S. Department of Health, Education, and Welfare (1969), in much the same way that Robert McNamara was applying the principles of goal-focused planning, cost-benefit analysis, and task-centered project management to the work of the U.S. Defense Department.

Other early pioneers in these movements included the economist Donald McGranahan (McGranahan, Richard-Proust, Sovani, & Subramanian, 1972) who, in his work with the United Nations Research Institute on Social Development (UNRISD) in Geneva, created a system of statistical *congruencies* for understanding the stages through which poorer countries moved in their efforts to achieve progressively high levels of social and economic development. Campbell, Converse, and Rodgers (1976) introduced qualitative assessments of life quality, including subjective *satisfaction with life measures,* into a field which, until that time, was dominated by approaches that used only objective measures to assess changes in development progress (Land & Spillerman, 1975; Morris, 1979; Streeten, 1981).

At the same time that the pace of work on social indicators and national systems of social reporting was quickening in the United States, parallel trends were occurring in Europe. Most notable among these efforts was the index construction work of Drenowski and Wolf (1966). One of the early accomplishments of both the U.S. and European efforts was the establishment on the part of the United Nations of what was to become a vast archive of easily accessible statistical data relating to the social and economic development of its member states (United Nations, 1975).

Unfortunately, the election of successive conservative governments in the United States brought the social indicators and social reporting movements to a virtual halt here, although individual American researchers continued work on the international dimensions of development. The effort continued uninterrupted, however, throughout much of Northern and Western Europe, with the result that today, the contributions of European social scientists to the measurement of national and international social progress are quite substantial (Beck et al., 1998; Berger-Schmitt & Jankowitsch, 1999; Christoph & Noll, 2003; Hagerty, Vogel, & Moller, 2002; Noll, 1996; Svallfors, 2003; Veenhoven, 1996; Vogel, 2003; Zumbo, 2002).

Part II

Social Indicators and Social Reporting in Contemporary Perspective

Monitoring and assessing changes in national and international development involves three discrete arenas of activity of interest to community practitioners: (a) social indicators, (b) social reporting, and (c) the construction of composite measures of social development. Fortunately, considerable work already has been accomplished in each of these areas, allowing practitioners to draw ideas for application to their unique community planning, research, and organization needs.

Social Indicators

Social indicators are (a) *direct measures* of phenomena they purport to measure (e.g., infant mortality rate, educational attainment level, divorce rates, the number of deaths or injuries associated with civil protest actions) and (b) *indirect measures* of other, always more complex phenomena that cannot be measured directly, or at least cannot easily be measured directly. For example, infant mortality rate often is used as a proxy for the quality of local or national health systems, divorce rate often is used as proxy for "family stability," and the number of deaths and injuries incurred in civil protest actions often is used as a proxy for "societal stability" or "societal cohesion." Thus, as direct measures of phenomena of interest to community practitioners, social indicators can serve as powerful measures of changes in development levels over time. When selected carefully, social indicators also can

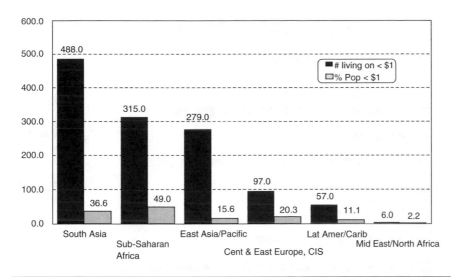

Figure 28.1   People Living on Less than $1 Per Day by Major Regions, 1999 ($N = 1,242$ Million)

Source: United Nations Development Programme, 2003, p. 41.

serve as powerful measures of phenomena that are too complex or would be too expensive to measure directly (e.g., the comparative effectiveness of alternative service systems, hidden crime rates, not yet fully seen but emerging community needs, etc.).

Social indicators fall into three basic categories: (a) *leading indicators*, which tend to show the direction of future economic or social activity, for example, increases in social cohesion in response to serious external threat; (b) *coincident indicators*, which tend to track social and economic cycles with comparatively little time lag time, for example, increases in crime rates during periods of growing unemployment or poverty; and (c) *lagging indicators*, which measure how the economy or society was rather than how it is or will be, for example, declines in social spending during periods of economic expansion. Figures 28.1 and 28.2 provide examples of lagging social indicators.

All three types of social indicators can contribute to the advancement of community practice, particularly in situations for which valid, reliable, and timely data are needed (e.g., needs assessment and planning) or for which the identification of pre-intervention baseline performance measures is desired (e.g., goal setting, pre- and postintervention assessments, cost estimation, etc.). Social indicators also are used to assess changes over time in the performances of even larger systems, including counties, states or provinces, nations, and the world as a whole.

Certain scientific criteria must be met in using social indicators for knowledge-based practice—the same criteria that apply to the use of indicators across all fields of scientific inquiry:

1. Indicators must have an a priori *clear and mutually agreed-upon operational definition.* These definitions must be in place prior to the collection of any data and, in any case, before the beginning of any analysis. Infant mortality rate,

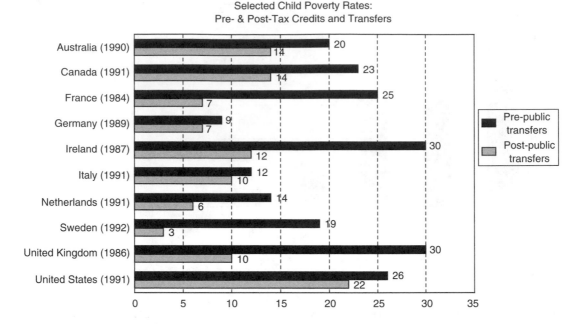

Figure 28.2   Childhood Poverty Rates for Selected Economically Advanced Societies Pre- and Post-Public Transfers

Source: Smeeding et al, 1998.

for example, can only refer to the number of children per 1,000 live-born who die sometime between birth and their first birthday. Variations in this operational definition cannot exist, least of all in the context of the same or related analyses.

2. Indicators must *validly* measure what they purport to measure. For example, per capita income should measure all sources of income to which the individuals have access (including public transfers and income from illegal sources) and not just those income sources that are reported by employers to public tax authorities.

3. Indicators must be *reliable,* meaning that the measures should produce the same results when applied by different researchers. For example, studies of women's access to contraception or to abortion services should produce the same results when the same concepts and the same methods are applied to the same population, regardless of who applies them.

4. Indicators must be *representative* of the population(s) for measures of the phenomena that are being sought (e.g., the degree of social cohesion or social cleavage among the residents of a given neighborhood).

5. Indicators must be *timely,* meaning that they should reflect the time period(s) of interest to the practitioner (e.g., specific days, weeks, months, or years). Measures that are too old or otherwise do not reflect the time periods under consideration are of little use for purposes of assessing time-related social progress.

6. Indicators must have the capacity to be *aggregated and disaggregated* at various levels of analysis (e.g., by year, for particular communities or neighborhoods, or for particular subgroups on which the indicators are based—gender, age, racial, ethnic, religious, nationality, political groups, etc.).

7. Indicators must be *easily interpreted.* Highly esoteric indicators (such as *racial-ethnic fractionalization index scores*) that are understandable only by a small cohort of specialists rarely have use in community practice.

8. Indicators must be *available* for purposes of analysis, meaning practitioners must be able to secure access to the indicators of particular interest to their communities. In situations where administrative, classified, or commercial data are needed, prior arrangements must be made to secure access to such data.

9. To be useful in helping to guide community practice, indicators must *reflect changes over time.* Examples of such change indicators include measures of quality of plumbing, housing, emergency services, communications, and other types of physical and social infrastructure available to the residents of particular communities.

10. The choice of indicators must have *policy relevance;* their collection and analysis must contain the potential for advancing different policy outcomes than those identified in the absence of such data.

11. The indicators selected to guide community practice must have the *capacity to reflect change(s),* such as social progress or failure, over time. Static indicators, or indicators that do not have the capacity to reflect change(s) over some designated time period, have little use in community practice.

Community workers practicing in economically advanced countries are fortunate in having a vast array of high-quality, socially relevant indicators available to them. The capacity for collecting still other indicators also exists for these practitioners; often, existing indicator collections can be enlarged by many of the same data collection organizations, once the need for such indicators manifests itself (e.g., selected governmental and nongovernmental organizations, including universities and commercial organizations that undertake public opinion polls, neighborhood surveys, and the like). Practitioners in less economically advanced countries (and less economically advanced communities in well-off societies) unfortunately have fewer established indicator sources available to them and, in many cases, have fewer opportunities for collecting representative indicators—albeit such efforts often are possible at the level of single neighborhoods, communities, cities, or other comparable levels of political organization. Research staff of local universities often co-operate with community practitioners in collecting and analyzing data in which both groups share a common interest.

Table 28.1 identifies major U.S. and international social indicator collection and dissemination organizations. The table includes both public and private organizations as well as highly specialized (e.g., Amnesty International, Stockholm International Peace Research Institute, the Office of International Policy of the U.S. Social Security Administration) and more broadly focused organizations (e.g., the

(Text continued on page 517)

Table 28.1   Selected Public and Private Sources of Social Indicators

Organization	Title	Frequency	Comments
Selected public data sources in the United States			
U.S. Central Intelligence Agency, Directorate of Intelligence	*CIA World Fact Book*	Annually	Provides comprehensive description of changing social, political, and economic situation of about 190 societies worldwide. http://www.odci.gov/cia/publications/ factbook/
U.S. Department of Commerce, Bureau of the Census	*Statistical Abstracts of the United States Population Statistics of the United States*	Annually	Provides access to thousands of time-series indicators related to all aspects of social, political, economic, and demographic development of the United States. Most indicators can be accessed without charge via the Internet. http://www.census.gov/prod/ www/statistical-abstract-us.html
U.S. Department of Commerce, Bureau of the Census	*Historical Statistical Abstracts of the United States*	Annually	Provides access to thousands of time-series indicators from 1790 to 1970. Many of these indicators may be accessed via the Internet. Data are available both at the national and state levels. http://fisher.lib.virginia. edu/census/
U.S. Department of Education, National Center for Education Statistics	*The Condition of Education The Digest of Education Statistics: 2001-2002 Education Indicators: An International Perspective Youth Indicators*	Continuously	Publishes social indicator data in four annually updated publications. Data may be disaggregated at the national, state and local levels. http://nces.ed.gov/
U.S. Department of Health and Human Services, Centers for Disease Control and Prevention, National Center for Health Statistics	*Vital Statistics of the United States Birth and Infant Death Data Set National Maternal and Infant Health Survey National Survey of Family Growth*	Monthly	Contains a comprehensive set of time-series data related to birth, mortality, fetal death, marriage and divorce, and so on. Data are quite detailed and can be used for national, state, and local analyses. Data also are linked to dozens of other data sets assembled by the Centers for Disease Control and Prevention that are of interest to health and social scientists. http://www.cdc.gov/scientific.htm

Organization	Title	Frequency	Comments
U.S. Department of Health and Human Services, Administration for Children and Families	*ACDY Data and Statistics*	Continuously	Publishes statistical national, state, and country data across a broad range of service sectors including: child care, child support, child welfare, Head Start, refugees, welfare caseloads. http://www.acf.dhhs.gov/
U.S. Department of Health and Human Services, Social Security Administration	*Social Security Programs Throughout the World*	Biannually	Publishes descriptive information concerning the existence, structure, funding mechanisms, and requirements of publicly managed social security programs worldwide. http://www.ssa.gov/statistics/ssptw99.html
U.S. Department of Housing and Urban Development	*HUD Statistics*	Continuously	Publishes housing-related data in a broad range of categories: housing, homelessness, affordable housing, urban planning, urban development, and so on. http://www.hud.gov/library/bookshelf03/index.cfm
U.S. Department of Labor, Bureau of Labor Statistics	*Various*	Continuously	Publishes a wide range of social indicators of interest to people at various levels of social organization: economic data, career guides, inflation and spending statistics, wage statistics, worker safety and health, productivity, international and comparative data. http://stats.bls.gov/
U.S. Department of the Treasury	*Statistics of the Internal Revenue Service*	Annually	Publishes time-series data concerning changes in income earned by aggregates of individuals, corporations, and other tax-paying and tax-exempt entities. For community organizers, the following statistical income series are particularly relevant: corporations, employment taxes, estate/wealth/gift taxes, international, tax exemptions, trusts, projections. http://www.irs.gov/taxstats/

Selected private data sources in the United States

Organization	Title	Frequency	Comments
Annie E. Casey Foundation	*Kids Count Data Book: State Profiles of Child Well-Being*	Annually	One of the most comprehensive statistical summaries of changing social, educational, and economic conditions of U.S. children in each of the nation's 50 states, the District of Columbia, and the U.S. Virgin Islands. Data are updated regularly and are presented for the nation as a whole, by state, and for many local communities. http://www.kidscount.org/
Children's Defense Fund	*The State of America's Children*	Annually	Contains an annual analysis of the changing social and economic status of U.S. children and families. Sections of the report provide national trend data concerning household

(Continued)

Table 28.1 (Continued)

Organization	Title	Frequency	Comments
			income, child health, child care, early childhood development, education, adolescent pregnancy, youth development and violence. http://www. childrensdefense.org/statesdata. htm
National Center for Charitable Statistics (of the Urban Institute)	*Charitable Statistics of the United States*	Continuously updated	Publishes a variety of continuously updated databases concerning all aspects of private philanthropy in the United States. http://nccs.urban.org/data.html
National Urban League	*The State of Black America*	Annually	Contains time-series data on the changing social, political and economic status of Americans of African ancestry in the United States. http://www.nul.org/publications/index.htm

Selected international data sources

Organization	Title	Frequency	Comments
Amnesty International	*Statistics on Human Rights Violations*	Continuously	Publishes both qualitative and quantitative analyses of the changing human rights situation for most countries of the world. Many of its most penetrating reports can be downloaded without charge from the Web site. http://www.amnesty-usa.org
Stockholm International Peace Research Institute (SIPRI)	*SIPRI Yearbook (of military and defense expenditures)*	Annually	Reports nearly 100 time-series indicators on all aspects of weaponry production, sales, and distribution around the world. http://www.sipri.org
United Nations Children's Fund (UNICEF)	*The State of the World's Children*	Annually	Reports about 100 indicators on a time-series basis for all member states of the United Nations. The report's primary focus is on children and families, including changing socioeconomic status of women. http://www.unicef.org/statis/
United Nations Development Programme (UNDP)	*Human Development Report*	Annually	Reports about 100 indicators on a time-series basis for all member states of the United Nations. The report's primary focus is on changing social and economic conditions in member countries, including gender issues. http://www.undp.org/toppages/statistics/
United Nations Educational, Scientific, and Cultural Organization (UNESCO)	*Statistical Yearbook*	Annually	Reports about 150 indicators on a time-series basis for all member states of the United Nations. Focus is on educational, scientific, and cultural performances of member countries. http://unescostat.unesco.org/

Organization	Title	Frequency	Comments
United Nations High Commissioner for Refugees (UNHCR)	*Refugees and Others of Concern to the UNHCR: Statistics*	Annually	Provides a large quantity of statistical data concerning the involuntary movement of people both within and across international borders, for example, people displaced by war, economic disasters, natural disasters, and so on. http://www.unhcr.org
World Health Organization	*World Health Report* *The Weekly Epidemiological Record*	Annually	Reports several hundred health, morbidity, and mortality indicators on a time-series basis for all member states of the United Nations. http://www.who.int/whosis/
World Bank	*World Development Report*	Annually	Reports several hundred indicators on a time-series basis for all member states of the United Nations. The report's primary focus is on comparative economic development including trade issues. http://www.worldbank.org/data/

U.S. Department of Labor, the U.S. Department of Health and Human Services). Nearly all of the data provided by these organizations are updated annually. Some organizations update their most sensitive indicators even more frequently (e.g., the U.S. Labor Department, the Centers for Disease Control, and so on).

Almost all of the data available from these organizations may be obtained either without cost or, in a few cases, for a nominal fee. Given their current electronic format, in most cases, data available from these organizations can be disaggregated at various levels of analysis according to the interests of particular users (e.g., by census tracts, neighborhoods, income groups, and so on). Data disaggregation for more detailed levels of analysis (such as data within a given community or communities for different combinations of age, gender, racial, income, religious, or other types of groups) often is possible with very large publicly gathered data sets, but typically a fee is imposed. Unlike the majority of national data sets, however, the social indicators contained in most international data sets rarely can be disaggregated at a level lower than the nation-state, although subnational data for extensively used indicators such as age, gender, and income are often available.

Comparable data collection organizations and social indicator data sets are available from major public and private data collection bodies located in virtually all economically advanced countries and in many larger developing countries as well. Many international organizations also collect and disseminate highly specialized cross-national indicators on a systemic basis. In virtually all cases, data collected at the national and international levels may be used for cross-national comparative purposes, but one always must check carefully for comparability of definitions and data collection methods (including time periods) across all the nations included in the analysis.

Social Reporting

As already noted, the international social reporting movement began at the same time as the international social indicators movement. Indeed, a very large reason why social indicators were collected at all was for their use in preparing social reports.

In their simplest form, social reports are no more than collections of social indicators put together between the two covers of a book. The *Statistical Abstracts of the United States* is a good example of a highly useful but primarily descriptive approach to the collection, reporting, and dissemination of time-series data related to virtually all aspects of collective life in the United States. Today, virtually every country of the world has a similar series of statistical reports that track critical social, political, and economic changes taking place in their society over time. Increasingly, these indicator collections are available in both print and electronic form, via CD-ROM or the Internet. Nearly all of these publicly gathered and disseminated data are now available to users without charge.

In their more sophisticated form, national social reports include a critical analysis of the nature, sources, and meaning of the broad-based changes that are taking place within their society. Many of these reports are far-reaching in conception; indeed, when implemented carefully, they can serve as the basis for realigning public policies toward the attainment of new societal goals (e.g., the Swedish, British, German, Italian, and Hong Kong national social reports). The tradition of European social reporting is particularly noteworthy with respect to its emphasis on the use of data to inform socially sensitive changes in administrative and legal policies.[1]

The situation of social reporting in the United States is at considerable variance with that found in other economically advanced countries. Although the United States collects and reports vast quantities of socially relevant data, the country's central government does not publish a formal state-of-the-nation social report. Rather, a plethora of highly specialized analyses emanate from departments and agencies of the central government, as well as from an array of researchers and policy analysts working in private research organizations that depend on federal sources for the bulk of their financial support. Owing to the varied purposes and methodologies of these investigations, their results typically cannot easily be integrated into the work of others. Consequently, an almost-always imperfect— certainly less complete and less timely—picture of critical social trends taking place in the United States emerges even from national analyses of critical social issues (e.g., changing patterns of poverty, changes in family structure and life, changes in community structure and life, increases or decreases in social solidarity, public attitudes toward various socially sensitive topics, etc.).

A variety of responses to the absence of a national social report for the United States have emerged over the past 15 years. Typically, and as suggested by the variety of social reports identified in Table 28.2, local communities have developed their own approaches to social analysis and social reporting. Many of these approaches are quite innovative. In every case, such reports tend to draw on a combination of social indicators collected at the federal and state levels in addition to original data collection that occurs at the local level. These processes also usually

Table 28.2   Selected Approaches to Community Social Reporting in the United States and Canada

Author/Creator	Title/Name	Frequency	Comments
Selected approaches to community social reporting in the United States			
Grand Traverse Regional Community Foundation	*Quality of Life for the Grand Traverse Region (Michigan)*	Annually	The Quality of Life Index is a community-based effort that attempts to identify, measure, and annually report on 10 different areas that affect the quality of life of everyone in the region. http://qualityindex.nmc.edu/toc.html
Critical Trends Assessment Program (CTAP)	*Critical Trends Report (Illinois)*	Annually	The CTAP is an ongoing process to evaluate changes in environmental quality in the State of Illinois. It also provides scientific support for the Ecosystems Program under Conservation 2000, a multiyear initiative to preserve and restore Illinois's ecosystems. http://dnr.state.il.us/orep/ctap/CTAPI.htm
Jacksonville Community Council	*Quality of Life in Jacksonville: Indicators for Progress (Florida)*	Annually	Trends in the local quality of life are tracked through 89 measurable indicators. Most come from publicly available data sources, but several come from a random telephone opinion survey. Data for most of the indicators are available starting with 1983, and all indicators are updated annually. The indicators measure the quality of life in nine areas: education, the economy, public safety, the natural environment, health, the social environment, government and politics, culture and recreation, and mobility. http://www.jcci.org/
North Carolina Progress Board	*2020 Draft Goals and Measures (North Carolina)*	In progress	The North Carolina Progress Board aims to form a data-based vision of North Carolina in the next 20 to 30 years. With goals and targets set, state leaders and agencies can work toward making that vision a reality—and helping communities and citizens attain the best quality of life possible. http://www.ncpb.state.nc.us/
City of Racine	*Sustainable Racine (Wisconsin)*	Annually	Throughout the Sustainable Racine planning process, an often-used visual tool of what sustainability means was a three-legged stool. For Racine, the "legs" on which development rests were the environment, the pursuit of equity, and growth of the economy. http://www.sustainable-racine.com/
Sustainable Seattle	*Indicators of Sustainable Community (Seattle, Washington)*	Annually	Sustainable Seattle is a citizen group working to improve the region's long-term health and vitality—cultural, economic, environmental, and social. The *Indicators of Sustainable Community* is the product of a community dialogue about the

(Continued)

Table 28.2 (Continued)

Author/Creator	Title/Name	Frequency	Comments
			region's future. Hundreds of Seattle-area volunteers have invested thousands of hours to design and research this integrated "report card." http://www.sustainableseattle.org/
Twin Cities East Metropolitan Area, Minnesota	*Social Outcomes for Our Community (Minneapolis and St. Paul, Minnesota)*	Annually	The report measures progress on five outcomes critical to the social health of the region's approximately 1 million residents: school readiness and success, affordable housing, economic opportunities, community safety, and healthy start for youth. http://www.cyfc.umn.edu/parenting/outcomes.html
Selected approaches to community social reporting in Canada			
Edmonton Social Planning Council	*Social Health Index (Edmonton, Canada)*	Annually	The Index is a composite of 15 local indicators used to create an overall assessment of the community's social health. http://www.edmspc.com/
City of Ontario	*Quality of Life Index Project (Ontario, Canada)*	Continuously	The Quality of Life Index Project (QLI) has been running for 2 years with funding from Health Canada. Results to date include three reports on the Quality of Life in Ontario (Fall 1997, Spring 1998, Fall 1998), several background papers, a Web site, and 20 community partners. This innovative approach to social reporting is based on hard data in a comparative framework with both provincial and local dimensions. http://www.osdc.org/socrep.html

involve the participation of large numbers of people drawn from all sectors of the local community. Thus, community approaches to social indicator and social report development tend to be highly participatory and, in the process, promote the development of a sense of ownership of the needs assessment, planning, goal-setting, and monitoring processes that occur all too rarely at higher, always more bureaucratic levels of political activity, that is, county, state/provincial, and federal.

Social Index Construction at the Local Level

A number of local initiatives also have resulted in the development of composite indexes of social progress that are used to monitor changes taking place in particular sectors of interest to local communities (e.g., housing, the environment, migration, poverty); see Table 28.2. Two efforts at creating composite indexes for use in measuring major social changes at the national level are Miringoff's *Index of Social Health* (Miringoff, Miringoff, & Opdyke, 1999) and the United Way of America's *State of Caring Index* (United Way of America, 2004).

Miringoff's Index of Social Health (ISH)

Miringoff and his associates at Fordham University's Institute for Innovation in Social Policy have been tracking social progress in the United States each year since 1985 (Miringoff et al., 1999). Using his own Index of Social Health (ISH), Miringoff monitors national performance on each of 16 social indicators, including child poverty, infant mortality rate, crime trends, access to health care, affordable housing, and so on. He combines performances on each indicator into a statistically weighted index and then uses the resulting composite scores to report on "the state of the nation's social health."

The results obtained from application of the ISH often are surprising, at least to the general public. Miringoff's team, for example, reports an inverse relationship between rates of economic expansion and advances in the nation's social health—sometimes with very dramatic losses occurring at the same time the economy is expanding rapidly. ISH scores plummeted from a high of 77 (out of a possible 100) earned in 1973 to only 38 in 1993. ISH scores recovered only slightly between 1993 and 1997, to 46. Increasing poverty rates (including child poverty) and rising crimes and suicide rates accounted for the most significant social losses on the ISH.

Miringoff's approach to social indexing raises many questions for methodologists, but its value to the public, including to politicians, is not questioned (Miller, 1997; Stille, 2000). National results obtained from the ISH have inspired a number of communities to develop versions of the ISH applicable to their local situation (see Table 28.2 for examples). The State of Connecticut, for which Miringoff has done extensive work, now even mandates that an assessment of the state's "social health" be conducted annually ("Connecticut's Social Health," 1998).

United Way of America's State of Caring Index (SCI)

The United Way of America's State of Caring Index (SCI) was developed in 1999 in response to a recognized need for more comprehensive measures of changing patterns of social cohesion and social caring within American society. Four goals were associated with the development of the SCI: (a) to highlight areas of social success for each state and for the nation as a whole, (b) to identify areas that need improvement, (c) to compare current conditions with past conditions, and (d) to compare conditions that exist in any one state with those found in other states and the nation as a whole (United Way of America, 2003).

In its present form, the SCI consists of 32 indicators divided across six sectors of development: the economy and financial well-being ($N = 6$), education ($N = 8$), health ($N = 8$), volunteerism/charity/civic engagement ($N = 5$), safety ($N = 2$), and natural environment and other factors ($N = 3$). Findings obtained from application of the SCI are presented in a variety of ways: (a) composite social caring scores are reported for the nation as a whole; (b) composite social caring scores are reported for each state of the United States; and (c) statistical and qualitative assessments are made of societal performance in each of the six sectors covered by the SCI. One of the most impressive features of this report is its use of clearly illustrated charts and diagrams to focus the reader's attention on critical areas in which social progress has and has not been made. The policy implications associated with each of the reports findings are both intuitive and compelling.

The United Way of America intends to publish updates to the national and state reports at regular intervals. Sectoral analysis will appear irregularly but always will accompany publication of the main report.

Social Index Construction at the International Level

Considerable work has been done on developing indexes for measuring social progress at the international level. The source of much of this work centers around various agencies of the United Nations (e.g., the United Nations Development Programme [UNDP], the United Nations Research Institute for Social Development [UNRISD]) and other organizations that invest heavily in international assistance to developing countries, such as the World Bank, the Organization for Economic Cooperation and Development (OECD), the U.S. Agency for International Development (USAID), and so on. A large number of academics also have taken up the challenge of developing composite measures of changes in national and international social progress.

In general, the international social index movement emerged side by side with the social indicator and social reporting movements. Indeed, many of the same people were involved in leadership positions for all three movements, including Jan Drenowski, Mabub al Haq, Kenneth Land, Donald McGranahan, Morris D. Morris, and Paul Streeten, among others. The goals of development assistance organizations and independent investigators working on the creation of international indexes of global social progress were the same: (a) to create new tools for use in monitoring changes in social progress throughout the world over time, (b) to establish baselines against which future changes in development could be measured, and (c) to serve as a basis for establishing new goals designed to advance world and national development objectives.

Table 28.3 identifies some of the most widely used composite measures of international development that have emerged since the mid-1970s. Each of the indexes has its own following, and each, in turn, has produced a body of empirical work that seeks to impact national and international development activities.

Physical Quality of Life Index (PQLI)

The Physical Quality of Life Index (PQLI) was developed in the mid-1960s by Morris David Morris and his colleagues at the Overseas Development Council (Morris, 1979; Streeten, 1981). Morris sought to achieve three purposes with the index: (a) to refocus the international debate on poverty and development to include more than just economic outcomes, (b) to focus international attention on the primacy of human development as the central goal of development work, and (c) to serve as a measure of changes over time in nations achieving their development priorities.

The PQLI consists of three indicators: infant mortality, life expectancy at age 1, and basic literacy. Country performances on each indicator are combined into

Table 28.3   Examples of Composite Measures of Social Progress Used in International and Comparative Research

Organization/ Author	Title/Name	Frequency	Comments
Overseas Development Council (ODC)	*Physical Quality of Life Index* (PQLI)	Irregularly	The PQLI was developed in the mid-1960s by Morris David Morris and his colleagues at the Overseas Development Council (Morris, 1979; Streeten, 1981). The PQLI consists of three indicators: (a) infant mortality, (b) life expectancy at age 1, and (c) basic literacy. Country performances on each indicator are combined into composite scores that range from 0 to 100. Reapplication of the PQLI allows for assessment over time of the changing capacities of governments to meet the basic needs of their populations.
Organization for Economic Cooperation and Development (OECD)	*Core Indicators for Measuring Development Progress*	Continuously	For nearly two decades, the OECD has sought to develop a set of core indicators closely associated with its international development assistance priorities (OECD, 1977). The organization's current set of 21 indicators is associated with a different development assistance goal: (a) reducing extreme poverty, (b) promoting universal primary education, (c) promoting gender equality, (d) reducing infant and child mortality, (e) reducing maternal mortality, (f) promoting reproductive health, and (g) protecting the natural environment (OECD, 1999). http://unstats.un.org/ unsd/mi/mi_goals.asp
Estes, Richard J.	*Index of Social Progress* (ISP; WISP)	Published every 5 years	Developed at the University of Pennsylvania (Estes, 1976), the ISP consists of 45 social indicators divided among 10 sectors of development: education, health status, status of women, defense effort, economic, demographic, geographic, social chaos, cultural diversity, and welfare effort. Statistically weighted versions of the index (WISP) are used to assess the changing social capacity of countries and major world regions. http://caster.ssw.upenn.edu/~restes/praxis/ dworld3.html
United Nations Development Programme (UNDP)	*Human Development Index* (HDI)	Annually	The HDI was introduced by the UNDP in 1990 as part of its now annual series of *Human Development Report(s)*. The HDI uses three indicators to assess national levels of human development: longevity, as measured by life expectancy at birth; educational attainment, as measured by adult literacy rates in combination with primary, secondary, and tertiary school

(Continued)

Table 28.3 (Continued)

Organization/Author	Title/Name	Frequency	Comments
			enrollment levels; and standard of living, as measured by real GDP or PPP. http://www.undp. org/dpa/publications/ hdro/98.htm
United Nations Development Programme (UNDP)	*Gender-Related Development Index (GDI)*	Annually	Introduced by the UNDP in 1995, the GDI makes use of the same indicators as those contained in the HDI. However, the GDI assigns different weights to the indicators in order to reflect inequalities in achievement between women and men. In effect, the GDI is simply the HDI adjusted downward for gender inequality.
United Nations Development Programme (UNDP)	*Gender Empowerment Measure (GEM)*	Annually	Also introduced by the UNDP in 1995, the GEM assesses the extent to which women are "empowered to take an active role in the economic and political life of a nation" (UNDP, 2003). The GEM tracks the percentage of women serving (a) in each country's parliament, (b) as administrators and managers, and (c) as professional and technical workers. The GEM also measures women's earned income as a percentage of the income earned by men.

unweighted composite scores that range from a low of 0 for countries with the least favorable development performances to 100 for those with the most favorable. Reapplication of the PQLI allows for assessment over time of the changing capacities of governments to better meet the basic needs of their populations.

Despite its initial influence in the field of development monitoring, the PQLI is rarely used today because of both the elementary nature of its indicators and the availability of other, more robust analytical tools.

The 1984 Index of Social Progress (ISP; WISP)

The Index of Social Progress (ISP) initially was conceptualized by this author in 1976 (Estes, 1976). In its present form, the ISP consists of 45 social indicators divided among 10 sectors of development: education, health status, women status, defense effort, economic, demographic, geographic, political chaos, cultural diversity, and welfare effort. Statistically weighted versions of the index (WISP) are used periodically to assess the changing capacity of the world as a whole and major world regions to provide for the basic social and material needs of their populations (Estes, 1984, 1988, 1998, 2003). Figure 28.3 illustrates the types of results that are obtained through application of the WISP to the analysis of worldwide social development trends over time.

In recent years, the author has adapted the ISP for use in monitoring social development trends occurring at the national level as well. Figure 28.4 illustrates

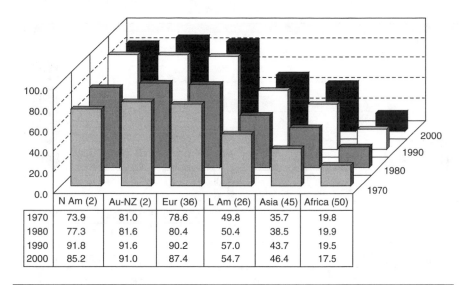

	N Am (2)	Au-NZ (2)	Eur (36)	L Am (26)	Asia (45)	Africa (50)
1970	73.9	81.0	78.6	49.8	35.7	19.8
1980	77.3	81.6	80.4	50.4	38.5	19.9
1990	91.8	91.6	90.2	57.0	43.7	19.5
2000	85.2	91.0	87.4	54.7	46.4	17.5

Figure 28.3   Average WISP Scores by Continent, 1970–2000 ($N = 161$)

Source: Estes, 2004.

the use of the ISP for analyzing development trends that occurred in the United States between 1970 and 2000. An even more tailored version of the ISP recently was created to monitor changes in social development for Hong Kong SAR (Estes, 2002; Estes, in press).

The United Nations Human Development Index (HDI)

The Human Development Index (HDI) was introduced by the UNDP in 1990 as part of its now annual series of *Human Development Report(s)*. The HDI builds on the conceptual legacy of both the PQLI and Drenowski and Scott's *Level of Living Index* (Drenowski & Wolf, 1966).

The HDI uses three indicators to assess national and international progress in human development: longevity, as measured by life expectancy at birth; educational attainment, as measured by adult literacy rates in combination with primary, secondary, and tertiary school enrollment levels; and standard of living, as measured by real Gross Domestic Product or Purchasing Power Parity. Country performances on each of these indicators are transformed into standardized scores, which, using a moderately complicated system of statistical weights, are combined to produce a single composite HDI score.

Like the previous indexes, the HDI attempts to focus international attention on both the economic and noneconomic aspects of development, including the persistence of global poverty, gender inequality, the relationship between social and economic development, and the need of people everywhere to participate more fully in framing both the goals and means of development. In 1995, the UNDP released two additional indexes that focus specifically on the changing status of women throughout the world, the Gender Related Development Index (GDI) and the Gender Empowerment Measurement (GEM).

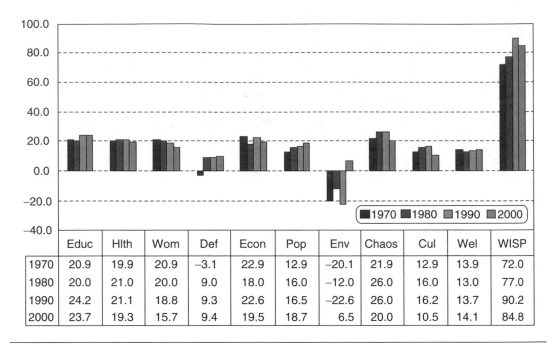

	Educ	Hlth	Wom	Def	Econ	Pop	Env	Chaos	Cul	Wel	WISP
1970	20.9	19.9	20.9	−3.1	22.9	12.9	−20.1	21.9	12.9	13.9	72.0
1980	20.0	21.0	20.0	9.0	18.0	16.0	−12.0	26.0	16.0	13.0	77.0
1990	24.2	21.1	18.8	9.3	22.6	16.5	−22.6	26.0	16.2	13.7	90.2
2000	23.7	19.3	15.7	9.4	19.5	18.7	6.5	20.0	10.5	14.1	84.8

Figure 28.4   WISP Subindex Scores for the United States, 1970–2000

Source: Estes, 2003.

The Contribution of Social Indicators to Community Practice

Social indicators, social reporting, and composite indexes of social progress can and do play an important role in community practice. When applied correctly, these tools can be used to advance community practice in at least five ways: (a) by providing an integrated conceptual framework into which diverse social, political, and economic phenomenon can be incorporated; (b) by helping to identify the goals toward which development activities can be directed and the means by which these goals can be attained; (c) by identifying specific targets that are to be achieved within designated time periods; (d) by providing a baseline against which subsequent success and failure can be assessed; and (e) by fostering active participation and a sense of ownership among and between all the stakeholders involved in the development and application of more knowledge-based approaches to practice.

The use of social indicators, social reports, and social indexes, of course, is not the answer to every challenge that confronts community practitioners. Their judicious use, however, can help both to further rationalize our practice and, at the same time, to promote progressively higher levels of goal attainment in our work with communities.

Note

1. Examples of especially noteworthy European social reports include: Belgo Data and Vrind (Belgium); Levevilkar I Danmark (Denmark); Donnees Sociales (France); Datenreport (Germany); Sintesi della Vita Sociale Italiana (Italy); Social and Cultural Report

(Netherlands); Sosialt Utsyn Leveka I Norge (Norway); Social Trends (United Kingdom); and Indicadores Sociales Panorama Social (Spain).

References

Andrews, J. H. (1996, September). Going by the numbers: Using indicators to know where you've been—and where you're going. *Planning Practice,* 14–18.

Balaswamy, S., & Dabelko, H. I. (2002). Using a stakeholder participatory model in a community-wide service needs assessment of elderly residents. *Journal of Community Practice, 10*(1), 55–70.

Bauer, R. A. (Ed.). (1966). *Social indicators.* Cambridge: MIT Press.

Beck, W., et al. (1998). *The social quality of Europe.* Bristol, UK: The Policy Press.

Bell, D. (1966). Toward a social report, I. *Public Interest, 15,* 72–84.

Berger-Schmitt, R., & Jankowitsch, B. (1999). *Systems of social indicators and social reporting: State of the art.* Mannheim, Germany: ZUMA.

Campbell, A., Converse, P., & Rodgers, W. (1976). *The quality of American life: Perceptions, evaluations, and satisfactions.* New York: Russell Sage Foundation.

Chow, J., & Coulton, C. J. (1996). Strategic use of a community database for planning and practice. *Computers in Human Services, 13,* 57–72.

Christoph, B., & Noll, H. H. (2003). Subjective well-being in the European Union during the 90s. *Social Indicators Research, 64*(3), 521–546.

Cohen, W. (1968, October). Social indicators: Statistics of public policy. *The American Statistician, 22,* 14–16.

Connecticut's social health on rise—but still far worse than 1970s. (1998, February 23). *The New-Times.*

Conner, R. F., Tanjasiri, S. P., & Easterling, D. (1999). *Communities tracking their quality of life.* Denver: The Colorado Trust.

Drenowski, J., & Wolf, S. (1966). *The level of living index.* Geneva, Switzerland: United Nations Research Institute for Social Development.

Drummond, W. J. (1995). The development of GIS-based small area social indicators. *Proceedings of the Third International Conference on Computers in Urban Planning and Urban Management, 1,* 185–209.

Estes, R. J., with J. S. Morgan. (1976). World social welfare analysis: A theoretical model. *International Social Work, 19*(2), 29–41.

Estes, R. J. (1984). *The social progress of nations.* New York: Praeger.

Estes, R. J. (1988). *Trends in world social development.* New York: Praeger.

Estes, R. J. (1998). Trends in world social development, 1970–95: Development prospects for a new century. *Journal of Developing Societies, 14*(1), 11–39.

Estes, R. J., in collaboration with C. H. Wai, J. Fung, & A. Wong). (2002). Toward a social development index for Hong Kong: The process of community engagement. *Social Indicators Research, 58*(1–3), 313–347.

Estes, R. J. (2003). The Index of Social Progress (ISP, WISP) Retrieved June 14, 2004, from The University of Pennsylvania, PRAXIS Web site: http://caster.ssw.upenn.edu/~restes/praxis/dworld3.html

Estes, R. J. (2004). Social development in the "new" Europe. *Social Indicators Research.*

Estes, R. J. (in press). *Social development in Hong Kong: The unfinished agenda.* London & New York: Oxford University Press.

Hagerty, M., Vogel, J., & Moller, V. (Eds.). (2002). Assessing quality of life and living conditions to guide national policy: The state of the art [Special issue]. *Social Indicators Research, 58*(1–3), 1–440.

Johnson, J. H. (2002). A conceptual model for enhancing community competitiveness in the new economy. *Urban Affairs Review, 37*(6), 763–779.

Land, K. C., & Spillerman, S. (Eds). (1975). *Social indicator models.* New York: Russell Sage Foundation.

McGranahan, D. V., Richard-Proust, C., Sovani, N. V., & Subramanian, M. (1972). *Contents and measurement of socio-economic development.* New York: Praeger.

Miller, D. (1997, November 20). Measuring our social health: Varieties of error. *The Yale Herald.*

Miringoff, M. L., Miringoff, M.-L., & Opdyke, S. (1999). *The social health of the nation: How America is really doing.* New York: Oxford University Press.

Morris, M. D. (1979). *Measuring the conditions of the world's poor: The physical quality of life index.* New York: Pergamon Press for the Overseas Development Council.

Noll, H. H. (1996). *Social indicators and social reporting: The international experiences.* Mannheim: ZUMA.

Organization for Economic Cooperation and Development (OECD). (1977). *Core indicators for rmeasuring development progress.* New York: Author.

Organization for Economic Cooperation and Development (OECD). (1999). *Core indicators for measuring development progress.* New York: Author.

Richmond, M. (1917). *Social diagnosis.* New York: Russell Sage Foundation.

Sawicki, D. S., & Flynn, P. (1996, Spring). Neighborhood indicators: A review of the literature and an assessment of conceptual and methodological issues. *Journal of the American Planning Association,* 165–183.

Schultz, J. A., et al. (2000). The community tool box: Using the Internet to support the work of community health and development. *Journal of Technology in Human Services, 17*(2/3), 193–215.

Smeeding, T., et al. (1998). *Poverty and parenthood across modern nations: Findings from the Luxembourg Income Study* (LIS Working Paper No. 193). Syracuse, NY: Syracuse University.

Stille, A. (2000, May 29). By all indications, we are pretty happy. *New York Times.*

Streeten, P. (1981). *First things first: Meeting basic human needs in developing countries.* New York: Oxford University Press for the World Bank.

Svallfors, S. (2003). Welfare regimes and welfare opinions: A comparison of eight Western countries, *Social Indicators Research, 64*(3), 495–520.

Telfair, J., & Mulvihill, B. A. (2000). Bridging science and practice: The integrated model of community-based evaluation. *Journal of Community Practice, 7*(3), 37–65.

United Nations. (1975). *Toward a system of social and economic indicators.* New York: Author.

United Nations Development Programme (UNDP). (2003). *Human development report, 2003: Millennium development goals—a compact among nations to end human poverty.* New York: Oxford University Press.

U.S. Department of Health, Education, and Welfare. (1969). *Toward a social report.* Washington, DC: Government Printing Office.

United Way of America. (2003). *United Way state of caring index.* Alexandria VA: United Way of America [http://national.unitedway.org/stateofcaring/about_faq.cfm].

Veenhoven, R. (1996). Happy life expectance: A comprehensive measure of quality of life in nations. *Social Indicators Research, 39,* 1–58.

Vogel, J. (2003). European welfare production: Institutional configuration and distributional outcome. *Social Indicators Research, 64*(3), 325–469.

Wong, Y. L. I., & Hillier, A. E. (2001). Evaluating a community-based homeless prevention program: A geographic information system approach. *Administration in Social Work, 25*(4), 21–45.

Zachary, J. (1995). *Sustainable community indicators: Guideposts for local planning.* Santa Barbara, CA: Community Environmental Council.

Zimbalist, S. (1977). *Historic themes and landmarks in social welfare research.* New York: Harper & Row.

Zumbo, B. D. (Ed.). 2002. Advances in quality of life research, 2001 [Special issue]. *Social Indicators Research, 60*(1–3), 1–334.

CHAPTER 29

Community Practice Challenges in the Global Economy

Michael Reisch

T he advent of economic globalization has dramatically transformed the
environment of community practice in both industrialized and developing
nations. It has fundamentally changed the relationship between the market
and the state, with serious consequences for low-income people and low-power
communities in the United States and throughout the world. The growing dominance of market mechanisms and ideologies has affected policy making at the
national and local levels in ways community practitioners are just beginning to
comprehend. Although the features of political democracy are spreading throughout the world, the potential impact of this trend is being undermined by the
concentration of transnational corporate power and the influence of such organizations as the World Bank, the International Monetary Fund (IMF), and the
World Trade Organization (WTO). Moreover, the usual marker of democratization, the holding of "free elections," has not produced truly representative governments and has frequently failed to unseat entrenched despotic leaders. As Fareed
Zakaria (2003) notes, there is increasingly a difference in the developing world
between the emergence of freedom as a concept and the creation of democratic
political markers. This chapter presents a critical analysis of these trends and
discusses current and potential social work responses on behalf of communities that
are increasingly excluded from and negatively affected by the new global political
economy.

The Assumptions of Community Practice

For the past century, community practice in the United States has been shaped by an integrated set of assumptions about the relationship among the economy, the state, and social welfare. As authors such as Fisher (1994) have pointed out, although ideological differences have existed among community practitioners, practitioners generally have shared the belief that state-sponsored social policies could be used to ameliorate the excesses and negative consequences of a market economy by collectivizing its social costs (Fisher & Karger, 1997; Kapp, 1971). They further assumed that there would be a gradual and continuing expansion of state responsibility for social provision, with modest redistributive results that would be of potential benefit to the residents of disadvantaged and disfranchised communities (Axinn & Stern, 2001; Jansson, 1997).

Particularly since the 1930s, this set of beliefs has led community practitioners to adopt a posture of cautious cooperation with the state, based on mutual self-interest. National and state governments would support the modest expansion of social welfare policies and programs to sustain the legitimacy of liberal democracy and the appearance of a pluralistic society. In turn, community practitioners would rely on government as a major source of funds and political validation in their efforts to balance the inequitable distribution of societal resources and power produced by a relatively untrammeled market economy (Reisch & Wenocur, 1986; Rothman, 1999).

Community practitioners further assumed that they could retain this delicate balance without compromising their ethical principles or abandoning their constituents. Finally, they assumed that solutions to community problems could be developed within local, regional, or national frameworks. (In fact, the primary emphasis of community practice during the 20th century was on organizing and development in neighborhoods or communities. This emphasis was based on the largely unquestioned belief that the sources of a community's problems are proximate to the arenas in which community practice strategies are implemented; Fisher, 1994; Rubin & Rubin, 2001.) Although such authors as Delgado (1994), Iglehart and Becerra (1995), and Rivera and Erlich (1998) have challenged this model, until recently, most texts on community organization, community practice, and even structural social work focused primarily on local arenas of struggle (Delgado, 2000; Fellin, 2001; Hardcastle, Wenocur, & Powers, 1996; Homan, 1999; Kahn, 1991; Mondros & Wilson, 1994; Mullaly, 1997; Rothman, 1999; Rothman, Erlich, & Tropman, 2001; Tropman, Erlich, & Rothman, 2001).

Economic globalization, however, has seriously challenged or invalidated many of these long-standing assumptions. Many observers claim that with the emergence of a well-integrated global market, national and local policymakers are increasingly being controlled—and spending on redistributive social benefits squeezed—by the flow of capital to sites where production costs are lower (Broadbent, 1998; George, 1998). This has dramatic implications for the economic stability and viability of communities in industrialized and developing nations. According to Fisher and Kling, "Global processes have disordered people's conceptions of who they are and to whom they are related and have undermined their bearing as to the nature of the social spaces in which their daily lives are grounded" (1993, p. xi).

Others have argued that to ensure that people's insecurity does not reach intolerable levels, there is a pressing need to expand the state's efforts to cushion the growing social risks, such as cyclical unemployment and underemployment, and the consequences of cutbacks in education, health care, and social service programs that accompany the vagaries of escalating globalization and rapid technological change (Deacon, 1998; Prigoff, 2001; Rodrik, 2001). From this perspective, the expansion of social security programs and social services, particularly those at the community level, can be a means of absorbing the risks of globalization. If community practice is to remain viable in the 21st century, it will need to adjust its conceptual frameworks, issue orientation, strategies, and tactics to this new political-economic reality.

The Nature of Economic Globalization

An understanding of the implications of economic globalization for community practice requires that it be distinguished from the internationalization of commerce and trade, which has existed for thousands of years. The key features of economic globalization, as it emerged in the late 20th century, are the rapid mobility and liquidity of capital; the short-term nature of investments; the interlocking connections of national currency systems; the speed of both capital and information transfer (including its effects on policy planning and analysis and the emphasis on short-term profit enhancement rather than long-term economic development); the growing power of multi- or transnational corporations, which organize production on a global scale; the promotion of specialized modes of production and knowledge; and the relative absence of countervailing political and ideological forces to direct, constrain, or control market-driven impulses. Other features include the shift of both manufacturing and service industries to areas of the world with the cheapest labor and least restrictive regulations; the increasing use of high technology in work, particularly in the fields of information and communications; the need for fewer workers with higher skills or for fewer hours of work to maintain the same level of productivity; a decline in the gender distinction of work, with its resultant impact on family and work relations; and a widening and rigidifying gap in income, wealth, education, skills, and status between classes and races. Whereas there is widespread agreement about what globalization is, there are serious differences of opinion about what the process of globalization represents and what its implications are for the future of state-sponsored social protection or the future of community life, particularly in urban areas (Bluestone, 1994; Economic Policy Institute, 2002; Federman et al., 1996; Friedman, 1999; Greider, 1997; Head, 1996; Madrick, 1995; Mishel, Bernstein, & Schmitt, 1996; Prigoff, 2001; Rifkin, 1995; Sasson, 1994; Soros, 1997; Wilson, 1996).

The Roots of Economic Globalization

The current pattern of economic globalization emerged in the early 1970s, although its origins lie in the immediate post–World War II era, particularly in the Bretton

Woods Agreement of 1944. For 25 years (from roughly 1945 to 1970), the combined effects of a global marketplace and the welfare state produced a "golden era" for the United States and other industrialized nations. Income inequality declined, and most groups saw their standard of living improve as a consequence of economic growth, a moderately progressive income tax, and the expansion of income transfer programs (Danziger & Weinberg, 1994; Sawhill, 1996). Even in the developing world, poverty and unemployment declined.

Since 1973, this picture has changed, with dramatic implications for community practice. During the 1980s and 1990s, a period of resurgent religious fundamentalism and ascendant Western neo-conservative politics—sometimes called Reaganism or Thatcherism—corporations that had once focused on the production of goods and services largely for local or regional consumption were transformed through merger, consolidation, and expansion into entities largely concerned with short-term profit enhancement. Previous loyalties to communities or even nations were replaced by allegiance to stockholders and investors. Economists have linked these phenomena to the growth of income and wealth inequality in the United States, other industrialized nations, and the developing world (Atkinson, 1998; Barlow & Clarke, 1998; Chossudovsky, 1997). Related factors include gaps in educational and job skill levels; the introduction of new technologies; the decline in the power of unions; the emphasis on foreign trade; changes in the wage scale and occupational structure of societies; the reorganization and transformation of work; the spread of regressive modes of taxation; and the stagnation or contraction of welfare benefits (Danziger & Weinberg, 1994; Madrick, 1995; Wilson, 1996).

Assumptions Behind Economic Globalization

Economic globalization is based on the assumption that capitalist institutions, ideology, and behaviors should pervade the world economy. This translates into the dominance of the market system, market values, and market mechanisms in all political and social institutions, including those at the community level (Barnet & Cavanagh, 1994). For example, since the 1980s, community development corporations (CDCs) have appeared to offer neighborhood residents the opportunity to gain greater control over their lives. Ironically, however, they often assume that common ground can be found between residents and the very corporate interests whose actions produced many of the community's problems (Fisher, 1994). Recognition of this contradiction has often disillusioned community residents and appears to have left them with few viable alternative strategies.

For example, community residents often feel powerless when faced with a choice between protecting their precarious economic status and protesting the degradation of their environment (e.g., the Love Canal environmental disaster of the 1970s near Niagara Falls, New York). Or, they may feel compelled to make fiscal, labor, and zoning concessions they can ill afford when major employers threaten to relocate their businesses. Successful efforts to fight the combined indifference to community problems of private sector interests and political leaders are few and require creative and sustained coalition work (Medoff & Sklar, 1994).

Economic reality at both the local and global levels, however, is much more complex. Certain countries still operate under socialist or mixed economies. Other nations, such as South Africa, are more protectionist in nature owing to their stage of economic development, and still others, like Japan, have a historical reluctance to open their society to free markets. Countries as varied as France, Malaysia, Mexico, and Russia reflect differing forms of capitalism, as the consequence of differences in their pace of institutional development, the pervasiveness of technology, local political issues, and distinct cultural and historical factors.

Some communities are more dependent on the vagaries of the global market than others. Consequently, at the local level, community practitioners confront the contradiction between consensus and conflict approaches (Mansbridge, 1980). It is not surprising, therefore, that differences in community practice within the United States and among the world's nations reflect significant variations in existing relationships among governments, the private sector, and community-based nongovernmental organizations (NGOs). Nor is it surprising that significant differences also exist based on variations in local history, culture, politics, and demographic mix (Rivera & Erlich, 1998; Rubin & Rubin, 2001). Despite these variations, the dominant assumptions that underlie economic globalization and their implications for policy have been particularly damaging to the poor nations of the world and to low-income or "disinvested" communities within the industrialized world.

By focusing on international integration, governments in poor nations divert human resources, administrative capabilities, and political capital away from more urgent development priorities, such as education, public health, industrial capacity, and social cohesion. This emphasis also undermines nascent democratic institutions by removing the choice of development strategy from public debate (Rodrik, 2001). Local protests regarding spending cuts on human capital infrastructure have erupted in many developing countries, such as South Africa, the Philippines, and Venezuela.

These socioeconomic trends have several implications for the field of community practice. First, the domestic market will become less significant to the profitability of corporations in the decades ahead. This will affect many of the social policies created from the 1930s to the 1970s to maintain a floor on consumption through income maintenance programs such as Social Security and economic subsidies to small farmers. Fiscal deficits in recent years have already led to funding cuts in the billions of dollars for education, health, and social service programs, and these cuts have direct and indirect effects on the quality of community life (Oxfam America, 1995; Prigoff, 2001; Reich, 2000). Recent attempts to "reform" welfare and privatize Social Security are just two examples of this trend. This means that the focus of community practice efforts at the local level will have to shift to take into account the changing priorities of national policies and their consequences.

Second, the lure of foreign markets, cheap overseas workers, and less restrictive labor and environmental policies means that employers can more easily carry out their threats to move production sites abroad or to other regions of the country. The availability of very inexpensive labor has weakened union organizing drives while promoting negotiations between labor and management focused on "givebacks," productivity, and job security issues. These negative effects of globalization also undermine the ability of community groups to extract certain concessions, such as respect for the area's environmental integrity, from corporations in their geographic area (Brecher & Costello, 1995; Falk, 1997; Gittell, 1998; Mander & Goldsmith, 1996; Martin & Schumann, 1997).

In the United States, the political imbalance of this new reality has already fragmented state policies by promoting interstate and even intrastate competition to attract corporate investment in an era of policy devolution (Larin, 1997). Communities are forced to sacrifice environmental quality, occupational safety, and, most important, a sense of control over their economic future. This diminishes the likelihood that the level of social provision found in more advanced welfare states since the early 20th century will be maintained (Barlow & Clarke, 1998; Bluestone, 1994). It also alters the "political mindset" of communities and changes the pattern of potential alliances and choice of coalition partners within them. In the wider political arena, globalization has contributed to the decline in social movements based on class solidarity by narrowing their focus, limiting their efficacy, and highlighting their failure to incorporate other disfranchised populations (Fisher, 1994).

Third, economic globalization has changed the nature of property, property relations, and work that was created by industrialization and the rise of industrial capitalism in the 18th, 19th, and early 20th centuries. Property itself is changing from money and other tangible commodities to credits. Consequently, trade agreements are now primarily about the protection of the property rights of investors. Despite recent protests, workers' rights and environmental protections have been largely ignored (Barlow & Clarke, 1998; Danaher, 1994; Prigoff, 2001). While these developments exacerbate the plight of low-income, low-power communities, they present opportunities for new interorganizational relationships that unite previously acrimonious groups.

In sum, the efficiency of the private sector is, more than ever, predicated on lowering the costs of production, especially wages and benefits, and shifting the social costs of market enterprise to the "inefficient" and increasingly cash-strapped public sector (Bello, 1994; Kapp, 1971). One implication of this development is that even under economic globalization, the social costs of production are indispensable aspects of a market economy and cannot be eliminated without a major revision of the system itself. All corrective measures to ameliorate the impact of these social costs (e.g., through income transfers and social services) do not address this fundamental issue (Deacon, 1998). Nevertheless, in today's economy, the short-term logic of the market system increasingly argues against the implementation or maintenance of these corrective measures (Caufield, 1996).

Proponents of globalization argue that the transfer of national resources from production for domestic use to production for export is required to promote economic development and to maintain competitiveness in the global market. Critics of globalization argue, however, that an emphasis on foreign trade, especially if overly reliant on foreign capital, results in the destabilization of long-standing institutions and communities, particularly in regions with established, subsistence model economies and social structures. The consequences of this shift include the destruction of local enterprises by transnational corporations, both in the United States and abroad, the privatization of unique national resources (often at bargain prices, as in Eastern Europe), the restriction of social spending on human capital investment, heavy debt burdens, and the overall shredding of long-standing social safety nets (Caufield, 1996; Chossudovsky, 1997; Danaher, 1994; Estes, 1998). Its effects can be seen from Rust Belt cities to abandoned rural areas.

The Role of the International Monetary Fund and the World Bank

Economic policy making in the industrialized world, then, reflects the logic of maintaining a system of global capitalism. A logical extension of globalization, especially but not exclusively in developing nations, is the shift of national resources from production for domestic use to production for export. Large multinational corporations, major banks, and international finance organizations such as the IMF and the World Bank support this approach and frequently employ its logic to extract political and social concessions from developing countries in need of credits and foreign investment. In the 1990s and the early 21st century, with the implementation of the North American Free Trade Agreement (NAFTA), General Agreement on Tariffs and Trade (GATT), and similar trade agreements, and with the growth in influence of the WTO, similar concessions have been extracted in industrialized nations particularly in the areas of labor and environmental policy (Atkinson, 1998; Broadbent, 1998; Prigoff, 2001).

This idea is best reflected in the so-called structural adjustment policies of the IMF and World Bank and the rules governing international commerce developed by the WTO (Greider, 1997; Soros, 1997). The major role of such policies has been to promote international conformity to the requirements of a global capitalist economy. This has affected community practice throughout the world, primarily through the limitations it places on public-sector spending, the privatization of public space (Fisher & Karger, 1997), and the promotion of NGOs as viable alternatives to state provision of social services, education, and health care. The growth of NGOs has occurred not only in the United States but also in developing countries with little or no tradition of such activities. This growth is occurring in areas of social welfare in which the nonprofit sector has never had the capacity to replace government-funded programs. In African nations, for example, substantial portions of the health and education sectors have been privatized and are now off-budget (Deacon, 1998; IMF, 1998). In the United States, nonprofit organizations including churches, which have few resources and whose programs have little or no demonstrated effectiveness, and private-sector organizations, which often are motivated more by profit than by altruism, are increasingly being asked to fill gaps in the social services, health care, and mental health fields (Cnaan, Wineburg, & Boddie, 1999).

Through the conditions attached to their loans to developing nations and the sheer volume of debt carried by these nations' economies (nearly $2 trillion), the World Bank and IMF wield enormous power. Since the 1980s, the debt burden of developing countries has intensified, resulting in the further contraction of welfare provisions, particularly in those nations (e.g., in Africa) where the economic plight of people and communities has worsened (IMF, 1998; World Bank, 1997). About 20% of these loans go to structural adjustment programs (SAPs), which countries receive only if they make draconian economic reforms that produce questionable benefits (Caufield, 1996; Danaher, 1994). Such "reforms" include currency devaluation, promotion of export-oriented production, cuts in social spending, privatization of state-owned industries, deregulation of the economy, and wage suppression. Ironically, by the end of the 20th century, the World Bank was taking in billions more dollars each year in repayments and interest than it loaned to developing nations. Recognition of the oppressive burden created by these loans was a major source of inspiration for the global debt reparations movement (Chandler, 1997; Prigoff, 2001). Prompted by persistent criticism from advocacy organizations and NGOs and even from staff inside the organization, the World Bank has recently taken some limited steps to make its policies more participatory and appropriate to the economic and social needs of developing nations. It is not clear at this time whether such changes will be expanded and sustained in the future.

The policies of the WTO, increasingly the focus of massive international protest activities at both the local and international levels, promote conditions such as the global movement of capital which benefit multinational corporations and investors. Under the guise of eliminating "restraints of trade," WTO tribunals have invalidated environmental, health, and worker safety laws. Simultaneously, WTO agreements have shielded economic elites from actual or potential liability for economic, social, or environmental damages they may cause in local communities (Galvin, Moch, & Prigoff, 2000). These developments alter the character and potential of community practice in the decades ahead. For example, they have already led to the formation of local, national, and international coalitions among organizations and groups of activists that have little or no history of such sustained collaboration. Sustaining such coalitions will require community practitioners to use technology, such as the Internet, in new and innovative ways; to integrate new knowledge about environmental conditions into long-standing concepts regarding economic and social development; and to recognize the role of international law in effecting local changes.

The Impact of Economic Globalization

Economic globalization and its attendant policy shifts have already had a sweeping impact on human well-being, particularly in the developing world, and on the ability of nations to respond to their socioeconomic problems through government or private-sector provision. In brief, they have widened the gap between rich and poor in industrialized nations and between rich and poor nations (i.e., the North/South dichotomy). They have forced local and state governments in the United States to alter their fiscal priorities to respond to market exigencies. Finally, they have essentially undermined the power of nation-states in the developing world and transferred power to a small number of international financial institutions that have no accountability to the people whose lives are affected by their decisions (Bello, 1994; Greider, 1997; Prigoff, 2001).

Growing Inequality and Its Political Consequences

On a worldwide scale, economic globalization has produced a growing gap in income and wealth; a decline in assets held by the majority of people; increased domestic migration and emigration, with disruptive effects on communities; a rise

in negative social indicators; the destabilization of cultures; growing social conflict; environmental degradation; loss of confidence in governmental institutions and political systems; and growing alienation and despair (Bello, 1994; Bluestone, 1994; Chossudovsky, 1997). In Fisher's words, "global capitalism destroys community at the same time it forces people back into it as their primary source of defense" (1994, p. 233).

Deacon has pointed out how globalization "sets welfare states in competition with each other and generates the danger of social dumping, deregulation and a race to the welfare bottom . . . [as it] raises issues of social redistribution, social regulation, [and] social empowerment to a regional and global level" (1998, p. 9). The consequence that is perhaps of greatest importance for community practice is that the supranational organizations spawned by globalization have revealed the increasingly anachronistic structure and function of national and state political institutions and social welfare organizations in an era when policy devolution has seemingly thrust more responsibility for community well-being onto state and local governments.

Ironically, this has occurred during a period in which the increased mobility of capital and information has affected the rapidity with which problems emerge, the ways they are perceived, and the speed with which institutions are expected to respond. In turn, new technologies promoted by globalization influence the development of social goals and the formation of institutional relationships needed to assess and resolve social problems. These developments have particular significance for community planning and development efforts at the local level because these methods of community practice assume the existence of a relatively benign state apparatus and the ability of targeted local actions to affect the sources of a community's problems.

The effects of globalization are also closely linked to demographic shifts resulting from the search for employment and the flight from political conflict. Indirectly, they have produced—at least in the short term—a decline in class consciousness and the growth of ethnic and religious strife at both the local and national levels in countries as diverse as Congo and Indonesia. Globalization has produced increased regional economic competition over resource development (e.g., in southeast Europe and central Asia around the exploitation of oil and gas reserves). It has also had an impact on patterns of national economic development, particularly in Eastern Europe, Latin America, and Africa. Developing nations have less ability to establish economic self-sufficiency (especially in terms of food production), to create social policies that promote the development of human capital, and to develop social safety nets (Caufield, 1996). On a lesser scale, the governments of such U.S. states as California, Michigan, and New York and many large or mid-size cities face similar fiscal restraints, particularly since the onset of the recent economic slowdown and the severe budget crises that have emerged in its wake (McNichol, 2003).

Nevertheless, the consequences of these trends are felt with particular severity in the developing world. The pressure to maintain high interest rates to attract foreign investment (these rates are often two to three times higher than in the United States) has had deleterious consequences on the growth of domestic industries, particularly small businesses, and the creation of domestic markets. The economic and social pressuses brought about by these trends have decreased the availability of resources for development of social infrastructure while increasing the need to

reduce the fiscal deficits that could help finance this investment. Since the disappearance of federal and state budget surpluses at the end of 2001 and the advent of huge deficits at all levels of government, large sections of the United States are experiencing similar pressures, often compounded by the legal requirement of producing a balanced budget and restrictions on how state and local governments can raise needed revenues. For example, to balance a projected $38.5 billion deficit for fiscal year 2004, the state of California imposed severe cuts in health, social service, and higher education programs and instituted a broad range of largely regressive taxes and fee increases (State of California, 2003).

Another major consequence of globalization is the exacerbation of the Global North/South dichotomy. Although nearly three quarters of the world's people live in the Global South, they share only one fifth of the world's wealth. According to the United Nations, the richest 20% of the world's population produces nearly 85% of the world's gross annual product, whereas the poorest 20% produces only 1.4%. The ratio of income of the top quintile to the bottom quintile has nearly tripled since 1960 (United Nations Development Programme, 1998; World Bank, 1997).

This growing inequality also appears in the United States, despite nearly a decade of unprecedented economic growth in the 1990s and the fleeting emergence of fiscal surpluses for the first time since the 1960s. In fact, the United States is now the most unequal of all industrialized nations in distribution of wealth and more unequal now than at any time since 1945, when such data began to be recorded (Office of Economic Cooperation and Development, 1996; U.S. Bureau of the Census, 2000). Recent tax cuts that disproportionately benefit a small minority of high-income taxpayers will considerably exacerbate this inequality.

In comparison with other, less prosperous countries, the state of human well-being in the United States lags behind (Estes, 1998; see also Estes, Chapter 28, this volume). For example, the United States ranks 21st in infant mortality; more than 13% of its population still lives in official poverty; and half of all U.S. adults are at economic risk in terms of literacy and educational proficiency. More than one sixth of the population lacks health insurance, and many millions more have inadequate coverage (Larin, 1997). Whereas 90% of Mexican children under the age of 5 are immunized against childhood diseases, this rate is below 50% in some U.S. cities (Annie E. Casey Foundation, 2003; Children's Defense Fund, 2003).

Social and Environmental Consequences

In sum, the effects of economic globalization are being felt in communities throughout the industrialized and developing world. These include

- environmental degradation through the exploitation of natural resources in the most profitable and least sustainable ways, such as the investment in dams and extractive industries such as mining;
- the social and fiscal costs of drug abuse, as farmers in the developing world frequently turn away from subsistence agriculture to more lucrative illicit cash crops such as coca or opium;

- the increased degradation of women and children through prostitution, international trafficking, and other forms of commercial exploitation including inhumane work conditions (Afshar & Barrientos, 1999);
- the costs of writing off the bad debts of developing nations, which have been estimated at more than $50 billion;
- a global economic slowdown, with such symptoms as rising unemployment or underemployment in key industries as a consequence of the export of jobs, and a decrease in trade due to the decline in consumption in developing nations;
- the economic, social, and political costs of increased immigration; and
- the rise in both international and interethnic conflict, fueled by competition for scarce resources, incursions to capture valuable resources, and government use of international loans to buy arms (Barlow & Clarke, 1998; Brown, Flavin, & French, 1997; Prigoff, 2001).

Implications for Community Practice

These consequences have serious implications for the future of community practice. First, they have provided community practitioners with a set of organizing issues that clearly link local problems to international developments. Using these issues as catalysts for organizing is not, however, without serious risks.

Economic globalization has also weakened the role of a historic ally of community practice efforts, organized labor (see Burghardt & Fabricant, Chapter 10, this volume), through its influence on the nature of work and the pressure to control wages. Particularly in the industrialized world, real wages have declined or stagnated, and work has become less stable (Reich, 2000). Globalization is transforming the workplace through so-called lean production, a range of strategies aimed at expanding productivity and reducing labor costs. These include the simplification of production, the replacement of skilled workers with unskilled employees, and the widespread use of outsourcing. These concepts have spread to the service sector, resulting in the displacement of many lower-level workers and middle-level managers. The introduction of managed care during the 1990s produced identical effects among social workers in health and mental health settings (Head, 1996; Strom-Gottfried, 1997; see also Scheyett & Drinnin, Chapter 23, this volume).

At the same time, economic globalization has spawned fiscal and monetary policies in many nations that primarily emphasize the creation of a climate suitable for investment rather than for the redistribution of societal goods. This has produced a propensity for budget and tax cuts, as well as increased reliance on private sector alternatives to state provision or funding of services. These policies have been accompanied by such persistent ideological attacks on the role of government in alleviating community problems that states' credibility and capacity as problem-solving institutions have been greatly undermined. As a result, growing attention is being paid in many nations to the role that nonprofit organizations can play in resolving community problems.

The Growth and Transformation of Nonprofit Organizations

In the United States and elsewhere, there has been a proliferation and promotion of NGOs and nonprofit organizations as a response to the withdrawal of state welfare intervention. This has produced major changes in the roles, responsibilities, expectations, and outcomes of nonprofits, even in those countries in which the nongovernmental sector has had vastly different histories, functions, contexts, and motives for formation (Cnaan et al., 1999; Eisenberg, 1998; Fisher & Karger, 1997; Gittell, 1998; Jacobson, 2001). Community-based planning is increasingly the responsibility of local NGOs, self-help groups, and volunteers (see Weil, Chapter 11, this volume), with professionals serving in various technical and consultative capacities (Prigoff, 2001). This development has serious implications for the future of community practice because the development of community-based organizations has long been an effective strategy used by practitioners to promote community and societal change. It provides both opportunities and challenges for community practitioners.

One noticeable effect has been the growing influence of market ideas on the culture of community-based organizations (Alexander, 1999). Market ideas have influenced these organizations' vocabulary, program emphases, staffing patterns, funding sources, and their relationship with constituents, even while nonprofits are increasingly expected to fill in the gaps created by cuts in government funding for social safety net programs. In this shifting climate, many scholars and activists have questioned the ability of nonprofit community-based organizations to survive and achieve their long-standing goals of community service and well-being (Abramovitz, 2002; Alexander, 1999; Gil, 1998; Reisch & Sommerfeld, 2001).

Emerging Strategies of Community Practice

There is an increasingly fractious debate among community practitioners as to how best to respond to the consequences of economic globalization. Ironically, most texts still give scant mention to the effects of global economic forces on the environment in which community practice occurs. Some activists even reject the idea of using globalization as the basis for analysis and strategic development (Blau, 1998). In different ways, some organizers seek to re-create a mythologized version of community, often based on conservative secular or religious values (Fisher & Kling, 1993). Some propose new approaches that go beyond a geographically centered model and that emphasize the resurgence of what Rivera and Erlich (1998) term *neo-Gemeinschaft* communities (Delgado, 1994, 2000; Iglehart & Becerra, 1995). Others promote the creation of alternative economic and political institutions at the local level, such as cooperatives and ecovillages, and focus on how communities can become self-sufficient centers of alternative, life-sustaining culture through grassroots empowerment (Brecher & Costello, 1995; Burbach, Nunez, & Kagarlitsky, 1997; Falk, 1997; Gil, 1998; Jacobson, 2001). There has also been a renewed emphasis on building social capital at the community level and on developing innovative models of philanthropy, such as online fund-raising, e-commerce among nonprofits, and the application of principles employed by venture capitalists to the development efforts of NGOs (Eisenberg, 1998; Gittell, 1998). Whether such approaches have long-term viability for community development in the current economic context has yet to be determined.

Despite these differences, many community practitioners now recognize that previous strategies, which viewed communities and even nations in isolation from the international environment, are no longer adequate. Nonetheless, while social action events and mass demonstrations from Seattle to Genoa have inspired a resurgence of community-based activism and protest, the persistence of diverse views, often based on identity politics, within contemporary movements and movement-based organizations hinders the ability of groups to develop coherent strategies or broad, effective coalitions (Fisher & Karger, 1997). While Gottdiener's observation that "no mechanisms currently exist that can aggregate neighborhood mobilization of needs into a viable public discourse" (1987, p. 285) is still basically valid, the explosive growth in the use of the Internet and the success of mass efforts like the Million Man and Million Woman Marches offer a glimmer of hope that the infusion of local needs into broader political debates may be possible in the future. For now, however, the formation of a viable, sustained community-based movement is hampered both by the existence of seemingly intractable racial, ethnic, and religious divisions and by the absence of organizational structures that could unite the multiple, disparate community organizing projects currently under way. Consequently, some community practitioners are grappling over how to combine long-standing class-, gender-, or race-based conceptual frameworks into effective strategies against the consequences of economic globalization (Afshar & Barrientos, 1999; Gittell, 1998; Naples, 1998; see also Gamble & Hoff, Chapter 8, this volume).

Sometimes this struggle is reflected in the agendas of activist groups that seek inclusion at the expense of clarity and fail to link proposed solutions to the problem—globalization—that sparked their initial mobilization (B. Manski, email communication, April 4, 2000). It may be difficult, for example, for displaced industrial workers in the United States or residents of a neighborhood threatened by the dumping of toxic wastes to connect their immediate problems with their roots in the decisions of elite financial institutions and with the suffering of people in the developing world. At other times, the struggle is reflected in the persistent tension between advocates of universal human rights and those who view such concepts as "self-interested attempts to protect the social welfare securities of the people in developed countries from being undercut by competition from the [developing world]" (Deacon, 1998, p. 24) and "instruments [that] only work to the advantage of the powerful and the dominant, and make the world more oppressive" (Raghavan, 1996).

Global organizations such as Bread for the World have attempted to overcome such divisions and organize a consensus around a strategy of sustainable human development. Such a strategy would incorporate the following elements:

- satisfaction of basic human needs for food, shelter, health care, education, and natural resources such as clean water
- expansion of economic opportunities for all people in ways that are environmentally and socially viable over the long term

- protection of the environment through future-oriented management of resources
- promotion of democratic participation, especially by poor people, in the fundamental economic and political decisions that affect their lives
- encouragement of adherence to internationally recognized human rights standards (Bread for the World, 1995)

Other organizations, including the International Forum on Globalization and the Other Economic Summit, are attempting to forge coalitions of community leaders, scholars, and service professionals into a "Community of Communities." Unfortunately, with a few notable exceptions, such as Arline Prigoff and the late Susan Kinoy, American social workers have not yet played visibly active roles in these antiglobalization efforts.

The development and sustenance of such coalitions will require cooperation between and among groups that have a long history of antagonistic relations or that are largely ignorant of one another's existence. They include international trade unions, environmental groups, civil and women's rights organizations, transnational NGOs, academic researchers, and even some liberal economists. In some countries, such as Canada, efforts to create such coalitions are much further along than in the United States (Deacon, 1998).

The Role of Social Work Education in a Global Economy

If the profession of social work is to retain its historic commitment to social justice and empowerment, the current generation of students will need to be prepared to work with communities whose economic plight will become increasingly desperate. To educate students to be effective community practitioners in this environment, social work educators, at a minimum, need to take the following steps:

- Provide students with a basic understanding of micro- and macroeconomics, so they can comprehend the impact of a global economy on the individuals, families, and communities with whom they work. In particular, students need to know how economic forces affect people's daily lives and self-concepts.
- Pay more attention to the changing nature of work, as well as the economic, social, psychological, and cultural effects of this change, especially at the community level.
- Emphasize the growing, yet often overlooked, significance of social class, without being drawn into divisive debates as to whether class, gender, or race is the primary source of oppression in our society.
- Integrate international perspectives throughout the curriculum and provide students with multicultural perspectives on social development.

In part, schools of social work can address the implications of economic globalization by incorporating content into their curricula on macroeconomics: the social implications of the shifting labor market, the legal and regulatory framework for employment, the philosophical and psychosocial dimensions of work in our society, and ethical issues for practice in this new environment. These recommendations emphasize the importance of a dual focus in social work education on (a) helping those in need of employment gain increased access to the workforce along with better conditions of work, and (b) improving the quality of life for workers, their families, and their communities.

To prepare students for the global economy of the future, Root (1997) suggests that social work education emphasize such content areas as organizational behavior and program innovation; the structure and dynamics of the labor market; assessment of and response to the special needs of workers; skills in cost-benefit/cost-effectiveness analysis; ethical issues involved in meeting conflicting demands; and legal issues that affect employment practices. Lewis (1997) has suggested such curricular enhancements as the development of practice skills to work with youth in school-to-work programs and with older workers in vocational rehabilitation and training programs; skills in evaluative research methods; and the ability to design and implement research projects and program interventions that reflect sensitivity to the differing needs of people in the workplace (e.g., women, people of color, individuals with disabilities).

Conclusion: The Future of Community Practice in a Global Economy

There are several reasons why economic globalization will have an impact on community practice in the United States and other nations for the foreseeable future. First, community practice, particularly in the United States, emerged in response to the social consequences of industrialization. The ideological roots, strategies, tactics, and organizational forms that characterize community practice are closely linked, therefore, to its relationship to the overall political economy and the consequences of that context and elitist decisions (Fisher, 1994; Patterson, 2000). Although the theories, focus, and methods of community practice have not yet adapted to these structural and cultural changes, the creation of effective community-level responses to globalization will become even more important if the worldwide economic slowdown of the first years of the 21st century continues.

Second, a persistent issue among community practitioners has been the importance of collectivizing the social costs of private enterprise through advocacy for increased public-sector responsibility for social and economic provision. Community practice has been most successful when it has integrated into its efforts issues of employment/unemployment, income distribution, equitable fiscal policies, occupational safety and health, and workers' political rights (Rose, 1997). In the 21st century, community practitioners will have to create new approaches to respond effectively to the new global economy and the growing gaps in employment, income, and wealth it has created (Reich, 2000; Rifkin, 1995). Among liberal economists, there is widespread acceptance of the premise that "socially regulated capitalism rather than unfettered capitalism and state socialism does better at meeting human needs" (Deacon, 1998, p. 16; see also Reich, 2000). Enacting needed approaches will require "a focus on broadly formulated issues and programs, articulated through multicultural coalitions and alliances, as central instruments for the achievement of policy goals, and the engagement of the state as an arena for struggle and change" (Fisher & Kling, 1993, p. 319). With their analytic, political, and group process skills, community practitioners are well-suited to play a critical role in such efforts.

Third, community practitioners have long emphasized the connections between private troubles and public issues, particularly issues associated with poverty and its consequences (Reisch & Andrews, 2001). The basic principles of community practice—social justice, self-determination, empowerment, democratic participation, and leadership development—are critically needed for the creation of viable alternative institutions (Hardcastle et al., 1996; Simon, 1994). Community practitioners need to incorporate these principles into new conceptual frameworks that synthesize global and local perspectives, include both class and identity politics, and balance the role of political-economic structures with a focus on human agency (Fisher & Kling, 1993). In the absence of such theoretical and practical integration, economic globalization as it is currently constructed "is likely to marginalize and exclude a majority of the world's population from participation in productive economic activity, and from its rewards" (Prigoff, 2001, p. 2).

Community practitioners can influence the direction of major economic and political trends by combining long-standing principles of self-determination, social justice, and democratic participation with updated skills and knowledge that reflect new social and technological realities. Neither resignation to the "inevitability" of the status quo nor nostalgia for a mythological past will create a more equitable world. As the South African proverb states, "We will learn the road by walking."

References

Abramovitz, M. (2002). *In jeopardy: The impact of welfare reform on nonprofit human service agencies in New York City.* New York: United Way of Metropolitan New York.

Afshar, H., & Barrientos, S. (Eds.). (1999). *Women, globalization, and fragmentation in the developing world.* New York: St. Martin's Press.

Alexander, J. (1999). The impact of devolution on nonprofits: A multiphase study of social service organizations. *Nonprofit Management and Leadership, 10*(1), 57–70.

Annie E. Casey Foundation. (2003). *Kids count 2003.* Baltimore, MD: Author.

Atkinson, A. B. (1998). *Equity issues in a globalizing world: The experience of OECD countries.* Paper presented at the International Monetary Fund Conference on Economic Policy and Equity, Washington, DC.

Axinn, J., & Stern, M. (2001). *Social welfare: A history of the American response to need* (5th ed.). Boston: Allyn & Bacon.

Barlow, M., & Clarke, T. (1998). *MAI: The Multilateral Agreement on Investment and the threat to American freedom.* New York: Stoddard.

Barnet, R. J., & Cavanagh, J. (1994). *Global dreams: Imperial corporations and the new world order.* New York: Touchstone.

Bello, W., with Cunningham, S., & Rau, B. (1994). *Dark victory: The United States, structural adjustment, and global poverty.* London: Pluto.

Blau, J. (1998). Globalization of the economy: A whole new world. *BCR Reports, 10*(1), 1.

Bluestone, B. (1994, Winter). The inequality express. *The American Prospect, 20*, 81–93.

Bread for the World. (1995). *Hunger 1995: The causes of hunger.* Washington, DC: Author.

Brecher, J., & Costello, T. (1995). *Global village or global pillage: Economic reconstruction from the bottom up.* Boston: South End Press.

Broadbent, E. (1998). The challenge to economic and social rights: Thoughts on citizenship in the welfare state in the North Atlantic world. *Global Society, 12*(1), 15–29.

Brown, L., Flavin, C., & French, H. (1997). *State of the world 1997: Worldwatch Institute report on progress toward a sustainable society.* New York: Norton.

Burbach, R., Nunez, O., & Kagarlitsky, B. (1997). *Globalization and its discontents: The rise of postmodern socialisms.* Chicago: Pluto.

Caufield, C. (1996). *Masters of illusion: The World Bank and the poverty nations.* New York: Henry Holt.

Chandler, D. (1997). Globalization and minority rights: How ethical foreign policy recreates the East-West divide. *Labour Focus on Eastern Europe, 58*, 15–34.

Children's Defense Fund. (2003). *The state of America's children.* Washington, DC: Author.

Chossudovsky, M. (1997). *The globalisation of poverty: Impact of IMF and World Bank reforms.* Washington, DC: International Monetary Fund.

Cnaan, R., Wineburg, R., & Boddie, S. (1999). *The newer deal.* New York: Columbia University Press.

Danaher, K. (Ed.). (1994). *Fifty years is enough: The case against the World Bank and the International Monetary Fund.* Boston: South End Press.

Danziger, S. H., & Weinberg, D. H. (1994). The historical record: Trends in family income, inequality, and poverty. In S. H. Danziger, G. D. Sandefur, & D. H. Weinberg (Eds.), *Confronting poverty: Prescriptions for change* (pp. 18–50). Cambridge, MA: Harvard University Press.

Deacon, B. (1998). *Towards a socially responsible globalization: International actors and discourses.* Sheffield, UK: University of Sheffield, Department of Sociological Studies.

Delgado, G. (1994). *Beyond the politics of place: New directions in community organizing in the 1990s.* Oakland, CA: Applied Research Center.

Delgado, M. (2000). *Community social work practice in an urban context: The potential of a capacity-enhancement perspective.* New York: Oxford University Press.

Economic Policy Institute. (2002). *State of working America.* Armonk, NY: M. E. Sharpe.

Eisenberg, P. (1998). Philanthropy and community building. *National Civic Review, 87*(2), 169–176.

Estes, R. (1998). Trends in social development, 1970–1995: Development prospects for a new century. *Journal of Developing Societies, 14*(1), 11–39.

Falk, R. (1997). Resisting "globalization from above" through "globalization from below." *New Political Economy, 2*(1), 17–24.

Federman, M., Garner, T. I., Short, K., Cutter, W. B., Kiely, J., Levine, D., McGough, D., & McMillen, M. (1996). What does it mean to be poor in America? *Monthly Labor Review, 119*(5), 3–17.

Fellin, P. (2001). *The community and the social worker* (3rd ed.). Itasca, IL: F. E. Peacock.

Fisher, R. (1994). *Let the people decide: Neighborhood organizing in America* (updated ed.). New York: Twayne.

Fisher, R., & Karger, H. J. (1997). *Social work and community in a private world: Getting out in public.* New York: Longman.

Fisher, R., & Kling, J. (Eds.). (1993). *Mobilizing the community: Local politics in the era of the global city.* Newbury Park, CA: Sage.

Friedman, T. (1999). *The Lexus and the olive tree: Understanding globalization.* New York: Farrar, Straus & Giroux.

Galvin, K., Moch, M., & Prigoff, A. (2000). Social workers participate in protest on global trade issues in Seattle. *NASW California News, 26*(6), 19.

George, V. (1998). Political ideology, globalization, and welfare futures in Europe. *Journal of Social Policy, 27*(1), 17–36.

Gil, D. (1998). *Confronting injustice and oppression: Concepts and strategies for social workers.* New York: Columbia University Press.

Gittell, R. J. (1998). *Community organizing: Building social capital as a development strategy.* Thousand Oaks, CA: Sage.

Gottdiener, M. (1987). *The decline of urban politics.* Newbury Park, CA: Sage.

Greider, W. (1997). *One world, ready or not: The manic logic of global capitalism.* New York: Simon & Schuster.

Hardcastle, D., Wenocur, S., & Powers, P. (1996). *Community practice.* New York: Oxford University Press.

Head, S. (1996, February 29). The new ruthless economy. *The New York Review of Books, 43,* 47–52.

Homan, M. S. (1999). *Promoting community change: Making it happen in the real world* (2nd ed.). Belmont, CA: Brooks/Cole.

Iglehart, A. P., & Becerra, R. M. (1995). *Social services and the ethnic community.* Boston: Allyn & Bacon.

International Monetary Fund (IMF). (1998). *Economic review.* Washington, DC: Author.

Jacobson, D. (2001). *Doing justice: Congregations and community organization.* Minneapolis, MN: Fortress Press.

Jansson, B. (1997). *The reluctant welfare state: Past, present, and future.* Pacific Grove, CA: Brooks/Cole.

Kahn, S. (1991). *Organizing: A guide for grassroots leaders* (Rev. ed.). Washington, DC: NASW Press.

Kapp, K. W. (1971). *The social costs of private enterprise.* New York: Schocken.

Larin, K. (1997). *Pulling apart: A state-by-state analysis of income trends.* Washington, DC: Center on Budget and Policy Priorities.

Lewis, B. M. (1997). Occupational social work practice. In M. Reisch & E. Gambrill (Eds.), *Social work in the twenty-first century* (pp. 226–238). Thousand Oaks, CA: Pine Forge.

Madrick, J. (1995). *The end of affluence.* New York: Random House.

Mander, J., & Goldsmith, E. (Eds.). (1996). *The case against the global economy—And for a turn toward the local.* San Francisco: Sierra Club.

Mansbridge, J. (1980). *Beyond adversary democracy.* New York: Basic Books.

Martin, H. P., & Schumann, H. (1997). *The global trap: Globalization and the assault on democracy and prosperity.* London: Zed Books.

McNichol, L. (2003). *The state fiscal crisis: Extent, causes, and responses.* Washington, DC: Center on Budget and Policy Priorities.

Medoff, P., & Sklar, H. (1994). *Streets of hope.* Boston: South End Press.

Mishel, L., Bernstein, J., & Schmitt, J. (1996). *The state of working America, 1996–1997.* Armonk, NY: M. E. Sharpe.

Mondros, J. B., & Wilson, S. M. (1994). *Organizing for power and empowerment.* New York: Columbia University Press.

Mullaly, R. (1997). *Structural social work* (2nd ed.). New York: Oxford University Press.

Naples, N. A. (Ed.). (1998). *Community activism and feminist politics: Organizing across race, class, and gender.* New York: Routledge.

Office of Economic Cooperation and Development (OECD). (1996). *Report on income inequality in industrialized nations.* Geneva: Author.

Oxfam America. (1995). *The impact of structural adjustment on community life: Undoing development.* Washington, DC: Author.

Patterson, J. (2000). *America's struggle against poverty in the 20th century.* Cambridge, MA: Harvard University Press.

Prigoff, A. (2001). *Economics for social workers: Social outcomes of economic globalization with strategies for community action.* Belmont, CA: Brooks/Cole.

Raghavan, C. (1996). *Barking up the wrong tree: Trade and social clause links.* Retrieved August 13, 2002, from http://www.twnside.org.sg/title/tree-ch.htm.

Reich, R. (2000). *The future of success.* New York: Knopf.

Reisch, M., & Andrews, J. (2001). *The road not taken: A history of radical social work in the United States.* Philadelphia: Brunner-Routledge.

Reisch, M., & Sommerfeld, D. (2001). *The impact of welfare reform on nonprofit organizations in Southeast Michigan: Implications for policy and practice.* Washington, DC: The Aspen Institute.

Reisch, M., & Wenocur, S. (1986). The future of community organization in social work: Social activism and the politics of profession building. *Social Service Review, 60*(1), 70–91.

Rifkin, J. (1995). *The end of work: The decline of the global labor force and the dawn of the post-market era.* New York: Tarcher/Putnam.

Rivera, F., & Erlich, J. (Eds.). (1998). *Community organizing in a diverse society* (3rd ed.). Needham Heights, MA: Allyn & Bacon.

Rodrik, D. (2001). Trading in illusions. *Foreign Policy, 123*(2), 55–62.

Root, L. (1997). Social work and the workplace. In M. Reisch & E. Gambrill (Eds.), *Social work in the twenty-first century* (pp. 134–142). Thousand Oaks, CA: Pine Forge.

Rose, N. (1997). The future economic landscape. In M. Reisch & E. Gambrill (Eds.), *Social work in the twenty-first century* (pp. 28–38). Thousand Oaks, CA: Pine Forge.

Rothman, J. (Ed.). (1999). *Reflections on community organization: Enduring themes and critical issues.* Itasca, IL: F. E. Peacock.

Rothman, J., Erlich, J., & Tropman, J. (Eds.). (2001). *Strategies of community intervention* (6th ed.) Itasca, IL: F. E. Peacock.

Rubin, H. J., & Rubin, I. S. (2001). *Community organizing and development* (3rd ed.). Boston: Allyn & Bacon.

Sasson, S. (1994). *Cities in a world economy.* Thousand Oaks, CA: Pine Forge.

Sawhill, I. (1996). The economy. In N. A. Winchester (Ed.), *Public policy and the new realities: A report of the NASW Presidential Forum* (pp. 1–5). Washington, DC: NASW.

Simon, B. L. (1994). *The empowerment tradition in social work practice.* New York: Columbia University Press.

Soros, G. (1997). The capitalist threat. *The Atlantic Monthly, 279*(2), 45–58.

State of California. (2003). *Governor's budget for the State of California, FY 2003–2004.* Sacramento, CA: Office of Fiscal Management.

Strom-Gottfried, K. (1997). The implications of managed care for social work education. *Journal of Social Work Education, 33*(1), 7–18.

Tropman, J., Erlich, J., & Rothman, J. (Eds.). (2001). *Tactics and techniques of community intervention* (4th ed.). Itasca, IL: F. E. Peacock.

United Nations Development Programme. (1998). *Human development report 1998.* New York: Oxford University Press.

U.S. Bureau of the Census. (2000). *Statistical abstract of the United States, 2000* (120th ed.). Washington, DC: Government Printing Office.

Wilson, W. J. (1996). *When work disappears: The world of the new urban poor.* New York: Knopf.

World Bank. (1997). *Having sustainable development: The World Bank and Agenda 21.* Washington, DC: Author.

Zakaria, F. (2003). *The future of freedom: Illiberal democracy at home and abroad.* New York: Norton.

CHAPTER 30

Supporting Women's Participation in Community Economic Development

The Microcredit Strategy

Salome Raheim

Helzi Noponen

Catherine Foster Alter

The economic health of a community is fundamental to the well-being of its members. In economically distressed areas, community economic development—efforts to improve the economic vitality of a community or region—is critical to promote access to resources and opportunities for subsistence, self-sufficiency, and self-determination. These efforts frequently include generating new businesses, stabilizing or expanding existing businesses, and attracting businesses from elsewhere to the community (see Rubin & Sherraden, Chapter 26, this volume).

Prior to the 1970s, gender issues were generally ignored in economic development efforts (Momsen, 1991). It was believed that men and women would benefit equally from economic initiatives. Unfortunately, gender-blind economic development efforts negatively affected women, perpetuating their exclusion from decision making and promoting their unequal access to resources (Momsen, 1991;

Stevenson, 1988). Within the past two decades, many planners, policymakers, and community practitioners have recognized that economic development efforts designed for women as participants and beneficiaries can have far-reaching effects on them, their families, and communities (Charlton, Everett, & Staudt, 1989; Young, Samarasinghe, & Kusterer, 1993).

Also during the past two decades, microcredit was being employed with promising results in developing countries as a strategy for poverty alleviation and economic development (Ashe, 1985) and gained attention in the United States (Servon, 1999). This strategy engages individuals in economic development by providing small loans for self-employment and the development of small enterprises. The popularity of the microcredit strategy is evidenced by the 1997 Microcredit Summit, at which hundreds of governmental and nongovernmental organizations (NGOs) began an international initiative to "reach 100 million of the world's poorest families, especially the women of those families, with credit for self-employment . . . by the year 2005" (Microcredit Summit, 1997, p. v; see also World Summit on Sustainable Development, 2002).

This chapter examines the advantages and limitations of microcredit as a strategy for expanding women's opportunities to participate in and benefit from economic development by discussing issues that are critical to the design of effective community economic development programs for women. The programs of two economic development organizations with a history of serving women, one in India and one in the United States, illustrate effective efforts. The chapter concludes with a discussion of considerations for planners, policymakers, and community practitioners in designing and implementing economic development initiatives that focus on women.

Women and Economic Development: Challenges to Gainful Participation

Women play a central role in the world's economy, and many poor women are essential to the economic survival of their families. Nevertheless, women's economic contributions are undervalued and often invisible. Women perform two thirds of the world's work, yet earn only 10% of the income and hold 10% of the property, despite their economic contributions. In 1995, most of the world's 1.3 billion absolute poor—people living on less than U.S. $1 a day—were women (U.S. Agency for International Development, 2000).

In both developed and developing countries, many challenges to women's gainful participation in the local economy persist. In industrialized countries, the lower status of "women's work," gender inequities in wages, and occupational segregation stifle women's earnings, economic opportunities, and progress. In developing countries, these factors may combine with the transition of local economies from subsistence production into an open global economy to create unique challenges to women's participation. In this transition, women's traditional roles have been disrupted as they have been thrust into new economic roles that have been poorly supported at best, and hampered at worst, by economic policies and community development programs.

Challenges in Developing Countries

Women have long been engaged in agriculture, artisan industries, and regional trade, but their roles in these sectors have declined significantly with the transformation of subsistence to capitalist economies tied to a global economic system (Boserup, 1970; Sen & Grown, 1987). Men's roles in these sectors have also been disrupted, but compared to women, they have found more opportunities in the changing economy (Banerjee, 1982). Women have fared worse because of relations of gender that disadvantage women, both in the private sphere within households and in the public sphere with employers and development bureaucracies (Sen & Grown, 1987).

Women continue to do unpaid subsistence production and reproduction work in the home, whether or not they have found work in the changing economy. Reproduction work consists of activities of home maintenance, cooking, cleaning, child care, and health care. Subsistence production work consists of activities of raising food crops, tending livestock, and gathering water, fuel, and forest products for family consumption. If not produced through women's labor, these items and services would have to be purchased in the market. Women's work contribution also includes unpaid labor in family enterprise units, typically in material preparation or packaging and finishing tasks. These activities are not considered productive work but only an extension of women's household chores (Momsen, 1991).

For poor households, the need to earn an income is high, and women, like men, seek jobs exchanging their labor services for payment in cash or kind. Compared with men, however, women face greater occupational segregation and wage discrimination. In agriculture and manufacturing, they tend to be concentrated into lower-paid, more labor-intensive, and female-specific operations, which are the first to become mechanized or altered by technological innovations. When technology is introduced, these positions are lost altogether or taken over by male workers (Sen & Grown, 1987).

In some industries, employers prefer to hire women and girls because they are perceived to be more adept (which could merely mean more disciplined) at tedious and monotonous tasks, as well as more dependable, more docile, and less likely to unionize than men (Beneria, 1989; Elson & Pearson, 1984). This is true for international employers producing goods for export, for example, high-tech semiconductor and electronics firms in Southeast Asia or the *maquiladoras* in export-processing zones in the Caribbean and along the U.S.–Mexican border, as well as for national employers producing basic wage goods. In addition, women's labor is preferred because it is cheaper. Women have fewer work alternatives and are responding to a household survival strategy, so they are willing to supply their labor for a lower price than men (Moser & Young, 1981). However, this type of formal-sector employment for women accounts for a very small percentage of total female employment, and it is often unstable in the highly competitive world market (Lim, 1990). In addition to layoffs and plant closings, disability owing to age, marriage, pregnancy, or work-related eye strain hinders women's participation in wage employment (Elson & Pearson, 1984).

Challenges in Developed Countries

In industrialized countries, women face economic challenges similar to those of their counterparts in the developing world, especially those who are poor or who have low incomes. Women make up 50% of the labor force but face many obstacles to reaping the full economic benefit of their work, including occupational segregation and wage discrimination. They are likely to work in the most vulnerable jobs, without health and other benefits. Women are more likely to work part-time, often holding several part-time jobs. Whether they work full- or part-time, many remain below the poverty line (Malveaux, 1990).

In the United States, the social welfare system may provide material support for women with children, but it creates additional challenges. Once supportive of female heads of household, the social welfare system has become increasing intolerant of women who rely on public assistance. Women with children who are not supported by a male wage earner are expected to be economically self-sufficient through participation in the wage labor market. Furthermore, the system sets standards for the quality of material support these women must provide for their children in order to keep their children with them, although the same system cannot assure them adequate wage employment or adequate child care while employed. As in developing countries, women's reproductive work in the United States is not valued, yet for those with children, their lives are increasingly regulated, often to the disadvantage of those with low income or in poverty.

Women, Self-Employment, and the Informal Sector

Given the challenges women face in the labor market, many women participate in self-initiated, income-generating activities—self-employment—to supplement wages or as an alternative to wage employment. These activities may occur in the formal (regulated) economy or in the informal (unregulated) sector. In either case, self-employment can help women circumvent obstacles to employment and facilitate their participation in the economy in ways that allow them to shape the conditions of their employment (Goffee & Scase, 1983; Raheim & Bolden, 1995).

The International Labour Organization's (1972) report on employment in Kenya was the first to draw attention to self-employment as a viable means of making a living. In developing economies, the informal or unorganized sector accounts for a substantial portion of employment—an estimated 20% to 50% of the total. In developed and developing countries, small business enterprises are the source of the majority of new employment opportunities. That report and subsequent research have shown that supporting productive self-employment, whether in the formal or informal sector, and microbusinesses can be a useful economic development strategy (Ashe, 1985; Benus, Johnson, Wood, Grover, & Shen, 1995; Raheim & Alter, 1998).

Supporting women's self-employment requires an understanding of their obstacles to entrepreneurship in formal and informal economies. A GEMINI study analyzed the constraints on women's enterprise activity for different business categories. Credit was an obstacle for 28% of start-ups, 29% of stagnant, 25% of small-growth, and 15% of high-growth activities (Liedholm & Mead, 1995, cited in Parker, 1996). In addition, a variety of other studies have identified lack of business knowledge and skills, lack of access to capital, and lack of access to business information and networks as the primary obstacles to women's successful entrepreneurship (Brush, 1990; Gould & Parzen, 1990; Keeley, 1990; Raheim, 1997).

Livelihoods Versus Microenterprises

The focus on the microenterprise concept and the subsequent program interventions of microcredit are attractive for economic development planners because of their market orientation. The livelihood system, however, is a better concept when thinking about women's roles in economic development. The livelihood system is a mix of individual and household survival strategies aimed at mobilizing current available resources and responding to changing needs over time (McKee, 1989). Resources consist of property or physical assets, human assets such as labor skills, and such collective assets as access to a common pool of resources or public sector entitlements. Opportunities are kin and friendship networks and institutional mechanisms, organizational and group memberships, and partnership arrangements (McKee, 1989).

The livelihood concept yields a fuller understanding of production and reproduction activities carried out by poor women in developing economies. According to McKee (1989), the livelihood concept permits a distinction between circumstances and goals. For example, a household may be in such a precarious economic situation that survival is the main goal. In such a household, securing adequate food and shelter is a primary concern. Acquiring a multiuse asset such as a milk cow, first for consumption within the household and then for earning income by selling extra milk, is one example of entrepreneurial activity supporting household survival (McKee, 1989). A similar example in a developed country is making clothing and doing alterations out of the home. Once survival is assured, a household's goal may shift from survival to security. The household may undertake additional earning activities or acquire assets that might yield a rental income stream, to diversify the livelihood mix with the aim of reducing risk and increasing flexibility. Growth is a third aim of a livelihood strategy. Having ensured survival and stability, a household may invest in riskier, higher-return activities. These include microenterprise production activities that require a significant investment in assets and equipment but can yield higher profits. The danger for women is that community economic development practitioners often focus solely on the third goal of growth, ignoring or failing to recognize the aims of survival and stability with which women are most concerned.

When designing appropriate interventions to support women in their economic roles, it is important to view the livelihood system as a whole: as a portfolio of assets and activities in which women play a key role in earning income as well as saving. Women may be primarily interested in income smoothing, that is, opting for a steady stream of income rather than fluctuating high and low incomes, Such income smoothing may, in turn, level out the highs and lows in income of casually employed male wage earners in their household (Noponen, 1991). Women may also be looking for flexibility in time so they can juggle income-earning activities with other household responsibilities. Women may also search for activities with low capital and low skill requirements or opt for few travel requirements in order to stay close to home and the site of their other work activities (Parker, 1996). This typically leads women to be concentrated in low-intensity, low-demand, and low-return activities located close to home. Finally, women tend to diversify their activities as a risk-reduction strategy, which results in lower investment into any single activity (Parker, 1996).

Microcredit as a Strategy for Supporting Women's Participation in Economic Development

The microcredit strategy emerged in recognition of the high proportion of the poor engaged in the informal employment sector. Access to credit at reasonable rates was viewed as the missing ingredient that could assist the poor, especially women, to establish, stabilize, and strengthen their economic activities, thereby increasing earnings and improving family welfare. Poor women, however, face obstacles in gaining access to credit in the formal sector. To overcome these barriers, microcredit programs have been designed to provide small loans, at reasonable rates, with easy application and repayment procedures in a supportive community-based delivery mechanism—the local self-help group (Stalker, Komvives, Noponen, & Das, 2000).

A self-help group is small group of village or neighborhood women who have been organized by NGO development organizations or microfinance institutions to save collectively and borrow individually from their pooled savings, which have been augmented by external loans from other sources (formal banks, intermediary microfinance lenders). The women act as the guarantor on the reliability of each borrower, removing the necessity of assets for collateral. Depending on the program model, the women themselves or NGO field officers handle savings collection, loan disbursements, and repayments. The self-help group, also known as a "solidarity group" or "peer lending circle," is also designed to act as a mutual support group helping individual women through business problems, economic distress, and repayment crises. It is also a useful entrée for NGOs to promote participation in other development programs such as education, training, and consciousness-raising. Because of these advantages, the self-help group model has proven to be the most common one employed by NGO providers of microfinance in developing economies (Stalker et al., 2000).

There are several micro- and macrolevel reasons for supporting women's microenterprises through microfinance. A significant percentage of households worldwide are headed by women and therefore dependent on the income of women for survival. Furthermore, after agriculture, women have been shown to be one of the main providers of jobs and income to other women (Parker, 1996). Mayoux (2002) conceptualizes three mutually reinforcing "virtuous spirals" to explain the assumptions of policymakers, NGOs, and funders about targeting women for microcredit interventions. It is argued that access to savings and credit leads to an "economic empowerment spiral," marked by women's control over credit, the investment of the credit in their enterprise, and increased income in their control. This has a mutually reinforcing effect on a "social and political empowerment spiral," marked by an increase in women's ability to negotiate a change in gender relations. This can result in increased status and changing roles in the home and community, as well as increasing mobility and access to wider networks and movements for social and political change. In a similar manner, there is a reinforcing effect on a "household well-being spiral," as women's ability to control the increased income results in their greater participation in decision making on consumption, involving more productive consumption decisions with greater gender equity.

Although microcredit is the most widely used economic development strategy designed to benefit women, Mayoux (1997) finds evidence that credit alone is insufficient to support women's gainful participation in the local economy. She examined several studies of programwide, disaggregated impact of increasing women's access to credit and found mixed results, which challenge the underlying assumptions of the virtuous spirals of microcredit and women's welfare.

The economic empowerment spiral may fail to take hold for many women whose husband or son uses the woman's loan to invest in their own business, leaving women with the burden of participating in the program and repaying the loan (Goetz & Sen Gupta, 1995). In this context, Goetz and Sen Gupta argue that women can become unpaid debt collectors for the NGO intermediary providers of credit. The authors further question the link between microcredit and women's empowerment, particularly increased decision making regarding the use of credit. They found that in a considerable percentage of cases in their sample, women do not have full or even significant decision-making control over the loan-supported microenterprise, when measured by control of the production process and marketing, labor management, and financial accounts. When they analyzed who controls the microenterprise among female participants in three Bangladesh microfinance programs, they found that women had full control in 17.8% of the cases and significant control in another 19.4% of cases of the enterprise. However, in 63% of cases, they had only partial, very limited, or no control.

Goetz and Sen Gupta (1995) found women's marital status, nature of the economic activity, loan size, and length of membership in the microcredit program were important explanatory factors in women's control over the enterprise. Widowed, divorced, or separated women had increased control. However, they still found that some female single heads of household would give their loans to external male family members such as nephews or sons-in-law in exchange for a steady food supply. Women who undertook traditional work activities, such as livestock rearing, agriculture, and fish processing, had greater control. The larger the loan size, the more likely that a substantial portion of the loan money—beyond what was invested in the woman's small activity—would be used by men, who were better able to exchange it in the market or public sphere.

Other researchers point to significant gains in empowerment for women borrowers including enhanced feelings of self-worth, improved gender relations, wider economic choices, and financial control (Hunt & Kasynathan, 2002). Others reject the notion of individualized control in favor of joint decision making and marketing by males as appropriate indicators of empowerment in some cultures (Kabeer,

1999). They further argue that while some loan money may leak to males when women are targeted, rarely if ever will loan money leak to women when males are targeted.

Some economic activities typically engaged in by women have limited potential for converting loan funds into a significant increase in either productivity or income. Low paying piece-rate production work in the home (e.g., bag stitching, incense rolling, box making), in which materials are supplied and goods are marketed by middlemen, is one example. Where middlemen dominate supply and product markets, the scope for women becoming independent producers is limited. There may be little reinforcing effect on the household well-being spiral, especially when increased credit can lead to increased workloads for women—for the borrowers themselves and perhaps for their daughters, who may be used as unpaid labor in the enterprise or replace their mothers' work in the household.

In addition, there may be a corresponding decrease in income contribution from male household members. In focus group discussions held in 2002, one of the authors (Noponen) noted that women in PRADAN (Professional Assistance for Development Action), an NGO-run rural livelihoods and microfinance program, reported that their husbands went less frequently for wage work, now that the women had an income from raising poultry. Studies report that compared with men, women spend a higher portion of their income on family welfare—health, nutrition, education, and housing improvements—diverting less to purchases for personal consumption such as tea, tobacco, liquor, and entertainment (Noponen, 1991).

The design of many microfinance programs, even those using self-help group models, may limit the reinforcing effects of access to credit on the social and political empowerment spiral. The poorest women may be overlooked entirely in microcredit programs because of their low resource base, lack of skills, and lack of market contacts (Mayoux, 1997). Rozario (2002) notes that the current focus on sustainability of microfinance programs and the resulting pressure on repayment discipline have caused an increase in aggressive peer pressure and competitiveness rather than mutual support among women borrowers in self-help groups. Because peer members perceive them as credit risks, the poorest women in the community are excluded from participating.

The trend of donors to emphasize the financial sustainability of programs and the profitability of the loan funds leads to an emphasis on large-scale, streamlined, "minimalist" programs that de-emphasize services that promote women's empowerment (Mayoux, 2002). Such programs do not address the issues of skill training, occupational and wage discrimination, unequal access to and treatment in supply and product markets, and mobility and empowerment in the public sphere, nor do they take into account such other constraints on women's economic participation as household work burdens. They provide credit to large numbers of poor women, but not the other resources that promote their success.

This trend also squeezes out small NGOs and those operating more comprehensive programs (e.g., credit plus training, consciousness raising, collective struggle against workplace problems) that may have a high success rate in empowering women to address local strategic rather than practical needs (Mayoux, 1997).

Some proponents of microcredit point to the high repayment rates (typically more than 90%) as proof that microcredit programs are meeting women's needs.

High demand for credit by poor women may represent desperation for low-interest loans, which are diverted away from intended use in the women's business toward urgent consumption or debt relief (Noponen, 1992). An unsecured microfinance program loan at between 16% and 24% interest is preferable to the typical unsecured moneylender's rate of 120%. Repayment rates also may be high because of the intense peer pressure from local women in microenterprise loan circles and the fear of community ostracism and disruption in traditional reciprocal exchanges of in-kind support. In some cases, high repayment rates often mask repayment from sources other than microenterprise income, such as sale or pledging of existing assets, taking additional loans from moneylenders (Noponen, 1991), or reduced food consumption.

Access to credit is not the only problem facing these entrepreneurs. Occupational segregation into low-growth, female-specific activities and lack of full mobility in the public sphere and wider economy are also constraining factors.

Case Examples

Case 1: Perspectives From India

PRADAN is a large rural livelihoods development NGO reaching 40,000 poor women and their households in seven of the poorest states in North India. PRADAN believes that microfinance is not an end in itself but a means for strengthening individual livelihood efforts and increasing the feasibility and effectiveness of PRADAN-initiated rural livelihood activities. Other activities include technological assistance in subsistence cultivation, market-based agriculture, forestry, animal husbandry, watershed improvements, and the development of nonfarm individual and group enterprises. Unlike other microfinance models, in which the NGO develops itself as the alternative microfinance institution, PRADAN seeks to develop the self-help group as the microfinance institution, while PRADAN becomes the field worker or promoter (Narendranath, 2001).

PRADAN's alternative approach to microfinance service delivery in India is to intervene from two directions. PRADAN applies pressure and incentives from the top on the existing banking industry to overcome its reluctance to lend to the rural poor. From the bottom, PRADAN promotes the formation of village self-help groups and their successful linkage with local banks by building capacities for independent functioning. This means going beyond the initiation and stabilization of groups that are able to carry out basic functions of regular and punctual attendance at meetings, on-time savings and loan repayment, record keeping, and election of leaders. It means increasing their functioning as a group so that members will be good partners with banks. PRADAN instills strong values of financial discipline (e.g., critical peer vetting of loans, quick group response to individual delinquencies and norms violation), tangible group mutual support for members, trust, and fair processes.

Focusing on livelihoods interventions, PRADAN promoters analyze the local economic base and identify potential economic activities for groups of producers. They may provide market solutions (e.g., outlets for marketing broiler chickens) or supply solutions (e.g., advanced mushroom spawn cultures). Often, PRADAN promoters are able to provide a technological solution (e.g., testing cocoons for disease for silk producers) to enhance production activities of groups of local producers. Where infrastructure is lacking, PRADAN cooperates with government and other banking institutions to help supply it (e.g., lift irrigation to facilitate production and marketing of vegetables).

PRADAN conceptualizes the following three realms for self-help groups (Narendranath, 2001). Although these realms were developed independently, they are remarkably similar to Mayoux's three mutually reinforcing spirals:

1. A self-help group for mutual support

2. A viable unit for external financial intermediation, leading to livelihood development

3. A vehicle for economic empowerment of the poor and marginalized households in the economy and for gender empowerment of women in the home, the work- and marketplace, and the wider community

Rather than seeking perpetual clients for their program services, PRADAN seeks ultimately to withdraw, as self-help groups become viable and sustainable on their own as mutual support groups, successfully linked to financial service providers and able to engage in a process of securing their strategic interests of overcoming structural constraints. As one means of promoting sustainability, PRADAN uses an Internal Learning System (Noponen, 2001, 2002a, 2002b) as a participatory impact assessment and planning system for community development programs (see Pennell, Noponen, & Weil, Chapter 34, this volume, for full discussion of PRADAN's Internal Learning System).

Case 2. Perspectives From the United States

The social, economic, technological, and policy contexts in the United States present a level of complexity that makes access to credit a necessary but often insufficient resource to support women's involvement in community economic development. Governmental regulation of business, tax laws, social welfare policies that limit income for continued eligibility for transfer payments, and competition from e-commerce are among the concerns and potential obstacles for the entrepreneur in the United States. Women often have limited access to the business information and support networks needed to negotiate the environment for successful business operation. Women living near or in poverty have especially limited access. Microenterprise development programs (MEDs) that go beyond the credit-only model can help women manage the complexities of business operation in the United States and meet the unique challenges of female entrepreneurship.

Of the 554 or more MEDs in the United States, 62% have a client base of more than 50% women (Clark, Huston, & Meister, 2002). The underlying philosophy of many of these MEDs is that women have the capacity to improve their economic well-being and that of their families through self-employment and small-business development and that several supports are needed to assist women to achieve these goals (Brush, 1990; Keeley, 1990).

Using lessons learned from Asia, Latin America, and other parts of the world, U.S. MEDs commonly provide a package of services. Most provide some combination of access to capital, information networks, and supportive services to promote women's participation in the economy (Clark et al., 2002; Keeley, 1990). These may include business training, technical assistance, business loans or assistance in securing business financing, peer support, and direct or brokered support services, such as child care and counseling. Although some U.S. MEDs (e.g., ACCION and Working Capital) focus primarily on lending, others that target women with low income, people receiving public assistance, or economically distressed communities tend to offer a more comprehensive package of services (Johnson, 1998; Servon, 1999).

The mission of the organization determines the combination of services MEDs provide. Those whose mission is poverty alleviation target women with low income and those receiving transfer payments (e.g., Temporary Assistance to Needy Families [TANF]). These programs usually provide or broker training, credit, and support services. MEDs whose mission is empowerment serve a broad range of women and provide support for business start-up, growth, or expansion (Servon, 1999). Although some programs principally focus on providing credit, almost all programs have a training component and provide access to support services (Clark et al., 2002). Whether the program focuses on providing credit or training, it may have a solidarity group or peer-lending component, instead of or in addition to individual lending.

Although the mission and combination of services MEDs provide vary, their common goal is to support women's participation in income generation in the formal economy. Similar to women in developing countries, women in the United States who are poor or have low incomes commonly engage in the informal economy (e.g., unlicensed child care or hair styling). Their self-employment efforts are frequently part of a livelihood or income-packaging strategy designed to meet their families' subsistence needs (Spalter-Roth, Soto, & Zandniapour, 1994). MEDs support women's livelihood strategies by helping them engage in expansion and minimal risk taking to grow their self-employment ventures. MEDs can also help women not already engaged in the informal sector to create viable small businesses for survival or stability of income flow. By facilitating women's participation in the formal economy, MEDs help women exercise a greater role in the economic development of their communities (Rodriguez, 1995).

Beyond promoting income generation through formal sector participation, MEDs that provide a broad range of services help women develop human capital, further increasing their capacity to participate in economic development. For example, training, mentoring, and business counseling increase women's knowledge, skills, and access to information and support networks. In addition, these approaches reduce women's isolation by connecting them to each other through group training and peer lending groups. In the absence of such programs, poor women are likely to have difficulty gaining entry to traditional, male-dominated networks for exchanging information and then getting support that is critical to business success (Raheim & Bolden, 1995; Rodriguez, 1995).

MEDs can facilitate relationships between women and organizations that build their human capital and strengthen their ability to participate in economic development. For many women with low incomes, the idea of joining the local chamber of commerce is foreign, and applying for a business loan seems out of reach. When MEDs provide women with the information and support they need to interact with local business organizations and public and private lenders, women are better able to participate in economic development activities. MEDs may help women develop relationships with other kinds of organizations, such as those that provide financial counseling services. In addition, MEDs can create interorganizational connections that build communities' capacities to involve women in economic development (Raheim, 2001; Servon, 1999).

One example of a U.S. MED organization that goes beyond credit to facilitate women's participation in economic development is the Institute for Social and Economic Development (ISED), located in Iowa. Since the mid-1980s, ISED has operated state-funded entrepreneurial projects for welfare recipients, as well as several federally funded microenterprise demonstration projects for people with low incomes. Although these projects are not exclusively for women, their target population is predominantly female. The ISED model and two projects are described here to illustrate how MEDs can facilitate women's involvement in economic development in their communities.

The ISED model has four program components, which combine human capital and economic development strategies: outreach and recruitment, training, business counseling, and ongoing technical assistance. First, much emphasis is placed on outreach and recruitment. Through various outreach methods, the program casts a wide net to reach low-income populations. Potential participants are recruited to attend an all-day orientation designed to encourage them to assess their strengths and development needs and to select into or out of the rigors of the program, based on this analysis. Thus, the model does not screen or select participants; rather, through self-assessment and counseling, it provides the opportunity for potential participants to decide (a) whether they have the personal resources to be successful entrepreneurs and (b) whether their business idea is worth the risk of time and money.

The second component is a structured 15-week training workshop that includes information and skill development in market research, planning, marketing, financial management, communications, and the legal and tax requirements for starting a small business. Eighty-four hours of training are provided in short sessions, with a heavy emphasis on skill development; in-class instruction is 5 to 6 hours per week, and out-of-class work takes about 20 hours per week. In this model, the process of training is given as much emphasis as the content of training. Building self-esteem, self-confidence, and control of one's life is seen as the foundation for making wise financial decisions, building technical skills, and achieving personal goals. Therefore, group process is central to the success of the training component because peer interaction enables participants to confront the feasibility of their ideas and their abilities to implement them. Peer support is a critical element in building participants' confidence and self-esteem. Participants "graduate" from the training component when they have completed their business plan.

Because this model does not select from a pool of applicants but enrolls all participants who elect to enter the program, business counseling, the third component, is as important as the training. Many participants are not well prepared to start a business: Some may be unable to read well, some may be unsure of their ability to write a successful business plan, and some may have personal barriers to overcome.

The ISED model requires its staff to join participants "where they are" in terms of their personal strengths and technical skills; through individualized business counseling and coaching, these participants gain the ability to use their natural creative and entrepreneurial talents to achieve their goals. Through counseling, the staff may help participants identify services offered by another agency that are needed to support their success, such as credit or family counseling.

When participants finish the workshop and complete an acceptable business plan, they have access to ongoing technical assistance as long as needed, including help with writing a loan application, coaching throughout the loan process, and assistance in linking themselves to community institutions and networks. The ISED model is based on the belief that to the greatest extent possible, participants should be imbedded in community relationships rather than marginalized through relationships with government welfare programs. Thus, commercial banks are preferred over state loan pools, and participants are strongly encouraged to become active members of their local chambers of commerce and women's business networks.

Evaluations of ISED's microenterprise initiatives have shown that these projects have successfully involved women in economic development in their communities. One of these, the Rivercities of Iowa/Illinois Self-Employment Program project (RISE), was funded by the U.S. Office of Community Services and was evaluated from 1991 to 1994 (Alter, 1994). It served 300 low-income women in both urban and rural areas. Evaluation findings showed several successful human capital and economic development outcomes, including comprehensive business plans, successful commercial loan applications, and stable new businesses.

Business survival rates were better than the national average. Of the 300 women who enrolled in RISE, 93 (31%) started a small business, 69 (23%) of these businesses survived 1 year, and 60 (20%) survived 2 years. This outcome is well above the less than 10% survival rate for small-business starts in the United States (Alter, 1994).

RISE participants were able to move off public assistance and toward economic self-sufficiency more quickly than comparison groups of women on Aid to Families with Dependent Children (AFDC), matched by county and date of first AFDC receipt. Evaluation findings showed that the microenterprise groups spent significantly fewer months on AFDC during the 3-year study than did the other two groups: ISED participants averaged 6.4 months after enrollment in the program, whereas the comparison groups averaged 9.6 months and 9.0 months during the same period.

Raheim and Friedman (1999) report similar outcomes and additional economic benefits from the Entrepreneurial Training (ET) project, also sponsored by ISED. This project is exclusively for recipients of TANF (formerly AFDC) and is funded by the Iowa Department of Human Services. The evaluation found that during the 6-year study period, 1,252 ET participants (76% of whom were women) exited TANF at higher rates and were off TANF for 4.3 more months than a matched comparison group (Raheim & Friedman, 1999). In addition to creating jobs for themselves through self-employment, ET participants' businesses created 50 additional jobs—18 full-time and 32 part-time. Thirty-eight of these 50 new jobs employed other people with low incomes. This result demonstrates how such programs can lead to further economic development through job creation.

The evaluation also documented increases in participants' human capital. Eighty-two ET participants were surveyed to assess the quality of the training. Most agreed that their knowledge and skills had increased in many areas, including how to obtain financing (87%), marketing (94%), business management (99%), and development of a business plan (97%).

An important strategy that ISED has used to implement its model is to form partnerships with business and community organizations. These organizations are diverse, including community action agencies, social service agencies, community colleges, neighborhood centers, banks, and chambers of commerce. These organizations participate in a wide range of MED implementation activities, including marketing, recruitment, business training, and mentoring. They also provide direct services to participants, such as credit counseling, family counseling, and child care. Through these community partnerships, ISED has created a large network of resource and service providers that support women with low incomes as they develop their human capital and participate in the economic life of their communities (Raheim, 2001).

Other studies have explored the profitability of businesses assisted by U.S. MEDs that use the "credit plus" model. The most notable of these is the Aspen Institute's Self-Employment Learning Project (SELP). This 5-year study of 405 business owners at five MEDs found that 72% of these entrepreneurs experienced income gains, with average household income rising by $8,484. Average household assets also rose, by an average $15,909. About 53% of these business owners moved out of poverty, many by combining business and wage income. For those who moved out of poverty, business income was a major factor, and household income nearly doubled (Clark, Kays, Zandniapour, Soto, & Doyle, 1999). Findings from SELP, the RISE demonstration, and the ET program indicate that microenterprise development models that go beyond credit provision can be valuable resources for promoting women's participation in community economic development in the developed world.

Conclusion

This chapter examines barriers to women's productive roles in the local economy and the advantages and limitations of microcredit as an economic development strategy to promote women's gainful participation. The chapter also presents examples of programs that overcome these limitations by providing access to credit along with training and other services. Here, we offer some considerations and resources for best practice for microenterprise development as a strategy to improve the lives of women and their families.

Mayoux (2002) argues that the problem is not microfinance per se but the dominant paradigm for its delivery—the large-scale, streamlined, minimalist microfinance institution, stressing financial sustainability and credit discipline over women's empowerment and other development goals. She and other researchers have offered some suggestions for improving "best practice" to achieve more gender-equitable outcomes. In terms of increasing the extent to which women control the loan and the income from it, Hunt and Kasynathan (2002) urge NGOs to improve the understanding and commitment of fieldworkers to gender issues and improve the monitoring of control-of-loan and other empowerment indicators. They suggest that NGOs provide popular education ("clear messages") on the importance of women's control of decision making on credit use and ownership of assets created. They also suggest that NGOs provide technical training to help women use their loans more productively. The case example of PRADAN illustrates the positive effects of the availability of credit for development of microenterprises on women's economic and social empowerment over time. PRADAN's use of the Internal Learning System shows how a system of self-evaluation at both individual and program levels can improve the productive use of loans and thereby help to improve women's and family's livelihoods (Noponen 2002b; see also Pennell, Noponen, & Weil, Chapter 34, this volume).

Researchers also point to the need for integration of complimentary business services for women, such as collective supply or marketing activities, with microfinance provision either through the NGO's own efforts or through interorganizational linkages with other providers (Hunt & Kasynathan, 2002; Mayoux, 2002). PRADAN has always viewed microfinance as one tool for its primary aim of livelihood improvement through interventions in the supply market, product market, or technology inputs. It is the group-formation aspect of the self-help group microfinance model that is the springboard for PRADAN's group livelihood activities. In this sense, PRADAN can be considered a "plus credit" model (primary livelihoods plus credit) rather than a "credit plus" (primarily credit plus some skill training or business or welfare services) or a "minimalist credit" (financial services only) program. Mayoux (2002) calls for rethinking of group structures and functions to go beyond the group as a microcredit repayment mechanism to one that is assisted in developing its own empowerment plans and agenda. The tracking of women's changing status in the home and community and the individual and group planning formats in the empowerment module of PRADAN's Internal Learning System are tools for sparking individual and group social change, especially those that result in women's fuller and more gainful participation in the economy (Noponen, 2002a).

In the United States, the Aspen Institute is operating the Microenterprise Fund for Innovation, Effectiveness, Learning and Dissemination (FIELD), a research and development effort designed to identify, develop, and disseminate best practices about microenterprise as an antipoverty strategy (Edgecomb, 2002). Initiated in 1998, FIELD has published numerous "best practice" guides for policy and program development and implementation, based on findings from demonstration projects and studies with MEDs across the United States (Aspen Institute, 2002).

FIELD's research has found that a strengths-based empowerment approach is most effective in promoting microenterprise development among MED clients, who are mostly women. FIELD's recommendations include strategies such as helping clients access their goals, skills, and the strengths of their support systems and incorporating skill development and experiences related to their assessment into the training program (Edgecomb, 2002).

FIELD has also recommended TANF policy changes that would promote women's participation in microenterprise as a means to leave TANF and achieve economic self-sufficiency. These recommendations include making self-employment preparation a countable work activity, removing limits on vocational education training, and making poverty reduction an explicit goal of TANF (Klein, 2002). In addition, Clark and colleagues (1999) recommend making health insurance accessible and affordable to those leaving TANF.

Community practitioners must view economic development as part of their practice in order to become effective advocates for interventions that improve the economic well-being of the communities they serve. Microenterprise development is one strategy for which practitioners can advocate. With an understanding of its potential and limitations, community practitioners can promote the policies and programs needed to make this strategy effective, especially for improving the lives of women and their families.

References

Alter, C. F. (1994). *Final report on the Rivercities of Iowa/Illinois Self-Employment program (RISE)*. Iowa City, IA: Institute for Social and Economic Development.

Ashe, J. (1985). *The PISCES II experience: Local efforts in micro-enterprise development*. Washington, DC: Agency for International Development.

Aspen Institute. (2002). *About microenterprise Fund for Innovation, Effectiveness, Learning and Dissemination (FIELD)*. Retrieved November 1, 2002, from http://www.fieldus.org

Banerjee, N. (1982). *Unorganized women workers: The Calcutta experience*. New Delhi: ICSSR.

Beneria, L. (1989). Subcontracting and employment dynamics in Mexico City. In A. Portes, M. Castells, & L. A. Benton (Eds.), *The informal economy: Studies in advanced and less developed countries* (pp. 173–188). Baltimore and London: The John Hopkins University Press.

Benus, J. M., Johnson, T. R., Wood, M., Grover, N., & Shen, T. (1995). *Self-employment programs: A new reemployment strategy, final report on the UI Self-Employment Program Evaluation*. Washington, DC: U.S. Department of Labor.

Boserup, E. (1970). *Women's role in economic development*. New York: St. Martin's Press.

Brush, C. G. (1990). Women and enterprise creation: Barriers and opportunities. In *Local initiatives for job creation: Enterprising women* (pp. 37–53). Paris: Organisation for Economic Cooperation and Development.

Charlton, S. E., Everett, J., & Staudt, K. (1989). *Women, the state and development*. Albany: State University of New York Press.

Clark, M., Huston, T., & Meister, B. (2002). *2002 Directory of microenterprise programs*. Washington, DC: Aspen Institute, Self-Employment Learning Project.

Clark, M., Kays, A., Zandniapour, L., Soto., E., & Doyle, K. (1999). *Microenterprise and the poor: Findings from the Self-Employment Learning Project five-year study of microentrepreneurs*. Washington, DC: Aspen Institute, Self-Employment Learning Project.

Edgecomb, E. (2002). *Improving microenterprise training and technical assistance: Findings for program managers*. Washington, DC: Aspen Institute, Microenterprise Fund for Innovation, Effectiveness, Learning and Dissemination.

Elson, D., & Pearson, R. (1984). The subordination of women and the internationalization of factory production. In K. Young, C. Wolkowitz, & Y. R. McCullagh (Eds.), *Of marriage and the market: Women's subordination internationally and it lessons* (pp. 18–40). London: Routledge and Kegan Paul.

Goetz, A. M., & Sen Gupta, R. (1995). Who takes the credit? Gender, power, and control over loan use in rural credit programs. *World Development, 24*(1), 45–63.

Goffee, R., & Scase, R. (1983). Business ownership and women's subordination: A preliminary study of female proprietors. *Sociological Review, 31*, 625–647.

Gould, S. K., & Parzen, J. (1990). Recommendations, conclusions, and plans for action. In *Local initiatives for job creation: Enterprising women* (pp. 37–53). Paris: Organisation for Economic Cooperation and Development.

Hunt, J., & Kasynathan, N. (2002, February). Reflections on microfinance and women's empowerment. *Development Bulletin, 57,* 71–75.

International Labour Organization (ILO). (1972). *Employment, incomes, and equality: A strategy for increasing productive employment in Kenya.* Geneva, Switzerland: Author.

Johnson, M. A. (1998). Developing a typology of nonprofit microenterprise programs in the United States. *Journal of Developmental Entrepreneurship, 3*(2), 165–184.

Kabeer, N. (1999). *The conditions and consequences of choice: Reflections on the measurement of women's empowerment.* Geneva, Switzerland: United Nations Research Institute for Social Development.

Keeley, K. (1990). The role of intermediaries in strengthening women's business expansion activities. In *Local initiatives for job creation: Enterprising women* (pp. 37–53). Paris: Organisation for Economic Cooperation and Development.

Klein, J. (2002). *Improving the climate for self-employment: Policy recommendations for TANF reauthorization.* Washington, DC: Aspen Institute, Microenterprise Fund for Innovation, Effectiveness, Learning and Dissemination.

Liedholm, C., & Mead, D. (1995). *GEMINI Action Research Program I: Final report: The dynamic role of micro and small enterprises in the development process.* Washington, DC: USAID.

Lim, L. Y. C. (1990). Women's work in export factories: The politics of a cause. In I. Tinker (Ed.), *Persistent inequalities, women, and world development* (pp. 101–122). New York: Oxford University Press.

Malveaux, J. (1990). Women in the labor market: The choices women have. In *Local initiatives for job creation: Enterprising women* (pp. 21–35). Paris: Organisation for Economic Cooperation and Development.

Mayoux, L. (1997, February). *The magic ingredient? Microfinance and women's empowerment.* Briefing prepared for the Microcredit Summit, Washington, DC.

Mayoux, L. (2002, February). Microfinance and women's empowerment: Rethinking "best practice." *Development Bulletin, 57,* 76–80.

McKee, T. (1989). Micro level strategies for supporting livelihoods, employment, and income generation for poor women in the Third World: The challenge of significance. *World Development, 17*(7), 993–1006.

Microcredit Summit. (1997). *The Microcredit Summit declaration and plan of action.* Washington, DC: RESULTS Educational Fund.

Momsen, J. H. (1991). *Women and development in the Third World.* London: Routledge.

Moser, C., & Young, K. (1981). Women of the working poor. *Institute of Development Studies Bulletin, 12*(3).

Narendranath, D. (2001, September 12–13). *PRADAN's self-help group methodology: Opportunities and challenges for empowerment.* Paper presented at the Participatory Methodologies Inception Workshop, hosted by PRADAN, New Delhi.

Noponen, H. (1991). The dynamics of work and survival for the urban poor: A gender analysis of panel data from Madras. *Development and Change, 22,* 233–260.

Noponen, H. (1992). Loans to the working poor: A longitudinal study of credit, gender, and the household economy. *International Journal of Urban and Regional Research, 16*(2), 234–259.

Noponen, H. (2001). The Internal Learning System for participatory assessment of microfinance, *Small Enterprise Development, 12* (4), 45–53.

Noponen, H. (2002a). The Internal Learning System (ILS): Impact assessment versus empowerment? In Linda Mayoux (Ed.), *Sustainable learning for women's empowerment—Ways forward in microfinance.* New Delhi: Sanskruti Press.

Noponen, H. (2002b). The Internal Learning System (ILS): A tool for participant and program learning in micro-finance and livelihoods interventions, *Development Bulletin, 57,* February, 106–110.

Parker, J. (1996, September 8). *Don't fall off the mountain: Business development strategies helping women microentrepreneurs compete.* Washington, DC: Association for Women in Development Forum.

Raheim, S. (1997). The problems and prospects of self-employment as an economic independence option for welfare recipients. *Social Work, 42*(1), 44–53.

Raheim, S. (2001). *Job Opportunities for Low-Income people (JOLI): Community Business Network Project final evaluation report.* Washington, DC: U.S. Department of Health and Human Services, Administration for Children and Families.

Raheim, S., & Alter, C. F. (1998). Self-employment as a social and economic development intervention for recipients of AFDC. *Journal of Community Practice, 5*(1/2), 41–61.

Raheim, S., & Bolden, J. (1995). Economic empowerment of low-income women through self-employment. *Affilia, 10*(2), 138–154.

Raheim, S., & Friedman, J. J. (1999). Microenterprise in the heartland: Self-employment as a self-sufficiency strategy for TANF recipients in Iowa 1993–1998. *Journal of Microfinance, 1*(1), 66–90.

Rodriguez, C. R. (1995). *Women, microenterprise, and the politics of self-help.* New York: Garland.

Rozario, S. (2002, February). Grameen Bank-style micro-credit: Impact on dowry and women's solidarity. *Development Bulletin, 57,* 67–70.

Sen, G., & Grown, C. (1987). *Development, crises, and alternative visions: World women's perspectives.* New York: Monthly Review Press.

Servon, L. J. (1999). *Bootstrap Capital: Microenterprises and the American poor.* Washington, DC: The Brookings Institution.

Spalter Roth, R., Soto, E., & Zandniapour, L. (1994). *Micro-enterprise and women: The viability of self-employment as a strategy for alleviating poverty.* Washington, DC: Institute for Women's Policy Research.

Stalker, L., Komvives, K., Noponen, H., & Das, V. (2000). *Should my organization start a micro finance program? A decision workbook for grassroots NGOs.* Ahmedabad, Gujarat, India: Friends of Women's World Banking.

Stevenson, L. (1988). Women and economic development: A focus on entrepreneurship. *Journal of Development Planning, 18,* 113–126.

U.S. Agency for International Development. (2000). *Women 2000: Beijing plus five, the USAID commitment.* Washington, DC: Office of Women and Development, GenderReach Project.

World Summit for Sustainable Development (2002). *Plan of implementation.* Retrieved November 1, 2002, from http://www.johannesburgsummit.org/html/documents/summit_docs/2309_planfinal.htm

Young, G., Samarasinghe, V., & Kusterer, K. (Eds.) (1993). *Women at the center: Development issues and practices for the 1990s.* Bloomfield, CT: Kumarian.

PART IV

Supports for Community Practice

Management, Monitoring, Research, and Evaluation

"Supports for Community Practice: Management, Monitoring, Research and Evaluation" presents a range of chapters outlining activities and approaches necessary to sustain community practice efforts and to build stronger skills in areas of research and evaluation. In Chapter 31, William Buffum raises significant challenges that must be considered and dealt with in community-based organizations. There is continued growth in the nonprofit sector with increased emphasis on development of community-based programs. Buffum argues that rather than rhetoric, definite strategies and commitment are needed to engage community members in the processes of service development and evaluation. Local organizations need to revisit community-based administration, program management, and monitoring to develop sound and inclusive governance processes and ensure that programs are responsive to the communities they serve.

Current directions in the political economy of human services and community practice make program and resource development strategies critical in the provision of services and development of supports. In "Fundraising, Programming, and Community Organizing: Working With Donors, Investors, Collaborators, and Purchasers," Armand Lauffer makes sense out of the processes used and the skills needed in these areas related to marketing, fundraising and sustaining organizations.

Julian Chow and Kelsey Crowe present a range of sophisticated approaches in "Community-Based Research and Methods in Community Practice." They argue that community-based research is both for communities and about them. Noting that the audience for this research is usually action oriented, they argue that the most relevant framework for research locates the methods of research within community practice objectives. They hold that all levels of community practice can benefit from use of both quantitative and qualitative methods and analyses and that there are at least eight different methodological approaches to analyzing findings that are of importance to members of communities and others who participate in the change process.

In "Empowerment Research and Program Evaluation," Joan Pennell, Helzi Noponen, and I argue for strengthening participatory research methods so that they are truly tools and strategies of empowerment. Building knowledge and the skills to use research data engages community members in understanding collective needs and can strengthen advocacy for needed changes. The processes involved engage constituencies in critically examining social conditions and problems, using participatory processes for data collection and analysis, and employing results in plans and action for positive community change.

Now and in the future, highly developed skills in the use of electronic technology are essential for community practice. In Chapter 35, "Practice in the Electronic Community," Roger Lohmann and John McNutt argue that the record to date is mixed and that there are real risks that the Internet could become primarily an extension of the marketplace or a means of reinforcing existing inequalities. There is, however, positive potential for supporting community and social justice issues in electronic communications. Among the opportunities available through the Internet is the ability for people with shared interests to exchange information in virtual communities. Advocacy groups are now able to use online communications for nearly immediate transmission of information about policies or issues. Internet communications can also be used to mobilize related social action taking place in different parts of the nation. The information gap between those with computer access and those without is a serious issue and one approach that can be maximized is making computer availability in organizations and communities a means of building access and increasing computer literacy and skills in low-income communities.

The final chapter of the *Handbook* provides another extremely useful methodology for use in analysis and application in planning for community and organizational improvements. Increasingly, citizens' groups are demanding access to information about the conditions in their communities—physical, economic, and social. Community-based organizations are now becoming increasingly sophisticated consumers of quantitative data to assist in planning. This chapter focuses on advances in use of small area administrative data, formatted to be user-friendly, that can be applied to make information useful and to support a range of community change efforts. Amy Hillier and Dennis Culhane discuss methods and a fascinating example of integrating and distributing administrative data to support community change.

CHAPTER 31

Revisiting Community-Based Administration, Program Management, and Monitoring

William E. Buffum

Although portions of the business sector have been consolidating into large megasystems, many agencies and community organizations are moving in the opposite direction toward greater localization, specialization, and collaboration with communities and organizations. This turbulent environment presents a special challenge to administrators and managers because meaningful control and authority are elusive in such community-based organizations. This chapter revisits the roles, strategies, and skills of administrators, managers, and supervisors who choose to make constituent groups the foundations of community-based organizations. It reviews some of the major issues that must be considered by those who wish to move either social agencies or community organizations to be more progressive in the ways in which they function to serve their constituencies. *Constituencies* perhaps is not the ideal term, but for this chapter, it is used to refer to the members of community organizations and the clients of social agencies. All such organizations have several constituencies beyond just their clients or members, of course. The thesis of this chapter is that far too much attention has been given to the more remote but powerful constituencies such as those that make funding decisions, and that too little attention is paid to the direct constituencies—members or consumers. To sharpen the necessary distinctions between approaches, some uncommon, extreme, and perhaps unfair propositions are put forth in this discussion. The reader should be aware that rarely is there a single correct way to structure and manage an organization, and that most settings require a blending of strategies.

A major theoretical foundation for management in community-based organizations emanates from the traditional business management literature. Although scholars in the field of social work have made important contributions to nonprofit and association management (e.g., Brody & Nair, 2000; Flynn, 1992; Follett, 1941; Hasenfeld, 1989; Patti, 2000; Skidmore & Rosenberg, 1994; Slavin, 1984; Weinbach, 1994; Weiner, 1990), their perspectives have not had substantial influence on the larger business management literature. As one example, Mary Parker Follett, an early (1868–1933) social work management scholar and settlement worker, was not widely recognized until after her death (Fox & Urwick, 1982). Still today there remains a belief in the general public (and indeed among some members of boards of directors of human service agencies) that people with MBA degrees are the most qualified managers for any and all organizations.

Many schools of social work continue to educate master's of social work (MSW) students for social work management positions through advanced concentrations and specializations; a small number of schools offer postgraduate certificates in nonprofit management, and at least one MSW program offers a dual degree program with their university's school of business administration (Council on Social Work Education, 2000; see also Weil, Chapter 1, this volume). However, if social work programs emphasize only traditional business management practices, they deprive their students of learning the realities of community-based nonprofit management and connection to direct constituencies. Emphasis on active grassroots participation is vital for the success of community agencies and organizations. The work of Grogan and Proscio (2000) and Medoff and Sklar (1994) are two exemplary models demonstrating how grassroots bottom-up organizations can be successful in the revitalization of decaying urban areas. In this chapter, several perspectives from traditional business management theory will be critically examined, and alternative conceptions for successful bottom-up management of agencies and community organizations are explored.

The Traditional Management Model

Hierarchy of Authority

A fundamental premise of traditional management theory is that there must be a clear line of authority, with links from the top administrators down to the lowest level of employee in an explicit chain of command (Taylor, 1947). This arrangement, it is argued, creates a climate in which people are clear about their jobs, their authority, and their roles so that conflict is minimized and efficiency enhanced. Those who fail to perform their roles well or who do not use appropriate authority are discharged. This process helps ensure that there is a good fit between employees and their actual jobs. Although the assumption is that those in organizations are paid employees, the field of volunteer management has adopted similar principles, arguing that volunteers may not work for money but that they work for other rewards and, therefore, should be treated much like any other employee (Fisher & Cole, 1993). Cnaan (1991) has presented a compelling critique demonstrating how community-based organizations tend to move over time toward centralized power.

Division of Labor

Another common view in management is that employees should have clear job descriptions that detail the tasks and requisite skills needed for various positions. Tasks should be differentiated according to groupings that are similar, an approach that attempts to realize benefits from greater specialization and more refined skill development (Weber, 1947). Furthermore, employees can better understand their individual jobs in contrast to the jobs of others. This makes functional differentiation possible. In human service organizations, functional differentiation is often seen in the form of separate divisions for intake, assessment, treatment, evaluation, and aftercare.

Planning and Decision Making

The field of business administration made great strides by recognizing the contributions that line workers can make through techniques such as quality circles, but the predominant view remains that top managers have more comprehensive perspectives, thereby making them uniquely qualified to make the best decisions (Martin, 1994). Many organizations have separate planning departments with personnel responsible for program planning, strategic or long-range planning, fund development, and implementation monitoring. The perspective is that these planning functions require specialized technical skills that typical employees do not possess (Brody & Nair, 2000).

Organization Goals

The goals of business organizations are usually stated in monetary terms. Similarly, charitable organizations and community associations are concerned with financial solvency, but their primary thrust is to benefit their constituents rather than their shareholders or owners. Charitable behavior in business organizations must contribute to overall profitability or the behavior is considered to be misdirected or reflective of goal displacement. Most charitable and community organizations have clear altruistic service and change goals, but frequently they find themselves hindered by financial constraints in achieving their goals. Thus, in the view of some, fundraising and development are necessary evils that can lead to goal displacement. Financial survival and strength may themselves become the real goals rather than strategies to break even (Lohmann, 1980).

Relations With External Environments

Much has been written in the management literature about the importance of the external environment to the success of business organizations (Pfeffer & Salancik, 1978). This environment is often described on a continuum that ranges from dependence to control over the critical players in the strategic environment of the organization. For example, Fabricant and Fisher (2002) documented in painstaking detail how current settlement houses in New York have been negatively affected by the increased external control of their fiscal resources and the policies that surrounded settlements' abilities to capture those resources, and Beverly Koerin (2003) documented current struggles of settlements to meet community needs. Similar concerns can be seen in many nonprofit organizations. One common response is to merge several small organizations into a larger megasystem that can have greater power in relation to its task environments. For example, one 501(c)3 corporation might oversee several children's services agencies such as family services, child guidance, work training, inpatient mental health, residential, special education, foster care, and adoptions. In the private sector, business organizations often attempt to gain market leverage through mergers, but at the same time, other organizations are choosing to specialize by controlling segments of a market by reverting to emphasis on a core technology. This strategic decision regarding expansion versus specialization is one that many local community organizations are tackling today.

Understanding Community-Based Management

These traditional management views should not be the basis for management in either charitable agencies or community organizations. There are several important reasons for this.

Domain Differences

Most organizations operate in three distinct domains. These domains may be described as the policy domain, the operational or production domain, and the consumer or constituent domain. The *policy domain* is characterized by parliamentary deliberations and voting, as is seen in the boards of directors of both for-profit and nonprofit corporations. Unincorporated associations likewise usually have some semblance of a board of directors with elected members. Relationships among policymakers may be in conflict at times, but board members have legitimate and largely equal power that has recognized legitimacy. They vote on issues and settle differences in a democratic manner. In contrast, the *operational domain*, or the production domain, is characterized by hierarchical roles and the use of formal authority. Those with positional power make the decisions, although the participation of others may be sought. These operational decisions must meet with the general approval of those in the policy domain or eventually top executive staff will be replaced. The third domain, the consumer or *constituent domain*, is usually more diffuse and disorganized, but with needs and wants that must be heard by operations staff. If the organization is not offering a product or service that consumers want, there will be problems. Some constituents are not organized and have a voice only through their behavior in the market. Others are highly organized with formal structures and identified spokespersons. In most for-profit corporations, this structure may be diagrammed using a pyramid with the policy domain at the top, operations in the middle, and constituents at the bottom, as is shown in Figure 31.1.

In some social agencies and community organizations, these three domains are present but the pyramid may be inverted, with the constituents playing a more significant controlling role and with their representatives occupying positions in the policy domain. This is the model that was espoused in the early work of Brager and Holloway (1978) and later developed by Rapp and Poertner (1992) with their

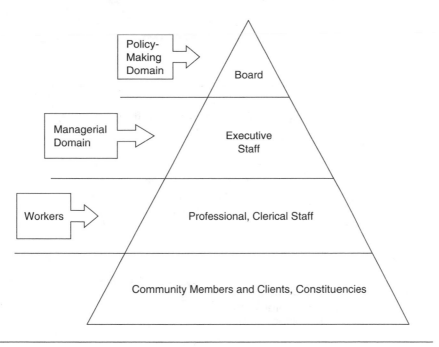

Figure 31.1   The Traditional Hierarchical Organization

focus on client-centered management. The model has even been promoted as a way of reengineering corporations in the more creative business management literature (Hammer, 1996; Hammer & Champy, 1993; Peters, 1994). In this organizational model, which is also called a model of flat organizations or alternative organizations, the operational domain is squeezed between constituents, who control two domains. Crossing boundaries further, constituents may also be actively engaged in the operations domain. With authority and decision making so diffuse, there are many unique challenges for community organizations.

Austin (2002) has developed a comparable conception, in which he described the traditional organization as being managed downward, the alternative being to manage upward. He added the idea of managing out, which he described as being a primary community practice skill. Regardless of how they are labeled, these three managerial activities occur differently within the domains of upper management, middle management, and external actors, as illustrated in Figure 31.2.

Elements of Progressive Community Organization Administration

Flat Hierarchy of Authority

One of the instrumental goals of community organizations should be the empowerment of constituent populations (Haynes & Mickelson, 2003). To reflect this goal in their own operations, organizations must distribute authority over as wide a spectrum as possible. This means that not only clients and workers are consulted, but that the broad target population also has legitimate, actual authority to

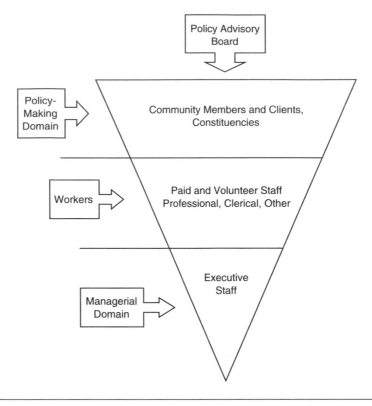

Figure 31.2   The Alternative Democratic Organization

meaningfully shape the organization. This goes beyond participation to actual control. Citizen and client advisory boards are a step in the right direction, but they will fall short if such entities lack real authority (Ginsberg & Keys, 1995; Perlmutter, 1988; Resnick & Patti, 1980).

To the extent that there is sharing of power and authority, there will be conflicts (Gummer, 1990). This is partially a consequence of the traditional ideas that both administrators and constituents have about their power, and their lack of experience in more egalitarian organizations. Some argue that people by their very nature strive for power and control and seek to attain dominance over others. That belief is supported by countless examples throughout history, but there are also many examples of selfless sharing and happiness resulting from beneficent acts. Because both scenarios have validity, there is no reason that only one model, the hierarchical control model of organizations, should be selected.

Little Division of Labor

In the progressive community organization, roles are cast broadly so that only a few members have specialized functions. This encourages the idea that there is equality among levels and members of the organization. Administrators, policymakers, and constituents contribute to the project in a collaborative style of interaction. The belief is that ability, leadership, and motivation are present in people at all levels, and that top administrators are not the sole repositories for such qualities. In the effective community organization, people work together to achieve desired ends, and no job is too unimportant to be shared by all (Homan, 1994; Mondros & Wilson, 1994). This idea is contrary to the usual viewpoints in the literature regarding status and the value of some jobs over others. It also is contrary to the views of those who argue that top administrators are wasting their valuable time by assisting line workers. This concern is less of an issue in organizations in which monetary compensation is not widely disparate, as it is in most organizations today.

Shared Planning and Decision Making

In the social work literature, planning is described as a rational process that requires training professionals who can design, guide, and interpret each step of the process (Brody & Nair, 2000; see also Brilliant, Chapter 12, this volume). Planning is a technical and analytical set of activities that requires specialized skills that are gained not simply through life experience but also through graduate-level coursework. However, planners are encouraged to seek broad consumer input as well as participation from all constituencies. United Way agencies do this quite well, frequently using techniques such as focus groups to involve different constituencies in planning. Although this process does introduce political dimensions in the interpretations and recommendations of community interest groups, the planning agency remains the primary decision maker.

The problem with this rational planning model is that in reality, it is not all that rational. Needs assessments, market studies, and consequent decisions are often a better reflection of the power of particular interest groups than of the constituencies that the agency or organization purports to serve (Gummer, 1990). A truly effective model would better emphasize the real, expressed needs of target populations and assessments of social problems as perceived by those most affected. This is most likely to be accomplished by a planning model that emanates from those experiencing the problem, collecting and understanding their qualitative voice, and using their perceptions to inform plans for effecting change (see Weil, Chapter 11, this volume). Agency and organization accountability should be to the members of the target population and only secondarily to groups such as social workers, agency directors, and funding sources. This approach is the essence of the conscientization process, as taught by Paulo Freire (2000).

Constituent Control of Goals

Although the literature clearly advises that there be constituent participation in setting organizational goals, this process is often weak, and the real directions are set by operations staff and boards of directors (Holland & Hester, 1999). This observation occasions a comment on boards. Most small nonprofit agencies have difficulty finding people who both possess desired skills and are willing to invest time on their boards. This is partially due to the reality that boards are legal entities whose members must assume financial liability and roles that require expertise in areas such as law, accounting, fundraising, and politics. As such, sought-after board members tend to be unrepresentative of the populations served by the agency but instead well-meaning and busy people in their own professions. Though these people make important contributions to agencies, they often lack the understanding of goals that are meaningful to the target populations and may not have the enthusiasm to see these goals through. Although not supported by current nonprofit corporate laws, and although it might raise concerns from benefactors, perhaps a better approach would be to put substantive program authority for setting goals in the hands of direct constituents and make the more technical group an advisory board to the agency. This is the reverse of much current practice in nonprofit agencies but is consistent with the general structure of grassroots community organizations, in which member control is primary.

Monitoring Processes and Outcomes

Funding sources influence the monitoring of program operations and the measurement of outcomes (Hasenfeld, 1982). In the public sector, there have been waves of emphasis on accountability and on the efficient use of scarce public dollars. The same has been true for nonprofit organizations, which typically report to several public contractors and private foundations. This reality has meant that agencies and funded community organizations must pay close attention to monitoring and evaluation activities as dictated by funders, although they may also evaluate activities and outcomes of importance to direct constituents. Monitoring can be described as a political process, in which an agency produces information that demonstrates the best aspects of the agency's performance (Hasenfeld, 1982). Information that is not positive may be set aside or interpreted in alternative ways to minimize harm. This sort of manipulation is often successful because the recipients of the evaluative information are external to the organization. If the recipients of this information were clients or members, such deception would be more difficult, because the beneficiaries of services are more likely to have substantive knowledge of the agency's performance due to direct experience.

The demand for external accountability to funding sources will not diminish in the foreseeable future. It is possible, however, to insist that there additionally be substantive evaluation that emerges from the concerns and interests of clients or members. The constituency interests of clients and members may vary widely and range from personal benefit to pride and investment in the agency's success in generating a greater sense of empowerment in a community. The major difference in approach is that the determination of desired outcomes and evaluation questions emerge from the direct constituents, and not from those who fund the agency. Similarly, the meaning of the information gathered rests with constituents, not with evaluation experts.

Challenges

The preceding discussion provides a set of principles that support more constituent-controlled organizations. There is no question, however, that organizations that wish to move in this direction face many barriers. Probably the most formidable of these barriers is a basic component embedded in Western organizational culture itself.

Managers, planners, citizens, and constituents alike have been raised in organizations that reflect the ideas of Henry Ford, whose production lines reduced worker involvement in the workplace, and Frederick Taylor, the father of scientific management, who viewed workers as part of the machinery. In contrast, Mary Parker Follett, an early social worker and management theorist who espoused more humanitarian views about organizations (see Follett, 1926/1978), was not widely recognized in the management literature until relatively recently, and in the human services literature, only Weiner (1982) gives significant attention to her contributions. A major part of the change must come from creative leaders who can break from the currently dominant paradigm of top-down control.

Several specific challenges warrant attention; if left unaddressed, they may hinder movement toward more progressive organizations. Unfortunately, there are no cookbook approaches to these challenges.

Internal Conflict

Arguing that conflict can be a source of creative energy in organizations is not difficult. Certainly those organizations that recruit or employ only like-thinking people will lack vitality and the motivation to keep abreast of changes occurring in their external environments. On the other hand, few people admit that they enjoy conflict, and most find conflict to be stressful, if not destructive. In the traditional management model, conflict is minimized or suppressed through hierarchy and linear authority structures. One might argue that some suppression is necessary so that an inordinate amount of time and energy is not directed away from achieving the organization's goals. Assuming that this is a real concern, the literature gives many examples of approaches for conflict management or resolution that do not require such hierarchical suppression. The skills of negotiation, collaboration, compromise, and concession are critical for building democracy from the bottom up, and these should be taught at all levels of organization.

That being said, there remain the inherent power struggles that will always be present in most organizations. These can be found between levels as well as within levels, but most major challenges seem to occur at the interfaces between levels: boards, operations, and constituents. Shifting from a model of top-down power to one of bottom-up authority will not be easy and likely will not happen in the absence of constituent organization for power. Initially, this client organization will have an overabundance of conflict, but to the extent that management and boards respond by sharing power, that overt conflict may move toward collaboration.

Leadership

The most common model for leadership is that of the charismatic person at the top who can use both learned and inherent personal characteristics to command the loyalty of followers. Although this model is largely discounted in the literature, alternatives remain unclear. The idea of shared or group leadership is vague, and ways in which leadership tasks, functions, and roles are either rotated or concurrently exercised requires understanding of complex group functions. Furthermore, the traditional hierarchical model of leadership is a structural component of most organizations, with the top leader holding most authority and usually earning the highest salary. Financial accounting standards, funding source requirements, and a host of other legal areas require that there be a person who assumes ultimate responsibility.

To move toward a more democratic model of shared leadership is difficult. Barriers to doing so, in addition to those mentioned previously, include the frequent lack of accountability by some organization members who function from an individualistic model and find group leadership to be cumbersome. Size is another important factor. When an agency or organization is small and people interact face-to-face regularly, it is more possible to have a flat structure that is more egalitarian. But as organizations grow in size, the need for integrating diverse activities grows and hierarchy is an understandable decision.

There are other ways to provide the integration that organizations need without increasing hierarchy and centralized leadership. These include electronic communications systems, face-to-face meetings, clarifying different work functions, training, professionalization, and standardization of work. The point is that there are several ways to encourage decentralized leadership, and increasing the number of levels of supervision is one way, but that approach fixes leadership roles in a few people, with the negative consequence of reducing the sense of mutual responsibility for leadership.

In addition to increasing the number of levels of supervision, there are other ways to provide the integration that organizations need without increasing hierarchy and centralized leadership. These include electronic communications systems, face-to-face meetings, clarifying different work functions, training, professionalization, and standardization of work.

Resources Acquisition

One of the more difficult problems faced by agencies and community organizations is fund development. All organizations need resources to survive and are to some extent dependent on those in the external environment who control these resources. This means that organizations are rarely able to operate to achieve goals without the support of funders. The movement toward greater privatization of public human services adds to this dilemma because nonprofit agencies often enter contractual agreements to provide specified services, thereby reducing their own autonomy to set goals and carve their own paths. In exchange for money, the agency agrees to give up its autonomy.

This is also implicit in funding for community organizations and indicates the central reason that ACORN, the Association of Community Organizations for Reform Now, has worked so hard to be fiscally self-sufficient. Saul Alinsky, former labor organizer beginning in the 1930s and later well-known community organizer in the Back of the Yards area in Chicago, was known for his harsh dealings with the churches that financially and otherwise supported his organizations, insisting that there be no strings attached to grants that were nonrefundable (Alinsky, 1972; Betten & Austin, 1990). He had the clout to demand money up front, but this is unheard of today.

The challenge is for agencies and organizations to strive for autonomy through a resource acquisition plan that emphasizes having low dependence on any single funder; maximizing revenue-producing activities, events, and services; and minimizing costs. Cost minimization can be a thorny issue, as there is a common assumption that the connection between quality and costs is linear and positive. Although this association is often overstated, attracting and retaining skilled staff members may well require competitive salaries. Organizations that rely on volunteers and member contributions may be less constrained, but even Alinsky (1972) emphasized the importance of a well-paid professional organizing staff. There seems to be no easy solution to this challenge other than to strive for lean organizations, eliminating components that are not critical to achieving goals.

Perceived Success

The success of an organization is largely a matter of perception. As Hasenfeld (1982) so masterfully asserted, the evaluation of goal achievement is determined in a political and economic context. As has been argued earlier, organizations have formal goals written to satisfy funders and the public, their members have expectations, and those who benefit from the agency's services also have needs and desires. Who defines success? What are the criteria? As previously stated, organizational success all too often is determined by funding sources that require information that is produced by management and filtered through a board of directors. Such evidence of success may include information generated by the clients or members of the organization via client satisfaction surveys, but the process is designed and implemented from the top of the hierarchy.

In progressive organizations, clients or members should be given the opportunity to design their own evaluation, from the bottom up, probably in addition to the more traditional assessments of outcomes and outputs (Latting & Leung, 2001). Such a client-generated evaluation likely would look at very different issues, attempt to answer different questions, use different methods, and assess the results in very different ways than would a traditional evaluation. The scope of this chapter does not allow a consideration of the alternatives, but the idea that truth is elusive, subjective, rooted in experience, and variously derived is now fairly well accepted by qualitative researchers. There are a range of models for qualitative and participatory research (see Pennell, Noponen, & Weil, Chapter 34, this volume) that could be effectively used for outcome evaluations by clients or members of organizations.

Conclusion

This chapter has provided a broad overview of traditional managerial perspectives and has argued that those wishing to develop more democratic, progressive organizations should free their thinking by seriously considering another paradigm. In environments that increasingly limit such experimentation, real courage is needed to follow another path. Democratizing our organizations should be a goal, one that can be approximated over time. Organizations that are inclusive can be developed by changing the structure of hierarchy to be more flat, by changing the division of labor to make work more holistic, and by making decision making more inclusive of various constituencies. Success is dependent on the strength of creative, capable, and iconoclastic leaders who are willing to work with their constituencies to find ways to overcome the obstacles.

References

Alinsky, S. D. (1972). *Rules for radicals: A practical primer for realistic radicals*. New York: Vintage Books.

Austin, M. J. (2002). Managing out: The community practice dimensions of effective agency management. *Journal of Community Practice, 10*(4), 33–48.

Betten, N., & Austin, M. J. (1990). The conflict approach to community organizing: Saul Alinsky and the CIO. In N. Betten & M. J. Austin (Eds.), *The roots of community organizing, 1917–1939* (pp. 152–161). Philadelphia: Temple University Press.

Brager, G., & Holloway, S. (1978). *Changing human service organizations: Politics and practice*. New York: Free Press.

Brody, R., & Nair, M. D. (2000). *Macro practice: A generalist approach* (5th ed.). Wheaton, IL: Gregory.

Cnaan, R. A. (1991). Neighborhood representing organizations: How democratic are they? *Social Service Review, 65*(4), 614–634.

Council on Social Work Education. (2000). *Summary information on master of social work programs*. Alexandria, VA: Author.

Fabricant, M. B., & Fisher, R. (2002). *Settlement houses under siege: The struggle to sustain community organizations in New York City*. New York: Columbia University Press.

Fisher, J. C., & Cole, K. M. (1993). *Leadership and management of volunteer programs: A guide for volunteer administrators*. San Francisco: Jossey-Bass.

Flynn, J. P. (1992). *Social agency policy: Analysis and presentation for community practice* (2nd ed). Chicago: Nelson-Hall.

Follett, M. P. (1941). The *Collected papers of Mary Parker Follett*. H. C. Metcalf & L. Urwick, Eds. New York: Harper.

Follett, M. P. (1978). The giving of orders. In J. M. Shafritz & P. H. Whitbeck (Eds.), *Classics of organization theory* (pp. 43–51). Oak Park, IL: Moore. (Original work published in 1926)

Fox, E. M., & Urwick, L. F. (Eds,).(1982). *Dynamic administration: The collected papers of Mary Parker Follett by Mary Parker Follett* (2nd ed.). New York: Hippocrene Books.

Freire, P. (2000). *Pedagogy of the oppressed* (30th ed.). New York: Continuum International.

Ginsberg, L., & Keys, P. R. (Eds.). (1995). *New management in human services*. Silver Spring, MD: NASW Press.

Grogan, P. S., & Proscio, T. (2000). *Comeback cities: A blueprint for urban neighborhood revival*. Boulder, CO: Westview Press.

Gummer, B. (1990). *The politics of social administration: Managing organizational politics in social agencies*. Englewood Cliffs, NJ: Prentice Hall.

Hammer, M. (1996). *Beyond reengineering: How the process-centered organization is changing our work and our lives*. New York: HarperCollins.

Hammer, M., & Champy, J. (1993). *Reengineering the corporation: A manifesto for business revolution*. New York: HarperCollins.

Hasenfeld, Y. (1982). *Human service organizations*. Boston: Allyn & Bacon.

Hasenfeld, Y. (1989). *Administrative leadership in the social services: The next challenge*. New York: Haworth.

Haynes, K. S., & Mickelson, J. S. (2003). *Affecting change: Social workers in the political arena* (5th ed.). Boston: Allyn & Bacon/Longman.

Holland, T. P., & Hester, D. C. (Eds.). (1999). *Building effective boards for religious organizations: A handbook for trustees, presidents, and church leaders.* San Francisco: Jossey-Bass.

Homan, M. S. (1994). *Promoting community change: Making it happen in the real world.* Belmont, CA: Brooks/Cole.

Koerin, B. (2003). The settlement house tradition: Current trends and future concerns. *Journal of Sociology and Social Welfare, 30*(2), 53–68.

Latting, J. K., & Leung, P. (2001). *Measures for evaluating community practice.* Englewood Cliffs, NJ: Prentice Hall.

Lohmann, R. A. (1980). *Breaking even: Financial management in human service organizations.* Philadelphia: Temple University Press.

Martin, L. L. (1994). *Total quality management in human service organizations.* Newbury Park, CA: Sage.

Medoff, P., & Sklar, H. (1994). *Streets of hope: The fall and rise of an urban neighborhood.* Cambridge, MA: South End Press.

Mondros, J. B., & Wilson, S. M. (1994). *Organizing for power and empowerment.* New York: Columbia University Press.

Patti, R. J. (Ed.). (2000). *The handbook of social welfare management.* Thousand Oaks, CA: Sage.

Perlmutter, F. (1988). *Alternative social agencies: Administrative strategies.* New York: Haworth.

Peters, T. (1994). *The Tom Peters seminar: Crazy times call for crazy organizations.* New York: Vintage.

Pfeffer, J., & Salancik, G. R. (1978). *The external control of organizations: A resource dependence perspective.* New York: Harper & Row.

Rapp, C. A., & Poertner, J. (1992). *Social administration: A client-centered approach.* New York: Longman.

Resnick, H., & Patti, R. (1980). *Change from within: Humanizing social welfare organizations.* Philadelphia: Temple University Press.

Skidmore, R. A., & Rosenberg, N. L. (1994). *Social work administration: Dynamic management and human relationships.* Boston: Allyn & Bacon.

Slavin, S. (1984). *Social administration: The management of the social services.* New York: Haworth.

Taylor, F. W. (1947). *Scientific management.* New York: Harper & Row.

Weber, M. (1947). *The theory of social and economic organizations* (A. M. Henderson & T. Parsons, Trans.). Glencoe, IL: Free Press.

Weinbach, R. W. (1994). *The social worker as manager: Theory and practice.* Boston: Allyn & Bacon.

Weiner, M. E. (1982). *Human services management: Analysis and applications.* Homewood, IL: Dorsey Press.

Weiner, M. E. (1990). *Human services management: Analysis and applications* (2nd ed.). Belmont, CA: Wadsworth.

CHAPTER 32

Fundraising, Programming, and Community Organizing

Working With Donors, Investors, Collaborators, and Purchasers

Armand Lauffer

A chicken is an egg's way of raising another egg.

—Anonymous

T o be effective programmatically, community organizers and their constituents must be able to manage in a complex funding environment populated by donors, investors, competitors and collaborators, and purchasers representing the private, voluntary, and public sectors.

Fundraising—whether through grant procurement, contracts, individual donor solicitation, campaigns, special events, or sales—has become a highly professionalized community practice activity, indistinguishable from community organizing program development. The term *fundraising* is used in this chapter to include both cash and non-cash (in-kind) contributions. The latter include donated or loaned real property, equipment and supplies, volunteer efforts, and other resources that have a cash equivalent. The fundraising environment for community practitioners has never been better. There are more dollars and non-cash resources available to them from a larger number of suppliers than ever before. However, there is also more demand for those resources from a growing number of competitors who are savvy in both locating potential suppliers and securing their support. It can be a very confusing environment for those new to fundraising.

To demystify the fundraising environment, we'll begin by exploring its characteristics, which include

1. a dramatic dollar growth in gifts from foundation and individual donors;

2. the expanding use of philanthropy as a business strategy by corporate investors;

3. the expanding range and activism of suppliers, competitors, and collaborators in the voluntary (nonprofit) sector;

4. the transformation of domestic government agencies from service providers to purchasers of these services via contracts with the nonprofit sector;

5. the professionalization of fundraising; and

6. an increasingly competitive fundraising environment for nonprofits.

We then examine the implications of this environment for resource and program development. The chapter concludes with recommendations on constructing a community organizer's electronic and print library that can be used by community groups and professionals to more effectively manage the funding environment.

The Fundraising Environment

The funding environment is populated by private donors, corporate investors, voluntary sector competitors and collaborators, and government purchasers of services. We will take them one at a time.

The Donors: Individuals and Foundations

The good news is that donors have more to give and are giving more than ever before. Private philanthropy has grown by more than 10% per year since 1995. The number of foundations and private trusts grew by about 30%, and their assets doubled during the 1990s.* Not even the economic slowdown of 2000 and 2001 and downturn of 2002 and 2003 seem to have dampened the enthusiasm of the well-to-do to do good. Nor is gift giving limited to the rich. Many campaigns have mass appeal, and grassroots fundraising methods, which community organizations employ, are often aimed more at "people-raising" than fundraising.

Dollars can be solicited through mass appeals or from specific individuals or members of identifiable groups. For example, an annual fundraising letter from the March of Dimes or the American Cancer Association is a direct appeal cast over a very large nationwide net. A telephone campaign seeking support for a regional health clinic is likely to be targeted only to residents of the area to be served. A one-time bricks-and-mortar campaign to expand a church's recreation center may appeal only to current parishioners. More time is spent per person, and the returns are likely to be greater in targeted rather than mass campaigns.

---

* The Foundation Center. (2004). *Highlights of the Foundation Center's* Foundation giving trends. Retrieved June 14, 2004, from http://fndcenter.org/research/trends_analysis/pdf/04fgthiltes.pdf.

Some organizations, such as universities, use parallel campaigns. The annual alumni campaign uses a modified mass appeal with letters and phone calls to both prospective and regular contributors. This is a relatively low-cost approach in which no more than one or two brief contacts are made. The focus is on the institution and its needs, and although the solicitation may be modified slightly to address presumed donor interest in academics, programs, athletics, and so forth, it is pretty much a one-size-fits-all approach. In contrast, the university's major gifts and endowment campaigns target only alumni and others with considerable wealth. The focus is on the donor rather than the institution. Institution-initiated, development-oriented interactions are designed to identify and address relevant donor interests. The process is both time- and labor-intensive; it may involve a number of one-on-one contacts over a period of years or even decades.

Why do people give their money to causes, programs, organizations, or population groups? Although the reasons vary with individuals and over time, motivations often include

1. doing good by promoting a cause, organization, or group;

2. knowing one's gift can make a difference;

3. receiving appreciation, esteem, or status as a result of one's donation or involvement in a "community of givers";

4. making it possible for some group or organizations (or even one's own name) to live on beyond the moment; and

5. benefiting personally as through a tax write off, securing one's economic future,[1] or receiving a "premium"[2] in return for the contribution.

Volunteers, who are themselves donors, often play critical roles in campaigns and other approaches to direct fundraising. For example, campaigns almost always involve some kind of authority structure that includes a steering committee, solicitors, co-ordinators, publicists, events chairs, and others. The professional community practitioner facilitates this process and may or may not be involved in direct solicitation.

Volunteers also play important roles in indirect fundraising, through such grassroots activities and events as organizing, managing, or participating in thrift shops, community fairs, bike-a-thons, bingo nights, picnics, holiday celebrations, and fundraising dinners. In indirect appeals, the benefit to the donor may overshadow the satisfaction of making the contribution. Visitors to the annual "Chocolate Extravaganza" may be totally unaware of what charities their $18 admissions fees support, and not really care. The "free" chocolate is its own reward. The volunteers involved may get more gratification from being part of the event than from knowing that money was raised for a good cause. Community organizers often use grassroots fundraising as much for community building as money making.

Community Building

It was the first time the H'mong people in Detroit had ever done anything as a community. The goal of the neighborhood fair was to raise scholarships so that H'mong women could go to college. But it turned out to be much more. Detroiters who had never heard of the H'mong community came out. We sold crafts and food, put on a concert that had old people playing native instruments and children dancing in costumes. It brought us together and gave us pride. (H'mong Program Volunteer)

In recent years, *planned giving* strategies have outdistanced other fundraising approaches in terms of dollars raised per contact hour. Gifts are made in the present, but their use is deferred to some time in the future. Examples include: (a) bequests to be paid when the donor's estate is settled; (b) *charitable gift annuities*, which are contracts between a donor and recipient organization in which the latter agrees to pay the donor a monthly income for life, in return for donated property or the remaining corpus of a cash gift; and (c) *trusts*, which are legal documents that specify what percentage of the income generated can be used in any given period.

Sometimes the establishment of a trust is the first step in organizing a *foundation*, which is a legal entity to which charitable gifts can be made and through which gifts and grants are made to other organizations. Foundations are required to have bona fide charitable purposes and must be governed by voluntary boards committed to overseeing operations.

Common Gifting Terms

Immediate Donation

- Donor makes cash or in-kind gift now.
- Donor receives full amount or value of gift as a tax deduction now.
- Foundation is free to use or invest the total now.

Charitable Gift Annuity

- Donor makes cash or in-kind gift now.
- Donor receives tax deduction now.
- Foundation pays the donor a fixed annual or monthly annuity on which the donor may have to pay taxes.
- At the end of annuity period, or when the donor dies, the foundation is free to use or invest the remaining funds.

Donor-Advised Fund

- Donor makes cash or in-kind gift now.
- Donor receives tax deduction now.
- Donor defers the decision of how the foundation will spend the money or to whom it will be allocated.

The nearly 44,000 philanthropic foundations in the United States allocate more than $8 million annually. Approximately 25 cents of every foundation dollar is spent on education.*

Fifteen cents go to health; another 15 cents go to human services. The rest is divided among research, international programs, and other priorities. Foundation priorities reflect the interests of a foundation's donors and its board of directors, which may be legally enjoined to fulfill or interpret the donor's directives. About 35,000 foundations are private or independent, a thousand or so are community foundations, and the remainder are corporate or operating foundations. Operating foundations are excluded from this discussion because they raise money primarily for their own operations rather than redistributing their income to other recipients.

Attracting Multiple Sources of Funding for Major Community Renewal

A 5-year, $90 million federal Renaissance Zone Grant to a coalition organized by the Cleveland Foundation generated more than $2 billion in investments by local banks, employers, real estate developers, individual donors, other foundations, and local units of government. Decay was reversed, unemployment and despair declined with minimal resident displacement, schools improved, and a revitalized downtown and waterfront gave Clevelanders a sense that they could control their own destiny as an urban community.

Some community foundations aggressively seek gifts from individuals, corporations, and other foundations to grow their endowments or to address needs in the service area reflected in the foundation's name or mission. Board members represent a wide variety of interests in the public, private, and voluntary sectors. They are likely to include both people who are influential in the community and those with specific expertise in areas the foundation funds. Many foundations are staffed by highly trained professionals, not a few of whom have extensive experience in community practice and nonprofit management.

Although overall funding priorities are set by the boards of community foundations, individual donors are permitted to specify the purposes for which their gift dollars may be spent. For example, an individual donor may wish her trust fund to be used in support of needy families, a corporate gift may be intended for cultural programs, and a private foundation's grant may be designated for the community foundation's administrative operations.

Community foundations often partner with other funders to leverage both dollars and expertise. The Cleveland Foundation's response to the federal government's Renaissance Zone Initiative is a good example. An Oakland, California, community foundation established a partnership with a failing school district and Lucas Films to create a successful family-centered approach to teaching and learning.

Most independent foundations are relatively small and staffed by volunteers, often the original donor or the donor's family and friends. Some expend only what they are able to raise in a given year. Some do not accept uninvited proposals.

---

*The Foundation Center. (2004). *Highlights of the Foundation Center's* Foundation giving trends. Retrieved June 14, 2004, from http://fndcenter.org/research/trends_analysis/pdf/04fgthiltes.pdf.

However, there are also megafoundations whose endowment-based annual expenditures dwarf the budgets of developing nations in several parts of the world. The largest among them—Gates, Ford, Pew, Hewlett, and Kellogg—have endowments of $5 billion to more than $30 billion. Today's 10 largest foundations spend as much as all philanthropic foundations did a decade ago.

Many private foundations are managed by qualified professionals who have access to a wide range of experts in the fields they fund. What distinguishes private foundations from others is that although their names may be associated with a founding family or corporate entity, their boards are independently selected. Frequently, funding priorities have expanded considerably beyond the vision of the founders.

A growing number of independent foundations advocate for the interests of specific population groups. For example, there are now more than 100 women's funds that support projects ranging from education to advocacy, and a growing number of African American, Native American, and other foundations whose grants are at least partially oriented to specific ethnic or sectarian populations.

Funding for Specific Populations

An Internet search for funding to support the training of indigenous health care advocates among migrant farm workers was unsuccessful until the terms *women* and *disadvantaged minorities* were substituted for *migrant farm workers* and the words *advocacy* and *leadership* were given primacy over *health care*. A positive funding matching with the Ms. Foundation led to a 3-year grant to train minority women with low incomes to take on leadership roles in their communities. In practice, this meant training a cadre of mothers from among the migrant families to become community advocates with both political savvy and information about where and how to get proper health care.

Although most private foundations do not distribute annual reports, the largest among them do have extensive written materials or Web sites on which they list funding criteria and provide grant application materials. Smaller, more local foundations may neither issue reports nor post on the Web; they are not legally required to do so. However, they are required to report income and expenditures to the IRS, and this information is in the public domain. Foundation tax returns are available on microfiche from The Foundation Center in New York. Large business enterprises are likely to set up their own foundations as ways of standardizing and professionalizing their strategic philanthropy. Because the boards of corporate foundations are almost always composed of corporate officers, the projects they support may be indistinguishable from those of companies that fund projects directly.

The Investors: Corporate Philanthropy

Both large corporations and small businesses increasingly integrate philanthropy and public service into their strategic planning and marketing. Strategic interests include making a profit, establishing or improving an image, advertising a product, and demonstrating good corporate citizenship by providing a public service to the community or communities in which the corporation does business. Stonyfield Farm, a New Hampshire–based dairy that supports family farms and sustainable farming methods, is more than merely a profitable corporation whose production methods and products are environmentally safe. Viewed from a community practice perspective, it is an example of a "non-service intervention." A *non-service intervention* is one in which a problem is addressed without recourse to a service program. For example, if a public utility reduces winter heating charges to residents of low-income neighborhoods, this obviates the need for the state or city to develop a heating subsidy program. Rather than addressing a problem by attempting a service solution, the corporation addressed the social needs of its primary beneficiaries (in this case, farmers and dairy employees) using business methods. In this example, consumers were also invited to become investors whose payoff was not monetary profit but instead the satisfaction of participating in community by proxy.

Non-Service Intervention

The founders of Stonyfield Farms established their company, now based in Londonderry, New Hampshire, at least in part because it cost local farmers more to raise a cow than they could get for its milk. By creating a healthy product—a premium yogurt produced from locally raised cows—the community's economic decline could be arrested. And by taking a personal tour of the factory, subscribing to a free newsletter (*Moos From the Farm*), or joining the Adopt-a-Cow club, consumers could share the satisfaction of belonging and contributing to the enterprise.

What motivates investors? Among the reasons for corporate philanthropy are

1. expanding profits by improving the company's position in the community;

2. the entrepreneurial urge to build something new;

3. making a difference by addressing the needs of employees and their families;

4. displaying good citizenship by improving the community in which the company does business; and

5. being identified with other public-minded agencies or with social causes such as the environment, research, and education.

Although the prime beneficiaries may be the company and its employees, corporate philanthropy can lead to some significant local benefits as well. For example, the Monsanto Corporation in St. Louis, Missouri, funded the St. Louis Zoo's world-famous Insectarium, which rivals the city's famed Botanical Gardens. Monsanto has also invested millions of dollars in early childhood programs, many of which serve their own employees.

The Dayton Hudson Corporation, the mass-market retailer that owns Target, follows a decentralized philanthropic policy. Managers of each Target store are encouraged to make small grants or gifts to worthy causes. Recently, the corporation listed all of Target's school-aid projects in a two-page ad in the *New York Times*, inviting other schools to "get on this list" by applying for funding through their community Target stores.

Non-Service Intervention

Foodgatherers, a collection and distribution partnership initiated by volunteers at Zingerman's Deli in Ann Arbor, Michigan, involves scores of area restaurants that distribute surplus meals to the needy in shelters and other settings in cooperation with social agencies, churches, and civic associations. Entering its third decade, Foodgatherers is one of hundreds of similar projects throughout North America.

Some companies do not normally fund social programs but are important resource providers nonetheless. For example, the Kroger Company, a Cincinnati-based grocery retailer, encourages its employees to tutor school children in the neighborhoods they serve. A public utility in Texas allowed some of its top executives release time to provide systems and budgeting consultation to the state's public welfare agency. The success of this effort soon led IBM and several other corporations to join a loose consortium of businesses offering similar aid to other public agencies and nonprofits. The result was both better management practice in the public and voluntary sectors and a new awareness of the importance of public services to disadvantaged populations on the part of the state's business elite.

Competitors and Collaborators in the Voluntary System

Both traditional and nontraditional civic associations and faith-based organizations are reemerging as significant players in funding social and community services. Many of these nonprofit, nongovernmental organizations are increasingly interdependent in both resource acquisition and program delivery. This interdependence is, in itself, not a new phenomenon. Voluntary social service agencies have long pooled their fundraising efforts though such federated structures as the United Way or its sectarian counterparts such as the Jewish Federation. Both government and foundation funders often require evidence of programmatic collaboration before grants are made. However, there are new imperatives that promote both collaboration and competition.

The expanding number of funders and funds appears to be dwarfed by demand fueled both by an exponential proliferation of social and community programs and issues. To cope with the demand, traditional suppliers seek new ways of reducing long-standing obligations, increasing the resources at their disposal, and requiring that recipients find matching funds or collaborate with others to reduce costs. Concurrently, petitioners for grants and gifts seek to free themselves from the risks inherent in single-source funding by seeking alternative funding sources or cost reductions through programmatic collaboration.

What has happened within the United Way and its members or recipients is a case in point. The United Way traces its origins to the early 20th century, during which local councils of social agencies became federated and created local community chests as their fundraising arms (see Brilliant, Chapter 12, this volume). Joint fundraising generated more funds than individual agency efforts and reduced the amount of agency staff and volunteer time devoted to the process. The income received was reallocated to member agencies according to agreed-on formulas.

Classic United Way fundraising is carried out through annual payroll deduction, an earlier community chest innovation, in which an employee's contribution is deducted by the employer from the paycheck and transferred to the federated fundraising structure. These fundraising drives are local in scope and conducted within the workplace with support from both labor and management. There are currently 1,900 United Way agencies that provide support to more than 50,000 local service agencies and chapters of the national organization. The funds raised are used to cover United Way costs and then redistributed to member agencies providing social, health, and educational services. Like those affiliated with the earlier community chest movement, local United Way member organizations could be relatively certain of receiving a similar allocation from year to year so long as there were no significant drops in campaign revenue or catastrophic events that required emergency funding. The process of becoming a member agency and thus of qualifying for an annual allocation could take several years.

This pattern began changing in the early 1980s when structural changes in the U.S. economy negatively affected local campaigns at the same time as newer kinds of federations began competing with the United Way for funds. Today, for example, all federal agencies sponsor a combined discretionary campaign that permits employees to designate that portions of their contributions go to the United Way and to several other federated funds. Included among these funds are International Service Agencies, Combined Health Appeals, National Voluntary Health Agencies, United Arts Funds, Environmental Federation of America, National Network of Women's Funds, and other minority or social action funds. Local and state governments are beginning to follow suit, as are a number of large corporations.

In response to such competition, local United Ways have developed their own approaches to donor choice: designated giving within the campaign and endowment giving outside the campaign. Within the campaign, donors may be permitted to designate on their pledge cards how much of their gifts should go to specific communities or neighborhoods, service categories (i.e., counseling or camping), populations to be served (i.e., children and youth or the elderly), or approved agencies named by the United Way. A few United Way communities, like those in Washington, DC, and Lansing, Michigan, have experimented with the use of competitive grants in lieu of annual allocations to distribute dollars generated by the annual drive. These grants are made without regard to agency membership. Any qualifying organization or program may apply.

Because income from local payroll deduction drives almost always falls short of the need, many United Ways now seek major gifts outside the annual campaign. However, the funds generated are not part of the annual allocation process. Instead, they may be managed by a local United Way foundation, which performs in much the same way a community foundation might—investing the gift and using the proceeds to seed innovation efforts, supplementing other sources of income, or making project grants to non–United Way agencies. In Los Angeles County, the United Way initiated a regional antipoverty effort in the late 1990s that, like the Cleveland Foundation's Renaissance project, involves scores of community groups, government agencies, schools, employers, and civic and faith-based organizations.

Both donor choice and the use of project grant funding instead of annual allocations to member agencies increase competition at the local levels. But they also can lead to collaboration between and among service providers. For example, a teen health clinic wishing to strengthen its position in a donor choice environment is likely to do all it can to increase its attractiveness to donors. By engaging in collaboration with other agencies, it demonstrates the regard of respected collaborators and its own commitment to efficiency through cost sharing.

Local service providers can also apply for funding from sectarian federations (such as Catholic Charities, Lutheran Social Services, the Jewish Federation, and Protestant Community Services) and from civic associations, mutual benefit organizations, or faith-based groups. Examples of civic associations include the Rotary and Lions Clubs, local chapters of the Junior League, Civitan, and Ruritan, and many others. Some of these organizations have national or international agendas for which they seek local service opportunities. For example, in addition to their international agenda of eradicating polio, local Rotary Clubs often recruit professional and businesspeople to provide pro bono assistance to area charities. Although Lions Club International supports a global vision program, local chapters are free to support services for the sight and hearing impaired and others in their own communities.

Program support may also be available from mutual benefit organizations. Many were founded a hundred or more years ago to provide social and economic assistance to their own members. Today they are more apt to function like civic associations responding to broader community needs. Among them are such familiar names as the Kiwanis, Variety Clubs, Knights of Columbus, B'nai B'rith, Shriners, Masons, Benevolent and Protective Order of the Elks, and the Loyal Order of the Moose. For example, the Shriners support a network of hospitals and Masons support local cultural programs. The Kiwanis run thrift stores in support of local agencies. These efforts may not yield large sums, but their grants often provide program support for which other funding is unavailable.

The most ubiquitous membership organizations in America are religious congregations and related faith-based organizations (see Cnaan, Boddie, & Yancey, Chapter 20, this volume). In 2000, these organizations raised about $12 billion for denominational charities such as sectarian federations and overseas assistance. However, more immediately relevant to community organizers is that congregations spent, in toto, $6 billion on local human service programs, $4 billion on health services, and $2 billion on community development and social justice programs. About half of this amount was linked to congregational activities and members' needs, leaving a generous $6 billion for other causes. Add volunteer involvement and in-kind support in the form of food, clothing, and housing, and this makes for a significant resource pool that is potentially available to nondenominational or interdenominational social services. Unfortunately, many community organizers are unfamiliar with the way in which churches support social programs or fearful that sectarian purposes will be attached to the funds given. That is not necessarily true; Habitat for Humanity and many shelter programs for the homeless or victims of domestic violence are cases in point.

Any of these organizations are potential competitors. But they are also potential suppliers and collaborators. What motivates potential competitors to become suppliers and collaborators with nonprofits? The motivations may include the following:

1. The organization's mission or goals fit with the nonprofit's.

2. Collaboration reduces dependence on a single source of supply.

3. The risk to a single funder is minimized and responsibility for funding and oversight of complex or costly programs is shared.

4. The likelihood that programs have support from multiple publics is increased.

5. When multiple organizations think and act in concert, new ideas are generated and the potential to bridge gaps between and among groups is expanded.

6. Some goals are realistic only if there is concerted action involving many players.

The Buyers: Governmental Funding Agencies and Others

The sums raised in the private and voluntary sectors are dwarfed by public spending, which accounts for almost $9 of every $10 allocated to social programs. Most government expenditures are designed to achieve goals that reflect legislative intent or administrative priorities. These may be narrowly targeted or relatively grand in scope. For example, a U.S. Department of Health and Human Services annual combined discretionary funding program provides grants of up to $100,000 to local agencies to promote particular programs or innovations in services to targeted populations: the elderly, the disabled, children at risk, and others.

In contrast, the Renaissance Grant to Cleveland was intended to fund a much more comprehensive program involving scores of interrelated interventions, dozens of local nonprofit and proprietary organizations, and large sums of money. In this case, the original grant was used as seed money to promote collaboration in investment and development at the local level.

Whether the projects funded are large or small, simple or complex, grants permit the awardees considerable latitude in the what and how of program development, whereas purchase of service contracts (POSCs) do not. POSCs give government agencies much more control over the work being done. Vendors are selected to conduct or modify existing programs, put new ones into effect, or extend them to previously unserved or underserved populations. Service contracting is not limited to governmental organizations. Corporations do it when engaging in *outsourcing*—contracting with a supplier to produce a process or conduct an activity which the corporation itself otherwise would have. The same is true of social agencies and advocacy coalitions that contract out for program evaluations or fundraising campaigns.

Why outsource? What are the presumed benefits of purchasing services? From the government's perspective:

1. It gets the job done better and faster.

2. Government has neither the competence nor the flexibility to perform all the tasks mandated by law, so it makes more sense to contract out to more specialized and flexible organizations.

3. It frees government up to do what it does best—plan, allocate, and support— rather than operate social programs.

4. It makes it easier for government agencies to initiate or cancel programs as new needs are uncovered and the public's program preferences or governmental policies change.

5. It is a cost-effective way of fulfilling the agency's mandate and the public interest.

From the contractee's perspective, POSCs provide new sources of funding and focused opportunities to innovate by doing it cheaper, better, and faster.

Responding to the Challenges in the Funding Environment

Connecting Program Development to Resource Development

So what comes first? The idea for a program or the possibility of funding? That's a badly phrased question, as unproductive as asking, What came first, the chicken or the egg? One might just as well conclude that a chicken is an egg's way of creating another egg as the other way around. A better way to examine the relationship between funding and programs is to think in terms of "opportunities." True, a good idea may engender opportunities, particularly if its framers can also introduce others to it and spark their enthusiasm. But then, the existence of an operating program may also suggest opportunities to a donor or a foundation that they might not have considered before. Moreover, the availability of grant funds may be just the opportunity a multicultural housing coalition needs to get itself moving. The operative word here is *opportunity*. The funding environment can be viewed as part of the community organizer's "opportunity environment," just as the community's voluntary organizations and coalitions might be viewed by funders as theirs. The trick is in finding the opportunities and then creating or exploiting them.

At the risk of oversimplifying, funding and other resource acquisition opportunities exist when a supplier (donor, investor, collaborator, or purchaser) is interested in and has the resources available for a program (so long as the supplier is not diverted by other competing opportunities that may be more interesting or less costly). Determining funders' interests is a first step in resource acquisition. Deciding which individual or foundation to approach is the fundraiser's call. However, what to invest in, to whom to donate, with whom to collaborate or to contract— that's the funder's call.

This is a hard lesson for some volunteers and even professional organizers to accept. Funders decide what to support, and they generally do so in relation to their own motivations. If their priorities match the petitioners' interests, the applicant's next steps include getting the application guidelines and forms, communicating with those who can provide necessary information on the donor's priorities and expectations (e.g., foundation program officers, recipients of other grants or contracts from the same funder, or fundraisers who have worked with the donor before or who have information on whether the supplier has the necessary funding available), writing the proposal, and submitting it to the funder. These are, short of elaboration, the steps outlined in many of the books on grant getting listed later. But they do not tell the whole story.

Donors' Choices

A well-to-do donor who had experienced a deprived childhood was so impressed by the literacy courses offered by his local community college at the county jail that he proposed a gift of $25,000 per year for 5 years to cover the cost of conducting three job-skills training courses in the jail each term. A local industrialist was so impressed by the job-skills courses that she engaged several other business leaders in funding an expansion of the program, leading to a threefold increase of the college's off-campus enrollment.

Hidden beneath the brief description of the community college's educational program for ex-offenders are a great many interactions that were necessary before a good fit of interests and capacities was established. The donor who made the 5-year gift had to be convinced that the college and the county jail were truly interested. College officials had to view the program as in the institution's best interest, and instructors had to be willing to teach in the jail. None of this would have worked had there not been receptivity on the part of prisoners and correctional authorities. What's more, the program had to be presented to the corporate givers as a public service that benefited their constituencies and advanced their corporate images.

The Professionalization of Fundraising

Both fundraising and funding have become increasingly sophisticated over the past two decades. Like other occupational groups that have achieved professional status, funders and fundraisers possess knowledge bases of their own, much of it transmitted through books and journals.[3] In addition to courses and workshops offered through the private sector and by occupational associations like The Foundation Center, it is now possible to major in fundraising, development, or applied philanthropy in a number of professional schools and even to receive a master's of arts and doctorate in the profession.[4]

There has been an information explosion in funding and fundraising. This is what has made it possible to recommend more then 100 books and other references for possible inclusion in the "Community Organizer's Grant Getting and Fundraising Print and Electronic Library" found at the end of this chapter. Most have been written since the late 1990s. These works, focused on fundraising, draw on and expand the scientific understanding of communities, organizations, and individuals and address both the contexts and methods of fundraising practice. A number of them focus explicitly on ethical and legal issues. Many link the terms *fundraising* and *development,* signaling a shift in focus from raising dollars to raising the level of community leadership and social responsibility.

Journals and newsletters, such as the *Chicago Philanthropy Quarterly,* the *Chronicle of Philanthropy,* the *Foundation News and Commentary, Grassroots Funding*

Journal, and the *Philanthropy Journal,* are dedicated to raising the knowledge base and standards of the profession. Philanthropy and development work are also addressed extensively in other journals that deal with more general issues affecting the nonprofit sector. Among them are *Nonprofit and Voluntary Sector Quarterly, Nonprofit Management and Leadership,* and *Nonprofit Times.*

There are a growing number of active listservs addressing one or more aspects of fundraising. They address such interests as deferred giving, ethical issues, and minority-oriented grant seeking. The National Council on Philanthropy has emerged as the premiere professional association in the field, although there are a number of more specialized associations, such as the Council of Foundations or the Jewish Funder's Network, that address the interests of more targeted constituencies. Many associations hold annual national meetings, conduct training workshops, and arrange mentoring relationships between experienced and novice funders or fundraisers. Community practitioners who do not take advantage of these information and networking resources are likely to be depriving their clients and constituents of important knowledge, know-how, and connections.

The Community Organizer's Grant-Getting and Fundraising Print and Electronic Library

These more than 100 books and scores of other print and electronic resources can be used to create a professional reference library. Recommended materials include how-to instruction, practice guidelines, analyses of emerging trends, and reports on best practices. A balanced library will include books, journals, and electronic references.

I. Books

Section I is divided into subcategories to help you locate appropriate books. Many can be found in community and university libraries throughout the United States. All can be ordered from local and electronic booksellers. See also the books described in Section III on how to use the Internet.

A. Grants, Contracts, Proposal Writing, and Project Design

Grant Getting: General

Bauer, D. G. (1999). *The "how to" grants manual: Successful grant seeking techniques for obtaining public and private grants* (4th ed.). Westport, CT: Greenwood.

Blum, L. (1996). *The complete guide to getting a grant: How to turn your ideas into dollars.* New York: John Wiley & Sons.

Burke, J., & Prater, C. A. (2000). *I'll grant you that: A step-by-step guide to finding funds, designing winning projects, and writing powerful proposals.* Philadelphia: Heinemann.

Carlson, M. (1997). *Winning grants: Step by step.* San Francisco: Jossey-Bass.

Lauffer, A. (1997). *Grants, etc.: Grant getting, contracting and fund-raising for nonprofits.* Thousand Oaks, CA: Sage.

Reiss, J. B., & Leukefield, C. J. (1995). *Applying for research funding: Getting started and getting funded.* Thousand Oaks, CA: Sage.

Proposal Writing

Coley, S. M., & Scheinberg, C. A. (2001). *Proposal writing.* Thousand Oaks, CA: Sage.

Gitlin, L. N., & Lyons, K. J. (1996). *Successful grant writing: Strategies for health and human service professionals.* New York: Springer.

Golden, S. L . (1997). *Secrets of sucessful grantsmanship: A guerilla guide to raising money.* San Francisco: Jossey-Bass.

Miner, L. E., Miner, J. T., & Griffith, J. (1998). *Proposal planning and writing* (2nd ed.). Phoenix: Oryx Press.

Robinson, A. (1996). *Grassroots grants: An activist's guide to proposal writing.* Berkeley, CA: Chardon Press.

Managing Grant Programs and Relationships

Bauer, D. G. (1999). *Successful grants program management.* San Francisco: Jossey-Bass.

Bernstein, S. R. (1991). *Managing contracted services in the nonprofit agency: Administrative, ethical and political issues.* Philadelphia: Temple University Press.

Demon, H. W., Jr., & Gibelman, M. (Eds.). (1989). *Services for sale: Purchasing health and human services.* New Brunswick, NJ: Rutgers University Press.

McIlnay, D. P. (1999). *How foundations work: What grantseekers need to know about the many faces of foundations.* San Francisco: Jossey-Bass.

Murray, V. (1991). *Improving corporate donations: New strategies for grantmakers and grantseekers.* San Francisco: Jossey-Bass.

Quick, J. A., & New, C. C. (1998). *Grant seeker's budget toolkit.* New York: John Wiley & Sons.

B. Fundraising and Development

Fundraising: General

Burlingame, D. F. (1997). *Critical issues in fund raising.* New York: John Wiley & Sons.

Carlson, M., & Clarke, C. (2000). *Team-based fundraising step by step: A total organization model.* San Francisco: Jossey-Bass.

Ciconte, B. K., & Jacob, J. G. (2001). *Fundraising basics: A complete guide* (2nd ed.). Gaithersburg, MD: Aspen.

Connors, T. D. (Ed.). (2000). *The nonprofit fundraising handbook.* New York: John Wiley & Sons.

Doyle, W. L. (1995). *Fund raising ideas: For all nonprofits: Charities, churches, clubs.* New York: American Fund Raising Institute.

Dunn, T. G. (1988). *How to shake the money tree: Creative fundraising for today's non-profit organization.* New York: Penguin Books.

Edles, P. L. (1993). *Fundraising: Hands-on tactics for nonprofit groups.* New York: McGraw-Hill.

Edwards, R. L., & Benefied, E. A. (1997). *Building a strong foundation: Fundraising for nonprofits.* Washington, DC: NASW Press.

Flanagan, J. (1992). *The grass roots fundraising book: How to raise money in your community.* Chicago: Contemporary Books.

Flanagan, L. (1994). *Raising capital: How to write a financial proposal.* Grants Pass, OR: Oasis Press.

Graham, C. (1999). *Keep the money coming: A step-by-step strategic guide to annual fundraising.* Sarasota, FL: Pineapple Press.

Greenfield, J. M. (Ed.). (1997). *The nonprofit handbook: Fund raising* (2nd ed.). New York: John Wiley & Sons.

Greenfield, J. M. (1999). *Fund raising: Evaluating and managing the fund development process.* New York: John Wiley & Sons.

Hodiak, D. L., & Ryan, J. S. (2001). *Hidden assets: Revolutionize your development program with a volunteer-driven approach.* San Francisco: Jossey-Bass.

Johnston, M. W. (2000). *Direct response fund raising.* New York: John Wiley & Sons.

Joyaux, S. P. (1997). *Strategic fund development: Building profitable relationships that last.* Gaithersburg, MD: Aspen.

Klein, K. (2001). *Fundraising for social change.* Oakland, CA: Chardon Press.

Mussoline, M. L. (Ed.) (1998). *Small nonprofits: Strategies for fundraising success.* San Francisco: Jossey-Bass.

Nichols, J. E. (1999). *Transforming fundraising: A practical guide to evaluating and strengthening fundraising to grow with change.* San Francisco: Jossey-Bass.

Nichols, J. E. (2001). *Pinpointing affluence in the 21st century: Increasing your share of major donor dollars.* New York: Bonus Books.

Reiss, A. H. (2000). *CPR for nonprofits: Creating strategies for successful fundraising, marketing, communications and management.* San Francisco: Jossey-Bass.

Schaff, T., & Schaff, D. (1999). *The fundraising planner: A working model for raising the dollars you need.* San Francisco: Jossey-Bass.

Seltzer, M., Klein, K., & Barg, D. (2001). *Securing your organization's future: A complete guide to fundraising strategies.* New York: The Foundation Center.

Shaw, S. C., & Taylor, M. (1995). *Reinventing fundraising: Realizing the potential of women's philanthropy.* San Francisco: Jossey-Bass.

Sommer, P. T. (1999). *Getting sent: A relational approach to support raising.* Downer's Grove, IL: InterVarsity Press.

Weinstein, S. (1998). *The complete guide to fund-raising management.* New York: John Wiley & Sons.

Fundraising Activities and Events

Amos, J. S. (1995). *Fundraising ideas: Over 225 money making events for community groups.* Jefferson, NC: McFarland & Co.

Brody, R. (1988). *Fund-raising events: Strategies and programs for success.* New York: Human Sciences Press.

Dove, K. E. (2000). *Conducting a successful capital campaign* (2nd ed). San Francisco: Jossey-Bass.

Freedman, H. A., & Feldman, K. (1998). *The business of special events: Fundraising strategies for changing times.* Sarasota, FL: Pineapple Press.

Kaitcher, C. R. (1996). *Raising big bucks: The complete guide to producing pledge-based special events.* New York: Bonus Books.

Kihlstedt, A., & Schwartz, C. P. (1997). *Capital campaigns: Strategies that work.* Gaithersburg, MD: Aspen.

Kuniholm, R. E. (1995). *The complete book of model fund-raising letters.* Englewood Cliffs, NJ: Prentice Hall.

Lindahl, W. E. (1992). *Strategic planning for fund raising: How to bring in more money using strategic resource allocation.* San Francisco: Jossey-Bass.

Lynn, D., & Lynn, K. (1996). *More great fundraising ideas for youth ministry: Easy-to-use money-makers that really work.* Grand Rapids, MI: Zondervan.

Nelson, D. T., & Schneiter, P. H. (1991). *Gifts-in-kind.* Rockville, MD: Fund Raising Institute.

Rice, J. A. (1997). *Let's party: How to plan special events and raise money in early childhood programs.* St. Paul, MN: Redleaf Press.

Stier, W. F. (1997). *More fantastic fundraisers for sport and recreation.* Champaign, IL: Human Kinetics.

Toler, S., & Towns, E. L. (2000). *Developing a giving church.* Kansas City, MO: Beacon Hill Press.

Warwick, M. (2000). *How to write successful fundraising letters.* San Francisco: Jossey-Bass.

Wendroff, A. L. (1999). *Special events: Proven strategies for nonprofit fund raising.* New York: John Wiley & Sons.

Williams, W., & Watson, C. E. (Eds.). (1994). *User-friendly fundraising: A step-by-step guide to profitable special events.* Alexander, NC: Creativity, Inc./Alexander Books.

Fundraising for Specific Occupational Settings

Bancel, M. (2000). *Fund raising for school staff.* San Francisco: Jossey-Bass.

Bauer, D. G. (1998). *The principal's guide to winning grants.* San Francisco: Jossey-Bass.

Bovich, E. H., & Bovich, J. P. (1998). *The art of fund-raising: What every health care trustee needs to know.* Chicago: American Hospital Association.

Callahan, K. L. (1997). *Effective church finances: A complete guide to budgeting, fund-raising, and setting and achieving financial goals.* San Francisco: Jossey-Bass.

Fitzpatrick, J. J., & Deller, S. S. (2000). *Fundraising for health and social service executives.* New York: Springer.

Holliman, G. N., & Holliman, B. L. (1997). *With generous hearts: How to raise capital funds for your church, church school, church agency, or regional church body.* Harrisburg, PA: Morehouse.

Hopkins, K. B., & Friedman, C. S. (1996). *Successful fundraising for arts and cultural organizations.* Westport, CT: Greenwood.

Lowenstein, R. L. (1997). *Pragmatic fund-raising for college administrators and development officers.* Gainesville, FL: University of Florida Press.

Steele, V., & Elder, S. D. (2000). *Becoming a fundraiser: The principles and practice of library development.* Washington DC: American Library Association.

Donor Empowerment and Development (Including Planned Giving)

Ashton, D. (1991). *The complete guide to planned giving.* Cambridge, MA: JLA.

Barrett, R. D., & Ware, M. E. (1997). *Planned giving essentials: A step by step guide to success.* Gaithersburg, MD: Aspen.

Campbell, B. (2000). *Listening to your donors.* San Francisco: Jossey-Bass.

Dillon, W. R. (1993). *People raising: A practical guide to raising support.* Westport, CT: Moody Press.

Jordan, R. R., Quynn, K. L., & Osteen, C. M. (1999). *Planned giving: Management, marketing, and the law.* New York: John Wiley & Sons.

Sturtevant, W. T. (1997). *The artful journey: Cultivating and soliciting the major gift.* New York: Bonus Books.

White, D. E. (1995). *The art of planned giving: Understanding donors and the culture of giving.* New York: John Wiley & Sons.

Williams, K. A. (1997). *Donor focused strategies for annual giving.* Gaithersburg, MD: Aspen.

C. Community Organization, Philanthropy, and Social Change

Philanthropy, Religion, Ethics, and the Law

Anderson, A., Burlingame, D. F., & Payton, R. L. (Eds.). (1996). *Ethics for fundraisers.* Bloomington, IN: Indiana University Press.

Arrossi, D., Satterthwaithe, D., Mitlin, J. E., Hardoy, F., & Bombarolo, R. (1994). *Funding community initiatives: The role of NGOs in the Third World.* London: United Nations Development Programme.

Brilliant, E. L. (1990). *The United Way.* New York: Columbia University Press.

Carson, E. D. (1989) *The charitable appeals fact book: How black and white Americans respond to different types of fund-raising efforts.* Washington, DC: Joint Center for Political and Economic Studies.

Elliott, D. (Ed.). (1995). *The ethics of asking: Dilemmas in higher education fund raising.* Baltimore: John Hopkins University Press.

Fischer, M. (2000). *Ethical decision making in fundraising.* New York: John Wiley & Sons.

Grace, K. S., & Wendroff, A. L. (2000). *High impact philanthropy: How donors, boards, and nonprofit organizations can transform communities.* New York: John Wiley & Sons.

Harris, T. (1999). *International fund raising for nonprofits: A country by country profile.* New York: John Wiley & Sons.

Hewa, S., & Hove, P. (1997). *Philanthropy in cultural context.* Lantham, MD: University Press of America.

Hodgkinson, V. A., Weitzman, M. S., & Kirsch, A. D. (1993). *From belief to commitment: The activities and finances of religious congregations in the United States.* Washington, DC: Independent Sector.

Hopkins, B. R. (1991). *The law of fund-raising.* New York: John Wiley & Sons.

Joseph, J. A. (1993). *Black philanthropy: The potential and limits of private generosity in a civil society.* Washington, DC: Association of Black Foundation Executives.

Kosmin, B., & Ritterband, P. (Eds.). (1991). *Contemporary Jewish philanthropy in America.* Savage, MD: Rowman & Littlefield.

Lichman, W. P., Katz, S. N., & Queen, E. L., II. (1998). *Philanthropy in the world's traditions.* Bloomington, IN: Indiana University Press.

Weisbrod, B. A., Cain, L., & Lama, C. L. (Eds.). (1998). *To profit or not to profit: The commercial transformation of the nonprofit sector.* New York: Cambridge University Press.

Wineburg, R. A. (2000). *A limited partnership: The politics of religion, welfare and social service.* New York: Columbia University Press.

Wuthnow, R., & Hodgkinson, V. A. (Eds.). (1990). *Faith and philanthropy in America: Exploring the role of religion in America's voluntary sector.* San Francisco: Jossey-Bass.

D. Partners in Development

America, R. F. (1995). *Philanthropy and economic development.* Westport, CT: Greenwood Press.

Brinkerhoff, P. F. (1996). *Financial empowerment: More money for more mission—An essential financial guide for not-for-profit organizations.* New York: John Wiley & Sons.

Cnaan, R. A. (1999). *The newer deal: Social work and religion in partnership.* New York: Columbia University Press.

Embley, L. L. (1992). *Doing well while doing good: The marketing link between business and nonprofit causes.* Englewood Cliffs, NJ: Prentice Hall.

Grace, K. S. (1997). *Beyond fundraising: New strategies for non-profit innovation and investment.* New York: John Wiley & Sons.

Himmelstein, J. (1997). *Looking good and doing good: Corporate philanthropy and corporate power.* Bloomington, IN: Indiana University Press.

Keegan, P. B. (1994). *Fundraising for non-profits: How to build a community partnership.* New York: HarperCollins.

Ostrander, S. A. (1997). *Money for change: Social movement philanthropy at Haymarket People's Fund.* Philadelphia: Temple University Press.

Ruskin, K. B., & Achilles, C. M. (1995). *Grantwriting, fundraising, and partnerships: Strategies that work.* Newbury Park, CA: Sage.

II. Start-Up List of Relevant Journals, Periodicals, and Directories

A. Journals and Periodicals

The Chronicle of Philanthropy is probably the single most comprehensive print source about trends in funding and philanthropy in the United States. However, one or more of the other items listed here may provide information more directly targeted to your work or organization. Some publish articles and summaries on the Web. Also, see Section III for a startup list of Web-based newsletters and relevant listservs.

Business and Society Review

Chicago Philanthropy Quarterly

*Chronicle of Philanthropy**

Currents (Council on Advancement and Support of Education [CASE])

Education Funding News

ERC [Ecumenical Resources Committee and Development Council] Newsbriefs

Federal Grants and Contracts Weekly

*Foundation News and Commentary**

Fund Raising Management Newsletter

Grant Advisor

Grants Magazine

Grantsmanship Center Magazine

Grassroots Fundraising Journal

Health Grants and Contracts Weekly

Minority Funding Report

Nonprofit Management and Leadership

Nonprofit and Public Sector Marketing

Nonprofit and Voluntary Sector Quarterly

*NonProfit Times**

Nonprofit World

*Philanthropy Journal**

Professional Fundraising

Public Economics

Religious Funding Monitor

Science

---

* Item with asterisks may also be found in part or in their entirety on the Web.

B. Directories

- Many public libraries, and all those affiliated with The Foundation Center, a national organization that collects, organizes, and communicates information about philanthropy in the United States, are likely to have one or more shelves set aside for a wide variety of sourcebooks that describe public and voluntary funding programs, associations, philanthropies, giving programs of corporations, and so forth. If your library does not, contact The Foundation Center (http:// fdncenter.org) to locate the nearest library with a collaborative grants collection. Be sure to look for the following two well-known documents about federal funding, plus your state's listing of grant and contract programs and procedures.
- The *Catalog of Domestic Federal Assistance* [*CDFA*], published by the U.S. Government Printing Office, Washington, DC 20407, is the most comprehensive single source of federal government funding programs. Formerly printed and distributed annually for free, it is now available electronically at http://www.cdfa.gov. Paper copies are available for a fee.
- The *Government Assistance Almanac,* written by Robert Dumouchel and published by OmniGraphics of Detroit, Michigan, reframes the content of the CDFA in a more accessible format.

Other directories from The Foundation Center and other publishers include the following:

Corporate Foundation Profiles

Corporate 500 Directory of Corporate Philanthropy

Foundation Directory

Guide to U.S. Foundations, Their Trustees, Officers and Donors

Matching Gift Details

National Director of Corporate Giving

Because of the difficulty and expense of updating these materials regularly, you may find them or similar information on the Web, often in Adobe or another downloadable format. In some cases, the information you are looking for may be available only on the Web.

III. Web-Based Resources

If you are new to the Web, you may want to begin by perusing one or more of the print sources listed here. They will lead you to government, corporate, and non-profit funding sites; instructions on proposal writing, budget design and grants management; matching services that link donors to organizations in need of funding or in-kind resources; electronic newsletters, and other services. If you are already familiar with the Web, you may find the Grants, Etc. website (http://www.ssw.umich.edu/grantsetc) to be a good place to start. Otherwise, locate and bookmark the sites you find most useful among those listed here.

A. Books on Using the Web for Raising Funds and Non-Cash Resources

Corson-Finnerty, A. D., & Blanchard, L. (1998). *Fundraising and friend-raising on the Web.* Chicago: American Library Association.

The Foundation Center. (2000). *The Foundation Center's guide to grantseeking on the Web.* New York: Author.

Johnston, M. W. (1998). *The fund raiser's guide to the Internet.* New York: John Wiley & Sons.

Peterson, S. (2000). *Grantwriter's Internet companion: A resource for educators and others seeking grants and funding.* Thousand Oaks, CA: Corwin Press.

B. Start-Up List of Internet Fundraising Resources

Government Information Sources

Catalog of Federal Domestic Assistance (http://www.gsa.gov/fdac/)

Federal Information Exchange (http://www.fie.com)

GrantsNet (http://www.os.dhhs.gov/progorg/grantsnet/)

NonProfit Gateway (http://www.nonprofit.gov/)

State Government Links (http://www.law.indiana.edu/law/v-lib/states.html)

Foundation Information Sources

Community Foundation Locator (http://www.cof.org/community/)

Community Foundations (http://fundsnetservices.com/commfoun.htm)

Council on Foundations (http://www.cof.org/)

The Foundation Center (http://fdncenter.org)

Foundations, Grants, and Trusts (http://people.delphi.com/mickjyoung/money.html)

Grantmaking Foundations (http://www.tgci.com/foundations/typefdn.htm)

Private Foundations in the United States (http://www.uwyo.edu/~prospect/found-us.html)

StateSearch (http://www.resources4evaluators.info/GovernmentsAgenciesFoundationsOrganizations.htm#Foundations)

Corporate Giving Sources

Corporate Giving (http://www.uwyo.edu/~prospect/corp-giv.html)

Corporate Grantmakers on the Internet (http://fdncenter.org/grantmaker/corp.html)

Directory of Corporate Community Involvement (charitynet.org/noframes/main.html)

Voluntary Sector Funding Sources

Catholic Charities USA (http://www.catholiccharitiesusa.org/)

Charities USA (http://www.charitiesusa.com/)

Independent Charities of America (http://www.independentcharities.org/)

Lions International (http://www.lions.org)

Mennonite Central Committee (http://www.mennonitecc.ca/mcc/index.html)

Nonprofit Sector Research Fund (http://www.aspeninst.org/dir/polpro/NSRF/NSRF1.html)

Presbyterian Church (U.S.A.) Foundation (http://www.fdn.pcusa.org/fdn/index.html)

United Jewish Appeal (http://www.uja.org/)

United Way of America (http://www.unitedway.org/)

How-To and Related Information Sites
Charitable Planning (http://www.netplanning.com/ch3.htm)

Funding Opportunities in the Behavioral and Social Sciences (http://cos.gdb.org/repos/fund/disc/behavioral.html)

Proposal Writing Short Course (http://fdncenter.org/fundproc/prop.html)

Social Statistics Briefing Room (http://www.whitehouse.gov/fsbr/ssbr.html)

Society for Nonprofit Organizations Funding Alert (http://danenet.wicip.org/snpo/funding.html)

Online Journals and Newsletters
Chronicle of Philanthropy (http://philanthropy.com)

Foundation News and Commentary (http://www.cof.org/fnc/fncindex.html)

FundRaiser Cyberzine (http://www.fundraiser.com)

Notes

1. Some tax-exempt gifts guarantee the donor an income for life, after which the corpus of the gift reverts to the recipient organization.

2. The premium may be provided in advance, as when a packet of wildflower seeds is included in a fundraising letter from an environmental group, or as an inducement to make a larger gift as when a public radio station offers a coffee mug in return for small donations, or access to a special event for those who make larger gifts. At some grassroots fundraising events, like community rummage sales or in thrift shops, the inexpensive purchase may be more motivating than the gift to charity.

3. For a general discussion of the professionalization process in occupations, see Lauffer, A., (1985), *Careers, colleagues, and conflicts: Understanding gender, race, and ethnicity in the workplace* (Chapter 4), Newbury Park, CA: Sage. For a discussion of professionalization in fundraising and philanthropy, see Burlingame, D. F., & Hulse, L. J. (Eds.), (1991), *Taking fund raising seriously: Advancing the profession and practice of raising money,* San Francisco: Jossey-Bass.

4. The best known of these programs is the Fundraising School, part of the Indiana Center on Philanthropy located cosponsored by Indiana University and Purdue University in Indianapolis. Others include: the Center for the Study of Philanthropy, Graduate Center, City University of New York; the Center for the Study of Voluntarism and Philanthropy, Duke University, Durham, NC; and the Institute for Nonprofit Organization Management at the University of California, San Francisco.

CHAPTER 33

Community-Based Research and Methods in Community Practice

Julian Chun-Chung Chow

Kelsey Crowe

I n recent years, community practice has generated a great amount of interest from social work scholars and practitioners. Broadly defined as actively engaging and working with people where they live, community practice has been recognized as a promising means for problem solving and capacity building at the local level (Weil, 1996).

One major component that characterizes this new form of practice is the call for better use of research to inform program and policy development (Coulton, 1995). However, despite the growing interest, the use of research in community practice has not received the same level of attention as the practice itself. In addition, there seems to be confusion regarding how research should be integrated into community practice. Therefore, the questions of what community-based research is and how to use it to guide practice must be better addressed.

Community-based research is as much about communities as it is for them. Unlike other forms of social science research that develop abstract theory or rigorously formulate cause-and-effect relationships for hypothesis-testing purposes, research that is community based aims to apply methods of data collection and analysis to generate findings that have highly practical results. The audience for such findings is typically made up of community members, practitioners, and local policymakers who wish to design an intervention that benefits a geography- or population-based community (Kingsley, McNeely, & Gibson, 1997). Typically, the goal of community-based research at this level of practice is to define problems and needs in a community and, increasingly, to define local resources for managing such needs (Tatian, 2000).

Traditional research approaches can be differentiated by methodological orientation. For example, quantitative data can be analyzed using simple descriptive or more complicated inferential statistical techniques, whereas technically sophisticated qualitative research analyses use theory-building approaches such as symbolic interactionism or grounded theory. Each approach to research is rooted in epistemological preferences about how we know what we know, the theoretical justifications of which can spiral upward toward even more abstract levels. Because community-based research is less concerned with epistemological differences than practical relevance, its objective is not only to produce and argue for the most "accurate" form of truth, but to ensure that whatever truth is sought is important to community members and policymakers who will organize around it. This practical objective of community-based research thus makes common distinctions of quantitative versus qualitative methods of data collection less relevant than for other forms of research overview.

We argue that a more relevant framework for comprehending community-based research is one that locates research methods within their practice objective. In community practice, such objectives vary widely. Based on the work of Chaskin, Venkatsh, Vidal, and Brown (2001), we identify three primary objectives of community practice that work to improve the lives of community members. Each of these practice objectives shapes the research question as well as the researcher's approach to data collection. This chapter first describes these three overall objectives in community work. It then describes various common sources of data that can be used across almost all three functions of community work, depending on suitability. Finally, it contextualizes methods of data collection and practical data analysis by outlining various uses for data and analysis that depend on the objective of practice.

Levels of Community Capacity-Building

Definitions of *community capacity* and *community development* abound, and creating other versions is not the thrust of this chapter. However, we do suggest an approach to looking at community capacity formulated by Chaskin and colleagues (2001) that helps identify functions of community practice, and corresponding research needs. In *Building Community Capacity,* Chaskin and his colleagues described community capacity as occurring on three levels: the realms of organizations, social networks, and individual leadership.

These realms benefit community life in somewhat different but highly inter-related ways. Communities with high organizational capacity are able to channel and distribute external resources to individual community members. Communities with high social networks share resources like information and equipment (Chaskin et al., 2001). Communities with strong individual leadership have the verbal, analytical, or charismatic ability to articulate their needs and access external change agents to get such needs met (Rubin & Rubin, 2000). Community practice taps into and seeks to improve at least one of these realms of community life. Community practice can mean improving access to local organizations providing important services, increasing social networks among organizational providers and community members to increase efficiency and enhance political leverage, or building the leadership skills of local community members who will advocate for culturally appropriate interventions. Community-based research is used to help practitioners achieve these overarching community-building capacity goals.

Community-based research assists organizational development in many ways. It can help determine what organizations are important to a community (Kingsley, 1999), what organizations in a community are working well (Rossi & Freeman, 1982), and what organizations are still needed in an area (Burch, 1996). Community-based research aids in building social networks by evaluating the progress of a collaborative partnership (Weiss, 1995), identifying community resources (Kingsley, McNeely, & Gibson, 1997), and assessing a community's likelihood of cooperative ties (Eng & Parker, 1994). At the individual level of community change, community-based research is called on to empower residents to lead as they work closely with researchers in all aspects of research (Minkler & Wallerstein, 1997; see also Pennell, Noponen, & Weil, Chapter 34, this volume).

Community-based researchers can select from among at least eight kinds of data collection methods for analyzing findings that are important to community members and community change participants. These findings can be relevant for change at the level of organizational and leadership development as well as for building social networks among important local and external actors.

Methods in Community-Based Research

Community-based research draws from the same toolbox of data collection methods as other types of research. These data sources can be secondary, in which case data have already been collected and the work of the community-based researcher is predominantly that of analysis. In other instances, new data may be required to better inform a particular practice objective, in which case primary data collection becomes part and parcel of community-based research. In many instances, researchers rely on a combination of primary and secondary data to perform a comprehensive community-based analysis. As already mentioned, the overarching goal of such analysis is to determine degrees of need, and in some cases, supplies of resources, within a community.

Examples of secondary data that help to inform researchers on community needs are census data and administrative data. The U.S. Bureau of the Census conducts a national census every 10 years. It enumerates the entire population and collects extensive demographic information about people living throughout the nation. Basic characteristics—such as age, sex, and race/ethnicity—about all individuals are gathered using the short form, and one of every six households is also surveyed about other characteristics—such as education level, income, and employment—using the long form. Basic census data from the short form can be analyzed at the small geographic block level, which corresponds to roughly one city block. More detailed information derived from the long form can describe block groups, which are a cluster of blocks (Tatian, 2000). The census provides information that can be used as a baseline for anticipating community-level needs, such as the percentage of non–English speakers or children younger than 5 years of age in a geographic region.

Administrative data is another source of secondary data used to determine the extent of need or problems in a community and to understand the level at which institutions are able to respond to such needs. Numerous county and municipal government agencies maintain records on community residents. Examples include local school districts, public assistance offices, child welfare offices, public health agencies, and police departments (Coulton, Nelson, & Tatian, 1997). From these sources, researchers can begin to understand community issues concerning children's academic attainment, the extent and location of local crimes, rates of child abuse reports per capita, and the number of teen pregnancies per adolescent, to cite a few examples. Such data can also serve as a proxy for other kinds of information, such as rates of disaffected youth who are committing crimes or the degree to which young people trade in career goals for early pregnancy. Such knowledge can assist in the determination of a community's possible service and economic needs. Data such as these are usually available at the zip code level and thus do not give as close an examination of community dynamics as can census data. However, administrative data are increasingly becoming available at a more local level as community-based organizations such as local Boys and Girls Clubs and neighborhood-based drug treatment programs are expected to maintain client records to demonstrate program effectiveness (Tatian, 2000). These records can assist with determining needs at a local level while also helping community researchers gauge how well institutions and organizations are responding to community members (see Hillier & Culhane, Chapter 36, this volume).

Census and administrative data in and of themselves are powerful tools for understanding community-level needs. The capacity for such data to inform researchers is greatly enhanced, however, with the development of computer software such as geographic information systems (GIS). GIS is a computer technology that allows researchers to identify spatial patterns among problems and resources. For example, the San Francisco Department of Health has used GIS with its administrative data to demonstrate that the majority of people in San Francisco who have HIV/AIDS are concentrated in two of the city's neighborhoods (Hardina, 2002). Such information suggests where to target AIDS prevention and other related services.

GIS relies on geocoding of administrative data and census data that is then mapped into spatial illustrations. These maps can be simple illustrations exhibiting only a single layer of information, such as the concentration of children younger than 5 years of age living in poverty within a particular radius. With more sophisticated software and a technologically sophisticated user, GIS can be used to produce analytical maps. These maps layer different kinds of information over each other. For example, the number of vacant buildings in an area can be overlaid with data on crime locations to illustrate possible relationships between land-use patterns and criminal activity (LisC and Policy Link, 2002).

Secondary data sources are useful for establishing the baseline of a problem or need, but they do little to reveal what people think about such problems or why such problems exist at all. Finding answers to these questions requires researchers to engage in primary data collection through one or more of the following methods: surveys, focus groups, key informant interviews, observation, and community forums. Using these methods, researchers can learn more about people's perceptions about a problem or pursue an in-depth exploration into the possible cause of a problem. As discussed previously, community-based research is not only about producing findings, but also about producing findings that matter to potential community actors. Consequently, primary data collection that involves assessing community members' opinions, ideas, and experiences with a particular problem can be a crucial aspect of conducting research that can be applied in efforts to solve community problems.

Surveys are a common method of primary data collection in community-based research. Survey data are used to gauge people's attitudes or beliefs about an issue. Because survey data are intended to be representative of a population, surveys should be widely distributed. They should be clear, easy to complete, and consist primarily of closed-ended questions to allow for administration by mail, over the telephone, door-to-door, or face-to-face (Dillman, 1978). The nature of such closed-ended questions means the researcher knows in advance what kind of answers he or she wants (Converse & Presser, 1986).

Focus groups, which are moderated discussions among people who share a common characteristic, are another method of primary data collection. Examples of common characteristics include participating in the same program, living in the same neighborhood, or sharing a similar circumstance, such as caring for an older parent. Questions typically asked in focus groups include: "What issues are most important?" and "How do feelings about this issue affect the problem of interest?" (Greenbaum, 1998). Focus groups are especially helpful for getting information about why or how something happens, rather than a simple list of what kinds of problems exist in a community (Hardina, 2002). Although focus group data cannot claim to be representative of a population, they provide an in-depth understanding of a population's attitudes, opinions, and concerns (Krueger, 1994).

Another source of primary data is the key informant interview. The key informant interview is an efficient and effective method for finding out about systemic and political barriers to solving community problems (Crabtree & Miller, 1995). Key informants are intentionally sampled from a select group of individuals who have expertise in a given area or who have formal or informal influence in an issue or with a population of interest. Examples of key informants include policymakers, staff members of community-based organizations, gang leaders, and well-respected members of a population of interest. Questions typically asked of key informants include, "What are the main obstacles to reducing this problem?" and "Which interventions are the most effective and why?" (Tatian, 2000).

Yet another method of primary data collection is observation. Observation is the most "naturalistic" method of data collection, because it studies people in their natural environments with minimal direction from or interference by the researcher (Crabtree & Miller, 1995). By using observation, researchers can record dynamics embedded in institutional forms, be they interpersonal relationships, relationships to space, or concrete institutions such as a public assistance office (Lofland & Lofland, 1995). Analysis of observational data can reveal subconscious experiences that subjects would not be able to account for in an interview or survey. This kind of data, although commonly used for theory-building research, is also useful in community-based research, in which questions about behavior such as client treatment, teenage loitering habits after school, or interactions between and among collaborating agencies, for example, can be examined as they occur naturally (Fortune & Reid, 1999).

A final method of information gathering described here is the community forum, perhaps the only method among all the rest that is particularly germane to community-based research. Community forums are public meetings in which information is exchanged and debated and strategies can be considered and critiqued. A community forum can be used to educate the public about an issue and to learn what the public thinks about an issue. Typically, forums are organized for the purpose of introducing research findings, proposing ideas for solving problems, and debating issues. Participants in a forum can include everyone who responds to announcements, be composed of members of the entire community, or be restricted to a limited number of individuals. The format usually consists of a formal presentation with a panel of experts and breakout sessions for attendees to reflect and debate about what has been presented and to add new ideas or concerns (Johnson, Grossman, & Cassidy, 1996; Witken & Altschuld, 1995).

In sum, researchers rely on both primary and secondary data to understand more about a community's needs and resources. The scope of need and the resources to be examined will depend on the overall target of community practice. Practitioners interested in organizational development may want to know what gaps in services exist in their communities, whereas those interested in enhancing political and economic leverage may wish to develop social networks between and among community, organizational, and institutional actors (Gray & Wood, 1991). Still other practitioners may want to develop grassroots leadership by focusing their efforts on individual capacity building. Methods of data collection and analysis in community-based research can help practitioners to achieve any one of these goals.

Organizational Development

Organizations are a vital resource in community life. They provide services such as education, counseling, recreation, cultural activities, and information about resources and referrals (Ferguson & Stoutland, 1999). Community practice is often concerned with the following kinds of organizational development questions: What kinds of programs does this community need? How well are existing programs being implemented? What kind of impact do programs have? (Rossi & Freeman, 1982). As we discussed earlier, community-based researchers can rely on a variety of data collection methods to answer these questions.

A community's need for organizational services can be examined by using at least one of the following kinds of data: administrative data, census data, survey data, focus group data, and key informant data. Administrative data reveal patterns of program and service utilization (Fortune & Reid, 1999) and demand for services (Burch, 1996). Program records, for example, can demonstrate demand for services by comparing the number of people who have requested a service with the number of people who received that service and why; common barriers include inability to pay, language problems, and staff shortages. Demand for service is a common indicator of an emerging community problem and documents need for services such as emergency shelters, soup kitchens, and housing (Hardina, 2002). By the same token, administrative data can reveal disinterest in a program if participants are not using the services regularly, if retention rates are low, or if few people are using services relative to the expected demand (Chambers, Wedel, & Rodwell, 1992).

Administrative agency data combined with census data also help government, nonprofit, and philanthropic foundations determine the need for more or different programs. Data on the incidence and prevalence of problems such as arrests, AIDS, or evictions per capita, for example, can provide insight into what programs might be helpful in a particular geographic area.

GIS mapping of administrative and census data can be especially powerful for illustrating gaps in services. In Cleveland, Ohio, a data intermediary group called CAN DO (Cleveland Area Network for Data and Organizing) examined characteristics of different cohorts of county public assistance recipients. Using mapping software, CAN DO easily determined that public assistance recipients vulnerable to time limits were concentrated in a few pockets of the city. At the same time, census data combined with other economic data revealed that most jobs were located outside these neighborhoods, thus making the need for auxiliary employment services such as transportation more clear to the local legislature (Tatian, 2000).

Census data analyzed by GIS also help existing programs to examine their degree of program coverage. Community-based researchers for Boys and Girls Clubs in Milwaukee, for example, geocoded client records to identify the range and degree of penetration that the organization had achieved in the surrounding neighborhood. By using ratios between the number of children in a census block area and the number of program participants in that block area, club officials were able to identify where outreach was weak and target their efforts appropriately (Urban Institute, 1999).

Community needs assessment surveys are another method for determining service needs for organizational development purposes. Ideally, survey findings are representative of a particular geographic or social population. The realities of high cost and low return rates, however, mean that community surveys are more likely than not to be statistically unrepresentative (Fortune & Reid, 1999). By their very nature, surveys rely on preconceived notions about what problems exist or what services are needed in a community. These concerns are listed as pre-established categories that are selected by community members. Although this feature of survey data is often criticized for its inherent bias in framing potential problems and service needs (Rubin & Babbie, 1997), results can still be surprising. Fortune and Reid (1999) described a 1996 study by Solomon and Mill in which HIV/AIDS researchers unexpectedly identified AIDS as a low-priority concern among mothers in a housing project. More significant to these women were issues concerning their children and crime. HIV/AIDS program planners thus redirected their program strategies to incorporate these concerns. In this instance, because the survey data in that study were fairly representative, program planners could be quite confident in their choice to refocus their program efforts.

In addition to identifying needs for more services, community-based practitioners are interested in how well an organization's existing programs and services are being implemented. This type of question often leads what is called a *process evaluation* (Steckler & Linnan, 2002). A process evaluation uses primary data collection methods such as key informant interviews, focus groups, and observation with clients, members, staff, and volunteers to examine how an organization is functioning. Interviewers ask for perspectives and opinions on aspects of organizational functioning as well as on how the organization can improve.

In addition to questions of service demand, coverage, and quality, organizations and their funders want summative evaluations to determine program outcomes (Rossi & Freeman, 1982). Answering these cause-and-effect questions with the greatest degree of accuracy requires sophisticated research designs using experimental and control groups (Chambers et al., 1992). Such research is costly and labor-intensive, however, so neighborhood-based programs often employ simpler, less statistically rigorous evaluation designs (Hardina, 2002). These simpler evaluation designs may be quasi-experimental, in which case the researcher exerts a degree of control over the sample through matching program participants according to variables that might influence the outcome, such as gender, age, or race. Effects of a program are often measured using pretests and posttests to document changes in behavior or attitudes based on the program's objectives. Other methods for summative evaluations rely on focus groups and key informant interviews with clients and possibly their immediate family to ask about changes in the nature or severity of the client's problems and other life issues as a result of their participation in the program (Fortune & Reid, 1999).

Whether aiming to determine service need, program quality, or program effects, community practitioners are engaged in a number of aspects of organizational development that lead to improved conditions for community members. Community-based researchers employ a range of methods for helping practitioners meet their goal of improving service delivery to the community through analyses and recommendations for appropriate organizational development.

Building Formal Social Networks

Community practitioners build neighborhood-based social networks that enhance a community's political, organizational, and financial capacity to implement a community-driven level of change (Fauri & Wernet, 2003). Typically, social network building takes the form of collaborative partnerships among organizations, city institutions, and residents (McKnight & Kretzman, 1993; Kingsley, McNeely, & Gibson, 1997). Funders and organizers of such partnerships may want community-based research to look into a community's capacity to work together (Cottrell, 1976; Eng & Parker, 1994). In other instances, sponsors of community building initiatives want to evaluate the process or impact of their collaborative building efforts (Rossi, 1999; Weiss, 1995). In helping practitioners pursue a project of community building, community-based researchers use a variety of primary data sources to gauge a community's capacity to engage in purposive relationships. In measuring this kind of community capacity, the unit of analysis shifts from the organization to the community (Eng & Parker, 1994).

A few assessment tools take a fairly calibrated look at what constitutes community capacity. These community capacity or civic infrastructure measurement tools are based on theoretically and, increasingly, empirically based assumptions about community conditions that make collaborations more or less productive. These conditions include community leaders' abilities to dialogue and see both sides of an issue, competently follow through on tasks, and have a high degree of trust in each other, as well as having a history of civic participation (Cottrell, 1976; Eng & Parker, 1994; Goodman et al., 1998; Gray & Wood, 1992; Kingsley, McNeely, & Gibson, 1997).

Surveys that investigate these kinds of capacities are often distributed to local residents or key participants in community life, including local, organizational, and institutional leaders. Eng and Parker (1994) developed a Likert-type survey measuring community competence that is administered to key community informants. Six dimensions of community work are included

1. level of participation among community members,

2. commitment of community members to their community as evidenced by volunteerism and community upkeep,

3. ability to manage conflict,

4. management of relations with the wider society,

5. ability to articulate one's demands, and

6. self-awareness and clarity of situational definitions (Eng & Parker, 1994).

Results are intended to help potential community-building participants anticipate strengths and weaknesses in their ability to collaborate as well as provide a baseline for measuring improvement in these areas.

Another highly publicized tool for assessing community capacity is called *asset mapping* (McKnight & Kretzman, 1993). Asset mapping begins from a perspective that communities are replete with strengths and talents that have long been overlooked by outsiders such as urban developers and business groups. This perspective of community strengths shifts much of the work done with community assessments away from needs and problems and toward strengths and resources. Asset mapping is an attempt to catalogue these strengths by distributing surveys that ask residents to describe their talents, interests, and professional skills that can be harnessed in a community-driven change effort. Additional assets such as citizen associations, through which local people come together to pursue common goals, and institutions present in the community, such as local government, hospitals, education, and human service agencies, are also inventoried as local resources. Surveys that measure community capacity or community resources are interested in understanding and thus contributing to the potential of building community-based social networks.

A second function of community-based research is to evaluate the implementation of a community-building initiative. Questions commonly asked in such evaluations concern the quality of collaborative leadership, the level of trust among participants, faith in partners' competence, the ability to complete tasks, shared interest in the mission, and the extent of full participation in decision making (Fawcett et al., n.d.).

Evaluations of this kind rely on a variety of methods. Observation of collaborative meetings, town hall meetings, and staff meetings reveal interpersonal working styles. Focus groups and interviews with collaborative participants, organizational partners, and neighborhood residents can reveal problems, challenges, and successes in collaborative work. Administrative records such as sign-in sheets for meetings and workshops, as well as points of contact for outreach, demonstrate the initiatives' efforts to penetrate the neighborhood and build community.

A large-scale study conducted by Chaskin, Chipenda-Dansokho, and Toler (2000) applied a wide range of methods to evaluate the implementation of the Ford Foundation's National Family Initiative. Relying on interviews with collaborative participants, organizational and institutional partners, and collaborative fiscal sponsors, as well as observational data from meetings and survey data from neighborhood residents and collaborative participants, the Chapin Hall Center was able to assess several aspects of the community-building initiative. The overall findings of the evaluation suggested numerous challenges, such as mistrust, insufficient support from resource providers, and a lack of clear goals. The results of this kind of process evaluation can help future funders and designers of community-building initiatives avoid similar pitfalls.

In addition to learning about the feasibility and quality of implementation of a community-building effort, sponsors and participants in such efforts want to know if collaborative work has any real effect on the community. Determining the effect or outcome of a community-wide initiative is a daunting task. As Connell, Kubisch, Schorr, and Weiss (1995) described, "CCIs [comprehensive community initiatives] are operating at so many levels (individuals, family, community, institutional, and system) and across so many sectors that the task of defining outcomes that can show whether the initiatives are working has become formidable" (p. 13). Outcome measurement is one of the most difficult tasks for a community researcher. Ideally, researchers would be able to use sophisticated research designs and employ sufficient controls over their experiments to draw tentative conclusions about the causes of community problems and effects of interventions in a quasiexperimental research model. As already mentioned, however, such procedures are difficult to implement even at the organizational level. At the community level, exerting experimental controls is all but impossible.

Communities vary in demographics, spatial patterns, and sociopolitical landscapes in known and unknown ways. Consequently, one cannot establish a "control group" or counterfactual to establish what would have happened in the community had a program not been there (Rossi, 1999). Moreover, the goals of a community initiative are often too numerous to measure. Examples range from providing more child care, to reducing teen violence, to increasing voter registration.

In an attempt to quantify results of such large-scale efforts, evaluators and practitioners have fashioned a method for evaluating community initiatives called a *theory of change approach*, which breaks down outcome evaluations into building blocks of success. Under the theory of change approach to evaluating community initiatives, assumptions behind what constitutes an effective intervention are made explicit and are tested. For example, if a community defines teenage violence as a primary problem and increasing after-school programs as its best solution, then the theory of change approach to evaluation will measure the extent to which a reduction in teenage violence is brought about by the specified intervention (Weiss, 1995). The success of this intervention is measured not once but over a series of stages. These stages of goal attainment are identified by community stakeholders and typically conceived as performance measures or intermediate goals (Rossi, 1999). These intermediate goals serve as building blocks toward the desired outcome. Using the same example of teenage violence and after-school programs, evaluators may work with stakeholders to craft intermediate goals such as increasing program enrollment, reducing peer-on-peer fighting among teens in the program, and creating an increased interest in school as steps toward their desired goal of reduced teen violence. Obtaining information regarding these intermediate goals may require a combination of administrative data and other data from interviews, observation, and surveys.

A theory of change approach to evaluating community initiatives shares similar principles with another community-building form of community-based research: the development of social indicators. Social indicators are a useful mechanism for facilitating discussion and focusing action by a range of community representatives around a particular goal. Social indicators are usually statistical representations or proxies of problems that interested stakeholders are concerned about changing. Social indicators can represent macro issues, such as the nation's economic health using the gross domestic product, or more local issues, such as the percentage of fifth graders in a community who are reading at or above the state average reading level (Hardina, 2002; see also Estes, Chapter 28, this volume).

Community-based researchers can work with community stakeholders such as residents, local policymakers, and organizational leaders to create social indicators that will mobilize these stakeholders to change their underlying conditions. Establishing the right indicator is a fairly technical process that requires experience and knowledge about what kinds of indicators can be measured over time, how they can be reliably measured (for example, using rates and percentages rather than absolute values), whether data are available, and which kinds of indicators are valid proxies for the issues being addressed (Meadows, 1998).

Community-based researchers can draw on any number of research methods to help in the goal of building social networks in communities. Researchers can use their measurement skills to help community stakeholders establish social indicators that bring about cooperation and meaningful results. They can use primary data collection methods such as observation, interviewing, and surveys to examine community-building processes for their successes and challenges and help community builders explore the feasibility of establishing cooperative social networks.

Developing Local Leadership

Local leaders are instrumental in organizing cultural events, spreading the word about community issues, and representing community interests through public hearings, tenant associations, and local crime watch groups. More formal leadership also exists at the community level and consists of religious clergy, local merchant representatives, or a councilperson.

Community-based researchers may be asked by a sponsoring body to further develop local leadership capacity, especially in economically marginalized communities whose members are marginalized from civil society and have little experience in using group processes to define and defend their interests (Freire, 1970/1998). Examples of leadership-building opportunities include development of resident councils in a public housing project, developing advocacy skills among members of a community affected by toxic wastes, or creating action groups among recipients of public assistance in a local neighborhood.

In building local leadership capacity, community practitioners work not just to understand a problem but also to help residents acquire skills that will enable them to understand the problem themselves and educate others about it. Community-based researchers can assist in this process by applying an approach known as *participatory research* or *action research*. This approach is based on the premise that "information is needed for change, and . . . for empowerment" (Minkler & Wallerstein, 1997, p. 36). The empowering results are achieved through strong collaboration between the researcher and community residents on all aspects of research design. This can include formulating the research question, developing procedures for data collection, and analyzing the results (Minkler & Wallerstein, 1997).

In participatory research, the required skills of the researcher expand in number to include interpersonal communication skills and cultural sensitivity in working with socioeconomically marginalized groups (Stoecker, 1999). For example, community-based researchers may work very closely with youth, who traditionally are not key architects in community-building initiatives. To guide the youth toward an understanding of basic research principles and skills, researchers must be attuned and responsive to what the young people are communicating and feel comfortable with different styles of communication and work patterns.

Researchers work with community members to enhance their interpersonal and technical skills and to build their understanding of research. These skills are applied toward the same purpose as other functions of community-based research—to get an assessment of needs and resources. Community-based researchers can work with community members to formulate research questions that are important to them, craft research designs, design and conduct interviews or surveys, and do "windshield tours" of a neighborhood to document obvious problems, such as broken streetlights or unsupervised children (Rubin & Rubin, 2000; Whyte, 1991).

A fairly straightforward and common data collection method for assessing needs and strengths in participatory research is called *mapping*. First designed for use in developing countries where there is often weak administrative data and low technological capacity, mapping is a visual exercise that asks people to map out community resources, needs, and dynamics (Whyte, 1991). Mapping is a highly tangible method of data collection that also permits community members to work together. For example, community members can map the composition of different households to enumerate the different age groups in a village, document how land-use and facility-use patterns differ by gender, or examine changes in their local landscape over time that might be related to social and environmental conditions (Narayan, 1996).

In the West, technological software is available to replicate a similar process. However, not all important community data are available online, and software does not always allow for analysis of the findings. One example of mapping in the United States is a participatory action research project called the Youth Mapping Project based out of the Academy of Educational Development (AED). Having been implemented in cities across the country, the youth mapping project asks youth to inquire after "places to go and things to do" in the neighborhood as a way of diagnosing community resources. After the young people tour and map their resources, they analyze their findings based on the following criteria: (a) the exact nature of the resources that are available to young people in their community; (b) where, how, when, and for whom resources are available; (c) which types of resources appear to be missing, inadequately available, inaccessible, or poorly provided; and (d) which parts of the community are resource poor

(AED, n.d.). Through this experience, youth develop analytic, educational, and leadership skills as they share information about needed resources.

Despite the greater sophistication required to produce GIS mapping, advances in technology have made hardware and software more affordable and more available in low-income neighborhoods in the United States. Many neighborhood organizations, libraries, and even some homes have access to this powerful computer technology. And with the amount of administrative and census data that are available online, GIS is becoming a highly effective way of "democratizing" information (Kingsley, McNeely, & Gibson, 1997).

Community-based researchers interested in building local leadership capacity can train community members to use GIS software so they can independently procure information as needed. One example of a successful community-led GIS project occurred with the help of a community-based church organization in Camden, New Jersey. Community leaders there believed that the growing number of abandoned and dilapidated units in their neighborhood was leading to increased crime rates. Training in GIS allowed these residents to present to the media and local politicians a visually compelling demonstration that blocks with more vacant units did indeed have more crime (Kingsley, Coulton, Barndt, Sawicki, & Tatian, 1997).

With building individual and group leadership as the goal of community practice, participatory action research can be a valuable tool for empowerment. By participating in their own fact finding, skill building, and overall learning, community residents become more confident about their worldview and are in a better position to advocate for the needs of their community. Community-based researchers draw from the same set of data collection methods as in other forms of research, be it surveys, interviews, or GIS with its access to administrative and census data. These same researchers also draw from an additional set of skills concerning the formation of respectful interpersonal relationships that facilitate the transfer of skills and knowledge between the researcher and the community members.

The Role of the Researcher

Community-based research relies on the same set of technical skills as other forms of research. Unlike other research, however, community-based research aims to produce findings that are practically relevant to community members, local political actors, and funders. Because the interest of community practice is to enhance community functioning, most community-based research pertains to designing interventions based on community identified needs and resources.

Some aspects of community research require more direct contact with local community members than do others (Marti-Costa & Serrano-Garcia, as cited in Hancock & Minkler, 1997). The amount of direct contact the researcher has with the community affects his or her role. On one extreme, the researcher barely works at all with the community, applying what Marti-Costa and Serrano-Garcia describe as *minimal contact methods.* Those conducting research about communities can rely on secondary data sources to extrapolate any number of "needs-based" conditions such as rates of poverty, language barriers, and early pregnancies, to name but a few examples. Such data are available online or through administrative agencies, though often those who collect these data may have little or no knowledge of or interest in the community. Typically, this focus would be designated as research on communities, rather than as community-based research.

On the other extreme, some researchers have extensive amounts of contact with community members, relying on what Marti-Costa (as cited in Hancock & Minkler, 1997) describes as *interactive contact methods*. The highest level of contact occurs in conducting participatory action research, when community members and researchers engage in a time-intensive process of collaboration over research design, implementation, and analysis. Other examples of interactive contact methods include focus groups, key informant interviews, and door-to-door surveys.

If sponsors of a community research project are primarily interested in developing local leadership, then community-based researchers should expect to select research methods that are appropriate to the time commitment of the group. Groups with little time may benefit from applying simpler methods such as mapping and windshield tours through a community to document its resources and attain a rough sense of needs. Individuals with more time and more sophisticated skills sets may wish to learn to use GIS software and conduct in-depth interviews.

If the sponsors of community research are interested primarily in getting a fairly accurate estimate of the need for services and have no time or interest in leadership development, then the community-based researcher can expect to draw from a wider array of methods that are most appropriate for answering their questions. This may mean relying more on administrative and census data and less on skill-transfer activities such as mapping.

Community-based researchers are directed in their choice of methods by the function of practice that brings them to the project. Minimal contact methods and interactive contact methods can also be categorized in epistemological terms as quantitative versus qualitative approaches to research. Quantitative data are found in administrative or census data sources, whereas qualitative data are retrieved through focus groups, interviews, and observation. As this chapter demonstrates, all levels of community practice can benefit from both kinds of data sources and analysis. Individual leaders can benefit from learning to retrieve secondary sources, and community needs assessments are often better informed and more likely to propel action when supplemented with primary data that are rooted in the particular dynamics of the community or organization being studied. What is of primary importance for the community-based researcher when crafting a research design and selecting research methods is not the epistemological concerns shared by the profession of research at large, but rather the function of community practice that is being served.

References

Academy for Education Development Center for Youth Development and Policy Research. (n.d.). *Mapping America: A curriculum for community YouthMapping.* Retrieved June 23, 2003, from www.communityyouthmapping.org/Youth/.

Burch, H. (1996). *Basic social policy and planning.* New York: Haworth.

Chambers, D., Wedel, K., & Rodwell, M. (1992). *Evaluating social programs.* Boston: Allyn & Bacon.

Chaskin, R., Chipenda-Dansokho, S., & Toler, A. (2000). *Moving beyond the neighborhood and family initiative: The final phase and lessons learned.* Retrieved June 15, 2003, from Chapin Hall Center for Children Web site, http://www.chapinhall.org/ProjectsGuide/

action.lasso?-database=publications&-layout=allfields&-response=publication_detail.html&-op='eq'&publication_id='CB-29'&-search.

Chaskin, R., Venkatsh, S., Vidal, A., & Brown, P. (2001). *Building community capacity.* New York: Aldine de Gruyter.

Connell, J. P., Kubisch, A. C., Schorr, L. B., & Weiss, C. H. (1995). *New approaches to evaluating community initiatives. Vol. 1: Concepts, methods, and contexts.* Washington, DC: Aspen Institute.

Converse, J. M., & Presser, J. (1986). *Survey questions: Handcrafting the standardized questionnaire. Quantitative applications in the social sciences series.* Newbury Park, CA: Sage.

Cottrell, L. S. (1976). The competent community. In B. H. Kaplan, R. N. Wilson, & A. H. Lighton (Eds.), *Further explorations in social psychiatry* (pp. 195–209). New York: Basic Books.

Coulton, C. J. (1995). Poverty, work, and community: A research agenda for an era of diminishing federal responsibility. *Social Work, 41,* 509–519.

Coulton, C. J., Nelson, L., & Tatian, P. (1997). *Catalog of administrative data sources: For neighborhood indicator systems.* Retrieved April 18, 2003, from the Urban Institute's National Neighborhood Indicators Partnership Web site, www.urban.org/nnip/pdf/catalog.pdf.

Crabtree, B. F., & Miller, W. L. (1995). *Doing qualitative research* (2nd ed.). Thousand Oaks, CA: Sage.

Dillman, D. A. (1978). *Mail and telephone surveys.* New York: John Wiley & Sons.

Eng, E., & Parker, E. (1994). Measuring community competency and the Mississippi Delta: Interface between program evaluation and empowerment. *Health Education Quarterly, 21,* 199–220.

Fauri, D. P., & Wernet, S. P. (Eds). (2003). *Cases in macro social work practice* (2nd ed.). Boston: Allyn & Bacon.

Fawcett, S. B., Paine-Andrews, A., Francisco, V. T., Schultz, J., Rishter, K. P., Patton, J. B., et al. (n.d.). *Our evaluation model: Evaluating comprehensive community initiatives.* Retrieved June 25, 2003, from the University of Kansas Web site, http://ctb.lsi.ukans.edu/tools/EN/sub_section_main_1007.htm.

Ferguson, R. R., & Stoutland, S. E. (1999). Reconceiving the community development field. In R. R. Ferguson & W. T. Dickens (Eds.), *Urban problems and community development* (pp. 33–75). Washington, DC: Brookings Institution Press.

Fortune, A. E., & Reid, W. J. (1999). *Research in social work* (3rd ed.). New York: Columbia University Press.

Freire, P. (1998). *Pedagogy of the oppressed* (Myra Bergman Ramos, Trans.). New York: Continuum. (Original work published 1970)

Goodman, R. M., Speers, M. A., McLeroy, K., Fawcett, S., Kegler, M., Parker, E., et al. (1998). Identifying and defining the dimensions of community capacity to provide a basis for measurement. *Health Education and Behavior, 25,* 259–278.

Gray, B., & Wood, D. (1991). Collaborative alliances: Moving from practice to theory. *Journal of Applied Behavioral Science, 27*(1), 3–22.

Greenbaum, T. (1998). *The handbook for focus group research.* Thousand Oaks, CA: Sage.

Hancock, T., & Minkler, M. (1997). Community health assessment or healthy community assessment. In M. Minkler (Ed.), *Community organizing and community building for health* (pp. 139–156). New Brunswick, NJ: Rutgers University Press.

Hardina, D. (2002). *Analytical skills for community organization practice.* New York: Columbia University Press.

Johnson, K., Grossman, W., & Cassidy, A. (Eds.). (1996). *Collaborating to improve community health: Workbook and guide to best practices in creating healthier communities and populations.* San Francisco: Jossey-Bass.

Kingsley, T. G. (1999). *Building and operating neighborhood indicator systems: A guidebook.* Washington, DC: Urban Institute.

Kingsley, T.G., Coulton, C. J., Barndt, M., Sawicki, D. S., & Tatian, P. (1997). *Mapping your community: Using geographic information to strengthen community initiatives.* Washington, DC: U.S. Department of Housing and Urban Development.

Kingsley, T. G., McNeely, J. B., & Gibson, J. O. (1997). *Community building coming of age.* Washington, DC: Urban Institute.

Krueger, R. (1994). *Focus groups: A practical guide* (2nd ed.). Newbury Park Oaks, CA: Sage.

LisC and Policy Link. (2002). *Mapping for change: Using Geographic Information Systems for community development.* Retrieved June 29, 2003, from www.liscnet.org/resources/2002/12/ information_991.html.

Lofland, J., & Lofland, L. (1995). *Analyzing social settings: A guide to qualitative observation and analysis* (3rd ed.). Belmont, CA: Wadsworth.

McKnight, J. L., & Kretzman, J. P. (1993). *Building communities from the inside out.* Chicago: ACTA.

Meadows, D. (1998). *Indicators and information systems for sustainable development.* Harland, VT: Sustainability Institute.

Minkler, M., & Wallerstein, N. (1997). Improving health through community organization and community building: A health education perspective. In M. Minkler (Ed.), *Community organizing and community building for health* (pp. 30–52). New Brunswick, NJ: Rutgers University Press.

Narayan, D. (1996). *Toward participatory research* (Technical Paper 0253-7494 WTP 307). Washington, DC: World Bank.

Rossi, P., & Freeman, H. (1982). *Evaluation: A systematic approach.* Beverly Hills, CA: Sage.

Rossi, P. H. (1999). Evaluating community development programs: Problems and prospects. In R. F. Ferguson & W. T. Dickens (Eds.), *Urban problems and community development* (pp. 521–568). Washington, DC: Brookings Institution Press.

Rubin, A., & Babbie, E. (1997). *Research methods for social work.* Belmont, CA: Wadsworth.

Rubin, H., & Rubin, I. (2000). *Community organizing and development.* Boston: Allyn & Bacon.

Steckler, A., & Linnan, L. (Eds). (2002). *Process evaluation for public health interventions and research.* San Francisco, CA: Jossey-Bass.

Stoecker, R. (1999). Are academics irrelevant? Role for scholars in participatory research. *American Behavioral Scientist, 42*(5), 840–854.

Tatian, P. A. (2000). *Indispensable information: Data collection and information management for healthier communities.* Retrieved April 25, 2003, from the Urban Institute's National Neighborhood Indicators Partnership Web site, www.urban/org/nnip/pdf/indispen.pdf.

Urban Institute. (1999). *Stories: Using information in community building and local policy.* Washington, DC: Author.

Weil, M. (1996). Community building: Building community practice. *Social Work, 41,* 481–500.

Weiss, C. H. (1995). Nothing as practical as good theory: Exploring theory-based evaluation for comprehensive community initiatives. In J. P. Connell, A. C, Kubisch, L. B. Schorr, & C. H. Weiss (Eds.), *New approaches to evaluating comprehensive community initiatives* (pp. 65–92). Washington, DC: Aspen Institute.

Whyte, W. F. (Ed.). (1991). *Participatory action research.* Newbury Park, CA: Sage.

Witkin, B. R., & Altschuld, W. (1995). *Planning and conducing needs assessments: A practical guide.* Thousand Oaks, CA: Sage.

CHAPTER 34

Empowerment Research

Joan Pennell

Helzi Noponen

Marie Weil

Empowerment research and *empowerment program evaluation* are forms of social inquiry that engage various constituencies in

- critically examining social conditions or social programs,
- affirmatively reflecting on their and others' contributions, and
- responsibly acting to advance individual and collective well-being.

Within such an empowerment framework, research and program evaluation can serve as supports and means of community practice. Congruent with the traditional mission and goals of community practice, these forms of social inquiry empower community residents, citizens groups, service users, workers, and other constituencies to examine and improve their individual and collective lives. Through their participation, these groups ensure that a study attends to their issues, is enriched by their experiences and contributions, and develops their research competence. Fundamentally, empowerment research and evaluation build civic capacities and promote community well-being. These strategies build collective efficacy within the group as well as individual self-efficacy (Bandura, 1997). Through participation in empowerment research processes, participants' experiences and perceptions—their local knowledge—are validated and they learn that their appraisals matter in the research and evaluation efforts.

Both empowerment research and empowerment program evaluation share the broad goals of social investigation. Like other types of social research, empowerment research seeks to generate "usable knowledge" to resolve social issues (Lindblom & Cohen, 1979). Like its counterparts, empowerment program evaluation is focused on gathering knowledge to improve social programming (Schalock, 1995; Shadish, Cook, & Leviton, 1991). Although the purposes of empowerment research and program evaluation are encompassed by these larger investigatory domains, their primary evaluative standard is whether the study promotes the empowerment of individuals and communities. The focus on empowerment helps to foster understanding not only of how inquiry constructs knowledge but how we create "formative narratives" to set the contingent and variable identities of diverse groups within a common cause (Giroux, 1991, p. 22).

From Kuhn's (1970) perspective, normal science is defined by the ascendency of a research community that determines the questions to be asked, the methods to employ in answering these questions, and the answers to accept as legitimate. For the findings to be collectively appraised, the research community must be informed of the study's design and relevant findings. Accordingly, scientific investigation refers to seeking answers to questions in a systematic manner subject to the evaluation of other researchers (Hammersley, 1992, p. 138). Flexibly adapting methods from participatory action research, empowerment studies include and affirm diverse people and groups among the research community and, thus, expand the group that specifies and reviews the research or evaluation's agenda, processes, and conclusions.

Empowerment studies are shaped by the participants' unique aspirations and contexts and therefore do not conform to one single model. Participants' level and type of involvement may vary; some participants may do all the research and evaluation on their own, or take on specific tasks, or act as consultants to the researchers. Finally, the structure of empowerment research is not limited to strictly quantitative or qualitative methods. Instead, it is characterized as a form of *social inquiry*, because this term encompasses the various intellectual legacies seeking to explain, understand, or criticize the social world (Dallmayr & McCarthy, 1977). Drawing on the history of social work in the United States, this chapter proposes the following distinguishing features of empowerment research and program evaluation:

- an *ontology* (theory of the world) of individual and collective empowerment,
- an *epistemology* (theory of knowledge) of cultural safety and indigenous knowledge, and
- a *methodology* (theory of research) of local and global significance and stewardship.

This chapter describes and explains each of these three aspects of empowerment inquiry and then illustrates them with a powerful example of program monitoring and evaluation among rural women in India. In conclusion, it outlines a series of steps for empowerment inquiry.

An Ontology of Individual and Collective Empowerment

> *Empowerment* is the process and product of realigning power so that people can direct their individual and collective destinies and better their lives.
>
> An *empowerment ontology* proposes a theory of change to guide social inquiry.

Dating back to the 1890s in the United States, social work in general and community practice in particular have a strong tradition of empowerment (Simon, 1994). Founded by an "equal partnership of women and men" (Chambers, 1986, p. 6), social work is characterized by a long-term commitment to creating an equitable, respectful, and responsible society, and social workers and community practitioners have long formed alliances with members of communities (although at times these alliances were perilously shaky) across class and culture to overcome the disempowerment of socially disadvantaged groups. Quite appropriately, the term *empowerment* was introduced to U.S. social workers by Barbara Solomon (1976) in her descriptions of work with African American communities.

The empowerment tradition emphasizes that social workers cannot grant power to their clients but can work with marginalized groups to develop and use their members' collective power to effect change (Staples, 1990). Social workers have viewed empowerment both as a process of building the capacity of participants to change their individual and collective destinies and as a product of such change (Gutiérrez, Parsons, & Cox, 1998; Parsons, 1991). Thus, for social workers, empowerment is not merely a tool to gain power and influence; it is at the heart of social work's core ethics of equity, respect, and responsibility.

Community practitioners in particular have learned about the meaning and significance of empowerment through their leadership and participation in emancipatory movements, including those advocating peace, civil rights, feminism, economic entitlements, and cultural affirmation (Mondros & Wilson, 1994). These involvements have highlighted that empowerment entails knitting an even tension between individual interests and collective causes (Pennell, 1990). Empowerment is advanced through including diverse populations, raising the awareness of inequities, affirming the efficacy of marginalized groups, and mobilizing these marginalized groups to counter oppression (Freire, 1968/1989; Lather, 1991; Rappaport, 1990). This critical analysis of power, reflective affirmation of participants' power, and responsible use of power are creatively shaped within local contexts in which people can identify their concerns and hopes (Foster-Fishman, Salem, Chibnall, Legler, & Yapchai, 1998). At the same time, these local aspirations are galvanized by emancipatory movements and, in turn, serve as the basis for global action.

Research and program evaluation in the empowerment tradition incorporate the investigatory process—from identifying the study agenda to using its results—to promote empowerment (Ristock & Pennell, 1996). Social work has a strong tradition of using social surveys and other types of investigation to foster progressive change (Zimbalist, 1977), and, as is the case in other disciplines (Fetterman, Kaftarian, & Wandersman, 1996), its theorists and practitioners continue to develop avenues to empowerment inquiry (Sohng, 1998). Empowerment inquiry draws on theories and methods developed by participatory and action researchers (Lewin, 1946; Stull & Schensul, 1987; Whyte, 1991), in particular, the emphases on addressing social inequities, relating collaboratively, learning together in an iterative process, validating on the basis of participants' realities, and building participants' research capacity (Altpeter, Schopler, Galinsky, & Pennell, 1999; McTaggart, 1997). These approaches diverge, however, in that empowerment of citizens, rather than their participation or use of action for change during the research process, serves as the touchstone for group capacity development and research tasks.

The empowerment tradition shapes the ontology or worldview of the research project or program evaluation. Commonly, social investigation reflects a conceptual model of reality or aspects of reality that provide a particular frame of reference and "a coherent, internally unified way of thinking about . . . events and processes" (Frank, 1968, p. 45). The selected frame of reference then directs attention to particular phenomena while others are considered to be of lesser importance to the research process (Fawcett, 1999, p. 3). Inquiry based within an empowerment tradition reflects a history of concern with social change and, thus, is oriented not by a "theory of reality" but instead by a "theory of practice"—how to act in the world (Friedmann, 1987, p. 186). Within this framework, then, the theory of empowerment practice addresses how people might act to change their world. An empowerment ontology is the context in which to develop the study's theory of knowledge and its theory of research.

An Epistemology of Cultural Safety and Indigenous Knowledge

Cultural safety refers to a context in which one can express and affirm one's own cultural beliefs and practices while extending oneself to understand and respect other worldviews. It is the necessary context for generating indigenous or local knowledge.

An *empowerment epistemology* justifies a theory of indigenous knowledge to guide social inquiry.

Social workers have enumerated obstacles to empowerment through their practice and research. These include systemic power imbalances based on authoritarian categories, inadequate social supports especially for caregivers, and internalized oppression preventing clients and other marginalized populations from identifying their own capacities (Simon, 1994). To surmount these hurdles, social workers in the United States have promoted a strengths perspective that reframes problems as assets, mobilizes and shares social supports, and dignifies people who have been labeled (Kretzmann & McKnight, 1993; Saleebey, 1997). A sense of strength or power comes from validation of one's identity and cultural ties.

For this reason, social workers have emphasized cultural competence or awareness: valuing multiculturalism, reflecting on one's own culture, responding sensitively to other cultures, and institutionalizing cultural respect (Green, 1995; Walker & Staton, 2000). The other side of cultural competence for social workers to consider is the necessity of a sense of cultural safety for service users or community members. *Cultural safety* is a term used in New Zealand to refer to human services practitioners' acknowledgment and affirmation of their clients' cultural and familial identities (Fulcher, 1998, p. 333).

Because of their inclusive nature, empowerment studies view obstacles to empowerment from the perspective of the participants. From this angle, cultural safety, rather than cultural competence, gains prominence. In a context of cultural safety, participants can express themselves without disparagement of their beliefs and practices, without forced assimilation into the dominant culture, or without the equally problematic misappropriation of aspects of their cultures to legitimate the dominant group (*Four Circles*, 1997; Havemann, 1992).

Cultural safety fosters research and evaluation relationships in which participants seek to learn from other cultures rather than impose their own notions of rationality as they study and evaluate other worldviews (Winch, 1964/1977). The process of learning means reaching out to understand and appreciate the logic of another culture within that culture's frames of reference and to recognize that one's own rationality is likewise an example of local or indigenous knowledge developed within specific contexts and historical relationships (Geertz, 1983). Extending oneself to another culture is less an act of appropriation or possession and more an act of "dispossession" of one's own knowledge claims (Ricoeur, 1981, pp. 18–19). Exploring another worldview does not require that one "approve" it; instead, it is an opportunity to acknowledge one's own traditions and reflect on one's stance (Gadamer, 1963/1979, p. 151). Thus, an empowerment theory of knowledge assumes that trustworthy knowledge is generated through creating the cultural safety that is needed for meaningful and truthful interactions among people with differing perspectives. These interactions promote respect of indigenous views, unsettle preconceptions, extend understanding, deepen commitments for change, and sustain an empowerment methodology.

Methodology of Local and Global Significance and Stewardship

Local and global significance refers to the meanings attributed to social conditions and programs by participants within local contexts and connected by global movements.

This multilevel process of attributing meanings fosters the assumption of stewardship or caretaking.

An *empowerment methodology* uses a theory of stewardship to guide social inquiry.

The often-quoted functionalist maxim of "starting where the client is" has guided generations of social workers in the formation of their initial agenda for their practice and research and the further development of this agenda with those variously referred to as clients, members, participants, or collaborators (Simon, 1994, p. 104). Drawing on such feminist research principles as validating women's perspectives (Harding, 1987; Smith, 1990), today's social work researchers within the empowerment tradition continue to advocate for orientating research and evaluation according to people's realities rather than relying solely on the researcher's theories (Parsons, 1998, p. 209).

In determining what issues to study and change, social work researchers have worked with others to discern which issues are most significant, thus developing a consciousness of what is relevant and important for this time and place (Gadamer, 1963/1979). *Relevance* reflects the degree to which the issue affects local conditions and relationships; *importance* resonates with values, concerns, and goals articulated by larger social movements. This message of local and global significance was conveyed by Catheryne Cooke Gilman to Settlement House workers in the motto, "Keep your fingers on the near things and eyes on the far things" (as cited in Chambers, 1963, p. 150). The agenda for empowerment inquiry is, thus, set through an oscillation between immediate situations and worldwide trends.

The local and global significance of empowerment inquiry encourages a stance of stewardship rather than ownership over the study's process and findings. Ownership refers to holding legal title over property as well as managing it and claiming its profits (Dahl, 1970). Empowerment inquiry is not "property" owned by its participants at the local and global levels but instead a common good over which they exercise stewardship. The root meaning of *ward* or *weard* is to "guard, watch, or protect" (Merriam-Webster, 2003), and this caretaking orientation is congruent with the social work role and with indigenous views (Debo, 1970, pp. 3–4; Little Bear, Boldt, & Long, 1984, p. 6) and ecological perspectives (Schumacher, 1973, p. 220) of people as the custodians of the land and its inhabitants. For a steward, inquiry is judged according to whether it contributes to local and global well-being.

Stewardship sets the methodological standards for empowerment research and program evaluation. From a caretaking stance, objectivity as "detached neutrality" is problematic and is viewed as both unrealistic and unethical. Instead, *objectivity* from the caretaking stance is defined as committed reasoning maximized by attending to diverse perspectives, reflecting on biases, and searching out what really helps. Stewards apply the validity and reliability norms appropriate for a particular research method, but the ultimate test of a study is its contribution to improving social conditions and social programs. The extent to which its findings assist others in bettering their lives sets the outside limits of the study's generalizability.

Empowerment Research and Evaluation in Action

Empowerment research then provides a model to assist members of a group or community in assessing their own assets and needs, documenting community conditions, identifying targets for action, planning strategies for change, and acting on that change. The research process, if it seriously engages people, can become a major means of working through differences or disagreements in perception about community issues or conditions. If a group can come together, often with a facilitator committed to empowerment strategies and community-based evaluation, and determine their methodology for documenting issues, conditions, and evidence, differences in perception can often be moderated and result in definitions and descriptions that more broadly represent the collective perspective rather than that of one or two members.

When definitions, questions, and approaches are agreed on, a group—even one that has not previously participated in community research—can carry out an assessment or an evaluation (see Raheim, Noponen, & Alter, Chapter 30, this volume). Depending on previous experience, however, the facilitative empowerment researcher engaged with a group can have roles that range from rather active teaching of techniques and methods, to coaching a group in implementation, to consultation as needed to complete a project, interpret results, or prepare a report to document need for community change.

Empowerment research and evaluation approaches are often specifically focused on community practice with disadvantaged or marginalized communities—partly as a way to help them make the playing field more accessible if not equal through the power of knowledge. Empowerment evaluation can also be employed within organizations and programs that serve such communities—as self-evaluation—through the design of research strategies that use staff's and, it is hoped, clients' knowledge about program issues to develop a research design that will render findings that are transparent and usable by staff to improve outcomes for clients and strengthen the design for service delivery (Usher, 1995). In *Foundations of Empowerment Evaluation,* Fetterman (2001) noted this utility for communities and organizations:

> Empowerment evaluation can create an environment that is conducive to empowerment and self determination. This process is fundamentally democratic in the sense that it invites (if not demands) participation, examining issues of concern to the entire community in an open forum. As a result the context changes: the assessment of a program's value and worth is not the endpoint of the evaluation—as it often is in traditional evaluation—but is part of an ongoing process of program improvement. (p. 3)

Empowerment research can be undertaken in many venues, but arguably, its most important use is in direct application in low-wealth communities as a precursor or accompaniment to organizing, community development, or work toward policy change. The Highlander Center in Tennessee has for decades developed and employed research methods useful for community empowerment through assisting residents in making changes in their social institutions or physical environment. The video "You Gotta Move" (Highlander Center, 1984) provides an exciting and validating example of citizen organizing and research in Appalachia to close down a toxic waste dump that was not only poisoning the physical environment, but leaching dangerous chemicals into the water supply and causing a variety of serious illnesses. Residents who had not thought of themselves as either organizers or researchers quickly learned means to research and understand complex chemicals, patterns of toxic waste dumping, evidence of cluster patterns of cancer related to environmental hazards, and means of presenting research evidence. They also learned how to use their research results to pursue successful court action.

Empowerment research and evaluation can be employed in disadvantaged communities throughout the world; good assessment research can be conducted by community members even without the benefits of literacy (Noponen, 1992, 2001). In a number of communities in South Africa, residents of impoverished townships are using these approaches in a variety of health care and promotion campaigns:

> One impoverished black community near Cape Town is implementing and evaluating smoking cessation, hypertension, and teenage pregnancy prevention programs. This progressive, self-reflective community mirrors the real spirit of hope for democracy and the reconstruction of South Africa. (Fetterman, 2001, p. 40)

A particularly broad-based and successful empowerment research program, Professional Assistance for Development Action (PRADAN), is being carried out in India. PRADAN, a large rural livelihoods and microfinance program, is operated through a nongovernmental organization (NGO) in seven of the poorest states in North India. Unlike many other microfinance programs, PRADAN works to apply pressure on the banking industry to open more lending opportunities to the poor. At the grassroots level, PRADAN facilitates the formation of self-help groups as their own microfinance institutions with NGO field staff to provide support to the groups (see Raheim, Noponen, & Alter, Chapter 30, this volume, for further discussion of PRADAN's program). One of the most interesting aspects of PRADAN is its Internal Learning System, which assists participants in project and program monitoring and embodies an empowerment evaluation approach.

PRADAN's Internal Learning System

PRADAN's Participant and Program Learning Tool—The Internal Learning System[1]

The Internal Learning System (ILS) is a participatory impact assessment and planning system for community development programs, especially those focused on microfinance and livelihoods, designed primarily to meet the learning needs of program participants, village groups, and operational field staff. The system is an empowerment tool for impoverished, illiterate participants and village groups to track and analyze changes in their lives and to use this understanding to alter their strategies as they participate in the economy and interact with individuals and institutions in the wider community.

The ILS extends the notion of participatory assessment into empowerment methods. The essence of the system is that it is participatory, internal, and capacity building. This internal focus does not mean that participants and staff are narrowly focused on the functioning of program operations. Participants use the system at each organizational level in a development program, from the individual participant, to participant groups, to field officers, to program managers. ILS users at each level, especially impoverished women's groups of borrowers, are the first to learn about the program's impact on performance and tailor their plans accordingly. These ILS users take on not only the data-gathering role for their project, but also the roles of data analysts, planners, documenters, and trainers. Because the sharing of knowledge is at the core of empowerment, findings from one community often can benefit many others (Noponen, 2001).

ILS uses multiyear pictorial diaries or workbooks, which bridge language barriers yet are suitable for long-term recordkeeping, to track the processes of development and change. By incorporating simple pictures or scenes to represent impact indicators ranging from rainy seasons and periods of high disease to holidays and harvest times, ILS allows users to keep a record of change over time by making tick marks to note quantities, as well as yes/no responses, and performance and satisfaction scale ratings. Use of the diaries or workbooks is ongoing; it is not a one-time or occasional event. Users should collect data at regular intervals, with additional notation (if possible) when a change occurs, and tally results periodically (at least once per year) over a multiyear period. These ILS activities and processes are designed to be integrated into daily life as seamlessly as possible.

ILS is truly empowering, in that participants work at several program levels, in contrast to other programs that at the top are steered by managers or outside investigators. To ensure that participation is even throughout, the system has been designed so that all users, especially women, carry out the same five ILS tasks. These include

- collecting data;
- assessing change;
- analyzing causes of change, or troubleshooting;
- planning and training; and
- documenting, sharing, and reinforcing program values.

At each program level, participants reflect on their findings, employ user-driven training input, outline plans, and document their experiences in their learning diaries. There is a direct and immediate link between changes and results recorded by participants and planning and training for subsequent programs. ILS is flexible in its structure, content, and processes. Each of these can be tailored to the learning needs, human resource capacities, and financial constraints of different organizations (see Noponen, 2002, for a more detailed description).

PRADAN's ILS Adaptation: "Life and Livelihood Workbooks"

PRADAN's "Boat of Life—the Family's Oar."[2] The overall theme of PRADAN's work is "Boat of Life—The Family's Oar," with the workbook itself cast as the oar or tool with which households can steer toward a better life. PRADAN has organized its pictorial workbook according to its conceptualization of the three realms of self-help groups (SHGs) to serve as

1. a mutual support group,

2. a unit for financial intermediation, and

3. a vehicle for empowerment.

Interwoven throughout this conceptualization are two themes common to Indian culture, "seven rivers to cross to reach a good life" and "the boat of life." The "seven rivers to cross" concept translated into a 7-point self-assessment scale with which members rate their overall social and economic progress. The "boat of life" concept is used in a series of pictures featuring favorable and unfavorable scenes to introduce and teach the values in each of the major workbook sections.

At the individual level, the scenes illustrate positive and negative aspects of living conditions, diversified livelihoods, crises and coping strategies, burden of debt versus savings, household dependency ratios, and good and bad gender relations. At the group level, the scenes include group efforts to solve the problems of individual households in distress, the efficacy of group versus individual approaches to securing credit from banks, and the pros and cons of group versus individual efforts to solve community problems. These scenes have proven to be quite popular among both participants, who use them for reflection and amusement, and organizing staff members, who use them as icebreakers and discussion starters. This success has prompted the addition of a "gender-bender" workplace scene to prompt discussion of nontraditional gender division of work activities.

At the heart of the PRADAN workbook is a finances and livelihood module. Participants are first guided through a process of analyzing their current financial situation by assessing normal household income and expenditure patterns by gender. Over time, PRADAN will be able to see whether there are reinforcing positive versus negative effects on a "household well-being spiral," noted by changing consumption patterns resulting from women being able to target their earning as they choose for family, educational, and business expenditures. Next, participants track the incidence of crises that disrupt or strain the normal household earnings and expenditure pattern and reflect on their current coping strategies and options for future deficit reduction. Participants then record annual debt and savings levels by source. This sets the stage for improving the household financial situation through improvement in livelihood activities.

Next, the effects of microfinance on an "economic empowerment spiral" are tracked by the women while greater understanding is promoted by facilitators. Using simple pictures, participants first describe their total livelihood "availabilities" (in land, livestock, and labor) and how they are currently using these resources. They assess their land (including forests, rivers, and soil suitable for farming), assets and improvements (such as livestock, labor, and buildings), and accompanying work conditions and practices. They track usage patterns over the year, note any problems experienced, and make decisions regarding changes in strategy. In a synthesis section, the women complete a livelihood production plan that prompts them to consider their total set of livelihood resources and options and to weigh the competing use of resources and production inputs to produce their chosen mix. Participants then make a credit investment plan that ties the infusion of credit to the livelihood production plan. The goal is to help participants learn to plan their way out of debt and vulnerability by strengthening their livelihood base over a period of several years. It is vital that women complete this process by themselves, with only the minimum necessary assistance from their husbands. This increases their knowledge about their livelihood situation, the tradeoffs of investing in different activities, and the importance of careful and strategic use of their loan money. Women who have used PRADAN's workbook report, "Our minds are being opened up" (Noponen, 2003).

Next, a well-being module addresses such practical needs as living conditions and material welfare, further reinforcing the positive effects of credit on the household well-being spiral. An empowerment module addresses strategic interests of women's empowerment issues in the home and community, tracking effects of the "social and political empowerment spiral" in a manner that also emphasizes analysis and planning options. The workbook concludes with a synthesis section that guides participants through reflection on their individual role in the SHG, summarizes the program, and allows participants to express satisfactions and dissatisfactions about the process.

Each section of the workbook is carefully sequenced to produce a logical whole. A woman first reflects on her living conditions and material welfare and ranks her position on the seven rivers scale. She then investigates why she is at this level by examining her financial situation. The participant is prompted to see the role of debt reduction, savings, and livelihood improvements in coping strategies and family welfare progress over time. The livelihood module that follows systematically guides her through analysis of her total availabilities and prompts her to make strategic use of credit and other scarce resources in improving them.

The next module focuses on the enhancing effects of better gender relations and women's fuller participation in decision making in the home, on livelihood and welfare improvement, and on mobility in the public sphere. The impact of the role of the woman and her participation in her SHG and PRADAN activities and her progress over time are explored in the concluding synthesis module. This linked set of modules, analysis, and planning exercises, each building on the lessons from the previous one, is akin to a pictorial rural livelihoods curriculum for very poor illiterate women and their households.

This case example shows how ILS can be a valuable learning tool for both participants and program managers to increase the productive use of loans, to improve livelihoods, and to improve women's economic and social empowerment over time. Researchers also point to the need for integration of complementary business services for women, such as collective supply or marketing activities, with microfinance provision, either through the NGO's own efforts or through interorganizational linkages with other providers (Hunt & Kasynathan, 2002; Mayoux, 2002). PRADAN has always viewed microfinance as a tool with which to accomplish their primary goal of livelihood improvement through interventions in the supply market, product market, or technology inputs. It is the group-formation aspect of the SHG microfinance model that is the springboard for PRADAN's group livelihood improvement activities. In this sense, PRADAN can be considered a "plus credit" model (primarily a livelihoods focus plus credit for loans) rather than a "credit plus" (primarily credit for loans plus some skill training or business or welfare services) or a "minimalist credit" (financial services only) program. Mayoux (2002) called for rethinking of group structures and functions to go beyond the group as a microcredit repayment mechanism to one that is assisted in developing its own empowerment plans and agenda. The tracking of women's changing status in the home and community and the individual and group planning formats in the empowerment module of PRADAN's ILS are tools for sparking individual and group social change, especially that which results in women's fuller and more gainful participation in the economy.

This example of grassroots microfinance SHGs using a pictorial workbook to learn how to strengthen support groups, improve financial skills, and to develop the self- and collective efficacy skills of empowerment presents a strong model for group learning and empowerment evaluation. The potential for application of empowerment research and evaluation in the Global South as well as in the northern hemisphere is unbounded. In PRADAN's instance and in many others, the results of empowerment-focused self-evaluation can lead to community improvement, development of adequate livelihoods, greater economic participation, and the increase of bases of social, political, and economic power for marginalized groups (Friedmann, 1992). Development of skills coupled with empowerment strategies can enable impoverished families to gain a foothold in the economy and to engage in civic participation. Greater use of these strategies for economic and social development employing research and evaluation methods as a tool of empowerment offers considerable hope for improved quality of life for the poor in many parts of the world. These research and evaluation approaches have much to contribute to the well-being of communities and are tools and methods that community practitioners should learn to use effectively with the communities they serve.

Fetterman (2001, pp. 34–41) described an empowerment evaluation process that assists groups in identifying their goals or outcomes, their strategies, and their evidence of achievement. He presented five facets or developmental stages of empowerment evaluation:

1. *Training:* teaching people "to conduct their own evaluation and thus become more self-sufficient."

2. *Facilitation:* coaching groups to conduct self-evaluations and to learn useful techniques, methods, and teamwork, and supporting them in their planning and implementation efforts.

3. *Advocacy:* working with groups to prepare their information to present their case for a community plan, a policy change, or an improvement in the community's environment. Assisting groups in preparing to speak or advocate for themselves.

4. *Illumination:* "an eye-opening, revealing, and enlightening experience" that can bring forward in a group's work new ways to help them become "a dynamic community of learners."

5. *Liberation:* "the act of being freed or freeing oneself from preexisting roles and constraints." Empowerment evaluation can be one means of enabling participants "to find new opportunities, see existing resources in a new light, and redefine their identities and future roles."

Empowerment research and evaluation thus can be powerful and perhaps transformative methods of inquiry providing opportunities to change aspects of one's life and a community's quality of life. The following steps are offered as one basic approach to this model of facilitation, learning, and development of skills for community change.

Steps for Empowerment Inquiry

Empowerment inquiry can be described as a series of community practice steps that conform more to a spiral than a line:

Setting the agenda. The agenda for empowerment research and evaluation emerges from the interaction of locally urgent issues and globally compelling causes that push for social change.

Diversifying participation. Diversity among participants and views is encouraged by fostering a context of cultural safety in which indigenous knowledge is respected, prejudices are recognized, and understanding is expanded.

Designing for change. The study is designed as a form of community practice in which participants draw on their strengths and learn by engaging in efforts to realize individual and collective empowerment.

Sharing findings. The research participants serve as stewards who share and use what they have learned for the good of themselves and others.

Notes

1. This section is adapted from Noponen (2002).
2. Adapted from Noponen (2003).

References

Aboriginal Corrections Policy Unit. *Four circles of Hollow Water.* (1997). Ottawa, Canada: Public Works and Government Services. Catalog Number JS 5–1/15–1997E.

Altpeter, M., Schopler, J. H., Galinsky, M. J., & Pennell, J. (1999). Participatory research as social work practice: When is it viable? *Journal of Progressive Human Services,10*(2), 31–53.

Bandura, A. (1997). *Self-efficacy.* New York: W.H. Freeman.

Chambers, C. A. (1963). *Seedtime of reform: American social service and social action, 1918–1933.* Minneapolis: University of Minnesota Press.

Chambers, C. A. (1986). Women in the creation of the profession of social work. *Social Service Review, 60*(1), 1–33.

Dahl, R. A. (1970). *After the revolution? Authority in a good society.* New Haven, CT: Yale University Press.

Dallmayr, F. R., & McCarthy, T. A. (Eds.). (1977). *Understanding and social inquiry.* Notre Dame, IN: University of Notre Dame Press.

Debo, A. (1970). *A history of the Indians of the United States.* Norman: University of Oklahoma Press.

Fawcett, J. (1999). *The relationship of theory and research* (3rd ed.). Philadelphia: F. A. Davis.

Fetterman, D. M. (2001). *Foundations of empowerment evaluation.* Thousand Oaks, CA: Sage.

Fetterman, D. M., Kaftarian, S. J., & Wandersman, A. (Eds.). (1996). *Empowerment evaluation: Knowledge and tools for self-assessment and accountability.* Thousand Oaks, CA: Sage.

Foster-Fishman, P. G., Salem, D. A., Chibnall, S., Legler, R., & Yapchai, C. (1998). Empirical support for the critical assumptions of empowerment theory. *American Journal of Community Psychology, 26*(4), 507–536.

Frank, L. K. (1968). Science as a communication process. *Main Currents in Modern Thought, 25*, 45–53.

Freire, P. (1989). *Pedagogy of the oppressed* (M. B. Ramos, Trans.). New York: Continuum. (Original work published 1968)

Friedmann, J. (1987). *Planning in the public domain: From knowledge to action.* Princeton, NJ: Princeton University Press.

Friedmann, J. (1992). *Empowerment: The politics of alternative development.* Cambridge, MA: Blackwell.

Fulcher, L. (1998). Acknowledging culture in child and youth care practices. *Social Work Education, 17*(3), 321–338.

Gadamer, H.-G. (1979). The problem of historical consciousness (H. Fantel, Trans.). In P. Rabinow & W. M. Sullivan (Eds.), *Interpretive social science: A reader* (pp. 103–160). Berkeley: University of California Press. (Original work published 1963)

Geertz, C. (1983). *Local knowledge: Further essays in interpretive anthropology.* New York: Basic Books.

Giroux, H. A. (1991). Modernism, postmodernism, and feminism: Rethinking the boundaries of educational discourse. In H. A. Giroux (Ed.), *Postmodernism, feminism, and cultural politics: Redrawing educational boundaries* (pp. 1–59). Albany: State University of New York Press.

Green, J. W. (1995). *Cultural awareness in the human services: A multi-ethnic approach.* Boston: Allyn & Bacon.

Gutiérrez, L. M., Parsons, R. J., & Cox, E. O. (Eds.). (1998). *Empowerment in social work practice: A sourcebook.* Pacific Grove, CA: Brooks Cole.

Hammersley, M. (1992). *What's wrong with ethnography? Methodological explorations.* London: Routledge.

Hancock, T., & Minkler, M. (1997). "Community health assessment or healthy community assessment? Whose community? Whose health? whose assessment?" In M. Minkler (Ed.), *Community Organizing and Community Building for Health,* (pp. 139–156). New Brunswick, NJ: Rutgers University Press.

Harding, S. (Ed.). (1987). *Feminism and methodology: Social science issues.* Bloomington: Indiana University Press.

Havemann, P. (1992). The indigenization of social control in Canada. In R. A. Silverman & M. O. Neilson (Eds.), *Aboriginal peoples and Canadian criminal justice* (pp. 111–119). Toronto, Canada: Harcourt, Brace.

Highlander Center & L. M. Phenix (Producer). (1995). You gotta move: Stories of change in the South [video recording]. Available from First Run Features, 153 Waverly Place, New York, NY 10014.

Hunt, J., & Kasynathan, N. (2002). Reflections on microfinance and women's empowerment. *Development Bulletin, 57,* 71–75.

Kretzmann, J. P., & McKnight, J. L. (1993). *Building communities from the inside out: A path toward finding and mobilizing a community's assets.* Evanston, IL: Institute for Policy Research, Northwestern University.

Kuhn, T. S. (1970). *The structure of scientific revolutions* (2nd ed.). Chicago: University of Chicago Press.

Lather, P. (1991). *Getting smart: Feminist research and pedagogy in the postmodern era.* New York: Routledge.

Lewin, K. (1946). Action research and minority problems. *Journal of Social Issues, 2,* 34–46.

Lindblom, C. E., & Cohen, D. K. (1979). *Usable knowledge: Social science and social problem solving.* New Haven, CT: Yale University Press.

Little Bear, L., Boldt, M., & Long, J. A. (Eds.). (1984). *Pathways to self-determination: Canadian Indians and the Canadian state.* Toronto, Canada: University of Toronto Press.

Mayoux, L. (2002). Microfinance and women's empowerment: Rethinking "best practice." *Development Bulletin, 57,* 76–80.

McTaggart, R. (Ed.). (1997). *Participatory action research: International contexts and consequences.* Albany: State University of New York Press.

Merriam-Webster. (Ed.). (2003). *Merriam-Webster's collegiate dictionary* (11th ed.). Springfield, MA: Merriam-Webster.

Mondros, J. B., & Wilson, S. M. (1994). *Organizing for power and empowerment.* New York: Columbia University Press.

Noponen, H. (1992). Loans to the working poor: A longitudinal study of credit, gender and the household economy. *International Journal of Urban and Regional Research, 16*(2), 234–259.

Noponen, H. (2001). The Internal Learning System for participatory assessment of microfinance. *Small Enterprise Development, 12*(4), 45–53.

Noponen, H. (2002). The Internal Learning System: A tool for participant and program learning in micro-finance and livelihoods interventions. *Development Bulletin, 57,* 106–110.

Noponen, H. (2003). The Internal Learning System: Impact assessment versus empowerment. In L. Mayoux (Ed.), *Sustainable learning for women's empowerment: Ways forward in microfinance.* New Delhi: Sanskriti.

Parsons, R. J. (1991). Empowerment: Purpose and practice principle in social work. *Social Work With Groups, 14*(2), 7–21.

Parsons, R. J. (1998). Evaluation of empowerment practice. In L. M. Guetiérrez, R. J. Parsons, & E. O. Cox (Eds.), *Empowerment in social work practice: A sourcebook* (pp. 204–219). Pacific Grove, CA: Brooks Cole.

Pennell, J. (1990). Knitting empowering configurations. In J. Turner (Ed.), *Living the changes* (pp. 188–195). Winnipeg, Canada: University of Manitoba Press.

Rappaport, J. (1990). Research methods and the empowerment social agenda. In P. Tolan, C. Keys, F. Chertok, & L. Jason (Eds.), *Researching community psychology: Issues of theory and methods* (pp. 51–63). Washington, DC: American Psychological Association.

Ricoeur, P. (1981). *Hermeneutics and the human sciences: Essays on language, action and interpretation* (J. B. Thompson, Ed. & Trans.). Cambridge, UK: Cambridge University Press.

Ristock, J. L., & Pennell, J. (1996). *Community research as empowerment: Feminist links, postmodern interruptions.* Toronto, Canada: Oxford University Press.

Saleebey, D. (Ed.). (1997). *The strengths perspective in social work practice* (2nd ed.). New York: Longman.

Schalock, R. L. (1995). *Outcome-based evaluation.* New York: Plenum Press.

Schumacher, E. F. (1973). *Small is beautiful: Economics as if people mattered.* New York: Harper & Row.

Shadish, W. R., Jr., Cook, T. D., & Leviton, L. C. (1991). *Foundations of program evaluation: Theories of practice.* Newbury Park, CA: Sage.

Simon, B. L. (1994). *The empowerment tradition in American social work: A history.* New York: Columbia University Press.

Smith, D. E. (1990). *The conceptual practices of power: A feminist sociology of knowledge.* Toronto, Canada: University of Toronto Press.

Sohng, S. S. L. (1998). Research as an empowerment strategy. In L. M. Guetiérrez, R. J. Parsons, & E. O. Cox (Eds.), *Empowerment in social work practice: A sourcebook* (pp. 187–203). Pacific Grove, CA: Brooks Cole.

Solomon, B. M. (1986). *Black empowerment: Social work in oppressed communities.* New York: Columbia University Press.

Staples, L. H. (1990). Powerful ideas about empowerment. *Administration in Social Work, 14*(2), 29–42.

Stull, D. D., & Schensul, J. J. (Eds.). (1987). *Collaborative research and social change: Applied anthropology in action.* Boulder, CO: Westview Press.

Usher, C. L. (1995). Improving evaluability through self-evaluation. *Evaluation Practice 16*(1), 59–68.

Walker, R., & Staton, M. (2000). Multiculturalism in social work ethics. *Journal of Social Work Education, 36*(3), 449–462.

Whyte, W. F. (1991). *Participatory action research.* Newbury Park: Sage.

Winch, P. (1977). Understanding a primitive society. In F. R. Dallmayr & T. A. McCarthy (Eds.), *Understanding and social inquiry* (pp. 159–188). Notre Dame, IN: University of Notre Dame Press. (Original work published 1964)

Zimbalist, S. E. (1977). *Historic themes and landmarks in social welfare research.* New York: Harper & Row.

CHAPTER 35

Practice in the Electronic Community

Roger A. Lohmann

John McNutt

Like community practice, the Internet has frequently been heralded as a force for progressive social change during its short but eventful life history. Its record to date, however, is decidedly mixed. The potential certainly exists for this powerful technology to advance the causes of human freedom, well-being, and community. At the same time, however, this extraordinary communication network, which in less than a decade has become nearly universal in scope and sweep, has also demonstrated the potential to become simply another extension of the global economic marketplace. Far worse, it could become a power tool for class domination or a simple reinforcement of existing and future inequalities.

The Internet was at its inception a commons rather than a marketplace (Lohmann, 1992). It was born of the collaborative interests of physicists around the world to find easier and more effective ways of sharing their research results. Scientists such as Tim Berners Lee, the author of HTML and the Web protocol "http," primarily were seeking ways to improve scientific collaboration. Very quickly, it became apparent that the ease of use that the World Wide Web granted scientists also could have major implications for enhancing democracy (as in the work of the Benton Foundation) or for improving communication between isolated members of a community.

Increasingly, however, these communitarian notions have been overwhelmed by images and ideas of the Internet as a single, enormous shopping arcade. It is good to remember here the difference between hype and reality. Even before the dot.com market meltdown of 2000, the actual track record of e-commerce and business-to-business solutions was just as spotty and equivocal as any of the assorted progressive experiments in promoting electronic democracy or community via the Internet. Dot-coms simply have larger advertising budgets. For every publicly celebrated Internet success story, there are 50 highly promising possibilities, 100 interesting innovations that did not pan out, and 10 workable innovations largely unknown to anyone but their creators.

The sudden growth of the Internet has meant that some old favorites, like the Foundation Center Library (www.foundationcenter.org) and the Grantsmanship Center (www.tgci.com) can now also be found online, along with newer or more local resources, such as Guidestar's online listing of tax-exempt organizations (www.guidestar.org) and the Maine Philanthropy Center (http://www.megrants.org). The Internet has also been a major boon to recent protest movements like the anti–World Trade Organization movement, which is linked by a variety of Web sites like www.wtowatch.org and www.tradewatch.org.

In this brief chapter, we examine several developments in online technology and resources that appear to hold great potential for advancing human well-being and social justice. Community organizations are already taking advantage of this technology and have achieved tangible results. The topics we will examine are electronic communication and networking, electronic advocacy, fundraising support, geographic information systems, and database management. We conclude with a brief discussion of information poverty and the growing disparity of information haves and have-nots.

The Electronic Community

Looking back to the early 1990s, few people were prepared for or had anticipated the powerful potential of the World Wide Web for social interaction, social integration, a sense of social solidarity, and building of social capital. There is an obvious mathematical allusion in the label *computer* and an astonishingly broad range of other functions associated with digital technology. However, there can be no denying that computer technology already ranks with the pen, the telephone, and the printing press as a fundamental aid to human communication. The networked computer now rivals the pen and the telephone for one-to-one communication. Moreover, like the printing press, the computer is well-suited to low-cost, one-to-many communications. But, unlike all previous technologies, the capabilities of a network of computers for many-to-many and many-to-one communications are unprecedented. It is the combination of these overlays of communications possibilities that have given rise to the idea of electronic or virtual community (Rheingold, 1993). *Electronic community* is a generic term that can be applied to a broad range of endeavors in cyberspace, such as e-mail, discussion lists (many-to-many e-mail), targeted mailings (one-to-many e-mail), telecommunities, portals, chat rooms, and other groupware, to name just a few.

E-Mail, Lists, and Electronic Community

One of the most important media of electronic community, if not the most technologically elegant, is the lowly but ubiquitous e-mail message. Its origins are in the combination of a text editor, a network connection, and a few simple, behind-the-scenes commands to manage the basic store-and-forward technology involved. From it we have gotten news groups, electronic discussion lists (almost universally mislabeled "listservs" after the software that distributes messages to such lists), chat rooms, and a host of other permutations on this basic idea. E-mail tends to come in two basic flavors: POP (Post Office Protocol), in which messages are automatically delivered to and stored on the user's desktop computer, and IMAP (Internet Message Access Protocol), in which messages remain on a central server and are read by the user's machine.

Some discussion lists (ARNOVA-L, created in 1991, and ACOSA-L, created in 1993) are, by design, venues for general discussion by a national or international community of academics and practitioners, sponsored by specific organizations, and used, in part, for membership recruitment purposes. Others, like the array of "charity channels" hosted by the conservative American Philanthropy Review (www.charitychannel.com), offer large lists on very narrow topics. Another completely different approach is that employed by professional historians, through which grant-funded networks of topical lists are moderated by specialists in each area. These moderators review and approve messages (mostly for civility, they claim; historians must be a testy bunch!) before they are forwarded to the list, thereby performing a function not unlike that of journal editors.

Despite its widespread use (or perhaps because of it), e-mail technology has remained a fairly static medium for the better part of a decade. Certainly there have been vast improvements in software for sending, retrieving, viewing, and storing e-mail messages. Qualcomm's Eudora; Microsoft's Outlook, Outlook Express, and Entourage; Netscape Communicator; and other latest-generation e-mail clients offer a broad array of support services for the convenience of the e-mail user. (Entourage, available only on the Macintosh at this writing, combines a unique feature by which clicking on any address in an online user's address book brings up a street map locating that address from the MSN Expedia service.) But the underlying POP3 (for messages placed directly on the user's machine) and IMAP (for messages left on a central server) technology represents mature, stable technologies that most users are unlikely to move away from anytime soon, despite a host of rival technologies, including NetMeetings, WebCams, and most recently, Groove.

Some users in large organizations and institutions now receive their e-mail through integrated groupware solutions like Notes and Groupwise, which combine enhanced e-mail service with group calendaring and other services. The centralized nature of groupware services makes them inherently more suitable for a single bureaucracy than for groups in a decentralized or pluralistic community, however. One possibility that could move community users away from basic e-mail is the Groove technology (www.groove.net) released by a group headed by Ray Ozzie, one of the original developers of Lotus Notes. The Groove browser is free, and the program is said to be a decentralized approach, like the Napster music-sharing phenomenon, and yet able to allow active collaborations like other groupware. Whether it will catch on and eventually replace existing e-mail or discussion lists remains to be seen.

The Telecommunities Movement

One electronically based social movement that was of particular importance for the history of community organization is the telecommunities movement of the mid-1990s (Schuler, 1996). A testament to the pace of social change on the Internet is the way this movement sprang up, flourished, and died in a space of less than five years. Before market realities brought a halt to such ventures, Apple Computer sponsored two national conferences on telecommunities in 1995 and 1996. The University of Victoria in Canada sponsored an international community networking conference. All that remains today of this movement, which in its prime had a heavy electronic democracy slant to it, is a variety of chamber of commerce–style Web sites marketing to local communities. One of the most interesting and far-reaching of these developments was the Blacksburg Electronic Village project (www.bev.net), which sought to wire and link all of the Virginia city's 50,000 inhabitants. Another interesting community-level effort of this type is the La Plaza Telecommunity (www.laplaza.org) in Taos, New Mexico. Still another was Charlotte's Web (www.charweb.org) in Charlotte, North Carolina, which is no longer operational. Many of the telecommunity ventures from the mid-1990s have simply ceased operations, whereas others have been folded into the chamber of commerce operations of local communities and become e-commerce sites for Main Street businesses.

Something of the spirit of this movement can still be discerned from the Web site of Nevada, Missouri, which once billed itself as "America's First Telecommunity" (see downloadable literature review online at http://www.oregontelcom.org/cctp/). Like Blacksburg, Nevada, and Taos, New Mexico, many of the communities that took part in the telecommunity movement were small or medium-sized cities. Austin, Texas, may have been one of the largest urban centers to develop this idea with its site (www.ci.austin.tx.us/telecom/intelcom.htm).

One telecommunity which operated on a statewide basis for nearly a decade was the West Virginia Information Service, or WISe, a statewide nonprofit funded by the Benedum Foundation and operated by the public television station in Morgantown, West Virginia. WISe linked community organizers and nonprofit organizations throughout the state of West Virginia and served as a primary e-mail post office for many of them until its demise in 2003. Its 800 numbers, easily con-figured First Class server, and widely disseminated client software made it feasible for even novice computer users.

There have been a number of ventures to create a sense of electronic community on the national level. One such group is the Organizers' Collaborative (www.organizenow.net), created in 1999. Their mission is to help nonprofit and activist groups all over the United States more effectively use computers and the Internet to achieve social change, primarily in three areas: creating Web sites to promote social change networking and resource sharing, studying the impact of the Internet on social justice efforts, and developing software tools and printed "how-to" resources.

Advocacy and Technology

Advocacy is a core function of community practice. In the past few years, technology has created a sea change in the nature of advocacy-related practice. Advocates of every stripe are creating Web sites, developing e-mail contact lists, and experimenting with new types of technology.

These new methods of advocacy are often referred to as *electronic advocacy* (Fitzgerald & McNutt, 1999; McNutt & Boland, 1999), *netactivism* (Schwartz, 1996), *virtual activism* (Krause, Stein, & Clark, 1998) and *cyberactivism* (Bennett & Fielding, 1999). All of these designations refer to the use of highly sophisticated communications technology to influence the decision-making process (McNutt & Penkauskas, 2000). Although in most cases this means Internet-related technology (also called *new media*), it can mean other types of interventions as well.

The most commonly used interventions appear to be e-mail strategies (including discussion lists and distribution lists) and Web-based strategies. Combined with earlier techniques, such as conference calling and faxing, they represent the current advocacy array. More sophisticated and adventurous organizations are experimenting with technologies like streaming video, online surveys, online fundraising, and even webcasting.

The advantages of these new technological methods include extending the reach of advocacy efforts, overcoming barriers of time and distance, and decreasing the transaction costs of organizing. Given the major policy decision making shifts that have occurred with processes of devolution of dollars and decisions to local levels and the phenomena of increasing decentralization, and so forth, these assets can carry considerable weight.

There is considerable evidence that electronic communication techniques are earning their place in the advocacy enterprise (McNutt, 2000). First, these techniques are the subject of considerable press coverage (Drinkard, 1999). This is especially true of pathbreaking efforts such as MoveOn.org, which began in 1998 as an online petition to "Censure President Clinton and Move On to Pressing Issues Facing the Nation" and later merged with the MoveOn Peace campaign to form MoveOn.org (www.moveon.org), a network of 1.7 million online activists. Second, material on these techniques has appeared in standard books on advocacy (Haynes & Mickelson, 2000; Smucker, 1999). Third, the political consulting community, many members of which have established Internet capability, has responded quite actively: In their well-known trade magazine *Campaigns and Elections*, a monthly section entitled "Bandwagon" deals solely with these issues. Fourth, a number of studies have established that these techniques are being used in advocacy practice (McNutt & Boland, 1999; Rees, 1999). Finally, groups such as the Benton (www.benton.org) and Markle (www.markle.org) Foundations, OMB watch (www.ombwatch.org), and others have created programs to promote this type of practice.

Because electronic advocacy is a practice in its formative stages, there is little theory to guide practitioners. McNutt and Penkauskas (2000) argued that there are four major processes in the practice of electronic advocacy: researching, organizing and collaborating, informing the public, and applying pressure to decision makers.

Research about issues, strategies, and opponents is fundamental to social action. It can be facilitated by the quick response of online databases and inquiries via e-mail. Technology can also facilitate online surveys and the analysis of data with statistical software, spreadsheets, and geographic information systems technology (see Hillier & Culhane, Chapter 36, this volume). Certainly, regular and accurate data collection is a critical step in establishing and maintaining a campaign of social action.

After data have been gleaned and interpreted, the next step is to inform the public about the nature of the findings. Web sites and e-mail are very good at reaching a large number of people quickly and inexpensively. In addition, some organizations are experimenting with video teleconferencing, webcasting, and streaming video (Turner, 1998).

Organizing and coordinating action are vital to any change effort. Traditionally, they have been among social advocates' most costly and time-consuming activities. Now, though, e-mail and Web sites provide the ability to organize quickly at minimal cost (Schwartz, 1996). Computer technology can also be used to create online fundraising networks to develop the funding base that is critical to any organizing effort (McNutt, Bartron, & Boland, 1999). Some organizations are developing secure Intranets (secure internal Internet-like systems) to facilitate coordination.

Finally, applying pressure to decision makers is a key part of social change. This often means sending multiple letters or faxes to decision makers (faxing can be done through a Web site). The evidence regarding the effectiveness of e-mail messages to decision makers is unclear. Three studies of national-level legislative offices paint a less than enthusiastic picture of the viability of e-mail compared to more traditional methods (Bonner, 1998; Davis, 1999; Lemmon & Carter, 1998). On balance, McNutt, Lima, Penkaukaus, and Rusoff (1999), in a study of state-level advocacy efforts in Massachusetts, found more positive results. This is perhaps the reason that many practitioners advocate the integration of these techniques with more traditional methods. Web sites offer some potential to influence decision makers by providing a ready source of information. Online petitions and report cards seem to be the emergent techniques in this area.

Developing an effort. Organizations that plan to develop electronic advocacy systems should realize that careful planning is essential to develop an effective operation (see Bennett & Fielding, 1999; Schwartz, 1996). Although this is a practice that depends on technology, it is primarily a people-oriented process as opposed to a technology-oriented process. It is essential to build two complementary structures: the human organization that conducts the advocacy and the technical system that supports this endeavor.

Creating the human organization requires integration with the overall operation of the parent group, particularly the government relations or advocacy function. It is important that strategies and tactics harmonize with overall planning. It is also important to incorporate the knowledge base that the organization has developed on the relevant political systems into the planning effort. For the technology to function effectively, good training and technical support are essential.

The technology arrangements should support the overall advocacy strategy and must be dependable and easy to use. Many of these technologies can and probably will support other functions of the organization, a fact that needs to be carefully considered in the planning effort. Less complex technologies that are similar to existing systems are more likely to be adopted (Rogers, 1995). It is probably better to start with a less-sophisticated system that can be scaled up than to begin with a cutting-edge system. Positive experience with these approaches can build the confidence needed for more sophisticated tasks.

Evaluating advocacy efforts is one of the most difficult research situations, because a multitude of factors contribute to any single outcome and advocacy goals can be complex and multifaceted. Given the open and public nature of advocacy efforts, the likelihood of unexpected intervening variables is quite high, and because of the multiplicity of actors, interveners, and responders, it can be difficult to determine direct causal relations. Despite these complexities, technology can revolutionize the practice of advocacy. It has the potential to promote social and economic justice in important and innovative ways.

Geographic Information Systems

Geographic information systems (GIS) offer planners and organizers new and unparalleled ways to present and analyze data (Hoefer, Hoefer, & Tobias, 1994). These systems combine mapping with powerful demographic and programmatic databases through a technology known as "geocoding," which allows the computer to integrate the two in a map that shows the distribution of a number of factors. There are two aspects of GIS that are of greatest interest to community practice. The first of these is to gather and correlate information with a spatial dimension or aspect. GIS technology can be used to create maps of the spatial distribution of social problems like child abuse from data sets of police arrest records, agency abuse complaints, school truancy reports, and so forth (all of which typically contain street addresses). The second involves the use of geosynchronous technology to assist and guide organizing efforts. For example, event data for a regional, national, or even local protest campaign might be plotted to show travel times and distances, sequencing, and other information.

One need not get involved in elaborate high-tech systems to benefit, at least minimally, from this technology. A number of companies, including Rand-McNally, market inexpensive CD-ROM disks that contain road and street maps of the entire United States, accessible by town name or zip code. A number of systems provide similar capacity over the Web, such as Mapquest and Yahoo! Maps. One new program, Microsoft's Entourage, builds such capabilities directly into its clients' e-mail accounts, and a number of automobile manufacturers offer geosynchronous map readers as (relatively expensive) new car options. These can be used by urban and rural community organizers or other social workers doing home visits to locate specific addresses and plan routes, and for numerous other purposes as well. These maps are generally as detailed and accurate as they are inexpensive. In one recent instance, a suburban neighborhood association used geosynchronous maps to supplement existing county maps submitted as part of a state highway redesignation project. Elsewhere, a colleague who once worked on the Navaho Reservation used these maps to trace a number of road connections with which he had been unfamiliar. At present, there are 22 fixed-position satellites in orbit around the earth which together make it possible to triangulate (within a precision of inches) any physical position on the planet. The existence of such powerful technology holds important political implications for community practitioners.

More sophisticated GIS software has a variety of additional capabilities. One can use these programs in combination with census and other similar data to plot the exact location and geographic distribution of low-income populations (Schlossberg, 1998). The painstaking labor that went into preparing the maps of the Halsted Street neighborhood published in *Hull-House Maps and Papers* (1895) would be reduced significantly if the same research were conducted today.

Online Fundraising

Another important facet of the relation between community practice and the Internet is the trend toward the development of online fundraising. From the 1920s, when current approaches to "federated financing" were initiated, to the present, fundraising for human services in the United States has been largely community based and under the control of nonprofit financial intermediaries like Community Chest and, more recently, United Way (see Brilliant, Chapter 12, this volume) and its various alternatives. Payroll deduction and other aspects of "workplace giving" have been important components (see Lauffer, Chapter 32, this volume).

With the emergence of the desktop computer in the early 1980s, we began to see the development of specialized fundraising software. Generally, these software products have tended to be relational databases with a range of appropriate fields suitable for storing and quickly referencing data on potential donors. A small number of companies also offer the capability of managing both donations and membership records in the same database. Several companies also supply specialized software to support the analytic, resource allocation, and complex data management of foundations, United Ways, and other grant agencies and financial intermediaries. At least some of these databases can be synchronized with handheld devices, which together with features such as wireless networking, make them potentially quite useful in community practice settings. As of this writing, the technological capabilities in this area far exceed actual use in many community practice settings.

Beginning about 1998, entirely new, non-community-based alternatives nested in the Internet presence of giant commercial entities like America Online and Fidelity began to evolve completely new forms of online fundraising. Since then, reports of a large number of successful campaigns carried out online have appeared in publications such as the *Chronicle of Philanthropy*. Within the United States, the American Red Cross has a particularly successful online fundraising operation, and the Red Cross raised millions of dollars following an earthquake in India.

In general, there have been four types of online fundraising, only three of which are legitimate, and one of which is fraudulent:

1. financial service companies, such as banks, brokerage houses, and investment services with existing electronic funds transfer capabilities, for whom donations were a simple addition to a "full range" of financial services;

2. Internet service providers and portals, for whom the ability to function as a financial intermediary for donations offered one of many ways for companies to distinguish themselves from their competitors in increasingly tight markets;

3. Internet startup companies (a number of which succumbed to the various "market readjustments" which started in early 2000); and

4. assorted online equivalents of the dubious and overtly fraudulent fundraising operations that have long plagued this field.

In almost all instances, the modus operandi of these new services is the same: In exchange for a "small fee," these firms will transfer donations from givers to designated 501(c)3 organizations. The fees charged can, in fact, vary widely, similar to credit card fees and, for that matter, local United Way administrative and fundraising costs.

As of this writing, the entire development of online fundraising is too new and unproven to be discussed in further detail. Theoretically, the ease of online contributing has the potential to completely replace workplace giving, conventional mail solicitations, and a variety of other, more traditional forms of fundraising. A single online intermediary (e.g., AOL's helping.org) conceivably could replace the fundraising operations of all 2,000+ United Ways in the United States with a system that is cheaper, is faster, and offers much more direct expression of donor preferences. In the process, much of what remains of the community social service planning network in the United States could also be seriously disrupted or undermined. Although such dire predictions are premature, community practitioners would be wise to keep an eye on this fascinating and volatile arena in which significant developments may be occurring in the next few years.

The Digital Divide

One of the key information issues that community practitioners must confront is the emerging digital divide between the information "haves" and "have-nots" (Cwikel & Cnaan, 1991; McConnaughey, Everette, Reynolds, & Lader, 1999; Tropman, Erlich, & Rothman, 1995; Wresch, 1996). In a knowledge-based economy, the lack of access to information may prove to be even more critical than limited financial resources in defining real poverty (Haywood, 1995; Lang & St. John's University, 1988). So far, the work of most community practitioners probably has not been significantly influenced by the growing recognition and attention to the emerging information theory of poverty. However, a number of practitioners and agencies are working to help members of low-income communities gain skills and computer literacy. In the near future, the information theory of poverty will have increased impact on the environment of community practice.

For example, in many states, governors and legislatures have endorsed or initiated projects to bring computers and network access to every school, and there have been a number of independent initiatives by nonprofit and community groups to widen the availability of information technology to disadvantaged populations.

The more challenging part of this effort is to develop serious know-how among members of disadvantaged populations. One such project is the Technology Opportunities Program (TOP; formerly TIIAP) funded by the U.S. Department of Commerce. To date, one TOP grant has been awarded to the Division of Social Work at West Virginia University to broaden the availability of information technology to information-poor populations in rural Appalachia. This is, as far as we know, the only project of its kind funded to a social work education program. (For a general discussion of community efforts to deal with the information poor, see McNutt, 1998.)

It is relatively clear already that electronic technology is a powerful and effective tool in the hands of the wealthy and powerful. It is also clear, however, that electronic technology in and of itself is class- and interest-neutral. If the opportunity is well used by social work practitioners and the nonprofit sector, it could become a class equalizer with regard to access of information.

Conclusion

As is true in so many facets of modern life, community practice is being changed in innumerable ways by the remarkable advance of Internet technology. Despite a veritable avalanche of publicity about its commercial potential, the market meltdown in the second half of 2000 revealed that the online universe is a far less purely commercial venue than once claimed. In particular, Internet technology still holds vast untapped potential for community practice aimed at advancing the cause of human well-being and social justice. One highly promising set of potentials are in the ability of Internet communications to escape the conventional limits of time and space and to supplement the conventional categories of face-to-face, small group, speaker-to-audience, traditional letter writing, and such one-way broadcast media as radio and television communications with an amazing new array of interactive capabilities.

One of the first venues in which some of these communications capabilities are being manifested is in the area of online advocacy. Another area with vast potential, but also significant implications for change, is the arena of online fundraising. Even as electronic communications may modify the traditional place-related confinements of traditional community practice, GIS technology makes it increasingly possible to do some interesting new things with conventional ideas of place. One of the major issues of social justice raised by these new technologies, however, is the large, and rapidly expanding, gap between information haves and have-nots.

References

Bennett, D., & Fielding, P. (1999). *The net effect: How cyber-advocacy is changing the political landscape.* Merrifield, VA: E-Advocates Press.

Bonner, J. (1998). The Internet and grassroots lobbying: The next wave. *Campaigns and Elections, 19*(9), 46–48.

Cwikel, J., & Cnaan, R. (1991). Ethical dilemmas in applying second wave information technology to social work practice. *Social Work, 36*(2), 114–120.

Davis, R. (1999). *The Web of politics: The Internet's impact on the American political system.* New York: Oxford University Press.

Drinkard, J. (1999, August 31). Internet transforming US politics. *USA Today.* Retrieved August 31, 1999, from http://www.usatoday.com/news/acovtue.htm.

Fitzgerald, E., & McNutt, J. G. (1999). Electronic advocacy in policy practice: A framework for teaching technologically based practice. *Journal of Social Work Education, 35*(3), 331–341.

Haynes, K. S., & Mickelson, J. S. (2000). *Affecting change* (4th ed.). New York: Longmans.

Haywood, T. (1995). *Info rich/info poor: Access and exchange in the global information society.* London: Bowker-Saur.

Hoefer, R. A., Hoefer, R. M., & Tobias, R. A. (1994). Geographic information systems and human services. *Journal of Community Practice, 1*(3), 113–28.

Hull-House maps and papers, by residents of Hull-House, a social settlement, a presentation of nationalities and wages in a congested district of Chicago, together with comments and essays on problems growing out of the social conditions. (1895). New York: Cromwell.

Krause, A., Stein, M., & Clark, J. (1998). *The virtual activist: A training course.* Available from http://www.netaction.org/training/.

Lang, J., & St. John's University. (1988). *Unequal access to information resources: Problems and needs of the world's information poor.* Ann Arbor, MI: Pierian Press.

Lemmon, P., & Carter, M. (1998). *Speaking up in the Internet age.* Washington, DC: OMB Watch.

Lohmann, R. A. (1992). *The Commons: New perspectives on nonprofit organization and voluntary action.* San Francisco: Jossey-Bass.

McConnaughey, J., Everette, D. W., Reynolds, T., & Lader, W. (1999). *Falling through the Net: Defining the digital divide.* Washington, DC: National Telecommunications and Information Administration, U.S. Department of Commerce.

McNutt, J. G. (1998). Ensuring social justice for the new underclass: Community interventions to meet the needs of the new poor. In B. Ebo (Ed.), *The cyberghetto, or cybertopia: Race, class, gender and marginalization in cyberspace* (pp. 33–47). New York: Praeger.

McNutt, J. G. (2000). Coming perspectives in the development of electronic advocacy for social policy practice [Electronic version]. *Critical Social Work, 1*(1). Available from http://core.ecu.edu/socw/csw/.

McNutt, J. G., Bartron, J., & Boland, K. M. (1999, November). *An empirical study of electronic fundraising activity in a group of non-profits.* Paper presented at the 28th Annual meeting of the Association of Voluntary Action Scholars, Arlington, VA.

McNutt, J. G., & Boland, K. M. (1999). Electronic advocacy by non-profit organizations in social welfare policy. *Nonprofit and Voluntary Sector Quarterly, 28*(4), 432–451.

McNutt, J. G., Lima, J., Penkauskas, K., & Rusoff, M. (1999, November). *A study of the impact of Internet-based technologies on the legislative process at the state level.* Paper presented at the 28th Annual meeting of the Association for Research on Nonprofit Organizations and Voluntary Action, Arlington, VA.

McNutt, J. G., & Penkauskas, K. (2000, April). *Electronic advocacy.* Paper presented at Getting Wired: Advocacy in Cyberspace, The First Boston College Conference on Electronic Advocacy in Social Work Practice, Chestnut Hill, MA.

Rees, S. (1999). Strategic choices for non-profit advocates. *Nonprofit and Voluntary Sector Quarterly, 28*(1), 65–73.

Rheingold, H. (1993). *The virtual community: Homesteading on the electronic frontier.* New York: Harper.

Rogers, E. M. (1995). *The diffusion of innovation* (4th ed.). New York: Free Press.

Schlossberg, M. (1998, November). *Asset mapping and community development planning with GIS: A look at the heart of West Michigan United Way's Innovative Approach.* Paper presented at the 27th Annual Meeting of the Association for Research on Nonprofit Organizations and Voluntary Action, Seattle, WA.

Schuler, D. (1996). *New community networks: Wired for change.* Reading, MA: Addison-Wesley.

Schwartz, E. (1996). *NetActivism: How citizens use the Internet.* Sebastopol, CA: O'Reilly.

Smucker, R. (1999). *The nonprofit lobbying guide* (2nd ed.). Washington, DC: Independent Sector.

Tropman, J. E., Erlich, J. L., & Rothman, J. (Eds.) (1995). *Tactics and techniques of community intervention* (3rd ed.). Itasca, IL: F. E. Peacock.

Turner, R. (1998). *Democracy at work: Non-profit use of Internet technology for public policy purposes.* Washington, DC: OMB Watch.

Wresch, W. (1996). *Haves and have-nots in the Information Age.* New Brunswick, NJ: Rutgers University Press.

CHAPTER 36

Integrating and Distributing Administrative Data to Support Community Change

Amy E. Hillier

Dennis P. Culhane

An increasing number of groups are demanding access to information about the physical, economic, and social conditions in their communities. In addition to researchers, community development corporations, neighborhood associations, social service agencies, and municipal agencies all are becoming consumers of quantitative data. More powerful desktop computers, sophisticated data management software, enormous data storage devices, and expanding Internet access have increased exponentially the capacity of even small organizations to handle large amounts of data. However, none of these advances guarantees that organization staff will be able to make sense of these mountains of data. Perhaps more important, the advances do not enhance access to the most useful types of data that frequently reside behind municipal agency firewalls and layers of bureaucratic red tape. The growing demand for small-area administrative data in useful formats makes essential the development of new tools to support a wide range of community change efforts.

Need for Small-Area Data

Data about the well-being of demographic groups, families, institutions, the built environment, the natural environment, and businesses play an increasingly important role in a number of efforts to improve communities. Analysis at the individual person or property level is often impractical and perhaps unethical because of limited access owing to concerns about confidentiality and the amount of information contained in individual-level data sets. Data aggregated by small geographic areas, such as census tracts, neighborhoods, and service districts, avoid problems with confidentiality and allow for easier recognition of patterns across space and time. Access to small-area data can facilitate needs assessments, program planning, site selection, and resource allocation by public or private agencies. Small-area data can also support long-term community planning, serving as the basis for forecasts of demographic and housing changes as well as models of the desired impact that various programs might have. The increasing emphasis on measurable outcomes by funders, including private foundations and the federal government, has also increased the need for trend data to evaluate the impact of programs. The ability of communities to monitor the impact of government and private actions, including their ability to mount Community Reinvestment Act challenges, also depends on their access to appropriate small-area data.

The demand for small-area data has increased over the past century along with the number of small geographic units available to serve as units of analysis. In his classic small-area study of housing and economic conditions, *The Philadelphia Negro,* W. E. B. DuBois used the political ward as his focus (1899). Responding to the need for new geographic units that were not politically based and were less subject to boundary changes, the Census Bureau introduced census tracts (originally called districts) in 1910. Concerned that cities did not recognize the value of these new geographic tabulations, the American Statistical Association established a Committee on Census Enumeration Areas in 1931 to promote census tracts and identify uses for tract-level data (U.S. Department of Commerce, 1994). President Hoover's Committee on Social Trends relied on a combination of ward-, municipal-, and county-level data for *Recent Social Trends,* the comprehensive account of social conditions it published in 1933 (President's Research Committee on Social Trends, 1933). On the other hand, the Works Progress Administration Real Property Surveys, conducted later that decade, used census tracts and blocks to report extensive information about households and housing conditions. The U.S. Bureau of the Census first provided data at the block level in 1940, followed by the block group in 1970.

The Social Indicators movement, encouraging the use of time-series data to monitor and effect social change, has increased considerably the demand for small-area data as it has gained momentum over the past 30 years (Bauer, 1966; Sawicki & Flynn, 1996). The Urban Institute's National Neighborhood Indicators Project has been supporting indicator projects in six cities—Atlanta, Boston, Cleveland, Denver, Oakland, and Providence—since the late 1980s (Kingsley, 1998). Additional projects in Jacksonville, Seattle, Pasadena, Milwaukee, and a host of other cities also have served to integrate and interpret small-area data to support community change efforts. Census data play an important role in these types of projects. However, the limitations imposed by the decennial nature of census data, lack of correspondence among local service areas and planning districts with the U.S. Bureau of the Census's standard geographic units, and the limited range of data elements made available have led researchers and community groups to look elsewhere.[1]

Municipal governments are perhaps the largest potential source of small-area data. City agencies are involved either directly or indirectly as conduits of city, state, and federal funding in nearly all areas of service delivery and community development, from public assistance, child welfare, education, and health care to housing inspections, rehabilitation, and demolition. With some notable exceptions, community organizations need to cajole or pay individual municipal agencies for administrative data or they have to appeal to their legal right to such information through Freedom of Information Act requests. In some cases, community organizations can acquire information about individual properties or areas but have much greater difficulty acquiring complete data sets that allow for citywide analysis.

Overview of Web-Based Information Systems

Web-based information systems that integrate and distribute administrative data aim to help fill the need left by the decennial U.S. Census. These systems take advantage of many technological advances in database administration, programming, and computer mapping. But they also depend on strong collaborations among their developers, data-providing agencies, and system users as much as on technical expertise. Although there are few limits to the forms these systems can take, there are a number of principles that distinguish them. Most important, they distribute data, making hard-to-acquire information accessible to a wide array of user groups. Although mapping may or may not play a large role in data displays, common geographic references—either street addresses or small-area units—provide the basis for data integration. These systems are both replicable and customizable. Much of the computer programming that creates the applications that serve up the data—including functionality to integrate, summarize, chart, map, and print the data—is transferable across applications that have different themes or serve different geographic areas. At the same time, these applications can adapt to specific data needs and data availability in individual municipalities. These systems are constantly maintained and updated. Data values are updated regularly to reflect continuous changes in local conditions. These systems are user-friendly, requiring minimal training for users who may have very limited computer experience and maximizing the ability of users to define their own queries and interpret the results accurately. Finally, the developers of these systems are accountable to funders, data providers, and system users.

Examples of Web-Based Information Systems and Partnerships for Information Collection and Distribution

Chicago's Neighborhood Early Warning System and Neighborhood Knowledge Los Angeles

Chicago's Neighborhood Early Warning System (NEWS) provides one of the earliest examples of an information system created to prevent housing abandonment by identifying at-risk properties. Started in 1984 when Harold Washington was mayor, NEWS originally relied on floppy disks to distribute data. Now on the Web and updated regularly, NEWS integrates property-level and area data on housing code violations, housing court cases, fires, tax assessments, and general housing characteristics for Chicago and Cook County (Center for Neighborhood Technology, 2003). Modeled on NEWS, Neighborhood Knowledge Los Angeles (NKLA) combines similar property-level and area housing data with U.S. Census data. In addition to generating tables based on inquiries about specific properties and areas, NKLA users can create maps and conduct queries to identify both the attributes of particular places as well as places with specified attributes (Community Information Technology Center, 2003).

The Cartographic Modeling Laboratory (CML) and Partnerships

The CML, a joint venture of the University of Pennsylvania School of Social Work and Graduate School of Fine Arts, has developed several similar applications that distribute a wide range of administrative data to community and municipal government partners in Philadelphia. The Neighborhood Information System (NIS) provides information about properties and the built environment, whereas the Services Utilization Monitoring System is focused on human services data relating to children.

Philadelphia Neighborhood Information System (NIS)

The Philadelphia NIS (Cartographic Modeling Laboratory [CML], 2003) integrates and distributes housing data from eight different municipal agencies along with 1990 and 2000 Census data through two different Web-based applications: ParcelBase and NeighborhoodBase. Agencies that provide data are the Office of Housing and Community Development, City Planning Commission, Department of Revenue, Department of Licenses and Inspections, Board of Revision of Taxes, Water Department, Philadelphia Gas Works, and U.S. Postal Service. Funding has been provided by the William Penn Foundation, the Pew Charitable Trusts, the University of Pennsylvania, and the city of Philadelphia.

The applications use Microsoft Visual Basic with ESRI's (Environmental Systems Research Institute's) ArcIMS (Arc Internet Map Server) to serve up various data displays in response to user requests. Data about property sales, ownership, housing vacancy, utility terminations, tax arrearages, housing code violations, and demolitions are featured. Data elements to be included were determined through discussions between the CML and data-providing agencies as well as through focus groups held with community organizations. The data-providing agencies are asked to provide data updates every three months.[2]

ParcelBase provides property-level data to registered users who consist of staff at city agencies and community organizations authorized to have an account by the city's Office of Housing and Community Development. Users identify a property by typing an address or property identification number, consisting of a five-digit street code and the house number, or by highlighting a property on a parcel map. A small screen pops up when a parcel is selected, displaying characteristics

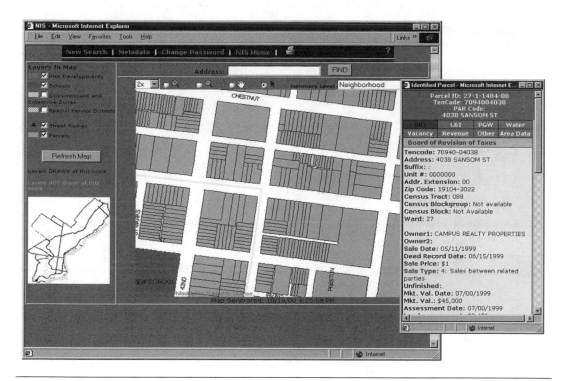

Figure 36.1   ParcelBase Application

Source: http://cml.upenn.edu/parcelbase/

Note: The ParcelBase application integrates property-level housing data from eight different municipal agencies in Philadelphia. Property characteristics are grouped according to their source agency using eight different tabs on a screen that pops up when a parcel is selected.

of the properties grouped according to their source agency using eight different tabs (see Figure 36.1). For properties identified as vacant through a foot survey conducted in certain parts of the city, a digital photograph of the property is also displayed. The query function allows users to create a list or map of properties that meet the criteria they identify. Users can generate and print reports that include a small map of the property and the characteristics from each of the agencies. ParcelBase went live in June 2000. As of this writing, there are more than 500 registered NIS users from more than 150 community organizations and 50 city agencies.

The NeighborhoodBase provides public access to the same data, aggregated by six different geographic units: Census tracts, Census block groups, councilmanic districts, neighborhoods, zip codes, and elementary school feeder areas. Data are aggregated using a georeference file that identifies the tract, block group, councilmanic district, neighborhood, zip code, and school area in which each address falls. The application then serves up the data from the preaggregated tables. Users can generate summary statistics, queries, tables, charts, or maps (see Figure 36.2). Through of series of drop-down menus, users then choose a general content area—housing characteristics, land use, property ownership, property taxes and revenue, real estate sales, utility information, vacancy and abandonment, and U.S. Census data—specific data element, year, and geographic unit. Neighborhood

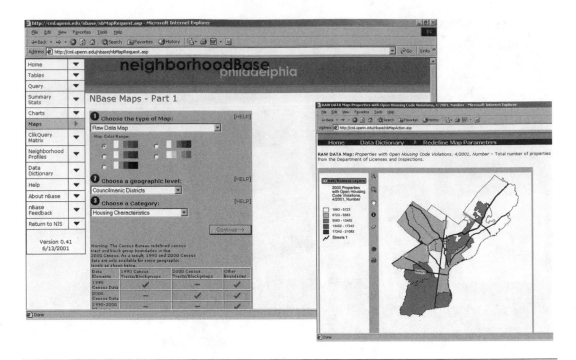

Figure 36.2   NeighborhoodBase Application

Source: http://cml.upenn.edu.nbase/

profiles provide maps identifying the location of each neighborhood (including boundaries, schools, libraries and recreation centers), neighborhood trivia, and summary data.[3]

NeighborhoodBase Application. The NeighborhoodBase allows users to create tables, charts, and maps with the same data included in ParcelBase aggregated at one of eight geographic units.

Services Utilization Monitoring System (SUMS)

SUMS grew out of discussions with the agencies that serve Philadelphia's children and families.[4] The participating agencies, including the school district and the city's public health and child welfare departments, were interested in sharing data to improve planning and interagency coordination, but they faced data-sharing restrictions due to confidentiality regulations. None of the agencies are permitted to release individual-level data to each other on a regular or periodic basis, but they are willing to share their data if the data are aggregated by Census blocks or larger geographic units.

The aggregation occurs through one of two methods. Agencies can install a geocoding and aggregation software created by the CML for this purpose, or they can enlist the CML to do the aggregation onsite and under their administrative control. The SUMS application is restricted to registered users, as is ParcelBase, but

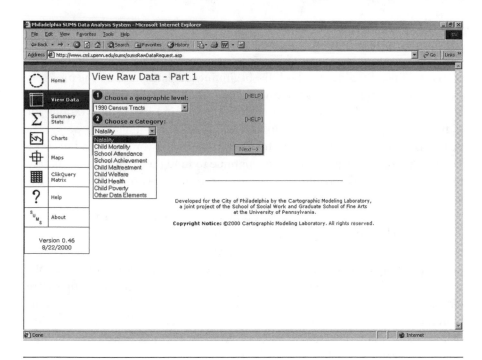

Figure 36.3   Services Utilization Monitoring System (SUMS) Application

Source: http://apollo.gsfa.upenn.edu/project_areas/philadelphia_sums.htm

Note: Users identify a geographic area, data category, then a specific data element to create a table, chart, or map in SUMS.

otherwise it is very similar to NeighborhoodBase. Users can opt to generate summary statistics, tables, charts, or maps. They then choose from one of eight categories—natality, child mortality, school achievement, school attendance, child maltreatment, child welfare, child health, and child poverty—through which the more than 150 specific data elements are organized (see Figure 36.3). Finally, users select a year and geographic unit: 1990 Census tracts, 1990 block groups, elementary school feeder areas, school district clusters, councilmanic districts, or public health districts.

Challenges in Developing and Maintaining Applications

Development of information systems like these involves a number of challenges. These range from building relationships with data-providing agencies, identifying appropriate data elements, and obtaining clear data documentation and regular updates, to assessing data quality, determining data access policies, developing and maintaining user-friendly applications, remaining accountable to supporters and users, developing long-range funding plans, and evaluating the processes and outcomes associated with the projects.

Establishing strong working relationships with data providers requires awareness of interagency dynamics. All or some of the municipal agencies that maintain housing data or information about children, for example, may not have a history of working together. From the beginning, the NIS had a strong advocate in the director of the Office of Housing and Community Development, who wrote letters of introduction encouraging various city agencies to participate in the project. Face-to-face meetings—at both the beginning and later stages of the project—provide critical opportunities for communicating the purpose of the project and remaining accountable to the data providers. Changes in local administrations and staff at participating agencies complicate the relationship-building process. The SUMS project was developed with the support of one mayor and his administration, but his replacement chose not to continue to fund the project. To be successful, information systems require long-term support from city officials, regardless of whether the city is involved in funding them.

Some of the challenges involved in building trust and consensus among city agencies may be avoided if an agency within the city serves as the developer. However, there may not be an agency with the time and staff appropriate for developing and hosting an integrated information system. Municipal firewalls may also make distribution of data outside city networks extremely difficult. Furthermore, city agencies may have little incentive to share data with community organizations. Universities or other private entities represent alternative host sites. Universities may be particularly interested in such a role, given that researchers have a direct interest in access to small-area data for research purposes. Universities may also have relatively greater flexibility for hiring staff and coordinating development contracts.

Identifying the data to be included also requires considerable thought. Agency staff members know the most about their own data and they may also be able to indicate what data maintained by other agencies would be helpful to them. Community organizations must also be involved in the process of deciding what is included in the application, either through focus groups or through some sort of advisory group. Face-to-face meetings and presentations to data providers and groups of system users also serve to keep developers accountable. Although initial planning should be as thorough and inclusive as possible, the process of updating and upgrading these information systems must also be flexible enough to incorporate suggestions for additions and improvements on an ongoing basis.

Even when there are strong relationships among developers and top officials at data-providing agencies, actually acquiring data regularly may still pose significant challenges. Relationships must be cultivated and maintained with the staff responsible for preparing the data in addition to those who authorize the data sharing. For both the NIS and SUMS, a schedule for updates was established up front and letters requesting data updates are sent several weeks prior to the expected transfer of data. Ideally, data updates would occur electronically and involve files in a standard format. But developers need to accept data in the medium and format available to data providers. Developers must also adapt to changes over time within the databases maintained by data providers, accepting that updates may not always include identical data.

Determining what level of data can be shared with which groups of users also involves some negotiation. For housing data, it may be appropriate to share address-level information with a wide array of groups. However, sharing very small-area aggregate human services data can pose threats to privacy. Care should be taken to ensure that data aggregated by small-areas such as city blocks do not allow for the identification of individuals. Once it is determined which user groups should have access to what level of data, data agreements should be formalized through letters of authorization from the data-providing agencies. The goal of these systems is to expand access to administrative data, and whenever possible, these systems should be available to the public. However, such access should not jeopardize the privacy of those who participate in city services—populations which by definition are generally vulnerable. Nor should it jeopardize relationships with data providers. Discussions of which administrative data is "public" and what that means in legal and ethical terms are an important by-product of the development of these information systems.

The goal of these Web-based applications is to increase access to information that can support community change efforts, not just to distribute raw administrative data. Therefore, users must be confident in the quality of the data. Some amount of random error is inevitable given the size of the data sets acquired; however, care should be taken to identify and resolve systematic errors. Some administrative data may be maintained for reporting purposes, but more likely they are part of a billing or service delivery system, further complicating the translation into useful formats for users outside the agency. Ideally, all agencies would use the same unique property identifier to facilitate data integration, but this may not be the case. The development team should include a database administrator who reviews all data for inconsistencies. Distributing administrative data also introduces an additional layer of quality control, and these systems should make it simple for users to report possible problems.

The applications distributing the data must also be user-friendly. Users should not be overwhelmed by the amount of data or the functionality, but the applications should be able to display the data in a number of formats including simple charts, tables, and maps. Online help systems that explain the different options are essential. Developers have a responsibility to encourage careful use of data, and users should be guided in their decisions to normalize and display data to prevent inappropriate choices. Data dictionaries should also be accessible, explaining the meaning of each of the data elements included. Such dictionaries rely on the establishment of clear metadata systems at the outset of development that indicate the source of various data sets, the date of acquisition, restrictions on access, and explanations of the variable names and values.

Given the emphasis they place on geography, these applications should allow users to choose from a number of geographic units. Just as with the identification of appropriate data elements, user groups should be consulted in deciding what geographic units should be included. These may range from standard census geographies, to local political subdivisions, to various service areas, planning districts, and neighborhood definitions. This may require time-consuming digitizing of paper maps, but the value of the small-area analysis depends on how meaningful the small-areas are to different users.

To ensure the sustainability of these systems, long-term funding plans need to be developed at the outset. Although private foundations may be appropriate sources of funding for initial development, user groups or city governments probably need to play a role in covering costs in the long run. This might be accomplished through a single contract with a municipal agency or a user fee based on the number of users or amount of time particular organizations require. However, city agencies and community organizations generally find funding for such services difficult given their limited budgets. Chicago's NEWS and NKLA have both relied on multiple sources of funding. The city of Chicago supported the NEWS project initially, and data updates are currently supported by a private foundation. NKLA has been funded through the National Telecommunication Information Administration, Fannie Mae Foundation, and the Los Angeles Housing Department, as well as the Microsoft Corporation. Funding for the first three years of the NIS came from two large private foundations, the Pew Charitable Trusts and the William Penn Foundation, as well as the University of Pennsylvania. Since then, the city of Philadelphia has joined the list of funders.

These systems also need to be evaluated on an ongoing basis using both process and outcome measures. Process evaluations might focus on the amount and extent of participation in developing the application. How cooperative were city agencies? Were they willing to dedicate staff time to identify appropriate data elements and transfer data regularly? How accountable was the developer to data providers and groups of users? Do potential users have an opportunity to influence the content, functionality, and levels of access to the information? These types of questions might be addressed through an outside evaluation or on an ongoing basis through discussions and online feedback forms. Measuring outcomes poses a greater challenge. In what ways did the application support community change efforts? How did community groups use the information generated? To what extent did the information save organizations time and money that otherwise would have been spent collecting data? To what extent did community and city agency staff develop skills for interpreting quantitative data? Initial development should spell out goals and how and by whom progress will be measured.

New Opportunities

Despite the significant challenges involved in their development, these information systems have tremendous potential for supporting community change efforts by efficiently distributing previously inaccessible data to large numbers of community change agents. Beyond merely sharing data, these systems can provide simple yet powerful tools for data analysis that help even those who have limited experience with quantitative data to identify and interpret the meaning of patterns in demographics, physical, economic, environmental, and health conditions, and service delivery. Geographic information system and data analysis software can be expensive and complicated. Online applications such as the Philadelphia NIS can deliver the necessary functionality without overwhelming and confusing users. Well-designed applications can help users generate and interpret summary statistics, such as frequencies and measures of central tendency. The inclusion of mapping functionality also encourages users to think spatially and recognize spatial clustering, sparseness, and associations. More sophisticated applications may also be able to introduce intermediate users to basic inferential statistics such as chi-square tests and linear regression. Universities are the appropriate teachers of basic quantitative data analysis skills, either through train-the-trainer programs with umbrella associations that provide technical assistance to community groups or through direct training programs and student internships.

There are no limits to the types of applications that might be developed beyond limits to funding and access to raw data. Web-based applications could be developed around a public safety theme and share information about nuisances, property crimes, and violent crimes, along with parking and housing violations. In addition to supporting the data needs of police and other public safety officials, these systems could support the work of police advisory groups, town watches, and other community organizations. In addition to providing information, they might provide opportunities for filing complaints, paying tickets, or communicating with public officials through virtual chat rooms. A public health application could integrate data about births and deaths, lead paint contaminations, immunizations, dangerous housing, communicable diseases, health insurance coverage, and access to health care facilities for all age groups. Local commerce departments, chambers of commerce, or community development corporations might sponsor an application focused on economic development. This could integrate information about types of businesses, business revenues, employment levels, commuting patterns, and day-care facilities, as well as locations of contiguous open land and brownfields for new development.[5]

These information systems need not be limited to administrative data. Community organizations can also contribute their own data based on foot surveys or questionnaires. With support from the CML and the Philadelphia Association of Community Development Corporations, several community organizations have conducted foot surveys of housing in their service areas. Surveyors used handheld computer devices programmed with survey questions and digital cameras to capture information about housing conditions not recorded by the municipal agencies. To facilitate integration into the system, NIS staff gave surveyors guidelines for the resolution and property identification for the digital photos. Community organizations can also generate and contribute more qualitative data to provide context for the quantitative administrative data, including photographs, interviews, and narratives.

At their best, these information systems provide opportunities for widespread understanding of current conditions that can be used to build consensus toward needed change. They empower individuals and organizations that might otherwise expend enormous effort to acquire small amounts of information, inviting them into broad discussions about the communities in which they live and work. They also provide objective standards for planning and evaluation, encouraging agents of community change to base decisions on empirical data rather than conjecture, anecdotal information, or political considerations. They also hold the potential to make municipal government more accountable to its citizens by sharing the information about the services it provides. This democratic ideal may not be realized in all existing distributed information systems, because developers face limits in funding and the willingness of city agencies to share information. However, this ideal represents the standard toward which developers should aim.

Notes

1. If the U.S. Bureau of the Census moves forward with more frequent administration of the long form through the American Community Survey initiative, Census data could prove more valuable, with annual information about population characteristics at the tract level. However, because it will depend on sampling, concerns about confidentiality will prevent small-area aggregation, such as block groups and Census blocks.

2. The one exception is the U.S. Post Office, which maintains information about vacant properties where mail is not delivered and provides data updates annually.

3. Neighborhood Information System (NIS) developers recognize that there are numerous ways to identify Philadelphia's neighborhoods. The NIS uses a map with 69 neighborhoods that were determined by the Temple University Social Science Data Library based on information gathered from the Philadelphia Police Department, the Philadelphia Inquirer, and historical research. Neighborhood boundaries are coterminus with 1990 Census tract boundaries.

4. The Cartographic Modeling Laboratory has developed a similar application for Palm Beach County, Florida, and is currently developing a system for Columbus, Ohio.

5. The Cartographic Modeling Laboratory developed a brownfields application that integrated vacant land information for part of North Philadelphia into a stand-alone mapping application for Philadelphia's Department of Commerce and the Pennsylvania Environmental Council.

References

Bauer, R. A. (Ed.). (1966). *Social indicators.* Cambridge, MA: MIT Press.

Cartographic Modeling Laboratory. (2003). *Philadelphia Neighborhood Information System.* Retrieved on April 29, 2003, from http://www.cml.upenn.edu/nis.

Center for Neighborhood Technology. (2003). *Chicago Neighborhood Early Warning System.* Retrieved on April 29, 2003, from http://www.newschicago.org.

Community Information Technology Center. (2003). *Neighborhood Knowledge Los Angeles.* Retrieved on April 29, 2003, from http://nkla.sppsr.ucla.edu.

DuBois, W.E.B. (1899). *The Philadelphia Negro.* Philadelphia: University of Pennsylvania.

Kingsley, G. T. (1998). *Neighborhood indicators: Taking advantage of the new potential.* Washington, DC: Urban Institute.

President's Research Committee on Social Trends. (1933). *Recent social trends.* New York: McGraw-Hill.

Sawicki, D. S., & Flynn, P. (1996). Neighborhood indicators: a review of the literature and assessment of conceptual and methodological issues. *Journal of the American Planning Association, 62*(2), 165–183.

U.S. Department of Commerce, Bureau of the Census. (1994). *Geographic areas reference manual* (10:2–10:3). Retrieved April 29, 2003, from http://www.census.gov/geo/www/garm.html.

Author Index

Subject Index

About the Editors

About the Editor

Marie Weil is Berg-Beach Professor of Community Practice and former Associate Dean at the University of North Carolina, Chapel Hill School of Social Work, where she teaches community practice, policy practice, and theory for social work intervention. She has led state-wide research and community-based planning and implementation initiatives in family support and family preservation and for adolescent family life programs, as well as consulting and conducting program evaluations for small nonprofits. Previously, she taught at the University of Southern California. She is the author or coauthor of thirteen books primarily focused on community practice; the author or coauthor of over thirty chapters related to community practice, feminist practice, and empowerment practice and service development for families and children; and more than 42 articles and monographs. She began her career working in community development in settlement houses in Philadelphia. She has served as Deputy Director of the Office of Economic Opportunity of Delaware and as Planning Director of the Wilmington Housing Authority. She is a founding member of the Association for Community Organization and Social Administration (ACOSA) and was the Founding Editor of the *Journal of Community Practice*, producing the first ten volumes. She is a recipient of ACOSA's Career Achievement Award.

About the Associate Editors

Michael Reisch is Professor and Director of the Multicultural Social Welfare History Project at the University of Michigan. He is the author or editor of more than 20 books and monographs, including *The Road Not Taken: A History of Radical Social Work in the U.S., From Charity to Enterprise,* and *Social Work in the 21st Century,* and more than 80 articles and book chapters on the history and philosophy of social welfare, community organization theory and practice, the nonprofit sector, and contemporary policy issues, particularly welfare reform. His work has been translated into French, Spanish, Italian, and Bulgarian, and he has lectured widely in Europe and Latin America. For more than 30 years, he has held leadership positions in national and state advocacy, professional, and social change organizations. He has directed or consulted on political campaigns at the federal, state, and local levels in four states and has been honored for his work by the Maryland State Legislature, the San Francisco Board of Supervisors, and numerous local and national nonprofit organizations, professional associations, and universities.

Dorothy N. Gamble is Clinical Associate Professor at the University of North Carolina School of Social Work at Chapel Hill. A member of the faculty since 1978, she currently teaches courses relating to citizen participation and sustainable development, and has led summer school abroad courses to Costa Rica, Honduras, Mexico, and South Africa. Within the university, she had been working for the past five years with an interdisciplinary network to provide guidance for ethically grounded community-based education. She is on the advisory board of the Center for Sustainable Enterprise at the Kenan Flagler Business School, and she is a Center Associate at the Duke-UNC Rotary Center for International Studies in Peace and Conflict Resolution. Her community service activities include numerous consultations with grassroots community groups and service on a number of public and nonprofit boards. She is a member of the editorial board of the *Journal of Community Practice* and has written extensively in the areas of community practice and development.

Lorraine Gutiérrez is a member of the faculty in the School of Social Work at the University of Michigan, where she teaches courses in multicultural practice and community work. She is an internationally recognized scholar in the area of multicultural practice in social work and has published more than 35 books, chapters, and articles on topics such as multicultural organizational development, working with women of color, group work, empowerment practice, and multicultural community organizing. In addition to her scholarship and teaching in this area, she has served as a consultant on this topic to large and small organizations including the Council on Social Work Education, the Swedish National Board of Health and Welfare, and schools of social work throughout the United States. She has a strong commitment to using her scholarship to improve services on the local level.

Elizabeth A. Mulroy is Professor of Management and Planning at the University of Maryland School of Social Work, Baltimore. Her research interests include organizations and their environments, and families in neighborhood poverty. Her current research is on "Networks That Work," a three-city study of diverse multisector collaborations and networks formed to collectively address large-scale social problems such as homelessness. Implications focus on the development of social environment theory to guide management and community practice. She is the author of numerous publications including the book *The New Uprooted: Single Mothers in Urban Life* (1995), is editor of *Women as Single Parents: Confronting Institutional Barriers in the Courts, the Workplace, and the Housing Market* (1988), and is writing a new book, *New Perspectives on Management and Community Practice.*

Ram A. Cnaan is Professor and Director of the Program for the Study of Organized Religion and Social Work at the University of Pennsylvania School of Social Work. He has published numerous articles in scientific journals on a variety of social issues and is the author of *The Newer Deal: Social Work and Religion in Partnership* and *The Invisible Caring Hand: American Congregations and the Provision of Welfare.* He is writing a book on the effect of congregations in urban America. He conducted the first national study on the role of local congregations in the provision of social services and has developed a related course. He is a national expert on nonprofit organizations and voluntary action with a specialty in the study of volunteerism and has studied the role of volunteers in human services, volunteer management, and volunteerism as a social construct. Most recently, he is studying the nexus between religion and volunteerism.

About the Contributors

Catherine Foster Alter is Dean and Professor at the Graduate School of Social Work at the University of Denver. From 1986-1992, she served as Director of the Iowa University School of Social Work. Her practice background in urban planning and social service administration led to a continuing interest in building theory and knowledge about interorganizational networks and collaborations as a strategy for social change. Her book with Jerald Hage, *Organizations Working Together* (1993) is used today by doctoral students in many disciplines. Her recent research focuses on alleviating poverty by using strategies such as micro-enterprise and self-employment programs that enable low-income women to move toward self-sufficiency. Most recently she was co–principal investigator on the evaluation of Colorado's welfare reform program.

Teiahsha Bankhead is Assistant Professor at California State University, Sacramento, in the Division of Social Work. She is coauthor with Jewelle Taylor Gibbs of *Preserving Privilege: California Politics, Propositions and People of Color.* Her research interests include social policy analysis and issues related to race, ethnicity, and gender.

Stephanie C. Boddie is Assistant Professor at the George Warren Brown School of Social Work at Washington University in St. Louis. She has coauthored (with Ram Cnaan) *The Newer Deal: Social Work* and *Religion in Partnership,* and *The Invisible Caring Hand: American Congregations and the Provision of Welfare.* She has also published several book chapters and articles on faith-based social services.

Eleanor L. Brilliant is Professor at Rutgers University School of Social Work. Her past work experience includes serving as Associate Executive Director (Planning, Allocations and Evaluation) for United Way of Westchester. She has also been Vice President/Secretary of the Association for Research on Nonprofit Organizations and Voluntary Action, and national Treasurer for the National Association of Social Workers. Her books include *The United Way: Dilemmas of Organized Charity* and *Private Charity and Public Inquiry: A History of the Filer and Peterson Commissions.*

William E. Buffum is Professor and Director of the George Williams College School of Social Work at Aurora University, Aurora, Illinois. Previously, he was Associate Dean at Barry University's School of Social Work and also at the University of Houston Graduate School of Social Work. His social work practice and research interests are in the areas of poverty organizing, community partnerships, and community mental health. He is a member of ACOSA, CSWE, NASW, NADD, SSWR, and the National Network for Social Work Managers. His current work is in forensic mental health.

Steve Burghardt is Professor of Community Organizing and Planning at the CUNY-Hunter College School of Social Work where he specializes in community organizing, community building, the political economy of social service work and innovative models of management, training and service. Author of *The Other Side of Organizing* and *The Welfare State Crisis and the Transformation of Social Services* (with Michael Fabricant), he has just completed *The Glass Is Always Full: Leadership Lessons From Everyday Folks for Lasting Executive Excellence* (with Willie Tolliver).

Iris Carlton-LaNey is Professor in the School of Social Work at the University of North Carolina at Chapel Hill. She has coedited two books and is the editor of *African American Leadership: An Empowerment Tradition in Social Welfare History.* She writes extensively about rural social work with elderly women and has been honored for her scholarship on African American social welfare history.

Paul Castelloe is Co-Executive Director of the Center for Participatory Change, a nonprofit organization in western North Carolina. His work focuses on supporting grassroots groups by integrating methods from community organization, popular education, and international participatory development.

Julian Chun-Chung Chow is Associate Professor at the School of Social Welfare, University of California, Berkeley. His research focuses on urban poverty issues, neighborhood services, and community practice, particularly responsive service delivery to culturally diverse populations.

Terry L. Cross is an enrolled member of the Seneca Nation of Indians and has served as Executive Director of the National Indian Child Welfare Association since 1983. He is the author of *Heritage and Helping,* an eleven-manual curriculum for tribal child welfare workers, *Positive Indian Parenting* curriculum, and *Cross-Cultural Skills in Indian Child Welfare.* He coauthored *Toward a Culturally Competent System of Care* (with Karl W. Dennis, Mareasa R. Isaacs, and Barbara J. Bazron). He is experienced in evaluation design and policy-related research, and he has organized culturally specific technical assistance programs for more than 15 years.

Kelsey Crowe is a doctoral student at the School of Social Welfare, University of California, Berkeley. Her research focuses on community capacity building and organizational development in low-income, multiethnic communities.

Dennis Culhane is Professor of Social Welfare Policy at the School of Social Work and Codirector of the Cartographic Modeling Laboratory at the University of Pennsylvania. His research on homelessness and housing makes extensive use of administrative data.

David Dempsey is the Manager of Government Relations/Political Action at the National Association of Social Workers (NASW). Previously, he served as Executive Director of the Washington State, Missouri, and Pennsylvania chapters. His publications include "Establishin ‘LAN (an Education, Legislation Action Network) in a State Chapter," in *Practical Politics,* and he is coauthor of the 1996 article "Political Practica: Educating Social Work Students for Policymaking." He has also presented at numerous social work education and social policy conferences on the subjects of politics and government.

Erin Drinnin is Adult Community Program Coordinator and Manager for The Homestead, an agency serving people with autism spectrum disorders in Des Moines, Iowa. She previously served as an intern for the North Carolina Commission for Mental Health, Developmental Disabilities and Substance Abuse.

John L. Erlich is Professor, Division of Social Work, California State University, Sacramento, and former Chair, Policy, Planning, and Administration. His coauthored publications include *Community Organizing in a Diverse Society, Strategies of Community Intervention, Tactics and Techniques of Community Intervention,* and *Taking Action in Organizations and Communities.* His scholarship focuses on grassroots organizing, diversity, and social action.

Richard J. Estes is Professor of Social Work at the University of Pennsylvania. He is the author of more than 100 articles and books on various aspects of international and comparative social welfare including *The Social Progress of Nations; Trends in World Social Development; Health Care and the Social Services; Internationalizing Social Work Education; Toward a Development Strategy for the Asia and Pacific Region; Resources for Social and Economic Development; Medical, Social, and Legal Aspects of Child Sexual Exploitation: A Comprehensice Review of Child Pornography, Child Prostitution, and Internet Crimes Against children; Social Development in Hong Kong: The Unfinished Agenda;* and *At the Crossroad: Development Challenges at the Beginning of a New Century.*

Michael Fabricant is the Executive Officer of the Doctoral Program in Social Welfare at the Graduate Center and Vice President for Senior Colleges of the Professional Staff Congress of the City University of New York. He is the author of five books and numerous articles. His most recent books include *The Crisis of the Welfare State and Transformation of Social Service Work* (with Steve Burghardt) and *Settlement Houses Under Siege: The Struggle to Sustain Community Organizations in New York City* (with Robert Fisher). A thread that runs through all of his work on homelessness, juvenile justice, and nonprofit community agencies is the extraction of praxis implications from both research findings and activist experience.

Walter C. Farrell, Jr., is Professor of Management and Community Practice in the Schools of Social Work, Public Health, and Public Policy, and Associate Director of the Urban Investment Strategies Center of the Kenan Institute in the Kenan-Flagler Business School at the University of North Carolina at Chapel Hill. He has published widely in the areas of urban social issues, minority economic development, social welfare policy, and workforce diversity.

Robert Fisher is Professor of Social Work and Director of Urban and Community Studies at the University of Connecticut. He is the author of a variety of books, including *Let the People Decide: Neighborhood Organizing in America* and, most recently, with Michael Fabricant, *Settlement Houses Under Siege: The Struggle to Sustain Community Organizations in New York City.* He is the recipient of two Fulbright fellowships and the Moses Distinguished Professorship at the Hunter College School of Social Work. He has been involved in community organizing and social justice efforts since the early 1970s.

Barbara J. Friesen is Director of the Research and Training Center on Family Support and Children's Mental Health, and Professor, Graduate School of Social

Work, at Portland State University in Portland, Oregon. Her research areas include family participation in mental health and other settings, the development and testing of a peer-based training program for families in early childhood settings, and evaluations of community-based systems of care.

Denise Gour, LCSW, is an entrepreneurial social worker with a strong preference for evidence-based models. As a Program Director at Metropolitan Family Service in Portland, Oregon, she established several successful family- and community-strengthening models serving thousands of children and adults each year. With Volunteers of America Oregon, she is directing a pilot program aimed at decreasing the recidivism rates of young felony offenders.

Amy E. Hillier is Research Associate at the Cartographic Modeling Laboratory and a lecturer in the Urban Studies program and School of Social Work at the University of Pennsylvania. Her research and teaching focus on the application of geographic information systems (GIS) to social welfare, urban history, and public health.

Marie D. Hoff is a retired social work professor, with faculty service at Saint Louis University and Boise State University; she taught social policy and macro-practice methods. Her major research focus has been the relationships between environmental concerns and human social welfare. She has published articles and two edited books on these topics: *The Global Environmental Crisis: Implications for Social Welfare and Social Work* (with J. G. McNutt), and *Sustainable Community Development: Studies in Economic, Environmental and Cultural Revitalization*. She is currently developing a Catholic Charities social services organization for the state of Idaho.

Cheryl Hyde is Associate Professor at the School of Social Work, University of Maryland-Baltimore, where she is Cochair of the Management and Community Organization Concentration and Assistant Director for Community-Based Research at the Social Work Community Outreach Service. Her areas of interest include community capacity building, social movements, feminist praxis, multicultural organizational development, and diversity learning strategies. She is on a number of editorial boards, including those of the *Journal of Community Practice* and *Administration in Social Work* and is Chair of the Association for Community Organization and Social Administration.

Bruce S. Jansson is the Driscoll/Clevenger Professor of Social Policy and Administration at the School of Social Work of the University of Southern California. He has written many articles and books including *Becoming an Effective Policy Advocate: From Policy Practice to Social Justice* (4th ed., 2003); *The Sixteen-Trillion-Dollar Mistake: How the U.S. Bungled Its National Priorities From the New Deal to the Present* (2001); and *The Reluctant Welfare State, American Social Welfare Policies, Past, Present, and Future* (5th ed., 2004).

James H. Johnson, Jr., is William Rand Kenan, Jr., Distinguished Professor of Management, Sociology, and Public Policy and Director of the Urban Investment Strategies Center of the Kenan Institute in the Kenan-Flagler Business School at the University of North Carolina at Chapel Hill. He has published widely in the areas of entrepreneurship and minority economic development, urban poverty, public policy, interethnic minority conflict in advanced societies, and welfare reform.

Armand Lauffer is Professor Emeritus of the School of Social Work at the University of Michigan. He now directs the MBA Program in Nonprofit Management and Jewish Communal Leadership at The Interdisciplinary Center, Herzliya, Israel. He initiated Michigan's Project STAR (Student Teacher Achievement Ratio) and its Continuing Education Program; Sage Publications' two Human Service series; and a process that led to establishment of the Association for Community Organization and Social Administration, from which he received a career achievement award in 2001. His more than twenty books include *Social Planning at the Community Level; Careers, Colleagues and Conflicts; Grants, Etc.; Strategic Marketing; The Practice of Continuing Education; Understanding Your Social Agency; Volunteers;* and *Getting the Resources You Need.*

Edith A. Lewis is Associate Professor of Social Work and Adjunct Associate Professor of Women's Studies at the University of Michigan. Her research and teaching interests include women and families of color, the lessons from parallel forms of social work practice in populations of color, international social welfare policy and services, and multicultural teaching.

Roger A. Lohmann is Professor of Social Work, Benedum Distinguished Scholar, and Director of the Nonprofit Management Certificate Program in the Division of Social Work, School of Applied Social Sciences, in the Eberly College of Arts and Sciences at West Virginia University. He created and operates nearly two dozen electronic discussion lists, including ARNOVA-L, which has been in continuous daily operation for the past 15 years, and the original ACOSA-L list. His current interest is in electronically enhanced communication.

Michelle Livermore is Assistant Professor of Social Work at The Ohio State University. She has published in the area of social development and edited *The Handbook of Social Policy* (with James Midgley and Martin Tracy). She continues to work in the areas of social capital, civic engagement, local capitalism, and employment.

Jacquelyn McCroskey is the John Milner Associate Professor of Child Welfare at the USC School of Social Work. She works actively with county, city, and school district policy makers in Los Angeles County, using data and scholarship to inform policy and guide improvements to service delivery systems for children and families. Her research includes analysis of service financing, organization and performance, and the impact of family-centered child welfare services.

John McNutt is Associate Professor of Social Work in the College of Social Work at the University of South Carolina. He initiated and continues to work with the Council on Social Work Education APM Technology Forum. He also created the original ACOSA Web site and operates the SWPolicy, NIRG, and other discussion lists. He has been a recognized national leader in advocating for the use of technology in community-level social work education. His principal interest is in electronic advocacy.

James Midgley is the Harry and Reva Specht Professor of Public Social Services and Dean of the School of Social Welfare at the University of California, Berkeley. He has published widely on issues of social development and international social welfare. His most recent books include *The Handbook of Social Policy* (with Martin

Tracy and Michelle Livermore), *Controversial Issues in Social Policy* (with Howard Karger and Brene Brown), and *Social Policy for Development* (with Tony Hall).

Terry Mizrahi is Professor at Hunter School of Social Work CUNY, Director of the Education Center for Community Organizing, and Chair of the Community Organizing and Planning concentration. She is the author of numerous books and articles related to community organizing, health advocacy, health policy and patients' rights. She was one of the founders of the Association for Community Organization and Social Administration and its publication the *Journal of Community Practice.* She is the coauthor of *Strategic Partnerships: Building Effective Coalitions and Collaborations* (ECCO) and coeditor of the book *Community Organization and Social Administration,* and she is engaged in other research, consultation, and training on coalition building. She is a national leader in the National Association of Social Workers and served as its President from 2001–2003.

Jacqueline Mondros is Professor and Associate Dean at University of Southern California School of Social Work. She has worked with social change organizations in Philadelphia, New York, and Miami, Florida, and has written extensively on community organizing and community work. Prior to her academic career, she was executive director of a settlement house. In Miami, she established the largest university-community partnership in the state, piloting community projects for children, families, and the elderly in Haitian and Latino communities.

Lynne Clemmons Morris is Associate Professor in the School of Social Work and Human Services at Eastern Washington University. Her current research interests are focused on impacts of destination resort development in rural western mountain communities and uses of information technology in the delivery and evaluation of rural human services.

John Morrison is Professor and former MSW Program Chair at Aurora University. He is a board member and past chair of the Association for Community Organization and Social Administration. He serves on the board of the Illinois Chapter of NASW and the Editorial Board of the *Journal of Community Practice.* He is coeditor, with Terry Mizrahi, of *Community Organization and Social Administration: Advances, Trends and Issues.* His current academic interests include international social work, prevention, and social development.

Susan Murty is Associate Professor and MSW Program Coordinator at the School of Social Work at the University of Iowa. Her research focuses on rural service delivery, rural community practice, network analysis, intergenerational service learning, and domestic violence. She is currently developing an end-of-life care curriculum in the MSW Program with support from a Social Work Leadership Development Award received from the Project on Death in America.

Biren (Ratnesh) A. Nagda is Associate Professor of Social Work and Director of the Intergroup Dialogue, Education and Action (IDEA) Training and Resource Institute at the University of Washington. His interests focus on cultural diversity, social justice, intergroup dialogue, and multicultural practice. He has done extensive research and published on intergroup dialogues in community settings, including a community-based research project examining practices in addressing race issues through small group dialogues.

Kristine E. Nelson is Professor at the Graduate School of Social Work at Portland State University in Oregon. She is coauthor of *Reinventing Human Services: Community- and Family-Centered Practice* and has conducted six federally funded studies of family preservation services and child neglect.

Helzi Noponen is an economic development planner who has been engaged in funded research, professional practice and university teaching activities in the fields of microfinance, gender and development, and sustainable livelihoods programs. She is a regional specialist in South Asia where she has been involved in field research and technical assistance projects for the past 24 years. Most recently, she has been involved in consultation with PRADAN—Professional Assistance for Development Action in India. Currently she is an external consultant to three Ford Foundation–funded Microfinance and Livelihood NGOs in India.

Yolanda C. Padilla is Associate Professor at the School of Social Work and Research Associate at the Populations Research Center, University of Texas at Austin. Her current projects examine health trajectories of Mexican American children from birth to age five, living conditions of children of immigrants, and the status of children along the U.S.-Mexico border.

Joan Pennell is Professor and Chair in the Department of Social Work at North Carolina State University. She is the principal investigator of the North Carolina Family-Centered Meetings Project and previously directed the North Carolina Family Group Conferencing Project. Previously she served as principal investigator for a Newfoundland and Labrador (Canada) demonstration of family group conferencing in situations of child maltreatment and domestic violence. Her publications focus on empowerment approaches to community practice, program development, and research. She coauthored *Community Research as Empowerment* and *Family Group Conferencing: Evaluation Guidelines.*

Salome Raheim is Associate Professor and Director of the University of Iowa School of Social Work. Economic empowerment, community development and culturally competent practice are major areas of her research, teaching, and practice. She has published numerous articles related to women, welfare, microfinance, and economic opportunity.

Beth Glover Reed is Professor at the University of Michigan-Ann Arbor with a joint appointment in Social Work and Women's Studies. Her research focuses on how social systems of various sizes create and sustain patterns of inequity and how these patterns can be changed towards a more socially just society. She teaches several courses in community organizing and community and social systems.

Maria Roberts-DeGennaro is Professor of Social Work at San Diego State University. She was the first President of the National Association for Community Organization and Social Administration. Her scholarship focuses on policy and interorganizational behavior. She was granted a Silberman Fund Award for her research related to the 1996 Welfare Reform Act. Her latest research interests have centered around

Web-based education. She is the recipient of an award for outstanding faculty contributions in the College of Health and Human Services at SDSU.

Herbert J. Rubin is Professor Emeritus of Sociology at Northern Illinois University. He is the author of *Applied Social Research* and (with Irene Rubin) three editions of *Community Organizing and Development*. He has written articles that explore rural development in Thailand, suburban land-use fights, cooperative housing, and economic and community development. Two of his publications, the monograph *The Dynamics of Development in Rural Development* and his book on community renewal in the United States, *Renewing Hope Within Neighborhoods of Despair: The Community-based Development Model*, explore issues of social change. He is currently studying national, Washington-based organizations that advocate for the poor.

Irene S. Rubin is Professor of Public Administration at Northern Illinois University. She is the author of *Running in the Red: The Political Dynamics of Urban Fiscal Stress, Shrinking the Federal Government, Class Tax and Power: Municipal Budgeting in the United States,* and *Balancing the Federal Budget: Eating the Seed Corn or Trimming the Herds*. She has written journal articles about citizen participation in local government in Thailand, how universities adapt when their budgets are cut, and fights between legislative staffers and elected and appointed officials about unworkable policy proposals. She is conducting an interviewing project on how local officials view and use contracts with the private sector and with other governmental units to provide public services.

Anna Scheyett is Assistant Clinical Professor of Social Work at the University of North Carolina at Chapel Hill, where she teaches health and mental health policy and practice in mental health and in organizations and communities. She also conducts training in mental health system reform. She has extensive experience working with people with severe and persistent mental illnesses and is the author of *Making the Transition to Managed Behavioral Healthcare: A Guide for Agencies and Practitioners*.

Robert Schneider is Professor at Virginia Commonwealth University School of Social Work and National Chairperson of Influencing State Policy (http://www.statepolicy.org). He is coauthor with Lori Lester of *Social Work Advocacy: A New Framework for Action* and coeditor with Nancy P. Kropf and Anne Kisor of the journal *Gerontological Social Work*.

Michael Sherraden is the Benjamin E. Youngdahl Professor of Social Development and Director of the Center for Social Development at the George Warren Brown School of Social Work at Washington University, St. Louis. He is author of *Assets and the Poor: A New American Welfare Policy* and coeditor of *Alternatives to Social Security: An International Inquiry*.

Margaret Sherrard Sherraden is Associate Professor of Social Work at the University of Missouri, St. Louis and Research Professor at the Center for Social Development at Washington University, St. Louis. Her books include *Community Economic Development and Social Work* with William Ninacs and *Kitchen Capitalism: Microenterprise in Low-Income Households* with Cynthia K. Sanders and Michael Sherraden.

Nancy Shore is a doctoral student in social welfare at the University of Washington. Prior to returning to school, she worked at a Head Start program. In addition to her commitment to child welfare, her other research and teaching interests include community-based participatory research and ethics.

Laura Wernick is in the Joint Doctoral Program in Social Work and Political Science and the Women's Studies Certificate Program at the University of Michigan. Her interest areas include urban politics, civic engagement, organizational theory, and intersectionality and power. Her dissertation research examines factors constraining and enabling community stakeholder participation and engagement in human service system and policy change. She works with Professor Robin Ely of the Harvard Business School on issues of diversity, pedagogy, and power within the workplace.

Gaynor I. Yancey is Assistant Professor of Social Work at Baylor University in Waco, Texas. She is the Associate Director of the FASTEN (Faith and Service Technical Education Network) national research project, a study of public and private sector collaboration in meeting the needs of the urban poor. She is coauthor with Ram Cnaan and Stephanie Boddie of the chapter "Bowling Alone But Serving Together: The Congregational Norm of Community Involvement" in *Religion, Social Capital, and Democratic Life*. Her research interest is in organizing and development through the work of faith-based organizations and congregations.